T0394346

Modernisation, National Identity and Legal Instrumentalism
(Vol. 1: Private Law)

# Legal History Library

VOLUME 35

*Series Editors*

C.H. (Remco) van Rhee, *Maastricht University*
Dirk Heirbaut, *Ghent University*
Matthew C. Mirow, *Florida International University*

*Editorial Board*

Hamilton Bryson, *University of Richmond*
Thomas P. Gallanis, *University of Iowa*
James Gordley, *Tulane University*
Richard Helmholz, *University of Chicago*
Michael Hoeflich, *University of Kansas*
Neil Jones, *University of Cambridge*
Hector MacQueen, *University of Edinburgh*
Paul Oberhammer, *University of Vienna*
Marko Petrak, *University of Zagreb*
Jacques du Plessis, *University of Stellenbosch*
Mathias Reimann, *University of Michigan*
Jan M. Smits, *Maastricht University*
Alain Wijffels, *Université Catholique de Louvain, Leiden University, CNRS*
Reinhard Zimmermann, *Max-Planck-Institut für ausländisches und
internationales Privatrecht, Hamburg*

The titles published in this series are listed at *brill.com/lhl*

# Modernisation, National Identity, and Legal Instrumentalism

*Studies in Comparative Legal History*

VOLUME 1: PRIVATE LAW

*Edited by*

Michał Gałędek
Anna Klimaszewska

BRILL
NIJHOFF

LEIDEN | BOSTON

Cover illustration: Katarzyna Kapica, Doodlestudio.tv.

This publication was supported with funds of University of Gdańsk's Vice-Rector for Research and Foreign Cooperation, Professor Piotr Stepnowski, and with funds of the Dean of Faculty of Law and Administration, Professor Jakub Stelina.

Library of Congress Cataloging-in-Publication Data

Names: Gałędek, Michał, 1978- editor. | Klimaszewska, Anna, 1984- editor.
Title: Modernisation, national identity and legal instrumentalism : studies
  in comparative legal history / edited by Michał Gałędek, Anna
  Klimaszewska.
Description: Leiden ; Boston : Brill Nijhoff, 2020. | Series: Legal history
  library ; volumes 35-36 | Includes bibliographical references and index. |
Identifiers: LCCN 2019038551 | ISBN 9789004395282 (vol. I ; hardback) |
  ISBN 9789004417151 (vol. II ; hardback) | ISBN 9789004417274 (vol. I ;
  ebook) | ISBN 9789004417359 vol. II ; (ebook)
Subjects: LCSH: Law--History.
Classification: LCC K160 .M63 2019 | DDC 340.09--dc23
LC record available at https://lccn.loc.gov/2019038551

Typeface for the Latin, Greek, and Cyrillic scripts: "Brill". See and download: brill.com/brill-typeface.

ISSN 1874-1793
ISBN 978-90-04-39528-2 (hardback)
ISBN 978-90-04-41727-4 (e-book)

Copyright 2020 by Koninklijke Brill NV, Leiden, The Netherlands.
Koninklijke Brill NV incorporates the imprints Brill, Brill Hes & De Graaf, Brill Nijhoff, Brill Rodopi, Brill Sense, Hotei Publishing, mentis Verlag, Verlag Ferdinand Schöningh and Wilhelm Fink Verlag.
All rights reserved. No part of this publication may be reproduced, translated, stored in a retrieval system, or transmitted in any form or by any means, electronic, mechanical, photocopying, recording or otherwise, without prior written permission from the publisher.
Authorization to photocopy items for internal or personal use is granted by Koninklijke Brill NV provided that the appropriate fees are paid directly to The Copyright Clearance Center, 222 Rosewood Drive, Suite 910, Danvers, MA 01923, USA. Fees are subject to change.

This book is printed on acid-free paper and produced in a sustainable manner.

# Contents

Tables   VII
Abbreviations   VIII
Notes on Contributors   X

1   Introduction: Modernisation, National Identity, and Legal
Instrumentalism   1
   *Michał Gałędek*

2   Prenuptial Agreements of the Hungarian Aristocracy in the Early
Modern Era   26
   *Zsuzsanna Peres*

3   Revolution and the Instrumentality of Law: Theories of Property in
the American and French Revolutions   49
   *Bart Wauters*

4   English Commercial Law in the *Longue Durée*: Chasing Continental
Shadows   73
   *Sean Thomas*

5   The Italian Destiny of the French *Code de commerce*   111
   *Annamaria Monti*

6   The Reception of the French Commercial Code in Nineteenth-Century
Polish Territories: A Hollow Legal Shell   143
   *Anna Klimaszewska*

7   Development of the Medical Malpractice Law and Legal
Instrumentalism in the Antebellum America   164
   *Marcin Michalak*

8   The Contractual Third-Party Notion Beyond the Principle of
the Relativity of Contracts: The Comparative Legal History as
Methodological Approach   191
   *Sara Pilloni*

9  Civilian Arguments in the House of Lords' Judgments: Regarding
   Delictual (Tortious) Liability in 20th and 21st Century   212
   *Łukasz Jan Korporowicz*

10  *Usucapio* in Era of Real Estate Title Registration Systems   237
   *Beata J. Kowalczyk*

11  In the Name of the Republic: Family Reform in Late Nineteenth and
   Early Twentieth-Century France and China   254
   *Mingzhe Zhu*

12  The Private Law Codification as an Instrument for the Consolidation
   of a Nation from Inside: Estonia and Latvia between Two World
   Wars   285
   *Marju Luts-Sootak, Hesi Siimets-Gross, Katrin Kiirend-Pruuli*

13  Reluctant Legal Transplant: United States Moral Rights as Late 20th
   Century Honor Law   311
   *Steven Wilf*

Index of Names   333
Index of Subjects   344
Index of Places   351

# Tables

11.1    Comparison of Family Laws in China     273
11.2    Divorces in Beijing from 1917 to 1928     277
11.3    Divorces claimed by the wives in Beijing and Tianjin     278

# Abbreviations

| | |
|---|---|
| 1st Cir. | United States Court of Appeals for the First Circuit |
| 2d Cir. | United States Court of Appeals for the Second Circuit |
| 3d Cir. | United States Court of Appeals for the Third Circuit |
| 5th Cir. | United States Court of Appeals for the Fifth Circuit |
| ABGB | Allgemeines Bürgerliches Gesetzbuch |
| AC | Appeal Cases |
| ANK | Archiwum Narodowe w Krakowie [National Archives in Krakow] |
| APW | Archiwum Państwowe w Warszawie [State Archive in Warsaw] |
| AWMK | Akta Wolnego Miasta Krakowa [Archives of the Free City of Krakow] |
| BGB | Bürgerliches Gesetzbuch |
| Binn. | Binney's Reports (Pennsylvania) |
| Burrow | Burrow's Reports |
| C. | Code of Justinian |
| Camp. | Campbell's Nisi Prius Cases |
| Car. & P. | Carrington & Payne's Nisi Prius Reports |
| CTh. | Theodosian Code |
| D. | Digest of Justinian |
| DALLOZ | *Jurisprudence générale...*, Victor Alexis Désiré DALLOZ et al. (eds.). |
| DPKP | Dziennik Praw Królestwa Polskiego [Journal of Laws of the Kingdom of Poland] |
| DPKW | Dziennik Praw Księstwa Warszawskiego [Journal of Laws of the Duchy of Warsaw] |
| E.R. | English Reports |
| ER | English Reports |
| E.D.N.Y. | United States District Court for the Eastern District of New York |
| Eng. Rep. | English Reports |
| F. 3d | Federal Reporter, Third Series |
| F. Supp. | Federal Supplement |
| F. Supp. 2d | Federal Supplement, Second Series |
| FIRA | Fontes Iuris Romani Anteiustiniani |
| G. | Institutes of Gaius |
| Greene | G. Greene's Reports (Iowa) |
| Kan. | Kansas Reports |

| | |
|---|---|
| KWH | Ustawa o księgach wieczystych i hipotece z dnia 6 lipca 1982 r. [Act of 6 July 1982 on Land and Mortgage Registers and on Mortgage] |
| Lloyd's Rep | Lloyds Law Reports |
| M. | MacPherson's Session Casses |
| Mass. | Massachusetts Reports |
| Mor. | Morrison's Dictionary of Decisions in the Court of Session, Scotland (1540–1808) |
| Ohio St. | Ohio State Reports |
| QB | Queen's Bench Reports |
| R. | Reports |
| S.C. (H.L.) | Court of Session Cases (Scotland) (House of Lords) |
| S.D. Ind. | United States District Court for the Southern District of Indiana |
| S.D.N.Y. | United States District Court for the Southern District of New York |
| SIREY | *Recueil général des lois...*, Jean-Baptiste SIREY et al. (eds.). |
| U.S. | Reports of Cases in the Supreme Court of USA |
| U.S.C. | United States Code |
| W.D. Mo. | United States District Court for the Western District of Missouri |
| WLR | Weekly Law Reports |
| ZGB | Schweizerisches Zivilgesetzbuch |

# Notes on Contributors

### Michał Gałędek
Ph.D. (2010), University of Gdańsk, is Professor in the Department of Legal History, Faculty of Law and Administration. In his research he focuses on the Polish administration, judiciary, codification, constitutionalism, and political thought at the beginning of 19th century and in the interwar period.

### Katrin Kiirend-Pruuli
PhD candidate, University of Tartu (Estonia), is also a judicial clerk at Tartu County Court. Her main area of research is Estonian Private Law in Interwar period.

### Anna Klimaszewska
Ph.D. (2011), University of Gdańsk, is Assistant Professor in the Department of Legal History, Faculty of Law and Administration. In her research she focuses on the influence exerted by the French law on the shape of the Polish legal system, commercial law, civil procedure and national legal identity in the 19th century.

### Łukasz Jan Korporowicz
Ph.D (2015), is Assistant Professor in the Department of Roman Law, Faculty of Law and Administration, University of Łódź. His main fields of research are: influence of the Roman law on English law (especially since 1700), English legal history and Roman law as an important factor in the developing of medieval canon law.

### Beata J. Kowalczyk
Ph.D. (2012), University of Gdańsk, is Assistant Professor in Department of Roman Law, Faculty of Law and Administration. She has published articles on Roman jurisprudence, Roman legal tradition, land law and comparative law including a monography USUCAPIO. *The Roman Origin of the Modern Institution of Usucaption* (UG Publishing, 2016).

### Marju Luts-Sootak
dr. iur. (2000), University of Tartu (Estonia), is a Professor of Legal History. Her main areas of research are History of Jurisprudence, Legal History of Estonia, History of the Faculty of Law of University of Tartu, Philosophy of Law and Methods of Legal Thinking.

NOTES ON CONTRIBUTORS

*Marcin Michalak*

Ph.D (2017), is an assistant professor at the Department of History of Law at the Faculty of Law and Administration of the University of Gdańsk. He focuses his research on the history of medical law and comparative analyses of the development of American and European law in the nineteenth century. He has published monographs, translations and many articles in this area.

*Annamaria Monti*

Ph.D. (1999), is Professor of Legal History at Bocconi University, Milan, Italy. She authored three books (*I formulari del Senato di Milano (secoli* XVI–XVIII), Milano, 2001; *Iudicare tamquam deus. I modi della giustizia senatoria nel Ducato di Milano tra Cinque e Settecento*, Milano, 2003; *Angelo Sraffa. Un antiteorico del diritto*, Milano 2011) and several essays and articles on the history of justice, the history of legal thought, the history of 19th-20th century commercial law and on comparative legal history.

*Zsuzsanna Peres*

Ph.D. (2009), National University of Public Service, is Associate Professor of Legal History at the Faculty of Science of Public Governance and Administration at that University. Previously, she was an Assistant Professor at the Legal Faculty of the University of Pécs, where she had earned her J.D. and Ph.D. Her current fields of research are comparative and Hungarian private law in the 16th to 18th centuries, Hungarian marriage property law of the aristocracy, the family fideicommissa, and the public administration of the feudal Hungarian state. She is fluent in five languages and author of approximately sixty academic publications.

*Sara Pilloni*

PhD in Comparative Law (curriculum Roman Law) at the University of Palermo, ESCLH member, since 2014 is teaching assistant and exam committee member for Roman Private Law Course at the University of Trieste, in collaboration with Prof. Mario Fiorentini. Her last article is "Actio aquae pluviae arcendae ed obbligo di patientiam praestare in presenza di un agger naturalis. Su Paul. 49 ad ed., D. 39, 3, 2, 5–6" (BIDR, 2018).

*Hesi Siimets-Gross*

*dr. iur.* (2011), University of Tartu (Estonia), is an Associate Professor of Roman Law and Legal History. Her main areas of research are Roman Private Law and its Reception, Estonian Legal History, Incipience and Abolition of Serfdom.

### Sean Thomas

Ph.D. (2008), Durham University, is Associate Professor at the Durham Law School (from September 2019, University of York, Reader at the York Law School). He has published on the historical development of commercial law in the long nineteenth century. More generally he is interested in the nature of ownership and ownership disputes in personal property. He also has interests in law and the circular economy, and the impact of smart technology on ownership.

### Bart Wauters

Ph.D. (2004), is assistant professor of European Legal History at IE Law School (Madrid). His latest book, co-authored with Marco de Benito, is *History of the Law in Europe: an Introduction* (Edward Elgar, 2017).

### Steven Wilf

J.D., Ph.D. (1995), Anthony J. Smits Professor of Global Commerce at the Law School of the University of Connecticut. His published books include *Law=s Imagined Republic: Popular Politics and Criminal Justice in Revolutionary America* (Cambridge University Press, 2010) and *Global Patent Cultures: Diversity and Harmonization in Historical Perspective* (edited with Graeme Gooday; Cambridge University Press, 2019).

### Mingzhe Zhu

Ph.D. (2015), is Associate Professor, China University of Political Science & Law, Beijing (100088).

CHAPTER 1

# Introduction: Modernisation, National Identity, and Legal Instrumentalism

*Michał Gałędek*

## 1 Approach

"Law is politics under another guise."[1] One of the approaches in historical legal research is to consider the history of law in the context of the aims which the law was supposed to serve. The instrumental application of legal tools in the implementation of certain aims may be connected with the execution of various political, social and economic programmes, be they short- or long-term, simple or complex, opportunistic or ideological. Every programme is based on an idea, a thought, a doctrine, on ideology and axiology, i.e. on the factors decisive in the process of establishing aims and their valuation. An attempt to distinguish modernisation or (national) identity aims is a capacious, general method of aim classification. In both cases we speak about aims which are, by nature, ideological, usually long-term and complex, and often based on extensive programmes for social, economic and political transformation (engineering). Legal instruments (tools) constitute not the sole, but a fundamental way of implementing modernisation or (national) identity ideology, as well as a natural consequence of the persons executing these programmes coming to power. In the case of legal modernisation, they first deem the existing reality (social, economic or political relations) unacceptable and obsolete, presenting the vision of a desirable new reality and selecting the tools, including legal ones, for transforming the current state of affairs. In this way they create a certain modernisation model. In turn, the executors of identity aims focus their attention on the needs of the community, with which they identify themselves, establishing the ways it can be consolidated and to strengthen its spirit and vitality. For this purpose, they try to define the values which should be promoted and the instruments which should be selected to create a friendly environment (conditions and mechanisms) for cultivating and developing identity ideas. The extent of the ideologisation of the law may therefore vary, depending

---

1  J.M. KELLY: *A Short History of Western Legal Theory*, Clarendon Press, Oxford, 1992, 432.

on the programme, strength and determination of the authority striving for modernisation, or on the degree of consolidation of a community.

## 2    Progressiveness of Modern Law

The history of law over the previous several centuries may be considered as the history of the increasing expansion of Western European legal and intellectual culture, reaching the most far-removed parts of the globe. One of the epochal turns of Western civilisation was the Enlightenment revolution in outlook which took place in the Western world and then began to spread to other regions, together with the dynamic technological development, capitalist economy, extension of the state apparatus and the development of science. All this resulted in a permanent change in the manner of perceiving the world, and in the consolidation of cosmopolitan ideas. Together with the economic and political expansion of the West accelerated in the 19th century, this resulted in the supremacy of the Western outlook on social, economic and political development. At the same time, modernisation and identity-national ideologies were also gaining popularity.

Moreover, as it was noticed in this book by Bart Wauters, who focused in his chapter on the issue of theories of property in the American and French Revolutions: "Especially in periods of political revolution, law often plays a highly instrumental role in giving shape to the new revolutionary society. Revolution means almost by definition a great change in the political and social conditions, and is often an opportunity to set up political and legal structures that supposedly improve the framework for political and legal decision-making. The law is the perfect instrument to capture the fundamental ideas that underlie the new revolutionary framework."[2]

The development of law, which took place over the last two centuries, also results from rapid post-Enlightenment transformations of legal systems and cultures, first in Western Europe (although these were rooted in previous periods), and then – with shorter or longer delays – across the world. It was a result of the increasing dominance of European legal culture on other continents, often connected with colonialism. Modern law, which was created as a result of those transformations, as well as the changing legal culture assumed

---

2    Bart WAUTERS: *Revolution and the Instrumentality of Law. Theories of Property in the American and French Revolutions*, Chapter 3 in this volume.

INTRODUCTION

characteristics different than those of traditional legal orders.[3] Hence the modern legal environment is, on principle, focused on the achievement of certain aims and, by its very nature, legitimises the actions of actors creating and interpreting law in order to implement a certain political, social and economic programme. While the traditional legal systems and traditional legal cultures are static, the modern paradigm assumes the progressiveness of systems characterised by dynamic changes determined by the pressures of modernisation, the latter increasing together with the expansion of the Western post-Enlightenment outlook on the world. At the periphery, this pressure results from the feeling of backwardness and the need to transform the social, economic or political spheres in accordance with the established Western modernisation model. The legal cultures of Western Europe and of the United States are regarded as being better developed and thus worth following for elites cherishing dreams about "successful passage from the periphery to the centre, from the backwardness to civilisation, from the feudality to modernity."[4]

## 3 Enlightenment Breakthrough

It was Enlightenment ideology that began to attach particular importance to law as the most important instrument for the realisation of progressive goals.[5] Belief in the significance of this tool was strengthened by the feeling that, in the rational (i.e. orderly and systematic) development of a legal order, particularly by way of the implementation of codification and constitutionalist ideas, this instrument may be almost perfect. Hence the legal system which serves to secure rights and freedoms of citizens should comprehensively regulate all areas of life, while the legislator should foresee all kinds of situations and, in particular, foresee all kinds of human behaviour, so that they can be directed towards implementation of the assumed ideological aim (social or political).[6]

---

3 Henry S. MAINE: *Dissertations on Early Law and Customs*, John Murray, London, 1883, 109–165.

4 Manuel GUȚAN: *The Legal Transplant and the Building of the Romanian Legal Identity in the Second Half of the 19th Century and the Beginning of the 20th century*, Romanian Journal of Comparative Law, 8(2017)/1, 64.

5 Michał GAŁEDEK: *Juridification as an Ideology of Polizeiwissenschaft in the 18th Century*, Journal on European History of Law, 8(2017)/1, 79–80. However, the early modern state was already "a legislative state" in the European centre (most developed West European countries). Michael STOLLEIS: *The Eye of the Law = idem, The Eye of the Law. Two Essays on Legal History*, Brickbeck Law Press, New York, 2009, 34.

6 Heikki PIHLAJAMÄKI: *Private Law Codification, Modernisation, and Nationalism: A View from Critical Legal History*, Critical Analysis of Law 135(2015)/2, 138; Aniceto MASFERRER:

Thus, Enlightenment ideology promoted the further development of modern law, "its positivism or rather its normative nature, concretely directing behaviour."[7]

Among the main determinants of the transformations ("vehicles of legal modernisation") taking place over the last two centuries, which are the issue of the Enlightenment revolution in outlook, it is necessary to include, on the one hand (1) modern constitutionalism (with the rule of law at the forefront), which crystallised mainly under the influence of liberalism, and (2) the ideology of codification,[8] and on the other hand, (3) growing juridification tendencies,[9] and (4) new techniques of legal interpretation[10] together with (5) the "vigorous development of legal scholarship."[11] The legal systems formed in accordance with this Western European model consist of constitutional law, legal philosophy and legal science, which also constitute the basis for the principles and rules of civil and criminal law and procedure.

The dynamic processes of transformation in the legal and juridical world, taking place under the influence of the driving forces mentioned above were also – or perhaps mainly – the result of an unprecedented progress in civilisation, of the expansion of capitalist markets and of democratisation processes accelerating since 19th century. They were accompanied by crystallisation of new ideological trends, as well as by the dynamic development, not only of

---

*Codification of Spanish Criminal Law. A Comparative Legal History Approach*, Journal of Comparative Law, 4 (2009), 96–104.

7     Kálmán KULCSÁR: *Modernization and Law*, Budapest, Akadémiai Kiadó 1992, 112.

8     PIHLAJAMÄKI: *Private Law Codification…, op. cit.*, 135–152; Aniceto MASFERRER: *Tradition and Foreign Influences in the 19th Century Codification of Criminal Law: Dispelling the Myth of the Pervasive French Influence in Europe and Latin America = The Western Codification of Criminal Law. A Revision of the Myth of its Predominant French Influence*, Aniceto MASFERRER (ed.), Springer, Cham, 2018, 5–11; Damiano CANALE: *The Many Faces of the Codification of Law in Modern Continental Europe = A Treatise of Legal Philosophy and General Jurisprudence*, Enrico PATTARO, Damiano CANALE, Paolo GROSSI, Hasso HOFMANN, Patrick RILEY (eds.), vol. 9: *A History of the Philosophy of Law in the Civil Law World*, Springer, Dordrecht-Heidelberg-London-New York, 2009, 136–142.

9     GAŁĘDEK: *Juridification as an Ideology…, op. cit.*, 76–84.

10    Michael STOLLEIS: *Judicial Interpretation in Transition from the Ancien Régime to Constitutionalism = Interpretation of Law in the Age of Enlightenment. From the Rule of the King to the Rule of Law*, Yasutomo MORIGIWA, Michael STOLLEIS, Jean-Louis HALPÉRIN (eds.), Springer, Dordrecht-Heidelberg-London-New York, 2011, 3–20.

11    *Legal Books in the Early Modern Western World = The Formation and Transmission of Western Legal Culture: 150 Books that Made the Law in the Age of Printing*, Serge DAUCHY, Georges MARTYN, Anthony MUSSON, Heikki PIHLAJAMÄKI, Alain WIJFELLS (eds.), Springer, Cham, 2016, 64; Jean-Louis HALPÉRIN: *Five Legal Revolutions since 17th Century. An Analysis of Global History*, Springer, New York-London, 2014, 23–30; PIHLAJAMÄKI: *Private Law Codification…, op. cit.*, 136, 139.

INTRODUCTION

legal science, but also of sociology, economics and political science. All of these exert a great influence on law. Another factor was the positive law system, continuously expanding and introducing into social reality an increasingly dense network of more and more elaborate and precise legal regulations. It has always constituted the foundation of 19th-century lawful liberal states and later of the 20th-century democratic states. The same holds true also for some authoritarian or totalitarian regimes, which formally also observed the rule of law or created the appearance of it being observed. This legal system was developed in individual countries in accordance with a certain model determined, on the one hand (as previously mentioned) by constitutionalism, and on the other hand by efforts of the codification movement. They went along with the need to proceduralise life in public space, as well as by, first and foremost, the need to put the tightest possible corset of legal norms on the activities of state bodies.

The ideological basis for that entire modern concept of state and law was formed in the Age of Enlightenment reconfiguring and adding new liberal or even democratic ideas as well as constitutional and codification themes to previously well-ordered early modern states.[12] This happened in accordance with the assumptions regarding the approach to the foundations of social life and the public sphere, that crystallised at that time. Afterwards, the social transformation which was concomitant with the transition from the feudal system to capitalism, and with the formation of new social classes (the middle class, the proletariat), accompanied by the necessity to redefine social needs, had its reminiscences directed towards revolutionary or evolutionary legal transformation.[13]

The universalistic progressive ideas of the Enlightenment era introduced new content into modern legal systems, which produced, at the time they were implemented, i.e. mainly during the Age of Revolution at the turn of the 19th century, "a sudden swing from one legal system to another" (mostly due to the liquidation of the feudal legal system, the secularisation of law and the political transformation of countries that resulted from the development of remoulded constitutionalism and cosmopolitan liberalism). Previously, starting with the Middle Ages, "Western legal systems had evolved without great ruptures."[14]

---

12  HALPÉRIN: *op. cit.*, 1–10.

13  Peter G. STEIN: *Legal Evolution: The Story of an Idea*, Cambridge University Press, Cambridge (UK), 1980, IX.

14  HALPÉRIN: *op. cit.*, x–xi.

Despite these fundamental changes, the continuity of development in Western legal culture was maintained.[15] The foundations of Western legal culture were firmly rooted in the heritage of the early modern era, although the common ideological-legal roots reached deeper – to the Middle Ages and the philosophical-legal thought of antiquity, which. It had been newly rediscovered at that time together with the achievements of Roman law. As a result, post-Enlightenment legal transition "did not occur at random, but proceeded by conscious reinterpretation of the past to meet present and future needs."[16] Therefore, the legal achievements of Western Europe from previous centuries were actually not rejected, but still constituted an important component of the modernised legal order in Western countries in the 19th century. The normative material from the pre-Enlightenment Ancien Régime was often, as in the case of Napoleonic codification, incorporated in the codes which officially repudiated the achievements of those times[17] Consequently, the revolution in outlook associated with popularisation of the Enlightenment thought changed the course of legal systems development, but "ultimately remained with it, thus deciding about the existence of ongoing historical continuity between past and future and [...] the organic development of legal institutions over generations of its predecessors."[18]

## 4      Legal Transformation at Revolutionary Times

The rational cosmopolitanism of the Enlightenment only served to strengthen the relatively homogeneous character of Western European legal culture,

---

15      Harold J. BERMAN: *Law and Revolution*, vol. 2: *The Impact of the Protestant Reformations on the Western Legal Tradition*, Harvard University Press, Cambridge (MA)-London, 2006, 2.

16      *Ibid.*, 3.

17      Rodolfo BATIZA: *The French Revolution and Codification: Comment on the Enlightenment, the French Revolution, and the Napoleonic Codes*, Valpariso University Law Review 18(1984), 680.

18      BERMAN: *op. cit.*, 2–3. As Berman noticed: the Western legal tradition formed on the on the basis of "the historically developing culture of the peoples of Europe, who, from the early twelfth to the early sixteenth centuries, shared a common and political subordination, as well as a common religious subordination, to the papal hierarchy of the Roman Catholic Church, and who from the sixteenth to the twentieth century experienced a series of great national Revolutions, each of which was directed partly against Roman Catholicsm and each of which had repercussions throughout of Europe." Compare: Michał GAŁĘDEK, Anna KLIMASZEWSKA: *A Controversial Transplant? Debate over the Adaptation of the Napoleonic Code on the Polish Territories in the Early 19th Century*, Journal of Civil Law Studies 11(2018)/2, 287.

INTRODUCTION                                                                                    7

although the division between common law systems and legal orders in continental countries, which had been clearly visible before, was maintained.[19] Afterwards, beginning in the 19th century, that Western European legal model – in its common law or continental legal systems – also was spread across the world by colonisation or by cultural and political affinity and interaction.[20] During the formative phase of the post-liberation of many new European as well as non-European postcolonial statehoods in the 19th and 20th century *modern* meant *European*.

> "Europe" could serve first, as a normative ideology; second, as legitimation strategy of [...] elites for generating support for legal reform and legal and political modernisation and thus as a source of political and legal argumentation and third, as a source of inspiration for transplantation, reception, institutional and idea migration and for conceptual legal reform.[21]

The revolutionary moments in the history of individual regions of the world were connected with different factors, like the establishment of autocratic regimes and their downfall followed by democratisation; colonisation and then decolonisation; or with the implementation of socialist ideology and then its bankruptcy. Due to these factors, some countries were suddenly pulled into the sphere of influence of Western European culture, which was coupled with attempts to destroy native culture. This, in turn, could bring about a revolutionary reaction to this sudden clash with a foreign social model and provoke the desire to restore "traditional values." All these sudden political and socioeconomic turns constituted breakthroughs in the development of the societies in which they took place, related to the intensified establishment of new aims for the restructuring of existing relations. Revolutions, understood in this way, aimed at "rapid advancement of the processes already unfolding, [and] were directed towards overcoming the disadvantages deriving from backwardness, towards the upgrading of economic development and the creation of qualitative changes in society and political order."[22]

Law is a traditional and basic tool for performing fundamental transformations. Material changes of the existing legal order during a revolution lead to

---

19   Cf. WAUTERS: *op. cit.*
20   BERMAN: *op. cit.*, 3.
21   Martin BELOV: *The Idea of "Europe" as a Factor in the Building of the Bulgarian Legal Identity*, Romanian Journal of Comparative Law 8(2017)/1, 44.
22   KULCSÁR: *op. cit.*, 174.

"a great shift," "an epochal turn" within the range of political, social and economic relations. This occurs due to the fact that there are two particular attitudes which may be observed not only in the wake of the Enlightenment revolution, but of all subsequent ones as well. The first is rejection of law, and the second is excessive trust in legal regulations. Following this assumption, "rejection of law was expressed partly by the theoretical refutation of old law," while the revolution "necessarily turns against the existing state organisation and legal system." On the other hand, the above-mentioned "trust in legal regulations associates illusions with the utilisation of law" and results in the "dominance of the law-maker's autocracy."[23]

However, revolution is characterised by different legal and socio-political conditions, and the attitude held toward it by the elites and societies of the European centre differs from that in other countries that adopted elements of Western legal tradition in the 19th and 20th centuries. It is true for semi-peripheral countries (such as those in Central-Eastern Europe or Latin America), which had previously been within the sphere of influence of Western Europe.[24] It is different still in peripheral states (dependent and colonial, mostly African and Asian[25]), which only encountered the Western European model of functioning of the legal order in the last two centuries. As a result, the consequences of legal revolutions are also different. Revolutionary reconstruction of the existing order has always occupied an integral place in the development (see the Bart Wauters chapter). However, in contrast to the Western European centre, the strenuous transformation of peripheral and semi-peripheral countries was, to a much greater extent, performed in an alien manner and directed against traditional values, as well as the existing foundations of socio-economic relations and political conditions.[26] What is more, semi-peripheral countries differed from the peripheral ones in that the law-making power was not completely alien to their citizens.[27] Hence it was not, sensu stricto, a colonial situation, but it constituted another model for the use of law as a tool of

---

23     *Ibid.*, 175.

24     It is depicted well in the chapter by Zsuzsanna PERES: *Prenuptial Agreements of the Hungarian Aristocracy in the Early Modern Era*, Chapter 2 in this volume.

25     Bertrand BADIE: *The Imported State. The Westernization of the Political Order*, Stanford University Press, Stanford, 2000, 146–156.

26     GUȚAN: *The Legal Transplant and the Building of the Romanian Legal Identity...*, *op. cit.*, 74–77; Michał GAŁĘDEK, Anna KLIMASZEWSKA: *The Implementation of French Codes on the Polish Territories as an Instrument of Modernization – Identifying Problems with Selected Examples = Le droit comparé et.../Comparative Law and... Actes de la conférence annuelle de Juris Diversitas*, Alexis ALBARIAN, Olivier MORÉTEAU (eds.), Presses Univérsitaires d Aix-Marseille, Aix-Marseille, 2015, 82–84.

27     KULCSÁR: *op. cit.*, 105, 143–145.

INTRODUCTION 9

development, more complex and employed, based on the principle of contrast and opposition between the local traditions and entirely foreign, new forms, to a much lesser degree.

In Central-Eastern Europe, in countries such as Poland (see chapters by Anna Klimaszewska and Michał Gałędek) or Hungary (see chapters by Zsuzsanna Peres and Judit Beke-Martos) or in South America, for example in Brazil (see chapter by Marjorie Carvalho de Souza), such phenomena could be observed in the 19th century, during the transformations wrought at that time.[28] They were modelled on Western European transformations and were connected with transplantation of basic elements of the Western legal order, such as codes or constitutional acts, onto new territories. A similar phenomenon could be observed in the 19th and 20th centuries in various other places in the world where, mainly, but not only through colonial expansionism, the processes of Europeanisation caused much greater shocks. Revolutionary transformations struck at the foundations of the existing social life, or at least were perceived as real threat to the basis of existence, on which the identity of a given community had hitherto been built. That is why they resulted in natural social resistance. It was much easier to neutralise that resistance and to assimilate the introduced changes if

> certain traditional elements were activated. Several factors reveal that processes of appropriation and adaptation are at work in the sphere of law more than elsewhere (like in politics or economy), and to such an extent as to produce more dysfunction. The rule of law belongs first of all to a domain were formalisation takes on a very particular operative importance: a written law or procedure reflects not only a system of values but also a more or less performative technical design that derives from a history and a culture.[29]

---

28 Manuel GUȚAN: *The Legal Transplant as Socio-Cultural Engineering in Modern Romania* = *Konflikt und Koexistenz. Die Rechtsordnungen Südosteuropas im 19. und 20. Jahrhundert*, Michael STOLLEIS, Gerd BENDER, Jani KIROV (eds.), Band 1: *Rumänien, Bulgarien, Griechenland*, Vittorio Klostermann, Frankfurt a.M., 2015, 500–503; GAŁĘDEK, KLIMASZEWSKA: *A Controversial Transplant?..., op. cit.*; M.C. MIROW: *The Power of Codification in Latin America: Simón Bolívar and the Code Napoléon*, Tulane Journal of International and Comparative Law, 93(2000), 90–97; M.C. MIROW: *Latin American Law: A History of Private Law and Institutions in Spanish America*, University of Texas Press, Austin, 2004, 128–129, 142; Agustin PARISE: *Ownership Paradigms in American Civil Law Jurisdictions: Manifestations of the Shifts in Legislation of Louisiana, Chile, and America (16th–20th Centuries*, Brill Nijhoff, Leiden-Boston, 2017, 267–268.

29 BADIE: *op. cit.*, 146.

Skilful policy which masked the revolutionary character of the introduced changes increased the adaptive capacity of the society and its capability to adjust to rapid changes. In other words, a law-maker involved in the fundamental transformation of the existing order, when interfering with the basis of prevailing relations, was constrained by the need to satisfy the identity expectations of the society and was not supposed to "mould the society towards the goal of modernisation only in accordance with the criteria of technical and economic efficiency."[30]

## 5    Between Modernisation and National Identity

In light of the above, one might ask what, generally speaking, is the characteristic feature of the process of the development of legal culture in Europe and in those regions of the world which have been under the influence of the expansionism of Western legal culture for the past two centuries. When preparing this volumes for publication, we were guided by the assumption that in the foreground one can observe two main determinants of legal development (which also facilitate classification of other features, usually deriving from and closely connected with them). On the one hand, it is the continuously felt pressure to modernise, to transform the existing reality, to wipe out backwardness in terms of civilisation with the use of modern tools, among which the modernised legal order played a key role. That trend was particularly deeply rooted in Enlightenment philosophy, in the feeling of backwardness, in the intellectual climate of that era, permeated with the optimistic belief in overcoming that state of affairs by way of rational selection of the means for social, political and economic transformation.[31] Enlightenment ideology consolidated the belief that mastering the law will somehow magically produce social change.[32] Afterwards, starting in the 19th century, pressure toward modernisation was activated by liberal doctrine and later by subsequent progressive ideologies, such as communism, socialism or human rights ideology, seeking to

---

30    KULCSÁR: *op. cit.*, 178–179; GUȚAN: *The Legal Transplant as Socio-Cultural Engineering...*, *op. cit.*, 504–505.

31    Paul HAZARD: *European Thought in the Eighteen Century: from Montesquieu to Lessing*, World Publishing Company, Cleveland, 1963, 442–444; Jerzy JEDLICKI: *A Suburb of Europe. Nineteenth-century Polish Approaches to Western Civilization*, Central European University Press, Budapest, 1999, 10–12.

32    GUȚAN: *The Legal Transplant as Socio-Cultural Engineering, op. cit.*, 499.

INTRODUCTION

reform the world and believing in the possibility of almost unlimited social engineering.[33]

In contrast to the programmes which aimed at thorough (revolutionary) transformation of the existing, unacceptable reality, conservatism as well as reactionary doctrines were being formed. It was the codification (as well as the constitution and other ideas and factors of the legal revolution from the early 19th century) to be "very much part and parcel of the liberalist agenda, whereas conservatives [and reactionaries] tended to oppose the idea because of its inherent threat of reform."[34] The traditionalists referred to the past, justifying either petrification of the existing state of affairs or, at the most, gradual evolution of social and economic relations, as well as of the political system, but without repudiating the national heritage or renouncing the elements constituting the native tradition.[35] Thus, more or less at the same time when the post-Enlightenment revolution in the legal world was beginning (at the turn of the 19th century), the preservative thought, focused on searching for national elements in legal culture, referring to the traditions of native law, promoting the idea of the organic growth of law and its evolutionary development, started to consolidate. This approach, defined by the maxim "for a rule to be a good law, it has to conform not to abstract reason, but to the spirit of the society to which it is to be applied," had previously been professed by Charles Montesquieu, and was later popularised mainly by the representatives of the German historical school of law from the early 19th century onwards. Their believe in the naturally evolved and ever-developing law of the people rooted in the *Volskgeist* and in the romantic idea of the German nation was shared by leaders of other nations.[36]

Referring to the tradition and national spirit of law, conservatism found common ground with nationalism as a movement and ideology which had grown on the ground of national ideas, and was strengthening its position in the process of building nation-state on a worldwide scale since the end of the

---

33   Markus D. DUBBER: *Colonial Criminal Law and Other Modernities* = *The Oxford Handbook of European Legal History*, Heikki PIHLAJAMÄKI, Markus D. DUBBER, Mark GODFREY (eds.), Oxford University Press, Oxford, 2018, 915–916.

34   PIHLAJAMÄKI: *Private Law Codification..., op. cit.*, 148.

35   STEIN: *op. cit.*, X.

36   R.C. VAN CAENEGEM: *European Law in the Past and the Future. Unity and Diversity over Two Millennia*, Cambridge University Press, Cambridge (UK), 2001, 94; Michał GAŁĘDEK: *The Problem of Non-Adaptability of National Legal Heritage. Discussion on the Reform of Civil Law in Poland in the Course of Work of Reform Committee in 1814*, Romanian Journal of Comparative Law 8(2017)/1, 12.

19th century.[37] Nationalism, to an even greater extent than conservatism, emphasised the necessity to cultivate the trends in identity which served to strengthen the national community. Focused on internal consolidation of a given national community, it searched for ways to achieve that goal, defining the components that constitute the national tradition. That determined the turn towards the past and towards the elements which were regarded as native. As a result, a negative attitude arose towards the law which came from the outside and, more generally, to any universally oriented ideas, accompanied by the emphasis placed on the values of old laws as the carrier of national legal tradition and the foundation of national legal identity.[38]

The issue of modernisation, as well as that of national identity may be understood, in relation to law, in two different ways. On the one hand, as law (legal norms), it may be perceived as an instrument used to modernise or nationalise reality (modernisation or consolidation of national identity performed through law). On the other hand, a legal system in itself may conform to the standards of what is considered to be progressive (modernisation or nationalisation of law). That is why both the formation and strengthening of national identity and the achievement of the goals of modernisation may be connected either with the way in which law is created, or with the specific character of how it is applied or taught. Both in the process of establishing laws and in the process of applying them implementation of widely understood national aims requires consideration and determination of specific national features, traditions, social relations, the degree of economic development, etc. In a word, everything that is perceived as unique for a given nationality, and particularly those things which are adjusted to its requirements and serve to strengthen the power and pride of the nation.

The need to strengthen the nation may result in affirmation of modernisation ideology among nationalists as well, who perceive in the progressive approach an opportunity to increase the nation's power and potential. However, modernisation was not supposed to jeopardise national goals, the internal integrity of the community or its basic values, in which a fundamental role was played by the history and traditions of a given nation. Progress and modernisation, therefore, had to remain in harmony with cultivation of national tradition and serve it. The problem with reconciling modernisation and identity aims resulted from the very nature of these, even though those two types of

---

37  GUȚAN: *The Legal Transplant as Socio-Cultural Engineering...*, *op. cit.*, 498; VAN CAENEGEM: *op. cit.*, 1, 33.

38  Lloyd S. KRAMER: *Nationalism in Europe and America: Politics, Cultures, and Identities since 1775*, University of North Carolina, Chapel Hill, 2011, 13–28.

INTRODUCTION

aims were not always necessarily in conflict. That antagonism resulted from the Enlightenment origin of modernisation ideology which, with its aspiration from the very beginning to universality, placed first conservatives and then nationalists in opposition to it.[39]

Popularisation of Enlightenment ideology[40] played a key role in relation to the pressure of modernisation, which emerged in modern times first in Europe and then in other areas of the world. Its advocates were, as a rule, focused on social transformation achieved in accordance with legal-natural standards – eternal, unyielding, general, same for all times, places and countries.[41] Enlightened intellectual elites and their followers in subsequent generations sought to elaborate a certain single supra-national universal measure of values and model for progress. Progressivists questioned the attempts at becoming closed within the borders of one's own nation and deprecated the need to care for a limited national community; moreover, they frequently renounced national historical tradition as obsolete and serving to maintain the existing state of affairs, which was seen as in need of change and modernisation.

The universal character of the "natural order of things," common to all of humanity and all nations, implied an assumption that transformation of reality, including that of legal systems and legal culture, should be achieved following one and the same direction for all countries and nations. In many cases, occidental legal transformation took place under both external political pressures (colonialism as well as geopolitical situation) and an underdeveloped nation surrendering;[42] however, one of these forces alone could be quite sufficient in particular conditions. It was therefore necessary not to look back, but to use foreign models and draw from the reformist achievements of those countries which had already managed to reach a higher stage in their development; that approach was therefore West-oriented. Enlightenment and post-Enlightenment universalism thus constituted the beginning of the ideological Westernisation of the world and, in a way, superseded Christianity in its mission to rebuild every corner or the world after its own fashion.

The theory of a "peculiar national spirit" may have constituted one extreme and a reaction to the uncritical universalist appeal of the Enlightenment. In the same way defining the direction of modernisation in accordance

---

39    PIHLAJAMÄKI: *Private Law Codification...*, *op. cit.*, 136.

40    Nonetheless "a great shift" in several Western countries – the most developed and those designing the path of global legal development – had already begun earlier, at least since the seventeenth century and the legal constructions of the first modern states. HALPÉRIN: *op. cit.*, xii, 1–10.

41    GAŁĘDEK: *The Problem of Non-Adaptability...*, *op. cit.*, 11.

42    GUȚAN: *The Legal Transplant and the Building of the Romanian Legal Identity...*, *op. cit.*, 64.

with foreign achievements, without taking into consideration specific local conditions, also raised doubts with regard to the uncompromising character of this reform strategy, which was implemented with the use of legal instruments or other tools serving to achieve either socio-economic or political transformations.

> The Enlightenment aimed at being universal, but instead it acquired the stigma of foreignness. Those who had the enthusiasm and skills to become the spiritual leaders of nations that were politically weak or fragmented, economically backward because of their feudal legacy, and culturally peripheral – the Spanish, the Germans, the Hungarians or the Poles – therefore faced a difficult dilemma. They could, of course, adopt the ready-made intellectual accoutrements, the contemporary European canon [...] and, clad in this armor, fight for [...] the reform of government, for a modern, developing society. [...] They could also do the reverse: they could shape the cultural make-up of their own people and their political system by drawing on the resources of their own petrified traditions, traditions which were opposed to the intellectual supremacy of the West – but in this case the price to be paid was the hampering of social change. [...] The true reformers of national culture had to opt for a middle course if they wanted to implant Western universalist ideas into minds that had been accustomed to different nourishment, and if they wanted to galvanize themselves and their compatriots into independent, creative action. The strategy of 'nationalizing progress,' so characteristic of the Late Enlightenment, meant a synthesis of the new and that which was native or had long been assimilated, a synthesis of the ideals of universal reason and the palpable reality of particular legacies, a synthesis which had to be constantly tested both in theory and social practice.[43]

Therefore, legal theories also sought an appropriate balance, for a strategy which, according to Rudolf von Jhering, could enjoy a finely balanced appreciation of conservative and progressive forces. Jhering, and then a large number of his followers, realised that law is directed to achieve certain aims and, consequently, it is orientated to the future as much as to the past. At a higher level of development, which law had reached particularly since the beginning of the 20th century, the tendencies to unify it on global scale and to proceed with its westernisation did not wane, but rather grew in strength. "Universal conceptions replace national ones, and legal institutions, like coins of standard

---

43    JEDLICKI: *op. cit.*, 8–9.

INTRODUCTION

value, circulate from country to country. Thus in progressive societies the law becomes less national and more universal as it develops."[44]

To sum up, it seems that it may be possible to characterise the dynamic development of civilisation that took place in the world over the last two centuries. This world was dominated by European culture which had been redefined by Enlightenment thought, through placing the aims established by the initiators of the development in question in one of the two categories – modernisation or national-identity, and sometimes in both. At the same time, starting from the Enlightenment era and throughout the 19th century, new legal ideologies became crystallised, which was followed by transformation of legal systems and legal cultures. The aims of and methods for achieving these transformations with the use of law were determined by one of two major theoretical-ideological trends, of which one was self-centred and retrospectively oriented, while the other was characterised by a cosmopolitan and progressive. The needs of modernisation, together with the accompanying tendencies to draw on foreign models overlapped with the identity requirements. They were defined through ideas concerning the unique characteristics of a given national spirit and through searching for it by way of referring to native legal tradition and rejecting foreign elements, particularly those perceived as non-assimilated ones.

This collaborative work, which is the result of the 4th Biennial ESCLH Conference "Culture – Identity – Legal Instrumentalism," held in Gdańsk and Gdynia from 28 June to 1 July 2016, consists of texts which concern research, following a common methodological approach, into the transformations taking place in legal cultures around the world. They are achieved under a strong influence of the pursuits of modernisation and identity, as well as of the conflicts. Regardless of the time or region under analysis, they resulted from the two mutually opposed ways of thinking about the goals which ought to be served by law, later determining the direction of that law's evolution.

This pattern becomes visible already in the only chapter of the book that focuses on the Early Modern times. Jiří Brňovják and Marek Starý, who in their text discuss changes in the legal institution of the Inkolat in the Bohemian Crown Lands during the Early Modern Period, analyse them within the context of the influence of the transformations occurring in legal institutions on the political circumstances and the modernisation of state and society. A similar research context underpins the text by Michał Gałędek, who devoted his chapter to the analysis of transformations that took place in the organisation of administration in the Polish territories in late 18th and early 19th centuries.

---

44   STEIN: *op. cit.*, 52, 67–68.

He summarizes his research within the paradigm of modernisation theory with an assessment of the reactions of the Polish political elite to the emergence of modern administration. The desire to return to the native tradition, identified mainly with administrative institutions set up in the late 18th century, clashed with the pragmatic modernizing vision, which dictated retention of the basic foundations on which the French administrative system was based. Also Imre Képessy discusses the practical issues of a national modernisation programme focusing on describing the circumstances surrounding the adoption of the April Laws by the Hungarian Parliament. The author notes how to a great an extent the programme of national modernisation, ushered in by the act, was entangled in the sociopolitical circumstances of Hungary. The modernizing paradigm also comes forward in the research by Tadeusz Maciejewski and Maja Maciejewska-Szałas. They delve into issues concerning political systems, by way of a comparative analysis of constitutional regulations in the Free European States of the inter-war period. The authors focused their attention on showing how the institution of independent cities, whose roots go to medieval Europe, especially Hanseatic towns and northern Italian city-states, in its modernized version found its application in modern Europe.

## 6 Instrumentality of Law

Comparative research in legal history requires definition of the planes on which it may be conducted. The authors considered the role of the law as a reality-forming instrument and focused on the universal issue of how this instrument works and what can be achieved with its aid. This is clearly visible for example in Bart Wauters' article "Revolution and the Instrumentality of Law. Theories of Property in the American and French Revolutions." It depicts how American and French revolutions instrumentalized pre-existing ideas to build a new political and legal framework. Wauters, departing from this assumption, noted that the theories of French and American revolutionary documents were instrumentalized to build a concept of property that made a sharper distinction between public power and private ownership. Similar to Bart Wauters' are the initial assumptions in the comparative research of Mingzhe Zhu. In analysing the legal reforms concerning the family structure during the republican moments of two countries: France (in the late 19th century) and China (in the early 20th century), Zhu points out the legal instrumentalism of both "reformists" and "revolutionaries," who sought to destroy the family, an ancient social institution protected by customs and traditional values. Zsuzsanna Peres tackled a similar research problem in her chapter. She devoted it to the issue of marriage property rights of Hungarian noble women in comparative context.

INTRODUCTION                                                                    17

Her text intends to prove the effect that the Austrian marriage property law
had on Hungarian law in the same legal area between the 17th and the 18th
century. Instrumental use of legal regulation for the achievement of specific
ideological and political purposes is also the focus of Simon Lavis, who presents probably the most glaring example of this problem in his chapter with
the telling title *Nazi Law as Pure Instrument: Natural Law, (Extra-)Legal Terror,
and the Neglect of Ideology*. The author shows how this totalitarian regime used
laws already in effect to pursue specific policies, by way of instrumentalizing
legal standards to serve its agenda. The way in which Lavis approaches his research topic seems to be very familiar to Thomas Mohr, although it could appear that the themes that occupy this latter author's attention have little to do
with the issues explored by Lavis. In his chapter, Mohr focuses on the problems
of instrumental application of law by courts with a view of achieving a certain
jurisprudential strategy. This author examines the evolution of the Judicial
Committee of Privy Council appeal as an instrument of British Imperial policy
during the 19th and early 20th centuries. Mohr argues that the judges of the
Privy Council held similar values and attitudes towards the British Empire as
the politicians who led successive British governments, indicating a number
of methods for the instrumental application of the law. Balázs Pálvölgyi notes
another situation connected with the instrumental application of law. He
turns his attention to Hungarian migration policy under the "direct impact of
the 1870 Agreement on Citizenship between US and Austria-Hungary" in the
period from the 1880s to 1914. Pálvölgyi indicated that in certain situations existing law may present an insurmountable obstacle to effective politics. In circumstances described by the author, the options of the Hungarian government
for pursuing a comprehensive migration policy were limited. Thus, the 1870
Agreement, instead of serving as an effective instrument in the hands of the
government, was indeed a factor that obstructed productive action.

## 7     Legal Transplants

One of the fundamental techniques of legal instrumentalism, keenly and frequently applied over the course of history especially with a view of accomplishing modernizing goals, is the transfer onto new ground of foreign legal
institutions borrowed from countries deemed paragons of modernity. The tur-
bulences that this may give rise to are depicted not only in the aforementioned
chapters by Gałędek and Wilf, but also in a few others.

From the perspective of techniques serving the construction of legal
institutions – or, more broadly – the shaping of legal order, of key importance
was the issue of borrowings (legal transfers) of specific codes, institutions, or

just concepts and ideas in contrast with the development of original solutions or retaining traditional elements of decisive importance for the features of a given legal culture and legal order, elements that had emerged and consolidated on native soil.[45] The key issue for the evaluation of legal transfer in those chapters that focused on this area was most frequently related to the adoption of a "foreign" loaned solution in another setting, under new political, social and economic circumstances and in another legal culture.

This perspective is shared by Annamaria Monti who in the chapter entitled *Italian Destiny of French Code de Commerce* turns her attention to the connections between French and Italian commercial law, studies the impact of foreign laws on the national trajectories and answers the question on how a legal system nourishes itself from exchanges, contacts and interactions with other legal systems. Similar is the nature of research conducted by Anna Klimaszewska in her chapter about reception of the French commercial law in nineteenth-century Polish territories. In Poland the differences stemming from the different practice of applying the French commercial law were much greater than in Italy, which was certainly connected to the specific socioeconomic circumstances and separate legal culture of not only Poland, but of all of Central Eastern Europe. Also Marjorie Carvalho de Souza devotes her chapter to the transfer of foreign patterns, in this case form Europe (Italy) to South America. She addresses the creation of the court of auditors in the First Republic in Brazil in 1889, examining this transplant from the perspective of a technical move enabling rapid establishment in a non-European peripheral territory of a European institution meant to be both a modern one and one satisfying universal standards, and thus suited for adaptation to new conditions.

The problem of adaptation of foreign law is of a universal nature. It comes as no surprise, then, that it constitutes the important research issue also in the chapter by Steven Wilf, even though he devoted it to the evolution of the concept of "moral rights" in the USA over the past quarter of a century, and so to a subject very distant to that of commercial law in the 19th century. It points to the specificity of the system of private law (its different fundamental tenets), as a result of which the transplant to a new system (the American) of legal acts created on the substrate of another (continental European) does not change the nature of the former, but rather results in a flexible absorption of a foreign law which, in isolation from its original background, loses its primary features

---

45    Cf. Sean Thomas' Chapter 4 in this volume: *English Commercial Law in the Longue Durée: Chasing Continental Shadows*. Thomas has undertaken an analysis of various factors affecting the development of English commercial law.

INTRODUCTION

and acquires a life of its own to fit in with the different logic of the American legal system. Marcin Michalak, in turn, focused on the problem of adoption of English common law in the United States of America in the first half of the 19th century. The author, using the example of doctors' liability for inappropriate treatment, attempted to show how local specificity forces creative implementation of legal norms originating from elsewhere, so that they can be of proper use in the new circumstances.

The authors of these chapters have explored the problem of legal transplant by analysing both the scope and method of reception, as well as by assessing the assimilation in the new setting by both society at large, and, even more importantly, by legal and political circles. A similar analytical method is applied by those authors whose research addresses the problem of using Roman law constructions in the process of building modern-era legal institutions. This group of chapters includes texts by Sara Pilloni, Łukasz J. Korporowicz and Beata Kowalczyk. Sara Pilloni focused in her comparative research on how the approach of legal science toward the institution of third-party contracts has evolved over the course of history. In this classic Romanistic approach to this research issue, the primary "creator" perceiving the law as a tool for the accomplishment of specific goals, and thus requiring an appropriately configured set of legal instruments, is first Roman jurisprudence, then the Medieval school of Roman Law (glossators), and then the modern doctrine of private law (Hugo Grotius) and the legislation of the 19th and 20th centuries (code-based solutions in France, Germany, Austria and Italy). Beata J. Kowalczyk's chapter, in turn, offers a comparative legal reflection on the evolution of the Roman institution of usucaption in modern and contemporary Europe. Similarly to Pilloni, Kowalczyk intends to prove that this legal institution is applicable in each legal system, while its detailed inner workings differ depending on the needs of the particular time and country. Łukasz J. Korporowicz, addressing the interactions between common law and continental systems, presents research on the House of Lords case law concerning delictual (tortious) liability. This chapter focuses on examples of using the authority of Roman law texts and ideas by the law lords as regards civilian arguments used in the delictual and tortious cases by the Appellate Committee of the House of Lords between 1932 and 2003.

## 8    How to Match Different Goals?

In the case studies presented, the issue of techniques, or the choice of paths and methods of building the legal order and creating individual institutions, could be determined on the one hand by the objectives that this law and its institutions were to serve. On the other hand, the very choice of methods for shaping the legal system may have been determined by political and ideological goals. Juxtaposing these two groups of mutual correlations between ideology and politics and the law proves that there is a feedback relation between them. In other words, the method for choosing solutions that make up the characteristics of a given legal order may have been ideologically determined in two ways. Thus, the law (code, institution, principle, etc.) may have been adopted or rejected, more or less favourably assessed, owing solely to its place of origin. In other cases, the overarching argument for the adoption of a given law was not its origin at all (and especially its native or foreign source), but the ideological purposes it was to serve. In such events, the decision-maker (primarily the legislator), focused on the aspect of the usefulness of the adopted legal solution and viewed it mainly as an instrument. In situations where the origins of the law were the paramount issue for the decision-maker, it was perceived as something more than a mere tool for the accomplishment of specific objectives. The features of such an instrument were of greater significance than how it would work in practice.

With a focus on axiological and teleological aspects, that is objectives and values that the creators of law expected to achieve with it, the scholars gathered here attempted to universalize their optics, choosing two main groups of objectives served by the law. As a result, while defining the goals achieved with the aid of legal instruments, chapter authors mentioned above (such as Wauters, Gałędek, Képessy, Carvalho de Souza, Klimaszewska or Monti), tried to examine the issue at hand from the perspective of the desire – deeply seated especially in Enlightenment thought – to set out on the path of progress, to "civilize" the world and its people, and to improve and modernize them.

On the other hand, what came to the fore in their texts are objectives aiming to strengthen the community that the stipulated law was to serve. Owing to the dominant tendency for communities and their formative legal orders to be built primarily in states, and for modern states to be built and consolidated around the ideas of national communities (leaving aside whether these are formed according to ethnic criteria or not), scholars assessed legal instruments from the angle of national objectives.

## 9 To Strengthen National Identity

Viewed from this perspective, attempts at strengthening national identity with the use of law as an instrument are clearly visible not only in the aforementioned chapters by Mingzhe Zhu or Jiří Brňovják and Marek Starý, but also in

INTRODUCTION

those authored by Marju Luts-Sootak, Hesi Siimets-Gross and Katrin Kiirend-Pruuli, Judit Beke-Martos, or by Sean Thomas, albeit in a different approach. Luts-Sootak, Siimets-Gross and Kiirend-Pruuli analyse the course of discussions about the Estonian Draft Civil Code 1936/40 from a comparative perspective. The main research goal is made clear in the title itself, since the scholars look at the Civil Code as an instrument for the consolidation of a nation from inside. Analysis of the works conducted over the codification has led the authors to conclude that "although the codification of Estonian private law was originally not motivated by the will to consolidate the nation and to shape the people's legal identity using the tool of codified private law, there was a change in the wake of the nationalistic ideology of the 1930s and those proposing the codification started to omit the goal of consolidation. The chapter by Judit Beke Mertos relates to an entirely different public law issue. Nevertheless, this author also connects her research with the context of strengthening and consolidating Hungarian national identity by way of tapping into tradition and rehashing it in the ceremonial and symbolic sphere. In her text devoted to the history of Hungarian constitutionalism, she focuses on the 1867 royal coronation, considered as the final element that restored the constitutional order in Hungary. National consolidation as the objective of a created legal institution is also the central research issue in the chapter by Ivan Kosnica. He concentrates on local citizenship in the Croatian-Slavonian legal area in the period from 1918 to 1941, pointing out its intimate relationship with the issue of shaping the national legal identity by Yugoslav authorities, under specific conditions typical of states that are not ethnically homogeneous, made up of regions with historically different legal and cultural traditions. As argued by Kosnica, the legal policies pursued by the authorities aimed to annul and separate Croatian legal identity and to promote the uniform Unitarian Yugoslav legal system. Finally, the law may be used an instrument of accomplishing national goals in the process of its natural long-term evolutionary transformation prompted by flexible adjustment to the changing reality. The English law, explored in the chapter by Sean Thomas, is a classic example of such developmental path. This author focused on the development of English commercial law to provide a complex answer to the question of how law, as an institution, can and does respond to commerce, itself an institution.

## 10    Conclusion

To sum up, in this book, the law of different states, various cultural circles, both in the trend-setting core of the world and of Europe, and on its peripheries striving to catch up, should be perceived primarily as a universal instrument for the transformation of reality, in order to accomplish two main desires of law-making elites: to solidify human relations primarily within the nation-state community, or to make the world a better place by reaching a greater degree of development, by transforming humanity and its social reality according to the chosen modernizing vision. It must be stressed that the authors of the texts in this publication argued that "national objectives" often have a retrospective vector, as they aim to nurture traditional solutions, while "modernizing objectives" are pursued with a view toward often fundamental (visionary) transformations of the extant reality, frequently with the aid of external models. Thus, the two groups of objectives were often mutually exclusive, and only rarely compatible. Which of these types of objectives came to the fore depended on the circumstances in the given cultural circle or on the sociopolitical and economic condition of a state or nation and on its dominant ideology. Both groups of objectives, national and modernising, were alluring in their own way, attracting attention like magnets and consequently pushing the opposite objectives out into the background. Thus, if the dominant vision was the modernizing one, it obscured the visions aiming to strengthen the national community and vice versa. Only rarely was there a true symbiosis between the two groups of objectives, accompanied by equal emphasis on both the conservative cultivation of domestic national tradition and changing the status quo so as to make it more modern.

Remembering the interplay and tensions continually arising from contrasting modernisation aims with the necessity to strengthen a community's own identity, the purpose of the chapters published in this collaborative work is to grasp the degree and specific character of legal development processes taking place in various places around the world, which are united by that common feature of the post-Enlightenment era itself, which can still be observed today.

In light of the above, individual chapters offer attempts to present and evaluate the ways in which the authors of projects for legal reforms strove to modernise their countries, borrowing from other legal cultures and, first and foremost, the ways in which they were trying to reconcile the universal desire to modernise the country with the endeavours made to consolidate and strengthen the nation. Strategies based on borrowing foreign models in order to realise goals of modernisation with the use of modern law were very often in opposition to traditionalistic strategies oriented to cultivating the domestic legal tradition and, in consequence, ill-disposed towards foreign borrowings. The basic question which the authors are trying to answer arises from the analysis of methods used by the elites of individual countries on how to deal with this "very touchy issue of national against foreign law"[46] or, in other words, to

---

46    VAN CAENEGEM: *op. cit.*, 94.

INTRODUCTION

strengthen a given country, modernising it with the use of legal instruments, without destroying the foundations on which its legal culture and community identity had grown.[47]

## Bibliography

Bertrand BADIE: *The Imported State. The Westernization of the Political Order*, Stanford University Press, Stanford, 2000.

Rodolfo BATIZA: *The French Revolution and Codification: Comment on the Enlightenment, the French Revolution, and the Napoleonic Codes*, Valpariso University Law Review 18 (1984).

Martin BELOV: *The Idea of "Europe" as a Factor in the Building of the Bulgarian Legal Identity*, Romanian Journal of Comparative Law 8(2017)/1.

Harold J. BERMAN: *Law and Revolution*, vol. 2: *The Impact of the Protestant Reformations on the Western Legal Tradition*, Harvard Univesrsity Press, Cambridge (Ma)-London, 2006.

Damiano CANALE: *The Many Faces of the Codification of Law in Modern Continental Europe = A Treatise of Legal Philosophy and General Jurisprudence*, Enrico PATTARO, Damiano CANALE, Paolo GROSSI, Hasso HOFMANN, Patrick RILEY (eds.), vol. 9: *A History of the Philosophy of Law in the Civil Law World*, Springer, Dordrecht-Heidelberg-London-New York, 2009.

Markus D. DUBBER: *Colonial Criminal Law and Other Modernities = The Oxford Handbook of European Legal History*, Heikki PIHLAJAMÄKI, Markus D. DUBBER, Mark GODFREY (eds.), Oxford University Press, Oxford, 2018.

Michał GAŁĘDEK: *Juridification as an Ideology of Polizeiwissenschaft in the 18th Century*, Journal on European History of Law, 8(2017)/1.

Michał GAŁĘDEK: *The Problem of Non-Adaptability of National Legal Heritage. Discussion on the Reform of Civil Law in Poland in the Course of Work of Reform Committee in 1814*, Romanian Journal of Comparative Law 8(2017)/1.

Michał GAŁĘDEK, Anna KLIMASZEWSKA: *A Controversial Transplant? Debate over the Adaptation of the Napoleonic Code on the Polish Territories in the Early 19th Century*, Journal of Civil Law Studies 11(2018)/2.

Michał GAŁĘDEK, Anna KLIMASZEWSKA: *The Implementation of French Codes on the Polish Territories as an Instrument of Modernization – Identifying Problems with Selected Examples = Le droit comparé et.../Comparative Law and... Actes de la*

---

47     The present chapter was prepared under the project "Administrative Thought in the Kingdom of Poland 1814–1831" financed by the National Science Centre (Narodowe Centrum Nauki) on the basis of decision no. DEC-2013/11/D/HS5/01901.

*conférence annuelle de Juris Diversitas*, Alexis ALBARIAN, Olivier MORÉTEAU (eds.), Presses Univérsitaires d Aix-Marseille, Aix-Marseille, 2015.

Manuel GUŢAN: *The Legal Transplant and the Building of the Romanian Legal Identity in the Second Half of the 19th Century and the Beginning of the 20th century*, Romanian Journal of Comparative Law, 8(2017)/1.

Manuel GUŢAN: *The Legal Transplant as Socio-Cultural Engineering in Modern Romania = Konflikt und Koexistenz. Die Rechtsordnungen Südosteuropas im 19. und 20. Jahrhundert*, Michael STOLLEIS, Gerd BENDER, Jani KIROV (eds.), vol. 1: Rumänien, Bulgarien, Griechenland, Vittorio Klostermann, Frankfurt a.M., 2015.

Jean-Louis HALPÉRIN: *Five Legal Revolutions since 17th Century. An Analysis of Global History*, Springer, New York-London, 2014.

Paul HAZARD: *European Thought in the Eighteen Century: from Montesquieu to Lessing*, World Publishing Company, Cleveland, 1963.

Jerzy JEDLICKI: *A Suburb of Europe. Nineteenth-century Polish Approaches to Western Civilization*, Central European University Press, Budapest, 1999.

J.M. KELLY: *A Short History of Western Legal Theory*, Clarendon Press, Oxford, 1992.

Lloyd S. KRAMER: *Nationalism in Europe and America: Politics, Cultures, and Identities since 1775*, University of North Carolina, Chapel Hill, 2011.

Kálmán KULCSÁR: *Modernization and Law*, Akadémiai Kiadó, Budapest, 1992.

*Legal Books in the Early Modern Western World = The Formation and Transmission of Western Legal Culture: 150 Books that Made the Law in the Age of Printing*, Serge DAUCHY, Georges MARTYN, Anthony MUSSON, Heikki PIHLAJAMÄKI, Alain WIJFELLS (eds.), Springer, Cham, 2016.

Henry S. MAINE: *Dissertations on Early Law and Customs*, John Murray, London, 1883.

Aniceto MASFERRER: *Codification of Spanish Criminal Law. A Comparative Legal History Approach*, Journal of Comparative Law, 4 (2009).

Aniceto MASFERRER: *Tradition and Foreign Influences in the 19th Century Codification of Criminal Law: Dispelling the Myth of the Pervasive French Influence in Europe and Latin America = The Western Codification of Criminal Law. A Revision of the Myth of its Predominant French Influence*, Aniceto MASFERRER (ed.), Springer, Cham, 2018.

M.C. MIROW: *Latin American Law: A History of Private Law and Institutions in Spanish America*, University of Texas Press, Austin, 2004.

M.C. MIROW: *The Power of Codification in Latin America: Simón Bolívar and the Code Napoléon*, Tulane Journal of International and Comparative Law, 93(2000).

Agustin PARISE: *Ownership Paradigms in American Civil Law Jurisdictions: Manifestations of the Shifts in Legislation of Louisiana, Chile, and America (16th-20th Centuries)*, Brill Nijhoff, Leiden-Boston, 2017.

Zsuzsanna PERES: *Prenuptial Agreements of the Hungarian Aristocracy in the Early Modern Era = Modernisation, National Identity, and Legal Instrumentalism. Studies in Comparative Legal History*, Michał GAŁĘDEK, Anna KLIMASZEWSKA (eds.), Brill Nijhoff, Leiden-Boston, 2020.

Heikki PIHLAJAMÄKI: *Private Law Codification, Modernisation, and Nationalism: A View from Critical Legal History*, Critical Analysis of Law 135(2015)/2.

Peter G. STEIN: *Legal Evolution: The Story of an Idea*, Cambridge University Press, Cambridge (UK), 1980.

Michael STOLLEIS: *The Eye of the Law* = idem, *The Eye of the Law. Two Essays on Legal History*, Brickbeck Law Press, New York, 2009.

Michael STOLLEIS: *Judicial Interpretation in Transition from the Ancien Régime to Constitutionalism* = *Interpretation of Law in the Age of Enlightenment. From the Rule of the King to the Rule of Law*, Yasutomo MORIGIWA, Michael STOLLEIS, Jean-Louis HALPÉRIN (eds.), Springer, Dordrecht-Heidelberg-London-New York, 2011.

Sean THOMAS: *English Commercial Law in the Longue Durée: Chasing Continental Shadows* = *Modernisation, National Identity, and Legal Instrumentalism. Studies in Comparative Legal History*, Michał GAŁĘDEK, Anna KLIMASZEWSKA (eds.), Brill Nijhoff, Leiden-Boston, 2020.

R.C. van CAENEGEM: *European Law in the Past and the Future. Unity and Diversity over Two Millennia*, Cambridge University Press, Cambridge (UK), 2001.

Bart WAUTERS: *Revolution and the Instrumentality of Law. Theories of Property in the American and French Revolutions* = *Modernisation, National Identity, and Legal Instrumentalism. Studies in Comparative Legal History*, Michał GAŁĘDEK, Anna KLIMASZEWSKA (eds.), Brill Nijhoff, Leiden-Boston, 2020.

CHAPTER 2

# Prenuptial Agreements of the Hungarian Aristocracy in the Early Modern Era

*Zsuzsanna Peres*

## 1 Introduction

This article forms part of a broader research intending to examine whether the Austrian marriage property law had a practical effect upon the Hungarian law of the same legal territory between the 17th and 18th centuries in the context of the Hungarian aristocrats and nobles. The article itself focuses on the Hungarian aristocracy with strong bonds to the court of Vienna and their difference from the so-called Hungarian common nobles pertaining to the noble counties, having no connections to the political groups of Vienna at all and being a factor only in the regional politics of the country. Within this subject the development of the Hungarian aristocracy should be examined in detail with special regard to their prenuptial agreements showing how they started to use in practice legal institutions foreign to the Hungarian legal system.

The methodology of the research as a whole, conducted for the fulfilling of the afore mentioned aim should be the examination of prenuptial agreements both between spouses coming from different nations and of those where both of the parties came from the same country and comparing the legal institutions used by the common nobles to the ones taking into practice by the Hungarian aristocrats.

## 2 The Hungarian Aristocracy and its "National Identity"

Before going in detail to the marriage property provisions of the Hungarian aristocracy we might get acquainted with the Hungarian aristocracy as a social layer in general.

Although the Hungarian Kingdom existed as a feudal state since the mid of the 13th century and the Hungarian nobles were promoters of the King's power since then, we cannot say that the Hungarian nobility formed an united and unchanged layer of the Hungarian society from its formation in the 13th century until the end of the feudal state in 1848. They were divided from a very

© KONINKLIJKE BRILL NV, LEIDEN, 2020 | DOI:10.1163/9789004417274_003

PRENUPTIAL AGREEMENTS OF THE HUNGARIAN ARISTOCRACY

early time to high nobles (the most important officials of the state and the king) and common nobles living in the so-called noble counties. The opportunity of becoming a high noble came by the protection of the country and the joining to the army. Defending the country was not only a duty of the Hungarian nobles, but at the same time an opportunity for a political raising. Those serving in the army could count on the grace of the King, could be awarded with royal donations and could even be invited to the royal court.[1] Of course, the high officials frequently changed on the side of the King when a new dinasty came to the Hungarian throne, as it happened several times after the last king of the Árpád dynasty, Andrew III (1265–1301) died in 1301. Following the Angevines, the Jagellonians, the Hunyadys, finally the Habsburg dinasty conquered the royal power in the Hungarian Kingdom. Ferdinand I Habsburg (1503–1564) was crowned as Hungarian King in 1527 after the defeat we suffered from the Turks at the battlefield of Mohács.[2] From then on the Hungarian Kingdom was living in a constant fight against the Turks who occupied the middle of the country's territory until their expulsion in 1687.[3]

---

1 Stephen Werbőczy (1458–1541) the famous Hungarian lawyer in his work called Tripartitum wrote about this in chapter. I.18. with the title "Why aren't women concerned in the possession of royal donations earned for the serving of the country?" He said: "...tell them that it is so because Hungary with all its belonging territories lies surrounded by enemies, close to their throat, and our predecessors always used to defend it with their swords and guns, and they used to obtain their properties for their military service and sheding of their blood, and so do they nowadays, too." *Tripartitum. Magyar Törvénytár = Corpus Juris Hungarici. 1000–1895*, Márkus DEZSŐ (ed.), Milleniumi Emlékkiadás, Franklin, Budapest, 1896.

2 The battle of Mohács in 1526 ended with a catastrophy for the Hungarians, significant number of the Hungarian nobles lost their lives in the battle and the territorial division resulting from the Turkish invasions changed significantly the political and state structure. During the period of the Turkish subjection, only the western part of the former country could be considered as the Kingdom of Hungary. The middle of the former territory was occupied by the Turks, the eastern part resulted in a new state called the Principality of Transylvania. By the death of King Louis II (1516–1526) the Habsburg dynasty ascended to the throne of the Kingdom of Hungary from the first half of the 16th century with its coronation centre in Pozsony (today Bratislava, Slovakia) and its royal court in Vienna.

3 The Hungarian nation with the help of the Austrian army managed to expulse the Turks from the middle territory of the country at the end of the 17th century. The biggest success was the reoccupation of the castle of Buda in 1686. After regaining the Capital of the country the army could reoccupy the whole territory that had been lost after the battle of Mohács. Although at the beginning of the 18th century the Habsburgs had to face the freedom war led by Ferenc Rákóczi II Prince of Transylvania, they managed to consolidate the country after repressing the revolution. A reorganisation process started in the country after 1723 that led to the adaptation of an – at that time modern – institution model in the public administration and judicature and established the grounds for the spreading of the enlightment's ideology. Cf. more about it Thomas WINKELBAUER: *Ständefreiheit und Fürstenmacht. Länder und Untertanen des Hauses Habsburg im konfessionellen Zeitalter.* Teil I = *Österreichische*

During these Habsburg times royal donations obtained for for service of the King became even more important for the Hungarian nobles who wanted to get closer to the new royal court freshly moved to Vienna by Ferdinand I. By earning properties they could plant their feet in the court and become officials of the King.[4] This is the way the new layer of the society, the Hungarian aristocracy was born. Of course, not only military endeavours led to the success of this upgrowing social layer, but more documents proove that those were also granted privileges who contributed with loans to the covering of the military expenses by taking into pawn royal properties. These loans provided for the King also contributed to the establishment of the wealthy Hungarian aristocracy. Actually, they were a fruitful opportunity, because all those to whom the King owed a debt had to be present in the royal court, and if he wanted to get his money back he had to keep strong relation to his Majesty by becoming a member of the Secret Council, or serving as an official either at the Hungarian Chancery, or the Hungarian Chamber.[5]

This newly forming Hungarian aristocracy during the reign of the Habsburgs, having the most economic power and political impact were only few families in number. The rest of the Hungarian nobles the so-called "common nobles" remained on the territory of the Hungarian Kingdom, far from the royal court. They were settled in the Hungarian territorial units, the counties, living with noble privileges but never having the luck of getting the position of a

---

*Geschichte 1522–1699,* Herwig WOLFRAM (ed.), Wirtschaftsverlag Ueberreuter, Wien, 2004, 123–172 and Karl VOCELKA: *Glanz und Untergang der Höfischen Welt. Repräsentation, Reform und Reaktion im Habsburgischen Vielvölkerstaat* = Österreichische Geschichte 1699–1815, Herwig WOLFRAM (ed.), Wirtschaftsverlag Ueberreuter, Wien, 2004, 58–67.

4 Among the literature dealing with the Hungarian aristocracy of the early modern times in general – with no aim of completeness – the works of Géza Pálffy should be mentioned. Géza PÁLFFY: *A bécsi udvar és a magyar rendek a 16. században* [The Viennese Court and the Hungarian Estates in the 16th century], Történelmi Szemle, 1999, 3–4 (epa.oszk.hu/00600/ 00617/00004/tsz99_3_4_palffy_geza.htm, accessed 03.04.2019); Géza PÁLFFY: *Der Adel aus den ungarischen Ländern am Kaiserhof 1526–1612* = *Die Weltliche und Kirchliche Elite aus dem Königreich Böhmen und Königreich Ungarn am Wiener Kaiserhof im 16.-17. Jahrhundert.* Anna FUNDÁRKOVÁ, István FAZEKAS (eds.), Publikationen der Ungarischen Geschichtsforschung in Wien, vol. 8, Wien, 2013, 37–76. Géza PÁLFFY: *A Magyar Királyság és a Habsburg Monarchia a 16. században* [The Hungarian Kingdom and the Habsburg Monarchy in the 16th century], MTA Történettudományi Intézet, Budapest, 2016 and the work of Katalin PÉTER: *Gyermek a koraújkori Magyarországon* [Children of the Early Modern Times' Hungary], MTA Történettudományi Intézete, Budapest, 1992. In addition to general works, there are several works focusing on the different noble families, as well.

5 Thomas WINKELBAUER: *Fürst und Fürstendiener. Gundacker von Liechtenstein, ein österreichischer Aristokrat des konfessionellen Zeitalters.* Oldenbourg Verlag, Wien-München, 1999, 163.

PRENUPTIAL AGREEMENTS OF THE HUNGARIAN ARISTOCRACY

high-ranking official close to the King's court. The new situation caused by the moving of the royal court to Vienna resulted in an even broader gap between the Hungarian aristocrats and common nobles.

We might also ask how the story of the Hungarian aristocracy can be linked to the main subject of the conference held at the University of Gdansk in 2016 with the title "Culture, Identity and Legal Instrumentalism"? Well, through the research of the afore mentioned nobles' documents we get a broader insight in the everyday life of the Hungarian aristocracy in Vienna as well, and we might also see how they could preserve or not their Hungarian character.

The period we examine (17th-18th centuries) is far earlier to the formation of the Hungarian nation.[6] Although many sources referred to the Hungarians using the word "*natio*," this time by nation something else was meant. As Jenő Szűcs wrote in his excellent and until nowadays gap-filling article with the title *Nationality and National Identity in the Middle Ages. Viewpoints to the Formation of a Unanimous Concept of Language,* by nation we mean a totally different thing in the middle ages than in the modern times.[7] The two notions shouldn't even be compared to each other.[8]

Before the birth of the modern, enlightened state notion, by nation – according to Werbőczy – that group of people should be meant which formed part of the political power.[9] They were those privileged groups who were part

---

6 The formation of the political nation was strongly linked to the recognition of the minority rights of minorities living on the territory of the Hungarian Kingdom and to the declaration of the Hungarian language as official one from 1844. Language played an immense role in the formation of the nation in almost every Eastern European country, such as in Hungary. Hans Koch explains it with the weakness of the towns' citizens. He says that in all those countries where the towns' citizens were weak politically even during the 19th century, the nationalism resulted in cultural movements and gave birth to the idea of forming a nation state. Hungary belonged to these states. Zoltán ÁCS: *Nemzetiségek a történelmi Magyarországon* [Nationalities of the Historical Hungary], Kossuth Könyvkiadó, Budapest, 1996, 134; Domokos KOSÁRY: *A magyar és európai politika történetéből* [From the History of the Hungarian and European Politics], Osiris, Budapest, 2001, 653.

7 Jenő SZŰCS: *„Nemzetiség" és „nemzeti öntudat" a középkorban. Szempontok egy egységes fogalmi nyelv kialakításához* ["Nationality" and "National Identity" in the Middle Ages. Viewpoints to the Formation of a Unanimous Concept of Language], Nemzetiség a feudalizmus korában. Értekezések a Történeti Tudományok köréből, 64, Akadémiai Kiadó, Budapest, 1972, 9–71.

8 József PERÉNYI: *A magyar „nemzeti öntudat" fejlődése a 11.-13. században,* [The Development of the Hungarian "National Identity" during the 11–13th Centuries], Nemzetiség a feudalizmus korában. Értekezések a Történeti Tudományok köréből, 64, Akadémiai Kiadó, Budapest, 1972, 83–101. in this case: 84.

9 *Tripartitum...,* op. cit., I, 3–4; Ágnes R. VÁRKONYI: *Magyarország keresztútjain. Tanulmányok,* [On the Crossroads of Hungary. Essays], Gondolat, Budapest, 1978, 326, 373; Emma BARTONIEK: *Corona és regnum.* [Crown and Regnum], Századok, 7–8/1934, 318–320, 327–329;

of the so-called „*corpus regni,*" the body of the state, also referred to as the members of the Hungarian "crown" possessing the power transferred to the King at the coronation. The loyalty to the King wasn't a manifestation of national feelings but of an absolute political loyalty towards the monarchy. It wasn't national identity even if we can find documents from the 17th century containing political argumentation counting on the Hungarian national feelings for the mobilisation of the Hungarians against the Turks.[10] Religious belief, society status, the territory each person came from (village, town, county, royal court) were more important nationforming factors than real national feelings.[11] This statement might be proven even by the census made during the reign of Joseph II (1780–1790) that contained no data collected regarding the nationality of the population.[12]

So, if we are searching for the national identity of the Hungarian aristocracy during the examined period, we might find the contrary. After the battle of Mohács those who went to serve in the royal court in Vienna wanted to become

---

Ferenc ECKHART: *A szentkorona-eszme története* [The History of the Holy Crown Theory], MTA, Budapest, 1941, 68–71. Latest literature: Károly KISTELEKI: *Magyar nemzet – magyar állampolgárság* [Hungarian Nation – Hungarian Citizenship] = *A kettős monarchia – Die Doppelmonarchie*, Gábor MÁTHÉ, Attila MENYHÁRD, Barna MEZEY (eds.), ELTE ÁJK, Budapest, 2018, 79–113, in this case: 91–93. The notion of the modern nation can always be examined in a context originated from the „volonté générale" defined by Rousseau or the „Volksgeist" defined by Herder. The birth of these theories cannot be dated earlier than the Enlightenment and the French Revolution. „Die Natur geht von Familien aus. Familien schließen sich einander; sie bilden einen Baum mit Zweigen, Stamm und Wurzeln. Jede Wurzel gräbt sich in den Boden und suchet ihre Nahrung in der Erbe, wie jeder Zweig bis zum Gipfel sie in der Luft sucht. Sie laufen nicht aus einander; sie stürzen nicht über einander. Die Natur hat Völker durch Sprache, Sitten, Gebräuche, oft durch Berge, Meere, Ströme und Wüsten getrennt; siet hat gleichsam alles, damit sie lange von einander gesondert blieben, und in sich selbst bekleibten." Johann Gottfried HERDER: *Briefe zur Beförderung der Humanität. J.G. Herders sämmtliche Werke. Zur Philosophie und Geschichte. Eilfter Theil. Briefe zur Beförderung der Humanität*, Johann VON MÜLLER (ed.), Büreau der deutschen Classiker, Carlsruhe, 1820, 320.

10    The modern notion of the nation can be determined only in the existence of the state sovereignty – claims Jenő Szűcs. SZŰCS: *op. cit.*, 9–71. in this case 31, 35, 63; Lajos RÁCZ: *A 15. század humanista magyar államelméletei*, [The Hungarian Humanist State Theories of the 15th Century] = *Tripartitum trium professorum. Három szegedi jogtörténész* [Tripartitum trium professorum. Three Legal Historians of Szeged], Elemér BALOGH, Mária HOMOKI-NAGY (eds.), Iurisperitus, Szeged, 2017, 74–86, in this case: 85.

11    SZŰCS: *op. cit.*, 27; Győző CHOLNOKY: *Állam és nemzet. Uralkodó nemzet- és nemzetiségpolitikai eszmék Magyarországon (1920–1941)* [State and Nation. Ruling National and Nationpolitical Theories in Hungary (1920 – 1941)], Hatodik Síp Alapítvány, Budapest, 1996, 13.

12    László KATUS: *A modern Magyarország születése. Magyarország története 1711–1914*, [The Birth of the Modern Hungary. The History of Hungary 1711–1914], Kronosz, Pécs, 2012, 122.

more similar to their Austrian fellows instead of differing from them. To stabilize their positions in Vienna they even tried to strengthen their relations to other wealthy and politically significant Austrian families by contracting marriages.

We might even say that based to the interference of the Viennese Court the educational level of the Hungarian aristocracy rose significantly and they started to differ even more from the common nobles. The closer interference with the Austrian hereditary provinces and the everyday correspondence with the foreign officials and acquaintances resulted in new habits and educational development. The knowledge they possessed before wasn't enough anymore because the world had opened for them. They started to copy the foreign aristocracy in behaviour and manners as well. Although the Hungarian aristocracy's general level of knowledge – except for some outstanding examples – stayed behind the level of the aristrocracies of other European countries (such as the Austrian or the French), it can be proven that from the 17th century on there was a general pressure on the members of the Hungarian aristocracy to be more educated and literate, to own a substantial library if they could afford to have one, and to know the world outside of their country well, which they could get to know by completing a so-called "*cavallierstour*" in the company of their teacher (*praeceptor*). They may not have had the same kind of education as today, but they were educated in a pragmatic way to be capable of handling their daily duties, to know how to converse, behave, dance and ride a horse and they also knew how to properly manage their properties.[13]

We cannot detect national feelings within the aristocracy for reasons of the language they had to speak, either. Although the Hungarian language existed already in the times before the foundation of the Hungarian state and was spoken by the Hungarians, Latin was the language that spread widely in official correspondence. The use of the Latin could be explained by the clerical dominance on the field of literacy and by the legally educated foreign clerical

---

13    With no aim of completeness, the following works written about the education of the Hungarian aristocracy were used for this article: István MONOK: *A művelt arisztokrata. A magyarországi főnemesség olvasmányai a XVI–XVII. században* [The Educated Aristocrat. The Readings of the Hungarian Aristocracy in the 16th–17th centuries], Kossuth Kiadó, Budapest-Eger, 2012 and Domokos KOSÁRY: *Művelődés a XVIII. századi Magyarországon* [Education in the 18th Century Hungary], Akadémiai Kiadó, Budapest, 1983. Among the articles dealing with the "*Cavallierstour*" – Katalin TOMA: *Nádasdy Istvan európai tanulmányútja: a Kavalierstour alkalmazása a magyar főuri nevelési gyakorlatban* [Stephen Nádasdy's European Study Trip: the Cavallierstour in the Education of the Hungarian Aristocrats.], *Idővel paloták... Magyar udvari kultúra a 16–17. században,* [Palaces by Time... Hungarian Court Culture in the 16th to 17th Centuries], Nóra G. ETENYI, Ildikó HORN (eds.), Balassi Kiadó, Budapest, 2005, 192–214.

intelligentsia moving to Hungary from the very early stage of the Hungarian state.[14] All the notaries and scribes working in the Royal Chancery established by Béla III (1148–1196) belonged to the church and were led by the Lord Chancellor who also used to be a churchman. The Lord Chancellor was usually the Archbishop of Esztergom (the leading clerical official in Hungary) appointed to this office by the King.[15] Moreover, the Church Chapters and Monasteries were the places entitled to issue documents under their own seals on the territories under their authority, so the Church became predominant on the field of literacy not only on the court but also on regional level.[16]

After the defeat at Mohács and the moving of the royal court to Vienna a new language started to appear in the state administration: the German. The reasons for the spreading of the German language lied in the reorganisation of the Hungarian administrative bodies by Ferdinand I right after his coronation in 1527. In his Hofstaatsordnung issued on 1st January 1527, the King established the new Austrian administrative bodies, such as the Court Council (*Hofrat*) and the Secret Council (*Geheimes Rat*) together with the Court Chancery (*Hofkanzlei*) and the Court Chamber (*Hofkammer*). In 1556 he added to these bodies the Military Council (*Hofkriegsrat*). By the reorganisation of the court structure, four important court officials were appointed: the Lord High Chamberlain (*Obersthofmeister*), the Master of Ceremonies (*Obersthofmarschall*), the Master of the Court Chamber (*Obersthofkammer*) and last but not least the Master of the Horse (*Oberststallmeister*).[17] Parrallel to the

---

14    György BÓNIS: *Jogtudó értelmiség a Mohács előtti Magyarországon*, [The Legally Qualified Intelligentsia of Hungary before Mohács], Akadémiai Kiadó, Budapest, 1971.

15    István FAZEKAS: *Humanisten und Juristen. Das Personal der Ungarischen Hofkanzlei in der Frühen Neuzeit. (1526–1690)* = Institutions of Legal History with Special Regard to Legal Culture and History, Gábor BÉLI, Diana DUCHONOVÁ, Anna FUNDÁRKOVÁ, István KAJTÁR, Zsuzsanna PERES (eds.), Publikon, Pécs, 2011, 321–331.

16    Irén ŐRINÉ BILKEI: *A hiteles helyek szerepe a feudáliskori magyar közigazgatásban* [The Role of the Loca Credibilia in the Hungarian Administration of the Feudal Era], Comitatus 3(1993)/3, 52–54.

17    The Master of the Horse was the fourth person in the rank among the court's high officials. He was the person to care for the horses, the royal journeys and the service of the page of honours of noble origin. The Master of the Court Chamber took care of the personal needs of the Ruler and handled his "personal matters." The Master of Ceremonies was the second official of the court right after the Lord High Chamberlain. He had jurisdiction over the residents of the court. The Lord High Chamberlain was the first in rank and position who had his own office. He took care of all affairs of the court such as the financial administration of the court, but he was also the person to take care of all the architectural investments, the court theatre and concerts, and the court chapel. The number of court officials and members of the royal household was continuously growing, especially during the times of Leopold I, Charles III, or Maria Theresa, from 1000 to 1760

PRENUPTIAL AGREEMENTS OF THE HUNGARIAN ARISTOCRACY          33

Austrian administrative reform Ferdinand I established in 1528 the Hungarian Chamber for the financial administration of the Hungarian Kingdom. This body became the most important state organ of the early modern Hungary.[18] In addition to this, the Hungarian Chancery was also established in 1540. The Chamber functioned in today's Bratislava and the Chancery functioned temporarily in Vienna while Esztergom was occupied by the Turks.[19] Both Hungarian state organs – although this caused several problems between the King and the Hungarian nobles – functioned under the supervision of the coinciding Austrian admnistrative organ.[20] Therefore, the official language to be used were the Latin and the German next to each other. If we take a look into the documents of the Court Chamber we might see that the Hungarian state organs usually led their correspondence in Latin but they got the official answer from the court in German. So all those people who wanted to have a state carreer had to know both of these languages besides of course being loyal to the Habsburgs.[21]

Opposite to the official documents, in the family archives we may find sources written in Hungarian, too, because the family correspondence usually went on in Hungarian. This could happen also because the women of the

---

      persons by the end of Maria Theresa's reign. Jakob WÜHRER, Martin SCHEUTZ: *Zu Diensten Ihrer Majestät. Hofordnungen und Instruktionsbücher am frühneuzeitlichen Wiener Hof,* Quelleneditionen des Instituts für Österreichische Geschichtsforschung, Wien-München, 2011, 17–19; WINKELBAUER: *Ständefreiheit..., op. cit.,* 39–41, 179–191; Győző EMBER: *Az újkori magyar közigazgatás története Mohácstól a török kiűzéséig* [The History of the Hungarian Administration from Mohács until the Expulsion of the Turks], Magyar Országos Levéltár kiadványai, Budapest, 1946, 48–72.

18    Lajos GECSÉNYI: *A döntést előkészítő hivatalnoki elit összetételéről. A Magyar Kamara vezetői és tanácsosai a 16. században* [About the Constitution of the Decision Preparing Administrative Elite. The Leaders and Councillors of the Hungarian Chamber in the 16th Century], *Magyar évszázadok. Tanulmányok Kosáry Domokos 90. születésnapjára,* [Hungarian Centuries. Publications for the 90th Birthday Anniversary of Domoks Kosáry], Mária ORMOS (ed.), Osiris, Budapest, 2003, 100–113, in this case: 100. Zoltán FALLENBÜCHL: *A Magyar Kamara tisztviselői a XVII. században* [The Clerks of the Hungarian Chamber in the 17th Century], Levéltári Közlemények, 39(1968), 233.

19    WINKELBAUER: *Ständefreiheit..., op. cit.,* 133–134; EMBER: *op. cit.,* 119–120, 124–126.

20    Theodor MAYER: *Das Verhältnis der Hofkammer zur ungarischen Kammer bis zur Regierung Maria Theresias = Mitteilungen des Instituts für österreichische Geschichtsforschung* (9 Band), Oswald REDLICH (ed.), Verlag Wagnerschen Universität, Innsbruck, 1915, 178–395.

21    Géza PÁLFFY: *A magyar nemesség bécsi integrációjának színterei a 16.-17. században* [The Stages of the Hungarian Nobility's Integration to Vienna in the 16th–17th century], *Tanulmányok Szakály Ferenc emlékére,* [Publication for the Memory of Ferenc Szakály], Pál FODOR, Géza PÁLFFY, István György TÓTH (eds.), MTA TKI, Budapest, 2002, 307–331, in this case 321–322, FALLENBÜCHL: *op. cit.,* 233–234.

family sometimes could only speak Hungarian and they had to face problems translating letters written in other languages.[22] We may also find documents, especially last wills in which the testator bound his heirs to be educated in Hungarian.[23] Of course there are examples for the contrary, too. Some Hungarian aristocrats considered the French as a language getting frequently used in Vienna and the German language more important than the Hungarian in the 18th century.[24] So, they decided to educate their children in these languages.[25]

The common nobles living in the counties judged the French and German speaking Hungarian aristocrats, they held them unpatriotic and they even said they don't deserve to be called Hungarians at all. They also judged the Hungarian aristocrats for the way they dressed. The common nobles instead of wearing suits according to the Viennese style they insisted wearing suits sewed according to Hungarian traditions and denied the wearing of whigs as well. This was how they wanted to protest against the so-called „náj modi" (Neue Mode) those followed who were living in the royal court of Vienna.[26]

---

22 Erzsébet Rákóczi (1654–1707) a noble woman wrote in her letter on 2nd June, 1695 to the that time Archbishop of Esztergom, Lipót Kollonich (1631–1707) that it was very hard to find someone to translate the Archbishiop's letter written in German. Iván BERKESZI: *A magyar nyelv a magánélet terén 1711–1790*. [Hungarian Language in the Private Life 1711–1790], Wunder Gyula nyomdája, Fehértemplom, 1885, 3–4.

23 Palatine Paul Pálffy's (1590–1653) testament. 3rd September 1653. ÖStA, HHStA, F.A. Pálffy, Arma I. Lad. 9. Fasc. III. Nr. 21. and Palatine Nicholas Esterházy's (1582–1645) testament. 22nd September 1624. MNL OL, F.A. Esterházy, Rep. 4. Fasc. E. Nr. 44. and Palatine Nicholas Esterházy's (1582–1645) testament. 14th August 1641. MNL OL F.A. Esterházy, Rep. 4. Fasc. E. Nr. 37. and cf. Lajos MERÉNYI: *Herceg Eszterházy Pál nádor*. [Palatine Prince Paul Esterházy], Magyar Történelmi Társulat, Budapest, 1895, 265–276 and Emma IVÁNYI: *Esterházy Pál nádor közigazgatási tevékenysége (1681–1713)* [Palatine Paul Esterházy's Administrative Function (1681–1713)], Akadémiai Kiadó, Budapest, 1991, 21.

24 Elisabeth LOBENWEIN: *Adelige Briefkultur am Beispiel der Privatkorrespondenz der Brüder Hyeronimus (1732–1812) und Gundaker (1731–1807) Colloredo. Adel im 18. Jahrhundert. Umrisse einer sozialen Gruppe in der Krise*, Gerhard AMMERER, Elisabeth LOBENWEIN, Martin SCHEUTZ (eds.), Studienverlag, Innsbruck-Wien-Bozen, 2015, 318–342, in this case: 322.

25 Count Ferencz Esterházy (1715–1785) had a French preceptress at his residence for the proper education of his daughters. His son was at the same time always accompanied by a French priest for the same reason. The daughters of Count Ferenc Károlyi (1705–1758) went to school to nowadays Kosice and Bratislava (Slovakia) and St. Pölten (Austria) in order to be taught to French. Count Sándor Károlyi (1669–1743) never forgot to mention in his letters written to his son how important is for his sons to be well educated in German and French. He wrote the children would have to start learning German at their age of eight because otherwise they "won't become a good German." BERKESZI: *op. cit.*, 7.

26 Endre ARATÓ: *A magyar „nemzeti" ideológia jellemző vonásai a 18. században* [Characteristics of the Hungarian "National" Ideology in the 18th century] = *Nemzetiség a feudalizmus korában* [Nationalities in the Era of Feudalism], Értekezések a Történeti Tudományok

# PRENUPTIAL AGREEMENTS OF THE HUNGARIAN ARISTOCRACY

## 3    Marriage Policy and Prenuptial Agreements of the Hungarian Aristocracy

Several documentary examples show how members of the Hungarian aristocracy with a fortune contracted marriages with foreign aristocrats, and their prenuptial agreements provide us a great research basis.

The members of the Hungarian aristocracy could be in general those to contract "international" marriages, meaning to marry someone outside of the Hungarian nobility. Moreover, they were those who owned a property valuable enough to be put into a written prenuptial agreement. The rest of the nobles and the non-nobles did not put emphasis on writing a detailed prenuptial agreement, they were content with having a simple agreement on the widow's remuneration for the end of the marriage and they could clarify other forthcoming issues later on in a last will or testament. It seems that more fortune one had the more interested he or she was in writing a prenuptial agreement.

Among the documentary sources most closely related to the subject of this article are the prenuptial agreements preserved in the National Archives in Vienna (*Haus- Hof- und Staatsarchiv*), mainly among the documents of the Lord High Chamberlain's Office (*Obersthofmeisteramt*). These documents contain the prenuptial agreements of the Ladies-in-Waiting attending to the Queen at the imperial court in Vienna. In the collection of documents preserved in Vienna, consisting of 335 prenuptial agreements, 38 are related to Hungarian aristocrats.

All the contracts made up in the Court of Vienna in the presence of the Lord High Chamberlain were prepared according to high standards and strict rules.[27] In contrast to the Viennese court's legal practice we can hardly find any details regarding the formal requirements of the prenuptial agreements according to the Hungarian laws and customs. Neither the *Tripartitum* (i.e. the main customary legal collection) nor the laws of the country contained any rules for the prenuptial agreements. There were no regulations regarding the content of these agreements either. Due to the lack of regulations some authors even wrote that the Hungarians were not that kind of a people who often put marital agreements into writing.[28] Researching the legal practice prooves us that

---

köréből. 64. György Spira (ed.), Akadémiai Kiadó, Budapest, 1972, 134, 137–140, 161; Várkonyi: *op. cit.,* 324.

27    Cf. more about Zsuzsanna Peres: *Marriage Property Rights of the Noble Women According to Their Prenuptial Agreements.* Journal on European History of Law 2(2018), 125–132.

28    György Jancsó a famous Hungarian lawyer in the era of the codification process of the Hungarian Private Law at the turn of the 19th and 20th centuries wrote in his renowned work that the prenuptial agreements were rare in the Hungarian legal practice because

they were wrong, because prenuptial agreements, maybe because of their general use in the Viennese court, became widely used on the territory of the Hungarian Kingdom as well and in these agreements each future spouse could stipulate whatever he or she wanted.

Reading these documents it is sometimes hard to define the legal background based on which they made their stipulations. Sometimes they referred to their stipulations as those that were in accordance with the laws of the country, but they did not quote exact legal chapters according to which they were provided specific property rights, so it is hard to identify what they meant by these statements.[29] Sometimes they quoted the *Tripartitum* but this usually happened when the case ended up in front of a court and the courts were bound to judge according to the laws and customs of the country. In these cases judges usually decided by referring to the specific existing laws and customs of Hungary.[30] In some prenuptial agreements they referred to the contract as an agreement made up "according to the existing laws of the country" or "according to the ordinary habits of honourable families."[31]

## 4 The Ruling Legal Customs on the Field of the Marriage Law

In contrast to the nuptial bond that belonged for centuries under the jurisdiction of the Church, marital property cases always belonged to the jurisdiction of the secular courts, so secular law regulated it. Some legal institutions related

---

Hungarians did not and still do not sympathize with this institution. They were only brought to us by the Austrian Civil Code entered into force in 1853. Cf. György JANCSÓ: *A magyar házassági és házastársi öröklési jog* [The Hungarian Marriage and Marital Succession's Law], Politzer, Budapest, 1901, 808.

29  As an example the prenuptial agreement of Paul Karl Pálffy and Mary Margareth Stubenberg can be quoted. They refer to the prenuptial arrangements as of those that were made according to the Hungarian and Austrian law and customs. „[...] daß hirumben nach Hungarisch und Österreichischen recht und gebrauch [...]" ÖStA HHStA FA. Pálffy Arma I. Lad. 9. Fasc. 2. No. 12. – Prenuptial agreement of Paul Karl Pálffy and Mary Margareth Stubenberg. 22 November 1718.

30  The case of the Esterházy widows at the beginning of the 18th century serve as an example, who received satisfaction according to the laws of the country and not according to their prenuptial agreements after the long legal procedure of their husbands. MNL (Magyar Nemzeti Levéltár) OL (Országos Levéltár) P 108 Esterházy Rep. 6. Fasc. 3. Nr. 125. – Contract between marquise Anna Margaretha Desanna et Rhodi, widow of Michael Esterházy and Maria Octavia von Gilleis, widow of Joseph Esterházy and Anna Eleonora Pálffy. 21 March 1722.

31  ÖStA HHStA FA. Pálffy Arma I. Lad. 9. Fasc. 2. Nr. 7. – Prenuptial agreement of Christoph Erdődy and Susanne Maria Pálffy. 28 February 1672.

PRENUPTIAL AGREEMENTS OF THE HUNGARIAN ARISTOCRACY

to marital property could be found in different acts of law, but a catalogue of the marital property rights, as the special rights of women, was assembled by Stephen Werbőczy in his previously mentioned work called *Tripartitum*. The *Tripartitum* was the customary legal collection prepared in 1514 that collected all the customs existing at that time and defining Hungarian private law over the subsequent centuries until the revolution of 1848. This collection had such a respect in its era that no codification attempts could erode its legal effect.

Werbőczy listed the following marital property rights in his collection: the quarter (*quarta puellaris*), the rights of the unmarried woman (*jus capillare*), the engagement gift and marital remuneration (*parapherna; dos*), the rights of the widow (*jus viduale*) and the inheritance of the widow (*successio vidualis*).[32] Some of these legal institutions had special Hungarian character while others were common in the legal systems of other countries. Although Werbőczy did not speak a word about the dowry, based on the practice we can state that this legal institution existed in the Hungarian legal practice as well. Of these rights, only the quarter, the rights of the unmarried woman and the marital remuneration require some further explanation because of their special Hungarian character.

The quarter (*quarta puellaris*) was the special part of the family property that the women, however many there were in the family, were entitled to inherit all together. They received their quarter after the death of the father together with their endowment. The quarter was the burden on the family property, the so-called *bona avitica* that usually belonged to and was inherited within the family through several generations. Those relatives, who inherited the family property after the death of the women's father had to provide the quarter for the women. The heirs were entitled to purchase the quarter in monetary form in order to keep the real estate properties within the family, but they had to provide it in one sum when the woman got married.[33] Documents often mentioned the quarter as part of the dowry, especially from the early modern period on.

The rights of the unmarried woman (*ius capillare*) consisted of the right to a decent maintenance and the right "to proper endowment." So, women could remain in the family residence even after the death of their father and they could not be forced to enter into an improper and indecent marriage. The right

---

32 *Tripartitum...*, *op. cit.*, Part I, title 88–91, 97; Rights of the unmarried woman: title 92; Engagement gift: title 93, 100; Marital remuneration: title 93–98, 103–111; Rights of the widow: title 99, 101.

33 Cf. more József HOLUB: *Néhány kérdés a leánynegyed köréből* [A Few Questions Regarding the Quarter], Értekezések a filozófiai és társadalmi tudományok köréből, Magyar Tudományos Akadémia, Budapest, 1936.

to proper endowment differed according to the fortune and status of the woman. While poor women contracted marriage in a plain wedding celebration, others with a fortune had a wedding lasting for several days and the serfs belonging to the family had to pay several exceptional taxes in order to cover the costs.[34]

The marital remuneration (*dos*) the wife received for the consummation of the marriage and loss of her virginity was a legal institution of a peculiar Hungarian character that existed until the end of the 19th century in Hungary. Although there were institutions with a similar character in other legal systems, such as the *Morgengabe* and the *Widerlag* or the German *dos*, the legal institution the Hungarians had in their legal system was something created from the mixture of these, having a special added Hungarian character. The amount of the marital remuneration could be paid for the woman only at the time of her husband's death and not earlier. Even if Werbőczy did not mention this in the Tripartitum, based on the practice we might state that women were paid the dos only for the case they decided to remarry after their husbands' death and this sum served as their dowry for the next marriage.[35] The sum of this remuneration was – if the husband did not stipulate more – according to the *Tripartitum* equivalent to the bloodwite of the husband.

The main reasons for the marital property provisions were the decent maintenance of the future widows. According to the that time rules the maintenance of the widow was the responsibility of the family the woman married into. So, after the death of her husband, the husband's next of kins had to take care of the widow until she decided to remarry someone else, or she died. The Hungarian customary rules did not contain detailed provisions for alimony or subsistence during the widowhood, they only stated in general that a widow is entitled to receive a proper subsistence after the death of her husband.

Finally, the property acquired in common during the marriage must be mentioned. According to the Hungarian customary law, among nobles the husband was the only acquirer of the property and the wife received half of this property only if she was mentioned by name in the acquisition contract.

---

34  Many sources describe such expensive weddings. Cf. more Béla RADVÁNSZKY: *Magyar családélet és háztartás a XVI. és XVII. században* [Hungarian Family Life and Households in the 16th and 17th Centuries], vol. 1, MTA, Budapest, 1896, 355–357.

35  Regarding the marital remuneration cf. more Zsuzsanna PERES: *Hitbérkikötések a magyar főúri családok körében a Werbőczy utáni időszakban* [Stipulations of Marital Remuneration among the Hungarian High Noble Families in the Post-Werbőczy Period] = *A jogi kultúrtörténet és a jogi néprajz új forrásai* [The Newest Sources of the Legal Cultural History and Legal Ethnography], Janka Teodóra NAGY (ed.), PTE Kultúratudományi, Pedagógusképző és Vidékfejlesztési Kar, Szekszárd, 2018, 281–300.

PRENUPTIAL AGREEMENTS OF THE HUNGARIAN ARISTOCRACY

The prenuptial contracts proove the contrary: all properties acquired during the marriage were considered as common property.[36] The children were those to inherit the common property but in the absence of children, the surviving spouse was entitled to receive the husband's share.

## 5 The Marital Property Provisions stipulated in Prenuptial Agreements

If we take a look into the prenuptial agreements concluded by Hungarian aristocrats, we may often find provisions differing from the legal institutions detailed in the Tripartitum. Sometimes also occurred that documents contained provisions for legal institutions unknown to the Hungarian customary law: such as the *Morgengabe*, or the *Widerlag* that could be considered as a counter-dowry given by the husband, or the *Spennadl Geld* which usually meant the covering of the household expenses by the husband. These were legal institutions in common use in the laws of the Austrian Hereditary Provinces in the early modern period, and not in the laws of Hungary thus they do not even have a proper translation. Documents usually referred to them by their original name. Nevertheless, they sometimes also obliged Hungarian nobles if they had promised to pay these in a marriage contract.[37]

In addition to these institutions all the prenuptial contracts of the aristocracy contained provisions for a specified amount of dowry (*Heyratts-gut*) the future wife brought to the marriage that she had to hand over into the possession of her future husband within one year and one day after the conclusion of the marriage. The amount differed according to the status of the spouses.[38]

---

36 "Was aber beede theile unter dem Göttlichen seegen hier nechst wehrender Ehe miteinander erringen und erwerben mögen, das ist als ein gemeinsammes Gutt zuachtenn und hat ieder theil mit der helffte dessen, es seyen Kinder verhanden oder nicht willkührlich zu disponieren." ÖStA, HHStA OMeA SR, Ehepakten des Hofstaates Karton 10, No. 28 – Prenuptial agreement of Johann Graf Pálffy and Anna Eleonora Gräfin Esterházy, 11 May, 1715.

37 For more, cf. Wilhelm BRAUNEDER: *Die Entwicklung des Ehegüterrechts in Österreich. Ein Beitrag zur Dogmengeschichte und Rechtstatsachenforschung des Spätmittelalters und der Neuzeit*, Peter Lang Verlag, Salzburg-München, 1973.

38 "[...] sollte aber die Gräffliche Fräule Brauth über kurz oder lang in den Fürsten Stand gelangen, so werden Ihr anstatt deren oben Puncto 6to begriffenen 3000 fl[oreni] zur Wittiblichen Unterhaltung sodan sechs tausend gulden, und anstatt deren in dem nemblichen Punct befindlichen 1000 fl[oreni] für die Wohnung, das Quartier in einem Stock in dem Fürst Esterházyschen Hauß in den Wallnerstrassen allhier, oder Statt dessen Jährlich zwey tausend gulden nach Ihrer Willkur dan über die oben Puncto 8to versprochene

The husband had to issue a receipt regarding the assignment of the dowry.[39] With a few exceptions, the dowry was specified as an amount of money usually between 2000 and 5000 Rhenish guilder, but it could also be more based on the party's will.[40] Depending on the provisions of the prenuptial agreement, this amount could be either returned to the wife after the end of the marriage, or inherited by the husband. As it has already been mentioned before, neither the Hungarian laws, nor the Tripartitum contained any regulation for the dowry, this institution appeared in the Hungarian practice meaning all the properties the women got to the marriage and handed over to her husband and in case the marriage remained childless, the dowry had to be repaid for the woman or her family. This property could be a movable one or a real estate as well, differing from the Austrian dowry that usually was paid in cash to the husband. The dowry as it existed in the prenuptial agreements of the Hungarian aristocracy was mainly similar to the dowry specified according to the Austrian customs, the families usually were more keen on providing money as a dowry than on giving real estates to the women.

As an expression of reciprocity to the dowry, the future husband always stipulated as *Widerlag* (counter-dowry) double the amount of the dowry.[41] The future fate of the *Widerlag* differed from that of the dowry. Half of it became the property of the wife after the marriage ended, the other half had to be inherited by the couple's children, or in the absence of children, reimbursed to

---

Mobilien, Pferd und Wagen annoch dreytausend gulden, Item anstatt deren Puncto 9no versprochenen 30000 fl[oreni] alß frey aigenes fünffzig tausend gulden und endlichen anstatt deren Puncto 5to erhaltenen 2000 fl[oreni] für Spennadel Geld, vier tausend Gulden Jährlich abgereichet und richtig verabfolget werden." ÖStA, HHStA OMeA SR, Ehepakten des Hofstaates Karton 12, No. 86 – Prenuptial agreement of Anton Fürst Esterházy and Theresia Gräfin Erdődy, 6 January 1763.

39 "[...] verspricht mehr benandte Freyle Brauth mit genehmhaltung Ihres wohlgemelten Herrn Vattern dem Herrn Bräutigams zu einem wahren und gewissen heyrathsguet in Jahr und Tag noch vollbrachter hochzeith gegen Quittung baar und richtig zubezahlen und zuerlegen fünff tausent gulden Rhein[isch]." ÖStA, HHStA OMeA SR, Ehepakten des Hofstaates Karton 10, No. 23 – Prenuptial agreement of Ludwig Ernst Batthyány and Theresia Gräfin Kinsky, 16 May 1717.

40 "[...] zu einem gewissen und rechten heyrath Gutt eine Summa von zwey taußent gulden Rheinis verheyratet worden." ÖStA, HHStA, OMeA SR, Ehepakten des Hofstaates Karton 10, No. 27 – Prenuptial agreement of Paul Karl Graf Pálffy and Maria Margaretha Gräfin Stubenbergh, 22 November 1718.

41 About the doubling of the amount: „[...] gedachter Herr Bräutigamb so benant fünff tausend gulden heyraths-gutt doppelt nemblich mit zehen taußent gulden Rheinisch: zu widerlegen gehalten und verbunden seyn [...]" ÖStA, HHStA OMeA SR, Ehepakten des Hofstaates Karton 10, No. 28 – Prenuptial agreement of Johann Graf Pálffy and Anna Eleonora Gräfin Esterházy, 11 May 1715.

PRENUPTIAL AGREEMENTS OF THE HUNGARIAN ARISTOCRACY 41

the husband's family. This occurred only if the wife survived her husband. In the reverse case, the husband was entitled to keep the *Widerlag* for himself. In this sense the *Widerlag* differed significantly from the marital remuneration existing in the Hungarian legal system, because in Hungary the husband had to transfer the amount not only to the wife but also to the wife's family, in case she died first. Of course, the *Widerlag* and the remuneration paid to the wife differed in their aim, too. The first was a counter-provision to the dowry, the second the prize for the marital virtues of the wife.

Prenuptial agreements often stipulated *Morgengabe*, even if it did not exist in the Hungarian legal system. This had been a valuable gift given to the wife right after the consummation of the marriage. These were pieces to be used by the wife during the marriage. The rings the future wives were entitled to get also constituted a necessary part of the gift.[42]

Aside from the gift, sometimes the future husband helped to cover the costs of the wedding too by paying the so-called *Hochzeits-Solennität, Hochzeits-Praesent* besides giving gifts and contributed to the adornation or so-called *Staffierung* of the wife. The amount of the latter provisions always depended on the social status of the spouses, so the expression *"standmässig"* (decent and proper) was always used as an attributive: *"standmässiger Subsistenz"* (decent and proper alimony), or *"Standt gemessener Außstaffierung"* (decent and proper endowment).

The other main part of the prenuptial agreement provisions were the provisions made in favour of future widows. Among these provisions, both life-estate and inheritance provisions can be found. Almost all prenuptial agreements entitled the future widow to put her late husband's property in escrow until she received her remuneration.[43]

---

42  "[...] nebst zweyen Diamant Ringen und tausend Ducaten in specie." ÖStA, HHStA OMeA SR, Ehepakten des Hofstaates Karton 10, No. 15 – Prenuptial agreement of Ferdinand Karl Graf Aspremond-Lynden and Theresia Gräfin Esterházy, 1 January 1730. "[...] mehrgedacht Fräulen Brauth neben zweyen Brauth Ringen anstatt des Geschmucks als mit welchem dieselbe von Ihro Frauen Mutter beraiths zur genüge versehen ist, und für andere eine Hoff Damen zuraichen gewöhnliche Brauth Regalien zwey taußent Ducaten in specie zugesagt worden." ÖStA, HHStA OMeA SR, Ehepakten des Hofstaates Karton 10, No. 27 – Prenuptial agreement of Paul Karl Graf Pálffy and Maria Margaretha Gräfin Stubenbergh, 22 November 1718.

43  "[...] das die Frau Wittib einen Jahrs frist nach ableben des Herrn Bräutigambs all solcher, vermög dises Heyraths contracts habender rechtmässiger Sprüchen und Forderungen wegen, vollständig beyfriediget werden [...]krafft dieser Ehe-beredung vollkommene macht und gwalt haben solle sine omni Juris strepitu per quemcunque Judicem pedaneum non obstante quocunque Juristitii tempore nec alio qualitercunque cogitabili impedimento, auß besagter Baimozischer herrschafft [...] Jährlich eine Summa von Sieben

The widow could live in the house of the husband and in case she did not wish to remain there, a specified amount had to be given to her for her annual subsistence to cover the costs of her residence. Usually the amount of this subsistence was 600 Rhenish guilder per year, but the husband could provide either more or less.[44] This amount was given in addition to the usual alimony of 3 000 Rhenish guilder. Moreover, the widow always received the brougham with the horses and the movables that served as appointments to her rooms.[45]

The common characteristics of these above mentioned legal provisions are that all of them were foreign to the Hungarian practice and they showed up in Hungarian prenuptial agreements only if one of the spouses came from the Austrian hereditary provinces.

## 6 Conclusion

The subject of marriage and marital property referring to nobles provides an outstanding opportunity for the examination of the interference of legal systems because the marital relations of the nobility belonging to the royal court did not stop at state borders but cut across the royal courts of the Kingdoms of Europe. Although prenuptial agreements often expressed that they were drawn up according to the laws and customs of Hungary, it is also proven that the use

---

tausent gulden [...] executive einzutreiben und Ihro einräumen zu lassen [...]" ÖStA, HH-StA OMeA SR, Ehepakten des Hofstaates Karton 10, No. 28 – Prenuptial agreement of Johann Graf Pálffy and Anna Eleonora Gräfin Esterházy, 11 May 1715.

44  „[...] die Wittibliche Wohnung Sechs hundert Gulden, die helffte von halb zu halb Jahren vorauß [...] in guetter gangbahrer Münz hier in Wienn bezahlt werde." ÖStA, HHStA OMeA SR, Ehepakten des Hofstaates Karton 10, No. 35 – Prenuptial agreement of Leopold Graf Pálffy and Antonia Gräfin Ratouit de Souches, 17 June 1708.

45  "Die Fahrnussen betreffend solle der Fräulen Brauth, im Fall Ihrer Verwittibung, alle Einrichtung von dreyen Wohnzimmern [...] aigenthumblich verbleiben. Ingleichen Ihro ein ganzer Zug der schönsten verhandenen Pferden und darzue gehörigen geschieren, sambt den besten Wagen, alles nach aigenen belieben zu erwehlen, dan ein Pferd für den aufwarter und ein Klepper für den Reitknecht verabfolgen werden." ÖStA, HHStA OMeA SR, Ehepakten des Hofstaates Karton 11, No. 56 – Prenuptial agreement of Franz Folch Fürst de Cardona and Antonia Gräfin Czobor, 22 April 1731. „Auß dreyen Zimmern des Gräfflich Pálffyschen haueß allhier in Wienn, benanntlichen aus dem Parada-Zimmer, dem Mitteren und ordinari Schlaffzimmer die bether und alle in selbigen sich befindende zugehörige Mobilien, ingleichen der beste Wagen und ein Zug Pferde verabfolget werden sollen." ÖStA, HHStA OMeA SR, Ehepakten des Hofstaates Karton 11, No. 42 – Prenuptial agreement of Niklas Graf Pálffy and Maria Anna Gräfin Althann, 11 January 1733.

of Hungarian legal institutions was not exclusive in the cases of Hungarian aristocrats either.[46]

Marriage contracts, dowry stipulations and last wills and testaments preserved in the various archives of Budapest and Vienna can serve as outstanding evidence to show how Hungarian officials who belonged to the court and married foreign persons experienced foreign legal institutions during their everyday life and started to use these institutions in the Hungarian legal practice for achieving their personal goals. These documents proove social interference in the development of the legal system and compared to other documents reffering to marriages contracted between common nobles of Hungary can give us an insight how foreign legal institutions could have an impact on the development of the Hungarian legal system.

Of course, the examination of these documents is not easy at all due to the methodology problems we are facing while reading the documents written in different languages. We must proceed very carefully when we are identifying the legal institutions the terminology was meant to cover.

This is of an immense importance if the foreign legal terminology on which the legal institution is named in the agreement, refers to a legal institution having an another character in the Hungarian legal practice. In most cases, the terminology fit to the proper meaning of the legal institution of the legal system to which the contracting party was bound, but there were some exceptions in the cases of Hungarian aristocrats, who wrote their documents in a language other than their mother tongue, or the officially used language. And of course we have to be very careful if the documents did not name an institution at all just explained the fulfilment of the specific duties.[47]

Through these documents we may also find proof of how the Hungarian aristocracy tried to get rid of his Hungarian character at the times when they had to fit in the court of Vienna. But this time lasted only until the end of the 18th century after which the Hungarian aristocrats – except of some families – tried

---

46 „[...] nach denen Hungarischen und Selbigen Wittiben zustehenden privilegierten Rechten [...]" – ÖStA, HHStA, OMeA SR, Ehepakten des Hofstaates Karton 1, No. 23 – Prenuptial agreement of Ludwig Ernst Batthyány and Theresia Gräfin Kinsky, 16 May 1717 or "[...] Vermög dieses Heirats denen löbl[ichen] Hungarischen Recht und Gewohnheiten zu folge [...]" ÖStA, HHStA OMeA SR, Ehepakten des Hofstaates Karton 10, No. 28 – Prenuptial agreement of Johann Graf Pálffy and Anna Eleonora Gräfin Esterházy, 11 May 1715.

47 "Elsőben: Minthogy emlétet Gróff Pálffy Miklós Uram az én kívánságomon kívül csak szintén proprio motu tíz ezer forintot megh nevezett jegyesemmel ad [...]" [First: the mentioned Count Nicholas Pálffy in addition to my request gives with my mentioned fiancee ten thousand florins for his own consideration [...]" ÖStA HHStA FA. Pálffy Arma I, Lad. 9, Fasc. 2, No. 7 – Prenuptial agreement of Christoph Erdődy and Susanne Maria Pálffy, 28 February 1672.

to get back to their Hungarian roots and contribute to the development of the Hungarian nation. During the 19th century most of these aristocratic families turned on the contrary, they took part in the national reform movements requesting the approval of the Hungarian language as the official state language. But these were different times with different aristocracy living in them.


## Bibliography

### Archival Sources

Magyar Nemzeti Levéltár [National Archives of Hungary], Family Archive of the Esterházy Family.

Österreichisches Staatsarchiv, Haus-, Hof- und Staatsarchiv Wien, Familien Archiv Pálffy.

Österreichisches Staatsarchiv, Haus-, Hof- und Staatsarchiv Wien, Familien Archiv Erdődy.

Österreichisches Staatsarchiv, Haus-, Hof- und Staatsarchiv Wien, Oberhofmeisteramt Sonderreihe, Ehepakten des Hofstaates.

### Literature

Zoltán Ács: *Nemzetiségek a történelmi Magyarországon*, [Nationalities of the Historical Hungary], Kossuth Könyvkiadó, Budapest, 1996.

Endre Arató: *A magyar „nemzeti" ideológia jellemző vonásai a 18. században*, [Characteristics of the Hungarian „National" Ideology in the 18th century] = *Nemzetiség a feudalizmus korában* [Nationalities in the Era of Feudalism], György Spira (ed.) Akadémiai Kiadó, Budapest, 1972.

Emma Bartoniek: *Corona és regnum* [Crown and Regnum], Századok, 7–8(1934).

Iván Berkeszi: *A magyar nyelv a magánélet terén 1711–1790*, [Hungarian Language in the Private Life 1711–1790], Wunder Gyula nyomdája, Fehértemplom, 1885.

György Bónis: *Jogtudó értelmiség a Mohács előtti Magyarországon* [The Legally Qualified Intelligentsia of Hungary before Mohács], Akadémiai Kiadó, Budapest, 1971.

Wilhelm Brauneder: *Die Entwicklung des Ehegüterrechts in Österreich. Ein Beitrag zur Dogmengeschichte und Rechtstatsachenforschung des Spätmittelalters und der Neuzeit*, Peter Lang Verlag, Salzburg-München, 1973.

Győző Cholnoky: *Állam és nemzet. Uralkodó nemzet- és nemzetiségpolitikai eszmék Magyarországon (1920–1941)* [State and Nation. Ruling National and Nation-political Theories in Hungary (1920 – 1941)], Hatodik Síp Alapítvány, Budapest, 1996.

Ferenc Eckhart: *A szentkorona-eszme története* [The History of the Holy Crown Theory] MTA, Budapest, 1941.

Győző EMBER: *Az újkori magyar közigazgatás története Mohácstól a török kiűzéséig* [The History of the Hungarian Administration from Mohács until the Expulsion of the Turks], Magyar Országos Levéltár kiadványai, Budapest, 1946.

Zoltán FALLENBÜCHL: *A Magyar Kamara tisztviselői a* XVII. *században* [The Clerks of the Hungarian Chamber in the 17th Century], Levéltári Közlemények, 39(1968), 233–268.

István FAZEKAS: *Humanisten und Juristen. Das Personal der Ungarischen Hofkanzlei in der Frühen Neuzeit. (1526–1690)* = *Institutions of Legal History with Special Regard to Legal Culture and History*, Gábor BÉLI, Diana DUCHONOVÁ, Anna FUNDÁRKOVÁ, István KAJTÁR, Zsuzsanna PERES (eds.), Publikon, Pécs, 2011, 321–331.

Lajos GECSÉNYI: *A döntést előkészítő hivatalnoki elit összetételéről. A Magyar Kamara vezetői és tanácsosai a 16. században* [About the Constitution of the Decision Preparing Administrative Elite. The Leaders and Councillors of the Hungarian Chamber in the 16th Century] = *Magyar évszázadok. Tanulmányok Kosáry Domokos 90. születésnapjára.* [Hungarian Centuries. Publications for the 90th Birthday Anniversary of Domokos Kosáry], Mária ORMOS (ed.), Osiris, Budapest, 2003, 100–113.

Johann Gottfried HERDER: *Briefe zur Beförderung der Humanität. J.G. Herders sämmtliche Werke. Zur Philosophie und Geschichte. Eilfter Theil. Briefe zur Beförderung der Humanität*, Johann VON MÜLLER (ed.), Büreau der deutschen Classiker, Carlsruhe, 1820.

József HOLUB: *Néhány kérdés a leánynegyed köréből* [A Few Questions Regarding the Quarter], Magyar Tudományos Akadémia, Budapest, 1936.

Emma IVÁNYI: *Esterházy Pál nádor közigazgatási tevékenysége (1681–1713)* [Palatine Paul Esterházy's Administrative Function (1681–1713)], Akadémiai Kiadó, Budapest, 1991.

György JANCSÓ: *A magyar házassági és házastársi öröklési jog* [The Hungarian Marriage and Marital Succession's Law], Politzer, Budapest, 1901.

László KATUS: *A modern Magyarország születése. Magyarország története 1711–1914* [The Birth of the Modern Hungary. The History of Hungary 1711–1914], Kronosz, Pécs, 2012.

Zoltán KÉRÉSZY: *Adalékok a magyar kamarai pénzügyigazgatás történetéhez* [Appendices to the History of the Hungarian Financial Administration], Benkő, Budapest, 1916.

Károly KISTELEKI: *Magyar nemzet- magyar állampolgárság* [Hungarian Nation - Hungarian Citizenship] = *A kettős monarchia – Die Doppelmonarchie*, Gábor MÁTHÉ, Attila MENYHÁRD, Barna MEZEY (eds.), ELTE ÁJK, Budapest, 2018, 79–113.

Domokos KOSÁRY: *A magyar és európai politika történetéből* [From the History of the Hungarian and European Politics], Osiris, Budapest, 2001.

Domokos KOSÁRY: *Művelődés a* XVIII. *századi Magyarországon* [Education in the 18th Century Hungary], Akadémiai Kiadó, Budapest, 1983.

Elisabeth LOBENWEIN: *Adelige Briefkultur am Beispiel der Privatkorrespondenz der Brüder Hyeronimus (1732–1812) und Gundaker (1731–1807) Colloredo = Adel im 18. Jahrhundert. Umrisse einer sozialen Gruppe in der Krise*, Gerhard AMMERER, Elisabeth LOBENWEIN, Martin SCHEUTZ (eds.), Studienverlag, Innsbruck-Wien-Bozen, 2015, 318–342.

Theodor MAYER: *Das Verhältnis der Hofkammer zur ungarischen Kammer bis zur Regierung Maria Theresias = Mitteilungen des Instituts für österreichische Geschichtsforschung*, vol. 9, Oswald REDLICH (ed.), Innsbruck, 1915, 178–395.

Lajos MERÉNYI: *Herceg Eszterházy Pál nádor* [Palatine Prince Paul Esterházy], Magyar Történelmi Társulat, Budapest, 1895.

István MONOK: *A művelt arisztokrata. A magyarországi főnemesség olvasmányai a XVI–XVII. században* [The Educated Aristocrat. The Readings of the Hungarian Aristocracy in the 16th–17th centuries], Kossuth Kiadó, Budapest-Eger, 2012.

Irén ŐRINÉ BILKEI: *A hiteles helyek szerepe a feudáliskori magyar közigazgatásban* [The Role of the Loca Credibilia in the Hungarian Administration of the Feudal Era], Comitatus 3 (1993)/3, 52–54.

Géza PÁLFFY: *A bécsi udvar és a magyar rendek a 16. században* [The Viennese Court and the Hungarian Estates in the 16th century], Történelmi Szemle 3–4/(1999).

Géza PÁLFFY: *A Magyar Királyság és a Habsburg Monarchia a 16. században* [The Hungarian Kingdom and the Habsburg Monarchy in the 16th century], MTA TKI, Budapest, 2016.

Géza PÁLFFY: *A magyar nemesség bécsi integrációjának színterei a 16.-17. században* [The Stages of the Hungarian Nobility's Integration to Vienna in the 16th–17th Century] = *Tanulmányok Szakály Ferenc emlékére* [Publication for the Memory of Ferenc Szakály], Pál FODOR, Géza PÁLFFY, István György TÓTH (eds.), MTA TKI, Budapest, 2002, 307–331.

Géza PÁLFFY: *Der Adel aus den ungarischen Ländern am Kaiserhof 1526–1612 = Die Weltliche und Kirchliche Elite aus dem Königreich Böhmen und Königreich Ungarn am Wiener Kaiserhof im 16.-17. Jahrhundert*, Anna FUNDÁRKOVÁ, István FAZEKAS (eds.), Publikationen der Ungarischen Geschichtsforschung in Wien, Wien, 2013, 37–76.

József PERÉNYI: *A magyar „nemzeti öntudat" fejlődése a 11.-13. században* [The Development of the Hungarian „National Identity" during the 11–13th Centuries] = *Nemzetiség a feudalizmus korában* [Nationalities in the Feudalism], György SPIRA (ed.), Akadémiai Kiadó, Budapest, 1972, 83–101.

Zsuzsanna PERES: *Hitbérkikötések a magyar főúri családok körében a Werbőczy utáni időszakban* [Stipulations of Marital Remuneration among the Hungarian High Noble Families in the Post-Werbőczy Period] = *A jogi kultúrtörténet és a jogi néprajz új forrásai* [The Newest Sources of the Legal Cultural History and Legal Ethnography], Janka Teodóra NAGY (ed.), PTE Kultúratudományi, Pedagógusképző és Vidékfejlesztési Kar, Szekszárd, 2018, 281–300.

Zsuzsanna PERES: *Marriage Property Rights of the Noble Women according to their Prenuptial Agreements*, Journal on European History of Law 9(2018)/2, 125–132.

Katalin PÉTER: *Gyermek a koraújkori Magyarországon* [Children of the Early Modern Times' Hungary], MTA Történettudományi Intézete, Budapest, 1992.

Lajos RÁCZ: *A 15. század humanista magyar államelméletei* [The Hungarian Humanist State Theories of the 15th Century] = *Tripartitum trium professorum. Három szegedi jogtörténész* [Tripartitum trium professorum. Three Legal Historians of Szeged], Elemér BALOGH, Mária HOMOKI-NAGY (eds.), Iurisperitus, Szeged, 2017, 74–86.

Béla RADVÁNSZKY: *Magyar családélet és háztartás a* XVI. *és* XVII. *században* [Hungarian Family Life and Households in the 16th and 17th Centuries], vol. 1, MTA, Budapest, 1896.

Jenő SZŰCS: *„Nemzetiség" és „nemzeti öntudat" a középkorban. Szempontok egy egységes fogalmi nyelv kialakításához* ["Nationality" and "National Identity" in the Middle Ages. Viewpoints to the Formation of a Unanimous Concept of Language] = *Nemzetiség a feudalizmus korában* [Nationalities in the Feudalism], György SPIRA (ed.), Akadémiai Kiadó, Budapest, 1972, 9–71.

Katalin TOMA: *Nádasdy Istvan európai tanulmányútja: a Kavalierstour alkalmazása a magyar főuri nevelési gyakorlatban* [Stephen Nádasdy's European Study Trip: the Cavallierstour in the Education of the Hungarian Aristocrats] = *Idővel paloták ... Magyar udvari kultúra a 16–17. században* [Palaces by Time... Hungarian Court Culture in the 16th to 17th Centuries], Nóra G. ETENYI, Ildikó HORN (eds.), Balassi Kiadó, Budapest, 2005, 192–214.

*Tripartitum. Magyar Törvénytár. Corpus Juris Hungarici. 1000–1895.* Márkus DEZSŐ (ed.), Franklin, Budapest, 1896.

Ágnes R. VÁRKONYI: *Magyarország keresztútjain. Tanulmányok* [On the Crossroads of Hungary. Essays], Gondolat, Budapest, 1978.

Karl VOCELKA: *Glanz und Untergang der Höfischen Welt. Repräsentation, Reform und Reaktion im Habsburgischen Vielvölkerstaat* = Österreichische Geschichte 1699–1815, Herwig WOLFRAM (ed.), Ueberreuter, Wien, 2004.

Thomas WINKELBAUER: *Fürst und Fürstendiener. Gundacker von Liechtenstein, ein österreichischer Aristokrat des konfessionellen Zeitalters.* Oldenbourg Verlag, Wien-München, 1999.

Thomas WINKELBAUER: *Ständefreiheit und Fürstenmacht. Lander und Untertanen des Hauses Habsburg im konfessionellen Zeitalter*, Teil I = Österreichische Geschichte 1522–1699, Herwig WOLFRAM (ed.), Wirtschaftsverlag Ueberreuter, Wien, 2004.

Jakob WÜHRER, Martin SCHEUTZ: *Zu Diensten Ihrer Majestät. Hofordnungen und Instruktionsbücher am frühneuzeitlichen Wiener Hof,* Quelleneditionen des Instituts für Österreichische Geschichtsforschung, Wien-München, 2011.

*Österreichisches Staatsarchiv, Haus-, Hof- und Staatsarchiv Wien, Familien Archiv Pálffy –* ÖStA, HHStA, F.A. Pálffy

*Österreichisches Staatsarchiv, Haus-, Hof- und Staatsarchiv Wien, Familien Archiv Erdődy* – ÖStA, HHStA, F.A. Erdődy

*National Archives of Hungary (Magyar Nemzeti Levéltár, Országos Levéltár), Family Archive of the Esterházy Family* – MNL, OL F.A. Esterházy

CHAPTER 3

# Revolution and the Instrumentality of Law: Theories of Property in the American and French Revolutions

*Bart Wauters*

Especially in periods of political revolution, law often plays a highly instrumental role in giving shape to the new revolutionary society. Revolution means almost by definition a great change in the political and social conditions and is often an opportunity to set up political and legal structures that supposedly improve the framework for political and legal decision-making. The law is the perfect instrument to capture the fundamental ideas that underlie the new revolutionary framework.

This chapter, will focus on the revolutionary era in North America and France at the end of the eighteenth century. It will focus on a single idea that was foundational in both countries, but apparently received different treatment: property. It will compare two basic legal instruments that captured the fundamental ideas underlying the two revolutions (the French Declaration of the Rights of Man and of the Citizen of 1789 and the US Declaration of Independence) and analyse to what extent these documents captured Enlightenment ideas on the nature of property.

It is widely known that the French Declaration of the Rights of Man and of the Citizen of 1789 listed property as one of the "natural," "sacred" and "inviolable" rights of man.[1] In the US Declaration of Independence, on the other hand, Thomas Jefferson did not include property as one of the "unalienable" rights of

---

1   The French Declaration did not include explicitly the idea of "unalienable" rights, but from the parliamentary debates ahead of the adoption of the text it becomes clear that the conception of "*inaliénabilité*" was what the National Assembly obviously had in mind; cf. for instance the interventions of deputies Mougin, Pélérin and d'André on 20 August 1789 in the National Assembly: *Archives Parlementaires de 1787 à 1860. Recueil complet des débats legislatifs et politiques des chambres Françaises*, Jérôme MAVIDAL, Émile LAURENT, Emile CLAVEL (eds.), Librairie Administrative de Paul Dupont, Paris, 1875, Première série, tome 8, 463: "Les représentants du peuple français [...] ont résolu d'exposer, dans une déclaration solennelle, les droits naturels, inaliénables et sacrés de l'homme [...] Les droits inaliénables et imprescriptibles de l'homme sont la liberté, la propriété, la sûreté, l'égalité des droits, la conservation de son honneur et de sa vie, la communication de ses pensées et la résistance à l'oppression."

---

© KONINKLIJKE BRILL NV, LEIDEN, 2020 | DOI:10.1163/9789004417274_004

man. Hence the obvious question arises: Why is there this difference in treatment? Was the difference meaningful?

It is not an indulgence to dwell on the appropriateness of these questions in the first place. Could it be expected that property was going to be included in Jefferson's Declaration? The answer is affirmative. There were other revolutionary constitutional texts in the young United States, drafted before or shortly after Jefferson's Declaration, that did list property as an unalienable right. The most notable is the *Virginia Declaration of Rights*, approved on 12 June 1776, only one month before the Declaration of Independence, and a direct source of Jefferson.[2] Moreover, John Locke, a more than likely source of Jefferson (more on that later), framed the triad "Lives, Liberties and Estates," which had to be preserved by governments.[3] Finally, William Blackstone, with whose *Commentaries of the Law of England* Jefferson, who was a lawyer, was well acquainted, also considered security, liberty and private property as the "principal" and "primary" rights of the English.[4] If Jefferson's most important sources all included the right to private property in the same breath as life and liberty, why didn't he include it? Was its omission significant?

## 1 Contextual Explanations

Scholars have pointed to the existence of chattel slavery in America as one of the reasons that explain the omission of private property in the Declaration of Independence. When human beings are legally considered as property, awarding property the status of an unalienable right would have given the impression

---

2 Article 1 reads: "That all men are by nature equally free and independent, and have certain inherent rights, of which, when they enter into a state of society, they cannot, by any compact, deprive or divest their posterity; namely, the enjoyment of life and liberty, with the means of acquiring and possessing property, and pursuing and obtaining happiness and safety," retrieved from Gunston Hall Website (gunstonhall.org/georgemason/human_rights/vdr_final.html, accessed 11.02.2016). Other state constitutions, such as those of Massachusetts, Pennsylvania or New Hampshire also made direct references to property as an unalienable right, cf. Luigi Marco BASSANI: *Life, Liberty, and ....: Jefferson on Property Rights*, Journal of Libertarian Studies, 18(2004), 31–87, 53.

3 John LOCKE: *Two Treatises of Government*, Peter LASLETT (ed.), Cambridge University Press, Cambridge (UK) 1988. Cf. e.g. II.87 (p. 323–324), II.123 (p. 350), II.209 (p. 404–405), II.222 (p. 412–414).

4 William BLACKSTONE: *Commentaries on the Laws of England*, J.B. Lippincott Company, Philadelphia, 1893, Book I, Chapter 1 (vol. 1, 100): "And these [rights of the people of England] may be reduced to three principal or primary articles; the right of personal security, the right of personal liberty, and the right of private property."

REVOLUTION AND INSTRUMENTALITY OF LAW 51

as to legitimize and perpetuate the institution of slavery. Jefferson, while a major slave-owner himself, did not approve of the institution and in his draft of the Declaration of Independence he included even a clause that contained an attack on the slave trade (the clause was removed in the final document).[5]

Apart from chattel slavery, the American revolutionaries also had to cope with their inconsistencies towards the "Indians" (or "Native Americans").[6] Even if there were some who argued that colonial settlers had honestly purchased the land from indigenous people,[7] it did not escape many observers that Native Americans were often forced to cede their lands under the threat of so-called "just wars." Moreover, Jefferson himself was very much aware that the "Indians" had rights too,[8] but that it would not suit the interests of white settlers if indigenous property rights were recognized as an unalienable.

Policy reasons should also be taken into account. Jefferson and the founding fathers were very aware that they had a unique opportunity to frame a society according to some pre-defined political ideals. The term "classical republicanism" has sometimes been used to style the political ideals of the initial phase of the American Revolution,[9] with a wide distribution of land ownership among

---

5  Peter GARNSEY: *Thinking about Property. From Antiquity to the Age of Revolution*, Cambridge University Press, Cambridge (UK), 2007, 222–223. The clause reads: "He has waged cruel war against human nature itself, violating its most sacred rights of life and liberty in the persons of a distant people who never offended him, captivating & carrying them into slavery in another hemisphere or to incur miserable death in their transportation thither [...]" = *The Papers of Thomas Jefferson. Vol. 1, 1760–1776*, Julien BOYD (ed.), Princeton University Press, Princeton, 1950, 243–247. The clause that was eventually removed to appease Northern slave traders and to convince Southern states, such as South Carolina and Georgia, to sign the Declaration.

6  GARNSEY: *op. cit.*, 223–224.

7  E.g. John Adams quoted in William B. SCOTT: *In Pursuit of Happiness: American Conceptions of Property from the Seventeenth to the Twentieth Century*, Indiana University Press, Bloomington, 1977, 40.

8  Anthony F.C. WALLACE: *Jefferson and the Indians. The Tragic Fate of the First Americans*, The Belknap Press of Harvard University Press, 162–165. "The attention which you pay to their [=Indians'] rights also does you great honor, as the want of that is a principal source of dishonor to the American character, the two principles on which our Conduct towards Indians should be founded, are justice and fear. After the injuries we have done them they cannot love us, which leaves us no alternative but that of fear to keep them from attacking us, but justice is what we should never lose sight of & in time it may recover their esteem," extract from a letter of Thomas Jefferson to Benjamin Hawkins, in reply to the latter's complaint about some states' dubious claims on Indian lands, quoted *ibidem*, 165. Cf. also Stanley N. KATZ: *Thomas Jefferson and the Right to Property in Revolutionary America*, Journal of Law and Economics, 19(1976) 467, 471.

9  Gordon S. WOOD: *The Radicalism of the American Revolution*, Vintage Books, New York, 1991; John G.A. POCOCK: *The Machiavellian Moment. Florentine Political Thought and the Atlantic*

individual farmers labouring independently and virtuously and upholding a republican form of government at its heart. For this wide distribution of land ownership, Jefferson succeeded in his native Virginia to abolish existing proprietary structures such as primogeniture or entail, while also favouring direct grants of small plots of land to "husbandmen."[10] Jefferson thus seemed to have taken for granted that government had far-reaching powers to regulate important aspects of the distribution of private property.

The last contextual element that might have been a practical obstacle to the inclusion of property as an unalienable right in the Declaration of Independence, was the fact that many revolutionary freeholders held their lands under colonial charters that were granted by the English crown. Loyalists stressed for instance that it would be inconsistent to claim "inherent and indefeasible" rights on the one hand, while at the same time to continue to make use of the common law to settle landed property dispute.[11] Some revolutionaries, including Jefferson, were of course quick to dismiss this, but others still felt uneasy about the feudal restraints in the colonial land charters and found that natural rights arguments undercut their own land claims.[12]

In France on the other hand, feudalism and the concentration of landowners in the National Assembly help to explain the inclusion of property into the Declaration of the Rights of Man and of the Citizen as a sacred and inviolable right. In spite of their divergences in opinion, moderates and radicals shared a belief in the defence of property rights against feudal and royal despotism.[13] Moreover, in the crazy days of August 1789, the countryside saw upheaval and violent unrest by peasants who wanted to dispose of the feudal regime, and the National Assembly was under pressure to produce quickly a document that

---

*Republican Tradition*, Princeton University Press, Princeton 1975 (re-edn 2003). Cf. also Bernard BAILYN: *The Ideological Origins of the American Revolution*, Harvard University Press, Cambridge (MA), 1992 (enlarged edition).

10 KATZ: *op. cit.*, 471–476.

11 Martin HOWARD, Jr.: *A Letter From A Gentleman at Halifax* (1765) = *Tracts of the American Revolution 1763–1776*, Merrill JENSEN (ed.), Hackett Publishing Company, Indianapolis-Cambridge (MA), 1966, 63–78, the alleged inconsistencies of the revolutionaries are highlighted on 69.

12 SCOTT: *op. cit.*, 39–40. Cf. also KATZ: *op. cit.*, 476–478.

13 Thomas E. KAISER: *Property, Sovereignty, the Declaration of the Rights of Man, and the Tradition of French Jurisprudence* = *The French Idea of Freedom. The Old Regime and the Declaration of Rights of 1789*, Dale VAN KLEY (ed.), Stanford University Press, Stanford, 1994, 300–339, 418–424; Rafe BLAUFARB: *The Great Demarcation. The French Revolution and the Invention of Modern Property*, Oxford University Press, Oxford, 2016, 13.

would vent some of the concerns of public opinion.[14] Some enlightened nobles on the National Assembly, while recognizing the need for reform of the feudal system, stressed that feudal rights were property rights and as such, they were as sacred and inviolable as other property rights. The Duke of Alguillon, one of France's largest landowners and politically linked to Lafayette, declared that:

> Les propriétaires des fiefs, des terres seigneuriales, ne sont, il faut l'avouer, que bien rarement coupables des excès dont se plaignent leurs vassaux ; mais leurs gens d'affaires sont souvent sans pitié, et le malheureux culti- vateur, soumis au reste barbare des lois féodales qui subsistent encore en France, gémit de la contrainte dont il est la victime. Ces droits, on ne peut le dissimuler, sont une propriété, et toute propriété est sacrée ; mais ils sont onéreux aux peuples, et tout le monde convient de la gêne contin- uelle qu'ils leur imposent.

He therefore proposed that vassals could buy back the feudal rights over fiefs and seigniorial lands at a price established by the Assembly, an idea that found its way to the final decree that abolished the feudal system.[15]

Declaring property rights sacred and establishing compensation when pub- lic necessity required expropriating someone was a way of bringing the nobil- ity on board of an adventure, the outcome of which was still largely unknown in August 1789.[16] Obtaining an as large consensus as possible in spite of obvi- ous differences was still the spirit by the end of August. The decision to include Article 17 seems to have been taken at the end of a long and exhausting session on the 26th of August; there was no similar article in the different drafts that were under the consideration of the Assembly, and it was introduced by Adrien Duport on the spot. The records of the debates on Article 17 are very succinct; it seems that impatience among many deputies to get over with the "preliminaries"

---

14    Cf. e.g. the intervention of Rabaud de Saint-Étienne in the morning session of 24 August: *Archives Parlementaires...*, *op. cit.*, 482.

15    *Archives Parlementaires...*, *op. cit.*, 344. Intervention of the Duke of Alguillon. Cf. 397 for the text of the final decree (art. 1).

16    Jean-Jacques CLERE: *L'abolition des droits féodaux en France*, Cahiers d'histoire, 94–95(2005), 135–157. Cf. also the conclusion of the evening session of 4 August 1789, *Archives Parlementaires...*, *op. cit.*, 350: "Faculté de rembourser les droits seigneuriales"; Article 2 of the draft of 5 August 1789, *ibid.*, 352, and the text finally adopted in the morning session of 6 August 1789 (*ibid.*, 356). Cf. also Article 1 of the consolidated text of the *Décret relative à l'abolition des privileges*, adopted on 11 August 1789, *ibid.*, 397.

of a Declaration and to proceed with the "real" work of drafting a constitution explains why the text of Duport passed without too much noise.[17]

It is possible that these contextual differences between the United States of America and France adequately explain why the French did include property and the Americans did not. After all, even documents such as Declaration of Independence or the Declaration of the Rights of Man and of the Citizen are the outcome of political discussion and compromise, and pragmatism is an important driver in politics, even in times of revolution.

## 2 Philosophical Considerations

But was the omission of Jefferson also significant on a deeper, philosophical level? Did the omission mean that for Jefferson property was not an unalienable right after all? Conversely, did the French inclusion mean that they had a different concept of the right of property? To what extent did the French, the Americans, or both capture or instrumentalise the Enlightenment ideas about property?

Recent authors such as Bassani are not impressed by the omission of property in the US Declaration of Independence and its substitution with "pursuit of happiness." They argue that "pursuit of happiness" includes the right to property and point to other writings by Jefferson that did list property as "unalienable." They also emphasize that "almost to a man, Patriots were agreed that the proper ends of government were to protect people in their lives, liberty and property," and as such, property was unmistakably included within the Bill of Rights of the Constitution. Their conclusion is that the omission does not mean that Jefferson did not consider property as an unalienable right.[18]

Other authors, however, think that the omission means just that: Jefferson's denial of property as an unalienable right. Allen Jayne thought that the rights of life and liberty for Jefferson were unalienable, in the sense that such rights

---

17    The report of the debate reads as follows: "Le plus grand nombre des membres veut passer enfin à la Constitution; d'autres veulent que l'on ne termine pas la déclaration des droits sans y insérer un article concernant la propriété. M. Duport en propose un qui réunit sur-le-champ beaucoup de suffrages, non qu'il n'y ait eu beaucoup d'amendements, qu'il n'ait été suivi d'une foule d'autres projets; mais qu'il a passé tel que le voici: [...]." *Archives Parlementaires..., op. cit.*, 489.

18    BASSANI: *op. cit.*, 49–59; the quote is from Forrest McDONALD: *Novus Ordo Seclorum. The Intellectual Origins of the Constitution*, University Press of Kansas, Lawrence, 1985, 1, quoted in BASSANI: *op. cit.*, 44–45.

could not be *internally* renounced or alienated, even though an individual could give them up *externally* under duress or when otherwise coerced. Property in the form of movable goods and land, on the other hand, was not part of one's internal self, and thus not an unalienable right.[19] Jayne's evidence on this point is rather weak, however, as he cites no document from Jefferson himself, only a text of the Scottish philosopher Henry Home, Lord Kames, the alleged source of Jefferson on the (un-)alienability of property; but then again, Kames' quote as reported by Jayne does not refer explicitly to this particular argument. Before Jayne, Morton White had reasoned along similar lines.[20] Jean Yarbrough also built on White's insights when she concluded that in Jefferson's opinion property was a natural right, but not an unalienable right.[21]

Given that we have no direct proof from Jefferson himself about why he substituted property with the pursuit of happiness,[22] scholars often look to the sources that might have been used by Jefferson. In doing so, they hope that a correct interpretation of the source will also lead to a correct interpretation of Jefferson's Declaration. But when looking at the historiography on Jefferson's sources of inspiration, the picture does not grow more clear. John Locke, James Harrington, Thomas Hobbes, Samuel Pufendorf, Lord Bolingbroke, Jean-Jacques Burlamaqui, Francis Hutcheson, David Hume, Lord Kames, William Blackstone and others have all been identified as possible influences or sources.[23] Jefferson himself would add Aristotle, Cicero and Algernon Sidney. Interpretations of the doctrines produced by all these thinkers have varied widely, so it is not to be hoped that a uniform conclusion can be drawn from them. We can even less hope to establish firmly and finally Jefferson's philosophical and conceptual framework regarding private property when he wrote the Declaration. But what we can do is show how legal doctrine has been instrumental on the level of the recurring patterns of thinking about the issues at stake. We will do that with the help of Locke, Burlamaqui and Blackstone.

Locke's influence on Jefferson has sometimes been questioned. In his book *The Machiavellian Moment*, John G.A. Pocock maintained famously that the Lockean concept of a natural society did not have the influence in colonial

---

19 Allen JAYNE: *Jefferson's Declaration of Independence. Origins, Philosophy & Theology*, The University Press of Kentucky, Lexington, 1998, 122.

20 Morton WHITE: *The Philosophy of the American Revolution*, Oxford University Press, 1978, 214.

21 Jean M. YARBROUGH: *Jefferson and Property Rights = Liberty, Property and the Foundations of the American Constitution*, Ellen F. PAUL, Howard DICKMAN (eds.), State University of New York Press, Albany, 1989, 65–84.

22 SCOTT: *op. cit.*, 41–42.

23 JAYNE: *op. cit.*, 128–129.

America that was traditionally ascribed to it. A few years later, Garry Wills formulated the hypothesis that Jefferson was almost an anti-Lockean, and had based his thoughts almost exclusively on the Scottish Enlightenment philosophers.[24] Be that as it may, it seems exaggerated to deny the influence of Locke on Jefferson. At least some Lockean ideas must have had at least a partial influence on Jefferson, if only as a reinforcement of opinions which had become commonplace by 1776.[25] However, another question is at least as important: *which* Locke was the one that influenced Jefferson?

Locke's ideas on private property as established in Chapter V of the *Second Treatise* have been scrutinized by a wide range of scholars. In the liberal / libertarian or "orthodox" interpretation, Locke establishes government in order to protect the pre-existing, natural rights of the individual, in particular the natural right to private property. Government is the outcome of a so-called possessive, self-interested individualism,[26] and it is labour that generates an entitlement to private property.[27] Other scholars have emphasized more the egalitarian aspects of Locke's property theory, with its premises of "original communism and original community,"[28] while still others are defending some kind of middle ground of "benign egoism."[29] Together with others, I argue that

---

24    POCOCK: *op. cit.*, 545. Garry WILLS: *Inventing America: Jefferson's Declaration of Independence*, Doubleday, New York, 1978 (re-edition 2002), eg. 238. Cf. also BAILYN: *op. cit.*, 27–28.

25    Convincing arguments for the influence of Locke on Jefferson have been elaborated by, among others, BASSANI: *op. cit.*, 43–48; WHITE: *op. cit.*, 48; JAYNE: *op. cit.*, 41–61. Michael ZUCKERT: *Natural Rights and the New Republicanism*, Princeton University Press, Princeton, 1994, 15–26.

26    Crawford B. MACPHERSON: *The Political Theory of Possessive Individualism: Hobbes to Locke*, Oxford University Press, Oxford, 1962, 263–270; cf. also BASSANI: *op. cit.*, 37–43.

27    Robert NOZICK: *Anarchy, State and Utopia*, Basic Books, New York, 1974, 174–178; ZUCKERT: *op. cit.*, 275–288; Richard A. EPSTEIN: *Takings. Private Property and the Power of Eminent Domain*, Harvard University Press, Cambridge (MA), 1985, 9–15.

28    The expression is from Jeremy WALDRON: *God, Locke, and Equality. Christian Foundations in Locke's Political Thought*, Cambridge University Press, Cambridge (UK), 2002, 154. Waldron's Locke places God at the centre of his account of basic equality. Other scholars also take the Christian framework of Locke very seriously and come to a radical-revolutionary reading, such as for instance James TULLY: *A Discourse on Property: John Locke and his Adversaries*, Cambridge University Press, Cambridge (UK), 1980. In Tully's line of thinking we find also Gopal SREENIVASAN: *The Limits of Lockean Rights of Property*, Oxford University Press, Oxford, 1995 and Matthew H. KRAMER: *John Locke and the origins of private property*, Cambridge University Press, Cambridge (UK), 1997. A revolutionary Locke is depicted by Richard ASHCRAFT: *Revolutionary Politics and Locke's Two Treatises of Government*, Princeton University Press, Princeton, 1986.

29    Jerome HUYLER: *Locke in America. The Moral Philosophy of the Founding Era*, University Press of Kansas, Lawrence, 1995, 120–148.

a straightforward libertarian reading of Locke is difficult to sustain and that our understanding of Locke's concept of private property would not be complete without taking into account its dimension of limited altruism.[30]

Locke's account of private property is an historical and evolutionary one. It is a description of how private property as a legal concept emerges gradually from a state of nature. Likewise, the institution of civil government is also an historical account, as the moment when individuals decide to hand over to the political society "the power to preserve the property, and in order thereunto, punish the offences of all those of that society."[31] There is a third evolutionary account, an economic one. It is the account of the evolution from an economy where each individual appropriates, within limits, the products of his labour, to an economy based on money, trade and "disproportionate" possessions. Locke was of course not the only one to make use of historical or evolutionary accounts. Other natural law theorists before and after him did make use of this methodology as well, because it allowed them to illustrate that some of their premises were not accidental but the result of logical and rational reasoning, and thus demonstrable.[32] The existence of large overseas dominions, in North America and elsewhere, with no evident traces of anything near a civil polity comparable to those existing in Europe, also added to the perception that the statements about original states of natures could somehow be demonstrated and checked "anthropologically."

The three historical accounts of property, civil government and economic progress are connected with each other.[33] In the state of nature, there are only "free, equal and independent" men.[34] To these men, "God has given the earth in common, for the support and comfort of their being."[35] Because each man has a property in his own person, the labour of his body is "properly his."[36]

---

30  For a useful oversight of the available literature on Locke's ideas on property, cf. Christopher Pierson: *Just Property. A History in the Latin West. Volume One: Wealth, Virtue and the Law*, Oxford University Press, Oxford, 2013, 220–231. A useful overview of the standpoints of modern researchers on Locke's thought in general can be found in Huyler: *op. cit.*, 1–28.

31  Locke: *op. cit.*, 11.87 (p. 323–324).

32  Duncan Forbes: *Hume's Philosophical Politics*, Cambridge University Press, Cambridge (UK), 1975, 18; Stephen Buckle: *Natural Law and the Theory of Property. Grotius to Hume*, Oxford University Press, Oxford, 2002, 6.

33  Locke provides historical accounts on other topics as well, such as marriage or paternal power, but a detailed consideration of these, though very interesting, would lead us too far.

34  Locke: *op. cit.*, 11. 95 (p. 330–331).

35  *Ibid.*, 11.26 (p. 286).

36  *Ibid.*, 11.27 (p. 288).

By mixing his labour with whatever he takes out of the state of nature, a man adds something of his own to it, and as a consequence excludes the common right of others.[37] He does not need the consent of others for appropriation and excluding them.[38] Moreover, self-preservation requires "of necessity" that man appropriates the fruits and the beasts of the earth, otherwise they would not be beneficial.[39] However, he can only take so "much as any one can make use of to any advantage of life before it spoils"[40] (the so-called "spoilation proviso"). Moreover, he can only do so "where there is enough, and as good, left in common" for others (the so-called "sufficiency proviso").[41] These limits on property holdings in the state of nature had as a consequence that it "could not be much" what an individual was capable of accumulating.[42] However, because of the "desire of having more than one needed,"[43] people by "mutual consent" agreed to attach a value to money, "some lasting thing that men might keep without spoiling."[44] It is in this state of nature, then, that individuals obtain a right to property and that, as a consequence of the introduction of money, "disproportionate and unequal" possessions come into being. For Locke, only when things are divided in the state of nature, "without compact,"[45] governments or civil societies are set up, "by the consent of every individual."[46]

The property rights that one acquires in a state of nature through labour and accumulation of money, before the setting up of governments, are moral rights. The individual proprietor is morally entitled to the things that belong to him. But he does not have the positive legal instruments to claim what is his or to settle disputes. Locke does not foresee many disputes because in the state of nature there is enough for everyone, and in any case the entitlement is subjected to the proviso that one could take only as much and as good as is left to others. However, in case conflicts do arise, every individual "hath by nature a power, not only to preserve his property, that is, his life, liberty and estate,

---

37    *Ibid.*

38    *Ibid.*, II.28 (p. 288).

39    *Ibid.*, II.26 (p. 286).

40    *Ibid.*, II.31, 37 (p. 290, 294–295).

41    *Ibid.*, II.27 (p. 288). For more information about the concepts of "spoilation limitation" and "sufficiency limitation" in Locke's theory, cf. MACPHERSON: *op. cit.*, 203–211; Gregory S. ALEXANDER, Eduardo M. PEÑALVER: *An Introduction to Property Theory*, Cambridge University Press, Cambridge (UK), 2012, 38–41; Jeremy WALDRON, *The Right to Private Property*, Clarendon Press, Oxford, 1988, 209–218.

42    LOCKE: *op. cit.*, II.37 (p. 293–294).

43    *Ibid.*

44    *Ibid.*, II.37, 47 (p. 294–295, 300–301).

45    *Ibid.*, II.50 (p. 301–302).

46    *Ibid.*, II.96 (p. 331–332).

REVOLUTION AND INSTRUMENTALITY OF LAW 59

against the injuries and attempts of other men; but to judge of, and punish the breaches of that law in others, as he is persuaded the offence deserves, even with death itself."[47] Of course, Locke knows that once land is made scarce because of the increase of people and stock, the risk of disputes increases, and as a consequence, communities settle the limits of their distinct territories, and "by laws within themselves regulate the properties of the private men of their society."[48] The setting-up of government and the development of positive regulation to protect property are thus intimately linked: "no political society can be, nor subsist, without having in itself the power to preserve the property."[49] When an individual consents to the setting up of a government, he hands over to it his natural power to punish offences.[50] Once the government is set up, the moral or pre-legal entitlements to private property become whatever the law makes of them and become entrenched in legal rules. "For in Governments the Laws regulate the right of property, and the possession of land is determined by positive constitutions."[51]

On the face of it, then, Locke's idea is that governments are set up and laws are promulgated to protect private property,[52] even when the distributive outcome in the state of nature has been "disproportionate and unequal." For Locke, this unequal distributive outcome is not morally wrong, as it is the consequence of the introduction of money by (tacit) *agreement* among people on attaching a value to "that little piece of yellow metal."[53] However, he is not insensitive to the fate of those persons most prejudiced by the resulting inequality. There are the spoilation and sufficiency provisos, of course, as well as his general conviction that the worst-off participant in the English economy, the day-labourer, is better offer than the best-off participant in the Native American economy.[54] But really interesting is the condition of charity that he imposes on property owners:

> As *justice* gives every man a title to the product of his honest industry, and the fair acquisitions of his ancestors descended to him; so *charity* gives

---

47   *Ibid.*, II.87 (p. 323–324).
48   *Ibid.*, II.45 (p. 299).
49   *Ibid.*, II.87 (p. 323–324).
50   *Ibid.*
51   *Ibid.*, II.50 (p. 301–302).
52   *Ibid.*, II.222 (p. 412): "The Reason why Men enter into Society, is the preservation of their Property."
53   *Ibid.*, II.37 (p. 294). Cf. WALDRON: *Right to Private Property...*, *op. cit.*, 224; also WALDRON: *God, Locke and Equality...*, *op. cit.*, 176–177.
54   *Ibid.*, II.41 (p. 297).

every man a title to so much out of another's plenty, as will keep him from extreme want, where he has no means to subsist otherwise.[55]

Furthermore, Locke stated that "every one, as he is bound to preserve himself, and not to quit his station wilfully, so by the like reason, when his own preservation comes not in competition, ought he, as much as he can, *to preserve the rest of mankind*."[56] He also quoted approvingly Hooker's *Laws of Ecclesiastical Polity*, with at its center the obligation to mutual love amongst men and from whence he derives "the great maxims of justice and charity."[57] In addition, elsewhere he referred to the "charity which we owe all one to another."[58] There certainly is thus a "charitable impulse" in Locke's writing, the only question remains how far it extends.[59] Locke could not have had in mind that a situation of extreme necessity would occur very often. After all, in his optimistic vision of productive growth in an economy based on labour and industry – of private appropriation that is – cases of extreme necessity would be very rare.[60]

Locke's title to charity is his version of what Grotius and Pufendorf, both sources of Locke, call the "right" or "privilege" of necessity. Grotius considers for instance that in case of absolute necessity for the preservation of one's own life the original use-right of the "state of community" revives in a way.[61] Pufendorf's privilege of necessity is not a pre-legal use-right that is revived because of the circumstances, as in Grotius; his is an "imperfect obligation" on the wealthy person to relieve him who's in need.[62] It is not entirely clear whether Locke has in mind the Grotian account of a revival of a pre-legal use-right to the common or the imperfect obligation of Pufendorf on the wealthy. There is something to be said for Jeremy Waldron's suggestion that for Locke the right of charity only entails a negative duty of the person with a surplusage of goods not to interfere when the poor person takes what is needed to save his life.[63]

---

55   *Ibid.*, 1.42 (p. 170).

56   *Ibid.*, 11.6 (p. 271). (original emphasis).

57   *Ibid.*, 11.5 (p. 270).

58   *Ibid.*, 11.93 (p. 328).

59   The expression is from HUYLERS: *op. cit.*, 145.

60   BUCKLE: *op. cit.*, 160; cf. LOCKE: *op. cit.*, 11.40–42 (p. 296–297).

61   Hugo GROTIUS: *The Rights of War and Peace*, Richard TUCK (ed.), Liberty Fund, Indianapolis, 2005 [based on the 1738 English translation of J. Barbeyrac's French translation], Book 11, Chapter 11, vi.2 (p. 434).

62   Samuel PUFENDORF: *Of the Law of Nature and Nations*, Basil KENNETT (transl.), Jean BARBEYRAC (notes), London, 1739, Book 11, Chapter VI, v–viii (p. 206–212).

63   WALDRON: *God, Locke and Equality...*, *op. cit.*, 185. A detailed discussion on the nature of the "right" or "privilege" of necessity in Grotius and Pufendorf would lead us too far. Cf. Dennis KLIMCHUK: *Property and Necessity = Philosophical Foundations of Property Law*,

REVOLUTION AND INSTRUMENTALITY OF LAW 61

The conclusion is that for Locke there are definitely some limits on private property, such as the limits of spoilation, of sufficiency and charity. That does not make him an egalitarian – the limits are hardly the effect of distributive justice or natural sociability.[64] Locke is struggling with some of the recurrent issues related to property that are at the center of our attention. At the heart of these recurrent issues there is the fact that a legal property right that is too absolute would in a way be self-defeating. As also the Grotian account regarding the right of necessity demonstrates, no individual owner of goods in a pre-legal community would consent to a civil society where in case of necessity he would no longer have the license to take what is needed for his own self-preservation.[65] Locke, as we saw, not only bases in labour the moral right of an individual to take the fruits of the earth, but also in the necessity of self-preservation.[66] It is this same idea of self-preservation that leads Locke to reject slavery. In a broad sense, Locke refers to property not only with material goods in mind but also to life and liberty.[67] Everyone has a "property in his own person."[68] When government is set up by consent, essentially to preserve and protect property, even the poor have an interest in the government; not because they have any material goods that they want the government to protect, but because they have a life and a liberty that need protection. Therefore everyone, including the poor, have a strong interest in the establishment and conservation of government, for their own preservation. Under a just government, slavery, both self-enslavement as well as enslavement by others, is not

---

James PENNER, Henry E. SMITH (eds.), Oxford University Press, Oxford, 2013, 47–67, 52–56; John SALTER: *Grotius and Pufendorf on the right of necessity*, History of Political Thought, 26(2005), 284–302; Steven FORDE: *The Charitable John Locke*, The Review of Politics, 71(2009), 428–458; Robert LAMB, Benjamin THOMPSON: *The Meaning of Charity in Locke's Political Thought*, European Journal of Political Theory, 8(2009), 229–252.

64 Richard TUCK: *The Rights of War and Peace. Political Thought and the International Order from Grotius to Kant*, Oxford University Press, Oxford, 1999, 179–181.

65 When he consents to the setting up of a government, a person relinquishes a portion of the right "to do whatsoever he thinks fit for the preservation of himself and others within the permission of the law of nature" (LOCKE: *op. cit.*, II.128 (p. 352)). What is given up extends "as far forth as the preservation of himself and the rest of society shall require" (*ibid.*, II.129 (p. 352–353)). There are some limits, however, including the limit that legislative power cannot be used to take property without the owner's consent (*Ibid.*, II.138 (p. 360–361)). Cf. A. John SIMMONS: *On the Edge of Anarchy. Locke, Consent, and the Limits of Society*, Princeton University Press, Princeton, 1993, 62.

66 Further elaborated in BUCKLE: *op. cit.*, 174.

67 Cf. e.g. LOCKE: *op. cit.*, II.87 (p. 323–324).

68 *Ibid.*, II.27 (p. 287–288). Cf. also Brian TIERNEY: *Dominium of self and natural rights before Locke and after = Transformations in Medieval and Early-Modern Rights Discourse*, Virpi MÄKINEN, Petter KORKMAN (eds.), Springer, Dordrecht, 2006, 173–203.

permissible.[69] Self-preservation is thus the main reason for the original appropriation by labour as well as for the compact that brings political society, including its legal relations, into being. In that sense, it is only logical that the pre-legal moral right to exclusive possession, as well as its legal right of property, are in a way limited by some constraints linked to the property right itself.

Jean-Jacques Burlamaqui, whose influence on Jefferson is not to be excluded,[70] considers property rights to be the consequence of a human convention. In the primitive or natural state, man has "a common right of use" and draws from the earth "whatever is necessary for the preservation and conveniences of life." He is in a situation of "indigence and incessant wants." God has implanted in him the "instincts and qualifications proper for applying these things [of the earth] to [his] advantage," something which must be done by "constant labour."[71] Property modifies this "natural power" by limiting and constraining it in order to distinguish what belongs to each individual. In that sense, property is an "adventitious state.".[72] Very interestingly, Burlamaqui distinguishes between different sorts of rights. The first distinction he makes is the distinction between natural rights and acquired rights. The former "appertain originally and essentially to man," while acquired rights are "those which he does not naturally enjoy, but are owing to his own procurement."[73] According to this classification, the primitive use-right is a natural right, while property rights are acquired rights. Burlamaqui's second classification of rights distinguishes between perfect and imperfect rights. Perfect rights are those which may be asserted rigorously, even by employing force, to obtain the execution, or to secure the exercise thereof in opposition to all those who attempt to resist or disturb us. Imperfect rights are those that cannot be enforced in order to secure their enjoyment. The adventitious property rights are examples of

---

69 LOCKE: *op. cit.*, II.23 (p. 284); SIMMONS: *op. cit.*, 48–55.

70 The first author to suggest the influence of Burlamaqui on Jefferson was Ray Forrest HARVEY: *Jean-Jacques Burlamaqui: A Liberal Tradition in American Constitutionalism*, University of North Carolina Press, Chapel Hill, 1937, 119–124; WHITE: *op. cit.*, 214; cf. also Petter Korkman's introduction to Jean-Jacques BURLAMAQUI: *The Principles of Natural and Politic Law*, Petter KORKMAN (ed.), Thomas NUGENT (transl.), Liberty Fund, Indianapolis, 2006, xviii; Petter KORKMAN: *Life, Liberty and the Pursuit of Happiness. Human Rights in Barbeyrac and Burlamaqui = Transformations in Medieval and Early-Modern Rights Discourse*, Virpi MÄKINEN, Petter KORKMAN (eds.), Dordrecht, Springer, 2006, 257–283, 274–275. BASSANI: *op. cit.*, 30. For opposing views, cf. JAYNE: *op. cit.*, 73–74, or BAILYN: *op. cit.*, 27–28.

71 BURLAMAQUI: *op. cit.*, 1.1.4.5 (p. 59–60).

72 *Ibid.*, 1.1.4.8 (p. 61).

73 *Ibid.*, 1.1.7.8 (p. 85–86).

perfect rights: it is permitted to use force to protect them; the right of necessity is an example of an imperfect right, because force or open violence is not allowed to enforce it.[74] It is his last distinction, however, that should draw most of our attention when considering the status of property in the Declaration of Independence. That is the distinction between rights that can be lawfully renounced or *alienated* and those that can not. Burlamaqui offers the creditor who forgives a sum due to him as an example of a right that can be renounced. Examples of rights that cannot be renounced are liberty, or the rights of a father over his children. The difference depends on whether the right in question is at the same time also a duty. Renouncing such a right would also imply the renouncement of our duty: A father cannot renounce his rights over his children, because of the duties he has towards them.[75] Where would property fit in this classification of unalienable and alienable rights? Burlamaqui himself does not help us explicitly. It is, however, very unlikely that he would consider the adventitious property right as *unalienable*, because obviously property rights can be alienated. He probably would have considered only the primitive use-right as unalienable, because man has not only a right but also a duty to preserve himself.[76] To return to the Jeffersonian triad of life, liberty and the pursuit of happiness as unalienable rights, we see that for Burlamaqui, liberty is unrenounceable. Life, or "the care for our self-preservation," is not alienable either.[77] And happiness is the ultimate end of man. "It is not in our power to change this," and is therefore a duty.[78] Life, liberty and happiness are thus at the same time rights and duties, the necessary connection of unalienable rights.[79] Property is not.[80]

As a trained lawyer, Jefferson was very familiar with common law scholars such as Coke and Blackstone, although he maintained a love-hate relationship with them.[81] Blackstone's theory of property is complex, and at first sight, has some internal contradictions. On the one hand, for example, the right of

---

74    *Ibid.* The right of necessity seems to become a mere right to "apply for succour to other men."

75    *Ibid.*, 1.1.7.5 (p. 83).

76    *Ibid.*, 1.2.4.22 (p. 161).

77    E.g. *ibid.*, 1.2.3.3 (p. 139); 1.2.4.9-10 (p. 150–151); 1.2.4.22 (p. 161).

78    *Ibid.*, 1.1.5.4 (p. 65) or 1.2.4.9 (p. 150). Cf. also Korkman's note at 134.

79    KORKMAN: *Life, Liberty and the Pursuit of Happiness...*, *op. cit.*, 264–265, 276.

80    That doesn't mean that for Burlamaqui, once a government is in place they should not respect "the life, property, and liberty of the subject." BURLAMAQUI: *op. cit.*, 2.1.7.18 (p. 312).

81    Thomas JEFFERSON: *Political Writings*, Joyce APPLEBY, Terence BALL (eds.), Cambridge University Press, Cambridge (UK), 1999, xiv.

property is "no natural, but merely a civil right."[82] There is "no foundation in nature or in natural law, why a set of words upon parchment should convey … dominion."[83] On the other hand, he acknowledges that "the original of property is probably founded in nature,"[84] and is an "absolute," "primary" and "principal" right.[85] This apparent contradiction can be solved by looking first into Blackstone's historical account of the development of private property, and afterwards by looking into his classification of rights.

Blackstone describes in great detail the development of private property from the beginnings of time to his present day of refined and civilized governments. Occupancy is the first step in this development, and he distinguishes between authors such as Grotius and Pufendorf on the one hand, who insist "that this right of occupancy is founded on a tacit and implied assent of all mankind that the first occupant should become the owner," and on the other hand authors such as Locke and Barbeyrac "holding that there is no such implied assent," occupancy by labour providing the only necessary title.[86] While he makes fun of this "dispute that savours too much of nice and scholastic refinement," he does acknowledge that occupation is the first step. In the time of "primeval simplicity," occupation generates only a temporary use-right, but "among the complicated interests and artificial refinements of polite and established governments," that is, when civil society was set-up, occupancy generated an "exclusive right to retain in a permanent manner."[87] Civil society and municipal law created thus the conditions of this right, "which is clearly a political establishment," protects it, and regulates the details of transmission of property.[88] In another part of the *Commentaries*, as we have seen, Blackstone had commented on the security, liberty and private property as the "principal" and "primary" rights of the English. But when he says so, that is because he considers these rights as political rights in the first place. Blackstone is familiar with the idea of natural rights as "rights inherent in us by birth," and which are partly given up when man enters into society.[89] He rather speaks of absolute

---

82 Blackstone: *op. cit.*, Book ii, Chapter i (vol. 1, 399).

83 *Ibid.*, Book ii, Chapter i (vol. 1, 393).

84 *Ibid.*, Book i, Chapter i (vol. 1, 107).

85 *Ibid.*, Book i, Chapter i (vol. 1, 100 and 107).

86 *Ibid.*, Book ii, Chapter i (vol. 1, 396).

87 *Ibid.*, Book ii, Chapter i (vol. 1, 396 and 398).

88 *Ibid.*, Book ii, Chapter i (vol. 1, 396 and 399): "Necessity begat property; and, in order to insure that property, recourse was had to civil society, which brought along with it a long train of inseparable concomitant, – states, government, laws, punishments, and the public exercise of religious duties."

89 *Ibid.*, Book i, Chapter i (vol. 1, 94).

REVOLUTION AND INSTRUMENTALITY OF LAW                                           65

rights, "which are such as appertain and belong to particular men, merely as individuals" and in opposition to relative rights, "which are incident to them as members of society."[90] These absolute rights "belong to their persons merely in a state of nature, and which every man is entitled to enjoy, whether out of society or in it.".[91] The principal aim of society is "to protect individuals in the enjoyment of those absolute rights, which were vested in them by the immutable laws of nature."[92] But even if nature has implanted these rights in each individual, it is government that defines those rights, "they are coeval with our form of government" and are "defined by several statutes."[93] There is still a *residuum* of natural liberty, "which is not required by the laws of society to be sacrificed to public convenience." In return for giving up part of his natural liberty, man receives in return "civil privileges, which society hath engaged to provide, in lieu of the natural liberties so given up by individuals."[94] It is among these civil privileges that he lists the "primary" and "principal" rights of security, liberty and private property. In the state of nature, property was for Blackstone a temporary use-right. Once a user stopped using a thing, another could come in and seize the vacant possession.[95] When entering into society, this natural, or indeed, absolute right was changed, and man in exchange for giving up part of this use right would receive a right of private property which included some modifications, such as "the method of *conserving* it in the present owner, and of *translating* it from man to man."[96] It is the permanent character of private property, which made it a civil right. The natural right of temporary use was not erased by the introduction and continuance of property, however, and there were still things that "belong to the first occupant, during the time he holds possession of them, and no longer," such as "elements of light, air and water."[97] In spite of some apparent contradictions then, Blackstone's idea on property is quite clear. There is a natural right of property in the state of nature, but that does not amount to much more than a temporary use-right to take from the public stock such things as the immediate necessities required. Private property in its developed, legal sense is a right completely defined by

---

90   *Ibid.*, Book I, Chapter 1 (vol. 1, 92).
91   *Ibid.*
92   *Ibid.*, Book I, Chapter 1 (vol. 1, 93).
93   *Ibid.*, Book I, Chapter 1 (vol. 1, 97 and 100).
94   *Ibid.*, Book I, Chapter 1 (vol. 1, 100).
95   *Ibid.*, Book II, Chapter 1 (vol. 1, 397).
96   *Ibid.*, Book I, Chapter 1 (vol. 1, 107) (my italics).
97   *Ibid.*, Book II, Chapter 1 (vol. 1, 401).

human law. That does not mean that government can violate private property at will, but essentially, for Blackstone, property is a "civil advantage."[98]

None of the authors above seems to have thought of private property as a straightforwardly unalienable right, at least not in its legal dimension within a civil society. An original, primitive use-right of the necessities of life is generally accepted as a faculty or power that is natural to man, but in a civil society such a primitive use-right would only appear again in emergency situations, not quite as the consequence of a natural right of property, but rather because of the natural right of self-preservation.

It is therefore interesting to investigate the philosophical foundations of the French Declaration as well, in order to determine which philosophical categories were used there that led them to declare property as a sacred and inviolable right. First of all, it must be observed that the Declaration did not include explicitly the idea of "unalienable" rights. However, from the parliamentary debates ahead of the adoption of the text it becomes clear that the conception of *"inaliénabilité"* had been considered. In one of the draft versions of a constitution, Rabaud de Saint-Étienne had called the right of self-preservation as the primitive, inalienable right of man.[99] Mirabeau had spoken of the *"droits inaliénables"* in his draft of the Declaration presented to the Assembly on 17 August, as well as in his intervention of 18 August.[100] In their interventions during the morning session of 20 August 1789, deputies Mougins, Pellerin and d'André reportedly spoke about natural, imprescriptible, sacred and unalienable rights, and included property among these.[101] Whether the disappearance of the term "unalienable" in the final version of the Declaration responds to doubts on their unalienable character is difficult to determine, because the published reports on the debates in the session where the final text was adopted may possibly be incomplete.[102] However, the aforementioned text of Rabaud de Saint-Étienne offers a clue. The first of the unalienable rights on his list was the right to self-preservation. From this primitive right were derived other fundamental and unalienable rights, such as liberty, property and equality. Liberty as a right

---

98    *Ibid.*, Book I, Chapter 1 (vol. 1, 107–109). For Blackstone, government cannot arbitrarily take the property of its subjects. In cases of public necessity (eminent domain) there must be a cause and just compensation, and in case of taxes there must be consent.

99    *Archives parlementaires…, op. cit.*, 403.

100   *Ibid.*, 438, 452.

101   *Ibid.*, 463: "Les représentants du peuple français […] ont résolu d'exposer, dans une déclaration solennelle, les droits naturels, inaliénables et sacrés de l'homme […] Les droits inaliénables et imprescriptibles de l'homme sont la liberté, la propriété, la sûreté, l'égalité des droits, la conservation de son honneur et de sa vie, la communication de ses pensées et la résistance à l'oppression."

102   Cf. footnote on 461 of the *Archives Parlementaires…, op. cit.*

REVOLUTION AND INSTRUMENTALITY OF LAW 67

was unalienable, so when someone willingly gave up his liberty, he was only giving up the exercise of liberty, not the right to liberty as such. Likewise, a person could alienate his possessions and goods, but this would not imply that he was giving up the right, only the exercise of it.[103] Not everyone agreed on this distinction between the inalienability of a right, and the alienability of its exercise, however. In his own draft of the Declaration, Sièyes included the inalienability of self-ownership:

> Art. 5. Tout homme est seul propriétaire de sa personne. Il peut engager ses services, son temps, mais il ne peut pas se vendre lui-même. Cette première propriété est inalienable.

This *primary* sort of ownership was different from the right to use and dispose of goods and income. This second kind of ownership, just like liberty and security, needed a higher degree of social protection, but he did not equate it with the *inalienable* right of self-ownership.

> Art. 10. Enfin tout homme est le maître de disposer et d'user de son bien et de son revenu, ainsi qu'il le juge à propos.

> Art. 11. La liberté, la propriété et la sécurité des citoyens doivent reposer sous une garantie sociale supérieure à toutes les atteintes.[104]

Sièyes' project was the one which received the second most votes of all the drafts for a Declaration that had been proposed to the Assembly as the basis for discussion for the final version.[105] The project that received the most votes, drafted by the sixth bureau of the Assembly under the direction of the archbishop of Bordeaux, Jérôme Marie Champion de Cicé, did not include the idea of inalienability at all, even if it was obviously inspired by the US Declaration of Independence.[106] The project of the sixth bureau proclaimed that nature had given man the right to life and the pursuit of happiness (art. 1). In order to reach these goals, nature had endowed man with faculties. Liberty consists in

---

103  *Ibid.*, 404.

104  *Ibid.*, 422–423.

105  *Ibid.*, 459.

106  For the text of the project of the sixth bureau, cf. *ibid.*, 431–432. For Jefferson's influence on the text, Cf. Ian McLean: *Thomas Jefferson, John Adams, and the Déclaration des droits de l'homme et du citoyen* = *The Future of Liberal Democracy: Thomas Jefferson and the Contemporary World*, Robert Fatton Jr., R.K. Ramazani (eds.), Palgrave Macmillan, New York, 2004, 13–30. Cf. also the remarks of Rabaud de Saint-Étienne on the similarities between the French and the American situations: *Archives Parlementaires…, op. cit.*, 452.

the free exercise of those faculties (Art. 2), the right of property being derived from the use of those faculties (Art. 3). Man had an equal right to liberty and to his own property (Art. 4). But man does not receive from nature the same means to make use of his faculties; that is the foundation of inequality. Inequality is a product of nature itself (Art. 5). Civil society is set up to protect the equality of rights in a situation of inequality of means (Art. 6).

The text is rather didactic, and "didn't meet the [Assembly's] expectations."[107] But it is remarkable that these articles, which in a heavily revised form would end up as Article 2 of the final version, seem to struggle with the same problems of property as the Declaration of Independence. Property as such was not a straightforward natural right but was the consequence of the use of some natural faculties. In a subsequent project, Mirabeau refined that the right of property consisted in the liberty to acquire, to possess, to produce, to trade and to dispose of one's goods.[108]

An interesting discussion on the limits of property rights took place in the debate over Article 16, which dealt with the state's power of taxation. One deputy, Jean-Antoine Teissier, Baron of Marguerites, proposed to include the idea that taxes were a subtraction from private property. But this was refuted by Mirabeau, who said that taxes were the price to be paid to enjoy one's possessions, an enjoyment that was common to all citizens.[109] The Assembly refused to continue this deeper philosophical debate on the nature of taxes, however, and focused instead on the question to what extent citizens had to have a voice in the decision to set the amount of taxes to be collected and to control expenditure.[110] This would result in the adoption of Articles 13 and 14.

The refusal of the Assembly to discuss what were repeatedly called "metaphysical niceties"[111] was a consequence of a combination of time pressure, impatience and a sense of pragmatism to produce a document that conveyed an image of consensus among deputies from a wide variety of backgrounds.

## 3    Conclusion

In this chapter, I have tried to answer two questions: why was there an apparently different treatment of property in the US Declaration of Independence

---

107    *Ibid.*
108    *Ibid.*, 439 (Article 11 of the Mirabeau Project).
109    *Ibid.*, 483.
110    *Ibid.*, 483–484.
111    Cf. e.g. *ibid.*, 231, 322–323, 420, 458, 462.

and in the French Declaration of the Rights of Man and of the Citizen? Was this difference meaningful from a theoretical perspective? The answers to these questions allow one to see how revolutions instrumentalize pre-existing ideas to build a new political and legal framework.

To answer the first question: why was there this apparent difference in treatment? Apart from the contextual differences related to slavery, Native Americans, colonial charters, policies favouring small land ownership and the abolishment of the feudal system, there is the undeniable circumstance that the two documents had a different type of genesis. The US Declaration was very much the creation of one dominant author, while the French Declaration was the product of parliamentary debate. The first document is more the result of principled reflection than the second one, which is more the outcome of a debate that explicitly left aside "metaphysical niceties."

Was the difference in the treatment of property meaningful? From what we know of the French debate, it seems not possible to conclude that the definition of property as a "sacred" and "inviolable" right in the French Declaration reflects a fundamentally different theoretical stance towards ownership than the US Declaration. On the contrary, a very few glimpses into the proceedings of the French debates indicate that at stake were the same philosophical issues on relationship between a pre-legal natural right to make use of the product of one's labour and legal property rights. These issues are basically two. On the one hand, there is the tension, in situations of extreme necessity, between the natural or pre-legal right of self-preservation of the person in need and the legal property rights of the affluent owner. On the other hand, there are the funding requirements of a civil government set up to protect the legal interests of its citizens. Both issues point to the relation between a pre-legal use right and legal property rights, which becomes self-defeating if this relation is considered to be too absolute. Jefferson's sources analysed in this article and the debate in the French National Assembly all point to this tension.

If the property theories of French and American revolutionary documents were approximately similar, that was because they made use of the same pool of ideas. These were instrumentalized to build a concept of property that made a sharper distinction between public power and private ownership. France, with the elimination of feudalism, implemented this distinction most visibly, but North America, with its policies favouring widespread landownership, did so as well. Moreover, following Locke and other natural law philosophers, there was increasingly an awareness on both sides of the Atlantic that property properly understood implied full, unshared ownership by a single person.

## Bibliography

Gregory S. ALEXANDER, Eduardo M. PEÑALVER: *An Introduction to Property Theory*, Cambridge University Press, Cambridge (UK), 2012.

*Archives Parlementaires de 1787 à 1860. Recueil complet des débats legislatifs et politiques des chambres Françaises*, Jérôme MAVIDAL, Émile LAURENT, Emile CLAVEL (eds.), Librairie Administrative de Paul Dupont, Paris, 1875, Première série, tome 8.

Richard ASHCRAFT: *Revolutionary Politics and Locke's Two Treatises of Government*, Princeton University Press, Princeton, 1986.

Bernard BAILYN: *The Ideological Origins of the American Revolution*, The Belknap Press of Harvard University Press, Cambridge (Ma), 1992 (enlarged edition).

Luigi Marco BASSANI: *Life, Liberty, and ...: Jefferson on Property Rights*, Journal of Libertarian Studies, 18(2004), 31–87.

William BLACKSTONE: *Commentaries on the Laws of England*, J.B. Lippincott Company, Philadelphia, 1893.

Rafe BLAUFARB: *The Great Demarcation. The French Revolution and the Invention of Modern Property*, Oxford University Press, Oxford, 2016.

Stephen BUCKLE: *Natural Law and the Theory of Property. Grotius to Hume*, Oxford University Press, Oxford, 2002.

Jean-Jacques BURLAMAQUI: *The Principles of Natural and Politic Law*, Petter KORKMAN (ed.), Thomas NUGENT (transl.), Liberty Fund, Indianapolis, 2006.

Jean-Jacques CLERE: *L'abolition des droits féodaux en France*, Cahiers d'histoire, 94–95(2005), 135–157.

Richard A. EPSTEIN: *Takings. Private Property and the Power of Eminent Domain*, Harvard University Press, Cambridge (MA), 1985.

Duncan FORBES: *Hume's Philosophical Politics*, Cambridge University Press, Cambridge (UK), 1975.

Steven FORDE: *The Charitable John Locke*, The Review of Politics, 71(2009), 428–458.

Peter GARNSEY: *Thinking about Property. From Antiquity to the Age of Revolution*, Cambridge University Press, Cambridge (UK), 2007.

Hugo GROTIUS: *The Rights of War and Peace*, Richard TUCK (ed.), Liberty Fund, Indianapolis, 2005.

Ray Forrest HARVEY: *Jean-Jacques Burlamaqui: A Liberal Tradition in American Constitutionalism*, University of North Carolina Press, Chapel Hill, 1937.

Jerome HUYLER: *Locke in America. The Moral Philosophy of the Founding Era*, University Press of Kansas, Lawrence, 1995.

Allen JAYNE: *Jefferson's Declaration of Independence. Origins, Philosophy & Theology*, The University Press of Kentucky, Lexington, 1998.

Thomas JEFFERSON: *Political Writings*, Joyce APPLEBY, Terence BALL (eds.), Cambridge University Press, Camridge (UK), 1999.

*The Papers of Thomas Jefferson. Vol. 1, 1760–1776*, Julien BOYD (ed.), Princeton University Press, Princeton, 1950.

Thomas E. KAISER: *Property, Sovereignty, the Declaration of the Rights of Man, and the Tradition of French Jurisprudence = The French Idea of Freedom. The Old Regime and the Declaration of Rights of 1789*, Dale VAN KLEY (ed.), Stanford University Press, Stanford, 1994, 300–339, 418–424.

Dennis KLIMCHUK: *Property and Necessity = Philosophical Foundations of Property Law*, James PENNER and Henry E. SMITH (eds.), Oxford University Press, Oxford, 2013, 47–67.

Stanley N. KATZ: *Thomas Jefferson and the Right to Property in Revolutionary America*, Journal of Law and Economics, 19(1976), 467–488.

Petter KORKMAN: *Life, Liberty and the Pursuit of Happiness. Human Rights in Barbeyrac and Burlamaqui = Transformations in Medieval and Early-Modern Rights Discourse*, Virpu MÄKINEN, Petter KORKMAN (eds.), Dordrecht, Springer, 2006, 257–283.

Matthew H. KRAMER: *John Locke and the origins of private property*, Cambridge University Press, Cambridge (UK), 1997.

Robert LAMB, Benjamin THOMPSON: *The Meaning of Charity in Locke's Political Thought*, European Journal of Political Theory, 8(2009), 229–252.

John LOCKE: *Two Treatises of Government*, Peter LASLETT (ed.), Cambridge University Press, Cambridge (UK), 1988.

Crawford B. MACPHERSON: *The Political Theory of Possessive Individualism: Hobbes to Locke*, Oxford University Press, Oxford, 1962.

Ian MCLEAN: *Thomas Jefferson, John Adams, and the Déclaration des droits de l'homme et du citoyen = The Future of Liberal Democracy: Thomas Jefferson and the Contemporary World*, Robert FATTON Jr., R.K. RAMAZANI (eds.), Palgrave Macmillan, New York, 2004, 13–30.

Robert NOZICK: *Anarchy, State and Utopia*, Basic Books, New York, 1974.

Christopher PIERSON: *Just Property. A History in the Latin West. Volume One: Wealth, Virtue and the Law*, Oxford University Press, Oxford, 2013.

John G.A. POCOCK: *The Machiavellian Moment. Florentine Political Thought and the Atlantic Republican Tradition*, Princeton University Press, Princeton, 1975 (re-ed. 2003).

Samuel PUFENDORF: *Of the Law of Nature and Nations*, Basil KENNETT (transl.), Jean BARBEYRAC (notes), London, 1739.

John SALTER: *Grotius and Pufendorf on the right of necessity*, History of Political Thought, 26(2005), 284–302.

William B. SCOTT: *In Pursuit of Happiness: American Conceptions of Property from the Seventeenth to the Twentieth Century*, Indiana University Press, Bloomington, 1977.

A. John SIMMONS: *On the Edge of Anarchy. Locke, Consent, and the Limits of Society*, Princeton University Press, Princeton, 1993.

Gopal SREENIVASAN: *The Limits of Lockean Rights of Property*, Oxford University Press, Oxford, 1995.

Brian TIERNEY: *Dominium of self and natural rights before Locke and after = Transformations in Medieval and Early-Modern Rights Discourse*, Virpi MÄKINEN, Petter KORKMAN (eds.), Springer, Dordrecht, 2006, 173–203.

*Tracts of the American Revolution 1763–1776*, Merrill JENSEN (ed.), Hackett Publishing Company, Indianapolis-Cambridge (MA), 1966.

Richard TUCK: *The Rights of War and Peace. Political Thought and the International Order from Grotius to Kant*, Oxford University Press, Oxford, 1999.

James TULLY: *A Discourse on Property: John Locke and his Adversaries*, Cambridge University Press, Cambridge (UK), 1980.

Virginia Declaration of Rights.

Jeremy WALDRON: *God, Locke, and Equality. Christian Foundations in Locke's Political Thought*, Cambridge University Press, Cambridge (UK), 2002.

Jeremy WALDRON: *The Right to Private Property*, Clarendon Press, Oxford, 1988.

Anthony F.C. WALLACE: *Jefferson and the Indians. The Tragic Fate of the First Americans*, Harvard University Press, Cambridge (MA), 1999.

Morton WHITE: *The Philosophy of the American Revolution*, Oxford University Press, Oxford, 1978.

Garry WILLS: *Inventing America: Jefferson's Declaration of Independence*, Doubleday, New York, 1978 (re-ed. 2002).

Gordon S. WOOD: *The Radicalism of the American Revolution*, Vintage Books, New York, 1991.

Jean M. YARBROUGH: *Jefferson and Property Rights = Liberty, Property and the Foundations of the American Constitution*, Ellen F. PAUL, Howard DICKMAN (eds.), State University of New York Press, Albany, 1989, 65–84.

Michael ZUCKERT: *Natural Rights and the New Republicanism*, Princeton University Press, Princeton, 1994.

CHAPTER 4

# English Commercial Law in the *Longue Durée*: Chasing Continental Shadows

*Sean Thomas*

## 1 Introduction

The general tenor of this book concerning modernisation is that it involves a shifting and a breakage with a prior legal regime; the clearest examples are the development and implementation of the civil codes of nineteenth century Europe.[1] English law, and history, is of course somewhat distinct.[2] This chapter questions whether there was anything especially modernising about the late Victorian changes to English commercial law. It does this by examining why institutions continued or changed. In doing so it also applies the theoretical framework of material civilisation developed by the French historian Braudel to the historical development of elements of English commercial law. This enables a critique of English commercial law based on the argument that such law is neither modern nor especially indicative of national identity. Instead, themes of continuity and communality across borders come to the fore, showing the influence of long standing commercial practices across jurisdictions.

The next section, "On the possibility of Big Legal History" addresses the possibility of analysing of commercial law in totality. The requirement to consider *why* there was change (if any), and not just *what* the change was, is acknowledged, and on this basis the two interconnected theses of this chapter are presented. First, there was at best *re*invention of commercial mechanisms over the *longue durée*. That is, by the mid-nineteenth century what was occurring was little different to practices from many centuries before. Second, the doctrinal forms that underpinned such commercial mechanisms can be seen as transmitting over the *longue durée* from one part of Europe to another, eventually landing in London by around the mid-nineteenth century. Thus whatever

---

1   Michał GAŁĘDEK: *Introduction: Modernisation, National Identity, and Legal Instrumentalism = Modernisation, National Identity, and Legal Instrumentalism: Studies in Comparative Legal History*, Michał GAŁĘDEK, Anna KLIMASZEWSKA (eds.), Brill Nijhoff, Leiden-Boston, 2020, 5–11.

2   Warren SWAIN: *Codification of Contract Law: Some Lessons from History*, University of Queensland Law Journal, 31(2012)/1, 39–54.

© KONINKLIJKE BRILL NV, LEIDEN, 2020 | DOI:10.1163/9789004417274_005

modernisation processes in progress at that point were susceptible to (unconscious) replication of much older practices. The use of the *longue durée* in the context of legal history is relatively novel, and there is thus some risk to this analysis in terms of methodology. Consequently, the third section, "Commerce: Vertical and Horizontal Shadows" provides a detailed explanation of Braudel's theory and its consequences for this chapter's argument. Essentially the idea is that the law's provision of credit mechanisms, connected to the sale process, has the effect of acting as nodal points connecting different layers of material civilisations. In particular credit mechanisms operate to transfer value from the middle economic layer to a shadow layer of financial capitalism. That financial capitalism reached a high point in nineteenth century England (where it coincided and interacted with the contemporary industrial revolutions) was due to the presence of institutional foundations that had been imported from various different other jurisdictions over the *longue durée*. Examining how law, as an institution, reacts to commerce, also an institution, reveals that the commercial law appeared to reinvent itself in the middle of the nineteenth century. The fourth section, "English Commercial Law: Chasing Shadows" considers this process, by showing how a reformulation of commercial law that emphasised its proprietary nature enabled correspondence with pre-existing credit mechanisms. The fifth section concludes.

## 2      On the Possibility of Big Legal History

Goode, the leading commercial lawyer, has described commercial law as "the totality of the law's responses to mercantile disputes".[3] He also implicitly recognised that this entailed, among other issues, a historical approach, acknowledging trade's role in world history,[4] and the role of change and the evidence of invention and reinvention in the area.[5] For Goode, a historical outline of English commercial law ties in initial continental developments of *lex mercatoria*, before nineteenth century crystallisation led to the contemporary position of a mature commercial jurisdiction.[6] This outline is expanded within Goode's Hamlyn lectures: English commercial law increased in "scope and sophistication," with various concepts and tools from law and equity helping create a

---

3  Roy GOODE: *Commercial Law in the Next Millennium*, Sweet & Maxwell, London, 1998, 8.
4  *Ibid.*, 1.
5  *Ibid.*, 3; Ewan MCKENDRICK: *Goode on Commercial Law*, Penguin, London, 2010, xxi.
6  Ewan MCKENDRICK: *Goode on Commercial Law*, Penguin, London, 2016, 3–8.

ENGLISH COMMERCIAL LAW IN THE *LONGUE DURÉE*

full-service commercial law.[7] Of equivalent importance to this narrative is how English commercial law developed in response to commercial practice, and by means – at least until modern times – of judicial rather than statutory intervention in a way that "[a] civil lawyer would surely find ... truly astonishing".[8]

However, Llewellyn, writing some seven decades before Goode, pointed out the following:

> History is barren if directed only to showing the course and change of institutions; equal attention must be paid to the more puzzling question of *why* one institution rather than another persisted, *why* one new variant rather than another has emerged. And legal history loses most of its value if it is obscured by an attempt to compress into one flat plane of analytical synthesis half a century of decisions that grow out of the one plane into another and another.[9]

Two distinct but ultimately interconnected points can clearly be seen here. Their application as critical lenses can reveal some intriguing possible responses to Goode's points about commercial law. First, that we can ask *why* was there change, and more interestingly, why was this change ultimately (or, more negatively, merely) reinvention rather than something truly novel. This chapter suggests that theorising commercial law through the *longue durée* perspective indicates the normalcy of reinvention of methods and mechanisms. Furthermore, this process of reinvention was necessarily one which crossed legal cultures. This is because of the particular focus for analysis here, commercial law regarding financing of sales, is an especially international phenomenon.[10] With movements of goods come the mechanisms that allow for such activity, such as financing. These practices crossed cultures over the *longue durée*.

---

7    GOODE: *Commercial Law...*, *op. cit.*, 9.

8    *Ibid.*, 11. Cf. Boris KOZOLCHYK: *The Commercialization of Civil Law and the Civilization of Commercial Law*, Louisiana Law Review, 40(1979)/1, 3–47; Geoffrey SAMUEL: *Civil and Commercial Law: a Distinction Worth Making?*, Law Quarterly Review, 102(1986)/3, 569–584. It is possible that legislation had an identifiable impact, such as the Warehousing Act 1803, which increased trade by shifting the liability for import duties from the point of importation to that of disposition, or the repeal of the Navigation Acts in 1849: Graeme J. MILNE: *Trade and traders in mid-Victorian Liverpool: Mercantile business and the making of a world port*, Liverpool University Press, Liverpool, 2000, 80–81, 147–148.

9    Karl Nickerson LLEWELLYN: *Cases and Materials on the Law of Sales*, Callaghan and Co., Chicago, 1930, xii.

10   Heikki PIHLAJAMÄKI: *Private Law Codification, Modernization and Nationalism: A View from Critical Legal History*, Critical Analysis of Law 135(2015)/2, 137.

Secondly, we can take Llewellyn's notion of planes of synthesis, and reformulate it as an analytical tool using Braudel's structural conceptualisation of material civilisation over the *longue durée* to evaluate English commercial law.[11] There is some indication of recognition of the value of a *longue durée* perspective in legal history,[12] and Braudel's work has had some slight influence in the legal literature in this area. Thus in Rogers' important work on the early history of the law of bills in English law, he recognised the value of Braudel's work for understanding the early merchant practices.[13] However, he did not engage with the theoretical aspect of Braudel's work concerning the layers of material civilisation, which this chapter does.

In *The Structures of Everyday Life*, Braudel argued that there are three levels of material civilisation: the shadow under-layer, concerning unrecorded transactions; the open middle layer, concerning market exchange; and the third "shadowy" over-layer, of global financial capitalism.[14] The connection between these layers is provided by exchanges of goods, and it is these connecting points (nodal points, in Braudel's terms) that will be the focus of this chapter. That is, there is focus on the points at which goods are exchanged between layers. More specifically, the focus is on the nodal points connecting the middle and upper layers. It is at those points that English law's doctrinal forms which regulate flows of value between the layers, as well as mechanisms to prevent risk from contaminating the layers, is most evident. It is at such points that we can see how doctrine expresses multiple dimensions of commercial interaction and connectivity. Moreover, it will be suggested that these doctrinal forms

---

11    There are probably infinite possible approaches to this task. Here, Braudel's approach was chosen for use; others were not. So be it.

12    Edward CAVANAGH: *Charters in the longue durée: the mobility and applicability of donative documents in Europe and America from Edward I to chief justice John Marshall*, Comparative Legal History, 5(2017)/2, 262–295, using the *longue durée* as justification for the period of time covered, but only very briefly acknowledging the methodological implications.

13    James Stephen ROGERS: *The Early History of the Law of Bills and Notes: A Study of the Origins of Anglo-American Commercial Law*, Cambridge University Press, Cambridge (UK), 1995, Ch. 2; 107–108.

14    Fernand BRAUDEL: *Civilization & Capitalism 15th–18th Century: The Structures of Everyday Life: The Limits of the Possible*, Siân REYNOLDS (trans.), Harper Row, New York, 1981. This theme of a shadow over-layer is common to historians from left- and right-wing persuasions: cf. e.g. Karl POLANYI: *The Great Transformation: The Political and Economic Origins of Our Time*, (1944), Beacon Press, Boston, 2001; Niall FERGUSON: *The World's Banker: The History of the House of Rothschild*, Weidenfeld & Nicolson, London, 1998. Cf. David GRAEBER: *Debt: The First 5,000 Years*, Melville House Publishing, London, 2014, 127, noting the similarities between modern and supposedly primitive non-commercial societies as to this layered structuring of dealing.

# ENGLISH COMMERCIAL LAW IN THE *LONGUE DURÉE* 77

and mechanisms for enabling inter-layer transactions can be comparatively historicised as being part of a *longue durée*.

There are of course many types of comparative legal analysis, and comparative legal history itself has many different forms.[15] This chapter moves away from the common practice examining the extent to which elements of doctrine can be traced to other jurisdictions. Little more can be said for example about the French origins of much of English contract law.[16] Instead, this chapter takes a much more theoretically inclined approach, and examines the institution that itself is subjected to the conceptual structures of law: commerce. This approach takes inspiration from Pihlajamäki's expression of one form of comparison: to "take a national or regional legal institution as the focus of interest, much as a traditional legal historian working within the boundaries of a national legal system would. However, unlike the traditional legal historian, the comparative legal historian would always position the research object in its international context."[17] Here the legal institution is that of commercial law, specifically concerning financing. Additionally, this chapter addresses another institution, that of commerce itself. The institution of commerce is placed in its international and historical context here. Following Gordley, this chapter rests on the idea that commercial law is not an "independent object of study" qua history.[18] Historical research can reveal how domestic doctrine is connected to other, foreign, formulations and systems. Moreover, such connections may necessarily run over time periods as well as spatial distance.

Here there are two institutions in focus: law, in particular the national law concerning financing in England; and commerce. Here the focus is on the historical aspect of legal history – commerce is the research object which is placed in its international context. Is this acceptable? It would appear so, in light of the specific reference to institutions as potential research objects in the quotation from Pihlajamäki noted above.[19] Additionally, Sacco's important work on

---

15    Cf. e.g. Olivier Moréteau, Aniceto Masferrer, Kjell A. Modéer: *Comparative Legal History*, Elgar, 2019. This excellent text unfortunately arrived too late to be incorporated into this chapter.

16    James Gordley: *Comparative Law and Legal History* = *The Oxford Handbook of Comparative Law*, Mathias Reimann, Reinhard Zimmermann (eds.), Oxford University Press, Oxford, 2006, 753, 758. Cf. also A.W.B. Simpson: *Innovation in Nineteenth Century Contract Law*, Law Quarterly Review, 91(1975), 247; Catharine MacMillan: *Mistakes in Contract Law*, Hart Publishing, Oxford, 2010.

17    Pihlajamäki: *Private Law Codification...*, op. cit., 137.

18    Gordley: *Comparative Law and Legal History...*, op. cit.,759.

19    Cf. also Aniceto Masferrer: *The Longing for Comparative Legal History*, glossae: European Journal of Legal History 9(2012) 206, 212 fn. 7: describing the aims of the journal Comparative Legal History: "this broad conception of comparative legal history may

legal formants also predicates the notion of comparisons as being of rules *and* institutions.[20] "Comparative law presupposes the existence of a plurality of legal rules and institutions … The primary and essential aim of comparative law as a science, then, is better knowledge of legal rules and institutions."[21] Institutions as used here are not a peculiarly legal concept. First we can note Sacco's introduction to the concept of legal formants proper, where he refers to *legal rules*, as that were the whole intellectual concept, rather than *legal rules and institutions*.[22] This is an important distinction. Without such a distinction it would be odd to talk, as Sacco otherwise rightly does, of legal formants being something more than doctrine, or practitioners, or legislators:

> The statements which are "legal formants" of the system, hortatory or not, may not be strictly legal. They may be propositions about philosophy, politics, ideology or religion. It would be as difficult to explain canon law without the notion of God as it would be to explain Soviet law without ideas taken from Marx or Engels or Lenin. It would not only be difficult, but inadequate and unfair. Whether strictly legal or not, the propositions that are one of the legal formants of a system may be true or false.[23]

Thus here we examine the legal formants of a specific aspect of an issue that has a common historical presence: financing goods transactions. Across different time periods, we can see the same basic structure of the doctrine that is

---

include: (1) focus on any substantive area of comparative legal history: public law, criminal law, commercial law, private law, etc. Articles may centre on "internal" legal history, exploring doctrinal and disciplinary developments in the law, or *on "external" legal history, setting legal ideas and institutions in a wider social and historical context*; (2) involve both temporal and geographical comparison. Contributors may explore the ancient world or the recent past, the historical East or West or the global North or South. Articles may involve Western and non-Western traditions, all internally diverse, and *state laws and non-state norms, including a wide variety of customary traditions*, from around the world. Indeed, the complex origins of all legal traditions often makes research in single modern systems comparative as *layers of autochthonous and borrowed laws and norms are uncovered*; and (3) discuss and develop comparative and *historiographical theory and methodology*. Indeed, in addition to crossing boundaries of time and space, the journal promotes, as appropriate, an interdisciplinary ethos that bridges disciplinary boundaries. *The theory and method of the humanities, the social sciences, etc. may all be relevant to our work*." The italicised elements are most relevant to this chapter's form of comparative legal history.

20    Rodolfo Sacco: *Legal Formants: A Dynamic Approach to Comparative Law*, American Journal of Comparative Law 39(1991)/1, 1.

21    *Ibid.*, 5–6.

22    *Ibid.*, 22.

23    *Ibid.*, 32.

encapsulated in the so-called "modern" English law on documentary credit. Notions of autonomy, and the capacity to divide a transaction according to its tangibility (goods versus documents representing goods), passed gently from one country to another, slowly moving at roughly the same time with the shifting poles of economic power in Europe. From the Italian city-states Genoa through to Venice, then via Antwerp and Amsterdam on to London, the march of the idea was consistent.

Is it really possible to put forward such a grand theory of commerce, methodologically speaking? Certainly, as Armitage and Guldi argue, a (re)turn to the *longue durée* has "great [...] critical potential ... [Its] return ... is imperative."[24] Shorter-term analyses are limited, and cannot "formulat[e] a turning point of consequence."[25] The problem of universality in legal history though is subject to a penetrating analysis by Sugarman and Rubin.[26] They examine the complexity and evidential uncertainty as to whether and to what extent law facilitated economic development in the approximate period concerned with in this chapter.[27] In particular, they question the claim (often presented as axiomatic) that legal certainty and predictability was both essential to and wanted by commercial actors. Thus regardless of the changes wrought throughout the nineteenth century to the complicated and contradictory doctrine and practice concerning commercial and corporate law, the practice of commerce often remained the same.[28] Yet claims as to the irrelevance of law to commercial behaviour may miss the point about how law can permeate throughout society.[29] Moreover:

---

24 Cf. David ARMITAGE and Jo GULDI: *The Return of the* Longue Durée. *An Anglo-American Perspective* (a translation of David Armitage, Jo Guldi, *Le retour de la longue durée: une perspective anglo-américaine*, Annales. Histoire, Sciences Sociales 2(2015) (70th Year), 289–318), 221 (cairn-int.info/article-E_ANNA_702_0289--the-return-of-the-longueduree. htm). Armitage and Guldi want to marry the conceptual basis of *longue durée* with the technological tools available to modern historians. Though an entirely laudable aim, it is not that of this chapter.

25 *Ibid.*, 221.

26 David SUGARMAN, G.R. RUBIN: *Towards a New History of Law and Material Society in England, 1750–1914 = Law, Economy and Society, 1750–1914: Essays in the History of English Law*, G.R. RUBIN, David SUGARMAN (eds.), Professional Books Ltd, Abingdon, 1984, 1. To a considerable extent that essay replicates and builds on David SUGARMAN: *Law, Economy and the State in England, 1750–1914: Some Major Issues = Legality, Ideology and The State*, David SUGARMAN (ed.), Academic Press, London, 1983, 213.

27 SUGARMAN, RUBIN: *Towards a New History...*, *op. cit.*, 3 et seq.

28 *Ibid.*, 6.

29 *Ibid.*, 7.

Facilitative laws are but one instance of a wider phenomenon, namely, the role of the law in the facilitation and legitimation of a plurality of semi-autonomous realms – a role which has yet to be fully chronicled. The law simultaneously exemplified such a realm and defined and reproduced a mode of thought and practice which promoted a variety of semi-autonomous realms ... [F]acilitative laws ... built upon as well as were imbricated within the long-standing tradition of semi-autonomous realms.[30]

This notion of a "semi-autonomous realm," and the role of laws, is particularly useful in conceptualising the issues at hand here. It is also valuable to remind ourselves that any legal authority (or, indeed, its absence) will invariably have involved "the marginalisation, suppression, qualification or consolidation of pre-existing social relations."[31] Here the consolidation of pre-existing social relations to be examined is that of commercial law. This chapter, in an attempt to "transcend the confines of lawyers' legal history,"[32] and provide an alternative to the twin manacles of legal history – empiricism and functionalism,[33] endeavours to look not just at the instrumentality of specific areas of doctrine, but instead take specific doctrinal examples contextualised within broader socio-economic structures, of being illustrative of a far broader trend.

English commercial law demonstrates continuity of practices, of commercial and legal institutions,[34] contextualised by long-term historical change. Yet for sale, its late arrival as a discrete area of law,[35] can be explained by a turning point in the *longue durée*: the changes evident in the eighteenth and nineteenth centuries. Whilst it is perhaps too much to talk of a "birth" of

---

30    *Ibid.*, 10.

31    *Ibid.*, 112.

32    *Ibid.*

33    *Ibid.*, 119: "The militantly positivist-empiricist methodology of orthodox legal history...."

34    E.g. GOODE: *Commercial Law...*, *op. cit.*, 5. Cf. John H. BAKER: *The Law Merchant and the Common Law before 1700*, Cambridge Law Journal, 8(1979)/2, 295–322; ROGERS: *Early History of the Law of Bills and Notes...*, *op. cit.* For a recent analysis of the failure of attempts to develop merchant courts, cf. Christian M. BURSET: *Merchant Courts, Arbitration, and the Politics of Commercial Litigation in the Eighteenth-Century British Empire*, Law and History Review, 34(2016)/3, 615–647. Cf. also Justin SIMARD: *The Birth of a Legal Economy: Lawyers and the Development of American Commerce*, Buffalo Law Review, 64(2016)/5, 1059–1134 (the ordinary practice of lawyers created the structures and institutions for economic development). This chapter focuses on other aspects of the development of commerce and commercial law.

35    Lawrence M. FRIEDMAN: *Formative Elements in the Law of Sales: The Eighteenth Century*, Minnesota Law Review, 44(1960)/3, 411–460, 413–419.

consumption,[36] there was a shift in consumption patterns: multiple things were bought and sold (exchanged) at markets serving radically different purposes to the fairs and markets that had been part of commercial life until this point.[37] Things also became more durable,[38] and consisted of more complex and different elements requiring equally complex supply chains. Things made other things, and things drew value not just from their use-value but from other intangible elements (such as brands).[39] This all led, eventually, to a quantitative explosion of things, and of exchange-value attached to (and generated by) things. These exchanges of things needed institutions – legal concepts, in order to properly situate them within material civilisation, and so the law was required to engage with contemporary commercial practice and policy.[40]

The creation of sale as a discrete body of doctrine prioritised a doctrinal structure, codified as the Sale of Goods Act 1893,[41] which was an ossification of legal responses to different consumption patterns resting on much older paradigms.[42] However, English commercial law was already structured to enable value-shifting from the middle layer to the upper law.[43] Sales law's crystallisation as a discrete topic would complement the more readily formed law on financing, by providing a strong property core to the sale concept,[44] as the property concept was central to financing.[45]

---

36    Cf. Neil McKendrick, John Brewer, J.H. Plumb: *The Birth of a Consumer Society: Commercialization of Eighteenth Century England*, Indiana University Press, Bloomington, 1982.

37    Frank Trentmann: *Empire of Things: How We Became a World of Consumers, from the Fifteenth Century to the Twenty-first*, Allen Lane, London, 2016, 1.

38    *Ibid.*, 29: "Possessions were becoming more numerous and refined [by the fifteenth century]."

39    *Ibid.*, Chapter 2.

40    Friedman: *Formative Elements in the Law of Sales..., op. cit.*, 460; Rogers: *Early History of the Law of Bills and Notes..., op. cit.*, 124.

41    For an instance of how the Sale of Goods Act 1893 merely replicated prior (error-ridden) doctrine, cf. e.g. Sean Thomas: *The Development of the Implied Terms on Quantity in the Law of Sale of Goods*, The Journal of Legal History, 35(2014)/3, 281–318.

42    Cf. e.g. Grant Gilmore: *On The Difficulties of Codifying Commercial Law*, The Yale Law Journal, 57(1948)/8, 1341–1358.

43    For analysis of a slightly earlier era: Donald O. Wagner: *Coke and the Rise of Economic Liberalism*, The Economic History Review, 6(1935)/1, 30–44.

44    For a classic, and still pertinent to English law, critique cf. Karl Nickerson Llewellyn: *Cases and Materials on the Law of Sales*, Callaghan and Co., Chicago, 1930; Karl Nickerson Llewellyn: *Through title to contract and a bit beyond*, New York University Law Quarterly Review, 15(1938)/2, 159–209.

45    Cf. Edward A. Purcell Jr.: *Capitalism and Risk: Concepts, Consequences, and Ideologies*, Buffalo Law Review, 64(2016)/1, 26: "One could usefully see the distinctive core of capitalism as three interrelated ideas about private property and the dynamic tendencies those

The argument herein is not that English law on sales financing shows one style of capitalist law. Rather, increased exchange-value attaining to goods was enabled by doctrinal structures and mechanisms drawing on pre-existing and long-standing practices. To some extent then, this can be understood as an attempt to historically frame the famous Horwitz-Simpson debate about the extent of change in contract law. Horwitz argued that contract law was in the eighteenth century "essentially antagonistic to the interest of commercial classes"[46] and that this changed in the following century to a body of law that favoured the commercial classes. Simpson's critique is preferred here. He suggested instead that there were continuations of much older social practices in material civilisation, and the law's tendency to favour commercial classes goes much further back. The contemporary perspective of eighteenth century England might well have been that people felt they were in an era of change,[47] and to some extent they were, but in Simpson's words: "the picture of a loss of primeval innocence appears most implausible."[48]

## 3    Commerce: Vertical and Horizontal Shadows

For Braudel, an appropriate metaphor for his analytical structure was that of a multi-storied house: the lowest levels were of material life, which sat underneath layers of "'economic life', before moving on to the highest level of all, the action of capitalism."[49] His aim was to study "the borderlines of the social, the political and the economic."[50] What he said about mid-eighteenth century Amsterdam pertains to the whole task:

---

ideas generated: first, the idea that property can be abstract and liquid, appear in a multitude of forms, and be exchanged systemically through numbers written on paper; second, the idea that individuals should use property to create commodities for sale and profit rather than for their own consumption; and third, the idea that individuals should pursue their own self interest and strive to amass the largest amount of property as possible because doing so is both a social and moral good." The chapter focuses on ideas one and two.

46    Morton J. HORWITZ: *The Historical Foundations of Modern Contract Law*, Harvard Law Review, 87(1974)/5, 927.

47    Cf. e.g. Paul LANGFORD: *A Polite and Commercial People: England 1727–1783*, (1989), Oxford University Press, Oxford, 1992.

48    A.W.B. SIMPSON: *The Horwitz Thesis and the History of Contracts*, University of Chicago Law Review, 46(1979)/3, 541.

49    Fernand BRAUDEL: *Civilization & Capitalism 15th-18th Century: The Wheels of Commerce*, *vol 2*, Siân REYNOLDS (trans.) (1979), Phoenix Press, London, 2002, 21.

50    BRAUDEL: *Wheels of Commerce..., op. cit.*, 21.

ENGLISH COMMERCIAL LAW IN THE *LONGUE DURÉE*                    83

> [We need] to see how this entire network, which I see as a superstructure, connected at lower levels with lesser economies. It is with these connections, meeting points and multiple links that we shall be particularly concerned, since they reveal the way in which a dominant economy can exploit subordinate economies, while not soiling its own hands with the less profitable activities or types of production, or even, most of the time, directly supervising the lesser links in the chain of trade.[51]

The questions are: can the nodal points be identified, and what can they tell us about the layers of material civilisation? Braudel wrote of how different layers have "thousands of humble points of intersection".[52] Every point of exchange involving explicit valuation of the goods exchanged is one where there is transference from one layer to the other. Thus the sale of goods in a shop involves the transfer of goods from outside of the middle layer of market economy into the under-layer of material life – coats to be worn, food to be eaten, computers to be played with and so on. At the same time, there is an intersection between the middle layer and the upper layer. A store keeper may use the money to pay off a loan secured against the shop, or there may be some sort of floor-plan stocking arrangement. Whatever occurs, there is a transfer of monetary value to the upper level of financial capitalism. The basic process can be extrapolated to more complex situations;[53] the connecting factor of price (money) in the role of exchange helps create a permeable interface between different layers of material civilisation.[54] Price enables under-layers of material transactions to become valued and thus move to the middle layer of open, market exchange.[55] The value aspect of that exchange then entails to the shadow over-layer of

---

51  *Ibid.*, 248.

52  *Ibid.*, 21.

53  *Ibid.*, 378: "This pyramid of trade, always identifiable, a society within a society, can be found anywhere in the West, and in any period. It had its own laws of motion. Specialisation and division of labour usually operated from the bottom up. If modernisation or rationalisation consists of the process whereby different tasks are distinguished and functions subdivided, such modernisation began *in the bottom layer of the economy*."

54  *Ibid.*, 432–433: noting capital's essential feature, the capacity to efficiently move towards a sector of high profit to obtain that money-flow for the higher layer.

55  Cf. Fernand BRAUDEL: *Civilization & Capitalism 15th-18th Century: The Perspective of the World*, vol. 3, Siân REYNOLDS (trans.), (1979), William Collins Sons & Co Ltd, London, 1984, 96: "Towns spelled money, the essential ingredient of the [12th century] commercial revolution." For a critical examination of money, cf. e.g. GRAEBER: *Debt...*, *op. cit.* (money existed in a formal, accounting, sense, but was not relevant in real commercial activity).

finance.[56] Yet there is in essence a hierarchy of power in these relationships, whereby an upper layer governs any lower layers by virtue of the money-exchange connection. The control obtained by the over-layer of finance is through occupation, as Braudel put it, of "the key sectors of accumulation."[57] This is not really a modern phenomenon, nor is it a revolutionary change in human activity. The Champagne fairs, which sat (geographically and economically) between the twelfth and thirteenth century poles of the Low Countries and the Italian Mediterranean, were less about the goods on sale as they were about the opportunity for credit markets.[58] Such fairs were arguably just an "interlude,"[59] but what followed in later centuries had the same basic structures, just on a different scale. They were nodal points, shifting value from middle to upper layers of exchange, and the shadows cast by such exchanges were small but growing.

The changes were slow, because the commercial and productive activity of the Mediterranean and northern Europe remained basically unchanged until, roughly, the eighteenth century.[60] Over the *longue durée* there was a growth in the volume of trade, but no significant change in the types of commodities imported into northern European ports. What changes that occurred were concerned with what Braudel termed the "superstructure": that aspect of society which is concerned with the fluidity of transactions, providing institutions of money, capital, debt.[61] Then around the mid-seventeenth to mid-eighteenth centuries there was an evident shift to imports from Asia and America, primarily resulting from colonialism.[62] The re-exporting trade, so long centred in Italy, shifted to northern Europe, where it would start to have substantial impact on

---

56    ROGERS: *Early History of the Law of Bills and Notes...*, *op. cit.*, 32–43: noting how trade circuits would involve use of commercial paper both as funds for the transaction itself, and as a distinct (though connected) finance mechanism for lending based on exchange rate differentials.

57    BRAUDEL: *Perspective of the World...*, *op. cit.*, 65.

58    *Ibid.*, 112.

59    *Ibid.*, 115.

60    *Ibid.*, 36: "The basic distances, routes, delays, production, merchandise and stopping places – everything or almost everything had remained the same." Niels STEENSGAARD: *The growth and composition of long-distance trade of England and the Dutch Republic before 1750* = *The Rise of Merchant Empires: Long-Distance Trade in the Early Modern World 1350–1750*, James TRACY (ed.), Cambridge University Press, Cambridge (UK), 1990, 106: "remarkable continuity"; TRENTMANN: *Empire of Things...*, *op. cit.*, 33: "There was more of everything ... but a household in 1600 still mostly had the same kind of things as two hundred years earlier."

61    BRAUDEL: *Perspective of the World...*, *op. cit.*, 36.

62    Cf. also TRENTMANN: *Empire of Things...*, *op. cit.*, Chapter 3 on the role of Empire on consumption.

ENGLISH COMMERCIAL LAW IN THE *LONGUE DURÉE*

consumption patterns,[63] in a similar manner to narrower but still profound changes wrought to consumption patterns of textiles in the mid-sixteenth to mid-seventeenth century following expansion of the English East Indian Company.[64] The effect of these long-term trends married to shorter-term changes was vast increases in volumes of trade.[65]

These broad changes can be observed (over the *longue durée*), in first Dutch, then British trade. Amsterdam was a world-city, perhaps *the* world-city, of the early eighteenth century.[66] World-cities are centres, focused on commerce, trade and exchange, sucking in assets and debt/credit. World cities operate at the primary nodal points of networks and circuits, and thus provide the best places to operate the translation function inherent in and necessary to the processing between the different layers of material civilisation. Amsterdam during the late seventeenth and early eighteenth century rested its wealth and power on non-specie commerce.[67] The mechanisms of commerce, the acceptance trade, were, however, transferable across the North Sea, not least because they were built on foundations developed long before the eighteenth century; the eighteenth century being merely a period of acceleration.[68] For Braudel, Amsterdam went "chasing shadows" by providing financial services at the expense of developing trade, and in doing so it "dropped the bird in the hand," i.e. the economics of entrepôt, leaving space for London.[69] From the mid-eighteenth century on, London became and remained preeminent and unchallenged until the start of the twentieth century, not least because London had the advantage of an enormous and growing domestic and colonial market (of production and consumption).

Cities such as London from the mid-eighteenth century effectively dominated by providing the conditions (the institutions and the concentration of wealth) to allow a mid-layer market economy as well as "an over-arching economy which seizes these humble activities from above, redirects them and

---

63    STEENSGAARD: *Growth and composition of long-distance trade..., op. cit.*, 151.

64    *Ibid.*, 123–128.

65    TRENTMANN: *Empire of Things..., op. cit.*, 23.

66    The focus here is necessarily restricted to the "Western" world.

67    Cf. Carla Rahn PHILLIPS: *The Growth and Composition of Trade in the Iberian Empires, 1450–1750 = Merchant Empires...*, TRACY op. cit., 34–101, 87 (noting the correspondence between the Dutch golden age and war and political disruption amongst their rivals).

68    Fernand BRAUDEL: *Afterthoughts on Material Civilization*, Johns Hopkins Press, Baltimore, 1977, 27–28.

69    BRAUDEL: *Perspective of the World..., op. cit.*, 246. London would itself later undertake the same shift from entrepôt to finance: Sean THOMAS: *The Origins of the Factors Acts 1823 and 1825*, 32(2011)/2, The Journal of Legal History, 151–187.

holds them at its mercy."[70] For Braudel, a vital point was the shifting nature of the pound sterling in the seventeenth and early eighteenth century. The overvaluation of gold relative to silver and the consequent export of silver to areas where it had an important function in commerce,[71] and the emerging de facto gold standard (long before a de jure gold standard) corresponding to the access to volumes of Portuguese-Brazilian gold following Lord Methuen's 1703 treaty with Portugal, put the British economy in a position to easily shift to a paper based-economy and thus reduce friction between the middle and upper layers of material civilisation. But this was only a subsidiary change, which helped provide some of the conditions necessary for the "real guarantee," which was the volume of goods produced in the British economy as a whole and the profits generated by accompanying trade which helped, alongside the metal valuation issues, to provide currency stability for sterling.[72] These specific issues are valuable, if only a very narrow illumination of the conditions impacting on Britain and London's economic status. There are of course a vast range of arguments about the conditions, factors and issues leading to the Industrial Revolution. However, the specific issues Braudel mentioned connect coherently to a more general mechanism allowing control of the lower layers in material civilisation: credit. How credit fits into this chapter's argument is thus: it is the mechanism that is the nodal connection between the layers.

The nodal points of connection and intersection between the layers are (at least partially) institutional.[73] One particular institution that needs examination is that of law: how law, as an institution, can and does respond to commerce, itself an institution.[74] It is a case of institutional interaction, in vertical and horizontal ways. The vertical interaction, the intersections between the different layers, meshes with horizontal interactions, between the different participants and actors within a particular layer. Sometimes one or the other is more visible: with the material and economic layers the circulation of goods is "visible on first observation without difficulty" and is the market economy.[75]

---

70  BRAUDEL: *Perspective of the World...*, *op. cit.*, 38.

71  Cf. e.g. Ward BARRETT: *World bullion flows, 1450–1800 = The Rise of Merchant Empires...*, *op. cit.*, 250–251 (noting the movement of silver to the Baltic).

72  BRAUDEL: *Perspective of the World...*, *op. cit.*, 364–365.

73  *Ibid.*, 27–31.

74  Cf. Ajay K. MEHROTRA: *A Bridge Between: Law and the New Intellectual Histories of Capitalism*, Buffalo Law Review, 64(2016)/1, 15: "Not only do legal rules and categories, like property and contract, come to define economic and social relations, legal institutions and processes provide the rational and routinized system of governance that is so critical to an effective market economy."

75  BRAUDEL: *Wheels of Commerce...*, *op. cit.*, 22. Cf. also, at 582: "The preconditions of any form of capitalism have to do with circulation."

ENGLISH COMMERCIAL LAW IN THE *LONGUE DURÉE*

The visibility of these interactions varies with one's perspective: it is arguably easy now to observe the circulation (or lack thereof) of non-material wealth – finance – between one and another layer.[76] Yet, legal doctrine can sometimes be blind to history.[77]

On the other hand, law can be revelatory: this is what an examination of the borderlines reveals following acknowledgment they are both created by and consist of law.[78] The presence and nature of borders and intersection matters, but so does understanding how connections were made between different state institutions and characters.[79] For Braudel, commercial paper, such as the bill of exchange, was central to the connectivity between the different institutions and layers, enabling the generation and importantly the closing up of networks and circuits that form the system.[80] There is a vast literature on networks, with evidence of many different types of network succeeding and failing. Sometimes strong institutions provide an appropriate framework of social closure,[81] sometimes weak, transitory ties operating to provide information flows will not require such institutional strength.[82] Here though the type of

---

76    *Ibid.*, 25–26. Cf. further e.g. William E. SCHEUERMAN: *Global Law in Our High Speed Economy = Rules and Networks: The Legal Culture of Global Business Transactions*, Richard P. APPLEBAUM, William L.F. FELSTINE, Volkmar GESSNER (eds.), Hart Publishing, Oxford, 2001, Chapter 3, 104–105.

77    Ron HARRIS: *The Encounters of Economic History and Legal History*, Law and History Review, 21(2003)/2, 340: "Each piece, or legal rule, interrelates with other, at times seemingly unrelated, pieces, in a thick legal-historical context." Cf. also Frederick POLLOCK: *Essays in Jurisprudence and Ethics*, MacMillan and Co., London, 1882, 198: "Lawyers, again, are for the practical purposes of their business concerned with the laws as they are, not as they have been."

78    Cf. MILNE: *Trade and traders...*, *op. cit.*, 114–115: "Historians have bemoaned" the volume of consignments to order; 153: a key area of inter-trader reliance was credit-worthiness, but this is an area "strangely invisible in much historical writing." Cf. also Frank TRENTMANN: *Introduction = The Oxford Handbook of the History of Consumption*, Frank TRENTMANN (ed.), Oxford University Press, Oxford, 2012, 15: "Historical engagement with ... law has been ... patchy."

79    Cf. BRAUDEL: *Wheels of Commerce...*, *op. cit.*, 419: "it was within the context of the modern economy that a certain capitalism and a certain version of the modern state first appeared," 515: the state had "to exert control over economic life, both near and far, to arrange for the circulation of goods, with as much coherence as possible"; GRAEBER: *Debt...*, *op. cit.*, especially 50–52: markets are bound up by violence, in an triangular relationship with institutions of states and taxation.

80    BRAUDEL: *Wheels of Commerce...*, *op. cit.*, 142–149, 168.

81    E.g. Avner GREIF: *Institutions and the Path to the Modern Economy: Lessons from Medieval Trade*, Cambridge University Press, Cambridge (UK), 2006.

82    E.g. Emily ERIKSON, Sampsa SAMILA: *Networks, Institutions, and Encounters: Information Flow in Early-Modern Markets*, Working paper, December 2015 (law.yale.edu/system/files/area/center/privatelaw/document/erikson_networks_market_expansion.docx).

network is of less interest than the connections within and between networks; the intersections between different layers of material civilisation. This is where law comes in, responding to the problems generated by transactions between different layers.

Law's capacity (and obligation) to respond to practical problems of commercial life emphasises the role of change in the history of commercial law; the more intricate issue is the extent and nature of this change. Certainly, the systemic revolution in litigation, from procedural to substantive disputes, needs accounting for.[83] Economy prevents this being discussed further. Additionally, whilst there is a need to acknowledge the diversity between ordinary sales and complex international commodity trades,[84] such differences are not really modern phenomena.[85] What therefore can we draw out about sales in the broader context of commerce, over the *longue durée*? We can say there have been changes, and that such changes are not all (if ever) novel. Rather, as Goode pointed out and as this chapter began by noting, *reinvention* is central to commercial law. For sales law this is also the case; the reinvention takes place by means of the development of a distinct body of sales law, resting on a foundation of property, that allows the use of forms of financing that are clearly evident as products of the *longue durée*.

It is tentatively suggested here that a key turning point was a shift in the nature and role of fixed capital (by which is meant tangible property, from goods to housing) in societies.[86] Braudel suggests that the transformation of fixed capital, in terms of becoming more durable (and thus also more costly) positively affected production within societies.[87] Such changes provided not

---

83   Cf. Robert B. FERGUSON: *The Adjudication of Commercial Disputes and the Legal System in Modern England*, British Journal of Law and Society, 7(1980)/2, 141–157.

84   Michael G. BRIDGE: *The evolution of modern sales law*, Lloyd's Maritime and Commercial Law Quarterly, (1991), 52.

85   GOODE: *Commercial Law...*, *op. cit.*, 4. Cf. also BRAUDEL: *Wheels of Commerce...*, *op. cit.*, 575: alongside the usual touchstone of double-entry bookkeeping, other commercial instruments were an accumulation of practice, yet "[m]ore significant than the innovating spirit of entrepreneurship were the increased volume of trade, the frequent inadequacy of the money supply, etc." As to the question of the changing complexity of doctrine, compare Patrick DEVLIN: *The Relation Between Commercial Law and Commercial Practice*, Modern Law Review, 14(1951)/3, 251 with Peter BIRKS: *English and Roman Learning in Moses v Macferlan*, Current Legal Problems, 37(1984)/1, 1–2.

86   Cf. e.g. Sean THOMAS: *Mortgages, fixtures, fittings and security over personal property*, Northern Ireland Legal Quarterly, 66(2015)/4, 343–365.

87   BRAUDEL: *Wheels of Commerce...*, *op. cit.*, 247, 338. Cf. also e.g. Judith FLANDERS: *The Making of Home*, Atlantic Books, London, 2014. The increased quality of goods is a possible reason for changes in quality obligations: Paul MITCHELL: *The development of quality obligations in sale of goods*, Law Quarterly Review, 117(2011)/3, 655. The story of goods at

ENGLISH COMMERCIAL LAW IN THE *LONGUE DURÉE* 89

just the opportunity for commercial growth, but they also identified with greater clarity potential targets, i.e. fixed capital, for a new form of financial-capitalist commerce. However, the capacity of things to hold value relative to their movement within the system, combined with existing and sophisticated ways of managing the transfer of things along networks and circuits, required close control of such processes of transfer. This much is clear from Milne's description of the port of Liverpool in the mid-nineteenth century. The increasing complexity of multilateral commodity trading, where the goods themselves may not ever been seen by the participants in the trade, meant that the extent of control traders could exercise over a supply chain was essential to the port's prosperity.[88] The central role played by traders is in line with the conceptual structure of nodal points of connection between the different layers of material civilisation. The trader is a character who operates within the nodal points. Their activity involves the transferring of value from one layer to another.

With greater commercial complexity came the division of control and ownership of the things moving: at different stages of the circuit exchanges between differing controllers and owners occur (whether through fair means or foul). Multiple methods were used to minimise the inevitable risk, such as financing using trusted personal/family connections,[89] or by using often location-specific (if not necessarily novel) work-arounds.[90] However, the capacity of exchanges in complex commercial transactions to provide a translating function, an institutional nodal point between different layers of material civilisation, matters. The process of exchange can shift value from one layer of material civilisation to another. Yet as Braudel notes, merchants used to continually change roles, following the highest profits, which hindered the growth the highest capitalist layer. This did not prevent financing from arising though; it was just that the lower layers of material civilisation were insufficiently secure or broad to support a coherent and consistent upper layer. Certainly there was considerable growth in the use of commercial paper as a result of economic change throughout the seventeenth and eighteenth century,[91] but it was

---

the lowest layer of material civilisation is admittedly more varied: Sara PENNELL: *Material Culture in Seventeenth-Century "Britain": The Matter of Domestic Consumption = Oxford Handbook...*, *op. cit.*; TRENTMANN, *op. cit.*, 64–84.

88  MILNE: *Trade and traders...*, *op. cit.*, 21.

89  *Ibid.*, 124–125.

90  *Ibid.*, 134–145 on the peculiar nature of joint ownership of ships, justified in Charles ABBOTT: *A Treatise of the Law Relative to Merchant Ships and Seamen*, London, 1802, 82–83. This sub-divided joint ownership mirrors Venetian practice 500 years before: BRAUDEL: *Perspective of the World...*, *op. cit.*, 129.

91  ROGERS: *Early History of the Law of Bills and Notes...*, *op. cit.*, 107–108.

only really during the first half of the nineteenth century period that the upper layer of financial capitalism became a fixture.[92] This was a consequence of the changes in fixed capital, which enabled effective reinvestment of funds into fixed capital which generated income.[93] Another form of reinvestment was in financing the sales transactions themselves.[94] In this context, the mechanisms of financial capitalism, such as bills of exchange, bearer and non-bearer documents, rules concerning endorsement and obligations, and so on, were *already in place.*

This aspect has recently been clearly demonstrated by De ruysscher in a series of important articles concerning the transmission of doctrine into (roughly) sixteenth century Antwerp from Italy,[95] and then the influences of Antwerp's doctrine in seventeenth century Amsterdam and German states.[96] In his analysis of how Antwerp dealt with these developments, he made the valuable point that generation of specific legal doctrine was in effect a scholarly replication in civilian jurisprudential language of merchant practices.[97] Thus by the sixteenth century Antwerp had developed "growing legal sophistication" corresponding to provisions regarding formation of commercial agreements (previously attention had almost entirely focused on enforcement).[98] This was connected to the increases in trade, but in particular that aspect of commerce that dealt with the parallel transactions to that of sale: financing, insurance, storage and so on.[99] By the later seventeenth century there is evidence of how commercial practices concerning financing were being implicitly

---

92    BRAUDEL: *Afterthoughts..., op. cit.*, 58–62. Cf. ROGERS: *Early History of the Law of Bills and Notes..., op. cit.*, 107–108

93    Cf. generally e.g. Thomas PIKETTY: *Capital in the Twenty-First Century*, Arthur GOLDHAMMER (trans.), Harvard University Press, Cambridge (MA), 2014.

94    BRAUDEL: *Perspective of the World..., op. cit.*, 246.

95    Dave DE RUYSSCHER: *Designing the Limits of Creditworthiness. Insolvency in Antwerp Bankruptcy Legislation and Practice (16th–17th Centuries)*, Tijdschrift voor Rechtsgeschiedenis, 76(2008), 307–327.

96    Dave DE RUYSSCHER: *Antwerp Commercial Legislation in Amsterdam in the 17th Century. Legal Transplant or Jumping Board?*, Tijdschrift voor Rechtsgeschiedenis, 77(2009), 459–479; Dave DE RUYSSCHER: *Innovating Financial Law in the Early Modern Netherlands and Europe: Transfers of Commercial Paper and Recourse Liability in Legislation and Ius Commune (Sixteenth to Eighteenth Centuries)*, European Review of Private Law, 19(2011), 505–518.

97    Dave DE RUYSSCHER: *From Usages of Merchants to Default Rules: Practices of Trade, Ius Commune and Urban Law in Early Modern Antwerp*, The Journal of Legal History, 33(2012)/1, 15–16, 25.

98    *Ibid.*, 11.

99    *Ibid.*, 12.

ENGLISH COMMERCIAL LAW IN THE *LONGUE DURÉE* 91

accepted in spite of clear prohibitions.[100] But this should not be taken as indicated that the doctrine had set against such capitalist behaviour. Instead, the limited references to mercantile custom and the relative rarity of arguments that stretched rather thin civilian conceptual structures to meet commercial practices is perhaps best understood as demonstrating how the "official urban rules, which were based on civil law, closely followed commercial practices."[101] For our purposes, it is of particular interest to note that De ruyscheer gave as an example of arguments stretching civilian concepts as that involved the interpretation of doctrines concerning *procurator* to allow holders of bills of exchange to sell those bills. He then notes that "this closely followed what in the early 1500s had been stated about the rights of holders of letters obligatory made out to bearer."[102] This indicates the potential importance of such transactions; these are the sort of transactions that exchange value from the middle to the upper layers of material civilisation. Moreover, it shows how the antecedents of such forms of capitalism can be discerned. So it would be no surprise to find that by the first half of the seventeenth century Antwerp had "completely acknowledged the newly developed method of indorsement,"[103] and yet at the same time there were only "relatively few commercial innovations that had to be promoted to the level of urban law."[104] It is suggested that this shows how the light was already there, but changes in commerce generally (increases in volumes of trade in goods) enhanced its lustre sufficiently to create the shadows in which the exchanges of value attending to the trades in goods, from the middle to the upper layer of material civilisation, could operate more effectively.[105]

---

100  *Ibid.*, 23 (bills of exchange on *ricorsa* terms).

101  *Ibid.*, 24.

102  *Ibid.*, 24.

103  *Ibid.*, 25.

104  *Ibid.*, 26.

105  It is worth briefly dealing with an important point made in DE RUYSSCHER: *Usages of Merchants...*, *op. cit.*, 26: "The rules acknowledging the usages were never presented as common principles applying in an area larger than the Antwerp jurisdiction, or as belonging to a distinct source of commercial law. The merchant witnesses underscored the local application of the attested norms." This is is easily accomodated by this chapter's argument. Such locality was not a problem for those introducing rules concerning commercial practices of financial capitalism. The relevant parties wanted the localism of Antwerp, because that was a world city. It was in Antwerp that such transactions would have meaning, that is, would be able to actually transfer value to the higher layer of capital, because it was at such times only in such world cities that such a layer would exist (and then, only in a rough and limited form compared to that found in nineteenth century London).

## 4 English Commercial Law: Chasing Shadows

The development of English commercial law is a story of incredible complexity affected not just by the massive changes of the Industrial Revolution, but by other regional and global historical trends (such as the shifts away from the Mediterranean towards northern Europe in the early modern period),[106] as well as by local peculiarities (such as the law/equity division;[107] the relationship between Scotland and England).[108] For Goode, three factors had (at least some) causal impact on the "pre-eminence" of English commercial law: the growth in commercial activity; political and social stability; and relative non-interference by the legislature combined with a pro-commercial judicial attitude.[109] A further factor that needs to be accounted for is the transformation of commercial practice and thought into doctrine,[110] and doctrine into dogma.[111]

One early key stage in this development was the shift in English law in dealing with bills of exchange. As Rogers has clearly demonstrated,[112] English

---

106 Cf. generally BRAUDEL: *Structures of Everyday Life...*, *op. cit.*; BRAUDEL: *Wheels of Commerce...*, *op. cit.*; BRAUDEL: *Perspective of the World...*, *op. cit.* Cf. also TRACY: *Merchant Empires...*, *op. cit.*

107 GOODE: *Commercial Law...*, *op. cit.*, 4.

108 As to the Scottish influence of Lord Mansfield, oft seen as the progenitor of modern English commercial law, cf. generally James OLDHAM: *The Mansfield manuscripts and the growth of English law in the eighteenth century*, University of North Carolina Press, Chapel Hill, 1992.

109 GOODE: *Commercial Law...*, *op. cit.*, 5–7; Robert B. FERGUSON: *Legal Ideology and Commercial Interests: The Social Origins of the Commercial Law Codes*, British Journal of Law and Society, 4(1977)/1, 18–38. PIHLAJAMÄKI: *Private Law Codification...*, *op. cit.*, 139: "A vigorous development of legal scholarship is necessarily almost always at work in the background [of codification]."

110 BRIDGE: *Evolution...*, *op. cit.*, 52: "the sale of goods ... has been formed by ideas drawn from mercantile dealings, with the market-place bulking large in its development." Contrast DE RUYSSCHER: *Usages of Merchants...*, *op. cit.*, 3 (what were often presented as customs were actually default (legal) rules); David LIEBERMAN: *Property, commerce and the common law: Attitudes to legal change in the eighteenth century = Early Modern Conceptions of Property*, John BREWER, Susan STAVES (eds.), Routledge, London, 1996, 144–158 (eighteenth century English commentators understood the impact and nature of commerce, and the division really stood as between real property and commercial law). This debate is part of the argument over whether there really was a *lex mercatoria*: Emily KADENS: *The Myth of the Customary Law Merchant*, Texas Law Review, 90(2012)/5, 1153–1206; Emily KADENS: *The Medieval Law Merchant: The Tyranny of a Construct*, Journal of Legal Analysis, 7(2015)/2, 251–289.

111 BRIDGE: *Evolution...*, *op. cit.*, 52–53: case-law provides a foundation for later commentary. Cf. also Alan RODGER: *The codification of commercial law in Victorian Britain*, Law Quarterly Review, 108(1992)/3, 570–590.

112 ROGERS: *Early History of the Law of Bills and Notes...*, *op. cit.*, 44–68.

ENGLISH COMMERCIAL LAW IN THE *LONGUE DURÉE* 93

courts prior to the seventeenth century were often dealing with transactions involving bills of exchange. However, they were dealing with disputes as regards the underlying transaction rather than on the bill itself. That is, the disputes were those concerning the actual debt obligation between the parties, or the obligations of factors and so on. The courts did not deal with and thus produce doctrine on the issue of a dispute on the bill itself; negotiability was thus not a developed concept in early English law. However, the seventeenth and eighteenth centuries altered this. This important change would help lay the foundations for further delineations between transactions involving goods and paper; a development that would have profound consequences when matched with the contemporary increases in goods transactions. There is an important point though to make here in the context of this chapter's thesis. Rogers rightly suggests that it would be anachronistic to treat the doctrinal treatment of bills transactions as evidence of the same practices as demonstrated by the doctrine which developed in the seventeenth, eighteenth and nineteenth century.[113] However, this is not the same as saying that the principle of division between commercial paper and underlying sales transactions was not recognised. The early courts were dealing with debt claims using mechanisms and processes of claim that were appropriate for the doctrinal context; that those debt claims involved similar sorts of instruments as were used in a variety of commercial claims is a different point. Furthermore, whilst the disputes concerned the underlying exchange transaction, and were not on the bases of the bill itself, this was merely the initial starting point for developing a process whereby the underlying transaction and the bill could form distinct obligations. This process would be very useful in commercial contexts where transactions involved more than a party and a counter-party, that is, where there were two distinct networks as between those connected through the underlying transaction and those connected through the associated commercial paper. Another element worth noting is that the sixteenth and seventeenth centuries saw the development of exchange transactions, which were concurrent to considerable discourse criticising such treatment of money as itself a commodity. Whether this criticism was (as often found in works coming out the European exchange centres such as Antwerp) on the basis that treating money as a commodity was sinful (as usury) or whether (as in the English context) it was harming the national interest (through the exporting of bullion),[114] it did not really matter as the point was that the successful opposition to these new forms of transactions "turned on seeing exchange dealings as

---

113  *Ibid.*, 67.
114  *Ibid.*, 90.

sales or exchanges of one form of property for another, that than as loans. Yet the property in question was money."[115] The task was for the law to catch up with this commercial treatment of money as potentially distinct from the underlying transaction. It achieved this in the specific context of bills through alteration in pleadings in the seventeenth century, which had the effect of enabling actions based on the bill itself.[116] The issue now to be examined is the later developments of the law of sale, and how that fitted into the pre-existing structures.

The initial English commercial texts (i.e. those going beyond mere records of mercantile practices[117]) including important works such as Chitty's 1799 text on bills of exchange,[118] and Abbott's 1802 text on shipping,[119] avoided sales as a discrete topic. Other less valuable compendia often merely offered sales as a single chapter.[120] The early formalism of English law meant the "substantive mercantile law ... had no existence as a coherent system of principles before the common law itself developed the means of giving it expression."[121] However, Blackburn's 1845 text on sale arguably changed this.[122] That text has been criticised though, with Bridge suggesting it was "not easy to reconcile with a commercial sales ethic" as it rejected "the historical values of personal property law," and involved an "enthronement of property represent[ing] an attempt to create a sophisticated intellectual structure" for sale.[123] However, Blackburn's property focus was not a "rejection" of historical practice,[124] but

---

115   *Ibid.*, 92.

116   *Ibid.*, Ch. 6.

117   Cf. e.g. BAKER: *Law Merchant...*, *op. cit.*, 296 fn. 7: "G. Maylnes, *Lex Mercatoria* (1622), which is not a law book but a compendium, of current practice compiled by a merchant." Baker later notes, at 297 that there was a "flood of textbooks on commercial law which followed [Lord Mansfield's] retirement [1793]."

118   Joseph CHITTY: *A Treatise on the law of Bills of Exchange, Checks on Bankers, Promissory Notes, Bankers' Cash Notes, and Bank-Notes*, London, 1799.

119   ABBOTT: *Law Relative to Merchant Ships...*, *op. cit.*

120   Cf. e.g. H.W. WOOLRYCH: *A Practical Treatise on the Commercial and Mercantile Laws of England*, London, 1829; J.W. SMITH: *A Compendium of Mercantile Law*, London, 1834.

121   BAKER: *Law Merchant...*, *op. cit.*, 321. Compare Roman law, which treated sale distinctly: cf. e.g. Reinhard ZIMMERMANN: *The Law of Obligations: Roman Foundations of the Civilian Tradition*, Oxford University Press, Oxford, 1996.

122   Colin BLACKBURN: *A Treatise on the Effect of the Contract of Sale, on the Legal Rights of Property and Possession in Goods, Wares, and Merchandize*, London, 1845.

123   BRIDGE: *Evolution...*, *op. cit.*, 63.

124   Cf. BAKER: *Law Merchant...*, *op. cit.*, 299: "Lord Mansfield's law was binding on his successors; and so, to the extent that it embodied mere current usage, it froze the practice of Georgian merchants as the permanent law of England." Or, did it merely replicate customs and practices that come up again and again in different contexts?.

ENGLISH COMMERCIAL LAW IN THE *LONGUE DURÉE* 95

arguably an illustration of the increasing importance of goods as stores of wealth,[125] and a useful touchstone to ascertain liability and interests.[126] By focusing on the concept of property, there was the possibility of distinguishing different types of commercial relationships vis-à-vis goods. Moreover, the identification of property became a clear way to work out the allocation of risk, as Llewellyn recognised.[127] This impacted on interconnections between layers of material exchange and financial capital.

Although other texts began appearing,[128] it was a monumental, career-rescuing,[129] 1868 tome that captured the market: Benjamin's *Treatise on the Law of Sale of Personal Property*.[130] It provided a conceptualisation of sale; one of such significance that the current English law on sale is merely a minor modification of Benjamin's scheme.[131] This is important due to the clear connection between Blackburn and Benjamin's texts. However, although Benjamin

---

125    That goods *could be* stores of wealth was not a new concept, Sir Frederick POLLOCK, F.W. MAITLAND: *The history of English Law before the time of Edward I*, Cambridge University Press, Cambridge (UK), 1898, 149: "the further we go back, the larger seems the space which the possession of chattels fills in the eye of the law." The change was in the quantity and nature of goods.

126    BLACKBURN, *Contract of Sale...*, *op. cit.*, 1–2. Cf. also SUGARMAN, RUBIN: *Towards a New History...*, *op. cit.*, 23–42.

127    Cf. supranote 30.

128    Such as George Joseph BELL: *Inquiries into the Contract of Sale of Goods and Merchandise as Recognised in the Judicial Decisions and Mercantile Practice of Modern Nations*, Edinburgh, 1845; William W. STORY: *A Treatise on the Law of Sales of Personal Property*, 1847; Leoni LEVI: *Commercial Law, Its Principles and Administration; or, the Mercantile Law of Great Britain*, William Benning & Co, London, 1850, which Goode rightly calls "a work of great erudition" (GOODE: *Commercial Law...*, *op. cit.*, 8 fn. 7). Cf. further G.R. RUBIN: *Levi, Leone (1821–1888) = Oxford Dictionary of National Biography*, Oxford University Press, Oxford, 2004 (oxforddnb.com/view/article/16551). Cf. also RODGER: *Codification of commercial law...*, *op. cit.*, 572–573. Levi's introductory plan of his *Commercial Law*, vol .1, refers to having based his outlining of the law of Great Britain to, inter alia, "Smith's Mercantile Law" (presumably SMITH: *A Compendium of Mercantile Law...*, *op. cit.*), and "Blackstone's Commentaries," giving further indication of the paucity of texts on commercial law at the time.

129    Catherine MACMILLAN: *Judah Benjamin: Marginalized Outsider or Admitted Insider?*, Journal of Law and Society, 42(2015)/1, 150–172.

130    Judah BENJAMIN: *A Treatise on the Law of Sale of Personal Property; With References to the American Decisions and to the French Code and Civil Law*, London, 1868.

131    The SGA 1893 merely replicated what was considered to be the law at the time: *Bank of England v Vagliano Bros* [1891] AC 107, 144–145 (Lord Herschell); HH Judge CHALMERS: *The Sale of Goods Act, 1893, including the Factors Acts, 1889 & 1890*, London, 1894, iii; LAW COMMISSION and SCOTTISH LAW COMMISSION: *Sale and Supply of Goods*, Law Com 160, Scot Law Com 104, 1987, paragraph 1.5; THOMAS: *Development of the Implied Terms on Quantity...*, *op. cit.*, 307.

justified his text by reference to the limitations with Blackburn's text,[132] like Blackburn he still took a property perspective.[133] Benjamin understood the broader commercial system,[134] rendering his focus on sale and property rather interesting as likely being an accurate representation of contemporary commercial practices and perspectives.[135]

A further explanation (and justification) for the late arrival of sale and its focus on property rests on long term developments from exchanges of goods to more complex commercial financing of such transactions. Britain (i.e. basically London) wrestled dominance of commerce – of financing – out of Dutch (i.e. basically Amsterdam) hands in the mid to late eighteenth century. At the same time rapid expansion in British domestic and international trade provided a foundation for utilisation of financial mechanisms to effectively translate the benefits of such trade – to move value from the middle market exchange layer to the upper layer of financial capitalism. The financial mechanisms deployed rested on the capacity of English law to draw property, as a concept, out of and away from tangible things, enabling wealth (in the form of "property") to move in much greater volumes, and more swiftly, between the layers of material civilisation. This can be seen with regard to various areas of commercial law;[136] here the focus (though this is an illustrative rather than exhaustive examination) is law governing the financing of transactions involving goods.[137]

Whilst specie/cash tended to have utility in lower-level exchanges,[138] non-specie payment mechanisms could be more efficient.[139] That this is

---

132 BENJAMIN: *Sale of Personal Property...*, *op. cit.*, iii.

133 In this sense, LEVI: *Commercial Law...*, *op. cit.*, was quite different.

134 MacMILLAN: *Judah Benjamin...*, *op. cit.*, 167.

135 Cf. FRIEDMAN: *Formative Elements in the Law of Sales...*, *op. cit.*, 419–443.

136 *Ibid.* Cf. also Ray B. WESTERFIELD: *Middlemen in English Business, particularly between 1660 and 1760*, Yale University Press, New Haven (CO), 1915 (1968 Reprint).

137 Cf. BRIDGE: *Evolution...*, *op. cit.*, 53 et seq. Bridge suggests delineation within the English case-law between the initial focus on small-scale transactions involving material integral to manufacturing processes, and the later developments of massively complex commodity transactions. It is tentatively suggested that there were more cases involving "small-scale" intra-supply-chain goods transactions, because they were more valuable. This meant that they became middle-layer exchanges, and that commodity transactions were themselves shifted up towards the shadow-layer of financial capitalism.

138 BRAUDEL: *Wheels of Commerce...*, *op. cit.*, 549: "Economic needs of the overwhelming everyday kind forced [states] to set great store by precious metals: without these, the economy [i.e. the under-layer] would only too often have been paralysed."

139 Stephen QUINN: *Money, finance and capital markets* = *The Cambridge Economic History of Modern Britain*, vol. 1: *Industrialisation, 1700–1860*, Roderick Floud, Paul Johnson (eds.), Cambridge University Press, Cambridge (UK), 2004, 151–154.

ENGLISH COMMERCIAL LAW IN THE *LONGUE DURÉE*

so is unsurprising, bearing in mind the long history of bills of exchange as money-payment mechanisms, which enabled long-distance, arms-length trading in paper to occur.[140] To some extent these activities were the preserve of small groups of merchants,[141] and states,[142] but by the later eighteenth century there was "enhanced public awareness of the economic utility of credit," for which circulation was fundamental: "So far as the great mass of property and business transactions was concerned, paper credit continued to flourish with the encouragement of the courts and without interference from government."[143]

Documentary credit exemplifies commercial systems of networks and circuits.[144] Although documentary credit can come in a wide variety of forms,[145] the basic point is that a sale financed by documentary credit involves two circuits, of goods and of documents relating to the financing of the sale. So although there must be compliance between the letter of credit and the underlying sales transaction, the sale is formally distinct from the documentary transaction.[146] This principle of autonomy, or independence principle, has the effect that when a documentary credit transaction takes off, it operates at a different velocity and is no longer tied to the underlying sale in quite the same fashion.[147] This had the effect of generating a commercial practice of treating the rights under documentary credit transactions as equivalent to cash, and a juridical policy of non-interference with this practice to enhance trust in international commerce.[148] The letter of credit thus functions as a carrier of the value of the underlying sales transaction.

---

140  Cf. e.g. BRAUDEL: *Perspective of the World...*, *op. cit.*, 241–245.

141  *Ibid.*, 66–67 (bills of exchange may cross continents, but not cultures).

142  QUINN: *Money, finance and capital markets...*, *op. cit*, 2004, Chapter 6; LANGFORD: *A Polite and Commercial People*, *op. cit.*, 692–693. For a critical examination of this process, cf. e.g. GRAEBER: *Debt...*, *op. cit.*, especially Chapter 11.

143  LANGFORD: *A Polite and Commercial People...*, *op. cit.*, 568.

144  William E. McCURDY: *Commercial Letters of Credit*, Harvard Law Review, 35(1922)/5, 539: "The commercial letter of credit has a long mercantile history ... [but] [i]t has a much shorter legal history." Rufus James TRIMBLE: *The Law Merchant and the Letter of Credit*, Harvard Law Review, 61(1947–48)/6, 982: "In the absence of adequate historical and archaeological research by persons trained in the law, the history of these instruments has been a controversial subject." More recently, cf. e.g. ROGERS: *Early History of the Law of Bills and Notes...*, *op. cit.*

145  Cf. McCURDY: *Commercial Letters of Credit...*, *op. cit.*, 542.

146  *Power Curber International Ltd v National Bank of Kuwait* [1981] 1 WLR 1233, 1241 (Lord Denning MR).

147  *RD Harbottle (Mercantile) Ltd v National Westminster Bank Ltd* [1978] QB 146, 155–156 (Kerr J).

148  *Intraco Ltd v Notis Shipping Corp (The Bhoja Trader)* [1981] 2 Lloyd's Rep 256, 257 (Donaldson LJ)

These modern understandings of documentary credit are continuities from earlier practices. Milne's examination of Liverpudlian commercial practices is revealing as to the general commercial practices in England in the early to mid-nineteenth century. Then mercantile and trading corporate forms and capitalisation thereof were particularly reliant on reputation and information. The primary credit relationships were between traders themselves rather than between traders and banks: the role of banks, including the Bank of England, was as "information brokers rather than lenders."[149] This had a dual effect:

> First, the entire system relied on a pool of information on the reliability and financial strength of trading firms, which enabled traders to decide whether those approaching them for extended credit where to be trusted or not. Secondly, bills of exchange, when discounted and signed on frequently in times of extreme financial speculation, could be used to construct houses of cards, liable to collapse should any of a number of parties involved in complicated transactions suffer a commercial setback.[150]

Since this would appear to contradict any principle of autonomy between banks and traders, a reasonable explanation might be that the notion of autonomy developed as a policy choice, based on a necessary fiction, for the protection of the parties (especially the financing parties). Thus the letter of credit transaction is founded on a policy of "instrumentality," of meeting the "desires of both the buyer and the seller" *as well as* the financier in the middle.[151] This much can be drawn from *Pillans v Van Mierop* in 1765,[152] which though flawed,[153] did set the foundations for the inexorable doctrinal development of the autonomy principle in bills of exchange and the more specific later concept of letters of credit.

The division between the different layers of market exchange and financial capitalism was thus conceptualised in terms of knowledge and information about the particular layers. If a party was involved with an aspect of a transaction that sat in one layer (market exchange – the sale) then they would not know – or would be deemed not to know – about those aspects of the same

---

149 MILNE: *Trade and traders..., op. cit.*, 154.

150 *Ibid.*

151 MCCURDY: *Commercial Letters of Credit..., op. cit.*, 542. Cf. generally Julian HOPPIT: *Risk and Failure in English Business 1700–1800*, Cambridge University Press, Cambridge (UK), 1987.

152 (1765) 3 Burrow 1663; 97 ER 1035.

153 In terms of the failed attempt to explain away consideration as merely an evidential requirement: cf. e.g. MCCURDY: *Commercial Letters of Credit..., op. cit.*, 565.

ENGLISH COMMERCIAL LAW IN THE *LONGUE DURÉE* 99

general transaction which resided in the other layer (financial capitalism – the financing of the sale). The division between merchant and financier was central to this: the different parties are on different vectors in the chain of transactions. These circuits do not flow in the same direction, and the networking of these circuits occurs at certain intersectional nodes. Such nodal points are where the tangible assets (goods) and intangible assets (documents) can efficiently and appropriately meet and be exchanged.[154] This is why it is perhaps best to explain documentary credit transactions as banks' lending credit, and not lending funds.[155] This process of exchange at the intersections of the different layers is not a fully free-flowing connection though. The autonomy principle at the core of bills of exchange, letters of credit, and later documents of title, operates as a sort of non-return valve in the intersectional nodes between the market exchange and financial capitalism layers. The value of the transaction can flow in either direction, but the risk element, which can (and if the risk crystalizes, *will*) reduce the transaction's value cannot be given such freedom to migrate from one layer to another. Information about credit-worthiness, the nature of the object of the transactions, or any other impact on the value of the transaction, is only useful if it is not corrupted. The autonomy principles thus help protect against the negative impact of bad information.

This outline of financing sales indicates first the extent of circularity and movement necessary to operate the system completely, and second the distinction between the financing transaction and the underlying sale. The importance of these elements becomes clearer when we consider the impact of a failure of a transaction. If the sales transaction is flawed, then the risk will fall as between buyer and seller depending on the nature of the flaw (in terms of explicit doctrine and the sales contract where pertinent). But this flaw does not impact so directly on the documentary transaction. It is only by impugnation of the documents themselves, and not implicitly by pointing to the goods, that documentary transactions can be susceptible to failure.[156]

This is not the only protective mechanism. Notions of commercial honour were often raised.[157] Participants in informal commercial clubs were willing to ignore apparent failures in a circuit in order to maintain capital flows. The interconnected nature of commercial actions meant there were rational reasons to act cooperatively to avoid failures, even if this may lead to greater losses and

---

154  BRAUDEL: *Wheels of Commerce...*, *op. cit.*, 343.
155  McCURDY: *Commercial Letters of Credit...*, *op. cit.*, 585, citing Frederick SILVER: *Commercial Banking and Credits*, New York, 1920, 190.
156  *Kwei Tek Chao v British Traders and Shippers Ltd* [1954] 2 QB 459, 480–481 (Devlin J.).
157  Philip W. THAYER: *Irrevocable Credits in International Commerce: Their Legal Nature*, Columbia Law Review 36(1936)/7, 1034.

resulted in a system potentially "open to abuse."[158] Correlatively, this cooperative system helped to avoid smaller traders being crushed, as they were seen as serving important purposes that larger firms could not achieve. This understanding may help to provide a more likely justification than mere honour for low volumes of disputes in this field, though of course there were multiple factors affecting litigation rates.[159] There is also a degree of correlation with the behaviour evident in the trade in corporate stock and sales in the nineteenth century, where there was considerable volumes of transactions that were technically illegal (such time sales of stock) or void for informality (under the Statute of Frauds 1677), but were not thrown up due to the strength of private ordering practices within commercial clubs such as the Stock Exchange.[160] Weisberg's extensive analysis of the early history of the voidable preference rule indicates a number of factors that impact on this analysis. Changes in cultural and regulatory responses to bankruptcy from the sixteenth century (which had a strict, rule-bound, complex, pro-creditor system which differentiated between trades and merchants), demonstrate an "ideology of commerce that took hold in the eighteenth century and turned the morally questionable and perceptually elusive phenomena of trade and credit into necessities, and then into virtues."[161] The practical if not necessarily legal uncertainty of credit rendered sympathetic what was once considered suspicious.[162] This shift was undergirded by the trend towards creating effective means of shifting value from the layer of market exchange to the financial capitalism shadow layer. The shifting morality of credit (and its twin, debt), specifically in a commercial context, was a precursor of specific doctrinal change, but was itself a reflection of commercial practices, developed over the *longue dureé*.

Graeber persuasively argues that as the core conceptual issue is debt, non-specie payment mechanisms provided better means to express longer-term relationships of debt and obligation. There have been shifts between credit and specie over time: the mid fifteenth century represented a shift from credit

---

158   MILNE: *Trade and traders...*, *op. cit.*, 159–160: traders could easily trade despite substantial losses.

159   BURSET: *Merchant Courts...*, *op. cit.*

160   Robert B. FERGUSON: *Commercial Expectations and the Guarantee of the Law: Sales Transactions in Mid-Nineteenth Century England = Law, Economy and Society, 1750–1914: Essays in the History of English Law*, G.R. RUBIN, David SUGARMAN (eds.), Professional Books Ltd, Abingdon, 1984, 192.

161   Robert WEISBERG: *Commercial Morality, the Merchant Character, and the History of the Voidable Preference*, Stanford Law Review, 39(1986)/1, 32. Cf. also HOPPIT: *Risk and Failure...*, *op. cit.*

162   WEISBERG: *Commercial Morality...*, *op. cit.*, 32.

ENGLISH COMMERCIAL LAW IN THE *LONGUE DURÉE* 101

to specie, with the current era being a shift back to credit.[163] This had interesting and often contradictory or even paradoxical effects: in a typical English village where trust was at the heart of communicative activity, cash was reserved for strangers. This lead to what Graeber calls "an increasing disjuncture of moral universes" between those who did not used cash and distrusted it, and those, in say the legal institutions, for whom cash transactions were normalised and instead the credit-debt relationship was treated as suspicious and even "tinged with criminality."[164] Yet the various elements of financial capitalism appeared to be present long before those elements of material capitalisms such as the factory and wage labour.[165] In other words, how come there was capitalism before capitalism?

This chapter analysed merely an obscure element of that question. The nineteenth century (with the usual fuzziness around the edges) saw the creation of dual credit/debt and specie economies, particularly in Britain. Cash began to be treated as entirely fungible and interchangeable, with explicit justifications of this based on the needs of commercial circulation.[166] Non-specie payment mechanisms like documentary credit, however, rested on long-term practices coalesced into a mentality or culture;[167] its soft-law status in contemporary law shows how little has changed.[168] A similar focus on long-term practices and cultures as generative bases can also be identified with documents of title;[169] there antecedents are classically (though not entirely accurately) identified in thirteenth century Italy and beyond.[170] Might this practice-focused development indicate how English commercial law was merely *enhancing* the

---

163   GRAEBER, *Debt...*, *op. cit.*, Chapters 8–11. Cf. also SIMARD: *The Birth of a Legal Economy...*, *op. cit.*, 1089–1090 (noting the "dearth of a medium of exchange" in the early US). Cf. LANGFORD: *A Polite and Commercial People...*, *op. cit.*, 449 (noting the growth in volume of available specie).

164   GRAEBER, *Debt...*, *op. cit.*, 328–339.

165   *Ibid.*, 345.

166   *Miller v Race* (1758) 1 Burrow 452; 97 ER 398.

167   Cf. e.g. Frederick Rockwell SANBORN: *Origins of the Early English Maritime and Commercial Law*, The Century Co., New York, 1930, 400; William MITCHELL: *An Essay on the Early History of the Law Merchant*, Cambridge University Press, Cambridge (UK) 1904, 157–158.

168   UCP 600, into force 1 July 2007. The first UCP was published in 1933.

169   *Lickbarrow v Mason* (1787) 2 TR 63; 100 ER 35 (bill of lading was a document of title because of mercantile usage).

170   Cf. generally ROGERS: *Early History of the Law of Bills and Notes...*, *op. cit.* Cf. also e.g. SANBORN: *Origins...*, *op. cit.*, 348–350, 397–399; TRIMBLE: *The Law Merchant and the Letter of Credit...*, *op. cit.* For a broader historical examination, BRAUDEL: *Wheels of Commerce...*, *op. cit.*, is replete with examples of such commercial practice throughout Europe and beyond, and GRAEBER: *Debt...*, *op. cit.*, Chapter 10, gives a good overview of the Islamic and Chinese developments in this field.

generation of shadow-layers of commercial activity?[171] Law created documentary payment mechanisms that limited the infectious nature of risk as well as preventing unnecessary diffusion of value between the layers, by restricting the directional flow of interconnections between the different layers of market exchange and the financial layer. This enabled the presentation of commercial law as being about speed:[172] this mentality had developed and stuck though long before the nineteenth century, before affecting later understandings of sale within commercial law.[173] As Baker suggests of the fourteenth century, records of clearly mercantile disputes provide insufficient detail about the "nature of the underlying transaction," but "mercantile instruments" were recognised. They could provide an evidential role in discharging a "pre-existing obligation," which had the benefit of flexibility and convenience. The absence of formal enforceability was a "secondary consideration."[174] As was noted above, De Ruysscher's research indicates that similar such practices were evident in Antwerp. Parallels with mid-nineteenth century English documentary credit practice are considerable; changes in contract formalities result in enforceable agreements but they remain as distinct obligations to the underlying (goods) transaction.

5       **Conclusion**

Braudel's suggestion of a layered relationship between non-market economy, market exchange, and a shadow-layer of financial capitalism, provides an appropriate normative framework for examining English commercial law. The focus here was on the specific nodal points of interconnection between the different layers of market exchange and financial capitalism. English law has particular commercial mechanisms operating as safety-valves, allowing value, but not risk, to travel swiftly up the layers. Yet this was neither novel nor unique to English law: it was the consequence of developments over much longer time periods and across wider space, encompassing various social, cultural and economic structures. Sale's arrival as a discrete topic in English law corresponded with the result of a long-term socio-economic process of enhancing the quality and durability of tangible things, along with the drawing out by commentators

---

171   Cf. generally Michael E. TIGAR, Madeline R. LEVY: *Law & the Rise of Capitalism*, Monthly Review Press, New York, 2000.

172   Cf. e.g. LIEBERMAN: *Property, commerce and the common law...*, op. cit., 151 (citing Chitty: *Bills of Exchange...*, op. cit.).

173   Cf. e.g. BRAUDEL: *Perspective of the World...*, op. cit., 155: "Discounting ... as established in eighteenth-century England, was in fact a revival of ancient practices."

174   BAKER: *Law Merchant...*, op. cit., 302–306.

and courts of property as a separable aspect of sale. This enabled abstract values to be extrapolated from things and then sent out into their own commercial network.

The inspiration for this study was serendipity: crossing Braudel's phraseology of shadows with literature on "shadow banking."[175] For example, Johnston considered the role of hedge funds in the repo market, where multiple recollateralisation of assets increases liquidity as well as interconnections in the network. The assets (such as bonds) in the hedge fund repo market were, however, flimsy and value-unstable. Yet a regulatory failure to govern considerable moral hazard shifted risk away from the hedge funds.[176] This story mirrors the earlier history of sales. The severity and brutality of the consequences seen in the hedge fund repo market is probably just a mere blip in what might be a much longer and slower process of network formulation between different layers of market civilisation. The layers of material civilisation, and the institutional structures, forms and intersections attendant to such layers and their nodal points, are to a considerable degree those created by long-term historical conditions. The shadows they create remain with us today.

The final words here are perhaps best left to Braudel:

> Venice was from the start trapped by the logic of its own success. The true doge of Venice, standing opposed to all the forces of change, was the city's own past, the precedents to which reference was made as if they were the tablets of the law. And the shadow looming over Venice's greatness was that of her greatness itself. This has some truth. Could the same not be said of twentieth-century Britain? Leadership of a world-economy is an experience of power which may one day blind the victor to the march of history.[177]

### Acknowledgements

This idea was presented at the European Society of Comparative Legal History conference, Gdańsk, June 2016, and I would like to thank the organisers of the panel on 19th and 20th century Commercial Law in Europe for their invitation. The anonymous reviewers deserve thanks for their valuable work, which has

---

175    Specifically Andrew JOHNSTON: *Regulating Hedge Funds for Systemic Stability: The EU's Approach*, European Law Journal 21(2015)/6, 758–786. This field of literature is considerable and growing, but economy precludes further analysis.

176    *Ibid.* Cf. generally PURCELL JR.: *Capitalism and Risk…, op. cit.*

177    BRAUDEL: *Perspective of the World…, op. cit.*, 132.

helped improve this piece. The editors of this volumes, Michał Gałędek and Anna Klimaszewska, deserve special praise for their unending patience and efforts.

## Bibliography

### Cases

*Miller v Race* (1758) 1 Burrow 452; 97 ER 398.
*Pillans v Van Mierop* (1765) 3 Burrow 1663; 97 ER 1035.
*Lickbarrow v Mason* (1787) 2 TR 63; 100 ER 35.
*Bank of England v Vagliano Bros* [1891] AC 107.
*Kwei Tek Chao v British Traders and Shippers Ltd* [1954] 2 QB 459.
*RD Harbottle (Mercantile) Ltd v National Westminster Bank Ltd* [1978] QB 146.
*Power Curber International Ltd v National Bank of Kuwait* [1981] 1 WLR 1233.
*Intraco Ltd v Notis Shipping Corp (The Bhoja Trader)* [1981] 2 Lloyd's Rep 256.

### Literature

Charles ABBOTT: *A Treatise of the Law Relative to Merchant Ships and Seamen*, London, 1802.

David ARMITAGE, Jo GULDI: *The Return of the Longue Durée. An Anglo-American Perspective*, Annales. Histoire, Sciences Sociales 2(2015) (70th Year), 289–318.

John H. BAKER: *The Law Merchant and the Common Law before 1700*, 8(1979)/2, Cambridge Law Journal, 295–322.

Ward BARRETT: *World bullion flows, 1450–1800 = The Rise of Merchant Empires: Long-Distance Trade in the Early Modern World 1350–1750*, James TRACY (ed.), Cambridge University Press, Cambridge (UK), 1990, 224–254.

George Joseph Bell: *Inquiries into the Contract of Sale of Goods and Merchandise as Recognised in the Judicial Decisions and Mercantile Practice of Modern Nations*, Edinburgh, 1845.

Judah BENJAMIN: *A Treatise on the Law of Sale of Personal Property; With References to the American Decisions and to the French Code and Civil Law*, London, 1868.

Peter BIRKS: *English and Roman Learning in Moses v Macferlan*, Current Legal Problems, 37(1984)/1, 1–28.

Colin BLACKBURN: *A Treatise on the Effect of the Contract of Sale, on the Legal Rights of Property and Possession in Goods, Wares, and Merchandize*, London, 1845.

Fernand BRAUDEL: *Civilization & Capitalism 15th–18th Century: The Structures of Everyday Life: The Limits of the Possible*, Harper Row, New York, 1981.

Fernand BRAUDEL: *Civilization & Capitalism 15th–18th Century: The Wheels of Commerce, vol 2*, (1979), Siân REYNOLDS (trans.), Phoenix Press, London, 2002.

Fernand BRAUDEL: *Civilization & Capitalism 15th–18th Century: The Perspective of the World, vol 3,* (1979), Siân REYNOLDS (trans.), William Collins Sons & Co Ltd, London, 1984.

Fernand BRAUDEL: *Afterthoughts on Material Civilization*, Johns Hopkins Press, Baltimore, 1977.

Michael G. BRIDGE: *The evolution of modern sales law*, Lloyd's Maritime and Commercial Law Quarterly, (1991), 52–69.

Christian M. BURSET: *Merchant Courts, Arbitration, and the Politics of Commercial Litigation in the Eighteenth-Century British Empire*, Law and History Review, 34(2016)/3, 615–647.

Edward CAVANAGH: *Charters in the longue durée: the mobility and applicability of donative documents in Europe and America from Edward I to chief justice John Marshall*, Comparative Legal History, 5(2017)/2, 262–295.

HH Judge CHALMERS: *The Sale of Goods Act, 1893, including the Factors Acts, 1889 & 1890*, London, 1894.

Joseph CHITTY: *A Treatise on the law of Bills of Exchange, Checks on Bankers, Promissory Notes, Bankers' Cash Notes, and Bank-Notes*, London, 1799.

Dave De RUYSSCHER: *Designing the Limits of Creditworthiness. Insolvency in Antwerp Bankruptcy Legislation and Practice (16th–17th Centuries)*, Tijdschrift voor Rechtsgeschiedenis, 76(2008), 307–327.

Dave De RUYSSCHER: *Antwerp Commercial Legislation in Amsterdam in the 17th Century. Legal Transplant or Jumping Board?*, Tijdschrift voor Rechtsgeschiedenis, 77(2009), 459–479.

Dave DE RUYSSCHER: *Innovating Financial Law in the Early Modern Netherlands and Europe: Transfers of Commercial Paper and Recourse Liability in Legislation and Ius Commune (Sixteenth to Eighteenth Centuries)*, European Review of Private Law, 19(2011), 505–518.

Dave De RUYSSCHER: *From Usages of Merchants to Default Rules: Practices of Trade, Ius Commune and Urban Law in Early Modern Antwerp*, The Journal of Legal History, 33(2012)/1, 3–29.

Patrick DEVLIN: *The Relation Between Commercial Law and Commercial Practice*, Modern Law Review, 14(1951)/3, 249–266.

Emily ERIKSON, Sampsa SAMILA: *Networks, Institutions, and Encounters: Information Flow in Early-Modern Markets*, Working paper, December 2015.

Niall FERGUSON: *The World's Banker: The History of the House of Rothschild*, Weidenfeld & Nicolson, London, 1998.

Robert B. FERGUSON: *Legal Ideology and Commercial Interests: The Social Origins of the Commercial Law Codes*, British Journal of Law and Society, 4(1977)/1, 18–38.

Robert B. FERGUSON: *The Adjudication of Commercial Disputes and the Legal System in Modern England*, British Journal of Law and Society, 7(1980)/2, 141–157.

Robert B. FERGUSON: *Commercial Expectations and the Guarantee of the Law: Sales Transactions in Mid-Nineteenth Century England = Law, Economy and Society, 1750–1914: Essays in the History of English Law*, G.R. RUBIN, David SUGARMAN (eds.), Professional Books Ltd, Abingdon, 1984, 192–208.

Judith FLANDERS: *The Making of Home*, Atlantic Books, London, 2014.

Lawrence M. FRIEDMAN: *Formative Elements in the Law of Sales: The Eighteenth Century*, Minnesota Law Review, 44(1960)/3, 411–460.

Michał GAŁĘDEK: *Introduction: Modernisation, National Identity, and Legal Instrumentalism = Modernisation, National Identity, and Legal Instrumentalism: Studies in Comparative Legal History*, Michał GAŁĘDEK, Anna KLIMASZEWSKA (eds.), Brill Nijhoff, Leiden-Boston, 2020.

Grant GILMORE: *On The Difficulties of Codifying Commercial Law*, The Yale Law Journal, 57(1948)/8, 1341–1358.

Roy GOODE: *Commercial Law in the Next Millennium*, Sweet & Maxwell, London, 1998.

James GORDLEY: *Comparative Law and Legal History = The Oxford Handbook of Comparative Law*, Mathias REIMANN, Reinhard ZIMMERMANN (eds.), Oxford University Press, Oxford, 2006, 753–772.

David GRAEBER: *Debt: The First 5,000 Years*, (2011), Melville House Publishing, London, 2014.

Avner GREIF: *Institutions and the Path to the Modern Economy: Lessons from Medieval Trade*, Cambridge University Press, Cambridge (UK), 2006.

Ron HARRIS: *The Encounters of Economic History and Legal History*, Law and History Review, 21(2003)/2, 297–346.

Julian HOPPIT: *Risk and Failure in English Business 1700–1800*, Cambridge University Press, Cambridge (UK), 1987.

Morton J. HORWITZ: *The Historical Foundations of Modern Contract Law*, Harvard Law Review, 87(1974)/5, 917–956.

Andrew JOHNSTON: *Regulating Hedge Funds for Systemic Stability: The EU's Approach*, European Law Journal 21(2015)/6, 758–786.

Emily KADENS: *The Myth of the Customary Law Merchant*, Texas Law Review, 90(2012)/5, 1153–1206.

Emily KADENS: *The Medieval Law Merchant: The Tyranny of a Construct*, Journal of Legal Analysis, 7(2015)/2, 251–289.

Boris KOZOLCHYK: *The Commercialization of Civil Law and the Civilization of Commercial Law*, Louisiana Law Review, 40(1979)/1, 3–47.

Paul LANGFORD: *A Polite and Commercial People: England 1727–1783*, (1989), Oxford University Press, Oxford, 1992.

LAW COMMISSION and SCOTTISH LAW COMMISSION: *Sale and Supply of Goods*, Law Com 160, Scot Law Com 104, 1987.

Leoni LEVI: *Commercial Law, Its Principles and Administration; or, the Mercantile Law of Great Britain*, William Benning & Co, London, 1850.

David LIEBERMAN: *Property, commerce and the common law: Attitudes to legal change in the eighteenth century = Early Modern Conceptions of Property*, John BREWER, Susan STAVES (eds.), Routledge, London, 1996, 144–158.

Karl Nickerson LLEWELLYN: *Cases and Materials on the Law of Sales*, Callaghan and Co., Chicago, 1930.

Karl Nickerson LLEWELLYN: *Through title to contract and a bit beyond*, New York University Law Quarterly Review, 15(1938)/2, 159–209.

Catharine MACMILLAN: *Mistakes in Contract Law*, Hart Publishing, Oxford, 2010.

Catherine MACMILLAN: *Judah Benjamin: Marginalized Outsider or Admitted Insider?*, Journal of Law and Society, 42(2015)/1, 150–172.

William E. MCCURDY: *Commercial Letters of Credit*, Harvard Law Review, 35(1922)/5, 539–592.

Ewan MCKENDRICK: *Goode on Commercial Law*, Penguin, London, 2010.

Ewan MCKENDRICK: *Goode on Commercial Law*, Penguin, London, 2016.

Neil MCKENDRICK, John BREWER, J.H. PLUMB: *The Birth of a Consumer Society: Commercialization of Eighteenth Century England*, Indiana University Press, Bloomington, 1982.

Aniceto MASFERRER, *The Longing for Comparative Legal History*, GLOSSAE: European Journal of Legal History 9(2012), 206–220.

Ajay K. MEHROTRA: *A Bridge Between: Law and the New Intellectual Histories of Capitalism*, Buffalo Law Review, 64(2016)/1, 1–22.

Graeme J. MILNE, *Trade and traders in mid-Victorian Liverpool: Mercantile business and the making of a world port*, Liverpool University Press, Liverpool, 2000.

William MITCHELL: *An Essay on the Early History of the Law Merchant*, Cambridge University Press, Cambridge (UK), 1904.

Paul MITCHELL: *The development of quality obligations in sale of goods*, Law Quarterly Review, 117(2011)/3, 645–663.

Olivier MORÉTEAU, Aniceto MASFERRER, Kjell A. MODÉER: *Comparative Legal History*, Elgar, Cheltenham, 2019.

James OLDHAM: *The Mansfield manuscripts and the growth of English law in the eighteenth century*, University of North Carolina Press, Chapel Hill, 1992.

Sara PENNELL: *Material Culture in Seventeenth-Century "Britain": The Matter of Domestic Consumption = The Oxford Handbook of the History of Consumption*, Frank TRENTMANN (ed.), Oxford University Press, Oxford, 2012, 64–84.

Heikki PIHLAJAMÄKI: *Private Law Codification, Modernization and Nationalism: A View from Critical Legal History*, Critical Analysis of Law 135(2015)/2, 135–152.

Thomas PIKETTY: *Capital in the Twenty-First Century*, Arthur GOLDHAMMER (trans.), Harvard University Press, Cambridge (MA), 2014.

Carla Rahn PHILLIPS: *The Growth and Composition of Trade in the Iberian Empires, 1450–1750 = The Rise of Merchant Empires: Long-Distance Trade in the Early Modern World 1350–1750*, James TRACY (ed.), Cambridge University Press, Cambridge (UK), 1990, 34–101.

Karl POLANYI: *The Great Transformation: The Political and Economic Origins of Our Time*, (1944), Beacon Press, Boston, 2001.

Frederick POLLOCK: *Essays in Jurisprudence and Ethics*, MacMillan and Co., London, 1882.

Sir Frederick POLLOCK, F.W. MAITLAND: *The history of English Law before the time of Edward I*, Cambridge University Press, Cambridge (UK), 1898.

Edward A. PURCELL JR.: *Capitalism and Risk: Concepts, Consequences, and Ideologies*, Buffalo Law Review, 64(2016)/1, 23–59.

Stephen QUINN: *Money, finance and capital markets = The Cambridge Economic History of Modern Britain*, vol. 1: *Industrialisation, 1700–1860*, Roderick FLOUD, Paul JOHNSON (eds.), Cambridge University Press, Cambridge (UK), 2004, Chapter 6.

Alan RODGER: *The codification of commercial law in Victorian Britain*, Law Quarterly Review, 108(1992)/3, 570–590.

James Stephen ROGERS: *The Early History of the Law of Bills and Notes: A Study of the Origins of Anglo-American Commercial Law*, Cambridge University Press, Cambridge (UK), 1995.

G.R. RUBIN: *Levi, Leone (1821–1888) = Oxford Dictionary of National Biography*, Oxford University Press, Oxford 2004.

Rodolfo SACCO: *Legal Formants: A Dynamic Approach to Comparative Law*, American Journal of Comparative Law 39(1991)/1.

Geoffrey SAMUEL: *Civil and Commercial Law: a Distinction Worth Making?*, Law Quarterly Review, 102(1986)/3, 569–584.

Frederick Rockwell SANBORN: *Origins of the Early English Maritime and Commercial Law*, The Century Co., New York, 1930.

William E. SCHEUERMAN: *Global Law in Our High Speed Economy = Rules and Networks: The Legal Culture of Global Business Transactions*, Richard P. APPLEBAUM, William L.F. FELSTINE, Volkmar GESSNER (eds.), Hart Publishing, Oxford, 2001, Chapter 3.

Frederick SILVER: *Commercial Banking and Credits*, New York, 1920.

Justin SIMARD: *The Birth of a Legal Economy: Lawyers and the Development of American Commerce*, Buffalo Law Review, 64(2016)/5, 1059–1134.

A.W.B. SIMPSON: *Innovation in Nineteenth Century Contract Law*, Law Quarterly Review, 91(1975), 247.

A.W.B. SIMPSON: *The Horwitz Thesis and the History of Contracts*, University of Chicago Law Review, 46(1979)/3, 533–601.

J.W. SMITH: *A Compendium of Mercantile Law*, London, 1834.

Niels STEENSGAARD: *The growth and composition of long-distance trade of England and the Dutch Republic before 1750 = The Rise of Merchant Empires: Long-Distance Trade in the Early Modern World 1350–1750*, James TRACY (ed.), Cambridge University Press, Cambridge (UK), 1990, 102–152.

William W. STORY: *A Treatise on the Law of Sales of Personal Property*, 1847.

David SUGARMAN: *Law, Economy and the State in England, 1750–1914: Some Major Issues = Legality, Ideology and The State*, David SUGARMAN (ed.), Academic Press, London, 1983, 213–266.

David SUGARMAN, G.R. RUBIN: *Towards a New History of Law and Material Society in England, 1750–1914 = Law, Economy and Society, 1750–1914: Essays in the History of English Law*, G.R. RUBIN, David SUGARMAN (eds.), Professional Books Ltd, Abingdon, 1984, 1–186.

Warren SWAIN: *Codification of Contract Law: Some Lessons from History*, University of Queensland Law Journal, 31(2012)/1, 39–54.

Philip W. THAYER: *Irrevocable Credits in International Commerce: Their Legal Nature*, Columbia Law Review 36(1936)/7, 1031–1060.

Sean THOMAS: *The Origins of the Factors Acts 1823 and 1825*, The Journal of Legal History, 32(2011)/2, 151–187.

Sean THOMAS: *The Development of the Implied Terms on Quantity in the Law of Sale of Goods*, The Journal of Legal History, 35(2014)/3, 281–318.

Sean THOMAS: *Mortgages, fixtures, fittings and security over personal property*, Northern Ireland Legal Quarterly, 66(2015)/4, 343–365.

Michael E. TIGAR, Madeline R. LEVY: *Law & the Rise of Capitalism*, Monthly Review Press, New York, 2000.

Frank TRENTMANN: *Introduction = The Oxford Handbook of the History of Consumption*, Frank TRENTMANN (ed.), Oxford University Press, Oxford, 2012, 1–19.

Frank TRENTMANN: *Empire of Things: How We Became a World of Consumers, from the Fifteenth Century to the Twenty-first*, Allen Lane, London, 2016.

Rufus James TRIMBLE: *The Law Merchant and the Letter of Credit*, Harvard Law Review, 61(1947–48)/6, 981–1008.

Donald O. WAGNER: *Coke and the Rise of Economic Liberalism*, The Economic History Review, 6(1935)/1, 30–44.

Robert WEISBERG: *Commercial Morality, the Merchant Character, and the History of the Voidable Preference*, Stanford Law Review, 39(1986)/1, 3–138.

Ray B. WESTERFIELD: *Middlemen in English Business, particularly between 1660 and 1760*, Yale University Press, New Haven, 1915 (1968 Reprint).

H.W. WOOLRYCH: *A Practical Treatise on the Commercial and Mercantile Laws of England*, London, 1829.

Reinhard ZIMMERMANN: *The Law of Obligations: Roman Foundations of the Civilian Tradition*, Oxford University Press, Oxford, 1996.

CHAPTER 5

# The Italian Destiny of the French *Code de commerce*

*Annamaria Monti*

## 1 Introduction

The very famous equestrian portrait of "Napoleon Crossing the Alps" painted by Jacques-Louis David (in five versions) in the early 19th century shows the First Consul returning to Italy to fight the Austrians. It offers an emphatic and idealised view of Bonaparte, who was going to take control of the entire Peninsula by force of arms. A few years later, in 1805, Andrea Appiani painted another well-known portrait of Napoleon, King of Italy: it depicts a self-confident young ruler, who, among a large series of reforms, put his codes into force in his Italian dominions.

As has been recently and most appropriately pointed out, European history is not only a history of freedom, equality and fraternity, but it is also a history of violence and conquests.[1] More specifically, within the countries conquered by French armies during the revolutionary and Napoleonic wars, it was also a history of clashes and encounters of different legal systems.[2]

In order to apprehend these phenomena, legal history has recently widened its fields of research and has begun to use new terms and concepts: normative entanglements, hybridisation, *métissage*, circulation, migration, traveling of law, legal transfers, or cultural translation.[3] The search for new instruments and tools is still under way, however, this appears to be a major historiographical renewal, leading to the development of new approaches. This does not mean that legal historians have abandoned their traditional research fields.

---

1  Thomas DUVE: *European Legal History – Concepts, Methods, Challenges = Entanglements in Legal History. Conceptual Approaches*, Thomas DUVE (ed.), Max Planck Institute for European Legal History Open Access Publication, Frankfurt a.M., 2014, 29–66.

2  Antonio GRILLI : *Il difficile amalgama. Giustizia e codici nell'Europa di Napoleone*, Vittorio Klostermann, 2012, Frankfurt a.M., 1–8.

3  Lena FOLJANTY: *Legal Transfers as Cultural Translation. On the Consequences of a Metaphor*, Max Planck Institute for European Legal History research paper series No. 2015–09 (ssrn.com/abstract=2682465); Lena FOLJANTY: *Translators: Mediators of Legal Transfers*, Rechtsgeschichte – Legal History 24 (2016), 120–121.

---

© KONINKLIJKE BRILL NV, LEIDEN, 2020 | DOI:10.1163/9789004417274_006

Yet, they henceforth question what happens when foreign law and traditional legal orders meet.[4]

Those research works tend to go beyond national histories and promote a comparative and transnational point of view. The point is in no way to juxtapose national histories, but to understand how a legal system nourishes itself from exchanges, contacts and interactions with other legal systems. This perspective includes the study of the impact of foreign laws on national trajectories, as well as the effect of the different waves of globalisation on those national paths.

In this perspective, the study of various aspects of attitudes toward French commercial law in different countries during the 19th century, especially those in the early stages of development in the first half of that century, such as the Polish or Italian territories,[5] seems to me consistent with this praiseworthy effort toward renewal of legal history's methods and goals. Furthermore, it seems to me consistent with at least one of the main themes of this book, that is "national identity": more precisely, my chapter deals with the impact of the French commercial code of 1807 on 19th century Italian commercial law, bearing in mind that the national unification of the country was achieved in 1861.

Concerning the Italian territories, very fruitful research work has been carried out for many years, searching the archives both in Italy and in Paris to apprehend the impact of the French revolution on the Italian Ancient States. Special attention has been paid to each different step of French military occupation, which was always supported by complex political action as proven by documentary sources.[6]

It all started in 1796. The French army led by Napoleon launched a campaign to invade the country. More specifically, it was an attack aimed at Habsburg Lombardy as part of the campaigns of the French revolutionary wars which were fought against the First and Second Coalitions. At that time, General Bonaparte was commander-in-chief of the Army of Italy (*Armée d'Italie*). Over the following years, First Consul Napoleon progressively defeated ancient Italian ruling princes and oligarchies. It was this period which the portrait by David

---

4  Cf. Mario Ascheri: *A final comment and request*, Rechtsgeschichte – Legal History 22 (2014), 270–273.

5  Concerning Spain, refer to Carlos Petit: *Historia del derecho mercantil*, Marcial Pons, Madrid, 2016.

6  Carlo Capra: *L'età rivoluzionaria e napoleonica in Italia 1796–1815*, Loescher, Torino, 1978, 15–22; Carlo Capra: *Gli italiani prima dell'Italia. Un lungo Settecento, dalla fine della Controriforma a Napoleone*, Carocci, Roma, 2014, 315–400. Cf. also Antonino De Francesco: *L'Italia di Bonaparte. Politica, statualità e nazione nella penisola tra due rivoluzioni, 1796–1821*, Utet, Torino, 2011.

THE ITALIAN DESTINY OF THE FRENCH *CODE DE COMMERCE* 113

referred to. As mentioned above, it was not only a question of battles and conquests: new political practices and new ideals began to be discussed and applied.

Initially, in the years 1796–1799, French Sister Republics were set up in the country, from the north to the south. It was a very short, though intensive period of social, juridical, and constitutional changes.[7] This was the time when Italy met the ideals of the French Revolution. Actually, this occurred at the sunset of the great Revolution, when the Directory was entering its last phase and Brumaire was approaching. Therefore, what was exported to Italy were the political and theoretical results of a Revolution "made in France" which had lost its extremism and was about to come to an end.[8]

Later on, first Piedmont (1800), then the Republic of Genoa (1805), the Duchies of Parma and Piacenza (1802), Tuscany (1807), and the Papal States (1809) were annexed directly by France,[9] while in the north-eastern part of the country, the Italian Republic succeeded the Cisalpine Republic (1802), where Napoleon himself served as president.[10] In 1805, the Italian Republic had to be transformed in Kingdom of Italy, as Bonaparte became Emperor of the French.[11] Consequently, he was crowned King of Italy in Milan cathedral (as shown in the portrait by Appiani).[12] In the South, Napoleon installed his brother Joseph as King of Naples (1806) and then, two years later, in 1808, when Joseph set off for Spain, the crown was handed to Marshal Joachim Murat.[13]

With regard to the transformation of earlier Italian legal systems, starting in 1796 major innovations came from the newly introduced principles of equality and liberty, which had been proclaimed by the French revolutionary

---

7   Carlo GHISALBERTI: *Le costituzioni giacobine (1796–1799)*, Giuffrè, Milano, 1957.

8   Refer to Adriano CAVANNA: *Codificazione del diritto italiano e imperialismo giuridico francese nella Milano napoleonica. Giuseppe Luosi e il diritto penale* in: Adriano CAVANNA: *Scritti (1968–2002)*, Jovene, Napoli, 2007, vol. 2, 833–927.

9   Recently, Virginie MARTIN: *Éduquer, civiliser, dominer ? Le rôle de Gérando dans l'annexion de la Toscane et des États pontificaux (1808–1810) = Joseph-Marie de Gérando (1772–1842): connaître et réformer la société*, Jean-Luc CHAPPEY, Carole CHRISTEN, Igor MOULLIER (eds.), Rennes, PUR, 2014, 129–142. For a partially different narrative, Michael BROERS: *The Napoleonic Empire in Italy, 1796–1814. Cultural Imperialism in a European Context?*, Palgrave Macmillan, Basingstoke-New York, 2005.

10  *Napoleone e la Repubblica Italiana, 1802–1805*, Carlo CAPRA, Franco Della PERUTA, Fernando MAZZOCCA (eds.), Skira, Milano, 2002.

11  *La formazione del primo Stato italiano e Milano capitale, 1802–1814*, Adele Robbiati BIANCHI (ed.), Istituto lombardo Accademia di scienze e lettere, Milano, 2006.

12  Carlo ZAGHI: *L'Italia di Napoleone dalla Cisalpina al Regno*, Utet, Torino, 1986.

13  Angela VALENTE: *Giacchino Murat e l'Italia meridionale*, Einaudi, Torino, 1965; Aurelio LEPRE: *Storia del Mezzogiorno d'Italia*, vol. 2: *Dall'Antico Regime alla società borghese (1657–1869)*, Liguori, Napoli, 1986, 163–216.

Declaration of the Rights of Man and of the Citizen. Regarding commercial law, this involved freedom of commerce and trade, and free enterprise. Commercial guilds were abolished.[14]

Key issues to French administration were administrative, judiciary and bureaucratic reforms to integrate Italian territories into the French orbit. These reforms and transformations were put into force over a number of years and in different ways, according to the corresponding French authoritarian political evolution towards the Consulate and the Empire.[15]

The enforcement of French codes, which started in 1806, was an *instrumentum regni* adopted by the Emperor. For sure, it was a significant example of normative transfer. Generally speaking, the transfer processes of these sets of norms and their reception in the Italian territories were more elaborate than one might imagine.[16] In fact, they were part of a sophisticated political planning process.[17]

More specifically, implementation of French texts in Italian territories was often preceded by a lively activity of legal drafting at national level in all fields of law: private law, civil procedure, commercial law, criminal procedure and criminal law.[18] Tentative projects written by Italian jurists were supported by the French government and in most cases by Napoleon himself.

In synthesis, historiography has made clear how the process of enforcing French codes in Italian territories was prepared by a very persuasive action aimed at gaining full approval.[19] In particular, in the northern part of the country, especially in the Kingdom of Italy, the transfer of French laws was preceded

---

14  Carlo GHISALBERTI: *Unità nazionale e unificazione giuridica in Italia*, Laterza, Roma-Bari, 1979, 97–105.

15  Alain PILLEPICH: *Napoleone e gli italiani*, Il Mulino, Bologna, 2005.

16  *Richterliche Anwendung des Code civil in seinen europäischen Geltungsbereichen außerhalb Frankreichs*, Barbara DÖLEMEYER, Heinz MOHNHAUPT, Alessandro SOMMA (eds.), Vittorio Klostermann, Frankfurt a.M., 2006; GRILLI, *Il difficile amalgama…, op. cit.*, 225–518. Cf. also Francesco MASTROBERTI: *Codificazione e giustizia penale nelle Sicilie dal 1808 al 1820*, Jovene, Napoli, 2001.

17  Adriano CAVANNA: *L'influence juridique française en Italie au XIXe siècle*, Revue d'histoire des Facultés de droit et de la science juridique, 15 (1994), 87–112. With regard to the Kingdom of Naples and in English, Aldo MAZZACANE: *A jurist for united Italy: the training and culture of Neapolitan lawyers in the nineteenth century* = Society and the Professions in Italy 1860–1914, Maria MALATESTA (ed.), Adrian BELTON (transl.), Cambridge University Press, Cambridge (UK), 1995, 80–110.

18  Melchiorre ROBERTI: *Milano capitale napoleonica. La formazione di uno Stato moderno 1796–1814*, vol. 2, Fondazione Treccani degli Alfieri, Milano, 1947.

19  CAVANNA, *Codificazione del diritto italiano e imperialismo giuridico francese nella Milano napoleonica…, op. cit.*, 847–852.

THE ITALIAN DESTINY OF THE FRENCH *CODE DE COMMERCE*                    115

by studies and discussion for Italian projects of codes which eventually did not succeed,[20] but in a single case, i.e. criminal procedure.[21] Everywhere, implementation of French texts was accompanied by translations into Italian of French legislative works, legal doctrine and case law, which were aimed specifically at law students and practitioners.[22]

In other words, Napoleon gave Italian jurists the chance to draft their own codes before directly implementing his codification, which was received gratefully and together with French legal works on it. This was part of Bonaparte's way of ruling to end the Revolution, thus looking for a compromise between tradition and Revolution. He recruited jurists who could help as his ministers. He did this in France. He did the same in Italy. Through his ministers, he acted balancing an authoritarian political approach and softer negotiation to achieve the "Frenchification" (*francisation*) of Italian Peninsula.[23]

This might also be considered part of a very complex and somehow ambiguous process of "appropriation and reproduction of normative options"[24] managed by Italian jurists and sponsored by the French Emperor, who acted with intent.[25]

---

20   One of the oldest of these projects was the draft of 1798 for a civil code for the Roman Republic: Filippo RANIERI: *Projet du Code civil de la Republique Romaine (1798). Paris, Bibl. Nat., Nouv. acq. fr. 21892*, Frankfurt am Main, Vittorio Klostermann, 1976. For a synthesis concerning codification of private law in the Italian territories, Ettore DEZZA: *Lezioni di Storia della codificazione civile. Il Code civil (1804) e l'Allgemeines Bürgerliches Gesetzbuch (ABGB, 1812)*, Giappichelli, Torino, 2000, 91–97. Cf. also Piergiorgio PERUZZI: *Progetto e vicende di un Codice civile della repubblica italiana (1802–1805)*, Giuffrè, Milano, 1971.

21   This was because of the jury. In fact, Napoleon was against the jury and thought that Italians were not ready for it. Italian code of criminal procedure of 1807 did not implement the jury. Cf. Ettore DEZZA: *Il Codice di procedura penale del Regno Italico (1807): storia di un decennio di elaborazione legislativa*, Cedam, Padova, 1983; Ettore DEZZA: *Le fonti del codice di procedura penale del Regno italico*, Giuffrè, Milano, 1985.

22   Maria Gigliola DI RENZO VILLATA: *Introduzione. La formazione del giurista in Italia e l'influenza culturale europea tra sette ed ottocento. Il caso della Lombardia* = *Formare il giurista. Esperienze nell'area lombarda tra Sette e Ottocento*, Maria Gigliola DI RENZO VILLATA (ed.), Giuffrè, Milano, 2004, 1–105.

23   Jean-Louis HALPÉRIN: *A proposito di alcune difficoltà nell'applicazione dei codici napoleonici nei dipartimenti francesi d'Italia* = *Giuseppe Luosi, giurista italiano ed europeo. Traduzioni, tradizioni e tradimenti della codificazione. A duecento anni dalla traduzione in italiano del Code Napoléon (1806–2006)*, Elio TAVILLA (ed.), Edizioni APM, Modena, 2009, 265–266.

24   Thomas DUVE: *Introductory remarks* = *Entanglements in Legal History. Conceptual Approaches*, Thomas DUVE (ed.), Max Planck Institute for European Legal History Open Access Publication, Frankfurt a.M., 2014, 3–25.

25   CAVANNA: *Codificazione del diritto italiano e imperialismo giuridico francese nella Milano napoleonica...*, *op. cit.*, 857–867.

Enforcement of the *Code de commerce* in Napoleon's Italian domains did not make any exception to this. The Commercial code was implemented in the territories annexed to French Empire as soon as it was implemented in France; in the Kingdom of Italy it was enforced after autonomous projects of commercial codes were rejected;[26] in the southern part of the Peninsula, i. e. in the Kingdom of Naples, the French Commercial Code was imposed in 1809 and debates came later.[27] Moreover, chambers of commerce were established in replacement of old commercial guilds and the stock exchange was regulated according to French standards.[28]

In synthesis, according to the most recent historiographical debate, this was the "backstage" of the implementation of French codification in Italy. This narrative is indeed supported by in-depth research in the archives.

Before moving on to the impact of the French commercial code of 1807 in the history of Italian commercial law, to better understand what happened one should start from the Italian tentative projects of commercial code drafted at the turn of the 19th century.

## 2    Drafts, Codes and Tentative Projects in 18th–19th Century Italy

Implementation of the *Code de commerce* in the Italian territories in 1808–1809 followed the very successful path of the implementation of the *Code civil* in 1806 and both codes were welcome and enjoyed long life in Italy. In particular, they served as a reference for Italian codes during the Restoration and also after Italian Unification.

Going back to the early nineteenth century, the *Code de commerce* was initially perceived on the Italian peninsula as a replacement for the ancient customary law and usages which varied from place to place. It was to be a law common to all based on reason, whose distant roots could be found in Savary's

---

26    Alberto Sciumè: *Gli usi commerciali nell'ordinamento del Regno Italico (1805–1814) = Diritto comune e diritti locali nella storia dell'Europa*, Giuffrè, Milano, 1980, 459–479; Alberto Sciumè: *I tentativi per la codificazione del diritto commerciale nel Regno italico (1806–1808)*, Giuffrè, Milano, 1982. For more reference, cf. below.

27    Saverio Gentile: *L'applicazione del Code de commerce in Calabria e l'emersione di un interessante tassello inedito relativo alla Commissione di Murat del 1814*, Historia et ius (historiaetius.eu) 5(2014), paper 5, 8–9.

28    Roberti: *Milano capitale napoleonica...*, *op. cit.*, vol. 3, 491–498.

THE ITALIAN DESTINY OF THE FRENCH *CODE DE COMMERCE*    117

*Ordonnance du commerce* of 1673 and *Ordonnance de la Marine* of 1681.[29] Both Napoleon and Italian jurists agreed on this.

According to the First Consul and his ministers, Italy needed a common commercial law. In fact, with regard to commerce and industry, profound changes occurred when old Italian legal systems and political institutions clashed with the French revolutionary order.

From then on, the Italian peninsula had its place within the French area of influence: the metric system was introduced, weights and measures made uniform and currency standardized. New commercial routes were opened.[30] On the one hand, the French political economy was to promote renovation in Italian territories, especially in respect to agriculture, and this mainly in favour of French economy. On the other hand, the economic consequences of the wars had a negative impact on Italian manufacturing and commerce, in particular the British naval blockade against the French and Napoleon's Continental Blockade against British trade.[31]

In this context, the harmonisation of commercial law was claimed to be in the name of prosperity of Italian territories. Through the abandonment of ancient customary rules and implementation of the French commercial code, commerce and trade were to improve. That was what Antonio Aldini, who was Paris' resident Secretary of State for the Kingdom of Italy, suggested to Napoleon in 1807.[32] This was in synthesis the French point of view.

On his side, Secretary of State Antonio Aldini was aware of similar needs expressed as well by the Italian drafts of commercial codes which had been previously discussed in the Kingdom of Italy. These tentative projects of 1806–1807 were not successful, however they showed to what point commercial law had (or had not) changed in Italy before the *Code de commerce* was enforced. They also testified how Emperor Bonaparte worked to make commercial

---

29    Ugo PETRONIO: *Un diritto nuovo con materiali antichi: il Code de commerce fra tradizione e innovazione* = *Negozianti e imprenditori: 200 anni dal Code de commerce*, Mondadori, Milano, 2008, 1–45.

30    CAPRA: *L'età rivoluzionaria e napoleonica in Italia 1796–1815...*, *op. cit.*, 190–238.

31    Concerning specifically Milan area, Alberto COVA: *Tradizione e innovazione nel mutato contesto politico e territoriale dell'età francese* = *Storia dell'industria lombarda*, 1, *Dal Settecento all'unità politica*, Sergio ZANINELLI (ed.), Edizioni Il Polifilo, Milano, 1988, 103–197.

32    Luigi BERLINGUER: *Domenico Alberto Azuni giurista e politico (1749–1827). Un contributo bio-bibliografico*, Giuffrè, Milano, 1966, 228.

118                                                                    MONTI

legislation uniform in all his dominions. Careful research on these projects has
been carried out by Italian scholars, therefore I will refer to their work.[33]

However, from the Italian point of view, one should consider that Italy had
a long and important legal tradition in regulating commercial transactions and
merchants. In fact, during the Middle Ages Italy was the cradle of many modern legal institutions and concepts at the basis of commercial law, from commercial papers to bankruptcy, from rudimentary forms of prohibition of unfair
competition, to limited liability of some business associates.[34] A large part of
these rules evolved through cross-border practices, especially across the Alps,
so that scholars speak of a French-Italian tradition for several commercial
rules.[35]

Around the 16th century, Italy lost its primacy in commerce and trade, because of geographical discoveries and new long-distance commercial routes
which bypassed the Mediterranean Sea. In that period, however, legal science
devoted to commercial law flourished precisely in Italy. Authors like Benvenuto Stracca,[36] Sigismondo Scaccia,[37] and Giuseppe Lorenzo Maria Casaregis[38]

---

33    Luigi BERLINGUER: *Sui progetti di codice di commercio del Regno d'Italia (1807–1808)*. Con-
      *siderazioni su un inedito di D. A. Azuni*, Giuffrè, Milano, 1970; Antonio PADOA-SCHIOPPA:
      *Le società commerciali nei progetti di codificazione del Regno Italico (1806–1807)*, now in id.,
      *Saggi di storia del diritto commerciale*, Led, Milano, 1992, 113–135; Arturo BRIENZA: *I pro-
      getti di codice commerciale nella Repubblica Cisalpina e nel Regno d'Italia*, Cisalpino-La
      Goliardica, Milano, 1978; SCIUMÈ : *I tentativi per la codificazione del diritto commerciale
      nel Regno italico…, op. cit.* These tentative projects have been edited by Alberto SCIUMÈ: *I
      progetti del codice di commercio del Regno italico (1806–1808)*, Giuffrè, Milano, 1999.

34    Umberto SANTARELLI: *Mercanti e società tra mercanti*, Giappichelli, Torino, 1998.

35    Jean HILAIRE: *Introduction historique au droit commercial*, Presses Universitaires de
      France, Paris, 1986, 39–43.

36    Benvenuto STRACCA: *De mercatura, seu mercatore tractatus*, Paolo Manuzio, Venetiis,1553.
      In English cf. Charles DONAHUE Jr.: *Benvenuto Stracca's De Mercatura: was there a Lex
      mercatoria in Sixteenth-Century Italy? = From lex mercatoria to commercial law, Compara-
      tive Studies in Continental and Anglo-America Legal History*, Band 24, Vito PIERGIOVANNI
      (ed.), Duncker and Humblot, Berlin, 2005, 69–120; Stefania GIALDRONI: *Tractatus de mer-
      catura seu mercatore, 1553, Benvenuto Stracca (Straccha) (1509–1578) = The formation and
      transmission of Western legal culture. 150 books that made the law in the age of printing*,
      Serge DAUCHY, Georges MARTYN, Anthony MUSSON, Heikki PIHLAJAMÄKI, Alain
      WIJFELLS (eds.), Springer, Cham, 2016, 96–99.

37    Sigismondo SCACCIA: *Tractatus de commerciis, et cambio*, Romae, sumptibus Andreae
      Brugiotti, ex typographia Iacobi Mascardi, 1619. In English, cf. Rodolfo SAVELLI: *Between
      Law and Morals: Interest in the Dispute on Exchanges during the 16th Century = The Courts
      and the Development of Commercial Law, Comparative Studies in Continental and Anglo-
      America Legal History*, Band 2, Vito Piergiovanni (ed.), Duncker and Humblot, Berlin,
      1987, 39–102.

38    Giuseppe Lorenzo Maria CASAREGI: *Discursus legales de commercio*, Genuae, typis Ioan-
      nis Baptistae Scionici, 1707. Cf. Vito PIERGIOVANNI: *Dottrina, divulgazione e pratica alle*

THE ITALIAN DESTINY OF THE FRENCH *CODE DE COMMERCE* 119

started composing treaties on issues of commercial law in the tradition of *mos italicus.* Their legal work also had an impact in other European countries such as Holland, Germany, England and, of course, in France.[39]

The evolution of commercial law was now linked to the rigorous *ius commune* frame of reference. Moreover, a few specialized Italian courts, such as the Florentine *Rota* and the Genoese *Rota* made a fundamental contribution to the rising science of commercial law at the European level. These mercantile high courts could count on the technical ability of learned lawyers which was soon adapted to the lively and demanding commercial practice.[40] In particular, appreciation of Genoese civil *Rota*'s case law was very high in legal practice, and this thanks to the innovative content, interpretation and systemisation of bankruptcy law, financial instruments, and insurance. The international success of a collection of its *Decisiones de mercatura* published in 1582, in Genoa and in Venice,[41] was confirmed by subsequent editions in Lyon, Frankfurt and Amsterdam.[42]

To sum up, around the 17th century, Italian commercial law was still at the core of new patterns of business and commerce. However, this was within the framework of the *ius commune* tradition. It is well known that it was only in the mid 18th century that the will to reform existing legal systems started to emerge at a legislative level. This also occurred in some parts of Italy: legislative and bureaucratic reforms were promoted in Lombardy, under the Habsburg rulers Maria Theresa, Joseph II and Leopold II; tentative reforms were put in place in Tuscany, under Lorena's rule or in Naples. These processes were to be continued over the 18th century.[43]

---

      *origini della scienza commercialistica: Giuseppe Lorenzo Maria Casaregi, appunti per una biografia, Materiali per una storia della cultura giuridica,* 9(1979), 289–327; Vito PIERGIOVANNI: *La 'Spiegazione' del Consolato del mare di Giuseppe Lorenzo Maria Casaregi, Materiali per una storia della cultura giuridica,* 36(2006), 15–27.

39    HILAIRE: *Introduction historique au droit commercial...*, *op. cit.*, 64–66. Cf. also Jean HILAIRE: *Droit du commerce et influences européennes dans le système juridique français,* Droits, 14(1991), 39–48: in France, 17th and 18th century Italian legal scholarship was still quoted in 19th century academic works.

40    Vito PIERGIOVANNI: *Courts and Commercial Law at the Beginning of the Modern Age = The Courts and the Development of Commercial Law...*, *op. cit.*, 11–21.

41    *Decisiones Rotae Genuae de mercatura et pertinentibus ad eam,* Venetiis, [Francesco Ziletti], 1582.

42    Vito PIERGIOVANNI: *The Rise of the Genoese Civil Rota in the XVIth Century: The 'Decisones de mercatura' Concerning Insurance = The Courts and the Development of Commercial Law...*, *op. cit.*, 23–38.

43    Giovanni TARELLO: *Storia della cultura giuridica moderna, I, Assolutismo e codificazione del diritto,* Il Mulino, Bologna, 1976.

In respect to commercial law, a few Italian States pursued codification of commercial law.[44] I will mention only here two main tentative projects which were drafted in Naples in 1781 and in Venice in 1786. Of course, these texts embraced a concept of codification different from the one adopted by the *Code de commerce*. In fact, these codifications were discussed earlier and in an older ideological frame. One should consider that these texts were prepared in Italy while in France the Minister of Justice, Hue de Miromesnil, presented a project to reform the 17th century *Ordonnance de commerce*.[45]

Discussions on Miromesnil's project started in 1782 and had not been concluded prior to the Revolution, so that they were interrupted. However, the *Projet Miromesnil* was to be used in drafting *Code de Commerce*. Something similar happened in Italy. The *Codice marittimo* by Michele De Jorio for the Kingdom of Naples[46] and *Codice per la Veneta mercantile marina*[47] for the Venetian Republic could not be enforced, but they were surely a reference for tentative project of commercial code under Napoleon. Both of them focused on commercial maritime law, which is not surprising if one considers Italian physical geography.

These initiatives were rooted in Italian Enlightenment critical reflection on economic and legislative topics. More specifically, the Neapolitan legislative text pursued a compromise between freedom of commerce and protection of local manufactures. It was conceived following other 18th century Neapolitan legislative reforms and was influenced by Physiocrats' economic thinking of the *Encyclopédie*.[48]

Its author, Michele De Jorio, was a disciple of Genovesi (the translator of Montesquieu).[49] He was a jurist, however, and his legal knowledge can be appreciated through reading his collection of commercial case law and doctrine published in Naples in 1799: his sources were Roman law and *ius commune*,

---

44 Similar efforts were carried out in Spain: PETIT: *Historia del derecho mercantile…, op. cit.*, 350–357.

45 HILAIRE : *Introduction historique au droit commercial…, op. cit.*, 81–82.

46 *Il codice marittimo del 1781 di Michele De Jorio per il Regno di Napoli*, vol. 1–2, Cesare Maria MOSCHETTI (ed.), Giannini editore, Napoli, 1979.

47 *Codice per la Veneta Mercantile Marina approvato dal decreto dell'eccellentissimo Senato 21 Settembre 1786*, [Venetiis], per li figlioli del qu: Z. Antonio Pinelli, stampatori ducali, 1786.

48 Cesare Maria MOSCHETTI : *Introduzione = Il codice marittimo del 1781 di Michele De Jorio…, op. cit.*, I, XIII–XC.

49 Massimo TITA, *De Jorio, Michele = Dizionario biografico dei giuristi italiani (XII–XX secolo)*, Italo BIROCCHI, Ennio CORTESE, Antonello MATTONE, Marco Nicola MILETTI (eds.), Il Mulino, Bologna, 2013, I, 683–684.

THE ITALIAN DESTINY OF THE FRENCH *CODE DE COMMERCE* 121

in particular Jacques Cujas[50] and Benvenuto Stracca,[51] but also decisions by the Genoese *Rota*, Jacques Savary[52] and customary commercial law. He "blended" this complex of legal references in the light of natural law and Enlightenment teachings.[53]

Concerning the Venetian codification of mercantile commercial law, a first project was complete already in 1777–1778 and the final version was promulgated in 1786, just one year before the Treaty of Campoformio which marked the end of independence for Venice. Articles of the code were clearly and precisely drafted, in a simple style. Its contents were inspired by the desire to protect Venetian commerce; in fact, the Venetian Republic intervened to protect Venetian ships and goods following ancient corporative patterns which had not changed. Generally speaking, the project had no revolutionary approach in respect to the legal and constitutional system of Venice, but on the contrary it was especially aimed at better defining traditional jurisdictional competence. The successful 17th century manual for maritime trades by Genoese jurist Carlo Targa[54] and the very famous old book of *Consolato del mare*[55] were a main reference.[56]

At the beginning of the 19th century, in a new political context, these legislative works were certainly an important background to start reforming commercial law in Italian territories. However, as mentioned above, Napoleon's political action involved the implementation of new legal principles: private ownership, freedom of commerce and trades, free enterprise, free competition.[57] New texts had to be drafted.

Proposals for a codification of commercial law based on freedom of commerce and trade were very soon presented in Milan, during the period of the

---

50 Recently, Xavier Prévost: *Jacques Cujas (1522–1590), jurisconsulte humaniste*, Librairie Droz, Genève, 2015.

51 Cf. above.

52 Jacques Savary: *Le parfait négociant, ou instruction générale pour ce qui regarde le commerce des marchandises de France, et des pays étrangers*, 2 voll., A Paris, chez la veuve Estienne et fils, 1749–1753.

53 Michele De Jorio: *La giurisprudenza del commercio umiliata a s. m. Ferdinando IV*, I–IV, In Napoli, nella Stamperia Simoniana, 1799.

54 Carlo Targa: *Ponderazioni sopra la contrattazione marittima*, Livorno, nella stamperia di Gio. Paolo Fantechi e compagni, 1755.

55 Il consolato del mare nel quale si comprendono tutti gli statuti, et ordini, disposti da gli antichi, per ogni caso di mercantia et di navigare … Con l'aggiunta delle ordinationi sopra l'armate di mare, sicurtà, entrate, et uscite, In *Venetia, Daniel Zanetti, & compagni, 1576*.

56 Giorgio Zordan: *Il codice per la Veneta Mercantile Marina*, Padova, Cedam, 1981.

57 Ferdinando Mazzarella: *Un diritto per l'Europa industriale. Cultura giuridica ed economia dalla Rivoluzione francese al Secondo Dopoguerra*, Milano, Giuffrè, 2016, 7–10.

Cisalpine and Italian Republics.[58] However, it was in April 1806 that the Minister of Justice of the Kingdom of Italy, Giuseppe Luosi[59] appointed Pompeo Baldasseroni chairman of a commission charged with drafting a commercial code.[60] Baldasseroni was a Tuscan jurist – and judge – who had already drafted a project of regulation of bills of exchange for the Tuscan Duchy of Massa and Carrara and had published a very successful book on the same topic.[61]

Baldasseroni drafted two projects in 1806: both of them were linked to the *ius commune* tradition and dealt mainly with maritime law.[62] In particular, following teachings of natural law, his second draft collected and put in order all the rules, norms, national and international customs referring to commercial law. The same ideas were expressed in a quite rich dissertation he published in 1807,[63] where he quoted a number of sources, starting with Montesquieu and including his own work on bills of exchange, *Consolato del mare*,[64] Valin's commentaries on the *Ordonnance de la Marine* of 1681,[65] Targa's manual,[66] the 18th century French jurist Emerigon on insurances,[67] his own brother Ascanio

---

58    For more reference, Sciumè: *I tentativi per la codificazione del diritto commerciale nel Regno italico…, op. cit.*, 26–34.

59    Refer to the collective book *Giuseppe Luosi, giurista italiano ed europeo. Traduzioni, tradizioni e tradimenti della codificazione…, op. cit.*

60    Berlinguer: *Domenico Alberto Azuni giurista e politico…, op. cit.*, 219–228; Sciumè: *I tentativi per la codificazione del diritto commerciale nel Regno italico…, op. cit.*, 19–26.

61    Pompeo Baldasseroni: *Leggi e costumi del cambio che si osservano nelle principali piazze di Europa e singolarmente in quella di Livorno*, In Pescia, nella stamperia di Gio. Tommaso Masi e compagni, 1784. For more reference, Maura Fortunati: *Baldasseroni, Pompeo = Dizionario biografico dei giuristi italiani…, op. cit.*, I, 147–148.

62    Sciumè: *I tentativi per la codificazione del diritto commerciale nel Regno italico…, op. cit.*, 34–40.

63    Pompeo Baldasseroni: *Dissertazione sulla necessita ed importanza della compilazione di un codice generale pel commercio di terra e di mare del Regno d'Italia, e sulle basi fondamentali sopra le quali debb'essere compilato*, Milano, dalla stamperia reale, 1807. Cf. Sciumè: *I tentativi per la codificazione del diritto commerciale nel Regno italico…, op. cit.*, 73–80.

64    Cf. above.

65    René Josué Valin: *Nouveau commentaire sur l'ordonnance de la marine, du mois d'août 1681*, vol. 1–2, A La Rochelle, chez Jerôme Legier, 1766.

66    Cf. above.

67    Balthazard-Marie Emerigon: *Traité des assurances et des contrats a la grosse*, vol. 102, A Marseille, chez Jean Mossy, imprimeur du Roi, de la Marine, et Libraire, à la Canebière, 1783.

Baldasseroni on maritime insurance as well[68] and of course the *Codice per la Veneta Mercantile Marina*.[69]

Minister Luosi appointed a committee of Italian jurists, magistrates, merchants and bankers to discuss the second draft by Baldasseroni. The Chairman was Giuseppe De Stefani, a Venetian judge. Both De Stefani and one of the other members, Giuseppe Compagnoni, Counsellor of State of the Kingdom of Italy, had to play a substantial role. As a result of the revision process, a third draft was published in 1807.[70]

This third tentative project of the commercial code, as well as the fourth and final one which was to follow, expressed the will to find a legislative compromise between the commercial law tradition and renewal of the legal system through state codification of the law. To this purpose, according to Napoleon's political legislative plan, the third (and fourth) draft adopted a different point of view in respect to Baldasseroni's drafts. More specifically, these tentative projects contained only private law rules on commerce and not those from public law. The main addressee was a new kind of merchant who participated in state political institutions as an individual. For him the state codified the law.[71]

This was surely a very important change in the way of thinking of commercial law codification. Italian jurists who participated in these legislative works were seizing the new ideas supporting Napoleon's codification. However, this change was not enough to arrive at an Italian commercial code different from the French one which was in preparation at the same time. Things went differently.

First, Domenico Alberto Azuni gave his legal advice on the third Italian draft.[72] Azuni, from Sardinia, had authored a tentative project on maritime law for the Kingdom of Sardinia in 1791.[73] His fame was however linked to his famous law dictionary of commercial case law and doctrine.[74] At the time, he

---

68    Ascanio BALDASSERONI: *Delle assicurazioni marittime*, vol. 5, Firenze-Livorno, nella stamperia Bonducciana, presso Giuseppe Gamba, 1801–1804.

69    Cf. above.

70    SCIUMÈ: *I tentativi per la codificazione del diritto commerciale nel Regno italico...*, *op. cit.*, 40–73.

71    SCIUMÈ: *I progetti del codice di commercio del Regno italico...*, *op. cit.*, 7–13.

72    BERLINGUER: *Sui progetti di codice di commercio del Regno d'Italia...*, *op. cit.*, 34–42; SCIUMÈ, *I tentativi per la codificazione del diritto commerciale nel Regno italico...*, *op. cit.*, 40–73.

73    BERLINGUER: *Domenico Alberto Azuni giurista e politico...*, *op. cit.*, 86 ff.

74    Domenico Alberto AZUNI: *Dizionario universale ragionato della giurisprudenza mercantile*, 3rd ed., vo. 1–2, Livorno, Tipografia Vignozzi, 1834.

was President of the Court of Appeals of Genoa. He had already made his name in France: in particular, he had taken part in the drafting of the Second Book of the *Code de commerce* devoted to maritime law as an external counsellor.[75]

In October 1807, Azuni wrote his report and compared the third Italian tentative project to the final version of the *Code de commerce*. Actually, he made specific reference to French project by Gorneau of 1801–1803.[76] He pointed out how the Italian text was more suitable for the Kingdom of Italy than the French text, especially concerning bankruptcy and sales. Moreover, he remarked how the Italian project was more appropriate from a scientific and technical point of view. He suggested, however, a series of changes to improve it, also from the point of view both of the legal language and legal drafting.[77] Clearly, he had learnt from his previous legislative experience when he was advisor to the French committee chaired by Gorneau.[78]

Notwithstanding that a fourth revised draft was prepared in late October 1807, Italian jurists were then well aware of the fact that this was no more a juridical question, but a political one. Napoleon's decision to put his *Code de commerce* into force had already been taken and was consistent with the Emperor's authoritarian political actions.[79]

Minister Luosi, with very little success, tried to negotiate some changes in the French text which was to be put into force in the Kingdom of Italy. Then he entrusted De Stefani and Azuni with the translation into Italian of French *Code de commerce*.[80] Finally, secretary of State Aldini signed the provision of

---

75    BERLINGUER: *Domenico Alberto Azuni giurista e politico...*, *op. cit.*, 184–187. Cf. also Riccardo FERRANTE: *Codification and lex mercatoria: the maritime law of the second book of the Code de commerce (1807) = From lex mercatoria to commercial law...*, *op. cit.*, 121–141.

76    Antonio PADOA-SCHIOPPA: *Napoleone e il 'Code de commerce'* = Antonio PADOA-SCHIOPPA: *Saggi...*, *op. cit.*, 89–112; Anne LEFEBVRE-TEILLARD: *Cambacérès et le code de commerce* = *Le code de commerce 1807-2007. Livre du bicentenaire*, Dalloz, Paris, 2007, 3-17; Fabien VALENTE: *La naissance du Code de commerce napoléonien = Qu'en est-il du Code de Commerce 200 ans après? Etats des lieux et projections*, Corinne SAINT-ALARY-HOUIN (ed.), Presses de l'Université des Sciences Sociales de Toulouse, Toulouse, 2009, 15–37.

77    A version of Azuni's report is edited by BERLINGUER: *Sui progetti di codice di commercio del Regno d'Italia...*, *op. cit.*, 87–145.

78    *Ibid.*, 29–34.

79    SCIUMÈ: *I tentativi per la codificazione del diritto commerciale nel Regno italico...*, *op. cit.*, 80–93. Cf. also CAVANNA: *Codificazione del diritto italiano e imperialismo giuridico francese nella Milano napoleonica...*, *op. cit.*, 886–888.

80    *Ibid.*, 93–101.

THE ITALIAN DESTINY OF THE FRENCH *CODE DE COMMERCE* 125

enforcement of the French commercial code on July 17, 1808.[81] It was then that the *Code de commerce* really began its Italian life.

Alternative Italian drafts, original and scientifically based, proved unachievable. It seems that this was not for a lack of understanding what codification meant to Napoleon, i.e. a state law based on principles of equality and freedom and, most important, a uniform, national legislation for all Italian territories. Nor was it because of lack of expertise, on the contrary, their contents were a testimony to a very rich legal tradition.

With specific respect to business organisations, these drafts were consistent with – or at least showed significant similarities to some types of commercial companies traditionally used by Italian merchants. In fact, during the medieval and modern periods different forms of commercial companies were developed in Italy: examples are merchants' and bankers' companies from Genoa, Venice and Florence and their international networks. These early business organisations were in substance similar to general partnerships and limited partnership, like the *commenda*. Echoes of such experience could be found in Italian tentative drafts.[82]

Napoleon's final political plan was that the *Code de commerce* had to become the uniform commercial legislation for all the territories under French rule. Italian drafts by Baldasseroni, De Stefani and Azuni proved, however, an effort to find alternative solutions, more suitable and consistent with local tradition.

Apart these tentative projects for the Kingdom of Italy and their destiny, historiography also draws attention to another tentative project drafted for the Papal States in 1801–1806, during the Papal restoration and before the Papal States were annexed to the French Empire in 1809.[83] The so-called *Codice di commercio per lo Stato ecclesiastico* was drafted by Monsignor Paolo Vergani and Vincenzo Bartolucci on the initiative of Pope Pius VII. Leaving aside further analysis, this text attested legislative works for a codification of commercial law that could be an alternative to the French one. Definitely, it was destined to be unsuccessful.[84]

---

81    *Codice di commercio di terra e di mare pel Regno d'Italia*, dalla stamperia reale, Milano, 1808.

82    Padoa SCHIOPPA: *Le società commerciali nei progetti di codificazione del Regno Italico…*, *op. cit.*, 120–132. Cf. also Paolo UNGARI: *Profilo storico del diritto delle anonime in Italia*, Bulzoni, Roma, 1974.

83    Cf. above.

84    Maura FORTUNATI: *Un progetto di codificazione commerciale nella Roma di Pio IX. Antonio Fabi ed il suo 'Codice di commercio per lo Stato pontificio' = Itinerari in comune. Ricerche di storia del diritto per Vito Piergiovanni*, Giuffrè, Milano, 2011, 121–124.

## 3 Reception of the *Code de commerce* in Italy

French codification can be regarded as a first moment of "transition" for Italian commercial law, which was "poured" into the French commercial code framework. It seemed to fit easily.

Thanks to Napoleon's strategy, the *Code de commerce* in his Italian dominions was not a completely foreign and new legal act. Certainly, it was an "imported" code.[85] However, a large part of its contents should not be considered foreign legal norms incorporating large elements of foreign legal systems. For example, recent research on commercial case law in Rome and Naples proved that commercial judges did not change their way of adjudicating, especially with respect to bills of exchange.[86] As mentioned above, commercial law in France and in Italy had common roots and the Italian "exercise" of legal drafting contributed to a better understanding of French commercial code committee work.

Outputs of French legal science and case law were taken advantage of to the greatest extent. After implementation of the *Code de commerce*, national legislative activity came to an end and Italian jurists started to focus on French doctrine and case law. The French Commercial code excluded other pertinent legislative sources, as was sanctioned in the promulgation law.

This also led Italian practitioners and commercial judges to look at French interpretations. Reports and discussions of the French *Code de commerce* committee were translated into Italian,[87] first of all Locré's s commentaries.[88] In parallel, collections of French Commerce Tribunals' decisions were edited in Italian.[89] Pardessus,[90] who largely contributed to implementation of the code

---

85  BERLINGUER: *Sui progetti di codice di commercio del Regno d'Italia..., op. cit.*, 74–84.

86  Massimo TITA: *Il giudizio dei pari. La giurisdizione commerciale a Roma e a Napoli tra Sette e Ottocento*, Arti Grafiche la Regione, Campobasso, 2012, 62–69, 91–100.

87  *Dei motivi del codice di commercio ovvero discorsi pronunciati al corpo legislativo di Francia dagli oratori del Consiglio di stato, e del Tribunato intorno al progetto della nuova legislazione commerciale. Traduzione italiana*, dalla tipografia di Francesco Sonzogno di Gio. Batt. stampatore e librajo ..., Milano, 1809.

88  Jean-Guillaume LOCRÉ: *Spirito del Codice commerciale ossia Commentario desunto dai processi verbali del Consiglio di Stato, dalle esposizioni dei Motivi e Discorsi ... e Complemento del Codice di commercio ... Versione italiana*, vol. 9, dalla tipografia di Francesco Sonzogno di Gio. B., Milano, 1811–1820.

89  Alberto SCIUMÈ: *Progetti legislativi tendenze dottrinali e prassi in tema di fallimento nell'Italia napoleonica = Confluences des droits savants et des pratiques juridiques, Actes du colloque de Montpellier (12–14 décembre 1977)*, Giuffrè, Milano, 1979, 549–578.

90  Jean HILAIRE: *Jean-Marie Pardessus = Dictionnaire historique des juristes français (XIIe–XXe siècle)*, Presses Universitaires de France, Paris, 2015, 793–795.

THE ITALIAN DESTINY OF THE FRENCH *CODE DE COMMERCE* 127

in France,[91] became a reference also for Italian jurists: his treaty on bills of exchange was immediately translated into Italian,[92] while his fundamental *Cours de droit commercial* circulated in French, at least at the beginning.[93]

Notwithstanding all this, during the Napoleonic era, Italian jurists also continued to be very attached to earlier legal doctrine and practice which were linked to the ancient legal system and remained an indispensable reference in issues of commercial law, as proven by the tentative projects of the commercial code mentioned above. Furthermore, continuity in interpretation was attested by the third edition of Azuni's Dictionary, which was published in Livorno in 1834. Its contents were the same as in the first 1786 edition, only the new principles emerging from French judicial implementation of the *Code de commerce* were added: sources were both ancient and recent case law and doctrine. Sirey's collection of French case law was a reference, together with Pardessus.[94] This continuity was remarkable, even during the Restoration.[95]

Furthermore, to improve the reception of his codes, Napoleon reformed law schools in the Italian territories, as he did in France.[96] With regard to the teaching of commercial law in French law schools, official teaching started in 1810, only in Paris, and the classes were conducted by Jean-Marie Pardessus.[97] In the Italian territories, the teaching of commercial law started earlier.[98] In the Kingdom of Italy, starting in 1808 commercial law according to the French commercial code was taught at Pavia University together with the older teaching of

---

91 Laura MOSCATI: *Dopo e al di là del Code de commerce: l'apporto di Jean-Marie Pardessus = Negozianti e imprenditori...*, *op. cit.*, 47–80. Cf. also Philippe NELIDOFF: *La naissance de la doctrine commercialiste au XIXe siècle = Qu'en est-il du Code de Commerce 200 ans après?...*, *op. cit.*, 39–56.

92 Jean-Marie PARDESSUS: *Trattato del contratto e delle lettere di cambio dei biglietti a ordine ed altri effetti di commercio secondo i principi de' nuovi codici ...Versione italiana*, vol. 1–2, dalla stamperia e fonderia di G.G. Destefanis, Milano, 1811.

93 The first Italian translation was published in Venice in 1821–1822. Further editions followed, for example, Jean-Marie PARDESSUS: *Corso di diritto commerciale... recato dal francese in italiano sulla sesta ed ultima edizione di Parigi ...per l'avvocato Francesco Galiani*, Stabilimento Tipografico, Napoli, 1858.

94 AZUNI: *Dizionario universale ragionato della giurisprudenza mercantile...*, 3rd ed., *op. cit.*

95 SCIUMÈ: *Progetti legislativi tendenze dottrinali e prassi...*, *op. cit.*

96 *Le università napoleoniche. Uno spartiacque nella storia italiana ed europea dell'istruzione superiore*, Piero DEL NEGRO, Luigi PEPE (eds.), Clueb, Bologna, 2008.

97 Jean HILAIRE: *Le droit les affaires e l'histoire*, Economica, Paris, 1995, 17–18 (siprojuris. symogih.org/ – accessed July 2018).

98 On the beginning of the teaching of commercial law in Napoleonic Law Schools, Riccardo FERRANTE: *Dans l'ordre établi par le Code civil. La scienza del diritto al tramonto dell'illuminismo giuridico*, Milano, Giuffrè, 2002, 102–113.

public economy. The same happened in Bologna, starting in 1808–1809.[99] Concerning the Italian Department annexed by the French Empire, teaching in Turin started already in 1807[100] and also the University of Genoa had commercial law classes. Both in Turin and in Genoa commercial law was taught as part of private law classes devoted to the *Code civil*.[101]

In respect to the implementation of commercial courts (*Tribunali di commercio*) in Italy and their case law, further research is really needed.[102] At the moment, one can count on some works devoted to commercial courts in Piedmont in the 18th and 19th centuries[103] and on a few essays on commercial case law in Italian territories under Napoleon.[104] Therefore, an evaluation of the impact of French commercial law in courts' practice is not yet possible. However, the French commercial code enjoyed a century-long life in Italy.[105] During the Restoration, the text of 1807 was revised in France, while in Italy it was still a reference in its original version.[106]

The Restoration was the moment of proliferation of commercial codes and regulations, and most of them were directly inspired by the French commercial

---

99   DI Renzo Villata: *Introduzione. La formazione del giurista in Italia…, op. cit.*, 67–68.

100  Ferrante: *Dans l'ordre établi par le Code civil…, op. cit.*, 110–111. Cf. also Gian Savino Pene Vidari: *Nota sull'inizio dell'insegnamento del diritto commerciale all'Università di Torino*, Bollettino storico-bibliografico subalpino, 1997, 511–531.

101  Riccardo Ferrante: *Università e cultura giuridica a Genova tra Rivoluzione e Impero*, Atti della Società Ligure di Storia Patria, 2002.

102  Commercial courts introduced by Napoleon were to be abolished in Italy in 1888: Cristina Ciancio: *Mercanti in toga. I Tribunali di Commercio nel Regno d'Italia (1861–1888)*, Bologna, Patron Editore, 2012.

103  Gian Savino Pene Vidari: *Tribunali di Commercio e codificazione commerciale Carloalbertina*, Rivista di storia del diritto italiano, 46–47 (1971–1972), 27–124; Gian Savino Pene Vidari: *Ricerche sulla giurisdizione commerciale negli Stati sabaudi*, Bollettino storico-bibliografico subalpino, 76(1978), 435–566; Gian Savino Pene Vidari: *Consolati di commercio e Tribunali commerciali = Dal Trono all'Albero della Libertà. Trasformazioni e continuità istituzionali nei territori del Regno di Sardegna dall'antico regime all'età rivoluzionaria*, Roma, Ministero per i Beni culturali e ambientali, 1991, I, 220–254.

104  Tita: *Il giudizio dei pari…, op. cit.*; Gentile : *L'applicazione del Code de commerce in Calabria…, op. cit.*

105  Cf. Béatrice Fournie: *L'influence à l'étranger du code de commerce français aux XIXe et XXe siècles: du declin du droit commercial français à l'emergence d'un droit des affaires francophone = Qu'en est-il du Code de Commerce 200 ans après?…, op. cit.*, 57–74.

106  Antonio Padoa-Schioppa: *Franckreich, Handelsrecht = Handbuch der Quellen und Literatur der neureren europäischen Privatrechtsgeschichte*, vol. 3/3, Helmut Coing (ed.), München, Beck, 1986, 3152–3187; Jean-Pierre Allinne: *Le développement du droit commercial en dehors du Code et l'influence des droits étrangers 1807–1925 = Qu'en est-il du Code de Commerce 200 ans après?…, op. cit.*, 75–104. Cf. also Hilaire: *Introduction historique au droit commercial…, op. cit.*, 95–134.

THE ITALIAN DESTINY OF THE FRENCH *CODE DE COMMERCE* 129

code of 1807. Even more than this: after the defeat of Napoleon, the *Code de commerce* continued to be in force in various part of the country. It was still implemented in former Republic of Genoa under Piedmont's government.

Gaetano Marré, professor of commercial law at the University of Genoa (starting in 1816), in 1822 published a course of commercial law which achieved great success among students and practitioners.[107] Besides the French commercial code, Locré and Pardessus, his references were Jousse, Savary, Valin Emerigon, Pothier, ancient Genoese *Rota* case law and contemporary French courts' case law, as well as Roman law and *ius commune* scholarship (from German scholar Heineccius (Heinecke)[108] to Scaccia and Casaregis). Furthermore, Marré regularly quoted the successful *Institutes de droit commercial français* by Claude Etienne Delvincourt,[109] lawyer, law professor for private law and dean at the Paris law school, whose work was also translated into Italian (in Naples).[110]

In Tuscany, codification of private law was rejected, but the French commercial code was kept in force as it was previously when the region was a French Department annexed by the French Empire.[111]

The Restoration was clearly a favourable time for codification and, during the first half of the 19th century, the States into which Italy was divided promulgated their own codes. Except for the Duchy of Parma, they all chose to codify commercial law and followed the French example. In Naples, for example, the codification of 1819 followed strictly the *Code de commerce* of 1807, with only a few variations.[112]

This meant that Neapolitan legal works devoted to commercial law continued to refer to French doctrine and, most interestingly, to French case law. Their authors were mainly practitioners and lawyers: a "mixed" legal practice

---

107 Gaetano MARRÉ: *Corso di diritto commerciale*, presso Fraticelli e c., Firenze, 1840.

108 Johann Gottlieb HEINECKE: *Elementa juris cambialis commoda auditoribus methodo adornata*, Rovereto, sumptibus Balleonianis, 1746. Cf. also Johann Gottlieb HEINECKE: *Elementi della giurisprudenza sul cambio mercantile... / dalla latina in lingua italiana trad. dall'avv. E. Cesarini*, G. Ferretti, Roma, 1838.

109 Claude Etienne DELVINCOURT: *Institutes de droit commercial français avec des notes explicatives du texte*, vol 1–2, chez l'Auteur aux Ecoles de Droit; Rondonneau et Decle, au Dépôt des Lois; Durand, Libraire; Eberhart, Imprimeur-Libraire, Paris, 1810.

110 Claude Etienne DELVINCOURT: *Istituzioni di diritto commerciale con annotazioni*, vol. 1–3, Dalla stamperia francese, Napoli, 1828.

111 Antonio PADOA-SCHIOPPA: *Italien, Handelsrecht*, in *Handbuch der Quellen und Literatur...*, vol. 3/3, *op. cit.*, 3209–3233.

112 Saverio GENTILE: *Gli ultimi fuochi dei napoleonidi. Il progetto di revisione della codificazione francese a Napoli (1814)*, Jovene, Napoli, 2015, 52–54.

emerged from thin manuals with an annex of models of judicial acts,[113] from extended commentaries which literally embodied French texts translated into Italian[114] and from rich collections of case law.[115]

In brief, at the beginning of the 19th century, commercial law – as well as private law – was codified and interpreted in Italy following the French example.[116] In the Papal States, commercial law was codified in 1821 and later, in 1842, this also occurred in the Kingdom of Sardinia. The French *Code civil* of 1804 was adopted in many areas in Italy after 1806, and it contributed to the creation of a legal environment particularly receptive to French law. Even after the Congress of Vienna, the French influence on Italian law continued to be very strong, in a mix of local traditions and foreign transplants. Of course, notwithstanding a general and quite widespread French influence, each Italian State had a few peculiarities.[117]

Even in the Kingdom of Lombardy-Venetia, which was established at the Congress of Vienna and put under the Austrian government, Book 1 of the French code of 1807 was kept in force. This, however, was true only for rules which were consistent with other Austrian laws, in particular with the Austrian Civil Code of 1811, the ABGB, and the civil procedure regulation of 1816.[118] Also here, commercial law doctrine and case law referred to France[119] and French commentaries continued to be translated into Italian.[120]

---

113   Gaetano Del Re: *Analisi della giurisdizione commerciale delle leggi di eccezione per gli affari di commercio, per lo Regno delle Due Sicilie, corredata di formole per i dovuti atti*, dai torchi di Luca Marotta, Napoli, 1823.

114   Domenico Balì: *Comentario del codice di commercio per lo Regno delle due Sicilie; ove si trovano esposti, lo spirito del codice di commercio di G. G. Locré*, vol. 1–2, dalla tipografia Vara, Napoli, 1825–1826.

115   *Dubbii e controversie in materie di commercio ultimamente agitate, e decise dalle primarie corti, e tribunali di Francia e d'Italia: opera dedicata ai signori giudici, avvocati, e negozianti*, Napoli, Dalla Tipografia Trani, 1838. Cf. also Michele Agresti: *Decisioni delle Gran Corti civili in materia di diritto*, vol. 1–6, dalla stamperia francese, dalla stamperia e cartiera del Fibreno, Napoli, 1827–1833.

116   Padoa-Schioppa: *Italien, Handelsrecht...*, *op. cit.*

117   *Ibid.*

118   *Ibid.*

119   For example, Michele Costi: *Codice di commercio di terra ossia il libro primo del codice di commercio di terra e di mare pel Regno d'Italia ora Regno Lombardo-Veneto*, coi tipi di G.A. Andruzzi, Venezia, 1841.

120   *Nuovo dizionario di diritto commerciale ossia riassunto di legislazione, di dottrina e di giurisprudenza di Devilleneuve e Masse: opera utilissima ai forensi, ai commercianti ed altre persone di affari; versione italiana a cura di Francesco Foramiti*, nel premiato stab. di G. Antonelli, Venezia, 1843; Claude-Alphonse Delangle: *Delle società di commercio. Opera confrontata coi trattati di Troplong, Vincens ...; prima versione italiana dell'avv. Giuseppe D'Angelo, con annotazioni*, presso Andrea Santini e figlio, Venezia, 1851; Fortuné Anthoine

THE ITALIAN DESTINY OF THE FRENCH *CODE DE COMMERCE* 131

The Kingdom of Lombardy-Venetia lasted until 1859, when Lombardy was annexed by Piedmont, while the region of Venetia and other parts of Northeastern Italy remained under Austrian rule. In 1863, in the Italian regions still under its domination, Vienna applied the German commercial code, the AD-HGB of 1861.[121]

For sure, Restoration seemed to be a golden age for the codification of commercial law in Italy. Italian jurists drafted a great number of texts and Italian legislators put in force a good number of commercial codes. However, one might wonder if this was a golden age also for commercial law in itself.

One should also consider that in each pre-unification state, internal tariff barriers and duties on trade were in force and different currencies were adopted. Thanks to a complex web of international trading agreements stipulated by each individual state, in the 1860s, just before unification, international commercial transactions were in fact smoother, and economically more convenient, with other European countries than within Italy.

The impression is that commercial law was somehow suffering this situation. Furthermore, it took a secondary role compared to civil law, and this was due to the fact that commercial law was codified. For commercial law, entering the stage of codified law meant subjection to the civil code.

In 1861, Italy was unified. A broad project of codification ensued, with the goal of adopting a national uniform set of laws for commercial law, private law, civil procedure, criminal law and criminal procedure underwent a process of national codification. Priority was however given to codifying private law, while commercial law was not perceived as a crucial issue.

At the time the Italian economy, but also the social and political structure, were still largely agrarian, and not surprisingly rules having a broader impact on this still largely pre-industrial or proto-industrial society, focusing on ownership rather than on modern business transactions and organisations, were perceived as more momentous to the creation of the nation and took precedence.

Notwithstanding a significant need for harmonisation (and modernisation), as mentioned above, after unification commercial law was not immediately

---

DE SAINT-JOSEPH: *Concordanza fra i codici di commercio stranieri ed il codice di commercio francese: opera contenente il testo dei codici e delle leggi commerciali di 44 stati...; prima trad. italiana con annotazioni e con un'appendice relativa all'attuale legislazione commerciale dell'Impero d'Austria e del Regno Lombardo-Veneto*, Dalla premiata Tip. di Pietro Naratovich Edit., Venezia, 1855.

121 MAZZARELLA: *Un diritto per l'Europa industriale...*, *op. cit.*, 50–74. Cf. also Johannes W. FLUME: *Law and Commerce. The Evolution of Codified Business Law in Europe*, Comparative Legal History 2(2014), 45–83.

reformed. After unification, in any case, a national market had to be developed. The Piedmont commercial code of 1842 was applied as it was from the former Kingdom of Sardinia to the other parts of the new country in order to standardize the highly fragmented commercial legislation existing across Italy. That code was, however, born old. It followed the French code of 1807 and did not consider any recent foreign reforms of commercial law, not even those that had been adopted in France in between 1807 and 1842.

Consequently, the first Unitarian commercial code promulgated in 1865 was unsatisfactory. However, only a few Italian jurists and politicians immediately voiced the need for a reform: among them, a well-known Italian jurist, Pasquale Stanislao Mancini, a lawyer and professor of International Law who was also a prominent politician and Minister of Justice. In 1869, he started his campaign for the adoption of a modern commercial law and the Commercial Code of 1882 can largely be seen as the result of his efforts.[122]

The Italian Code of 1882, composed of four books like the French Code of 1807, was inspired by the most recent foreign legislations such as the abovementioned German Commercial Code of 1861. Generally speaking, the new Italian commercial code was greeted with enthusiasm by jurists in Europe. Very positive opinions were expressed, as that of the president of the French *Cour de Cassation*, Gabriel Massé, and the Italian commercial code of 1882 sanctioned the end of *Code de commerce*'s long hegemony in the country.

## 4 Conclusion

Certainly, the *Code civil* "proved the most successful code of the century."[123] With regard to the Italian legal system and society, historiography has made clear how the *Code civil* had a long-lasting influence in the country.[124]

With regard to the reception of the *Code de commerce*, instead, the question has not yet received the attention it deserves and further research is needed.

---

122 Antonio PADOA-SCHIOPPA: *La genesi del codice di commercio del 1882* = PADOA-SCHIOPPA: *Saggi...*, *op. cit.*, 157–203.

123 Franz WIEACKER: *A history of private law in Europe: with particular reference to Germany*, Tony WEIR (transl.), Reinhard ZIMMERMANN (foreword), Oxford, Clarendon Press, 1995, 273–275.

124 Adriano CAVANNA: *Mito e destini del 'Code Napoléon' in Italia. Riflessioni in margine al 'Panegirico a Napoleone Legislatore' di Pietro Giordani* = CAVANNA: *Scritti...*, *op. cit.*, vol. 2, 1079–1129.

However, it is clear that it was a code which put commercial law under the rule of private law. Furthermore, its contents were not entirely new: it was a sort of "compromise," as well as with the *Code civil,* and was conceived in a pre-industrial country.

Generally speaking, through the codification commercial law was affected by Napoleon's political action: new legal principles were implemented, such as equality, private ownership, freedom of commerce and trades, free enterprise, free competition. According to Wieacker, the *Code de commerce* was "a product of the early economic liberalism of the First Empire."[125]

In this perspective, the *Code de commerce* definitely sanctioned the final objectification of commercial law, which was no longer a personal law of merchants, but a law of the state based on equality and freedom. In this sense, it contributed to the construction of the Italian juridical identity after the political unification of the country in 1861. However, I believe, commercial law always proved (and still proves) to be a complicated issue for legislators, depending on the underlying political choices.

Around 1950, Italian jurist Tullio Ascarelli[126] considered how the *Code de commerce* marked the beginning of a new age for commercial law in continental Europe, the third one since the Middle Ages. Previously, during the medieval period, commercial law was made by merchants through guilds and customary law. Later, during the modern era (sixteenth-nineteenth century), princes started to legislate on issues of commercial law. Therefore, commercial law gradually overcame its corporative origins and became part of the common law of the state.[127]

Furthermore, in this third period which was opened by French commercial code, commercial law was to gain wider application in every citizen's economic activities, as far as imposing changes on private law rules in the late 19th century. This last phenomenon was called the "commercialisation" of private law by French jurist Georges Ripert and this was exactly what the *Code de commerce* had rejected.[128] Social and economic transformations made the difference.

---

125  WIEACKER: *A history of private law in Europe, op. cit.,* 271.

126  Mario Stella RICHTER JR.: *Ascarelli, Tullio = Il contributo italiano alla storia del Pensiero – Diritto,* Istituto della Enciclopedia Italiana, Roma, 2012, 707–711.

127  Tullio ASCARELLI: *Sviluppo storico del diritto commerciale e significato dell'unificazione* (1953), now in Id., *Saggi di diritto commerciale,* Giuffrè, Milano, 1955, 7–33.

128  Georges RIPERT: *Aspects juridiques du capitalisme moderne,* Libraire générale de droit et de jurisprudence, Paris, 1946.

## Bibliography

Michele AGRESTI: *Decisioni delle Gran Corti civili in materia di diritto*, vol. 1–6, dalla stamperia francese, dalla stamperia e cartiera del Fibreno, Napoli, 1827–1833.

Jean-Pierre ALLINNE: *Le développement du droit commercial en dehors du Code et l'influence des droits étrangers 1807–1925* = *Qu'en est-il du Code de Commerce 200 ans après ? Etats des lieux et projections*, Corinne SAINT-ALARY-HOUIN (ed.), Presses de l'Université des Sciences Sociales de Toulouse, Toulouse, 2009, 75–104.

Tullio ASCARELLI: *Sviluppo storico del diritto commerciale e significato dell'unificazione* (1953) = Tullio ASCARELLI: *Saggi di diritto commerciale*, Giuffrè, Milano, 1955, 7–33.

Mario ASCHERI: *A final comment and request*, Rechtsgeschichte – Legal History 22(2014), 270–273.

Domenico Alberto AZUNI: *Dizionario universale ragionato della giurisprudenza mercantile*, 3rd ed., Tipografia Vignozzi, Livorno, 1834.

Ascanio BALDASSERONI: *Delle assicurazioni marittime*, vol. 1–5, nella stamperia Bonducciana, presso Giuseppe Gamba, Firenze-Livorno, 1801–1804.

Pompeo BALDASSERONI: *Dissertazione sulla necessita ed importanza della compilazione di un codice generale pel commercio di terra e di mare del Regno d'Italia, e sulle basi fondamentali sopra le quali debb'essere compilato*, Milano, dalla stamperia reale, 1807.

Pompeo BALDASSERONI: *Leggi e costumi del cambio che si osservano nelle principali piazze di Europa e singolarmente in quella di Livorno*, nella stamperia di Gio. Tommaso Masi e compagni, Pescia, 1784.

Domenico BALÌ: *Comentario del codice di commercio per lo Regno delle due Sicilie; ove si trovano esposti, lo spirito del codice di commercio di G. G. Locré*, vol. 1–2, dalla tipografia Vara, Napoli, 1825–1826.

Luigi BERLINGUER: *Domenico Alberto Azuni giurista e politico (1749–1827). Un contributo bio-bibliografico*, Giuffrè, Milano, 1966.

Luigi BERLINGUER: *Sui progetti di codice di commercio del Regno d'Italia (1807–1808). Considerazioni su un inedito di D. A. Azuni*, Giuffrè, Milano, 1970.

Arturo BRIENZA: *I progetti di codice commerciale nella Repubblica Cisalpina e nel Regno d'Italia*, Cisalpino – La Goliardica, Milano, 1978.

Michael BROERS: *The Napoleonic Empire in Italy, 1796–1814. Cultural Imperialism in a European Context?*, Basingstoke, New York, Palgrave Macmillan, 2005.

Carlo CAPRA: *Gli italiani prima dell'Italia. Un lungo Settecento, dalla fine della Controriforma a Napoleone*, Carocci, Roma, 2014.

Carlo CAPRA: *L'età rivoluzionaria e napoleonica in Italia 1796–1815*, Loescher, Torino, 1978.

Giuseppe Lorenzo Maria, CASAREGI, *Discursus legales de commercio*, typis Ioannis Baptistae Scionici, Genuae, 1707.

THE ITALIAN DESTINY OF THE FRENCH *CODE DE COMMERCE* 135

Adriano CAVANNA: *Codificazione del diritto italiano e imperialismo giuridico francese nella Milano napoleonica. Giuseppe Luosi e il diritto penale* = Adriano CAVANNA: *Scritti (1968–2002)*, vol. 2, Jovene, Napoli, 2007, 833–927.

Adriano CAVANNA: *L'influence juridique française en Italie au* XIX*e siècle*, Revue d'histoire des Facultés de droit et de la science juridique, 15(1994), 87–112.

Adriano CAVANNA: *Mito e destini del 'Code Napoléon' in Italia. Riflessioni in margine al 'Panegirico a Napoleone Legislatore' di Pietro Giordani* = Adriano CAVANNA, *Scritti (1968–2002)*, vol. 2, Jovene, Napoli, 2007, 1079–1129.

Cristina CIANCIO: *Mercanti in toga. I Tribunali di Commercio nel Regno d'Italia (1861–1888)*, Patron Editore, Bologna, 2012.

*Codice di commercio di terra e di mare pel Regno d'Italia*, dalla stamperia reale, Milano, 1808.

*Codice per la Veneta Mercantile Marina approvato dal decreto dell'eccellentissimo Senato 21 Settembre 1786*, per li figlioli del qu: Z. Antonio Pinelli, stampatori ducali, [Venetiis], 1786.

Michele COSTI: *Codice di commercio di terra ossia il libro primo del codice di commercio di terra e di mare pel Regno d'Italia ora Regno Lombardo-Veneto*, coi tipi di G.A. Andruzzi, Venezia, 1841.

Alberto COVA: *Tradizione e innovazione nel mutato contesto politico e territoriale dell'età francese* = *Storia dell'industria lombarda*, vol. 1, *Dal Settecento all'unità politica*, Sergio ZANINELLI (ed.), Edizioni Il Polifilo, Milano, 1988, 103–197.

Antonino DE FRANCESCO: *L'Italia di Bonaparte. Politica, statualità e nazione nella penisola tra due rivoluzioni, 1796–1821*, Utet, Torino, 2011.

Michele DE JORIO: *La giurisprudenza del commercio umiliata a s. m. Ferdinando* IV, vol. 1–4, nella Stamperia Simoniana, Napoli, 1799.

*Dei motivi del codice di commercio ovvero discorsi pronunciati al corpo legislativo di Francia dagli oratori del Consiglio di stato, e del Tribunato intorno al progetto della nuova legislazione commerciale. Traduzione italiana*, dalla tipografia di Francesco Sonzogno di Gio. Batt. stampatore e librajo ..., Milano, 1809.

Gaetano DEL RE: *Analisi della giurisdizione commerciale delle leggi di eccezione per gli affari di commercio, per lo Regno delle Due Sicilie, corredata di formole per i dovuti atti*, dai torchi di Luca Marotta, Napoli, 1823.

*Decisiones Rotae Genuae de mercatura et pertinentibus ad eam*, [Francesco Ziletti], Venetiis, 1582.

Claude-Alphonse DELANGLE: *Delle società di commercio. Opera confrontata coi trattati di Troplong, Vincens ... ; prima versione italiana dell'avv. Giuseppe D'Angelo, con annotazioni*, presso Andrea Santini e figlio, Venezia, 1851.

Claude Etienne DELVINCOURT: *Institutes de droit commercial français avec des notes explicatives du texte*, vol. 1–2, chez l'Auteur aux Ecoles de Droit ; Rondonneau et Decle, au Dépôt des Lois; Durand, Libraire; Eberhart, Imprimeur-Libraire, Paris, 1810.

Claude Etienne Delvincourt: *Istituzioni di diritto commerciale con annotazioni*, vol. 1–3, Dalla stamperia francese, Napoli, 1828.

Ettore Dezza: *Il Codice di procedura penale del Regno Italico (1807) : storia di un decennio di elaborazione legislativa*, Cedam, Padova, 1983.

Ettore Dezza: *Le fonti del codice di procedura penale del Regno italico*, Giuffrè, Milano, 1985.

Ettore Dezza: *Lezioni di Storia della codificazione civile. Il Code civil (1804) e l'Allgemeines Bürgerliches Gesetzbuch (ABGB, 1812)*, Giappichelli, Torino, 2000.

Maria Gigliola, di Renzo Villata: *Introduzione. La formazione del giurista in Italia e l'influenza culturale europea tra sette ed ottocento. Il caso della Lombardia* = *Formare il giurista. Esperienze nell'area lombarda tra Sette e Ottocento*, Maria Gigliola di Renzo Villata (ed.), Giuffrè, Milano, 2004, 1–105.

Charles Donahue, Jr.: *Benvenuto Stracca's De Mercatura: was there a Lex mercatoria in Sixteenth-Century Italy?* = *From lex mercatoria to commercial law, Comparative Studies in Continental and Anglo-America Legal History*, Vito Piergiovanni (ed.), vol. 24, Duncker and Humblot, Berlin, 2005, 69–120.

*Dubbii e controversie in materie di commercio ultimamente agitate, e decise dalle primarie corti, e tribunali di Francia e d'Italia: opera dedicata ai signori giudici, avvocati, e negozianti*, Dalla Tipografia Trani, Napoli, 1838.

Thomas Duve: *European Legal History – Concepts, Methods, Challenges* = *Entanglements in Legal History. Conceptual Approaches*, Thomas Duve (ed.), Max Planck Institute for European Legal History Open Access Publication, Frankfurt a.M., 2014, 29–66.

Thomas Duve: *Introductory remarks* = *Entanglements in Legal History. Conceptual Approaches*, Thomas Duve (ed.), Max Planck Institute for European Legal History Open Access Publication, Frankfurt a.M., 2014, 3–25.

Balthazard-Marie Emerigon: *Traité des assurances et des contrats a la grosse*, vol. 1–2, chez Jean Mossy, imprimeur du Roi, de la Marine, et Libraire, à la Canebière, Marseille, 1783.

Riccardo Ferrante: *Codification and lex mercatoria: the maritime law of the second book of the Code de commerce (1807)* = *From lex mercatoria to commercial law, Comparative Studies in Continental and Anglo-America Legal History*, vol. 24, Vito Piergiovanni (ed.), Duncker and Humblot, Berlin, 2005, 121–141.

Riccardo Ferrante: *Dans l'ordre établi par le Code civil. La scienza del diritto al tramonto dell'illuminismo giuridico*, Giuffrè, Milano, 2002.

Riccardo Ferrante: *Università e cultura giuridica a Genova tra Rivoluzione e Impero*, Atti della Società Ligure di Storia Patria, Genova, 2002.

Johannes W. Flume: *Law and Commerce. The Evolution of Codified Business Law in Europe*, Comparative Legal History 2(2014), 45–83.

Lena FOLJANTY: *Legal Transfers as Cultural Translation. On the Consequences of a Metaphor*, Max Planck Institute for European Legal History research paper series No. 2015–09.

Lena FOLJANTY: *Translators: Mediators of Legal Transfers*, Rechtsgeschichte – Legal History 24(2016), 120–121.

*La formazione del primo Stato italiano e* Milano capitale*, 1802–1814*, Adele ROBBIATI BIANCHI (ed.), Istituto lombardo Accademia di scienze e lettere, Milano, 2006.

Anthoine de Saint-Joseph, FORTUNÉ: *Concordanza fra i codici di commercio stranieri ed il codice di commercio francese: opera contenente il testo dei codici e delle leggi commerciali di 44 stati...*; prima trad. italiana con annotazioni e con un'appendice relativa all'attuale legislazione commerciale dell'Impero d'Austria e del Regno Lombardo-Veneto, Dalla premiata Tip. di Pietro Naratovich Edit., Venezia, 1855.

Maura FORTUNATI: *Baldasseroni, Pompeo* = *Dizionario biografico dei giuristi italiani* (XII–XX *secolo*), Italo BIROCCHI, Ennio CORTESE, Antonello MATTONE, Marco Nicola MILETTI (eds.), vol. 1, Il Mulino, Bologna, 2013, 147–148.

Maura FORTUNATI: *Un progetto di codificazione commerciale nella Roma di Pio* IX. *Antonio Fabi ed il suo 'Codice di commercio per lo Stato pontificio'* = *Itinerari in comune. Ricerche di storia del diritto per Vito Piergiovanni*, Giuffrè, Milano, 2011.

FOURNIEL, Béatrice: *L'influence à l'étranger du code de commerce français aux* XIX*e et* XX*e siècles: du declin du droit commercial français à l'emergence d'un droit des affaires francophone* = *Qu'en est-il du Code de Commerce 200 ans après ? Etats des lieux et projections*, Corinne SAINT-ALARY-HOUIN (ed.), Presses de l'Université des Sciences Sociales de Toulouse, Toulouse, 2009, 57–74.

Saverio GENTILE: *L'applicazione del Code de commerce in Calabria e l'emersione di un interessante tassello inedito relativo alla Commissione di Murat del 1814*, Historia et ius (historiaetius.eu) 5(2014), paper 5.

Saverio GENTILE: *Gli ultimi fuochi dei napoleonidi. Il progetto di revisione della codificazione francese a Napoli (1814)*, Jovene, Napoli, 2015.

Carlo GHISALBERTI: *Le costituzioni giacobine (1796–1799)*, Giuffrè, Milano, 1957.

Carlo GHISALBERTI: *Unità nazionale e unificazione giuridica in Italia*, Laterza, Roma-Bari, 1979.

Stefania GIALDRONI: *Tractatus de mercatura seu mercatore, 1553, Benvenuto Stracca (Straccha) (1509–1578)* = *The formation and transmission of Western legal culture. 150 books that made the law in the age of printing*, Serge DAUCHY, Georges MARTYN, Anthony MUSSON, Heikki PIHLAJAMÄKI, Alain WIJFELLS (eds.), Springer, Cham, 2016, 96–99.

Antonio GRILLI: *Il difficile amalgama. Giustizia e codici nell'Europa di Napoleone*, Vittorio Klostermann, Frankfurt a.M., 2012.

Jean-Louis, HALPÉRIN: *A proposito di alcune difficoltà nell'applicazione dei codici napoleonici nei dipartimenti francesi d'Italia = Giuseppe Luosi, giurista italiano ed europeo. Traduzioni, tradizioni e tradimenti della codificazione. A duecento anni dalla traduzione in italiano del Code Napoléon (1806–2006)*, Elio TAVILLA (ed.), Edizioni APM, Modena, 2009, 265–274.

Johann Gottlieb, HEINECKE: *Elementa juris cambialis commoda auditoribus methodo adornata*, sumptibus Balleonianis, Rovereto, 1746.

Johann Gottlieb HEINECKE: *Elementi della giurisprudenza sul cambio mercantile… / dalla latina in lingua italiana trad. dall'avv. E. Cesarini*, G. Ferretti, Roma, 1838.

Jean HILAIRE: *Droit du commerce et influences européennes dans le système juridique français*, Droits, 14(1991), 39–48.

Jean HILAIRE: *Jean-Marie Pardessus = Dictionnaire historique des juristes français* (XI-Ie–XXe siècle), Paris, Puf, 2015, 793–795.

Jean HILAIRE: *Introduction historique au droit commercial*, Paris, Puf, 1986.

Jean HILAIRE: *Le droit les affaires e l'histoire*, Paris, Economica, 1995.

*Il codice marittimo del 1781 di Michele De Jorio per il Regno di Napoli*, Cesare Maria MOSCHETTI (ed.), vol. 1–2, Giannini editore, Napoli, 1979.

*Il consolato del mare nel quale si comprendono tutti gli statuti, et ordini, disposti da gli antichi, per ogni caso di mercantia et di navigare … Con l'aggiunta delle ordinationi sopra l'armate di* mare, *sicurtà, entrate, et uscite*, appresso Daniel Zanetti, & compagni, Venetia, 1576.

Anne LEFEBVRE-TEILLARD: *Cambacérès et le code de commerce = Le code de commerce 1807–2007. Livre du bicentenaire*, Dalloz. Paris, 2007, 3–17.

Aurelio LEPRE: *Storia del Mezzogiorno d'Italia*, vol. 2, *Dall'Antico Regime alla società borghese (1657–1869)*, Liguori, Napoli, 1986.

Jean-Guillaume, LOCRÈ: *Spirito del Codice commerciale ossia Commentario desunto dai processi verbali del Consiglio di Stato, dalle esposizioni dei Motivi e Discorsi … e Complemento del Codice di commercio … Versione italiana*, 9 vol., dalla tipografia di Francesco Sonzogno di Gio. B., Milano, 1811–1820.

Gaetano MARRÉ: *Corso di diritto commerciale*, presso Fraticelli e c., Firenze, 1840.

Virginie MARTIN: *Éduquer, civiliser, dominer ? Le rôle de Gérando dans l'annexion de la Toscane et des États pontificaux (1808–1810) = Joseph-Marie de Gérando (1772–1842): connaître et réformer la société*, Jean-Luc CHAPPEY, Carole CHRISTEN, Igor MOULLIER (eds.), PUR, Rennes, 2014, 129–142.

Francesco MASTROBERTI: *Codificazione e giustizia penale nelle Sicilie dal 1808 al 1820*, Jovene, Napoli, 2001.

Aldo MAZZACANE: *A jurist for united Italy: the training and culture of Neapolitan lawyers in the nineteenth century = Society and the Professions in Italy 1860–1914*, Maria

THE ITALIAN DESTINY OF THE FRENCH *CODE DE COMMERCE*  139

MALATESTA (ed.), Adrian BELTON (trans.), Cambridge University Press, Cambridge (UK), 1995, 80–110.

Ferdinando MAZZARELLA: *Un diritto per l'Europa industriale. Cultura giuridica ed economia dalla Rivoluzione francese al Secondo Dopoguerra*, Giuffrè, Milano, 2016.

Melchiorre ROBERTI: *Milano capitale napoleonica. La formazione di uno Stato moderno 1796–1814*, vol. 2, Fondazione Treccani degli Alfieri, Milano, 1947.

Laura MOSCATI: *Dopo e al di là del Code de commerce: l'apporto di Jean-Marie Pardessus = Negozianti e imprenditori: 200 anni dal Code de commerce*, Mondadori, Milano, 2008, 47–80.

*Napoleone e la Repubblica Italiana, 1802–1805*, Carlo CAPRA, Franco DELLA PERUTA, Fernando MAZZOCCA (eds.), Skira, Milano, 2002.

Philippe NELIDOFF: *La naissance de la doctrine commercialiste au XIXe siècle = Qu'en est-il du Code de Commerce 200 ans après ? Etats des lieux et projections*, Corinne SAINT-ALARY-HOUIN (ed.), Presses de l'Université des Sciences Sociales de Toulouse, Toulouse, 2009, 39–56.

*Nuovo dizionario di diritto commerciale ossia riassunto di legislazione, di dottrina e di giurisprudenza di Devilleneuve e Masse: opera utilissima ai forensi, ai commercianti ed altre persone di affari; versione italiana a cura di Francesco Foramiti*, nel premiato stab. di G. Antonelli, Venezia, 1843.

Antonio PADOA-SCHIOPPA: *La genesi del codice di commercio del 1882* = Antonio PADOA-SCHIOPPA: *Saggi di storia del diritto commerciale*, Led, Milano, 1992, 157–203.

Antonio PADOA-SCHIOPPA: *Le società commerciali nei progetti di codificazione del Regno Italico (1806–1807)* = Antonio PADOA-SCHIOPPA: *Saggi di storia del diritto commerciale*, Led, Milano, 1992, 113–135.

Antonio PADOA-SCHIOPPA: *Napoleone e il "Code de commerce"* = Antonio PADOA-SCHIOPPA: *Saggi di storia del diritto commerciale*, Led, Milano, 1992, 89–112.

Antonio PADOA-SCHIOPPA: *Franckreich, Handelsrecht = Handbuch der Quellen und Literatur der neureren europäischen Privatrechtsgeschichte*, Helmut COING (ed.), vol. 3/3, Beck, München, 1986, 3152–3187.

Antonio PADOA-SCHIOPPA: *Italien, Handelsrecht =, Handbuch der Quellen und Literatur der neureren europäischen Privatrechtsgeschichte*, Helmut COING (ed.), vol. 3/3, Beck, München, 1986, 3209–3233.

Jean-Marie PARDESSUS: *Corso di diritto commerciale ... recato dal francese in italiano sulla sesta ed ultima edizione di Parigi ... per l'avvocato Francesco Galiani*, Stabilimento Tipografico, Napoli, 1858.

Jean-Marie PARDESSUS: *Trattato del contratto e delle lettere di cambio dei biglietti a ordine ed altri effetti di commercio secondo i principi de' nuovi codici ...Versione italiana*, vol. 1–2, dalla stamperia e fonderia di G.G. Destefanis, Milano, 1811.

Gian Savino, PENE VIDARI: *Consolati di commercio e Tribunali commerciali = Dal Trono all'Albero della Libertà. Trasformazioni e continuità istituzionali nei territori del Regno di Sardegna dall'antico regime all'età rivoluzionaria*, vol. 1, Ministero per i Beni culturali e ambientali, Roma, 1991, 220–254.

Gian Savino, PENE VIDARI: *Nota sull'inizio dell'insegnamento del diritto commerciale all'Università di Torino*, Bollettino storico-bibliografico subalpino, 95(1997), 511–531.

Gian Savino, PENE VIDARI: *Ricerche sulla giurisdizione commerciale negli Stati sabaudi*, Bollettino storico-bibliografico subalpino, 76(1978), 435–566.

Gian Savino, PENE VIDARI: *Tribunali di Commercio e codificazione commerciale Carloalbertina*, Rivista di storia del diritto italiano, 46–47(1971–1972), 27–124.

Piergiorgio PERUZZI: *Progetto e vicende di un Codice civile della repubblica italiana (1802–1805)*, Giuffrè, Milano, 1971.

Carlos PETIT: *Historia del derecho mercantil*, Marcial Pons, Madrid, 2016.

Ugo PETRONIO: *Un diritto nuovo con materiali antichi: il Code de commerce fra tradizione e innovazione = Negozianti e imprenditori: 200 anni dal Code de commerce*, Mondadori, Milano, 2008, 1–45.

Vito PIERGIOVANNI: *Courts and Commercial Law at the Beginning of the Modern Age = The Courts and the Development of Commercial Law, Comparative Studies in Continental and Anglo-America Legal History*, vol. 2, Vito PIERGIOVANNI (ed.), Duncker and Humblot, Berlin, 1987, 11–21.

Vito PIERGIOVANNI: *Dottrina, divulgazione e pratica alle origini della scienza commercialistica: Giuseppe Lorenzo Maria Casaregi, appunti per una biografia*, Materiali per una storia della cultura giuridica, 9(1979), 289–327.

Vito PIERGIOVANNI: *La 'Spiegazione' del Consolato del mare di Giuseppe Lorenzo Maria Casaregi*, Materiali per una storia della cultura giuridica, 36(2006), 15–27.

Vito PIERGIOVANNI: *The Rise of the Genoese Civil Rota in the XVIth Century: The 'Decisones de mercatura' Concerning Insurance = The Courts and the Development of Commercial Law, Comparative Studies in Continental and Anglo-America Legal History*, vol. 2, Vito PIERGIOVANNI (ed.), Duncker and Humblot, Berlin, 1987, 23–38.

Alain PILLEPICH: *Napoleone e gli italiani*, Il Mulino, Bologna, 2005.

Xavier PRÉVOST: *Jacques Cujas (1522–1590), jurisconsulte humaniste*, Librairie Droz, Genève, 2015.

Filippo RANIERI: *Projet du Code civil de la Republique Romaine (1798). Paris, Bibl. Nat., Nouv. acq. fr. 21892*, Vittorio Klostermann, Frankfurt a.M., 1976.

*Richterliche Anwendung des Code civil in seinen europäischen Geltungsbereichen außerhalb Frankreichs*, Barbara DÖLEMEYER, Heinz MOHNHAUPT, Alessandro SOMMA (eds.), Vittorio Klostermann, Frankfurt a.M., 2006.

Georges RIPERT: *Aspects juridiques du capitalisme moderne*, Librarie générale de droit et de jurisprudence, Paris, 1946.

THE ITALIAN DESTINY OF THE FRENCH *CODE DE COMMERCE* 141

Umberto SANTARELLI: *Mercanti e società tra mercanti*, Giappichelli, Torino, 1998.

Jacques SAVARY: *Le parfait négociant, ou instruction générale pour ce qui regarde le commerce des marchandises de France, et des pays étrangers*, 2 voll., chez la veuve Estienne et fils, Paris, 1749–1753.

Rodolfo SAVELLI: *Between Law and Morals: Interest in the Dispute on Exchanges during the 16th Century = The Courts and the Development of Commercial Law, Comparative Studies in Continental and Anglo-America Legal History*, vol. 2, Vito PIERGIOVANNI (ed.), Duncker and Humblot, Berlin, 1987, 39–102.

Sigismondo SCACCIA: *Tractatus de commerciis, et cambio*, sumptibus Andreae Brugiotti, ex typographia Iacobi Mascardi, Romae, 1619.

Alberto SCIUMÈ: *Progetti legislativi tendenze dottrinali e prassi in tema di fallimento nell'Italia napoleonica = Confluences des droits savants et des pratiques juridiques, Actes du colloque de Montpellier (12–14 décembre 1977)*, Giuffrè, Milano, 1979, 549–578.

Alberto SCIUMÈ: *I progetti del codice di commercio del Regno italico (1806–1808)*, Giuffrè, Milano, 1999.

Alberto SCIUMÈ: *I tentativi per la codificazione del diritto commerciale nel Regno italico (1806–1808)*, Giuffrè, Milano, 1982.

Mario STELLA RICHTER Jr., *Ascarelli, Tullio = Il contributo italiano alla storia del Pensiero – Diritto*, Istituto della Enciclopedia Italiana, Roma, 2012, 707–711.

Benvenuto STRACCA: *De mercatura, seu mercatore tractatus*, Paolo Manuzio, Venetiis, 1553.

Giovanni TARELLO: *Storia della cultura giuridica moderna*, vol. 1: *Assolutismo e codificazione del diritto*, Il Mulino, Bologna, 1976.

Carlo TARGA: *Ponderazioni sopra la contrattazione marittima*, nella stamperia di Gio. Paolo Fantechi e compagni, Livorno, 1755.

Massimo TITA: *De Jorio, Michele = Dizionario biografico dei giuristi italiani (XII–XX secolo)*, vol. 1, Italo BIROCCHI, Ennio CORTESE, Antonello MATTONE, Marco Nicola MILETTI (eds.), vol. 1, Il Mulino, Bologna, 2013, 683–684.

Massimo TITA: *Il giudizio dei pari. La giurisdizione commerciale a Roma e a Napoli tra Sette e Ottocento*, Arti Grafiche la Regione, Campobasso, 2012.

Paolo UNGARI: *Profilo storico del diritto delle anonime in Italia*, Bulzoni, Roma, 1974.

*Le università napoleoniche. Uno spartiacque nella storia italiana ed europea dell'istruzione superiore*, Piero DEL NEGRO, Luigi PEPE (eds.), Clueb, Bologna, 2008.

Angela VALENTE: *Giacchino Murat e l'Italia meridionale*, Einaudi, Torino, 1965.

Fabien VALENTE: *La naissance du Code de commerce napoléonien = Qu'en est-il du Code de Commerce 200 ans après ? Etats des lieux et projections*, Corinne SAINT-ALARY-HOUIN (ed.), Presses de l'Université des Sciences Sociales de Toulouse, Toulouse, 2009, 15–37.

René Josué VALIN: *Nouveau commentaire sur l'ordonnance de la marine, du mois d'août 1681*, vol. 1–2, chez Jerôme Legier, La Rochelle, 1766.

Franz WIEACKER: *A history of private law in Europe: with particular reference to Germany*, Tony WEIR (transl.), Reinhard ZIMMERMANN (foreword), Clarendon Press, Oxford, 1995.

Carlo ZAGHI: *L'Italia di* Napoleone *dalla Cisalpina al Regno*, Utet, Torino, 1986.

Giorgio ZORDAN: *Il codice per la Veneta Mercantile Marina*, Cedam, Padova, 1981.

CHAPTER 6

# The Reception of the French Commercial Code in Nineteenth-Century Polish Territories: A Hollow Legal Shell

*Anna Klimaszewska*

## 1 Introduction[1]

In his 1902 speech to the American Bar Association, Sir Mackenzie Chalmers said:

> A code should be founded on a firm basis of experience. You then know what you are doing. A practical and working code cannot spring from the head of the draftsman, as Pallas Athene is fabled to have sprung, fully equipped, from the head of her father Zeus. In legislation, as in other sciences, the "a priori" road is a dangerous one to tread. When the principles of law are well settled, and when the decided cases that accumulate are mere illustrations of accepted general rules, then the law is ripe for codification. A code can usefully settle disputed points, and fill up small lacunae in the law, but it should always have its feet on the ground. If you go above and beyond experience, you are codifying in the air, and will probably do more harm than good to commerce and mercantile law.[2]

These words entail a metaphor which applies perfectly to what happened in the Polish territories in the early 19th century in commercial law. From the head of the Polish legislator, admittedly somewhat forced by the circumstances, sprang, like Pallas Athene from the head of Zeus, the French *Code de commerce*. In 1807, Napoleon established the Duchy of Warsaw, as a result of which,

---

1 The present paper has been prepared under the project "Implementation of the Rules of French Commercial Law in the Duchy of Warsaw, the Constitutional Kingdom of Poland and the Republic of Krakow- *Code de Commerce* in Clash with the Polish Reality" financed by the National Science Centre (Narodowe Centrum Nauki) on the basis of decision no. DEC-2013/09/B/HS5/02617.

2 Mackenzie Dalzell CHALMERS: *Codification of Mercantile Law = Report of the Twenty-Fifth Annual Meeting of the American Bar Association held at Saratoga Springs, New York, August 27, 28 and 29, 1902*, Dando Printing and Publishing Company, Philadelphia, 1902, 283.

---

© KONINKLIJKE BRILL NV, LEIDEN, 2020 | DOI:10.1163/9789004417274_007

besides e.g. the Civil Code and the Code of Civil Procedure, the Commercial Code of 1807 was also promulgated. It was "thrown," however, into a legal reality whose character was feudal and, to a great extent, customary; a reality where no commercial code had existed before.

How, then, was its potential put to a use? Did the Polish legislator employ the *Code de commerce* consciously and purposely to change the existing economic reality? What was the reaction of the Polish society to the new institutions, which emerged suddenly, without time for gradual development? And what was the mechanism of adopting the French commercial law into Polish circumstances?

In trying to find the answers to these questions, I will focus on the reaction to the *Code de commerce* on three planes: the legislative (I), that of legal science (II) and that of application of law – the practical (III). Analysis of these will make it possible to understand whether the French Commercial Code served to modernise Polish reality.

## 2 Legislative Plane – Cracks in the Legal Shell

Despite the fact that the Commercial Code was formally adopted in 1809,[3] already nearly a year before (10 months), by virtue of the *Provisions concerning the organisation and attribution of judicial authorities and members of the judiciary* [hereinafter: *Provisions*] dated 23 May 1808, the application of certain provisions of the *Code de commerce* had been sanctioned, provided that the Civil Code of 1804 made reference to them.

Moreover, even though the adoption of the *Code de commerce* occurred without the reluctance articulated in regard to other French acts, it was also accompanied by an almost complete lack of interest, haste and the absence of any deeper reflection, which was visible along the entire legislative path. Already at the Council of State session in February 1809, the main focus was on the necessity to introduce the *Code de commerce* as an inseparable element and addition to the *Code civil* and on the problem of its effectiveness in relation to the aforementioned *Provisions*.[4] A report by Karol Fryderyk Woyda and

---

3   The *Code de commerce* was introduced in the Duchy of Warsaw based on a bill passed by the Sejm on 24 March 1809: *Prawo stanowiące przyjęcie Kodexu Handlowego Francuzkiego dla Księstwa Warszawskiego* [The Law on Adoption of the French Commercial Code in the Duchy of Warsaw], dated 24 March 1809, Dziennik Praw Księstwa Warszawskiego [Journal of Laws of the Duchy of Warsaw] (hereinafter: DPKW), vol. 1, 239;

4   Session 271 at the Royal Palace, held on 14 February 1809; *Protokoły Rady Stanu Księstwa Warszawskiego* [Minutes of the Council of State of the Duchy of Warsaw], Bronisław PAWŁOWSKI, Tadeusz MENCEL (eds.), TNT, Toruń, 1965, vol. 2/1, 84 et seq.

A HOLLOW LEGAL SHELL

Stanisław Staszic, recommending the adoption of the Code, excluding Book II (*Of maritime commerce*), was presented at the session held on 21 February 1809, to which the Council agreed "not having sufficient time to bring such a voluminous work before the Sejm for examination."[5] Once the draft was submitted to the Sejm, the core of substantive work was transferred to the Commission of Civil Legislation. It was appointed on 11 March, but its personnel composition changed subsequently.[6] And so, its permanent members had 8, and the newly appointed one 3 days (*sic*!) to acquaint themselves with the act that was to be adopted. On 19 March, copies of the draft were handed out to some deputies, while discussions over this draft were scheduled for the 20 March Chamber session. In the meantime, the position of the Council of State changed as regarded the draft contents. On 17 March, at the evening session no. 299 of the Council of State at the Royal Palace, based on establishments of the Minister of Justice Feliks Łubieński made with members of the Commission of Civil Legislation presented by the former and in the presence of the latter, it was decided that the *Code de commerce* would have to be implemented *en bloc* owing to the lack of an official translation.[7] What is more, Sejm deputies were mostly landed gentry, not much interested in this subject.[8] There were also many organisational problems: 48 copies of the draft were distributed among 107 deputies one day prior to its adoption and before voting only one commission member offered broader content-related remarks – Ignacy Stawiarski. Another commission member, Tomasz Byszewski, confused commercial matters with tax matters.[9]

Additional problems were generated by the fact that the Code was adopted officially, in its entirety, in the French language. It should be noted that, by the order of the Minister of Justice, Feliks Łubieński, the translation of the Code by Walenty Skorochód-Majewski was published in the year preceding its

---

5    *Ibid.*, 101. At session no. 289, held on 11 March 1809, the Council decided to bring the draft to the Sejm agenda in this shape, after having introduced only redaction corrections.

6    The originally appointed members of the commission were T. Byszewski, W. Lalewicz, M. Stokowski, S. Jarociński and I. Stawiarski, but at the sixth session, it was noted that W. Lalewicz and S. Jarociński would be unable to serve due to illness. They were replaced with M. Skrzypiński and A. Bielski. *Dyariusze Sejmów Księstwa Warszawskiego, zeszyt 1, Dziennik posiedzeń izby poselskiej sejmu r. 1809* [Sejm Transcripts of the Duchy of Warsaw, fascicule 1, Journal of the Sessions of the Sejm Deputy Chamber of 1809], Marceli Handelsman (ed.), nakł. Towarzystwa Naukowego Warszawskiego, E. Wende i s-ka, Warsaw, 1913, 16.

7    *Protokoły Rady Stanu...*, *op. cit.*, 177.

8    Fryderyk Skarbek: *Dzieje Księstwa Warszawskiego z przedmową Piotra Chmielowskiego* [History of the Duchy of Warsaw with a Preface by Piotr Chmielowski], Drukarnia Artystyczna Saturnina Sikorskiego, Warsaw, 1898, vol. 2, 109.

9    *Dyariusze Sejmów...*, *op. cit.*, 29–31.

adoption.[10] However, its quality left much to be desired; it was prepared in a great hurry and the author himself admitted having poor knowledge of commercial relations.[11] Missing also was any type of remark on the repealment of the heretofore binding rules and customs, both in the transitional provisions (unlike in the case of the Civil Code[12]), and in the Act that implemented the *Code de commerce* in the Duchy.[13]

Various institutions were not fully regulated in the code. Such issues were governed and developed in France by separate legal acts, not binding in the Polish territories,[14] and supported by the centuries-long output of *jurisprudence* (Fr.). In consequence, Polish entrepreneurs were left on their own with regard to numerous matters, which in turn resulted in a rather flexible approach to the norms of the Code. What is more, by the decision of 11 January 1817, issued by the *Namiestnik* (Viceroy) of the Kingdom of Poland as *Merchant Law* (*Urządzanie kupiectwa*),[15] whose authors not only ignored the fact that the

---

10   *Kodex handlowy z zlecenia JWgo Ministra Sprawiedliwości przetłumaczony przez Walentego Majewskiego wezwanego iako Notaryusza Publicznego* [Commercial Code Commissioned by the Minister of Justice and Translated by Walenty Majewski Called Upon as Notary Public], Druk. Zawadzkich, Warsaw, 1808.

11   *Ibid.*, Cf: preface.

12   Instruction from the Minister of Justice of 23 May 1808 r. Published, among others, in *Prawo cywilne obowiązujące w Królestwie Polskim* [Civil Law Binding in the Kingdom of Poland], Stanisław ZAWADZKI (ed.), nakł. wydawcy w druk. Karola Kowalewskiego, Warsaw, 1863, vol. 3, 347–348.

13   Supra n. 3.

14   E.g. those that regulated formalities in connection with issuing governmental permissions to set up stock companies (*sociétés anonymes*): Regulation of 21 December 1807 (*Règlement de son excellence le ministre de l'intérieur, du 21 décembre 1807, sur l'exécution de l'article 37 du Code de Commerce, relatif aux sociétés anonymes*) or ministerial circulars of 22 December 1817 and 9 April 1819, or the regulations of 19 March 1801, 19 April 1801 and 16 June 1802, that governed the issues of the stock exchange in France. The issue of the Warsaw Mercantile Exchange (*Giełda Kupiecka w Warszawie*) was not regulated until a decision was issued by the *Namiestnik* of the Kingdom of Poland on 12 April 1817. In the first years however, the indexes of the Mercantile Exchange contained only the listings of bills of exchange and of currencies. The first security introduced on the listings were covered bonds of the Land Credit Society (*Towarzystwo Kredytowe Ziemskie*) in the Kingdom of Poland. The first listed stocks were the stocks of Warsaw-Vienna Rail Road Company. They were, however, removed from the index in 1844, "as the company had not been effectively established" – it had not managed to raise enough capital to finance the costs of railway construction. Interest in the listing of stocks began in the 1870s, when sixteen companies began to trade their stock. The Act of 1872, which conferred much greater autonomy to the Mercantile Exchange, also contributed to its development.

15   Decision of the *Namiestnik* of the Kingdom of Poland dated 11 January 1817 (Merchant Law); *Dziennik Praw Królestwa Polskiego* [Journal of Laws of the Kingdom of Poland] (hereinafter referred to as: DPKP), vol. 4, 159–177.

A HOLLOW LEGAL SHELL

*Code de commerce* had been implemented in the territory of Poland and did not refer to it in any way, but also drafted provisions contrary to those of the *Code*, the corporate organisation of trade was introduced, as well as paid business licences. This was in clear opposition to the freedom of commercial activity expressed in the flagship Article 1 of the *Code de commerce*, according to which it was sufficient to conduct commerce and make it one's habitual profession (*Sont commerçants ceux qui exercent des actes de commerce, et en font leur profession habituelle*).

All this points to the absence of a conscious and well-thought out strategy of the legislator as regards the use of what was a ready commercial act to shape Polish reality. It was noted, as the Minister of Justice Feliks Łubieński underscored, "how strongly commerce drives the enrichment of a country, how consolidated commerce anchored in law must thrive" (*jak daleko handel wpływa na zbogacenie kraju, jak handel ugruntowany i prawem dokładnie objęty koniecznie w górę iść musi*).[16] At the same time, a number of circumstances made the adoption of the *Code de commerce* seem like a natural choice to the authorities.[17] Among said circumstances were the establishment of the Duchy of Warsaw as a French protectorate, the sudden necessity to build new state structures, the adoption of the *Code civil* (guaranteed by the Constitution), the growing political strength of Łubieński, who promoted French solutions (and who, despite protests, introduced the *Code de procédure civile* as effective in an unconstitutional mode), the absence of strong resistance to the French commercial act (which had subsequently led to the rejection of the *Code pénal* and the *Code d'instruction criminelle*). Nevertheless, chaos, haste, and the lack of content-related preparation in the course of legislative works resulted in that, instead of a French Commercial Code, whose contents was built and shaped not only by the sentences stipulating its provisions, but also the constantly growing body of laws related to the commercial law that existed outside of the code, the output of legal science and judicial decisions, the adopted act was damaged goods – a shell full of holes through which the contents could freely seep out.

---

16    *Dziennik posiedzeń..., op. cit.*, 29.

17    Jonathan M. Miller has coined the term *bricolage* to designate using whatever is available by legislators in going through with legal transplants, and by this term he means "[...] simply pasting together whatever one has at hand, and the results may appear to have ludicrously little link to the drafter's society, because the drafter did not take the time or lacked the technical competence to anchor the transplanted norm in local reality." Cf: Jonathan M. Miller: *A Typology of Legal Transplants: Using Sociology, Legal History and Argentine Examples to Explain the Transplant Process*, The American Journal of Comparative Law, 51(2003)/4, 845.

## 3     Legal Science[18]

Scholars exhibited a lack of interest in the introduction of the French Commercial Code. It was not until the 1840s that some animation could be observed, albeit a minimal one. The code was translated again, and its provisions were analysed also in reference to the additional French legislation[19] (not in force in the Polish territories), as well as the judicial decisions of French courts. The French commentaries were starting to be translated, too. The core of the discussion, however, revolved primarily around terminological doubts caused by the lack of Polish institutional equivalents and terminology.

The breakthrough moment as regards the interest of scholars in the commercial law did not arrive until the 1860s. From then on, 62 of the total of 82 publications ever issued in the 19th century Kingdom of Poland (i.e. 75.6%) appeared in the form of monographs, studies, articles, translations, reviews, lectures, collections of laws and judgements, etc.[20] Throughout the existence of the Duchy of Warsaw, five works concerning commercial law (6.09%) were published, and in the period of the constitutional Kingdom of Poland, a mere three short articles (3.66%). In the period of rule of Ivan Paskevich (1832–1856), known as "the night of Paskevich" owing to the intensified political repressions and economic sanctions of the Russian Empire toward the Kingdom of Poland following the fall of the November Uprising, twelve of them were published (14.63%).

The situation was similar in Galicia,[21] where six (8.45%) publications connected with the field of commercial law appeared in the years 1834–1856

---

18    This is the revised version of the research results that have been published in: Anna KLI-MASZEWSKA: *Influence of French legalese on the development of Polish legal language within the area of commercial law = Multilingualism and law*, Emőd VERESS (ed.), Sapientia Hungarian University of Transylvania – Forum Iuris – Robert Schumann Association, Cluj-Napoca – Kolozsvàr, 2016, 175–184.

19    This, for example, was the case of amendments to Art. 42 of the Commercial Code, introduced by way of the Act of 31 March 1833, of the law of 10 April 1825 on the safety of sailing and maritime trade or of the reform of the *Code de commerce* of 28 May 1838 regarding bankruptcies and insolvencies (gradual process of decodification of commercial law).

20    For full bibliography cf. Anna KLIMASZEWSKA: *Nauczanie i nauka prawa handlowego w okresie paskiewiczowskim* [Teaching and Science of Commercial Law in the Times of Ivan Paskevich] = *Królestwo Polskie w okresie namiestnictwa Iwana Paskiewicza (1832–1856). System polityczny, prawo i statut organiczny z 26 lutego 1832 r.* [The Kingdom of Poland During the Governorship of Ivan Paskevich; Political System, Law and Organic Statute of 26 February 1832], Lech MAŻEWSKI (ed.), von Borowiecky, Radzymin, 2015, 219–231.

21    It should be mentioned that from 1815–1855 the French Commercial Code was not binding in the entire territory of Galicia, but only in Krakow. The provisions which were applied in Galicia with regard to this area of law were issued for the German crown states, and also locally, by the administrative authorities of the Lvov Governorate.

A HOLLOW LEGAL SHELL 149

(including those on the Austrian Act on bills of exchange of 25 January 1850), while from the '60s onward (1863–1900), sixty-five items were published (91.55%).

In the part of Poland annexed by Prussia[22] only four titles were published, all of them in the second half of the 19th century (one in 1855, the remaining three in 1876, 1881 and 1899 respectively).

Can we say, then, that the *Code de commerce* provided an impulse for the development of commercial law science? It evidently did, but its impact was delayed. It is also difficult to find connections between the development of commercial law science and the political situation of Poland, since they were (as evidenced by the available data) completely independent of each other. The development of commercial law science was impaired neither by the repressive rule following the fall of the November Uprising, nor by the stricter policy enforced by the Russian Empire against Poland after the fall of the January Uprising in 1864. However, it should be noted that in the lands annexed by Prussia, where the Code never really took effect as it was promptly repealed, the Polish commercial law science did not really develop at all.

It should not be forgotten that commercial law, in contrast to other areas of law, was obviously regarded by censorship as a relatively safe area. Starting from the 1860s, we can observe significant progress in the knowledge displayed by individual authors with regard to foreign publications, commentaries, legislation and judicial decisions, not only of French origin. In Galicia, the majority of titles concerned Austrian, and sometimes German law; in the Kingdom of Poland, despite the fact that the French subject-matter was in the centre of attention there, works on German, Austrian, English, Russian and Swiss legal issues were written as well. There was also significant development with regard to the way in which individual institutions were understood and commented on, as there was much more flexibility and the scientific discussion was at a decidedly higher level than before. Despite the fact that the political conditions during the period of both the Duchy of Warsaw and the Constitutional Kingdom of Poland were much more favourable, the interest in commercial law was considerably hampered by lack of knowledge and fledgling terminology. However, it must be remembered that the authors writing in the second half of the 19th century had begun to study commercial law much earlier, and their publications were often the fruit of many years of explorations of this topic.

---

22    Where the *Code de commerce* was binding for only a few years and only in the territory constituting the Grand Duchy of Poznań established in 1815. After the fall of the Duchy of Warsaw, on 1 January 1816, the Code was repealed and the Prussian *Landrecht* was reinstated.

# 150 KLIMASZEWSKA

## 4 Plane of Application of *Code de commerce*

Thus, in a situation of a clear lack of preparation to adopt the *Code de commerce* on the part of both the legislator and of the representatives of legal science, what about the practice of application of law, especially in the first years after the code took effect? How did Polish merchants and entrepreneurs deal with this? How did the judges manage? These two issues should be separated:

(1) First of all, entrepreneurs, merchants, dealt with this situation in various ways. Part of commercial activities were transacted in full respect for the rules of *Code de commerce*,[23] but there were also numerous breaches of its norms, attesting to a fairly careless approach to its application.

For example, the protest at the demand of an enterprise operating under the business name of Piotr Steinkeller, drafted by the Krakow notary Antoni Matakiewicz in breach of a number of provisions of *Code de commerce*.[24] The obligation to use two notaries, or one notary and one court bailiff with two witnesses to participate jointly in the drawing of the protest (Art. 173) was not

---

23 One such positive example was certainly the contract concluded between Count Jan Nepomocen Kwilecki and Ludwik Hirschman and Jan Chryzostom Kijewski, which took effect on 1 January 1830. Archiwum Państwowe w Warszawie [State Archive in Warsaw] (hereinafter referred to as: APW), Kancelaria Aleksandra Engelke notariusza w Warszawie [Notary Office of Aleksander Engelke, notary in Warsaw], 39, 5358, 216–221v.

24 "At the demand of the trade here in Krakow under the business name of Piotr Steinkeller existing at Szczepańska Street [...] the Notary [...] set out to the trade of Franciszek Buchelt, Krakow merchant, to whom I presented the [...] bill of exchange of the following content, along with a demand for immediate payment, as he had accepted it on 25 June 1824 for payment within 4 weeks. [...] in response, Buchelt stated that he demanded an extension of another 8 days, as he is not at present able to pay this debt, while in a week's time he may pay at least a part thereof. As a result of this refusal to pay the bill, the undersigned notary, with a view to secure the return of capital, interest due, opportunities lost and possible costs that may arise on behalf of the executing trade, protested against such refusal in the name of his clients. The present deed of protest was drafted by [...]" („Na żądanie handlu tu w Krakowie pod firmą Piotr Steinkeller egzystującego a to przy ul. Szczepańskiej [...] Notariusz [...] udał się do handlu Franciszka Buchelt kupca krakowskiego, gdzie temuż [...] weksel osnowy następującej okazałem, z wezwaniem zapłacenia go natychmiast, gdy takowy przez niego jeszcze 25 czerwca 1824 roku do zapłacenia w 4 tygodniach akceptowany został. [...] w odpowiedzi Buchhelt oświadczył, iż żąda jeszcze mieć przedłużony termin do dni 8, gdyż na teraz nie jest w stanie zapłacić ten dług; za tydzień zaś przynajmniej część onego opłaci. W skutku w ten sposób odmówionej wypłaty wekslu podpisany notariusz w celu zabezpieczenia interesantom zwrotu kapitału, należnych procentów, straconych korzyści i ponieść się mogących kosztów, w imieniu handlu rekwirującego, przeciwko takowemu odmówieniu wypłaty wekslu protestował. Tegoż protestu akt niniejszy spisał [...]"). Archiwum Narodowe w Krakowie [National Archives in Krakow] (hereinafter: ANK), Akta notariusza Antoniego Matakiewicza w Krakowie [Archives of Notary in Krakow Antoni Matakiewicz], 40, notarial deed (n.d.) no. 23 of 26 January 1825.

A HOLLOW LEGAL SHELL

observed, as Matakiewicz went to see the drawee on his own. He demanded that the drawee pay the bill of exchange (issued on 25 June 1824, accepted for payment within four weeks, which lapsed on 23 July 1824) with a delay of over six months (23 January 1825 instead of 24 July 1824), thus breaching the provisions of Art. 161 and 162.

The companies law also presented many opportunities for abuse. It was common practice not to indicate the type of company established.[25] Not always were the formalities needed to set up the company satisfied.[26] Some very strange legal constructions were created, such as the one based on a contract concluded between a Warsaw merchant Józef Dyzmański, Teodor Weichhan and Ignacy Neumark,[27] whereas one party to the contract were Dyzmański and Weichhan jointly, and the other party was Neumark. The relations between Dyzmański and Weichhan were regulated by a non-terminated company deed from 1826, while the mutual rights and obligations of Dyzmański and Weichhan jointly towards Neurmark were governed by another company deed concluded in 1827. Pursuant to its contents, Neumark did not join the existing company, but established a whole new one with the other two men. "Profits and losses," based on this contract, were to be "enjoyed and borne in equal parts" by them on the one part and by Neumark on the other part.[28] Similarly "advances shall be provided by the parties as need may be and according to the speculations accepted by both parties, and the contingency taxes shall be borne by them proportionally to half of deposit."[29] Also "all profits received or possible to be received from the government shall belong in half to Ignacy Neumark and in half to Józef Dyzmański and Teodor Weichhan."[30]

Some very interesting material for analysis is provided by a contract concluded on 14 May 1826 between a Belgian entrepreneur, John Cockerill, and

---

25    E.g. APW, Kancelaria Teodora Czempińskiego notariusza w Warszawie [Notary's Office of Teodor Czempiński, Notary in Warsaw], 15, n.d. no. 1880 of 15 December 1813 or 60, n.d. no. 7761 of 11 February 1828, as well as APW, Kancelaria Jana Wincentego Bandtkie notariusza w Warszawie [Notary's Office of Jan Wincenty Bandtkie, Notary in Warsaw] 52ª, n.d. no. 5121 of 7 June 1826 or 64, n.d. no. 5312 of 23 March 1827.

26    E.g. company set up between "Krystian Bichterl, a citizen [...] of Krakow [...] and Wojciech Konrady producer of candles and soap"; ANK, Akta Wolnego Miasta Krakowa [Archives of the Free City of Krakow] (hereinafter: AWMK), WM 236, 143–164.

27    APW, Notary's Office of Jan Wincenty Bandtkie, notary in Warsaw, 54ª, 5312, 40–47v.

28    *Ibid.*, 43v.

29    „[...] awansów równie dostarczać powinny strony w miarę potrzeby i spekulacji przez obydwie strony uznanej, również do liwerunków po połowie kaucji stanić mają." *Ibid.*

30    „[...] wszelkie korzyści uzyskane i uzyskać się mogące od rządu należeć będą w połowie Ignacego Neumarka, a w drugiej połowie do Józefa Dyzmańskiego i Teodora Weichhana." *Ibid.*, 43v–44.

Counsellor of State Franciszek Ksawery Kossecki.[31] The company "established with the purpose of setting up a wool spinning mill and a textile factory in Przedbórz [...] [was to be] run as a limited partnership (commandite partnership) between John Cockerill and Xawery Kossecki"[32] in such a way that

> partners shall remain [solely] simple partners, with no liability beyond the share capital contributed to the partnership by each of them, and without any liability for the partnership being secured by their personal liability, real property or chattels [...], nor even by any valuables or credits, which remain separate and divisible from the partnership and whose disposal and administration the parties reserve as their own.[33]

Therefore, the status of Cockerill and Kossecki was clearly established as the status of limited partners (*commanditaires*), while – as should be emphasized – they were the only partners mentioned in the concluded contract. The problem consisted in that a limited partnership required a general partner (*associé responsable et solidaire*), an issue precisely stipulated in Art. 23 of the French Commercial Code. Meanwhile, the contract between Cockerill and Kossecki did not stipulate the establishment of a partner who would secure the partnership's liabilities with his personal assets without limitation. What is more, the same Art. 23 also provided that the business name of a limited partnership could only be formed of the names of general partners. From the relevant notary's deed it follows, however, that the company set up between Cockerill and Kossecki would be run "under the trade name of Karol Ludwik Hamann and Co."[34] – a proxy of Cockerill in the signing of this contract, who was to act in the capacity of a plant director in Przedbórz, against a salary and the obligation to submit quarterly balance sheet and activity reports.[35] Moreover, the contract clearly expressed the intention for Cockerill to act in a managerial

---

31    APW, Notary's Office of Jan Wincenty Bandtkie, notary in Warsaw, 52ª, 5110, 23–48v.

32    „[...] umówiona względem założenia przędzalni wełny i fabryki sukna w Przedborzu [...] prowadzić się [miała] sposobem komandytowym ze strony Johna Cockerilla i ze strony Xawerego Kosseckiego." *Ibid.*, 25v.

33    „[...] wspólnicy są i zostawać będą [jedynie] prostymi komandytariuszami, bez żadnej innej odpowiedzialności, jak tylko jedynie tej, które nadają ich kapitały zakładowe, do współki tej przez każdego z nich wniesione, tudzież bez obowiązku odpowiadania w jakikolwiek inny sposób za zobowiązania dotyczące, ani zatem osobami swymi, ani majątkami i mieniem swym [...], ani nawet wartością lub kredytem jakimkolwiek, które i owszem zupełnie pozostaną odrębnymi i oddzielnymi od niniejszej współki i których tedy zupełnie wolne urządzenie i użycie warują sobie wzajemnie." *Ibid.*, 26–26v.

34    *Ibid.*, 25v.

35    APW, Notary's Office of Jan Wincenty Bandtkie, notary in Warsaw, 52ª, 5110, 28.

A HOLLOW LEGAL SHELL

capacity, from which limited partners were clearly barred by Art. 27 of the *Code de commerce*.[36] The construction adopted by Cockerill and Kossecki, characterized by partners liable only up to the limit of the contribution made, with a management board or, as in this case, a director appointed for its management and reporting on the handled matters, was typical of a stock company (*société anonyme*) in the French code. Pursuant to Art. 31 stock company "is managed by agents or directors, who are either stockholders or not, with or without salary, and removable from office at a certain period,"[37] which matched the role and function of Karol Ludwik Hamman as stipulated in the company's articles of association. However, the requirement of this type of company to have a government-issued authorisation, revocable at any time, discouraged entrepreneurs in France as well.[38]

The discussed articles of association were so starkly contradictory to the provisions of the French Commercial Code that its interpretation without fail leads to the suspicion of intentionality not only of the parties, aiming to circumvent these provisions, especially since Cockerill had been accused of all types of fraud and unlawful activities on the market of Congress Poland. Significant within this context is the participation of the well-connected Franciszek Ksawery Kossecki. Any coincidences are highly doubtful, as is a lack of knowledge of the acting notary regarding the contents of a law which had been in effect for over seventeen years, regardless of whether this was Jan Wincenty Bandtkie himself – Dean of the School of Law and Administration and of the Faculty of Law and Administration of the Royal University of Warsaw (!), or another employee of such a fine office. The same applies to the witnesses to the conclusion of the articles of association: Karol Księżyk, merchant and

---

36   In the event of breaching the prohibition of a limited partner acting as a management board, stipulated in Art. 27 – and such intention was clearly stated in the articles of association as regarded Cockerill – and his representation of the Company's interests even on the basis of a power of attorney, the French code provided for an extension of his liability to that of a general partner (Art. 28). In France, the reform within this scope did not take place until the adoption of the Act of 6 May 1863 (Loi qui modifie les art. 27 et 28 du Code du commerce), published in: *Collection complète des lois, décrets, ordonnances, règlements et avis du Conseil d'État (de 1788 à 1836 inclusivement, par ordre chronologique), publiée sur les éditions officielles, continuée depuis 1836 et formant un volume chaque année*, Jean Baptiste DUVERGIER (ed.), Charles Noblet, Paris, 1863, vol. 63, 214–228.

37   John RODMAN: *The Commercial Code of France, with the Motives, or Discourses of the Counsellors of State, Delivered before the Legislative Body, Illustrative of the Principles and Provisions of the Code, Translated from the French, with Explanatory Notes, and a Complete Analytical Index*, C. Wiley, New York, 1814, 95.

38   Cf: Jean HILAIRE: *Introduction historique au droit commercial*, Presses Universitaires de France, Paris, 1986, 213–243.

judge of the Commercial Tribunal and Jan Dawid Ebert, Secretary of the State Council (who additionally acted, as clearly stated, in the capacity of an interpreter,[39] from which it follows that he spoke French). It also merits a mention that Karol Księżyk was also a witness to the conclusion of the contract between Neumark and Dyzmański and Weichhan.[40] This seems to confirm the hypothesis that the notary's office of Bandtkie was consciously used to circumvent the provisions of the Commercial Code, which is attested to, besides the discussed contracts, by the notary deed no. 5465 drafted on 27 November 1827 (file no. 55a), which directly cites articles of the *Code de commerce* right next to provisions of the company deed that are in clear opposition to them.

(2) What was the situation as regards the application of the French Commercial Code by courts?

Many issues aroused doubts and disputes in France itself, not to mention the Polish territories, especially since the Polish ruling judges, unlike was the case in France, in the event of any uncertainty, could not avail themselves of the rich *jurisprudence* (Fr.), of the doctrine's output or of the constantly growing body of laws related to the commercial law, which was not received in Poland along with the Code.

The case files I have gone through so far indicate a number of issues as follows. First of all, it is not possible to recreate the full picture of the activities of the Polish judiciary within this scope, owing to the incomplete court files held in Polish archives. The only surviving records are those of the Kalisz Civil Tribunal[41] (*Archiwum Główne Akt Dawnych* [AGAD], Central Archives of Historical Records), and court records of the Free City of Krakow (ANK), as well as records of commercial cases adjudicated by the Civil Tribunal in Bydgoszcz, which had been left without examination upon the collapse of the Duchy of Warsaw, and which still had to be resolved pursuant to the provisions of *Code de commerce* when the Bydgoszcz region constituted part of the Prussian state. The rest have been destroyed. The files of Commercial Tribunals which operated in the Polish territories[42] no longer exist. Therefore, generally the activities

---

39    APW, Notary's Office of Jan Wincenty Bandtkie, notary in Warsaw, 52ª, 5110, 48v.

40    He has also collaborated with Bandtkie on many other occasions. For example, in the drafting of the articles of association of a company whose purpose was to produce cast iron and build machines in Warsaw, set up by Tomasz Moore Evans, Józef Morris and Andrzej Birch Evans, dated 10 October 1823, published in: *Rocznik warszawski*, 2(1961), 334–338.

41    They also contain a few cases examined by the Commercial Tribunal of the Kalisz Department before it was closed.

42    From 1815, only the Commercial Tribunal in Warsaw was included in the budget draft of the Kingdom of Poland. In the remaining areas, commercial cases were examined by Civil

A HOLLOW LEGAL SHELL

of professional judges, and not of merchants who also adjudicated in Commercial Tribunals, may be subject to assessment. It must be also emphasized that it is difficult to directly trace the train of thought followed by the court in any given case, as the case files do not provide reasons for judgment; they only hold argumentations of the parties and the ruling. Thus, it allows us only to deduce, although with high probability, which arguments of the parties the ruling judges found convincing.

One of the most interesting examples were the judgements of the Appellate Court of the Free, Independent and Strictly Neutral City of Krakow (*Sąd Apelacyjny Wolnego, Niepodległego i Ściśle Neutralnego Miasta Krakowa*) regarding the jurisdiction of commercial tribunals, to which the appellate court referred in connection with the activities of the coal mines in the town of Dąbrowa.

In 1816 – seven years after the implementation of the *Code de commerce* in the central territories[43] and six years after its binding force was extended also to the newly-incorporated post-Galician departments[44] – a case was filed with a court concerning the partners in the Dąbrowska Coal Company.[45] The case, among other issues, referred to the lack of jurisdiction of the Commercial Tribunal that had examined it in the first instance, connected on the one hand with the absence of commercial character of sales of the extracted coal, and on the other hand with the fact that the partners in said company did not have the status of traders (*commerçants*). The representatives of the parties exchanged various interpretations of individual articles in the French Commercial Code in their argumentation,[46] yet the crux of the problem was that its provisions did not address this issue directly. The code lacked a legal definition of commercial acts; it only listed a catalogue of such in Book IV (Of Commercial jurisdiction), Title II (Of the Competency of the Tribunals of Commerce), which enumerated, among others, the purchase of goods with the purpose of their resale or enterprise of manufactures (*entreprise de manufactures*) (Cf: Art. 632 and subsequent). Provisions of the code, however, did not apply to the sale of

---

Tribunals; Cf: *Postanowienie, że Trybunały Cywilne na prowincyi mają się zajmować i czynnościami Trybunałów Handlowych* [Decision that Civil Tribunals in the Province are to Handle the Tasks of Commercial Tribunals], published in: *Zbiór przepisów administracyjnych Królestwa Polskiego. Wydział Sprawiedliwości*, [Collection of Administrative Provisions of the Kingdom of Poland. Justice Department], vol. 4, 113–115.

43 Supra n. 3.

44 *Dekret z 9 czerwca 1810 r. o wprowadzeniu Kodeksu Handlowego do prowincyi nowowcielonych* [Decree of 9 June 1810 on introduction of the Commercial Code in newly incorporated provinces], DPKW, vol. 2, 220.

45 ANK, Akta Wolnego Miasta Krakowa [Archives of the Free City of Krakow] (hereinafter: AWMK), WM 236, 15–50.

46 It must be underscored that the knowledge of the effective provisions of the proxies of both parties was impressive.

coal directly; nevertheless, in both French and Polish judicial decisions an expansive interpretation of the code's catalogue of commercial acts was sometimes adopted. At the time, in France the sale of coal extracted by a mine's owners or licence holders was not, in principle, regarded a commercial act within the meaning of the Commercial Code, as an effect of implementation of a mining law of 21 April 1810,[47] but this latter law was not in effect in the Polish territories.

The Legislative Body Commission, in the grounds for the final wording of the provision, underscored:

> Cette rédaction est proposée pour plus grande clarté. Elle fera cesser les contestations qui s'élèvent fréquemment sur la question de savoir si les sociétés qui exploitent une mine sont de la compétence des tribunaux de commerce. La mine étant une propriété foncière, le particulier ou la société qui l'exploite fait valoir son héritage et rien de plus. Il faut donc exprimer clairement qu'il n'y a pas lieu à le traduire devant les tribunaux de commerce.[48]

---

47    Pursuant to Art. 32 of this law, "Exploitation des mines n'est pas considérée comme un commerce, et n'est pas sujette à patente."; Loi du 21 avril 1810 concernant les mines, les minières et les carrières, published in: *Collection complète des lois, décrets, ordonnances, réglemens, et avis du Conseil-d'État, publiée sur les éditions officielles du Louvre; de l'Imprimerie Nationale, par Baudouin; et du Bulletin des lois, de 1788 à 1824 inclusivement, par ordre chronologique, avec un choix d'Instructions ministérielles, et des Notes sur chaque Loi, indiquant, 1° les Lois analogues; 2° les Décisions et Arrêts des Tribunaux et du Conseil-d'État; 3° les Discussions rapportées au Moniteur; suivie d'une table analytique et raisonnée des matières*, Jean Baptiste Duvergier (ed.), A. Guyot et Scribe et Charles-Béchet, Paris, 1826, vol. 17, 90–98. For more on earlier legislation, cf. Ernest Lamé-Fleury: *De la législation minérale sous l'ancienne monarchie, ou Recueil méthodique et chronologique des lettres patentes, édits ordonnances, déclarations, arrêts du Conseil d'État du roi, du parlement de la Cour des monnaies de Paris, etc., concernant la législation minérale*, Auguste Durand, Paris, 1857; *Recueil des lois, arrêtés et instructions sur les mines, minières, carrières et usines; contenant toute la législation en cette matière, depuis et compris la loi du 28 juillet 1791 jusqu'à ce jour; divers Extraits des Chartes du Hainaut; les Décisions ministérielles intervenues et les Dispositions générales prises par l'Autorité provinciale en fait des Mines*, Monjot, Mons, 1824, especially *Motifs du projet de loi sur les mines, adopté par le Corps Législatif de France en séance du 21 avril 1810*, 199 et seq. Compare also Art. 13 of the law of 25 April 1844: "Ne sont pas assujettis à la patente: [...] les concessionnaires de mines pour le seul fait de l'extraction et de la vente des matières par eux extraites."

48    *Observations de la Commission du Corps Législatif, du 17 mars 1810*; Jean-Guillaume Locré: *La législation civile, commerciale et criminelle de la France*, Treuttel et Würtz, Paris, 1827, vol. 9, 465.

A HOLLOW LEGAL SHELL

French commentators also addressed this issue, among others Count Philippe-Antoine Merlin in his famous *Recueil alphabétique*, who explained this matter as follows:

> Pour extraire de sa mine le charbon de terre qu'elle renferme dans son sein, le propriétaire à qui elle appartient, est obligé d'acheter une grande quantité de bois, de fers et de cordages; cependant la loi du 21 avril 1810 déclare expressément qu'il ne fait pas acte de Commerce; pourquoi? Parce-qu'il ne vend pas les objets qui lui servent de moyens pour extraire son charbon des entrailles de la terre.[49]

At first, judicial decisions also confirmed that, pursuant to Art. 32 of the Act of 21 April 1810, a company set up with the purpose of running a licenced mine was of a civil, and not commercial, nature (Cf: among others, judgements of the Cassation Court of 7 February 1826,[50] 15 April 1834[51] and 10 March 1841,[52] as well as decision of the Council of State of 7 June 1836[53]). Restrictions in the application of this principle only began to emerge in the judgements of the Cassation Court in late '20s and early '30s (judgements of 30 April 1828[54] and 15 December 1835[55]). However, it was not until a judgement dated 26 March 1855 that the Cassation Court admitted that a company set up with the purpose of mining

---

49    Philippe-Antoine MERLIN: *Recueil alphabétique de questions de droit qui se présentent le plus fréquemment dans les tribunaux; ouvrage dans lequel l'auteur a fondu et classé un grand nombre de ses plaidoyers et réquisitoires, avec le texte des arrêts de la cour de cassation qui s'en sont ensuivis*, Garnery, Paris, 1827, vol. 2, 294.

50    Published in: *Journal du Palais, présentant la jurisprudence de la Cour de cassation et des cours d'appel de Paris et des autres départemens, sur l'application de tous les codes français aux questions douteuses et difficiles*, 1826, vol. 2, 542; *Jurisprudence générale du Royaume, en matière civile, commercial et criminelle, ou Journal des Audiences, contenant dans la première partie les arrêts de la Cour de cassation; dans la deuxième les arrêts des Cours royales du Royaume; et dans la troisième les lois, ordonnaces et décision du Conseil-d'État et autres qui peuvent intéresser les jurisconsultes, année 1829*, Victor Alexis Désiré DALLOZ et al. (eds.), Paris, (hereinafter: DALLOZ) 1826, I, 157. Cf: also judgement of the Cassation Court dated 24 June 1829 (DALLOZ: 1829, I, 280).

51    DALLOZ: 1834, I, 195; *Recueil général des lois et des arrêts en matière civile, criminelle, commerciale et de droit public*, Jean-Baptiste SIREY et al. (eds.) (hereinafter: SIREY) 1834, I, 650.

52    DALLOZ: 1841, I, 175.

53    DALLOZ: 1837, III, 135.

54    SIREY: 1828, I, 418. Cf: also the judgement of the *Cour royale de Bordeaux* of 22 June 1833; SIREY: 1833, II, 547.

55    SIREY: 1836, I, 333.

may be, depending on the case, deemed a civil or a commercial one,[56] which was also reflected in the works of commentators.[57]

However, when the case in question between Helena Żółtowska and Katarzyna Hügerle and administrators of the mine company in Dąbrowa was being examined before the Krakow court, according to the French extra-codical legislation, the sale of coal extracted by owners or license holders of mines, or by their employees, was not a commercial act, and a company run in connection with this activity did not have a commercial nature. The Krakow court ruled in line with this position, finding that the Commercial Tribunal that ruled in the first instance, was not competent.[58] It did so despite not having found a clear and unambiguous answer in the Commercial Code, not having any support of other legal acts related to the commercial law that existed outside of the code, which were not binding in the Polish territories, and without any help from the Polish school of commercial law, which did not even exist at the time.

The issue of jurisdiction of Commercial Tribunals also became the focus of considerations in the case between "Tomasz de Ruhmfeld Chromy, Józef de Geppert, doctors of medicine, Antoni Kiesewetter, a road commissary, Marcin Schestarum, prefect of a salt storage in Wieliczka, a hard coal mining company and alum factory in the village of Dąbrowa [...] and Józef Zwierzyna, active in various branches of commerce."[59] The examining Appellate Court in Krakow ruled differently than in the first example, as administrators of the mine had hired a commission agent (*commissionnaire*) for the sale of coal. This confirmed the jurisdiction of the Commercial Tribunal in the case, once again in line with the French spirit.

These, of course, are just examples. However, from the remaining court files in commercial cases up until 1830[60] it follows, amazingly, that the majority of cases in many complicated matters (already in the first decade after the

---

56    "Une société formée pour l'exploitation d'une mine peut, d'après les circonstances, être considérée comme une société commerciale, et non comme société civile."; SIREY: 1856 (2 ser.), I, 504. A company established to exploit a mine may, depending on the circumstances, be considered a commercial, not a civil company.

57    Cf: Charles Bonaventure Marie TOULLIER, Jean Baptiste DUVERGIER: *Le droit civil français, suivant l'ordre du Code, ouvrage dans lequel on a réuni la théorie a la pratique*, Société Typographique Belge, Aldolphe Wahlen et Cie, Bruxelles, 1841, vol. 9, 167; Émile VINCENS: *Des societes par actions. Des banques en France*, Madame Huzard, Paris, 1837, 47 et seq.

58    ANK, AWMK, WM 236, 12–14.

59    ANK, AWMK, WM 237, 137–152.

60    The temporal boundaries of the research conducted by Michał Gałędek and myself with the grant listed in footnote 1 are delimited by the breakout of the 1830 November Uprising and the simultaneous process of limiting the autonomy of the Republic of Krakow. Following the collapse of the uprising, not only did the political circumstances change

reception of the Commercial Code) were ruled on in accordance with the French line, even though the additional French commercial legislation was not implemented on the Polish territories, and even though access to French subject literature or collections of judgements must have been difficult (there is a possibility that they were available, but matters were certainly not made any easier by the fact that representatives of Polish legal science were disinterested in commercial law at the time). In a number of cases extensive statements made by representatives of the parties, including a lot of valuable additional information which Polish judges could not obtain either from the legislator or from Polish scientists, were extremely helpful. So, even though the *Code de commerce* was the eponymous "hollow legal shell" at first ignored by the legislator, by the representatives of legal science and by some part of entrepreneurs and merchants, the judges guaranteed the durability of this shell.

These 19th century experiences, then, show that even if the legislator does not fulfil his role appropriately, there may still be judges able to effectively watch over correct application of the law. This is particularly comforting within the context of the shake-up in the relations between the legislative and judicial powers that has recently taken place in Poland.

## 5      Conclusion

Did the *Code de commerce* serve as a tool in the modernisation of Polish reality, then? Despite the absence of a well-thought-out strategy of the Polish legislator to use it to its fullest potential, the answer is certainly "yes." It led to the birth of the Polish science of commercial law. Its adoption also propelled the rapid development of Polish legal language in this scope, as it was necessary to come up with new terms for the new solutions and hithertofore unknown institutions, which had no equivalents in Polish. It remained in effect in the Polish territories until 1933, and from long-term perspective it is possible to assess its impact on the shape of economic relations in the Polish territories, on the development of legal institutions and, most importantly – on the birth of commercial law in Poland as a separate branch of law.

considerably, but the new political situation left a lasting mark on the overall sociopolitical life in the country, including commercial relations.

## Bibliography

### Archival sources

Archiwum Narodowe w Krakowie, Akta notariusza Antoniego Matakiewicza w Krakowie, 40.

Archiwum Narodowe w Krakowie, Akta Wolnego Miasta Krakowa, WM 236.

Archiwum Narodowe w Krakowie, Akta Wolnego Miasta Krakowa, WM 237.

Archiwum Państwowe w Warszawie, Kancelaria Notarialna Jana Wincentego Bandtkie, notariusza w Warszawie, 52ᵃ.

Archiwum Państwowe w Warszawie, Kancelaria Notarialna Jana Wincentego Bandtkie, notariusza w Warszawie, 54ᵃ.

Archiwum Państwowe w Warszawie, Kancelaria Notarialna Jana Wincentego Bandtkie, notariusza w Warszawie, 64.

Archiwum Państwowe w Warszawie, Kancelaria Notarialna Teodora Czempińskiego, notariusza w Warszawie, 15.

Archiwum Państwowe w Warszawie, Kancelaria Notarialna Teodora Czempińskiego, notariusza w Warszawie, 60.

Archiwum Państwowe w Warszawie, Kancelaria Notarialna Aleksandra Engelke, notariusza w Warszawie, 39.

### Literature

Mackenzie Dalzell CHALMERS: *Codification of Mercantile Law = Report of the Twenty-Fifth Annual Meeting of the American Bar Association held at Saratoga Springs, New York, August 27, 28 and 29, 1902*, Philadelphia, Dando Printing and Publishing Company, 1902, 282–291.

*Collection complète des lois, décrets, ordonnances, règlements et avis du Conseil d'État (de 1788 à 1836 inclusivement, par ordre chronologique), publiée sur les éditions officielles, continuée depuis 1836 et formant un volume chaque année*, Jean Baptiste DUVERGIER (ed.), imprimé par Charles Noblet, Paris, 1863, vol. 63.

*Collection complète des lois, décrets, ordonnances, réglemens, et avis du Conseil-d'État, publiée sur les éditions officielles du Louvre; de l'Imprimerie Nationale, par Baudouin; et du Bulletin des lois, de 1788 à 1824 inclusivement, par ordre chronologique, avec un choix d'Instructions ministérielles, et des Notes sur chaque Loi, indiquant, 1° les Lois analogues; 2° les Décisions et Arrêts des Tribunaux et du Conseil-d'État; 3° les Discussions rapportées au Moniteur; suivie d'une table analytique et raisonnée des matières*, Jean Baptiste DUVERGIER (ed.), A. Guyot et Scribe et Charles-Béchet, Paris, 1826, vol. 17.

*Dyariusze Sejmów Księstwa Warszawskiego, zeszyt 1, Dziennik posiedzeń izby poselskiej sejmu r.*, Marceli HANDELSMAN (ed.), nakł. Towarzystwa Naukowego Warszawskiego, E. Wende i s-ka, Warsaw, 1913.

*Dziennik Praw Królestwa Polskiego*, Drukarnia Rządowa, Warsaw [s.a.], vol. 4.

*Dziennik Praw Księstwa Warszawskiego*, W Drukarni Xięży Pijarów, Warsaw, 1810–1811, vol. 1–2.

Jean HILAIRE: *Introduction historique au droit commercial*, PUF, Paris, 1986.

*Journal du Palais, présentant la jurisprudence de la Cour de cassation et des cours d'appel de Paris et des autres départemens, sur l'application de tous les codes français aux questions douteuses et difficiles*, 1826, vol. 2.

*Jurisprudence générale du Royaume, en matière civile, commercial et criminelle, ou Journal des Audiences, contenant dans la première partie les arrêts de la Cour de cassation; dans la deuxième les arrêts des Cours royales du Royaume; et dans la troisième les lois, ordonnaces et décision du Conseil-d'État et autres qui peuvent intéresser les jurisconsultes, année 1829*, Victor Alexis Désiré DALLOZ et al. (eds.), Imprimerie de Béthune, Paris, 1829.

*Jurisprudence générale du Royaume, en matière civile, commercial et criminelle, ou Journal des Audiences de la Cour de cassation et des Cours royales. Avec un supplement contenant les lois, ordonnaces et decision diverses, année 1826*, Victor Alexis Désiré DALLOZ et al. (eds.), Imprimerie de J. Smith, Paris, 1826.

*Jurisprudence générale du Royaume, recueil périodique et critique de legislation, de doctrine et de jurisprudence, en matière civile, commercial, criminelle, administrative et de droit public; contenant: Première partie – Les Arrêts de la Cour de Cassation; Deuxième partie – Les Arrêts des Cours Royales; Troisième partie – Lois, Ordonnaces, Décision du Conseil-d'État, Dissertations, Délibération de la régie, et autres documens qui peuvent intéresser les Jurisconsultes, année 1837*, Victor Alexis Désiré DALLOZ et al. (eds.), Imprimerie de Madame Veuve Poussin, Paris, 1837.

*Jurisprudence générale du Royaume, recueil périodique et critique de legislation, de doctrine et de jurisprudence, en matière civile, commercial, criminelle, administrative et de droit public, contenant: Première partie – Les Arrêts de la Cour de Cassation; Deuxième partie – Les Arrêts des Cours Royales; Troisième partie – Lois, Ordonnaces, Décision du Conseil-d'État, Dissertations, Délibération de la Régie, et autres Documens qui peuvent intéresser les Jurisconsultes, année 1841*, Victor Alexis Désiré DALLOZ et al. (eds.), Imprimerie de Crété, Paris, 1841.

*Jurisprudence générale du Royaume, recueil périodique et critique de legislation, de doctrine et de jurisprudence. Première partie – Jurisprudence de la Cour de Cassation; Deuxième partie – Jurisprudence des Cours Royales; Troisième partie – Lois, Ordonnaces, Décision du Conseil-d'État, dissertations et autres documens qui peuvent intéresser les Jurisconsultes, année 1834*, Victor Alexis Désiré DALLOZ et al. (eds.), Imprimerie de M^me V^e Poussin, Paris, 1834.

Anna KLIMASZEWSKA: *Influence of French legalese on the development of Polish legal language within the area of commercial law = Multilingualism and law*, Emőd VERESS (ed.), Sapientia Hungarian University of Transylvania – Forum Iuris – Robert Schumann Association, Cluj-Napoca - Kolozsvàr, 2016, 175–184.

Anna KLIMASZEWSKA: *Nauczanie i nauka prawa handlowego w okresie paskiewiczowskim*, = *Królestwo Polskie w okresie namiestnictwa Iwana Paskiewicza (1832–1856)*. *System polityczny, prawo i statut organiczny z 26 lutego 1832 r.* Lech MAŻEWSKI (ed.), von Borowiecky, Radzymin, 2015, 219–231.

*Kodex handlowy z zlecenia J Wgo Ministra Sprawiedliwości przetłumaczony przez Walentego Majewskiego wezwanego iako Notaryusza Publicznego*, Druk. Zawadzkich, Warsaw, 1808.

Ernest LAMÈ-FLEURY: *De la législation minérale sous l'ancienne monarchie, ou Recueil méthodique et chronologique des lettres patentes, édits ordonnances, déclarations, arrêts du Conseil d'État du roi, du parlement de la Cour des monnaies de Paris, etc., concernant la législation minérale*, Auguste Durand, Paris, 1857.

Jean-Guillaume LOCRÉ: *La législation civile, commerciale et criminelle de la France*, Treuttel et Würtz, Paris, 1827, vol. 9.

Philippe-Antoine MERLIN: *Recueil alphabétique de questions de droit qui se présentent le plus fréquemment dans les tribunaux; ouvrage dans lequel l'auteur a fondu et classé un grand nombre de ses plaidoyers et réquisitoires, avec le texte des arrêts de la cour de cassation qui s'en sont ensuivis*, Garnery, Paris, 1827, vol. 2.

Jonathan M. MILLER: *A Typology of Legal Transplants: Using Sociology, Legal History and Argentine Examples to Explain the Transplant Process*, The American Journal of Comparative Law, 51(2003)/4, 839–885.

*Prawo cywilne obowiązujące w Królestwie Polskim*, Stanisław ZAWADZKI (ed.), nakł. wydawcy w druk. Karola Kowalewskiego, Warsaw, 1863, vol. 3.

*Protokoły Rady Stanu Księstwa Warszawskiego*, Bronisław PAWŁOWSKI, Tadeusz MENCEL (eds.), TNT, Toruń, 1965, vol. 2/1.

*Recueil des lois, arrêtés et instructions sur les mines, minières, carrières et usines; contenant toute la législation en cette matière, depuis et compris la loi du 28 juillet 1791 jusqu'à ce jour; divers Extraits des Chartes du Hainaut; les Décisions ministérielles intervenues et les Dispositions générales prises par l'Autorité provinciale en fait des Mines*, Monjot, Mons, 1824.

*Recueil général des lois et des arrêts en matière civile, criminelle, commerciale et de droit public*, Jean-Baptiste SIREY et al. (eds.), de l'Imprimerie de La Chevadière, Paris, 1828.

*Recueil général des lois et des arrêts en matière civile, criminelle, commerciale et de droit public*, Jean-Baptiste SIREY et al. (eds.), Imprimerie de Casimir, Paris 1833.

*Recueil général des lois et des arrêts en matière civile, criminelle, commerciale et de droit public*, Jean-Baptiste SIREY et al. (eds.), Imprimerie de Bacquenois, Paris, 1834;

*Recueil général des lois et des arrêts en matière civile, criminelle, commerciale et de droit public*, Jean-Baptiste SIREY et al. (eds.), s.n., Paris 1836.

*Recueil général des lois et des arrêts en matière civile, criminelle, commerciale et de droit public*, L.M. DEVILLENEUVE et al. (eds.), Imprimerie de Cosse et J. Dumaine, Paris, 1856.

# A HOLLOW LEGAL SHELL

John RODMAN: *The Commercial Code of France, with the Motives, or Discourses of the Counsellors of State, Delivered before the Legislative Body, Illustrative of the Principles and Provisions of the Code, Translated from the French, with Explanatory Notes, and a Complete Analytical Index*, C. Wiley, New York, 1814.

*Rocznik warszawski*, Państwowy Instytut Wydawniczy, Warsaw, 1961, vol. 2.

Fryderyk SKARBEK: *Dzieje Księstwa Warszawskiego z przedmową Piotra Chmielowskiego*, Drukarnia Artystyczna Saturnina Sikorskiego, Warsaw, vol. 2, 1898.

Charles Bonaventure Marie TOULLIER, Jean-Baptiste DUVERGIER: *Le droit civil français, suivant l'ordre du Code, ouvrage dans lequel on a réuni la théorie a la pratique*, Société Typographique Belge, Aldolphe Wahlen et Cie, Bruxelles, 1841, vol. 11.

Émile VINCENS: *Des sociétés par actions. Des banques en France*, Madame Huzard, Paris, 1837.

*Zbiór przepisów administracyjnych Królestwa Polskiego. Wydział Sprawiedliwości*, Part 1, W Drukarni Jana Jaworskiego, Warsaw, 1866, vol. 4.

CHAPTER 7

# Development of the Medical Malpractice Law and Legal Instrumentalism in the Antebellum America

*Marcin Michalak*

## 1 Introduction

The announcement of the Declaration of Independence in Philadelphia,[1] on the 4th of July 1776, followed by the signing, on the 3rd of September 1783, of the Treaty of Paris, by virtue of which the Kingdom of Great Britain formally recognised the sovereignty of the United States of America, fulfilled the ambitions for independence of many inhabitants of the British colonies in North America. One of the greatest challenges faced by the Americans at that time was to provide the new state with a political system.[2] The enactment of the Federal Constitution in the year 1787 was a symbolic culmination of activities undertaken in that area. At the same time, the establishment of a constitutional order was only the first step on the way of constructing a legal system in the newly-created state. The issue concerning adoption of concrete solutions with regard to private law was no less important than the form of the government. Despite the opinions that, after breaking free of the rule of Great Britain, English common law should also be renounced, the arguments for maintaining that law in the newly-established state prevailed. However, multidimensional differences between England and the United States made the direct implementation of common law impossible. That law had to be adopted in such a way as to take into consideration the unique character of the new state. The institutions and principles which conformed to American society were to be adopted, whereas those which did not comply with the character of the new state were to be discarded.

Roscoe Pound, in describing the process of implementing English common law in the United States, used the term "juristic chemistry."[3] He wrote: "The

---

1 The author of the publication obtained financial resources for the preparation of a doctoral dissertation from the National Science Center in the form of a doctoral scholarship based on Decision No. DEC-2015/16 / T / HS5 / 00432.
2 Lawrence M. FRIEDMAN: *A History of American Law*, Simon and Schuster, New York, 2005, 65.
3 Roscoe POUND: *The formative era of American law*, Boston, Little, Brown, 1938, 96.

---

© KONINKLIJKE BRILL NV, LEIDEN, 2020 | DOI:10.1163/9789004417274_008

DEVELOPMENT OF THE MEDICAL MALPRACTICE LAW

chemist does not make materials which go into his test tube. He selects them and combines them for some purpose and his purpose thus gives form to the result".[4] Analogous actions were undertaken by judges, selecting "English rules, doctrines and institutions," taking as the criterion their "applicability to American conditions" and, in consequence, adopting them as common law of the United States, or "in case they were not applicable, determining what should be obtained in their place".[5]

The comparison used by Roscoe Pound is confirmed by another prominent American legal historian Morton Horwitz, who adds that the American judges in the 19th century modeling common law creatively used it as a tool for "framing general doctrines based on a self-conscious consideration of social and economic policies".[6] He indicates that "this increasing preoccupation with using law as an instrument of policy is everywhere apparent in the early years of the nineteenth century".[7] Horwitz points out that "in the whole variety of the areas of law, ancient rules were reconsidered from a functional or purposive perspective."[8]

One of the interesting examples of the use of law by American judges as a tool for adapting old English common law to the new American reality – so that it could be consistent with American conditions and the emerging American identity – is the medical malpractice law. In the discussed context, two principles adopted in the area of physicians' liability for malpractice, the so called *locality rule* and *school of practice doctrine*, deserve special attention.

## 2 English Common Law in the New Republic

Rejection of the rule of Great Britain by the Americans in the second half of the 18th century raised the question whether the law originating from that monarchy should also be discarded.[9] Consideration of that problem was justified, especially due to the fact that the antagonisms which had grown in the area of politics also had a strong influence on the English legal heritage.[10]

---

4    *Ibid.*

5    *Ibid.*

6    Morton J. Horwitz: *The transformation of American law, 1780–1860*, Harvard University Press, Cambridge (MA) 1977, 2.

7    *Ibid.*, 3.

8    *Ibid.*, 3.

9    *Ibid.*, 65–66.

10   Pound: *op. cit.*, 7.

Aversion to English law was visible in numerous studies published at the end of the 18th and at the beginning of the 19th century.[11] In 1792, François-Xavier Martin wrote about English law, still binding in North Carolina, that it was the "last seeming badge and mortifying memento" of the dependence on Great Britain and, as such, should be replaced as soon as possible with native American legislation.[12]

In turn, Charles Warren states that, at dinners and meetings following the American Revolution, the following toast was often raised: "The Common law of England: may wholesome statutes soon root out the engine of oppression from America."[13]

The antipathy towards English law was also increased by the fact that a significant number of older and renowned members of the legal community were, in the course of the Revolution, on the side of the party favouring the English, the so-called Loyalists, also referred to as the Royalists or Tories.[14] In consequence, after the War of Independence, aversion and lack of trust shown towards lawyers as a professional group was clearly visible.[15] That aversion towards the community whose members, in considerable numbers, supported the King during the Revolution, was naturally extended onto their basic working tool, i.e. English common law.[16]

Apart from political arguments, it was stated that English law was not suitable for the American reality, also due to the fact that it was anachronistic and over-formalised. It was indicated that the legal system formed in the conditions of a monarchical system did not accord with the needs of a developing new republican society.[17]

The opponents to the adoption of English law were not content merely with criticising it; they also proposed alternative solutions concerning the issue of forming a legal system in the new state. Some members of the political class expressed the opinion that a formalised system of legal norms was, in itself, an obstacle in implementation of true justice.[18] Hence the suggestion that the old

---

11    *Ibid.*, 7.

12    *A collection of the statutes of the Parliament of England in force in the state of North-Carolina*, Francois Xavier MARTIN (ed.), From the Editors Press, Newbern, 1792, VI.

13    Charles WARREN: *A history of the American bar*, Little, Brown, and Company, Boston, 1911, 227.

14    FRIEDMAN: *op. cit.*, 66; Thomas B. ALLEN, *Tories: Fighting for the King in America's First Civil War*, Harper Collins, New York, 2011.

15    WARREN: *op. cit.*, 212.

16    Bernard SCHWARTZ: *The Law in America: A History*, Tata McGraw Hill Publishing Company, New York, 1974, 10.

17    POUND: *op. cit.*, 6.

18    FRIEDMAN: *op. cit.*, 66.

DEVELOPMENT OF THE MEDICAL MALPRACTICE LAW

common law should be replaced with the principles of equity or of "natural" justice.[19] The idea of replacing the existing law with an abstractedly worded system of natural justice may have seemed attractive from a theoretical point of view, yet in practice such an assumption was, for obvious reasons, a utopian one. The United States, entering an era of social, economic and technological development, did not need a vague vision, but a legal order which would be able to meet the challenges posed by the American reality, which was becoming more and more complex.[20]

In those circumstances it was necessary to find secure and verified solutions. It can be said that the occurrences on the other side of the Atlantic met those expectations. The post-revolutionary antipathy of American society towards England went hand in hand with its growing sympathy towards France. At first, this resulted mostly from the support given to the United States in the course of their fight for independence, and was later additionally intensified by a feeling of solidarity, when the French had begun their own revolution.[21] The approval of the actions undertaken on the Seine also concerned those connected with legislation. The codification movement in Europe and the successes in that area naturally attracted the attention of the United States. Codification constituted the symbol of clarity, coherence and order.[22] Against this background, common law was perceived by part of the legal community as a system which was highly uncertain, unstructured and difficult to apply efficiently.[23] It was not an accident that Jeremy Bentham, a great English lawyer of that era, was a keen supporter of codification. Taking into account the disadvantages of his native system, he warned the Americans: "Yes, my friends, if you love one another – if you love, each one of you, his own security – shut your ports against common law, as you would shut them against the plague."[24] In the 19th century, in his letters addressed to President Madison, Bentham still suggested that a complete code of law for the United States of America should be created.[25]

Despite the existing rationale that the legal system of the United States should be constructed on a different basis than English common law, the

---

19    SCHWARTZ: *op. cit.*, 11–12; FRIEDMAN: *op. cit.*, 69.

20    SCHWARTZ: *op. cit.*, 12; FRIEDMAN: *op. cit.*, 69–70.

21    SCHWARTZ: *op. cit.*, 12.

22    FRIEDMAN: *op. cit.*, 69–70.

23    *Ibid.*, 66; Maurice Eugen LANG: *Codification in the British Empire and America*, H.J. Paris, Amsterdam, 1924, 34.

24    LANG: *op. cit.*, 35.

25    Daniel J. BOORSTIN: *The Americans: The National Experience*, Knopf Doublday Publishing Group, New York, 2010, 36.

position of English law as the main source of reference in that respect was not seriously endangered[26] for a few reasons. Firstly for the English-speaking legal community in the United States at the end of the 18th century, common law was, naturally, the system in which they had been educated and which they were using in everyday practice.[27] Young students of law derived their knowledge, in the libraries of their patrons, from English law textbooks, in particular from William Blackstone's *Commentaries*. Common law was the system which was well-known and applied in practice. Its dominant status was supported by the fact that few representatives of the bar were able to use, easily and effectively, French or Latin texts, not to mention any comprehensive knowledge of foreign law.[28] Therefore, despite the aversion towards England and everything connected with the British heritage, with the simultaneous sympathy towards France and the codification movement developing in Europe, English common law remained, for American lawyers, a natural and obvious reference point.

The legal system inherited from Great Britain, apart from its practical dimension, constituted another important value for the Americans. Together with the increase of the aspirations toward independence in the 18th century, the inhabitants of the colonies regarded common law as the source of their inviolable rights.[29] The allegation that those rights were not respected by the monarch constituted one of the main axes of the controversy which led to the War of Independence. It was in common law that the fundamental norms of natural law, the concept found at the centre of the American Revolution, were perceived. In that respect, common law constituted a valuable inheritance for the Americans.[30] In the minds of many citizens of the United States, English law, though perhaps slightly outdated, unstructured and chaotic, was still the source of the rights and freedoms for which they fought in the course of the Revolution.

Due to the above circumstances, it was common law that for the Americans became the foundation for constructing the legal system of their new state.

---

26    FRIEDMAN: *op. cit.*, 66.
27    *Ibid.*
28    SCHWARTZ: *op. cit.*, 14–15.
29    FRIEDMAN: *op. cit.*, 67.
30    David S. BOGEN: *Privileges and Immunities: A Reference Guide to the United States Constitution*, Greenwood Publishing Group, Westport, 2003, 9–11.

# DEVELOPMENT OF THE MEDICAL MALPRACTICE LAW

## 3    Americanisation of Common Law

The decision to adopt English common law in the newly-established state was by no means an easy task. It soon became clear that the law adopted from Great Britain had to be adjusted to an entirely new reality. It was impossible and inadvisable to implement it in the same form in which it had been functioning in England. Common law had to be Americanised, i.e. adjusted to conditions and circumstances materially different from those on the other side of the Atlantic.[31] The core of the process which was to take place in the first decades following the proclamation of independence by the United States, was aptly characterised in 1813 by William Tilghman, a judge of the Supreme Court of Pennsylvania, who stated:

> When our ancestors emigrated from England, they took with them such of the English principles as were convenient for the situation in which they were about to place themselves. It required time and experience to ascertain how much of the English law would be suitable to this country. By degrees, as circumstances demanded, we adopted the English usages, or substituted others better suited to our wants [...][32]

The Supreme Court of the United States issued a similar statement at that time, indicating:

> The common law of England is not to be taken in all respects to be that of America. Our ancestors brought with them its general principles, and claimed it as their birth right. But they brought with them, and adopted only that portion which was applicable to their situation.[33]

In short, English common law implemented by the Americans had to be modified and creatively adjusted to new circumstances.

The institutions and principles which would be of service to American society had to be adopted, whereas those which were anachronistic and irrelevant in relation to the republican reality of the new state had to be rejected. As the Supreme Court of Ohio indicated in 1853:

---

31    FRIEDMAN: *op. cit.*, 67; SCHWARTZ: *op. cit.*, 15–18.

32    *Poor v. Greene*, 5 Binn. 554.

33    *Van Ness v. Packard*, 27 U.S. 137.

> The English common law, so far as it is reasonable in itself, suitable to the condition and business of our people, and consistent with the letter and spirit of our federal and state constitutions and statutes, has been and is followed by our courts [...]. But wherever it has been found wanting in either of these requisites, our courts have not hesitated to modify it to suit our circumstances, or, if necessary, wholly to depart from it.[34]

It was this process of adopting English common law in the United States of America that Roscoe Pound described as the "juristic chemistry."[35] Adjusting English common law, by American courts, to the conditions in which the new state and society were functioning was particularly intensive in the first decades following the proclamation of independence by the United States of America. The literature indicates the exceptional importance of the period from the 1780s to the 1860s. These few decades are defined as the *formative era* or the *golden age* of American law.[36]

As Morton Horwitz points out, the phenomenon of legal transformations that occurred in the *golden age* of American law consisted in the fact that the judge's initiative in remodeling former principles was calculated to achieve specific goals.[37]

The two examples below show how particular American conditions contributed to the transformation of old English common law, while creating a space for introducing changes that were intended to achieve peculiar social or economic goals.

It is emphasised in the literature that the main factors determining the directions for the development of American law included, among other factors, the geographical differences between both countries, as well as the specific social conditions in which the legal system of the newly-created state was developing.[38]

Therefore, the implementation of English common law in the United States of America required, first and foremost, that the differences in the geographical conditions of England and the United States be taken into consideration.[39] Compared to the British Isles, America offered almost unlimited land resources.

---

34   *Bloom v. Richards,* 2 Ohio St. 387.

35   POUND: *op. cit.,* 96.

36   Charles M. HAAR: *Golden age of American Law,* G. Braziller, New York, 1965; HORWITZ: *op. cit.*

37   HORWITZ: *op. cit.,* 3.

38   James Willard HURST: *The Growth of American law. The law makers,* Little, Brown, and Company, Boston 1950, 6–15; POUND: *op. cit.,* 7.

39   HURST: *op. cit.,* 6–7; SCHWARTZ: *op. cit.,* 16–18; POUND: *op. cit.,* 8.

The feudal origin of common law resulted in the situation where land law was a maze of detailed rules concerning the transfer of property rights and the inheritance rules.[40] They fossilised, to a great extent, the situation where property in land was held by a small group of landlords, constituting the source of their wealth and power.[41] In this respect, American conditions were entirely different. The main problem of the society was not the concentration of land among a narrow group of owners, but the need to manage enormous territories stretching west beyond the borders of the federation constituent states. Due to its availability, land was regarded as a good, as capital which might constitute the subject of trade.[42] The essence of this phenomenon was aptly described by Tocqueville, who wrote: "almost all the farmers of the United States combine some trade with agriculture; most of them make agriculture itself a trade. It seldom happens that an American farmer settles for a good upon the land which he occupies; especially in the districts of the Far West, he brings land into tillage in order to sell it again, and not to farm it; he builds a farmhouse on the speculation that, as the state of the country will soon be changed by the increase of population, a good price may be obtained for it."[43] The change of the way in which the role of land was perceived in society, arising from geographical conditions, was translated directly into modification of law in this area. Both the practice and legislation aimed at simplifying the law of trade in land.[44] By virtue of the statutes enacted and judicial decisions, numerous solutions of English common law, inapplicable in American conditions, were repealed. The old forms of property rights transfer, characteristic for feudal relations, such as, for example, inheritance based on the principle of primogeniture, or English forms of fee tail, naturally had to be removed from the American legal system.[45]

Secondly, as was indicated by James W. Hurst, during the "formation period" of American law: "the most creative, driving and powerful pressures upon our law emerged from the social setting."[46] Indeed, the most pressing need to adjust common law to the new reality was connected, first and foremost, with the

---

40  FRIEDMAN: *op. cit.*, 171–172; SCHWARTZ: *op. cit.*, 17.

41  FRIEDMAN: *op. cit.*, 167.

42  Gregory S. ALEXANDER: *Commodity and Propriety: Competing Visions of Property in America Legal Thought, 1776–1970*, Chicago University Press, Chicago, 1997.

43  Quote from James Willard HURST: *Law and the conditions of freedom in the nineteenth-century United States*, University of Wisconsin Press, Madison, 1956, 13.

44  FRIEDMAN: *op. cit.*, 173.

45  More on this subject, cf. HURST: *Law and the conditions of freedom...*, *op. cit.*, 12–13; FRIEDMAN: *op. cit.*, 171–186.

46  HURST: *The Growth...*, *op. cit.*, 11.

requirements of the "pioneer society," born in the United States of America.[47] Gordon S. Wood, in his book *The Radicalism of the American Revolution*, described those transformations in a vivid way, when he wrote:

> In 1760 America was only a collection of disparate colonies huddled along a narrow strip of the Atlantic coast – economically underdeveloped outposts existing on the very edges of the civilized world. The less than two million monarchical subjects who lived in these colonies still took for granted that society was and ought to be a hierarchy of ranks and degrees of dependency, and that most people were bound together by personal ties of one sort or another. Yet scarcely fifty years later these insignificant borderland provinces had become a giant, almost continent-wide republic of nearly ten million egalitarian-minded bustling citizens, who not only had thrust themselves into a vanguard of history but had fundamentally altered their society and their social relationships.[48]

As the author further concludes: "[...] Americans had become, almost overnight [...] the most modern people in the world."[49]

The legal system of the United States of America, developing in the first half of the 19th century, had to respond to the needs and meet the expectations of that new society, while common law, with its medieval, feudal origin was, in many respects, unsuitable to those conditions. In England, it mostly served the needs of the *gentry*.[50] It was only that small part of society, which owned the land and was subject to legal relations connected with it. The majority of the inhabitants of the Kingdom used, on everyday basis, the rules of local customary law. As a result, the true number of recipients of common law was quite limited. American society in the first half of the 19th century, formed by the spirit of revolutionary changes, based on the principles of individualism and egalitarianism, where possession of land was not an exclusive characteristic, but was enjoyed by a growing group of citizens, required a law which would be truly common.[51] In order to function as the legal system regulating everyday problems of millions of citizens of the United States, common law had to become more flexible and accessible. As Friedman indicates:

---

47    POUND: *op. cit.*, 11.
48    *Ibid.*, 6–7.
49    *Ibid.*, 6.
50    FRIEDMAN: *op. cit.*, 70.
51    *Ibid.*, 70.

DEVELOPMENT OF THE MEDICAL MALPRACTICE LAW

What happened to American law in the nineteenth century, basically, was that it changed dramatically, fundamentally, to conform to the needs, wants, and pressures coming from the vast increase in the numbers of consumers of law.[52]

The law, serving a multitude of its new "consumers," had to perform other functions than it had before. Instead of fossilising the existing order, it was to become a useful tool, an instrument used to realise specified goals.[53] When such goals changed, the ways of achieving them also had to change. In the face of the radical transformations which occurred in American society at the time of the Revolution, the task of reconstructing common law, so that it might serve in the new reality, was undertaken by both the state legislatures and the courts.[54] As briefly phrased by Daniel Boorstein, it was all about reconstructing the old English common law to meet the requirements of "[...]a new society now changing with unprecedented speed[...]."[55]

## 4 Adaptation of English Common Law in the United States of America and the Issue of Doctors' Liability

It is interesting that the need to remodel English common law in such a way that it might properly serve American society also concerned an apparently universal issue, namely the doctor-patient relationship. This is reflected in two principles concerning doctors' liability for malpractice developed by judicial decisions of American courts in the 19th century, i.e. the so-called *locality rule* and the *school of practice doctrine*.

## 5 Locality Rule

A publication by Charles Lowell, titled *An authentic report of a trial before the Supreme Judicial Court of Maine, for the county of Washington, June term, 1824: Charles Lowell v. John Faxon & Micajah Hawks* appeared in 1825 in Portland.[56]

---

52    *Ibid.*

53    *Ibid.*

54    *Ibid.*, 71.

55    Boorstein: *op. cit.*, 36.

56    Charles LOWELL: *An authentic report of a trial before the Supreme Judicial Court of Maine, for the county of Washington, June term, 1824 : Charles Lowell v. John Faxon & Micajah Hawks, surgeons and physicians, in an action of trespass on the case, for ignorance and*

In a few dozen pages, the author related in detail the course of court proceedings which he himself instigated against two physicians, John Faxon and Micajah Hawks, for medical malpractice. It could be concluded from the facts of the case, presented in the contents of the publication, that Lowell was thrown by a horse and, as a result, suffered a serious injury to his hip. As the event occurred in Lubec, a small town in Maine, John Faxon, the only local doctor, was summoned to attend the injured man.[57] He established that the hip was dislocated and that he was able to render the necessary help, and then began to set the patient's leg. An acquaintance of Charles Lowell, present during the surgery, advised him to summon a different doctor, as he thought that the leg, despite the physician's assurances, had not been properly set.[58] In that situation, Dr Hawks, practising in the nearby town of Eastport, was sent for. He arrived in Lubec and, having examined the patient and consulted Dr Faxon, decided that the surgery should be repeated. Then the two physicians together set the leg again.[59]

After the surgery the doctors advised the patient to remain in bed for at least two weeks. During the convalescence Dr Faxon attended him on a day-to-day basis. For a few days after the surgery, Lowell complained of intense pain and was wholly deprived of strength. He got out of bed for the first time fifteen days after the surgery.[60] He was worried about a depression, visible on the outside part of his hip, so he summoned Dr Hawks in order to consult him in that matter. Having examined the patient, the doctor said that it was a natural consequence of the hip dislocation, and that the depression would disappear when the limb had regained its strength and the body weight was evenly distributed. However, there was no improvement and, apart from the visible depression, it occurred that the treated leg was longer than the healthy one. Since Dr Hawks did not feel competent enough to deal with the case further, he summoned yet another physician, Dr Whipple.[61] The latter decided that, after the limb had been set, another dislocation must have occurred. For that he blamed Dr Faxon,

---

     *negligence in their professional treatment of the plff's dislocated hip : with observations on the prejudices and conduct of the inhabitants of Eastport, in regard to this cause : the character and testimony of the several witnesses, and the novel, and extraordinary positions assumed by the court*, Portland, 1825.

57    *Ibid.*, 3–4.
58    *Ibid.*, 9.
59    *Ibid.*
60    *Ibid.*, 10.
61    *Ibid.*, 4–5.

# DEVELOPMENT OF THE MEDICAL MALPRACTICE LAW

who had attended Lowell every day. Dr Whipple stated that, in those circumstances, the patient would probably be crippled for the rest of his life.[62]

Charles Lowell, not reconciled with the diagnosis, decided to seek help in Boston, more than 300 miles away from his town. There he consulted with several renowned surgeons, practising in Massachusetts General Hospital. They were all of the opinion that, as a result of his accident, the patient had suffered from a simple dislocation of the hip joint.[63] The injury could have been easily treated directly after the accident, but a few months later, as in Lowell's case, the chances of a successful cure were considerably lower. Despite this unfavourable prognosis, the patient decided to undergo yet another surgery in Boston, which, however, failed to produce the desired results.[64]

Following his consultations with the physicians from Massachusetts General Hospital, Charles Lowell came to the conclusion that his current state of health was the result of mistakes made in the course of treatment by Dr Faxon and Dr Hawks. Consequently, he decided to file a claim against them.[65] He alleged that the physicians lacked the proper skills, which was manifested in inappropriate setting of the leg; he also accused them of *carelessness*, when, after the surgery, they did not compare the length of the healthy leg with that of the injured one.[66]

In the course of the proceedings, the claimant's attorney appointed doctors from Boston to act as experts with regard to treatment of that kind of injury. They stated that

> a surgeon with usual skills and prudence could not make a mistake as to whether the limb had been properly set or not; if it had been properly set in the first place, the patient could not dislocate it again while lying in bed.[67]

In their opinion, a prudent surgeon, possessing suitable skills, would also have compared the length of the healthy legs with that of the injured one. Finally, the appointed doctors indicated that, in the case in question, it was impossible to perform the surgery without a traction device, which the defendants had not used.[68]

---

62    *Ibid.*, 4.
63    *Ibid.*, 5.
64    *Ibid.*
65    *Ibid.*, 6.
66    *Ibid.*, 18.
67    *Ibid.*, 12.
68    *Ibid.*

Having heard the witnesses and the opinion of experts, the presiding judge instructed the jurors on the binding law. The judge indicated that the claimant sought damages in connection with the *"negligence"* and *"unskilfulness"* of the defendants. Relating to the level of skills which the defendants ought to possess, the judge indicated that the law did not require a physician to apply any extraordinary, special skills, but an *ordinary degree of skill*, represented by other members of the profession. What is important, however, the judge added that, when speaking about other members of the profession, one ought to have meant the doctors practising in the same area as the defendants. To explain that standpoint, the judge indicated that it would be unjustified to expect from a surgeon practising in the country or in a small town to possess the same skills as a surgeon practising in London or another large city. The judge indicated that patients in cities were able to choose among doctors with different specialisations, whereas in a small town, where there are few physicians, it could not be expected that specialists in every area of medicine would be found.[69] This remark is particularly important in the context of further argumentation, when the judge, in relation to Dr Faxon, recalled that the latter was not a surgeon and only sporadically dealt with cases requiring surgical treatment. He undertook to treat the claimant as the physician who attended his family on a daily basis. Thus, the judge seemed to imply that it could not be expected from Dr Faxon to possess the same skills as those of, for example, the physicians from Boston, specialising in surgery.

The report from the court proceedings in the case of *Charles Lowell v. John Faxon & Micajah Hawks* is one of the first documents where the rule ordering that the place of practice be taken into consideration when assessing the

---

69  *Ibid*: "In this case, the Plaintiff demands damages for the negligence and unskilfulness of the Defendants, in the management of his lameness. The Plaintiff has declared in various manners, but the amount of all the charge is, that they treated him unskilfully and negligently. Now, in making your verdict, you may find them both guilty, or both not guilty, or one guilty, and the other not guilty, according as you have found the evidence, which you have heard. For the Plaintiff to support his case on the charge of unskilfulness, it is necessary for him to make it appear, that the Defendants did not manage with competent skill. The skill required in this case is not the greatest possible skill, neither will the best possible skill be sufficient. You should compute- the skill according to the state of practice, in the country where the Defendants live. It is not to be expected of a Surgeon or Physician in a country or obscure village, that he will possess the skill of a Surgeon in the city of London, or any other large city – this, it would be unreasonable to expect; because in large cities, where there are a great many Surgeons and Physicians, a person may have his choice, there is always competition. The patronage of Surgeons in such places, is great; in small villages, the patronage being small, we must not expect a very great degree of skill – No, gentlemen, all that is required in skill, is an ordinary degree of skill, compared with that of others in the country where they reside."

DEVELOPMENT OF THE MEDICAL MALPRACTICE LAW

appropriate skills and diligence of a doctor is articulated.[70] It is possible to find more examples of such instructions given by judges of jury courts at that time. For instance, in 1857 in Ohio, one of the courts there adjudicated the case of *McMillen v. Hewitt, Sprague and Rodman*, in which a patient sued his oculists, accusing them that, as a result of their negligence, he was weak-sighted for two years.[71] When instructing the jury in that case, the judge also related to the place where the physicians were practising, indicating that: "To require the highest degree of skill would deprive all places, except large cities, of medical men."[72] By that remark the judge clearly implied that the level of skills of doctors practising in large urban centres is different than that of physicians in the country, hence a universalised model of required skills could not be applied to all. Similarly to the case of *Lowell v. Faxon & Hawks*, the judge also seemed to draw attention to the fact that the number of doctors and, in consequence, the degree of specialisation in cities resulted in the situation where the skills of individual physicians dealing with concrete areas of medicine were higher than those possessed by doctors in small towns dealing with all medical cases.

Apart from some judges, the issue of the place where doctors' practises in the context of liability for inappropriate treatment was also raised by scholars. For example, John Elwell, considering how the phrase *"an ordinary degree of skill"* should be understood in the context of appropriate practice standards, wrote:

> In large cities and towns, are always found surgeons and physicians of the greatest degree of skill and knowledge [...]. In the smaller towns and country, those who practice medicine and surgery, though often possessing a thorough theoretical knowledge of the highest elements of the profession, do not enjoy so great opportunities of daily observation, and practical operations; where the elementary studies are brought into everyday use; as those who reside in the metropolitan towns; and though just as well informed in the elements and literature of the profession, they should not be expected to exercise that high degree of skill and practical knowledge possessed by those having greater facilities for performing

---

70 Marc D. Ginsberg: *The locality rule lives! Why? Using modern medicine to eradicate an unhealthy law*, Drake Law Review 61(2013), 325; Kenneth A. DeVille: *Medical Malpractice in Nineteenth Century America. Origins and Legacy*, New York University Press, New York, 1992, 54–55.

71 DeVille: *op. cit.*, 56.

72 John J. Elwell: *A Medico-legal treatise on malpractice and medical evidence*, J.S. Voorhies, New York 1860, 162.

and witnessing operations, and who are, or may be, constantly observing the various accidents and forms of disease[73]

Milo McClelland in his *Civil malpractice: a treatise on surgical jurisprudence* drew attention to the same problem, indicating that:

> Reasonably, as much cannot be expected of physicians in remote localities, where he is cut off from opportunities of improvement, as from physicians living in communities where opportunity is afforded of seeing diseases and accidents under more varied forms[...][74]

Similarly, Thomas Shearman and Amasa Redfield in the elaboration *A treatise on the law of negligence*, emphasised that

> In country towns, and in unsettled portions of the country remote from cities, physicians, though well informed in theory, are but seldom called upon to perform difficult operations in surgery, and do not enjoy the greater opportunities of daily observation and practice which large cities afford. It would be unreasonable to exact from one in such circumstances that high degree of skill which an extensive and constant practice in hospitals or large cities would imply a physician to be possessed of.[75]

Raising the issue of the place of practice in the context of required skills was particularly understandable in the United States of America. Marked differences in the development of large urban centres on the East Coast and of sparsely populated, still little explored territories in the west, resulted in the situation where the possibility of gaining experience, as well as access to the newest achievements of medicine and advanced facilities was incomparably greater for doctors in large cities than for those practising far away in the country. In consequence, as scholars indicated, people could not expect the same from a Boston surgeon, who gained his knowledge and experience in a big metropolis, offering great possibilities, and from a doctor practising on the western frontier of the United States, with very limited assess to the current achievements of science and technology.

---

73     *Ibid.*, 23.

74     Milo A. McClelland: *Jurisprudence: with chapters on skill in diagnosis and treatment, prognosis in fractures, and on negligence*, Hurd and Houghton, New York, 1877, 18–19.

75     Thomas G. Shearman, Amasa A. Redfield: *A treatise on the law of negligence*, Baker, Voorhis & Co., Publishers, New York 1870, 508; DeVille: *op. cit.*, 211.

DEVELOPMENT OF THE MEDICAL MALPRACTICE LAW

The conviction growing in the first half of the 19th century and expressed by both judges of jury courts and by scholars, namely that the place of practice should be taken into account while assessing the level of skills which a doctor ought to possess, was sanctioned by judicial decisions of appellate courts in the second half of the 19th century.

One of the first rulings discussing the issue in question was that in the case of *Teft v. Wilcox* from 1870.[76] When considering what due diligence of a doctor means in given circumstances, the judges indicated that he should act in accordance with current medical knowledge, taking into account the general development in medical sciences. However, the court emphasised that such a requirement may be applied to different members of the profession to a varying degree. The judges indicated that the conditions in which some doctors practise "may be many times more favorable than those of others," which may occur "by reason of locality."[77] They heavily relied on the textbook by J.J. Elwell, citing the excerpt concerning the differences in access to achievements in medical knowledge between doctors practising in big cities and those working in the country. Although these considerations clearly indicated that the court was aware of the problem, they were not decisive for the outcome of the case, and merely constituted the *obiter dictum* of the ruling, without assuming the character of precedent.[78]

Nevertheless, it was just a matter of time before the court had to deal directly with the issue of place of practice in the context of doctors' liability. In January 1880, the Massachusetts Supreme Judicial Court examined the case of *Small v. Howard*.[79] The claimant in that case was a patient who had seriously injured his hand on broken glass. As the sued doctor testified: "the cut throughout the whole inside of the wrist extended to the bone, severing all the arteries and tendons."[80] The treatment undertaken by the surgeon did not lead to full recovery and the hand remained disabled. The doctors appointed by both parties indicated before the jury court that the cut, from a medical point of view, was a complicated one and required a high level of skill in treating such kind of wounds.[81] The defendant was a surgeon practising in Chelmsford, a small town in Massachusetts. In his instructions to the jury, the judge indicated that the doctor was obliged to possess knowledge, skills and experience at an appropriate level, usually represented by other members of the profession. He was also

---

76    *Tefft v. Wilcox*, 6 Kan. 46.
77    *Ibid.*, 63–64.
78    DeVille: *op. cit.*, 211.
79    *Small v. Howard*, 128 Mass. 131.
80    *Ibid.*, 132.
81    *Ibid.*

obliged to act in accordance with the principle of due and usual care and diligence in treating the case entrusted to him.[82] The judge further indicated: "The defendant, undertaking to practise as a physician and surgeon in a town of comparatively small population, was bound to possess that skill only which physicians and surgeons of ordinary ability and skill, practising in similar localities, with opportunities for no larger experience, ordinarily possess."[83]

Having taken into account the judge's instructions, the jury decided in favour of the defendant, stating that the doctor was not guilty of inappropriate treatment. The claimant appealed that decision. The claimant's representative indicated that instructing the jurors with regard to the level of skill which a surgeon ought to possess was a mistake. In his opinion, the judicial decisions to date indicated that such a standard was established in a more general way, and a doctor was obliged to possess at least such skills as an average surgeon anywhere in the country, not just such skills as were normally displayed by physicians from small towns. The representative argued that adopting such logic lowered the standards of knowledge and skills expected from physicians and, consequently, constituted a threat to patient safety.[84]

In January 1880, the appeal was decided by the Massachusetts Supreme Judicial Court. Relating to the claims in the appeal, the judges indicated:

> It is a matter of common knowledge that a physician in a small country village does not usually make a speciality of surgery, and, however well informed he may be in the theory of all parts of his profession, he would, generally speaking, be but seldom called upon as a surgeon to perform difficult operations. He would have but few opportunities of observation and practice in that line such as public hospitals or large cities would afford. The defendant was applied to, being the practitioner in a small village, and we think it was correct to rule that "he was bound to possess that skill only which physicians and surgeons of ordinary ability and skill, practising in similar localities, with opportunities for no larger experience, ordinarily possess; and he was not bound to possess that high degree of art and skill possessed by eminent surgeons practising in large cities, and making a speciality of the practice of surgery."[85]

---

82  *Ibid.*

83  *Ibid.*

84  *Ibid.*, 133–134.

85  *Ibid.*, 136.

DEVELOPMENT OF THE MEDICAL MALPRACTICE LAW

This excerpt from the ruling issued by the Massachusetts Supreme Judicial Court for a number of years remained an important precedent for American courts adjudicating with regard to doctors' liability for inappropriate treatment. It indicated that, while assessing whether a doctor failed to comply with the required standard of skill and care in a given case, reference should be made to the model of a physician practising in *similar local conditions*. In the doctrine it was emphasised that the above principle had been established in order to protect doctors practising in the country and to ensure that expectations towards them would not be the same as those towards city physicians, who have wider possibilities for gaining experience, greater access to the newest achievements of medicine, and better technical infrastructure.[86]

## 6    School of Practice Doctrine

Apart from the rule which made it obligatory to take into consideration, in defining the standard of appropriate conduct of a doctor, the place where he was practising, American jurisprudence in the 19th century elaborated one more principle modifying English law in such a way that it could be used in American conditions. That principle was defined in the doctrine as the *school of practice doctrine*.

During its June 1848 term, the Supreme Court of Iowa examined an appeal of the ruling in the case of *Bowman v. Woods*.[87] The proceedings were initiated by Mr and Mrs Woods against Dr Bowman. The facts of the case cited in the content of the ruling showed that the defendant had acted in the capacity of doctor in Mrs Woods' delivery of a child. In the course of the delivery he advised that, following the birth of the child, the placenta should be left in the body of the patient until it had been expelled "by efforts of nature."[88] Contrary to the physician's expectations, the placenta was not expelled naturally, and the condition of the woman was gradually deteriorating. "About thirty-six hours after the delivery" another doctor was summoned.[89] Dr Coffin, who visited the patient at that time, testified before the jury court that, on his arrival, the placenta was still in Mrs Woods' body. This condition resulted in a significant loss of blood and, in consequence, led to the patient's prostration. It was

---

86    Jon R. WALTZ: *The rise and gradual fall of the locality rule in medical malpractice litigation*, De Paul Law Review 18(1969), 410.

87    *Bowman v. Woods*, 1 Greene 441.

88    *Ibid.*, 442.

89    *Ibid.*

the doctor's opinion that Dr Bowman should have removed the placenta much earlier, and that any delay might have resulted in puerperal fever. Several other doctors appointed by the claimants as experts shared Dr Coffin's opinion. As a result, the first-instance jury court found for the injured patient and awarded compensation in the amount of 50 dollars.[90] Dr Bowman appealed the decision.

In his appeal against the ruling the doctor stated that the allegation of inappropriate conduct in the course of delivery, which had been formulated against him, was entirely unjustified. Leaving the placenta in the patient's body until the time of its natural delivery, he acted in complete accordance with the principles of the school of medicine which he was practising, i.e. *botanic medicine*.[91] In other words, Dr Bowman was of the opinion that he could not be charged with *malpractice* since, being a *botanic physician*, he had acted from the beginning in accordance with the standard established by that "system of practice."

Analysis of the decision issued in the case in question by the Supreme Court of Iowa shows clearly how the norms concerning doctors' liability were developing as a result of English common law colliding with American reality in the first half of the 19th century.

First of all, in the justification of the decision issued by the appellate court, it is possible to discern extensive references to English legal heritage. This is visible in several areas. In the introduction to their consideration of the issue of dispute, the judges, characterising the subject of the claim, already indicated that: "The proceedings below were against Bowman for malpractice as a physician, in a case of accouchement."[92] The term *malpractice* used there had been taken directly from the *Commentaries on the Law of England* by William Blackstone.[93]

The concept of *malpractice* used by the court in Iowa had been defined in the third volume of the *Commentaries*. In the section devoted to personal injuries, Blackstone indicated that

> Injuries, affecting a man's health, are where by any unwholesome practices of another a man sustains any apparent damage in his vigour or

---

90    *Ibid.*

91    *Ibid.*

92    *Bowman v. Woods*; "The proceedings below were against Bowman for malpractice as a physician, in case of accouchement."

93    William BLACKSTONE: *Commentaries on the laws of England*, vol. 3, Printed for the subscribers, by Robert Bell, at the late Union Library, in Third-Street, Philadelphia 1771–1772, 122.

DEVELOPMENT OF THE MEDICAL MALPRACTICE LAW

constitution. [...] by the neglect or unskilful management of physician, surgeon or apothecary. For it hath been solemnly resolved ... that *mala praxis* is a great misdemeanour and offence at common law, whether it be for curiosity and experiment, or by neglect; because it breaks the trust which party had placed in his physician, and tends to the patient's destruction.[94]

The direct use by the Supreme Court of Iowa of a concrete term functioning in English common law, was obviously not limited only to a language influence, but was connected with referring to the entire English acquis, related to the legal institution behind that term. This is clearly visible in further considerations of the court. Although the judges did not refer, at any time, *explicite* to any judicial decision issued by an English court with regard to *malpractice*, the phrases cited in the contents of justification unambiguously indicate that they were familiar with those decisions. The statement included there, namely that "on the part of every medical practitioner, the law implies an undertaking that he will use ordinary degree of care and skill in medical operation" is particularly noteworthy.[95] That phrase was taken directly from the ruling in the case of *Lanphier v. Phipos*, issued by an English court in London in 1838. Judge Tindal, adjudicating in that case, stated that "Every person who enters into a learned profession undertakes to bring to the exercise of it a reasonable degree of care and skill."[96] A similar clear reference to the concepts elaborated on the basis of English judicial decisions was the following statement applied by the Supreme Court of Iowa: "the regular physician is expected to follow the rules of the old school in the art of curing."[97] It is impossible not to notice here an analogy to the principle established in the case of *Slater v. Baker and Stapleton*, namely that malpractice means "to do contrary to the rule of the profession, what no surgeon ought to have done."[98]

The Supreme Court of Iowa had to confront those solutions concerning liability for malpractice, elaborated on the basis of English doctrine and judicial

---

94  *Ibid.*, 122.

95  *Bowman v. Woods.*

96  *Lanphier and Wife v. Phipos*, 8; F.A. CARRINGTON, Joseph PAYNE: *Reports of Cases argued and ruled at Nisi Prius, in the Courts of King's Bench, Common Pleas, & Exchequer; together with Cases tried on the Circuits, and in the Central Criminal Court: From Hilary Term, 7 Will. IV., to Easter Term, 2 Vict.*, vol. 8, Andrew Milliken, Dublin, 1839, 475–480.

97  *Bowman v. Woods.*

98  *Slater v. Baker and Stapleton*, 2; George WILSON: *Reports of cases argued and adjudged in the King's courts at Westminster* [1742–1774], E. and R. Brooke and J. Rider, London, 1799, 359–362.

decisions, with the arguments put forward in his appeal by Dr Bowman. Here a significant problem arose. The defendant indicated in his appeal that he was a *botanic physician*. The courts in England, stating that "Every person who enters into a learned profession undertakes to bring to the exercise of it a reasonable degree of care and skill" and that the gauge of appropriate conduct is acting in accordance with "the rule of the profession," related to a precisely defined group of people and to a concrete set of rules. That resulted from the way in which the medical professions in England were functioning in the 18th century. Persons engaged in medicine were divided there into three basic groups: *physicians, surgeons* and *apothecaries*. Each of those "medical orders" had its own organisational structure, tasks and privileges. Physicians, as members of a learned profession, constituted a small elite, clearly separated from surgeons, who were engaged in a sort of craftsmanship, as well as from apothecaries, who were traders.[99] In contrast to surgeons, physicians did not do any physical work. Their task was to "observe, speculate and prescribe" appropriate medicines.[100] They represented the group described as a *status profession*, as opposed to an *occupational profession*. The position of physicians was defined through the prism of the privileges to which they were entitled, and not only on the basis of simple classification by virtue of the work they performed. They constituted a small group of persons living mostly in London and belonging to the Royal College of Physicians, among whose members were solely graduates of Oxford or Cambridge.[101] Hence, practising as a doctor on the British Isles was subject to heavy restrictions. The tradition of defining the requirements whose fulfilment was necessary to practise that profession dated back to the 15th century in England.[102] Therefore, English courts, when defining what appropriate conduct in practising a "learned profession" was referred to a concrete group of people who, in their activities, should observe the principles elaborated on the basis of medical science.

The appellant, Dr Brown, who described himself as a *botanic physician*, did not resemble an English physician in any way. That resulted from radically different conditions in which medical professions were functioning in the United States of America. As John Ordronaux, one of the most eminent American specialists in the area of legal-medical issues, indicated in the late 1860s, "In

---

99   Paul STARR: *The social transformation of American medicine*, Basic Books, New York 1982, 37–38.

100   *Ibid.*, 38.

101   *Ibid.*

102   John H. RAACH: *English medical licensing in the early seventeenth century*, Yale Journal of Biology and Medicine 16 (1944)/4, 267–288; Richard Harrison SHRYOCK: *Medical licensing in America, 1650–1965*, Johns Hopkins Press, Baltimore, 1967, 27.

DEVELOPMENT OF THE MEDICAL MALPRACTICE LAW

England there are three orders in the medical profession, viz., physicians, surgeons, and apothecaries. These orders are the creatures of statutory enactments, defining and prescribing the qualifications, rights, duties and liabilities of such corporate bodies and their members, as also the limits within which their franchise may be exercised. In the United States, these distinctions do not obtain, being considered as essentially opposed to that spirit of the common law which favours the right of every man to practice in any profession or business in which he is competent."[103] The American way in which the medical profession was functioning, characterised by Ordronaux, boiled down to the principle that "medical services" can be rendered by anyone who regards himself as a competent person. In fact, in the first half of the 19th century all the forms of licensing access to practising as a doctor almost completely disappeared in the United States of America. The law, compliant with the spirit of liberalism, did not impose any formal requirements on persons rendering medical assistance, provided they found "clients" interested in their "services" on the open market. That situation was connected with intensive development of alternative methods of treatment, represented, for example, by Dr Bowman.

The conditions in which medical professions were functioning, so radically different in England and the United States in the first half of the 19th century, made it necessary for the court in Iowa, when examining the case of *Bowman v. Woods*, to adopt an entirely different perspective than that of London judges when dealing with the issue of liability on the part of persons providing medical treatment. The judges in Iowa, drawing their knowledge from William Blackstone's *Commentaries* as well as from case law of English courts, were aware of the fact that a doctor should be expected to proceed with "due care," acting in accordance with the "rules established by the practised profession." However, the question how to deal with a person who "treats" patients based on methods other than those of conventional medicine, at the same time taking into consideration the fact that such a person was given, by law, full freedom in his activities, still remained open.

Taking all the above circumstances into account, the Supreme Court of Iowa stated in their ruling as follows:

> As yet there is no particular system of medicine established or favored by the laws of Iowa. And as no system is upheld, none is prohibited. The

---

103 John ORDRONAUX: *The jurisprudence of medicine in its relations to the law of contracts, torts, and evidence: with a supplement on the liabilities of vendors of drugs*, T. & J. W. Johnson & Co., Philadelphia, 1869, 5–6.

regular, the botanic, the homœopathic, the hydropathic, and other modes of treating diseases, are alike unprohibited; and each receives more or less favor and patronage from the people. Though the regular system has been advancing as a science for centuries, aided by research and experience, by wisdom and skill, still the law regards it with no partiality or distinguishing favor; nor is it recognized as the exclusive standard or test by which the other systems are to be adjudged [...]. A person professing to follow one system of medical treatment, cannot be expected by his employer to practice any other [...] The law does not require a man to accomplish more than he undertakes, nor in a manner different from what he professes. Therefore, if in this case, the defendant below could show that he was employed as a botanic physician, and that he performed the accouchement with ordinary skill and care, in accordance with the system he professed to follow, we should regard it as a legal defense [...].The people are free to select from the various classes of medical men, who are accountable to their employers for all injuries resulting from a want of ordinary diligence and skill in their respective systems of treating diseases.[104]

The justification issued by the Supreme Court of Iowa is unambiguous in its form. The principles elaborated on the basis of English common law, namely that a doctor is expected to act with "due care," whose standards are established by the "rules of practised profession" had to be confronted with the reality of Iowa, where medicine could be practised by anyone who wanted to undertake such activities, without the necessity to fulfil any requirements in that area. Therefore, because law in Iowa allowed "in the same degree, different ways of curing diseases," conventional medicine could not be regarded as the only model of appropriate conduct. That led the court to the conclusion that persons rendering medical assistance are liable towards their patients for any damage resulting from lack of ordinary care, but assessed from the perspective of a given way of treatment, practised by them (the so-called *school of practice doctrine*).

## 7  Summary and Conclusions

The achievement of independence by the United States of America presented the local elites with an important question concerning the form of the legal

---

104    *Ibid.*, 443–444.

system in the new country. With regard to systemic law, it was decided to depart from the English model and create a written constitution in the form of one document, regulating the organisation of the federation. At that time, there were postulates that there should also be a new opening in the area of private law. It was argued that achieving independence was the right moment to reject English common law, which was criticised for its anachronisms and permanent state of uncertainty. Furthermore, it was indicated that a legal system derived from a monarchy was not suitable for the republic. Additionally, the postulate for rejecting common law was strengthened by the fact that the codification movement in Europe scored successes in France, particularly favoured by the Americans. However, those arguments proved to be insufficient in the face of rational reasons and the symbolic meaning of common law for the inhabitants of the former colonies. First of all, English law was well-known and applied in practice. Consequently, it was still used in a natural way in the newly-created state. Secondly, the allegation that common law was not observed constituted the main axis of the conflict between the Empire and the colonists. As a result, on the threshold of independence, the Americans perceived common law as the redoubt of their basic rights and freedoms, and in that symbolic meaning it constituted a valuable heritage, worthy of being preserved. Hence common law ultimately became the law in the United States of America.

The main differences between England and the United States did not allow, however, for direct adoption of common law. That law had to be implemented in the newly-created country with its specific character taken into account. Adjusting common law to American conditions made it necessary to take into consideration a number of factors, from differences in the geographical conditions of England and the United States to fundamental issues, such as the completely new social-economic reality in which American statehood was being developed.

The process of creative adaptation of English common law to the conditions and needs of the new society and state was thorough and comprehensive in character. It concerned, among others, such a specific area of law as liability of doctors for inappropriate treatment. The norms regulating this issue also had to be modified in such a way as to be suitable for the conditions and needs of the new country and society. That was evidenced in the 19th century by adopting two principles connected with the liability of doctors for malpractice i.e. the locality rule and the school of practice doctrine.

The specific character of the geographical conditions in the United States of America made it necessary to clarify the rules concerning doctors' liability, known to English common law, in such a way that they would take into account the disproportions in the potential for medical care in different parts of the new state, which varied with regard to their development. People could not expect the same from a Boston surgeon, who gained his knowledge and experience in a big metropolis, offering great possibilities, and from a doctor practising on the western frontier of the United States, with very limited assess to the current achievements of science and technology. This resulted in the development of a principle, in accordance with which the place of practice had to be taken into consideration when assessing the standard of doctors' appropriate conduct.

In turn, adopting the principle that concrete actions by physicians had to be examined in the light of the "school of treatment" practised by them, was closely connected with social transformations which took place at the end of the 18th century and in the first half of the 19th century in the United States of America. In the spirit of liberalism and egalitarianism, i.e. the values which had formed the basis for the new state, all the forms of regulations restricting the possibilities of rendering medical services were abandoned. As as result, patients could be treated by doctors who applied various methods of diagnosis and therapy. Such a situation led to the necessity of modifying the rules of English common law, concerning liability for *medical malpractice*. The standard of due diligence had to be established taking into consideration a concrete school of treatment, represented by the physician sued for malpractice.

The process of creative adjustment of common law norms concerning the liability of doctors for malpractice to the conditions and needs of the American society in the 19th century shows how deeply the factors which are unique in a given country and society influence the form of legal norms, so that they can perform their function as well as possible. The adoption of the locality rule and the school of practice doctrine by American courts in the 19th century demonstrates that, when creating legal solutions based on foreign models, it is necessary to adjust the adopted norms carefully to the conditions and specific character of the environment in which they are to be applied. American judges creating the so-called "school of practice doctrine" and "locality rule" used the law as a tool, an instrument to effectively and rationally regulate the doctor-patient relationship in the American conditions.

## Bibliography

### *Cases*

*Poor v. Greene*, 5 Binn. 554.

*Van Ness v. Packard*, 27 U.S. 137.

*Bloom v. Richards,* 2 Ohio St. 387.

*Tefft v. Wilcox*, 6 Kan. 46.

*Small v. Howard*, 128 Mass. 131.

*Bowman v. Woods*, 1 Greene 441.

*Lanphier and Wife v. Phipos*, 8 Car. & P. 475.

*Slater v. Baker and Stapleton*, 95 E.R. 860.

### *Literature*

Gregory S. ALEXANDER: *Commodity and Propriety: Competing Visions of Property in America Legal Thought, 1776–1970*, Chicago University Press, Chicago, 1997.

Thomas B. ALLEN, *Tories: Fighting for the King in America's First Civil War*, Harper Collins, New York, 2011.

William BLACKSTONE: *Commentaries on the laws of England*, vol. 3, Printed for the subscribers, by Robert Bell, at the late Union Library, in Third-Street, Philadelphia 1771–1772.

David S. BOGEN: *Privileges and Immunities: A Reference Guide to the United States Constitution*, Greenwood Publishing Group, Westport, 2003.

Daniel J. BOORSTIN: *The Americans: The National Experience*, Knopf Doublday Publishing Group, New York, 2010.

*A collection of the statutes of the Parliament of England in force in the state of North-Carolina*, Francois Xavier MARTIN (ed.), From the Editors Press, Newbern, 1792.

Kenneth A. DEVILLE: *Medical Malpractice in Nineteenth Century America. Origins and Legacy*, New York University Press, New York, 1992.

John J. ELWELL: *A Medico-legal treatise on malpractice and medical evidence*, J.S. Voorhies, New York 1860.

Lawrence M. FRIEDMAN: *A history of American Law*, Simon and Schuster, New York, 2005.

Marc D. GINSBERG: *The locality rule lives! Why? Using modern medicine to eradicate an unhealthy law*, Drake Law Review 61(2013).

Charles M. HAAR: *Golden age of American Law*, G. Braziller, New York, 1965.

Morton J. HORWITZ, *The transformation of American law, 1780–1860*, Harvard University Press, Cambridge (MA) 1977.

James Willard HURST: *Law and the conditions of freedom in the nineteenth-century United States*, University of Wisconsin Press, Madison, 1956.

James Willard HURST: *The Growth of American law. The law makers*, Little, Brown, and Company, Boston 1950.

Maurice Eugen LANG: *Codification in the British Empire and America*, H.J. Paris, Amsterdam, 1924.

Charles LOWELL: *An authentic report of a trial before the Supreme Judicial Court of Maine, for the county of Washington, June term, 1824 : Charles Lowell v. John Faxon & Micajah Hawks, surgeons and physicians, in an action of trespass on the case, for igno-*

*rance and negligence in their professional treatment of the plff's dislocated hip : with observations on the prejudices and conduct of the inhabitants of Eastport, in regard to this cause : the character and testimony of the several witnesses, and the novel, and extraordinary positions assumed by the court*, Portland, 1825.

Milo A. McClelland: *Jurisprudence: with chapters on skill in diagnosis and treatment, prognosis in fractures, and on negligence*, Hurd and Houghton, New York, 1877.

John Ordronaux: *The jurisprudence of medicine in its relations to the law of contracts, torts, and evidence: with a supplement on the liabilities of vendors of drugs*, T. & J.W. Johnson & Co., Philadelphia, 1869.

Roscoe Pound: *The formative era of American law*, Boston, Little, Brown, 1938.

John H. Raach: *English medical licensing in the early seventeenth century*, Yale Journal of Biology and Medicine 16 (1944)/4.

Bernard Schwartz: *The Law in America: A History*, Tata McGraw Hill Publishing Company, New York, 1974.

Thomas G. Shearman, Amasa A. Redfield: *A treatise on the law of negligence*, Baker, Voorhis & Co., Publishers, New York 1870.

Richard Harrison Shryock: *Medical licensing in America, 1650–1965*, Johns Hopkins Press, Baltimore, 1967.

Paul Starr: *The social transformation of American medicine*, Basic Books, New York 1982.

Jon R. Waltz: *The rise and gradual fall of the locality rule in medical malpractice litigation*, De Paul Law Review 18(1969).

Charles Warren: *A history of the American bar*, Little, Brown, and Company, Boston, 1911.

CHAPTER 8

# The Contractual Third-Party Notion Beyond the Principle of the Relativity of Contracts: The Comparative Legal History as Methodological Approach

*Sara Pilloni*

## 1 Introduction

In the last few years, the discipline concerning third-party contractual protection has changed substantially, due to both an extension of contractual liability rules and a limitation of the principle of the relativity of contracts.

At the same time, this change has caused great juristic, legal and doctrinal intervention on the third-party as legal notion in different European legal systems and new interesting studies have been carried out concerning the role of the third-party according to contractual law.[1]

Generally speaking, this interest on the topic of third-parties represents an excellent opportunity for legal scholars to describe and explain the development of the issue of the protection of the contractual third-party from different points of view, especially from a historical and comparative one, in order to identify the main instruments as well as legal techniques, which have distinguished the long process of acknowledgement of the third-party as a relevant legal notion. According to this multi-level approach, legal historians can consider this issue from a privileged global perspective, because, starting from the analysis of the Roman law sources regarding the *stipulatio alteri*, one can

---

1  A fine sample of this renewed interest for the third-party as a juridical subject is the study promoted in 2015 by the *Association Henri Capitant des amis de la culture juridique française* focused on the relevance of this legal notion from four different points of view: third-party and contract, third-party and property, third-party and legal procedure, third-party and public law. According to the comparative approach adopted, this study outlines many questions which have traditionally interested the third-party issue in most of Western civil law systems. The conference proceedings have now been published as ASSOCIATION HENRI CAPITANT: *Les tiers. Journées panaméennes de Panama et Chitré, Tome LXV, année 2015*, Bruylant et LB2V, Paris, 2016.

---

© KONINKLIJKE BRILL NV, LEIDEN, 2020 | DOI:10.1163/9789004417274_009

reconstruct the basis of the legal debate on this fundamental topic in the History of private law and the solutions eventually adopted.

Indeed, the topic here proposed is particularly suitable for a scientific and historical analysis involving issues of private law and history of law: it represents an ideal paradigm of the development of private law movements from the ancient Roman discipline to the present, in other words, from the ancient rules and solutions of Roman law to the modern civilian tradition.

The main changes in the acknowledgement of the third-party legal notion will be briefly pointed out and underlined in the following paragraphs, in order to identify the most important issues linked to these changes; the comparative, historical analysis will involve three typical European legal systems, such as the French, the German and the Italian legal systems, which have been interested by a similar evolution in terms of the third-party legal notion, even mutually influenced as regards some peculiar features of the problem.

Despite many undeniable similarities in the evolution of this legal notion in the typical legal systems selected, some differences might be underlined in the process of acknowledgement of the third-party as a relevant legal notion; starting from the common Roman law heritage, a different interpretation of the most relevant sources was at the basis of a huge heterogeneity in the modern configuration of the problem.

Different legal formants[2] had a strong impact on the evolution of the third-party notion in the three legal systems considered: first of all, in a legal instrumentalism perspective, the Roman law sources have been interpreted according to different theoretical and practical issues during middle ages, influencing at the same time each single legal tradition about the evolution of the principle of the relativity of contracts during the modern age.

For this reason, primarily special attention will be devoted to certain classical and epiclassical sources of Roman law as pivotal steps in the building of the relevance of a third-party in European contract law: through the analysis and a brief exegesis of these selected sources, an attempt will be offered to indicate the juridical reasoning at the basis of the long process, which has led to the acknowledgement of the third-party as a relevant legal notion.

The historical analysis will involve only a few selected instances of the whole, complex history concerning the development and acknowledgement of the legal notion of a third-party. As outlined in the following paragraphs,

---

2   On this legal concept, cf. Rodolfo SACCO: *Legal Formants: A Dynamic Approach to Comparative Law* (*Installment I of* II), The American Journal of Comparative Law 39(1991)/1, 1–34 and Rodolfo SACCO: *Legal Formants: A Dynamic Approach to Comparative Law* (*Installment II of II*), The American Journal of Comparative Law 39(1991)/2, 343–401.

THE CONTRACTUAL THIRD-PARTY NOTION                                    193

attention will be focused on specific legal sources and doctrinal movements, which might point out interesting aspects of the subject proposed here without redundantly repeating broad historical analyses, which have already been carried out by some of the most important scholars of legal history.[3]

According to the methodological approach here proposed, specific attention will be given to the Roman Law sources and to the related juridical solutions: these will be functional for a better comprehension of the contractual third-party's protection issue and its development through the history of law.

For this reason, the bird's eye's view on the selected issue befits the diachronic approach adopted hereby: the historical dynamics and process through which the third-party legal notion has been given relevance and acknowledgement are composite and cover a wide range of time, thereby requiring a quick and clear legal historical overview for better understandig the main line of research.

## 2    *Obligatio est iuris vinculum*: The Lack of Relevance in the Acknowledgement of a Third-Party Legal Notion

Historically speaking, Roman law scholars have always analysed the third-party notion as if it were related to the law of contracts in terms of validity and subsequent acknowledgement of the third-party contract, intended as the main exception to the principle of the relativity of contracts.

This approach, focused on the recognition of a *stipulatio alteri* general model and structure, finds its justification on the legal notion of *obligatio* and its discipline as was developed in the Roman law of obligations:[4] indeed, this traditional way of interpreting the third-party issue is probably affected by an

---

3   Reference here is made to some important works which have analysed the third-party issue from both an historical and comparative point of view; among others, cf. Reinhard ZIMMER-MANN: *The law of obligations: Roman foundations of the civilian tradition*, Oxford University Press, Oxford, 1996, 34–45; *Gli effetti del contratto nei confronti dei terzi nella prospettiva storico-comparatistica. IV Congresso Internazionale ARISTEC Roma, 13–16 settembre 1999*, Letizia VACCA (ed.), G. Giappichelli, Torino, 2001; *Ius quaesitum tertio*, E.J.H. SCHRAGE (ed.), Duncker & Humblot, Berlin, 2008; *Contracts for a third-party beneficiary. A historical and comparative account*, Jan HALLEBEEK, Harry DONDORP (eds.), Martinus Nijhoff Publishers, Leiden-Boston, 2008.

4   For a general overview on the Roman law of obligations as related to the third-party issue and the relevant bibliography until the 1970s cf. Mario TALAMANCA: *Obbligazioni (Dir. rom.)* = *Enciclopedia del diritto*, Giuffrè, Milano, 1979, vol. 29, 24–28.

improper overlap concerning contractual obligation between the schemes of the modern law of contracts and the rules of Roman law, giving a false perspective to all the sources concerning the *stipulatio alteri* issue.

In order to better understand the terms of the third-party issue since the development of private law in ancient Rome, the analysis must necessarily begin with the definition of the term *obligatio* according to the only reference available of the entire *Corpus Iuris Civilis*, and more precisely that contained in the *Institutes* of Emperor Justinian.

> I. 3. 13 pr: *Obligatio est iuris vinculum, quo necessitate adstringimur alicuius solvendae rei secundum nostrae civitatis iura.*[5]

Thus, the *obligatio* was conceived as a *iuris vinculum*, i.e. a legal and voluntary bond between the parties that had formed the stipulation: through this legal bond, the parties were obliged by necessity to pay something, according to the law of the Roman *civitas*.[6]

The typical and classical legal structure was indeed bilateral (creditor/obligee/promisee/stipulator, on one side, and debtor/obligor/promisor, on the other side), which did not allow the introduction of a trilateral legal structure (creditor/obligee/promisee/stipulator, debtor/obligor/promisor and third-party).

Consequently, on the one hand, the effects connected to the contractual obligation according to Roman law arose only for the parties involved in this voluntary bond and, on the other hand, only the parties had the power as well as the right to dissolve the bond, i.e. *solvere obligationem*.

This conventional and bilateral structure finds its confirmation in a general rule established to deny the validity of a particular kind of contractual obligation, i.e. the *stipulatio*, when the parties used the contractual obligation to secure the performance for the benefit of a third-party; this rule is known under

---

5 This definition of the term *obligatio* has represented one of the most typical elements in the Roman law tradition, which has influenced juridical science, particularly the civil law codifications, between the 19th and 20th centuries; cf. Massimo Brutti: *Il diritto privato dell'antica Roma*, G. Giappichelli Editore, Torino, 2011, 423–426.

6 The translation here proposed is based on the one suggested by David Ibbetson: *Obligatio in Roman Law and Society = The Oxford Handbook of Roman Law and Society*, Paul J. Du Plessis, Clifford Ando, Kaius Tuori (eds.), Oxford University Press, Oxford, 2016, 573; the author agrees with the intepretation of I. 3. 13 pr proposed by Giovanni Falcone: *Obligatio est iuris vinculum*, G. Giappichelli Editore, Torino, 2003, 173. This definition of the term *obligatio* is now generally ascribed to Gaius' *Res Cottidianae*, accordingly to the exegesis and the attribution proposed in *ibid.*, 30–71.

THE CONTRACTUAL THIRD-PARTY NOTION 195

the name of *alteri stipulari nemo potest* principle[7] and is reported in the Digest

> Ulpianus, libro 49 *ad Sabinum*, D. 45. 1. 38. 17: *Alteri stipulari nemo potest, praeterquam si servus domino, filius patri stipuletur: inventae sunt enim huiusmodi obligationes ad hoc, ut unusquisque sibi adquirat quod sua interest: ceterum ut alii detur, nihil interest mea* (...).

as well as in the *Institutes* of Emperor Justinian

> I. 3.19.19: *Alteri stipulari, ut supra dictum est, nemo potest: inventae sunt enim huiusmodi obligationes ad hoc, ut unusquisque sibi adquirat quod sua interest: ceterum si alii detur, nihil interest stipulatoris* (...).

In more general terms, according to this rule, the parties could not stipulate in favour of a third-party nor could they charge the third-party with a duty, because the rule was established to deny the effect of both the *stipulationes alteri* and the *stipulationes in alterum*.[8]

Concerning the *stipulationes in alterum*, this was not allowed because charging someone with a duty without the assumption of the corresponding liability was considered "inappropriate" according to the principles of Roman law; regarding the *stipulationes alteri*, instead, the promisee was not considered to have any actionable interest in the conclusion of a *stipulatio* whose effects were in favour of a different subject (*nihil interest mea/stipulatoris*).

From another point of view, the reason for such a strict prohibition could also be found in the formal distinctive features behind the contract of a *stipulatio*, which did not give the third-party the right to demand fulfillment of the obligation: these features were conceived to exclusively allow parties to pronounce the ritual *formula*, according to the bilateral structure of the Roman *obligatio*, so that no possibility was given to a third-party to enter the stipulation, not even in the form of a benefit.[9]

---

7   For a general overview on the *alteri stipulari nemo potest rule* and its implications cf. ZIM-MERMANN: *op. cit.*, 34–40 and Jan HALLEBEEK: *Ius Quaesitum Tertio in Medival Roman Law = Ius quaesitum tertio*, E.J.H. SCHRAGE (ed.), Duncker & Humblot, Berlin, 2008, 63–65.

8   This distinction is adopted by Paolo VOCI: *Istituzioni di diritto romano*, Giuffrè Editore, Milano, 2004, 367–368 and Antonio GUARINO: *Diritto privato romano*, Jovene Editore, Napoli, 1992, 837.

9   The *alteri stipulari nemo potest* issue is part of the more general problem concerning the impossibility to acquire something through an *extraneus*, meaning that no one could act for another but had to act only for himself: the *per extraneam personam nobis adquiri non posse*

Since room for the third-party as the centre of its own rights, arising from the *obligatio* itself, was hardly recognisable, according to this conventional and binding general model of obligation, the legal concept and notion of third-party, used to identify a specific category of subjects who are not part of the contract and are not directly interested by its legal effects, was not considered worthy of attention.

After all, Roman jurists, according to their practical case-by-case approach, always showed a clear lack of interest for merely abstract legal problems:[10] notions and general categories of subjects were only introduced much later and belong to the modern doctrinal approach to legal problems, which it would be improper to use for the understanding and interpretation of the issues behind Roman obligations.

However, despite the limits that lay at the basis of Roman private law for the lack of relevance of the third-party legal notion, especially in the contract law, as part of the law of obligations, it was possible to identify certain specific "legal" positions according to which, even if the coinciding subjects remained unrelated to the contract, the corresponding interests had a sort of relevance to Roman law, no matter the nature of the reasons that were at the basis of the contract, whether these were material or legal.

The fact that certain particular cases of *stipulatio alteri* probably became the prevalent practice required a specific juristic intervention and subsequent acknowledgement of the exceptions to the *alteri stipulari nemo potest* rule. Although compilers adapted some classical and epiclassical sources in order for these exceptions to be allowed, the norm was still to adopt the classical, formal rule and include the *alteri stipulari nemo potest* principle in the *Corpus Iuris Civilis*.[11]

---

rule as reported in Gaius, Inst. 2.95 and in the *Pauli sententiae* 5.2.2, and then adopeted in the Justinianic Institutes at I. 2.9.5 and Codex at C. 4.27.1, did not allow direct representation in Roman private law Also related to the *alteri stipulari nemo potest* rule is the general prohition of *emere vendere contrahere, ut alter suo nomine recte agat* as reported in Paulus, libro 12 *ad Sabinum*, D. 44.7.11 and Quintus Mucius Scaevola, *libro singulari "hóron,"* D. 50.17.73.4, which represents an adaptation of that rule to a specific type of contracts, as clearly shown by the use of the verbs *emere, vendere* and *contrahere*. About these principles cf. HALLEBEEK: *op. cit.*, 65–66.

10    Biondo BIONDI: *Contratto e stipulatio*, Giuffrè, Milano, 1953, 3, speaks about a lack of interest in "juridical architecture" problems.

11    The reference is here to a group of sources in which a direct action was granted to a subject who did not take part to the conclusion of the *stipulatio*: using modern terms which belong to the German private law doctrine, we should speak here about *Echter Vertrag zugunsten Dritter* cases, i.e. cases in which the third-party emerges as a relevant, juridical subject.

THE CONTRACTUAL THIRD-PARTY NOTION                                    197

The legal positions and related sources have often been linked to Roman law in the attempt to find some legal precedents of the modern third-party contract from the time of ancient Rome. Indeed, the sources at the basis of these case studies have mostly been interpolated by Emperor Justinian's compilers in order to adapt the classical sources to the innovations of Justinian's age. Thus, it is rather complicated to reconstruct what the authentic solution found by classical jurists was as well as the original purpose they pursued in the regulation of the case studies considered.

For this reason, the sources and the case studies regulating them should be considered from two different perspectives: classical and epiclassical Roman law on the one side, and the Roman law of Justinian's time on the other. The latter, in particular, could provide the legal historian with a first, concrete approach to the doctrinal issue concerning the third-party legal notion and its evolution.

3      The Grant of an Action to a Third-Party According to Certain Classical and Epiclassical Sources: Is this a Real, Systematic Intervention or Rather a Modern, Doctrinal Overinterpretation?

According to Justinian's Chancellery policies, an *actio utilis* was granted for certain specific and controversial cases in order to guarantee the right to sue those subjects who were not originally an active party to the contract; as a partial exception to this intervention fom the Justinian age, we can take one epiclassical constitution into account, which is reputed to be original and to concern the *donatio sub modo* as a possible case of third-party contract

> C. 8.54.3, Impp. Diocletianus et Maximianus AA. Iuliae Marcellae, a. 290: pr. *Quotiens donatio ita conficitur, ut post tempus id quod donatum est alii restituatur, veteris iuris auctoritate rescriptum est, si is in quem liberalitatis compendium conferebatur stipulatus non sit, placiti fide non impleta, ei qui liberalitatis auctor fuit vel heredibus eius condicticiae actionis persecutionem competere. 1. Sed cum postea benigna iuris interpretatione divi principes ei qui stipulatus non sit utilem actionem iuxta donatoris voluntatem*

---

One cannot find a specific space in this brief analysis for the cases of *Unechter Vertrag zugunsten Dritter*, in which the possibility of granting an action to a third-party was absolutely denied, but the *stipulatio alteri* was considered to be valid at least for the promisee if it corresponded to a particular and patrimonial interest of the promisee himself.

*competere admiserint, actio, quae sorori tuae, si in rebus humanis ageret, competebat, tibi accommodabitur.*

According to the rescript of Emperor Diocletian, an *actio utilis* could be granted as a result of the Emperor's *benigna iuris interpretation*, i.e. in case of a donation in which an object was transferred after a certain period of time to another person, i.e. a second donee: in this way, a trilateral operation (donor – first donee – second donee) was performed and, although the second donee did not have any right to ask the fulfillment of the *modus*, according to ancient Roman law, Diocletian's Chancellery admitted granting of an action *iuxta donatoris voluntatem*.[12]

From the point of view of Roman law, the structure of the juridical operation as well as the action granted to the second donee, as third-party, relate this case study to the modern idea of third party-contract much more than other sources, which have been considered to be linked to that institution;[13] indeed, if in this case of *donatio sub modo* we can gather the structure of a general trilateral operation, in the other case studies involved in the third-party issue this abstraction does not seem to be as suited.

Other case studies, which have been supposed to be likely legal precedents of the modern third-party contract, concern relevant legal positions and might be classified into three different categories: the restitution and/or constitution of the dowry[14], the deposit (or commodate) accomplished by a restitution

---

12      The rescript has also been preserved as *Fragmenta Vaticana* nr. 286, in Theodor MOMMSEN: *Iuris anteiustiniani fragmenta quae dicuntur vaticana = Collectio librorum iuris anteiustiniani in usum scholarum*, Paul KRUEGER, Theodor MOMMSEN, Wilhelm STUDEMUND (eds.), Apud Weidmanoss, Berolini, 1890, vol. 3, 91 (http://droitromain.upmf-grenoble.fr/Responsa/FragVat.htm, accessed: 10.03.2017).

        The Fragmenta Vaticana text presents only few differences from the subsequent compilers' text; about this fundamental source in the history of third-party rights cf. Mario TALAMANCA: *Diocl. et Max. C. 8. 54. 3* = FV. 286: *«donatio sub modo», «datio ob rem» e contratto a favore di terzi = Studi in onore di Antonino Metro*, C. RUSSO RUGGERI (ed.), vol. 6, Giuffré, Milano, 2010; Giovanni FINAZZI: *Il contratto a favore di terzo proprio nell'esperienza giuridica romana = Studi in onore di Antonino Metro*, C. RUSSO RUGGERI (ed.), vol. 2, Giuffré, Milano, 2010, 464–467; ZIMMERMANN: *op. cit.*, 39–40; HALLEBEEK: *op. cit.*, 72.

13      In this sense cf. the considerations developed in TALAMANCA: *Diocl. et Max....*, *op. cit.*, 282.

14      Different epiclassical Imperial constitutions are related to this first category: C. 5.14.4, Imp. Gordianus A. Torquatae, a. 239; C. 5.14.7, Impp. Diocletianus et Maximianus AA. et CC. Phileto, a. 294; C. 5.12.26, Impp. Diocletianus et Maximianus AA. et CC. Demostheni, a. 294; C. 5.12.19 pr., Impp. Diocletianus et Maximianus AA. et CC. Achilli, a. 294. The particular object of these sources (the dowry and its constitution and/or restitution) is at the basis of the interesting circumstance that the third-party was mostly a woman: the

THE CONTRACTUAL THIRD-PARTY NOTION                                        199

agreement in favour of a third-party[15] (in which the controversial case of the *depositum in publicum*[16] might be included) and the sale of the pledge by the pledgee accomplished by a restitution agreement in favour of the pledgor, who is considered as a third-party in respect to the sale contract.[17]

All these legal positions and their classification into the aforementioned categories are based on the attempt in the related sources to try and find a solution in favour of a subject who, however, does not figure as a party in the main stipulation: Justinian's Chancellery considered the third-party, in these cases, as a juridical subject worthy of granting an *actio* in order to give him/her the right to sue on the agreement.

In the case of the *donatio sub modo* mentioned above, other than Diocletian's Chancellery, the compilers also recognised both the peculiarity of these specific legal positions, in which the general aim was not to benefit the obligee/promisee/stipulator but the third-party beneficiary, and the reason for an intervention based on the *aequitas* as a source of integration and effective justice in case of a lack of appropriate and conventional solutions.

The large diffusion of contractual praxis to stipulate in favour of specific third-parties in exceptional cases, such as the four categories described above, likely determined the need in both Imperial chancelleries for a direct intervention, in order to protect these specific positions and harmonise and make uniform the discipline behind these particular agreements.

In this sense, the innovative intervention seems to be not related to a systematic reformulation of the *alteri nemo potest* rule, but rather appears to be linked to the specific cases, which, time by time, were considered, and, which, however, were suitable to compile to the legal positions, as classified in the four categories already described.

In fact, this abstract classification is the result of the exegetical work of the doctrine on the relevant Roman sources from the time of the scholars of medieval Roman law. For this reason, there is no room for a generalisation from these specific cases, which rather represent a typical feature of a doctrinal approach of these juridical issues by Roman jurists.

This approach shows all its limitations when it also leads modern scholars to misinterpret these cases: indeed, the integrative interventions during Justinian's time (epiclassical in the *donatio sub modo* case) were based on the typical

---

     peculiar, personal *status* of women in ancient Rome caused in practice the development
     of specific, juridical solutions in order to protect their interests.

15     Cf. C. 3.42.8, Impp. Diocletianus et Maximianus AA. et CC. Photino, a. 293.

16     Cf. C. 4.32.19, Impp. Diocletianus et Maximianus AA. et CC. Aureliae Irenae.

17     Cf. Ulpianus, libro 38 *ad edictum*, D. 13.7.13 pr.

Roman case-by-case approach, which means that the acknowledgement and definition of a third-party legal notion were not characterised by a real, systematic intervention.

Rather, this idea represented an improper doctrinal overinterpretation of a modern legal issue applied to the Roman sources so that their original range and relevance was missing, which caused a general misunderstanding regarding the third-party issue in the Roman law of obligations and contracts.

## 4 The Exceptions to the *Alteri Stipulari Nemo Potest* Rule beyond Roman Law: The Emergence of the Third-Party Relevance in the Law of Obligations and Contracts According to the Medieval Roman Law

As briefly pointed out above, the classification into specific categories of the limited cases of granting an action to the third-party represents the result of the doctrinal interpretation of the Roman private law system from the time of the scholars of medieval Roman law.

Indeed, even if this exegetical and interpretational work does not completely respect the *ratio* and meaning of the Roman legal solutions, as considered in their own context, it has played a pivotal role in the construction of a dedicated space for the third-party as legal notion in the European civil system.

The sources of Roman law have been studied since the 12th century and since the development of the Law School of the University of Bologna in order to identify their relation with the formal rule, which denied the validity to the *stipulatio alteri*: the *Quatuor Doctores* generally adopted a case-by-case approach based on the bilateral relationship "formal rule – strict exceptions", without trying to extrapolate those exceptions into a general principle.

Among the jurists and glossators of Roman law, Bulgarus, in particular, whose teaching and work of interpretation can be read in the *Casus Codicis* by his pupil Wilhelmus de Cabriano,[18] strictly denied that any *stipulatio alteri*, outside of the recognised exceptions, could be considered valid, according to

---

18    The *Casus Codicis* has been recently edited by Tammo WALLINGA: *The Casus Codicis of Wilhelmus de Cabriano*, Vittorio Klostermann Verlag, Frankfurt a. M., 2005.

THE CONTRACTUAL THIRD-PARTY NOTION                                    201

the "prohibition of analogy" as internal *ratio* of the Digest.[19] For the scholar,
any violation of this prohibition represented a direct violation of the law:[20]

> Gl. excepta, C. 4.27.1, ll. 18–40: *Ceterum ea que iuris sunt ex procuratoris*
> *contractu plerumque nobis queruntur. "Queruntur" dico utiliter, non direc-*
> *to: utiles enim actiones interdum nobis ex contractu procuratoris dantur, ut*
> *in deposito et in quibusdam aliis casibus, que maxime circa iudicia reperit-*
> *ur. Ex tali itaque stipulatione nec procuratori queritur cum eius non intersit,*
> *nec domino: nam cum alteri quis stipulatur non ei cui fit set ei qui facit stip-*
> *ulationem actio queritur, isque solus ex tali contractu agit, si eius intersit.*
> *Sunt tamen casus in quibus et ei cui stipulatio st facta actio quesita creditur.*
> *Ubi ergo cuius interest alii dari poterit alteri stipulari, ut interdum directa*
> *actio nascatur, interdum utilis detur, id est: vel directa competat ei qui stipu-*
> *latus est, vel utilis datur ei cui stipulationem fecit. Interesse autem estima-*
> *tur vel ratione persone vel etiam propter affectionem.*
>
> *Quedam etiam stipulationes alii facte subsistunt speciali ratione: ratione*
> *persone, ut si creditori procuratorive suo quis stipulatus sit, quo casu ei qui*
> *stipulatus est actio competit affectionis ratione, cum pater nepotibus stipu-*
> *latus est, quando cui stipulatio facta est, actio danda est, ut infra de pactis*
> *dotalibus Pater [C.5.14.7] et ff. Sol. matri. Gaius [D.24.3.45]; ratione singu-*
> *lari, ut C. ad exhibendum l. penult. [C. 3.42.8] et ff. de pignorat. Si cum*
> *[D.13.7.13] et de donationibus que sub modo Quotiens [C. 8.54.3], quius casi-*
> *bus et ei cui stipulatio facta est actio danda est. Ubi ergo reperieris ex alte-*
> *rius contractu alteri actionem dari, cum certi sint casus in iure nostro com-*
> *prehensi in quibus debeat decerni, ibi dandam merito dixeris. Ceterum si*
> *passim hoc ad consequentias trahere volueris, vereor ne legem offendas.*

The exceptions acknowledged by epiclassical and late Roman law were considered to be based on a *ratio singularis*, which deviated from the general *ratio*
*iuris* and allowed granting a direct action (*actio directa*) to the third-party in
contrast to the prohibition described by the *alteri stipulari nemo potest* rule.

---

19 Paulus, libro 54 *ad edictum*, D. 1.3.14 = D. 50.17.141 pr: *Quod vero contra rationem iuris recep-*
   *tum est, non est producendum ad consequentias.*

   About the principle of analogy in the glossators' thought cf. Gerhard OTTE: *Dialektik*
   *und Jurisprudenz, Untersuchungen zur Methode der Glossatoren*, Vittorio Klostermann,
   Frankfurt a.M., 1971, 203–204.

20 Cf. WALLINGA: *op. cit.*, 274.

Martinus Gosia, indeed, in contrast to the other *Doctores*, followed the opposite path and tried to generalise the use of equity at the basis of the epiclassical interventions and those of Justinian's time in order to overcome the conventional limits of the *strictum ius* and consequently consider a *stipulatio alteri* as a valid contractual obligation,[21] according to his interpretation of Roman *aequitas*, which was clearly expressed in the Accursian gloss at section C. 4.27.1[22]

> Gl. nulla, C. 4.27.1: *Nulla de stricto iure, sed de aequitate, sic. M(artinus), quod Io (hanni) non placet.*

As can be read in Hugolinus de Presbyteris' *Dissensiones dominorum*, Martinus Gosia acknowledged a general use of the *actio utilis* and consequently allowed the third-party to sue on the agreement in its favour, which was not affected by invalidity:[23]

> *item dicit M.(artinus), quod ex alieno pacto utilis actio datur ei, in cuius persona conceptum est, et hoc exemplo C. ad Exhib. L. Penult. (C. 3.42.8) C. de Donat.(ionibus), quae sub modo L. Quotiens (C. 8.54.3). Bul.(garus) vero et U.(go) et Iac.(obus) dicunt, non dari, nisi expressim dixit, quum iuris regula sit, ex alieno pacto actionem non dari.*

Thus, Martinus Gosia channeled both the *actio directa* and the *actio utilis* towards the achievement of the same result, i.e. to give the third-party the right to sue on the agreement in case of failure of the promisor to follow it, uniforming all the exceptions of the *Corpus Iuris Civilis* in a general "equity" rule.[24]

---

21      About Martinus Gosia's position among the *Quatuor Doctores* cf. HALLEBEEK: *op. cit.*, 75–77.

22      Cf. *Codicis domini Iustiniani sacratissimi principis perpetui Augusti. iuris enucleati ex omni veteri iure collecti repetitae praelectionis*. Al colophon finale: "Explicit feliciter. Anno domini Millesimo cccclxxxij die xxij mensis Novembris per magistrum Johannem Syber," Lugduni, N 9r-v-.

23      Cf. HUGOLINI DE PRESBYTERIS: *Diversitates sive dissensiones dominorum sive controversiae veterum iuris romani interpretum*, Ed. Haenel, Lipsia, 1834, §256, 428–429.

24      The generalisation for Martinus Gosia is based on the acknowledgement of a *nudus pactum* in the cases described at C. 3.42.8 (deposit or commodate accomplished by a restitution agreement in favour of a third-party) and C. 8.54.3 (*donatio sub modo*), from which an action was admitted in order to allow the third-party to sue on the *pactum*. In this sense cf. Jan HALLEBEEK: *Contracts for a third-party beneficiary: a brief sketch from the Corpus Iuris to present-day civil law*, Fundamina, 13(2007)/2, 15.

THE CONTRACTUAL THIRD-PARTY NOTION                                        203

Historically speaking, since the debate started among the *Quatuor Doctores*, the emergence of a general consideration for the third-party issue can be discovered. Although the object of the *Quatuor Doctores'* study was not the identification of a general third-party notion, their work conducted on the exceptions of the *Corpus Iuris Civilis* to the *alteri stipulari nemo potest* rule paved the way towards the acknowledgement of the relevance and validity of third-parties' stipulations and contracts.

Moreover, Martinus Gosia pioneered the idea of a generalisation and abstraction of the *stipulatio alteri* structure: by demolishing the concept of the third-party issue as a mere exception to the *alteri stipulari nemo potest* rule, he tried to give the *alter* juridical relevance.

The doctrinal heritage which these scholars have left us, i.e. this duality of perspective in considering the *stipulatio alteri* issue, has drawn the attention of the entire debate on the relevance of the third-party, the relativity of contract rules as well as the long process to acknowledge the third-party contract as a general contractual structure.

Even if the coherence of the *stipulatio alteri* as a general contractual structure with the contractual system and its accordance to the *ius naturae* was to be acknowledged for the first time only much later with the work of Hugo Grotius, as illustrated in the *De jure belli ac pacis libri tres*,[25] the duality of perspective described above by previous authors certainly had a pivotal role in the building of a theoretical and doctrinal approach to the third-party issue.[26]

---

      About the concept of *aequitas* in Martinus Gosia's doctrine cf. HALLEBEEK: *Ius Quaesitum Tertio...*, *op. cit.*, 77 and Hans ANKUM: *Die Verträge zugunsten Dritter in den Schriften einiger mittelalterlicher Romanisten und Kanonisten = Sein und Werden im Recht. Festgabe für Ulrich von Lübtow zum 70. Geburtstag am 21. August 1970*, Walter G. BECKER, Ludwig SCHNORR VON CAROLSFELD (eds.), Dunker & Humblot, Berlin, 1970, 559–560.

25    HUGONIS GROTTII: *De jure belli ac pacis libri tres, in quibus jus naturae & gentium, item juris publici praecipua explicantur = The Classics of International Law*, J.B. SCOTT (ed.), vol. 1, Carnegie Institution of Washington, Washington., 1913, 224–227.

26    About the the role of Hugo Grotius in the acknowledgement of a general model of third-party contract cf. Harry DONDORP, Jan HALLEBEEK: *Grotius' Doctrine on adquisitio obligationis per alterum and its Roots in the Legal Past of Europe = Panta rei. Studi dedicati a Manlio Bellomo*, Orazio CONDORELLI (ed.), Il Cigno GG Edizioni, Roma, 2005, vol. 2, 205–244; Harry DONDORP: *The Seventeenth and Eighteenth Centuries = Contracts for a third-party beneficiary. A historical and comparative account*, Jan HALLEBEEK, Harry DONDORP (eds.), Martinus Nijhoff Publishers, Leiden-Boston, 2008, 55–58.

## 5 The Modern Approach to the Third-Party Issue: Some General Considerations from the Third-Party Contract to the Modern Discipline of Third-Party Protection

Starting from the acknowledgement of coherence of the *stipulatio alteri* with the general contractual system, as illustrated by Hugo Grotius, the *alteri stipulari nemo potest* principle could be dogmatically overcome and the validity of the third-party contract definitely admitted, finding its own specific place in modern civil law codifications.

In this sense, the long process which took place up to the recognition of the third-party and its legal notion culminated with the reception of a general structure of the *stipulatio alteri* in the 19th century codifications, although this did not occur in a uniform way. Two different models, in fact, in contrast to each other were proposed, i.e. the French Civil Code (1804) and the German Civil Code (1900), which showed a different approach both in terms of the principle of the relativity of contracts and in terms of the third-party contract as general, contractual institute.

The authors of the French Civil Code, under the influence of Pothier's exegesis of the related Roman law sources,[27] adopted a conservative approach and retained the *alteri stipulari nemo potest* rule,[28] as stated in the previous Art. 1165:[29]

> *Les conventions n'ont d'effet qu'entre les parties contractantes; elles ne nuisent point au tiers, et elles ne lui profitent que dans le cas prévu par l'article 1121.*

---

27 Cf. Robert Joseph POTHIER: *Traité des obligations. Tome premier*, Chez Debure l'aîné, Paris, Chez Rouzeau – Montaut, Orléans, 1761, 67–92.

28 About the development of the *alteri stipulari nemo potest* rule in the French private law system under an historical and comparative perspective, cf. René-Marie RAMPELBERG: *Brève perspective comparative sur les destinées de la règle «alteri stipulari nemo potest»* = *Les concepts contractuels français à l'heure des principes du droit européen des contrats*, Pauline RÉMY-CORLAY, Dominique FENOUILLET (eds.), Dalloz, Paris, 2003.

29 Cf. also the previous art. 1119 of the *Code Civil*, according to which *On ne peut, en général, s'engager, ni stipuler en son propre nom, que pour soi-même.*

  Recently, the *Ordonnance n° 2016-131 du 10 février 2016 portant réforme du droit des contrats, du régime général et de la preuve des obligations* modified a great part of the French Civil Code and also reformulated the relativity of contracts' principle and its exceptions. According to the new art. 1199 of the *Code civil*: *Le contrat ne crée d'obligations qu'entre les parties. Les tiers ne peuvent ni demander l'exécution du contrat ni se voir contraints de l'exécuter, sous réserve des dispositions de la présente section et de celles du chapitre III du titre IV.*

THE CONTRACTUAL THIRD-PARTY NOTION                                   205

Only two exceptions were admitted and codified in Art. 1121:

> *On peut pareillement stipuler au profit d'un tiers lorsque telle est la condition d'une stipulation que l'on fait pour soi-même ou d'une donation que l'on fait à un autre. Celui qui a fait cette stipulation ne peut plus la révoquer si le tiers a déclaré vouloir en profiter.*

These deviations from the strict prohibition of stipulating in favour of a third-party were based on the idea of an actionable interest as a condition for a valid stipulation (*condition d'une stipulation que l'on fait pour soi-même*), according to Ulpianus (libro 49 *ad Sabinum*, D. 45.1.38.17), and on the case of the *donatio sub modo*, as provided in Diocletian's rescript C. 8.54.3 (*condition ... d'une donation que l'on fait à un autre*).[30]

In contrast to the French model, the authors of the German Civil Code opted for a different and more complete discipline of the third-party contract: without providing a specific, binding rule for the relativity of contracts, they naturally acknowledged a direct action in favour of the third-party and the third-party contract as a general institute within German contract law also drawing a distinction between the *Echter Vertrag zugunsten Dritter* and the *Unechter Vertrag zugunsten Dritter*:[31]

> § 328 BGB, Vertrag zugunsten Dritter: *1. Durch Vertrag kann eine Leistung an einen Dritten mit der Wirkung bedungen werden, dass der Dritte unmittelbar das Recht erwirbt, die Leistung zu fordern.*
>
> *2. In Ermangelung einer besonderen Bestimmung ist aus den Umständen, insbesondere aus dem Zweck des Vertrags, zu entnehmen, ob der Dritte das Recht erwerben, ob das Recht des Dritten sofort oder nur unter gewissen Voraussetzungen entstehen und ob den Vertragschließenden die*

---

30   Cf. ZIMMERMANN: *op. cit.*, 44. Regarding the role of Roman sources in the French legal system and the development of the *stipulatio alteri* doctrine cf. also Harry DONDORP: *The Reception of Institutes 3. 19. 19 in France = Ex iusta causa traditum; Essays in honour of Eric H. Pool (Fundamina nummer: editio specialis)*, Rena VAN DEN BERGH (ed.), University of South Africa, Pretoria, 2005, 59–68.

31   Regarding the historical development until the codification of the third-party contract in the German BGB at §§ 328–335 cf. among others Martin PENNITZ: *Ius quaesitum tertio: German Legal Doctrine and Practice in the 18th and 19th Century = Ius quaesitum tertio*, E.J.H. SCHRAGE (ed.), Duncker & Humblot, Berlin, 2008.

On the general structure of the Vertrag zugunsten Dritter according to the German contract law cf. among the others Walter BAYER: *Der Vertrag zugunsten Dritter: neuere Dogmengeschichte – Anwendungsbereich – dogmatische Strukturen*, Mohr, Tübingen, 1995.

*Befugnis vorbehalten sein soll, das Recht des Dritten ohne dessen Zustimmung aufzuheben oder zu ändern.*

Only the interpretive work carried out by French courts on the idea of an actionable interest, which regarded the condition of a valid stipulation in terms of a profit, at least moral, for the *stipulator*, paved the way for a third-party contract in French contract law,[32] which was close to the German model.

The Italian codification appears to be quite different from the two aforementioned general models, which can be considered, together with the Austrian Codification, as original archetypes in the processing of codification. The Italian Civil Code, instead, was not conceived as a first-generation code, but rather a derived one, since its first redaction, from the French and German models.

The third-party contract discipline in the Italian Civil Code was broadly based on both the models described above, according to the peculiar nature of the code itself. If the Italian codification of 1865 concerning the third-party contract discipline was perfectly in line with the Napoleonic Code,[33] the new Civil Code of 1942 opted for the German solution, preferring the general and abstract model of the third-party contract and corresponding right for the third-party to sue on the contract itself:[34]

> Art. 1411 of the Italian Civil Code: *1. È valida la stipulazione a favore di un terzo, qualora lo stipulante vi abbia interesse.*
>
> *2. Salvo patto contrario, il terzo acquista il diritto contro il promittente per effetto della stipulazione. Questa però può essere revocata o modificata*

---

32    The reform also interested the specific issue of third-parties contractual effects and introduced at the Artt. 1205–1207 a more detailed discipline for the *stipulation pour autrui*, broadly based on the interpretation of Art. 1121 of the *Code civil* given by the French courts; actually, according to the new Art. 1205: On peut stipuler pour autrui, i.e. the *stipulation pour autrui* is now formally allowed without imposing any other condition.

      This new regulation appears to be closer to the solutions generally adopted in the other civil law systems.

33    Art. 1128 Codice Civile 1865: *Nessuno può stipulare in suo proprio nome, fuorché per sé medesimo. Tuttavia può ciascuno stipulare a vantaggio di un terzo, quando ciò formi condizione di una stipulazione che fa per se stesso, o di una donazione che fa ad altri. Chi ha fatta questa stipulazione, non può rivocarla, se il terzo ha dichiarato di volerne profittare.*

      Art. 1130 Codice Civile 1865: *I contratti non hanno effetto che tra le parti contraenti: essi non pregiudicano nè giovano ai terzi, fuorchè nei casi stabiliti dalla legge.*

34    On the third-party contract in the Italian Civil Code of 1942 cf. among the others Lucio Valerio MOSCARINI: *Il contratto a favore di terzi. Artt. 1411–1413*, Giuffrè, Milano, 2012.

*dallo stipulante, finché il terzo non abbia dichiarato, anche in confronto del promittente di volerne profittare.*

*3. In caso di revoca della stipulazione o di rifiuto del terzo di profittarne, la prestazione rimane a beneficio dello stipulante, salvo che diversamente risulti dalla volontà delle parti o dalla natura del contratto.*

Eventually, the brief itinerary through the third-party contract, just outlined, shows how the generalisation of the *ratio*, under the exceptions of the Roman law to the *alteri stipulari nemo potest* rule, was accepted as main rule by the doctrine, by the legislation and even by the jurisprudence in most European civil law systems, although, as we briefly pointed out, with substantial differences. Whereas the German BGB admitted the general validity of third-party contracts, in other systems this process took place through different channels, i.e. the courts in the French system and the doctrine in the Italian system, opening the way towards the acknowledgement of a uniform, abstract structure of the *stipulatio alteri* that was beyond the strict limits of the formal, binding rule.

However, in more recent times, the third-party protection issue has been the subject of deep change, which actually has passed through the acknowledgement of the third-party as a sort of relevant contractual subject outside the limits of the relativity of contract rules.

This fundamental change in the consideration of the third-party corresponds to a new interest and importance of the third-party itself as a centre of economic and legal interest; a circumstance, this last one, which is in need of something different and more effective than a simple intervention on the traditional relativity of the principle of contracts.

In this sense, a pivotal role has been played by the reconsideration of the field of the application of the contractual liability rules in order to also extend the advantages connected to this type of liability to specific third-parties against the extra-contractual liability, while trying at the same time to assimilate the third-party itself to the contractual structure through the use of doctrinal or jurisprudential schemes as, for instance, the "contract with protective effects towards third-parties", i.e. the German private law institute *Vertrag mit Schutzwirkung zugunsten Dritter*.[35]

---

35   Especially the "contract with protective effects towards third-parties," as an independent and specific contractual institute, has had a certain influence on the Italian third-party protection issue, thanks to the work of Paolo Castronovo on the notion of "obblighi di protezione," i.e. protective effects and duties in favour of the third-party.

The *ratio* according to which the third-party legal positions, which deserve increased protection, are identified is quite similar to the one at the basis of the valid *stipulationes alteri* of Roman law together with their interpretation by the scholars of medieval law. A sense of equality inspires the idea of more effective protection of particularly weak categories of subjects, whose position in relation to a valid contract concluded between two contracting parties is considered worthy of the maximum degree of protection provided by the law of contracts, i.e. the extension of contractual liability.

Both functional approaches, although temporally far apart from each other, have in common the way they approached the relevant problems and developed an appropriate solution in order to go beyond the strict limits of the formal, binding rule: first the *alteri stipulari nemo potest* rule and then the basic conditions for the application of the contractual liability rules, by becoming a real and effective party of a contract.

## 6    Conclusion

According to all the above considerations and the general overview of certain sources of Roman law as well as different events that occurred in the history of the third-party issue, the scholar, especially the legal historian, is provided with a wealth of knowledge to identify problems and trends in the protection of third-parties as they evolved in similar civil law systems, despite the different methodological approach to the issue.

As we have noted at the beginning of this brief analysis, the third-party issue is still considered a current, important topic in the study of movements in private law; more specifically, the tendency to study and reformulate the fundamental rules of private law is mostly caused by changes and reforms of those legal institutes, which normally were considered to be part of the civil tradition, as the recent reform of the French law of obligations has clearly shown.

Through the analysis of the historical evolution of the relevance and acknowledgement of the third party in the law of contracts, we could have stressed that the third-party issue has often been related to the third-party

---

Also Italian courts recognised in few, specific cases the application of this contract, for example in case of birth injuries and damages and medical malpractice, even if now we can consider this exegetical aproach as almost set apart.

For an overview on the "contract with protective effects towards third-parties" issue in the Italian private law system and some bibliographical suggestions cf. Giovanni VARANESE: *Il contratto con effetti protettivi per i terzi*, Edizioni Scientifiche Italiane, Napoli, 2004.

contract, but actually this assimilation does not cover all the possible ways to look at the third-party as a relevant legal notion.

The sources considered and the interpretational work, which historically has been carried out by scholars and commentators through the history of private law, have shown how the third-party can also be considered from a different point of view, i.e. a subject who is not a party of the contract and must be considered worthy of protection only in exceptional and specific cases.

Furthermore, the analysis has revealed how a uniform interpretive approach can be identified: we are speaking about the case-by-case approach, which has characterised both Roman law and the subsequent doctrine until the modern extension of the rules of contractual liability to the third-party and which has allowed to identify the real and appropriate role played by this legal subject under the perspective of the history of private law.

The trend to generalise its discipline, giving it an abstract nature, normally corresponds to an increase in the praxis of considering the third-party position as relevant, even if it is touched by the effects of the contracts only indirectly; nevertheless, a case-by-case approach, which suggests regulation of the position of subjects involved only in similar, relevant cases appears to be the most appropriate approach to follow, since it is able to adapt the law to the demands of everyday life.

In this way, a pivotal role has been played by the different legal formants, with a special attention to the creative contribution assured by the jurisprudence; also in the civil law systems considered, the legal instrumentalism approach has revealed to be more effective then an interpretation based on the mere legal formalism, adopting a new perspective on the strict application of the principle of the relativity of contracts.

Therefore, the bird's eye's view on the selected issue and the diachronic perspective adopted has been revealed as the optimal solution for better understandig the connection line between the composite and different legal experiences through centuries. This global and historical approach can make many comparative issues and considerations possible, which are certainly functional to a better comprehension of the role of third-parties and to their relevance in the history and development of private law in various European legal systems.

### Bibliography

Hans ANKUM: *Die Verträge zugunsten Dritter in den Schriften einiger mittelalterlicher Romanisten und Kanonisten = Sein und Werden im Recht. Festgabe für Ulrich von Lübtow zum 70. Geburtstag am 21. August 1970,* **Walter G.** BECKER, **Ludwig** SCHNORR VON CAROLSFELD (eds.), Dunker & Humblot, Berlin, 1970.

ASSOCIATION HENRI CAPITANT: *Les tiers. Journées panaméennes de Panama et Chitré, Tome LXV, année 2015*, Bruylant et LB2V, Paris, 2016.

Walter BAYER: Der Vertrag zugunsten Dritter: neuere Dogmengeschichte – Anwendungsbereich – dogmatische Strukturen, Mohr, Tübingen, 1995.

Biondo BIONDI: *Contratto e stipulatio*, Giuffrè, Milano, 1953.

Massimo BRUTTI: *Il diritto privato dell'antica Roma*, G. Giappichelli, Torino, 2011.

Harry DONDORP: *The Seventeenth and Eighteenth Centuries = Contracts for a third-party beneficiary. A historical and comparative account*, Jan HALLEBEEK, Harry DONDORP (eds.), Martinus Nijhoff Publishers, Leiden-Boston, 2008, 47–68.

Harry DONDORP, Jan HALLEBEEK: *Grotius' Doctrine on adquisitio obligationis per alterum and its Roots in the Legal Past of Europe = Panta rei. Studi dedicati a Manlio Bellomo*, Orazio CONDORELLI (ed.), Il Cigno GG Edizioni, Roma, 2005, vol. 2, 205–244.

Harry DONDORP: *The Reception of Institutes 3. 19. 19 in France = Ex iusta causa traditum; Essays in honour of Eric H. Pool (Fundamina nummer: editio specialis)*, Rena VAN DEN BERGH (ed.), University of South Africa, Pretoria, 2005, 59–68.

Giovanni FALCONE: *Obligatio est iuris vinculum*, G. Giappichelli, Torino, 2003.

Giovanni FINAZZI: Il contratto a favore di terzo proprio nell'esperienza giuridica romana = Studi in onore di Antonino Metro, C. RUSSO RUGGERI (ed.), Giuffré, Milano, 2010, vol. 2.

Fontes Iuris Romani Anteiustiniani, Florence 1940, vol. 1–3.

Gli effetti del contratto nei confronti dei terzi nella prospettiva storico-comparatistica. IV Congresso Internazionale ARISTEC Roma, 13–16 settembre 1999, Letizia VACCA (ed.), G. Giappichelli, Torino, 2001.

Antonio GUARINO: *Diritto privato romano*, Jovene, Napoli, 1992.

Jan HALLEBEEK: *Contracts for a third-party beneficiary: a brief sketch from the Corpus Iuris to present-day civil law*, Fundamina 13(2007)/2, 1–22.

HUGOLINI DE PRESBYTERIS: Diversitates sive dissensiones dominorum sive controversiae veterum iuris romani interpretum, Ed. Haenel, Lipsia, 1834.

HUGONIS GROTTII: *De jure belli ac pacis libri tres, in quibus jus naturae & gentium, item juris publici praecipua explicantur = The Classics of International Law*, J.B. SCOTT (ed.), Carnegie Institution of Washington, Washington D.C., 1913, vol. 1.

David IBBETSON: *Obligatio in Roman Law and Society = The Oxford Handbook of Roman Law and Society*, Paul J. DU PLESSIS, Clifford ANDO, Kaius TUORI (eds.), Oxford University Press, Oxford, 2016.

Ius quaesitum tertio, E.J.H. SCHRAGE (ed.), Duncker & Humblot, Berlin, 2008.

Theodor MOMMSEN: Iuris anteiustiniani fragmenta quae dicuntur vaticana = Collectio librorum iuris anteiustiniani in usum scholarum, Paul KRUEGER, Theodor MOMMSEN, Wilhelm STUDEMUND (eds.), vol. 3, Apud Weidmanoss, Berolini, 1890.

Lucio Valerio MOSCARINI: Il contratto a favore di terzi. Artt. 1411–1413, Giuffrè, Milano, 2012.

Gerhard OTTE: Dialektik und Jurisprudenz, Untersuchungen zur Methode der Glossatoren, Vittorio Klostermann, Frankfurt a.M., 1971.

Robert Joseph POTHIER: *Traité des obligations. Tome premier*, Chez Debure l'aîné, Paris, Chez Rouzeau – Montaut, Orléans, 1761.

René-Marie RAMPELBERG: *Brève perspective comparative sur les destinées de la règle «alteri stipulari nemo potest» = Les concepts contractuels français à l'heure des principes du droit européen des contrats*, Pauline RÉMY-CORLAY, Dominique FENOUILLET (eds.), Dalloz, Paris, 2003.

Rodolfo SACCO: *Legal Formants: A Dynamic Approach to Comparative Law (Installment I of* II), The American Journal of Comparative Law, 39(1991)/1, 1–34.

Rodolfo SACCO: Legal Formants: A Dynamic Approach to Comparative Law (Installment II of II), The American Journal of Comparative Law, 39(1991)/2, 343–401.

Mario TALAMANCA: *Obbligazioni (Dir. rom.) = Enciclopedia del diritto*, Giuffrè, Milano, 1979, vol. 29, 24–28.

Mario TALAMANCA: *Diocl. et Max. C. 8. 54. 3 =* FV. 286: *«donatio sub modo», «datio ob rem» e contratto a favore di terzi = Studi in onore di Antonino Metro*, C. RUSSO RUGGERI (ed.), vol. 6, Giuffré, Milano, 2010.

Giovanni VARANESE: Il contratto con effetti protettivi per i terzi, Edizioni Scientifiche Italiane, Napoli, 2004.

Paolo VOCI: Istituzioni di diritto romano, Giuffrè Editore, Milano, 2004.

Tammo WALLINGA: The Casus Codicis of Wilhelmus de Cabriano, Vittorio Klostermann Verlag, Frankfurt a.M., 2005.

Reinhard ZIMMERMANN: The law of obligations: Roman foundations of the civilian tradition, Oxford University Press, Oxford, 1996.

CHAPTER 9

# Civilian Arguments in the House of Lords' Judgments: Regarding Delictual (Tortious) Liability in 20th and 21st Century

*Łukasz Jan Korporowicz*

## 1 Introduction

In the long history of the judicial branch of the House of Lords, one is likely to find many examples of the use of authority of foreign texts and ideas by the Law Lords. These texts were used by the justices as a comparative (in the broad sense) approach to the problem with which they were dealing in the particular case. Even if these comparisons were not directly exploited in the judgments, they were treated as an instruments of judicial analogies and debates. Among them, the examples derived from Roman law can be treated as the most interesting. It is commonly believed that the law of the Romans little impact on the development of English law. It can be even said that the lack of Roman influences was an "injector" in the mental propulsion of legal national identity of English law. It should be remembered however, that the House of Lords was not only the supreme judicial entity of England, but its jurisdiction covered also other territories of the United Kingdom, including Scotland. The development of the Scots law owed much to the *ius commune* tradition and therefore also to Roman law. The judicial panels – the Law Lords' who were deciding the particular cases – were not chosen according to the jurisdiction within which they practised. Consequently, many Scottish judges decided English cases and conversely, many English judges were deciding Scottish cases.

In such situation it seems to be reasonable to ask some crucial questions. First, whether the Roman law was in fact used by the Law Lords. Second, it is possible that the use of Roman references was limited to sole authority of the ancient legal order or they did appear as a some sort of *terra comparationis*. The final question is, how far the references were deliberate. The main aim of this article is to answer these questions and provide a reader with at least general knowledge about the influence of Roman law in the jurisdiction of the House of Lords.

Although the House of Lords functioned as a top court of the United Kingdom for very long period of time, it is sensible to limit the time frame of this

© KONINKLIJKE BRILL NV, LEIDEN, 2020 | DOI:10.1163/9789004417274_010

CIVILIAN ARGUMENTS IN THE HOUSE OF LORDS' JUDGMENTS     213

analysis, as well as the analysed subject. The choice fell upon delictual or tortious liability. It seems that civilian concepts that refer to this issue were used quite frequently by the Law Lords. Due to one of the main themes of this volumes – modernisation – only the cases that could be labelled as modern were a subject of analysis. This precondition was fulfilled by the cases decided following the great reform of the British judicature which occurred between 1873 and 1876 when the Appellate Jurisdiction Act 1876 was issued. The cease of the jurisdiction of the House of Lords in 2009, instead, was ruled by the Constitutional Reform Act 2005. In addition, the modern cases are also understood as the one which are still valid points of reference for the lawyers practicing in the British courts.

To sum up, the article is an analysis of the cases decided between 1932 and 2002 regarding the tortious liability. In each of the examined cases the Roman law appeared. It is even possible to divide the aforementioned references into two groups: those concerning the Roman delict of *iniuria* and those concerning the Roman delict of *damnum iniuria datum*.

It may seem at first that the below research is a case-note or an anthology of the precedents. In fact, the detailed presentation of the arguments approach has been purposely rendered. It is important not only to focus on the terms which were quoted by the Justices, but it is significant to identify wider perspectives. The one which refers to the circumstances as well as the quality of the quotation. For this reason, close analysis of the particular judgments will be discussed.

## 2     The References to the Concept of Roman *Iniuria*

The very first use of Roman legal provisions regarding the delict of insult can be witnessed in the judgment of the House of Lords issued in 1943 in case *Stewart v. London, Midland and Scottish Railway Co.*[1] The case was started by Margaret Elizabeth Stewart bringing an action as executrix for her late sister Mary Hellen. On 20 September 1940 both women were travelling as passengers by train owned and operated by the London, Midland and Scottish Railway Co. Due to the fault of one of the company's workers, an accident occurred. As a consequence, the plaintiff was injured while her sister sustained a mortal wound. In March 1941, Miss Margaret Elizabeth Stewart brought an action against the Railway Company for payment to the pursuer as an individual the sum of £750 and payment to the pursuer as executrix for her sister's estate of £1000. The

---

1    *Stewart v. London, Midland and Scottish Railway Co.* 1943 S.C. (H.L.) 19.

Company admitted that the accident had been caused by its employee and agreed to pay damages for personal injury. The representatives of the Railway Company constantly refused, however, Miss Stewart's right to damages as executrix. The case was decided by the *Court of Session* in 1941.

In the House of Lords, four of five judges[2] referred to the authority of Roman law. The first judgment was delivered by the Lord Chancellor Viscount Simon (in office 1940–1945). At the very beginning he noted that the general rule of Scots law as well as Roman law did not extinguish the causes of the action in case of a death of any of the parties. The legal successors of the deceased parties are allowed to participate in the case as potential litigants who have the right to institute and pursue an action or to defend. Viscount Simon pointed out, however, that there is an exception to that general rule. In case of personal injury, the litigation could be continued by the legal successors of the wrongdoer, but not of the injured party. This seems reasonable in as far as this claim has essentially a personal character. The Lord Chancellor observed that dealing with this type of actions in such a manner was already characteristic for the Romans and their *actio iniuriarum*. Such an exception allowed another one, i.e. the victim's representatives continue the litigation if the action had already been brought by the sufferer himself who subsequently died.[3] The Lord Chancellor then noted that this rule in Roman law and Scots law are similar, but not the same. In case of Roman law, the transmissibility was allowed if the litigation was already at the *litis contestatio* stage. To prove his opinion, the Lord Chancellor quoted a passage from the Digest attributed to Paulus: *litis contestatione et poenales actiones transmittuntur ab utraque parte, et temporales perpetuantur.*[4] The Law Lord explained that the *litis contestatio* in Roman law could be treated as a kind of termination of the obligation and additionally as the reason to enter into a new obligation between plaintiff and the defendant. He stated that "the theory was that the stage of *litis contestatio* there arose a sort of novation."[5] To support his argument, the Lord Chancellor referred to the authority of Gaius,[6] but at the end he mentioned that in the different stages of the history of Roman litigation *litis contestatio* took place at different stages of the procedure. To compare Scots and Roman regulations,

---

2  Lord Clauson agreed only with the argumentation presented earlier by the Lord Chancellor and he refrained from giving his own reasoning (*Stewart v. London, Midland and Scottish Railway Co.* 1943 S.C. (H.L.) 19, 47).

3  *Stewart v. London, Midland and Scottish Railway Co.* 1943 S.C. (H.L.) 19, 25.

4  D. 27, 7, 8, 1 (*Paulus libro nono responsorum*). Lord Chancellor noticed also that the analogues provision could be found in I. 4, 12, 1.

5  *Stewart v. London, Midland and Scottish Railway Co.* 1943 S.C. (H.L.) 19, 25.

6  G. 3, 180.

CIVILIAN ARGUMENTS IN THE HOUSE OF LORDS' JUDGMENTS                    215

Viscount Simon explained that the Scots law did not know a simple equivalent
of the Roman *litis contestatio*, but "if process has been actually raised by the
pursuer in his lifetime, his representative may ‹insist›, *i.e.*, stand in his shoes
and carry on the litigation for the benefit of the estate."[7] The aforementioned
query of the provisions of Roman law seems to be rather rudimentary from the
civilian perspective.[8] Nevertheless, treating them simply as a citing of *regula
iuris*, it is acceptable and it is difficult not to notice their solidity and usefulness
for further reasoning.

In a further part of the judgment, the Lord Chancellor concentrated on the
method of using in English as well as in Scottish law the maxim *actio personalis
moritur cum persona*. He proclaimed that the rule had not been developed – as
it had sometimes been suggested – as an offspring of the Roman or canoni-
cal legal tradition.[9] In his opinion, it was fully demonstrated in two scholarly
works. The first was an article published in 1913 and written by Henry Goudy[10]
while the second was a passage from P.H. Winfield's *A Textbook of the Law of
Tort* in which the author dates the first use of the maxim to 1479.[11] Contemporary scholarship has since argued for the *a quo* date of respecting the maxim
even earlier to the late 13th or early 14th century.[12]

The second Law Lord who presented his judgment was Lord Thankerton (in
office 1929–1948). He referred to Roman law just on two occasions, but both of
them regarded one of the cited case *Bern's Executor v. Montrose Asylum.*[13]

The third judgment was issued by Lord Macmillan (in office 1930–1939 and
1941–1947). He started with the short overview of the history of delictual liability in Scots law. The Law Lord proclaimed that the final shape of that liability
was given to this branch of law no earlier than 1795, when "a claim of damages
for personal injuries due to negligence was for the first time held relevant in
the Court of Session."[14] He placed that event in the context of the final separation of the crime and delict, which occurred in the 18th century. It is interesting
that Lord Macmillan added casually that "the law of Scotland was then [i.e. in

---

7   *Stewart v. London, Midland and Scottish Railway Co.* 1943 S.C. (H.L.) 19, 25.

8   Cf. e.g. William W. Buckland: *A Text-book of Roman Law from Augustus to Justinian*, 3rd
    ed., Cambridge University Press, Cambridge (UK), 1966, 591.

9   *Stewart v. London, Midland and Scottish Railway Co.* 1943 S.C. (H.L.) 19, 26.

10  Henry Goudy: *Two Ancient Brocards* = *Essays in Legal History*, Paul Vinogradoff (ed.),
    Oxford University Press, Oxford, 1913, 215–232.

11  Percy H. Winfield: *A Textbook of the Law of Tort*, 2nd ed., Sweet and Maxwell, London
    1943, 201.

12  Jan Halberda: *Dzieje doktryny actio personalis moritur cum persona w angielskim com-
    mon law*, Krakowskie Studia z Historii Państwa i Prawa 3(2010), 40.

13  *Bern's Executor v. Montrose Asylum* (1893) 20 R. 859.

14  *Stewart v. London, Midland and Scottish Railway Co.* 1943 S.C. (H.L.) 19, 38.

the 18th century] still in a formative stage, and the influence of the Roman law in shaping the development of its doctrines was still potent."[15] He is explaining that the reason of this influence can be traced back in the phenomenon of massive scholarly journeys undertaken by Scottish students in the 17th and 18th centuries to the continental universities, especially to the Netherlands. The Law Lord had mentioned several distinguished lawyers of the era who had undertaken such voyages: Lord Stair (1619–1695), who had studied in Leiden from 1682 until 1688, Lord President Forbes (1685–1747; in office 1737–1747), who studied in Leiden as well, and Lord President Dundas (1685–1783; in office 1748–1753), who undertook his studies in Utrecht.[16] Lord Macmillan noted also that none of the good legal libraries of the era was complete if it did not hold works of such authors as Grotius, Vinnius, the Voets, Heineccius or other famous civilians.[17] This last statement of the Law Lord seems to be very important. Although he was proclaiming the importance of the pure Roman law in the process of the development of the Scots law, his mention of the Dutch studies of the Scottish lawyers as well as their libraries illustrate the significance of the *ius commune* tradition in Scotland. After all, his deliberations seem to be closer to the recent statements presented by John W. Cairns about the Humanist reception of Roman law in Scotland and the use of the *ius commune* sources for the proper interpretation of Scots law.[18]

For this reason, Lord Macmillan stated that it should not be surprising Scots law had taken over Roman regulations regarding the *actio iniuriarum*. It is interesting that the Law Lord attempted to present the character of the Roman action by quoting a passage taken not from the original ancient sources, but the treatise by Vinnius. He noticed that the *actio iniuriarum* was used originally as an instrument of remedy for an insult rather than for the damage itself (*in ea non principaliter de damno sarciendo sed de contumelia vindicanda agitur*[19]). In his opinion, the *utilis actio legis Aquiliae* would be a better comparison for the modern action of reparation for personal injury, but historically Scottish

---

15    *Ibid.*

16    More about Scots who were studying law in Netherlands in 17th and 18th centuries cf. Robert Feenstra: *Scottish-Dutch Relations in Seventeenth and Eighteenth Centuries = Scotland and Europe 1200–1850*, T.C. Smout (ed.), John Donald Publishers, Edinburgh, 1986, 128–142.

17    *Stewart v. London, Midland and Scottish Railway Co.* 1943 S.C. (H.L.) 19, 39.

18    J.W. Cairns: *Historical Introduction = A History of Private Law in Scotland*, vol. 1, eds. Kenneth Reid, Reinhard Zimmermann, Oxford University Press, Oxford, 2000, 162–163.

19    Arnold Vinnius: *Institutionum Imperialium Commentarius & Jurisprudentiae Contractae*, vol. 4, Ex Typographia Baleoniana, Venetiis, 1740, 12.

CIVILIAN ARGUMENTS IN THE HOUSE OF LORDS' JUDGMENTS 217

jurists based their argumentation on the *actio iniuriarum*.[20] Finally, at the end, Lord Macmillan noted – casually again – that owing to this method of reasoning Scottish jurisprudence treated the term *iniuria* more broadly than English lawyers who owed the transplantation of the term into its own legal vocabulary to Henry Bracton (13th c.).[21] It should be noted that the introduction of the term into the vocabulary itself was not equal with the reception. Bracton, who had written his work in Latin, had instinctively used Latin legal lexicon. Coincidently, it was very often derived from Roman law. It dost not mean that Bracton was intentionally contaminating the common law with civilian ideas. Such an impact was accidental.

After these introductory remarks, Lord Macmillan finally referred to the meritum of the case. He noted, just as the Lord Chancellor before him, that Roman law knew the general rule that allowed legal successors to bring an action "on behalf" of their dead relatives. Additionally, he noted that the exception to that rule appeared in case of the *actio iniuriarum*. An explanation for this exclusion was connected with the aim of the action. The Law Lord based his argumentation again on the authority of Dutch lawyers. He pointed out that according to Vinnius the aim of the action was *contumeliam vindicare*, while for Heineccius it was *quia ad vindictam tendit*. In the opinion of the Law Lord, this kind of thinking about personal injury was inherited by Scots law. In the later part of his judgment, Lord Macmillan focused on the exceptional possibility of continuing the action when the litigation was already started. This time he called upon the authority of Heineccius (*"una est exceptio si lis ante mortem contestata sit. Per litis contestationem enim fit novatio et quod antea ex delicto debebatur jam debetur ex quasi contractu"*[22]) and he supplemented it with a short passage from Vinnius (*"quia judicio accipiendo nova contrahitur obligatio judicati"*[23]). Differently than the Lord Chancellor, Lord Macmillan emphasized predominantly the novative character of the *litis contestatio*.[24] He quoted the passage from John Erskine's (1695–1768) work: "both by the Roman law and

---

20   *Stewart v. London, Midland and Scottish Railway Co.* 1943 S.C. (H.L.) 19, 39.

21   Lord Macmillan refers to F.W. Maitland's commentary of the Bracton's treatise: Frederick W. MAITLAND: *Select Passages from Bracton and Azo*, Selden Society 8, London, 1895, 218.

22   Johann Gottlieb HEINECCIUS: *Recitationes in Elementa Iuris Civilis Secundum Ordinem Institutionum*, Typis Crapelet, Pariisis, 1810, vol. 4, 1111. It is important to note that Henineccius's textbook was a very popular source of knowledge about Roman law in 18th century Scotland, cf. J.W. CAIRNS: *Rhetoric, Language, and Roman Law: Legal Education and Improvement in Eighteenth-Century Scotland*, Law and History Review 9(1991), 41; 43; 55, n. 90.

23   VINNIUS: *op. cit.*, 4, 12.

24   *Stewart v. London, Midland and Scottish Railway Co.* 1943 S.C. (H.L.) 19, 40.

ours ... in consequence of the judicial contract implied in it, there arises a *nova causa obligationis*."[25]

In the final part of his judgment, Lord Macmillan referred to another question, which was raised by the parties – the possibility of using an action for solatium. The Law Lord had declared that such an action did not exist in the Roman legal system, because it did not allow bringing an action for the death of a free man *quia liberum corpus nullam recipit aestimationem*. The quoted passage can be attributed to Gaius and may be find in the ninth book of Justinian's Digest.[26] Lord Macmillan emphasized also that the same rule is effectual also in English law. As a confirmation for his own words he referred to Lord Ellenborough's statement in the case *Baker v. Bolton*.[27]

The last judgment was issued by Lord Wright (in office 1932–1964) – an English judge. His reasoning shall be treated predominantly as an addendum to the earlier judgments. Among the issues, which were – in the Law Lord's opinion – not fully explained, Lord Wright enumerated the problem of the consequences of the *litis contestatio*. It is quite surprising to read an honest statement of the Law Lord who is declaring that to him it was "not clear" how the *litis contestatio* worked in the frame of Roman private law procedure.[28] This honesty might be explained by the fact that he was trained in English law. It would clarify his unawareness in the field of Roman law.

The further reasoning of the Law Lord is also quite astonishing. He decided to comment on the presence of the maxim *actio personalis moritur cum persona* in Scotland. He believed that the rule had never been accepted in Scotland in the same manner as it had been in England. In his opinion, the earliest example of its use in England could be dated to the times of Lord Coke C.J. (1552–1634). It is difficult to understand such a belief while the legal historians of English law had been placing the use of maxim in a much earlier period. It is also difficult to come to terms with the following statements of the Law Lord. He proclaimed that the maxim *actio personalis moritur cum persona* was not a

---

25 John ERSKINE: *An Institute of the Law of Scotland*, Edinburgh, Ediburg Legal Education Trust, 1773, vol. 3, 8, 51.

26 D. 9, 3, 7 (*Gaius libro sexto ad edictum provinciale*).

27 *Baker v Bolton* (1808) 1 Camp. 493; 170 Eng. Rep. 1033. Lord Ellenborough stated that "in a civil Court, the death of a human being could not be complained as an injury." In the opinion of some authors, the English judge in speaking these words referred to the tradition of Roman law, but in the opinion of others such a statement would be an exaggeration, cf. e.g. William Searle HOLDSWORTH: *The Origin of Rule in Baker v. Bolton*, Law Quarterly Review 32(1916), 431–437 or Frederick Parker WALTON: *Actio personalis and the French Law*, Journal of Comparative Legislation and International Law 18(1916), 51.

28 *Stewart v. London, Midland and Scottish Railway Co.* 1943 S.C. (H.L.) 19, 44.

CIVILIAN ARGUMENTS IN THE HOUSE OF LORDS' JUDGMENTS

rule of Roman law. In his opinion, Roman law would not use the term *personalis* as a denomination of the delictual action. In his opinion, the term *poenalis* would fit more and the term *personalis* could be understand only from the perspective of the *actiones in personam*.[29] It is honestly difficult to understand what Lord Wright wanted to proclaim. Such a separation of the terms *personalis* and *poenalis* as the Law Lord suggested can hardly be found in the Roman law sources. It is possible, however, that a kind of odd inspiration for the aforementioned divagation of the judge may be found in W.S. Holdsworth's *History of English Law*. The English legal historian mentioned the penal character of the actions used in case of inheritance debts.[30]

At the end, all the Law Lords confirmed the reception of the Roman concept of *actio iniuriarum* into Scots law, although they differed in the estimation of its scale. The reference to *actio* was treated instrumentally by the particular judges who wanted to refer to the term. Each of them, however, was willing to prove a bit different aspect of its use.

Nonetheless, it is important to explain that there is a good reason why the case *Stewart v. London, Midland and Scottish Railway Co.* is regarded as a one of the key precedents of the Scottish law of delicts. The decision of the House of Lords was a judicial approval of the beliefs of the doctrine of the law concerning the importance of the Roman delict of insult on the grounds of Scots law. As Niall R. Whitty observed, although delict of *iniuria* was transplanted into the Scottish legal system in the 18th century, only the so-called "neo-Civilian reaction" that occurred in the 20th century allowed it to be fully exploited.[31]

Analysis from the same perspective of other decisions issued by the Appellate Committee of the House of Lords after the end of the Second World War is required. Although these were linked with the concept of Scottish solatium, alien to Roman law, their analysis was also chiefly based on the Roman delict of *iniuria*. It shows clearly how the Roman ideas was comparatively used to develop a national-based doctrine of law. The first such case was *Cole-Hamilton v. Boyd*, decided by the House of Lords in 1963.[32]

The dispute occurred following a traffic accident involving three vehicles – one car and two motorised bicycles. The pillion passenger on one of these was a young woman who sustained serious harm. When the car driver was informed about the claim against him he decided to pay a certain sum of money

---

29  *Ibid.*, 46.

30  William Searle HOLDSOWRTH: *History of English Law*, vol. 3, Methuen & Co. Ltd., London 1923, 577–580.

31  Niall R. WHITTY: *Rights of Personality, Property Rights and the Human Body in Scots Law*, Edinburgh Law Review (2004–2005), 200.

32  *Cole-Hamilton v. Boyd 1963* S.C. (H.L.) 1.

to the *curator bonis* of the girl and additionally he made an assignation of a claim[33] against the second motorised bicycle driver. He had not, however, discharge any of the girl's right to reparation in respect to the accident. When the action for solatium was brought against the driver of the motorised bicycle, the car driver became additional pursuer, while the defendant questioned the fact whether the action *ex delicto* could be assigned in Scots law and that the full compensation of the girl's loss was achieved by the car driver's payment.

The lawyers who were representing the girl recalled the arguments of the personal character of the action for solatium which had already appeared in the judgments of the Lords in the case *Stewart v. London, Midland and Scottish Railway Co*. They stated that the "critical point [for the aforementioned action] was not a matter of evidence of the intention of the injured party, but the personal nature of the claim."[34] They added also that "the personal character of the claim was what counted in Roman law."[35] Nevertheless they noticed that the quotation by the Lord President of the Court of Session of Sohm's textbook of Roman law was incorrect,[36] because it did not refer to the problem of the claim for damages, but rather to the problem of inheritance law.[37]

In a further part of their argumentation, the representatives of the injured victim questioned their opponents' arguments. Firstly, the dispute referred to the passage from Erskine's *An Institute of the Law of Scotland*. The respondent's party quoted the paragraph which dealt with the problem of the assignation,[38] but the lawyers of the appellant pointed out that just one paragraph earlier Erskine had clearly stated that the assignation may be considered just from the perspective of the debts or movable goods.[39] Secondly, the lawyers noted that their opponents wrongly called over the constitutions inserted in the Code of Justinian. The constitution was issued by Diocletian and Maximian in 294 A.D. The Emperors were dealing with the problem of buying pledged property (*pignus*) and the question who shall be sued for the recovery of any surplus – the heir of the creditor or the heir of the purchaser who is in

---

33 "Assignment of the claim" was at first unknown in common law, but it was acknowledged by equity. It is kind of transfer of the right to bring an action on another person, cf. more Elizabeth A. MARTIN: *Oxford Dictionary of Law*, Oxford University Press, Oxford 2003, 35–36, *s.v. assignment*.

34 *Cole-Hamilton v. Boyd* 1963 S.C. (H.L.) 1, 3.

35 *Ibid.*

36 Rudolph SOHM: *The Institutes of Roman Law*, J.C. LEDLIE (transl.), Oxford University Press, Oxford, 1892, 426–427.

37 *Cole-Hamilton v. Boyd* 1963 S.C. (H.L.) 1, 4.

38 ERSKINE, *op. cit.*, vol. 3, 5, 2.

39 *Cole-Hamilton v. Boyd* 1963 S.C. (H.L.) 1, 5. More about the "assignation" in Erskine's work, cf. Klaus LUIG: *Assignation = A History of Private Law…, op. cit.*, vol. 2, 416–417.

CIVILIAN ARGUMENTS IN THE HOUSE OF LORDS' JUDGMENTS          221

possession of the property. According to the Emperors, the right person to be sued is the heir of the creditor. The representatives of the victim noted that passage from the Code refers to "a different chapter of the Roman law".[40] They suggested also that the given passage may be compared with several fragments of the Digest.[41]

It is interesting to note that the civilian arguments were presented just by the parties' representatives. None of the Law Lords referred to their Roman law excursions. Still the argumentation of the respondents allowed them to declare that the assignation of the action for solatium *inter vivos* was acceptable according to Scots law.

Personal injury was the subject of another case heard by the House of Lords in 1972 – *M'Kendrick v. Sinclair*.[42] The facts of the case regarded another fatal accident. While at work, a factory employee was electrocuted. His siblings decided to bring an action of assythment. It was a type of action known to Scots law, which originated in feudal law and was similar to the Anglo-Saxon concept of wergild.[43] It is emphasised that the main aim of assythment shall be seen as prevention of a family vendetta.[44]

In the opinion of the relatives of the deceased, the manager of the factory culpably and recklessly knew about the defective condition of the machine, especially that one of the other workers in the factory had already received electric shocks while using it. Nevertheless, the manager ordered the late worker to continue working. The defendant party attempted to prove that the action of assythment was no longer is use in Scots law because it had fallen into desuetude.

Two of five Law Lords recalled the authority of civilian tradition. Lord Reid (in office 1948–1975) noticed that the action brought to the court by the pursuers was an "archaic remedy."[45] Due to this fact, the Law Lord decided to present the history of its use in Scots law.[46] Upon the information derived from the *Practicks* of James Balfour (1525–1583), the Law Lord pointed out the popularity of the action in the 16th century and its common use in Scottish

---

40     *Cole-Hamilton v. Boyd* 1963 S.C. (H.L.) 1, 5.

41     D. 27, 7, 8 (*Paulus libro nono responsorum*) and D. 47, 10, 28 (*Ulpianus libro 34 ad Sabinum*).

42     *M'Kendrick v. Sinclair* 1972 S.C. (H.L.) 25.

43     For more about the assythment, cf. Robert BLACK, *A historical survey of delictual liability in Scotland for personal injuries and death*, Comparative and International Law Journal of Southern Africa 8(1975), 52–70 and Kenneth McK. NORRIE: *The Intentional Delicts = A History of Private Law...*, *op. cit.*, vol. 2, 484–488.

44     McK. NORRIE: *op. cit.*, 484.

45     *M'Kendrick v. Sinclair* 1972 S.C. (H.L.) 25, 49.

46     *Ibid.*, 50.

courts.[47] He then showed the ways of using the action of assythment in 17th and 18th century Scotland by quoting passages from the works of Lord Stair[48] and Lord Bankton (1685–1760).[49] The judge had observed finally that the afore-mentioned action was in earlier periods linked with criminal liability. He illustrated that opinion by quoting an extensive passage from the textbook by Erskine.[50] Finally, he mentioned some precedents based on the action of assythment.[51] He noticed also that action was successfully used in the Court of Session in 1752 in the case *Lady Leith-Hall v. Earl of Fife*.[52]

The reason for describing the action so widely was connected with its later replacement by a new remedy based on the concept of quasi-delict of negligence which could be linked with a certain influence of Roman law on Scots law.[53] The process began already in the late 18th century. Lord Reid opposed, however, the statement of the pursuers who suggested that the action of assythment had vanished and was no longer present in the system of Scots law. The Law Lord pointed out that very often the process of displacing the action was accompanied by skilful merging of the titles of liability. The judge had evoked the case of *Black v. Caddell*[54] which was heard by the Scottish courts as well as in the House of Lords at the beginning of the 19th century. It is interesting to note that the plaintiff in the named case at first based his claim on the doctrine of assythment, while at the House of Lords he additionally raised a claim based on the Roman *obligatio quasi ex delicto*.

The example recalled by the judge seems to be an important proof which affirms the reception of Roman law in Scotland already in the early 19th century. It is important also to emphasise that the reception does not have to be understand only as a simple transition of the foreign legal provisions into another legal system. Scottish lawyers managed to join two different legal orders in such a manner that they created a certain new value.

The second Law Lord who analysed the civilian arguments which appeared in the case was a Scottish judge – Lord Kilbrandon (in office 1971–1989). He evaluated approvingly the facts regarding the history of assythment presented

---

47  *The Practicks of Sir James Balfour of Pittendreich*, P.G.B. McNeil (ed.), Star Society 21–22 (1963), 516.
48  Lord Stair: *Institutions of the Laws of Scotland*, Edinburgh 1681, 1, 9, 7.
49  Lord Bankton: *An Institute of the Laws of Scotland*, Edinburgh 1752, 1, 10, 15.
50  Erskine, *op. cit.*, vol. 4, 4, 105.
51  *M'Kendrick v. Sinclair* 1972 S.C. (H.L.) 25, 50–51.
52  *Lady Leith-Hall v. Earl of Fife* (1768) Mor. 13904.
53  *M'Kendrick v. Sinclair* 1972 S.C. (H.L.) 25, 53.
54  *Black v. Caddell* (1804) Mor. 13905.

CIVILIAN ARGUMENTS IN THE HOUSE OF LORDS' JUDGMENTS          223

earlier in the judgments of the Court of Session judges.[55] He believed that the most noteworthy was the fact that the action of assythment functioned not only as a demand for revenge, but it recalled the civilian idea of *reparatio damnorum*.[56] Further, Lord Kilbrandon pointed to an explicit tendency, characteristic of both Scottish institutional writers as well as Scottish judges, toward gradual separation of the private and public forms of assythment. The private one started to steer into the form of civilian construction of reparation of damages.[57] He noticed also that the process had already begun in the 18th century and he quoted a passage by Erskine to verify his beliefs.[58] The Law Lord also mentioned that Erskine's deliberation was well-connected with the Roman maxim *alterum non laedere*, which was marked by the judge as "Justinian's."[59]

Later in his judgment, Lord Kilbrandon continued the discussion about the separation of the private form of the assythment. He recalled the authority of the scholarly works as well as court decisions.[60] He quoted an extensive part of an article by D.M. Walker in which the Scottish scholar observed that in the 19th century the term assythment started to be identified with such terms as damages, civil reparation, or solatium. The scholar had noted also that it is impossible to show when the separation of the civil and criminal form of the assythment precisely occurred. Nevertheless, it is certain that the civilian form gave birth to the modern use of Scottish *actio iniuriarum*.[61] This analysis enabled the Law Lord to move swiftly to the reference to the *Stewart v. London, Midland and Scottish Railway Co.* case where Lord Macmillan – as mentioned above – presented the history of the creation of the Scottish emanation of the Roman delict of *iniuria*.[62] It is interesting to note Lord Kilbrandon's grumbling about the incorrect choice of the arguments used in the *Stewart v. London, Midland and Scottish Railway Co.* case. In his opinion, a much better field of the reference would be *lex Aquilia*.[63]

---

55   *M'Kendrick v. Sinclair* 1972 S.C. (H.L.) 25, 63–64.

56   Regarding the liability in the civilian tradition, cf. Reinhard ZIMMERMANN: *Usus Modernus Legis Aquiliae and Delictual Liability Today*, Stellenbosch Law Review 1(1990), 67–93.

57   *M'Kendrick v. Sinclair* 1972 S.C. (H.L.) 25, 65.

58   ERSKINE: *op. cit.*, vol. 3, 1, 12.

59   D. 1, 1, 10, 1 (*Ulpianus libro secundum regularum*).

60   *M'Kendrick v. Sinclair* 1972 S.C. (H.L.) 25, 66.

61   David M. WALKER: *Solatium*, Juridical Review 62(1950), 156. More recently in the same manner: ERIC DESCHEEMAEKER: *"Solatium" and Injury to Feelings: Roman Law, English Law and Modern Tort Scholarship = Iniuria and the Common Law*, Eric DESCHEEMAEKER, Helen SCOTT (eds.), Hart Publishing, Oxford-Portland, 2013, 76.

62   *M'Kendrick v. Sinclair* 1972 S.C. (H.L.) 25, 66.

63   To verify his opinion, Lord Kilbrandon referred to three scholarly works: Thomas B. SMITH'S: *Strange Gods: Crisis of Scots Law as a Civilian System* = Thomas B. SMITH: *Studies*

Finally, the Law Lords dismissed the pursuers' request, but they declared simultaneously that the assythment as such had not vanished from the system of Scots law. They explained that both in England and Scotland, the rule of law may not fall into desuetude. It is interesting to mention, however, that just a few years later, in 1976, the *Damages (Scotland) Act* was promulgated and it officially abolished the existence of assythment in Scotland.[64]

As to the desuetude, it may be added that although in general terms the Justices were right, in practice, certain exceptional instances of the desuetude has been accepted by judges both in England and Scotland. The difficulties in achieving the desuetude effect was well described by Lord Mackay:

> desuetude requires for its operation a very considerable period, not merely of neglect, but of contrary usage of such a character as practically to infer such completely established habit of the community as to set up a counter law or establish a quasi repeal[65]

Somewhat different were the circumstances which were the impetus for the *Dick v. Burgh of Falkirk* case heard by the Law Lords in 1975.[66] The case regarded another labour accident which was a consequence of the negligent behaviour of the employers (the provost, magistrates and councillors of the Burgh of Falkirk). An injured workman brought an action of damages on 31 May 1972. He died, however, on 22 March 1973. His wife became executrix of his estate. She was established also as a party pursuer. Independently she brought another action for solatium. Due to the circumstances, the opposite party argued that the woman was not entitled to bring it. The case had been heard by the House of Lords in 1975. Two Law Lords referred to the Roman legal tradition. In the final part of his judgment, Lord Wilberforce (in office 1964–1982) noticed that the representatives of the respondents referred to the concept of *litis contestatio* understanding that "the moment that the injured person commences an action for damages, he transmutes or novates his claim in delict

---

> *Critical and Comparative*, W. Green, Edinburgh, 1962, 78, David M. Walker's article and Frederick H. LAWSON's: *A Common Lawyer at the Civil Law*, University of Michigan School of Law, Ann Arbor, 1953, 155, n. 121. The judge pointed out that he is referring to D.M. Walker's article published in the 1970 volume of Juridical Review. In that volume, however, the mentioned scholar did not publish any article about delictual liability. It is possible there is an error in the official version of the law report. It is plausible that Lord Kilbrandon was referring to the D.M. Walker's article on solatium, previously quoted.

64    Sec. 8 Damages (Scotland) Act 1976 (c. 13). Cf. also McK. NORRIE, *op. cit.*, 488.

65    *Brown v. Magistrates of Edinburgh* 1931 S.L.T. 456, 568.

66    *Dick v. Burgh of Falkirk* 1976 S.C. (H.L.) 1.

CIVILIAN ARGUMENTS IN THE HOUSE OF LORDS' JUDGMENTS 225

into one of a quasi-contractual nature and that by so doing he effectively excludes any action by his relatives in the event of his death."[67] Lord Wilberforce stated that he "applaud[ed] the ingenuity of this argument, but ingenuity is all that it possesses."[68] He declared also that *litis contestatio* was then understood in Scots law differently than in Roman law and only the "Latinity" of the used term lends itself to observation of the resemblance of the concepts.

The second Law Lord who mentioned the authority of Roman law was Lord Kilbrandon. He pointed out that the death of an injured party causes in Scots law the exclusion of the use of the solatium. In his opinion that rule is similar to the prohibition known in Roman law according to the action of injury.[69]

As to the *litis contestatio*, Lord Kilbrandon quoted the passage from one of the works of Heineccius[70] which was previously quoted by Lord Macmillan in the case of *Stewart v. London, Midland and Scottish Railway Co.*[71] The German scholar explained that one of the consequences of the *litis contestatio* was the creation of a new legal relation between the parties which could be labelled as quasi-contract.[72] The judge noted that such a consequence appeared in Roman law but not in Scottish private law. He explained that *litis contestatio* occurred in Roman law after the last act undertaken by the praetor at this stage of the procedure (the *in iure* stage) i.e. the appointment of a judge and sending the case to him. The Law Lord added that this order of events occurred when the controversy had a factual character. When the controversies had only a legal character, the case was decided by the praetor himself.[73] This last statement by Lord Kilbrandon raises a question about his knowledge of Roman law. It is true that the formulary procedure acknowledged the possibility of ending the case at the *in iure* stage, but only in several precise circumstances, i.e.: when the praetor denied an action (*denegatio actionis*), when the defendant

---

67    *Dick v. Burgh of Falkirk* 1976 S.C. (H.L.) 1, 20.

68    *Ibid.*

69    *Ibid.,* 26.

70    HEINECCIUS: *op. cit.*, vol. 4, 4, 1111.

71    *Dick v. Burgh of Falkirk* 1976 S.C. (H.L.) 1, 26.

72    The question of the contractual character of the *litis contestatio* shall be connected with the postulates suggested at the turn of the 19th and 20th century by M. Wlassak. They became the subject of severe criticism and one can see their rejection in the scholarly works published since the mid-20th century. It is quite strange then that Lord Kilbrandon referred to the contractual concept of *litis contestatio* in the 1970s, especially given that the British scholarly literature already possessed at least two well-known books in which that rejection occurred: BUCKLAND: *A Text-book...*, *op. cit.*, 695–696 and Herbert F. JOLOWICZ, Barry NICHOLAS: *Historical Introduction to the Study of Roman Law*, 3rd ed., Cambridge University Press, Cambridge (UK), 1972, 177.

73    *Dick v. Burgh of Falkirk* 1976 S.C. (H.L.) 1, 27.

accepted the plaintiff's claim (*confessio in iure*), when an oath was taken (*iusiurandum*), or when the parties compounded (*transactio*).

Regardless of these doubts, Lord Kilbrandon had finally denied the possibility of using the Roman concept of *litis contestatio* in modern Scots law. He summed up his deliberations by quoting W.A. Hunter's opinion about Roman *litis contestatio* that it was "unfair and capricious"[74] and he noted that Erskine declared that the Scots "are strangers to the Roman *formulae*."[75] The Law Lord explained that in Scots law the right of action can be extinguished by decree of the Court, settlements by the parties, or a unilateral act of abandonment by the pursuer.[76]

Finally, the Law Lords decided that the woman's claim was compatible, and she was entitled to claim damages both as an individual and as the executrix-dative of her deceased husband.

A similar case – *Robertson v. Turnbull*[77] – was heard by the Appellate Committee in 1981. Due to the analogous facts, the cases are discussed quite often jointly. A matter analysed regarded the subjective range of the applicability of the solatium. The pursuer brought an action of solatium as a consequence of an accident suffered by his wife. Her health condition prevented her from continuing her previous duties, and it also rendered her employment impossible. Her husband recognised himself as being in the right to bring an action of solatium. The Law Lords had univocally declared, however, that this claim was groundless. They pointed out that in the *Dick v. Burgh of Falkirk* case it had been decided that the aforementioned claim had arisen from the death of the injured party.

Roman law arguments were raised by the counsels of the pursuer.[78] The only Law Lord who reacted to them was Lord Fraser of Tullybelton (in office 1975–1989). After he discussed the previous judgments of the Scottish courts as well as the House of Lords, he declared that there were no reasons which would permit the solatium claim of the relatives when the injured party is still alive. He pointed out that already in the 1870 case of *Eisten v. National British Railway Co.*[79] one can find similar argumentation. It is interesting, however, that the Law Lord recalled the opinion proclaimed in 1870 by Lord President Inglis, who declared that one of the sources of his reasoning was the Roman

---

74    William A. Hunter: *A Systematic and Historical Exposition of Roman Law in the Order of a Code*, 4th ed., Sweet & Maxwell, London, 1903, 984.

75    Erskine, *op. cit.*, 4, 1, 65.

76    *Dick v. Burgh of Falkirk* 1976 S.C. (H.L.) 1, 27.

77    *Robertson v. Turbull* 1982 S.C. (H.L.) 1.

78    *Ibid.*, 2.

79    *Eisten v. National British Railway Co.* (1870) 8 M. 980.

CIVILIAN ARGUMENTS IN THE HOUSE OF LORDS' JUDGMENTS 227

construction of *actio iniuriarum*. In the opinion of Lord Fraser, the Scottish provisions regarding the delictual liability originated in the Roman *lex Aquilia*. He justified his opinion by calling on the authority of scholarly works and judgments.[80] This opinion was parallel to the aforementioned opinion by Lord Macmillan in the *Stewart v. London, Midland and Scottish Railway Co.* case.

Further in his judgment, Lord Fraser mentioned that the development of the Scottish solatium was also connected with the changes in the understanding of the legal character of the assythment. Finally, aiming to show the Roman roots of the delictual liability, the Law Lord recalled the authority of South African cases decided in the 1920s and 1930s concerning the same subject.[81]

## 3    The References to the Concept of Roman *Damnum Iniuria Datum*

As previously mentioned, one of the most crucial objections rendered against the development of solatium in Scots law was ill-considered enclosure with the Roman delict of insult. In the opinion of many judges as well as representatives of Scottish legal doctrine, more suitable would be grounding that development on the pattern offered by Aquilian liability. In fact, however, the *lex Aquilia* was exploited in the Scots law, but in relation to different circumstances.

It is important to remember, however, that the evaluation of the scale of the influence of the Roman legal provisions on the Scots law shall be considered carefully. The process of using Roman patterns by Scottish lawyers is a very long one. Sometimes, it is possible to believe that we may observe an example of the reception, while in fact we are dealing with the Romanised institution of the Scots law since several centuries. A good illustration of such a phenomenon would be the 1931 case of *Kolbin & Sons v. Kinnear & Co.*[82] which regarded a cargo of flax and tow shipped during the First World War from Archangel to Dundee. The Romanists would pay attention to Lord Atkin's (in office 1928– 1944) reference to the three degrees of the gravity of negligence in Roman law: *culpa lata*, *cupla levis* and *culpa levissima*.[83] All of them, however, were already known by Scottish lawyers before the decision in the *Kolbin & Sons v. Kinnear & Co.* case and it is not possible to consider them as an example of the reception of Roman law by the House of Lords. In fact, this is very well visible in Lord

---

80    *Robertson v. Turnbull* 1982 S.C. (H.L.) 1, 8.
81    *Ibid.*, 9.
82    *Kolbin & Sons v. Kinnear & Co.* 1931 S.C. (H.L.) 128.
83    *Ibid.*, 138.

Atkin's attitude. He mentioned the degrees of *culpa*, but did not comment on them.[84]

An unusual instance of referring to the concept of Aquilian liability can be seen through the example of the famous case *Donoghue v. Stevenson*.[85] The lack of direct reference to the Roman law sources did not preclude the civilian foundation of the ruling and arguments presented by the Lord Macmillan.

The case regarded the liability of a producer of ginger-beer. During the process of manufacturing the beverage, a snail was enclosed in one of the bottles. In August 1928, the appellant drank a bottle of the ginger-beer and found inside the decomposed remains of a snail. As a result, she "suffered from shock and severe gastro-enteritis"[86] as Lord Buckmaster stated in his judgment. The case became a subject of interest to the Law Lords in 1931 and in May 1932 they decided with the majority of three out of five that the manufacturer was liable for negligence. In a few years, the case came to be known as one of the most important precedents in both English and Scottish law. When the judgments of the Law Lords are read it is difficult to find any references to Roman law or the civilian tradition. Nevertheless, it is clear that the solution proposed by the judges brings to mind the general provisions of the delictual liability characteristic for Roman law and based on the *lex Aquilia*. It is true, especially when the judgment of the Lord Macmillan is read. Until recently, those similarities could be treated as a coincidence. But in 1992, the late Lord Rodger of Earlsferry (Law Lord 2001–2009; Justice of the Supreme Court of the UK 2009–2011) published an original version of Lord Macmillan's judgment which included some references to Scottish institutional writers and the tradition of *ius commune*.[87]

The change in the version of the judgment was likely connected with the efforts undertaken by Lord Atkin. He agreed essentially with Lord Macmillan's argumentation, but he was hoping for the universalisation of the judgment and in consequence for the common use of the precedent both in Scottish courts as well as in English courts. In order to achieve that, he had likely asked

---

84 Sceptical of the use of the term *cupla* in Scots law and the possibility of its reception from Roman law was Geoffrey MacCormack: *Culpa in Scots Law of Reparation*, Juridical Review (1974), 13–29.

85 *Donoghue v. Stevenson* [1932] AC 562.

86 *Ibid.*, 566.

87 Alan Rodger: *Lord Macmillan's Speech in Donoghue v. Stevenson*, Law Quarterly Review 108(1992), 236–259. Cf. also Alan Rodger: *Mrs. Donoghue and Alfenus Varus*, Current Legal Problems 41(1998), 1–22; David J. Ibbetson: *A Historical Introduction to the Law of Obligations*, Oxford University Press, Oxford, 1999, 190–195; Robin Evans-Jones: *Roman Law in Britain = Quaestiones Iuris. Festschrift für Joseph Georg Wolf zum 70. Geburstag*, Ulrich Manthe, Christoph Krampe (eds.), Duncker & Humblot, Berlin, 2000, 97–108.

CIVILIAN ARGUMENTS IN THE HOUSE OF LORDS' JUDGMENTS

Lord Macmillan to remove all the "Scottish" quotations.[88] The judgment was modified predominantly in its first part. After the introduction (the same in both versions), Lord Macmillan attempted to present the rules of delictual (tortious) liability in English and Scots law. He pointed out that the origins of both delictual systems are different, but this is of no account in the context of *Donoghue v. Stevenson* case.[89] Later, the Law Lord accounted for the applicability of the claim and the appeal.[90] To do so, he quoted the passages from the work of Lord Stair regarding the nature of the delict[91] and then he cited an extensive passage from Erskine, in which the 18th century jurist defined the character of delictual liability: "every fraudulent contrivance or unwarrantable act by which another suffers damage (…) subjects the delinquent to reparation. (…) Wrong may arise not only from positive acts of trespass or injury, but from blameable omission or neglect of duty."[92] At the end, Lord Macmillan referred to the fragments from Bell's *Principles*[93] and he recalled the maxim *alterum non laedere*[94] which he described as recognised by all civilised legal systems.[95]

Although, Lord Macmillan did not directly recall the authority of Roman law in his unpublished judgment, but it is noteworthy that all quoted passages authored by Lord Stair, Erskine, and Bell were based on the longstanding Roman legal tradition. It is important to notice also that since the final version of the judgment was devoid of these references, the presented idea remained untouched.[96]

It is true that any of the judgments delivered in the *Donoghue v. Stevenson* case did not contain the elements of Roman law, still English lawyers were aware of the similarities of Roman solutions and the one presented in Lord Macmillan's decision. It was difficult, however, to locate these similarities. For example, Lord Denning (Law Lord 1957–1962; Master of the Rolls 1962–1982) in a judgment delivered in 1960 in the case *Watson v. Fram Reinforced Concrete Co.* referred to the *Donoghue v. Stevenson* case which was already a well-established precedent in English law at that time. He ascertained that the rule expressed

---

88  EVANS-JONES: *op. cit.*, 102–103.

89  RODGER: *Lord Macmillan's…*, *op. cit.*, 248–249.

90  *Ibid.*, 249.

91  LORD STAIR, *op. cit.*, 1, 8, 9; 1, 9, 1; 1, 9, 6.

92  ERSKINE, *op. cit.*, 3, 1, 13.

93  George J. BELL: *Principles of the Law of Scotland*, William Blackwood, Edinburgh 1829, sec. 553.

94  D. 1, 1, 10, 1 (*Ulpianus libro secondo regularum*).

95  RODGER: *Lord Macmillan's…*, *op. cit.*, 250.

96  About the legal background that preceded the delivery of the final decision in the case cf. IBBETSON: *op. cit.*, 188–189.

in the 1932 case "applies to all cases where damage is the gist of the action" and added that "it is a principle not only of English law, but also of the Civil law."[97] To reaffirm this opinion, he referred to the authority of the great English Romanist, William W. Buckland, who had written "so too the careless conduct without damage, or the damage without anything making it imputable, would have no import at civil law. The breach of duty is the wrongful infliction of damage. And so the Romans put it – *damnum iniuria datum*."[98] As a summary of his deliberations Lord Denning ascertained that if the same principle stood in English law as well as in Roman law, there could be no doubt that the same rule applies also in Scots law.[99]

The aim of Lord Atkin's actions in 1932 was to transplant confidently the pattern of Roman-based Scottish delictual liability into English law. This concept was successfully achieved. A good example of that success may be the case of *Fairchild v. Glenhaven Funeral Services Ltd.*, decided by the Appellate Committee in 2002. Three men – Arthur Eric Fairchild, Thomas Fox and Edwin Matthews, due to the character of their work, were exposed to contact with and inhalation of asbestos fibres. The first and the second men died in 1996 after they were diagnosed with mesothelioma. The third man was diagnosed with the same type of cancer in 2000. The families of Fairchild and Fox as well as Matthews himself decided to claim damages. The key problem during the litigation was to indicate who would be directly liable for causing the injury.

The crucial judgment in the case was delivered by Lord Rodger of Earlsferry. The Scottish judge pointed out that the problem of arrogating the liability to the substantial person already engaged the interest of Roman lawyers in the context of *lex Aquilia*.[100] The judge mentioned an article published a few years earlier by Jeroen S. Kortmann[101] which regarded the same issue and then he had presented his own interpretation of the two passages from the Digest. At first, he quoted the passage by Julian[102] who had presented the case of a slave beaten by two different people and who eventually died. The owner of the slave was entitled to bring an action based on the first chapter of *lex Aquilia*. The problem, however, was how to indicate the responsible attacker. In the opinion of the Roman jurist, both of them were equally liable. Julian had

---

97    *Watson v. Fram Reinforced Concrete Co.* 1960 S.C. (H.L.) 92, 116.
98    William W. BUCKLAND: *Some Reflections on Jurisprudence*, Cambridge University Press, Cambridge (UK), 1945, 113.
99    *Watson v. Fram Reinforced Concrete Co.* 1960 S.C. (H.L.) 92, 116.
100   *Fairchild v. Glenhaven Funeral Services Ltd.* [2003] 1 AC 32, 113.
101   Jeroen S. KORTMANN: *Ab alio ictu(s): Misconceptions about Julian's View on Causation*, Journal of Legal History 20(1999)/2, 95–103.
102   D. 9, 2, 51, pr. (*Iulianus libro 86 digestorum*).

shown that his opinion is agreeable with the authority of the old jurists, the so called *veteres*.[103] The entire passage was quoted in Latin as well as in English translation by Charles H. Monro.[104] Next the Law Lord referred to the similar fragment hand on the account of Ulpian. Lord Rodger finished his deliberation about the Aquilian liability, writing that:

> the exact scope of these decisions can, of course, no longer be ascertained and it is likely that different jurists held differing views: the sixth-century compilers of the Digest may well have altered the texts to some extent, if only by abbreviation, cutting out the cut and thrust of debate.[105]

Finally, the Law Lords confirmed the arguments presented by Lord Rodger and they decided similarly as the Roman jurist almost two thousand years before. It was decided that in extraordinary circumstances, when it is impossible to settle who shall be considered liable for causing the injury, it is possible to bring an action against all the parties who could have contributed. It should be ascertained also that the aforementioned ruling would not be possible if there had been no transplantation of the Scottish delictual liability into the English law in 1932.[106]

At the end, it is worth mentioning another English case that can be taken up in the same perspective as the previous one. In the previous case, the problem reflects the possibility of bringing an action against several potential liable parties. In the *Heaton v. Axa Equity & Law Assurance Society Plc.*[107] case – also decided in 2002 – there were two liable entities, but one of them had already settled an agreement with the defendant.[108] Additionally, it needs to be indicated that the damage was caused by the breach of a contract and not a delict. All the Law Lords declared unanimously, however, that the bases of the liability are unimportant and the decision declared by them may be used either in the context of the breach of a contract or in the case of the delictual liability as well.

---

103 D. 9, 2, 51, 1 (*Iulianus libro 86 digestorum*).
104 Charles H. Monro: *The Digest of Justinian*, vol. 2, Cambridge University Press, Cambridge (UK), 1909, 140–141.
105 *Fairchild v. Glenhaven Funeral Services Ltd.* [2003] 1 AC 32, 113–114.
106 Lord Rodger's decision became a source of inspiration for Helen Scott's article *Killing and Causing Death in Roman Law*, Law Quarterly Review 123(2013), 101–122.
107 *Heaton v. Axa Equity & Law Assurance Society Plc.* [2002] 2 AC 329.
108 This was possible according to the ruling in *Jameson v. Central Electricity Generating Board* [2000] 1 AC 455.

The difficulties connected with the analysed case were emphasised by Lord Rodger. He asserted, however, that they may not be treated as something new. He had pointed out that already Roman lawyers were forced to deal with similar problems.[109] As an example, the judge presented the case recorded in Paulus' commentary on the writings of Plautius. The parties in the case were a creditor, a debtor, and a surety. The question regarded the possibility of suing a surety by the creditor when the same creditor had settled an agreement with the debtor that he would not bring an action against him.[110]

Indeed, the aforementioned reference had no impact on the final decision of the Law Lords, but it shows certain attitude to seek similar legal solutions in the Roman, English and Scottish systems of law. There is a chance that such a reference was possible due to the earlier custom to place those different legal orders together in the context of delictual (tortious) liability.

## 4    Conclusions

The above-presented judgments issued by the House of Lords may be considered solely as a judicial anthology. This supposition, however, is wrong. The main aim of the aforementioned discussion was to create a detailed portrayal of the types and quality of the civilian arguments used in delictual and tortious cases by the Appellate Committee of the House of Lords between 1932 and 2002. In addition, the analysis shows how Roman law could be used as an instrument of legal argumentation.

It should not be surprising that most of the civilian references appeared in Scottish appeals. Only two English cases appeared in the above-presented analysis. In both, however, the Scottish judges played an important role. The civilian references were not only connected with the activity of the judges. Also, counsel were eagerly quoting the authority of early modern jurists of the widely understood *ius commune*. The original Roman law sources were rather marginal.

The question that may arise following the aforementioned analysis would be whether or not these cases could be treated as an example of the doctrinal reception of Roman law by the House of Lords. The general answer would be "no," but one must always remember the civilian heritage of Scots law. Constant judicial troubles with approaching ancient *iniuria* and *damnum iniuria datum* are fascinating stories regarding how these institutions could be

---

109    *Heaton v. Axa Equity & Law Assurance Society Plc.* [2002] 2 AC 329, 356.
110    D. 2, 14, 32 (*Paulus libro tertio ad Plautium*).

CIVILIAN ARGUMENTS IN THE HOUSE OF LORDS' JUDGMENTS

instrumentally treated and interpreted. The analysis of the Justices' judgments, however, allow to call them "Romanised." The appearance of such references in the House of Lords can be considered as some sort of verification of the existence of the tradition and an example of what can be called an intellectual reception. It is additionally interesting that such reception occurred in the sphere of the jurisdiction that rather commonly rejected the importance and influence of ancient Roman law tradition (in case of England) as well as in the sphere of jurisdiction which constantly conflicts as to the size of reception of Roman law (in case of Scots law).

As to the English cases, it may be observed that the 1932 case of *Donoghue v. Stevenson* introduced civilian elements into the English legal discussion on the tort of negligence – today the most important and well-developed tort in English tort law. This was affirmed, instinctively, by Lord Denning in *Watson v. Fram Reinforced Concrete Co.* in 1960. It is also possible that Lord Rodger would not have been so eager to cite Roman jurists in his judgments, if there had been no earlier precedent of such behaviour among judges. Although it is possible to observe a tendency to quote civilian arguments in English cases, this may not be considered as a reception in the commonly understood manner.[111] But it is important to see that this practice was deliberate.

In this situation it is possible to place the civilian influences into the wide scope of using Roman law as an old and good authority, and source of fair legal principles. In other words, this is what can be called comparative legal history in action.[112]

## Acknowledgements

I would like to express my sincere gratitude to Professors Hector MacQueen and Paul J. du Plessis (both from Edinburgh Law School) for all their helpful comments and suggestions that improved the final version of this chapter.

---

111   Cf., however, the final paragraph in Maria F. CURSI's chapter, *Roman Delicts and the Constructions of Fault*, = *Obligations in Roman Law. Past, Present, and Future*, T.A.J. MCGINN (ed.), The University of Michigan Press, Ann Anbor 2012, 316.

112   It is worth mentioning that Lord Mance in his contribution published in memory of Lord Rodger classified the references to Roman law as an example of using "foreign laws" by the Scottish judge in his judgments, cf. Lord MANCE: *Foreign Laws and Languages = Judge and Jurist. Essays in Memory of Lord Rodger of Earlsferry*, Andrew BURROWS, David JOHNSTON, Reinhard ZIMMERMANN (eds.), Oxford University Press, Oxford, 2013, 85–97.

## Bibliography

### Cases

*Baker v Bolton* (1808) 1 Camp. 493; 170 Eng. Rep. 1033
*Bern's Executor v. Montrose Asylum* (1893) 20 R. 859
*Black v. Caddell* (1804) Mor. 13905
*Cole-Hamilton v. Boyd* 1963 S.C. (H.L.) 1
*Dick v. Burgh of Falkirk* 1976 S.C. (H.L.) 1
*Donoghue v. Stevenson* [1932] AC 562
*Eisten v. National British Railway Co.* (1870) 8 M. 980
*Fairchild v. Glenhaven Funeral Services Ltd.* [2003] 1 AC 32
*Heaton v. Axa Equity & Law Assurance Society Plc.* [2002] 2 AC 329
*Jameson v. Central Electricity Generating Board* [2000] 1 AC 455
*Kolbin & Sons v. Kinnear & Co.* 1931 S.C. (H.L.) 128
*Lady Leith-Hall v. Earl of Fife* (1768) Mor. 13904
*M'Kendrick v. Sinclair* 1972 S.C. (H.L.) 25
*Robertson v. Turbull* 1982 S.C. (H.L.) 1
*Stewart v. London, Midland and Scottish Railway Co.* 1943 S.C. (H.L.) 19
*Watson v. Fram Reinforced Concrete Co.* 1960 S.C. (H.L.) 92

### Literature

Robert BLACK: *A historical survey of delictual liability in Scotland for personal injuries and death*, Comparative and International Law Journal of Southern Africa 8(1975), 52–70.

George J. BELL: *Principles of the Law of Scotland*, William Blackwood, Edinburgh 1829.

William W. BUCKLAND: *Some Reflections on Jurisprudence*, Cambridge University Press, Cambridge (UK), 1945.

William W. BUCKLAND: *A Text-book of Roman Law from Augustus to Justinian*, 3rd ed., Peter STEIN (rev.), Cambridge University Press, Cambridge (UK), 1966.

John W. CAIRNS: *Rhetoric, Language, and Roman Law: Legal Education and Improvement in Eighteenth-Century Scotland*, Law and History Review 9(1991), 31–58.

John W. CAIRNS: *Historical Introduction = A History of Private Law in Scotland*, Kenneth REID, Reinhard ZIMMERMANN (eds.), Oxford University Press, Oxford 2000, vol. 1, 14–184.

Maria F. CURSI: *Roman Delicts and the Constructions of Fault = Obligations in Roman Law. Past, Present, and Future*, T.A.J. McGINN (ed.), University of Michigan Press, Ann Anbor, 2012, 296–319.

Eric DESCHEEMAEKER: *"Solatium" and Injury to Feelings: Roman Law, English Law and Modern Tort Scholarship = Iniuria and the Common Law*, Eric DESCHEEMAEKER, Helen SCOTT (eds.), Hart Publishing, Oxford-Portland 2013, 67–95.

John ERSKINE: *An Institute of the Law of Scotland*, Edinburgh, Ediburg Legal Education Trust, 1773.

Robin EVANS-JONES: *Roman Law in Britain = Quaestiones Iuris. Festschrift für Joseph Georg Wolf zum 70. Geburstag*, Ulrich MANTHE, Christoph KRAMPE (eds.), Duncker & Humblot, Berlin, 2000, 83–110.

Robert FEENSTRA: *Scottish-Dutch Relations in Seventeenth and Eighteenth Centuries*, = *Scotland and Europe 1200–1850*, T.C. SMOUT (ed.), John Donald Publishers, Edinburgh 1986, 128–142.

Henry GOUDY: *Two Ancient Brocards = Essays in Legal History*, Paul VINOGRADOFF (ed.), Oxford University Press, Oxford, 1913, 215–232.

Jan HALBERDA: *Dzieje doktryny actio personalis moritur cum persona w angielskim common law*, Krakowskie Studia z Historii Państwa i Prawa, 3(2010), 37–49.

Johann Gottlieb HEINECCIUS: *Recitationes in Elementa Iuris Civilis Secundum Ordinem Institutionum*, Typis Crapelet, Pariisis, 1810.

William Searle HOLDSWORTH: *The Origin of Rule in Baker v. Bolton*, Law Quarterly Review 32(1916), 431–437.

William Searle HOLDSWORTH: *History of English Law*, vol. 3, Methuen & Co. Ltd., London 1923.

William A. HUNTER: *A Systematic and Historical Exposition of Roman Law in the Order of a Code*, 4th ed., Sweet & Maxwell, London 1903.

David J. IBBETSON: *A Historical Introduction to the Law of Obligations*, Oxford University Press, Oxford 1999.

Herbert F. JOLOWICZ, Barry NICHOLAS: *Historical Introduction to the Study of Roman Law*, 3rd ed., Cambridge University Press, Cambridge (UK), 1972.

Jeroen S. KORTMANN: *Ab alio ictu(s): Misconceptions about Julian's View on Causation*, Journal of Legal History 20(1999)/2, 95–103.

Frederick H. LAWSON: *A Common Lawyer at the Civil Law*, University of Michigan School of Law, Ann Arbor, 1953.

Klaus LUIG: *Assignation = A History of Private Law in Scotland*, Kenneth REID, Reinhard ZIMMERMAN (eds.), Oxford University Press, Oxford 2000, vol. 2, 399–419.

Geoffrey MacCORMACK: *Culpa in Scots Law of Reparation*, Juridical Review (1974), 13–29.

Frederick W. MAITLAND: *Select Passages from Bracton and Azo*, Selden Society 8, London 1895.

Lord MANCE: *Foreign Laws and Languages = Judge and Jurist. Essays in Memory of Lord Rodger of Earlsferry*, Andrew BURROWS, David JOHNSTON, Reinhard ZIMMERMANN (eds.), Oxford University Press, Oxford, 2013, 85–97.

Elizabeth A. MARTIN: *Oxford Dictionary of Law*, Oxford University Press, Oxford, 2003.

Charles H. Monro: *The Digest of Justinian*, Cambridge University Press, Cambridge (UK), 1909, vol. 2.

Kenneth McK. Norrie: *The Intentional Delicts = A History of Private Law in Scotland*, vol. 2, Kenneth Reid, Reinhard Zimmermann (eds.), Oxford University Press, Oxford, 2000, 477–505.

Alan Rodger: *Lord Macmillan's Speech in Donoghue v. Stevenson*, Law Quarterly Review 108(1992), 236–259.

Alan Rodger: *Mrs. Donoghue and Alfenus Varus*, Current Legal Problems 41(1998), 1–22

Helen Scott: *Killing and Causing Death in Roman Law*, Law Quarterly Review 123(2013), 101–122.

Thomas B. Smith: *Strange Gods: Crisis of Scots Law as a Civilian System* = Thomas B. Smith: *Studies Critical and Comparative*, W. Green, Edinburgh, 1962, 72–88.

Rudolph Sohm: *The Institutes of Roman Law,* J.C. Ledlie (transl.), Oxford University Press, Oxford, 1892.

*The Practicks of Sir James Balfour of Pittendreich*, P.G.B. McNeil (ed.), Star Society 21–22 (1963).

Arnold Vinnius: *Institutionum Imperialium Commentarius & Jurisprudentiae Contractae*, vol. 4, Ex Typographia Baleoniana, Venetiis, 1740.

David M. Walker: *Solatium,* Juridical Review 62(1950), 144–168.

Frederick Parker Walton: *Actio personalis and the French Law*, Journal of Comparative Legislation and International Law 18(1916), 40–59.

Niall R. Whitty: *Rights of Personality, Property Rights and the Human Body in Scots Law*, Edinburgh Law Review (2004–2005), 395–400.

Percy H. Winfield: *A Textbook of the Law of Tort*, 2nd ed., Sweet and Maxwell, London 1943.

Reinhard Zimmermann: *Usus Modernus Legis Aquiliae and Delictual Liability Today*, Stellenbosch Law Review 1(1990), 67–93.

CHAPTER 10

# *Usucapio* in Era of Real Estate Title Registration Systems

*Beata J. Kowalczyk*

## 1 Introduction

Roman law contains numerous universal, supranational and timeless elements, which have largely contributed to its global reach.[1] The world is characterized today by virtual economic unity, as well as – owing to the increased importance of international treaties and arbitration – by political unity, an example of which is the European Union. Thus, it is no wonder that attempts at unifying private law have been undertaken for a number of years. At the same time, models are sought which could serve as a mould for working out a common solution. Unification within the scope of public law has invoked the concept of *ius commune*, widespread in Ancient Rome.[2] Most likely, there is no better model for such unification within private law than the institution of acquisitive prescription, or usucaption, regarding which there exists a time-honoured, unwritten and global agreement as to its structure and functioning. This is confirmed by the inclusion of a regulation regarding usucaption in the Draft Common Frame of Reference document.[3] Thus, it would not be an exaggeration to state that the institution of acquisitive prescription belongs to the common legal heritage of all humanity, as its many variations may be found in nearly all legal cultures of the world. To prove this point, it is sufficient to

---

1  Katarzyna SÓJKA-ZIELIŃSKA: *Drogi i bezdroża prawa. Szkice z dziejów kultury prawnej Europy* [On and Off the Paths of Law. Sketches on the History of Europe's Legal Culture], Ossolineum, Wrocław, 2010, 35–36.

2  H. Patrick GLENN: *On Common Laws*, Oxford University Press, Oxford, 2007, 16 et seq.; Åke MALMSTRÖM: *The System of Legal Systems. Notes on a Problem of Classification in Comparative Law*, Scandinavian Studies in Law 13(1969), 147 et seq.; Joan CHURCH, Christian SCHULZE, Hennie STRYDOM: *Human Rights from a Comparative and International Law Perspective*, Unisa, Praetoria, 2007, 24 et seq.

3  *Principles, Definitions and Model Rules of European Private Law. Draft Common Frame of Reference*, Christian VON BAR, Eric CLIVE, Hans SCHULTE-NÖLKE (eds.), vol. 1, European Law Publishers, Münich, 2009.

© KONINKLIJKE BRILL NV, LEIDEN, 2020 | DOI:10.1163/9789004417274_011

indicate that usucaption, aside from continental Europe and the common law countries, is known in Republic of South Africa,[4] Japan[5] and China.[6]

From its very establishment, usucaption as an original institution, heretofore unknown by the Greek or medieval German laws, contributed to the simplification and ordering of legal relations by way of doing away with states of uncertainty, and also led to consistency between the facts and the legal status, which is desirable in all legal systems. In practical legal transactions, however, states of uncertainty are unavoidable. What is important is to ensure that they do not stretch on forever, as this may cause disputes and evidence-related difficulties in court proceedings. The structure of usucaption shaped in the Roman system was transplanted into contemporary legal systems. Even though nearly twenty-five centuries have passed since its very first regulation in the Law of the Twelve Tables, the institution of usucaption is still applied in many countries, regardless of their legal or socio-economic system.

However, it must be emphasized that currently in many countries, the function of protection of transactions has been taken over by the generally accepted good faith acquisition from a non-owner, and in the case of real property, by the principle of public credibility of land and mortgage registers, which is closely connected to the system of registration of real property titles. For this reason, in countries where this institution functions, i.e. in German (§ 892 of the BGB), Austrian (Allgemeines Grundbuchgesetz of 1871), Swiss (Art. 973 of the ZGB), and Polish law (Art. 5–9 of the KWH), the application of usucaption is limited to cases of Justinian extraordinary usucaption, which waives the need for a just title, or for good faith, as in the case of the 30-year usucaption regulated under Art. 172 §2 of the Civil Code. Even though usucaption has lost the clear functional connection Polish derivative acquisition that it had under Roman law, it still maintains its significance as a statutory method of acquisition of ownership.[7] Considering the above, it seems important to check

---

4   Daniel VISSER: *Obligations arising neither from Contract nor from Delict = Southern Cross: Civil Law and Common Law in South Africa*, Reinhard ZIMMERMANN, Daniel VISSER (eds.) Clarendon Press, Oxford, 1996, 530 et seq.

5   Hiroshi ODA: *Japanese Law*, London, Butterworths, 1992, 163 et seq. The Japanese law has both the institution of extinctive and acquisitive prescription. The general rule allows for the acquisition of ownership upon the lapse of 20 years of peaceful possession. If possession is accompanied by good faith, the acquisitive prescription takes effect upon the lapse of 10 years. The principle of *accessio possessionis* also applies.

6   YONGMIN Shin: *Maintenance or Discard on Acquisitive Prescription System: Also on the Missing and Construction of Acquisitive Prescription in Property Law in China*, Journal of Fujian Administration Institute 1(2009); YIFEI Zhong: *The necessity of establishing positive prescription system in China*, Journal of Harbin Institute of Technology 1(2005).

7   Wojciech DAJCZAK, Tomasz GIARO, Franciszek LONGCHAMPS DE BÉRIER: *Prawo rzymskie. U podstaw prawa prywatnego*, Wydawnictwo Naukowe PWN, Warszawa, 2009, 408 et seq.

whether a system of registration of real property titles, adopted by a given country, exerts an influence on the functioning of acquisitive prescription. The analysis of this issue will be completed in respect to various systems of registration of real property titles or only registering the legal transactions aiming to transfer the legal deed to real property. As a consequence, the role of acquisitive prescription in ensuring consistency between the facts and legal status of a real property under different title registration systems will be examined. Finally after comparative analysis the chapter will able to answear the question if development of IT technology allowed for such modernisation of real estate registration systems and the introduction of legal solutions that in practice usucaption is impossible, and whether the consequence of this situation will not be *desuetudo* of *usucapio*.

## 2 Evolution and Application of *Usucapio* in Roman Law

The eponymous issue requires consideration of two factors, namely the division into acquisitive prescription (*praescriptio adquisitiva*) and extinctive prescription (*praescriptio extinctiva*), as well as the division into ordinary and extraordinary acquisitive prescription, and, as regards real property, whether it functions within a positive or negative system of title registration. In the last stage of development of Roman law, next to the prescription of acquisitive character, that is usucaption, there also functioned the extinctive prescription that led to the loss of a right, contemporarily known as limitation.

In both these cases, the occurrence of the result provided for by the law hinged on the satisfaction of certain prerequisites, although in the absence of good faith, it was known right away that the lapse of time could not lead to the acquisition of ownership, but only to blocking the claim of the plaintiff. As a consequence, *usucapio* led to the acquisition of rights as a result of the passage of time, while the extinctive prescription led to the loss of the right to press effective legal action. In Roman law, these two institutions were treated as separate, with the exception of the period of vulgar law, when *usucapio* was erroneously classified as a limitation. The reform conducted by Constantine and Theodosius inclined Justinian to introduce a new regulation in the form of extraordinary usucaption, in the medieval period referred to as *longissimi taemporis praescriptio*, which led to the acquisition of ownership even without a lawful title and regarding stolen things upon the lapse of 30, and in some cases, 40 years.[8]

---

8    C. 7, 39, 8, 1.

Even in old common law, the institution of *praescriptio* was viewed uniformly, yet it was divided into that serving the acquisition of things and rights – *praescriptio acquisitiva*, and into that resulting in the limitation of claims and complaints – *praescriptio extinctiva*. A similar unanimous regime was adopted in French (Art. 2219 of the Civil Code) and Austrian legislation (§1451 of the ABGB). In the German (§ 194, 937) and Swiss (Arts. 661 and 728) codes, as a result of the influence of the Pandectist school, the concept of usucaption was defined with greater precision, and it was limited to the ownership of material things. Limitation, on the other hand, resulted in the loss of claims. This solution was also transplanted to the Polish Civil Code (Arts. 117–125 and Arts. 172–176).

*Usucapio*, as a method of acquisition of ownership following a specified period of continuous possession and the satisfaction of the remaining prerequisites stipulated by the law, was originally applied as a remedy measure in two situations. Firstly, when the formal legal requirements were not fulfilled, and more precisely when the *res mancipi* was transferred to the acquirer with circumvention of mancipation or *in iure cessio*.[9] Secondly, in the situation of acquisition of any thing, even through a formal procedure, but from a person who was not entitled to dispose of it, if the circumstances did not indicate *furtum* (G. 2, 43). Another important function of *usucapio* was that it made it easier for the owner to prove his ownership in vindication actions. This was very difficult, practically impossible, as it was necessary to prove the title of one's predecessors, theoretically all the way back to the original owner (the so-called *probatio diabolica*).[10] In practice, the owner could also quote acquisition of title through usucaption in order to succeed in bringing about vindication.[11] After Justinian's reform, as a result of which the differences between quiritarian and bonitarian ownership were abolished, usucaption mattered only in the event of acquisition of a thing from a non-owner.

---

9     In this case, *usucapio* was to put an end to the interim state that was bonitarian ownership and made it possible to acquire quiritarian ownership. Had it not been for usucaption, the possessor would never be able to become an owner of this thing within the meaning of *ius civile*. G. 2, 41.

10     Jerzy PIEŃKOS: *Praecepta iuris*, Iuris, Warsaw-Poznań, 2010, 51, as well as Györgyo DIÓSDI: *Ownership in Ancient and Classical Roman Law*, Akademiai Kiado, Budapest, 1968, 162; Cf. Heinrich Hackfeld PFLÜGER: *Ueber die probatio diabolica*, Archiv für die civilistische Praxis 77(1891), 16–27 and Hans KIEFNER: *Klassizität der 'probatio diabolica'?*, Zetschrift der Savigny Stiftung für Rechtsgeschichte, Romanistische Abteilung 81(1964), 212–232.

11     Gaius does not mention this function of usucaption in his textbook. Vindication actions were so widespread in Rome, that it was obvious and most frequently applied. This is most likely why the jurist omitted this function. Cf. Władysław ROZWADOWSKI: *Prawo rzymskie. Zarys wykładu wraz z wyborem źródeł* [Roman Law. An Outline of Lecture with Selection of Sources], Ars boni et aequi, Poznań, 1992, 129.

*Longi temporis praescriptio* as a procedural institution of usucaption defence did not emerge until 199 A.D., when it appeared in the rescriptum issued by Emperors Septiumius Severus and Caracalla.[12] Its primary function was on provincial lands, which excluded private property, where it could be used against vindication claims of quasi-owners. Despite the formal nature of *longi temporis praescriptio*, the requirement of good faith and of just title held in this case. The time limit for raising this defence was 10 years if the plaintiff and defendant resided in the same community (*inter praesentes*) and 20 years if they resided in different communities (*inter absentes*). The procedural institution that thus functioned, interestingly, did not lie at the foundation of the procedural institution of extinctive prescription, as in the post-classical period, *longi temporis praescriptio*, from a defence of limitation that extinguished claims morphed into one with the acquisition by usucaption.[13] The statute of limitations on claims, which resulted in the ability to raise the defence of extinctive prescription, and thus led to numerous difficulties in pursuing one's rights, was not introduced until the times of Constantine the Great for real claims (40 years),[14] and then of Theodosius II in 424 A.D.[15] for all claims (30 years).

## 3     Registration of the Legal Title to the Real Estate from Historical Point of View

The choice of a topic related to real property as the subject of analysis is not accidental. Suffice it to mention the distinctive character of real property that sets it apart from other objects of legal transactions. Firstly, real property is immovable, and thus its ownership cannot be physically transferred from one person onto another, and as regards land real property we should also mention features such as durability or uniqueness.

From the historical point of view, the legal title to real property already played an important role in the early agricultural economies. Contracts concluded as early as 3000 B.C. indicate that people needed official protection for the land they acquired. Even the Bible, in the Book of Jeremiah, offers a description of an early transaction involving land. In 578 B.C., Jeremiah bought

---

12    FIRA, vol. 1, 437.

13    Beata RUSZKIEWICZ: *Longi temporis praescriptio jako zarzut długiego okresu posiadania* [Longi temporis praescriptio as a defence of a long period of possession], Zeszyty Prawnicze, 11(2011)/1, 235 et seq.

14    FIRA, vol. 3, 101.

15    CTh. 4, 14, 1.

from his cousin Hanamel a field, closing the transaction with respect of the legal requirements.[16] As per the Book of Jeremiah, the deal was registered in two copies of written deeds, of which one was sealed and the other remained open. Both copies were given for safekeeping to a priest, who placed them in a clay pot kept in the central temple. Without a doubt, the clay pot in the care of a priest is the equivalent of the register of real estate titles kept in the form of deeds confirmed by witnesses.[17]

Nevertheless, official documents containing information on the ownership status of land date even earlier than 3000 B.C. Ancient Egyptian rulers maintained a Royal Register to record land titles for tax purposes. Much later in Europe, registers of land titles were also kept for the same reason. The first European ruler who, following the establishment of cadastre, encouraged the development of similar systems all over the continent was the Emperor of France, Napoleon I.[18]

At first, the introduction of systems for the registration of real estate titles was motivated solely by tax-related reasons, but soon it turned out that there exists another important element, that is the need to register the titles of buyers, who saw this as a facilitation of the transfer of the legal title to acquired land.[19] It seems that this solution may have meant that buyers wanted to be certain that the person entered in the register as owner was indeed entitled to effectively transfer the ownership title. Or it expressed the will for the state, which was the de facto creator of the register, to guarantee that such transfer of title, even if the person on record was not the true owner, would still be effective. As a consequence, this would lead to the situation in which the legal status of the real property as disclosed in the register, and its actual legal status were the same, and this is the most desirable situation from the perspective of the safety of legal transactions.

---

16  The Book of Jeremiah 32, 9–12. *Biblia Starego i Nowego Testamentu* [Bible of Old and New Testament], Kazimierz JACASZEK (ed.), Warsaw-Poznań 2011, 701. The transaction concluded between Jeremiah and his uncle's son was executed according to the requirements of the Roman law concerning the transfer of ownership of *res mancipii*, that is through *in iure cessio*, a symbolic act of transfer before witnesses, with silver weighed on a scale.

17  Gershon FEDER, Akihiko NISHIO: *The benefits of land registration and titling: Economic and social perspectives*, Land Use Policy, 15(1998)/1, 25–26.

18  Pierre CLERGEOT: *The Origins of the French General Cadastre*, PSI Cadastre, FIG Working Week 2003 (http://formesdufoncier.org/pdfs/Clergeot-OriginesENGLISH.pdf, accessed 28.06.2017).

19  Tim HANSTAD: *Designing Land Registration Systems for Developing Countries*, American University International Law Review 13(1998)/3, 647–703.

Rational aspects prove, however, that the complete elimination of inconsistencies between the legal status disclosed in the register and the true legal status is not possible.[20] When there is no register, in certain specific circumstances, effective acquisition of a real estate title by the acquirer would only be possible as a result of usucaption, but if a register does exist, it may successfully provide safety of transactions by introducing relevant legal regulations concerning the consequences of entries in the register.

One example is the institution of public credibility of land and mortgage registers,[21] provided by the Polish legislator. The Act on Land and Mortgage Registers and Mortgages (Journal of Laws of 2017, item 1007, uniform text) contains a specific legal regulation which aims to protect parties acting in trust of the register (land and mortgage register), to thus ensure safety of the legal transactions involving real properties. Pursuant to Art. 5 of the cited Act,

> in the event of divergences between the legal status of real property disclosed in the land and mortgage register and the true legal status, the contents of the land and mortgage register shall be interpreted in favour of the party who, by way of a legal transaction with a person entitled as per the land and mortgage register, acquired the ownership or another property right.

Thus, a third party, based on the records in the land and mortgage register, may acquire the right disclosed in it or render a performance to the benefit of the entity that is disclosed as the entitled party, even if this is not the true case. Thus, the essence of public credibility of land and mortgage registers boils down to the effective acquisition of the right disclosed therein, even if the disposing party is not entitled to transfer such right. Therefore, it is an exception to the general rule of Polish law, according to which no one may transfer onto another more rights than he himself has, that is *nemo plus iuris in alium transefrre potestas quam ipse habet*.[22]

---

20 Daniel Jakimiec: *Rękojmia wiary publicznej ksiąg wieczystych a wadliwe wykreślenie wpisu wieczystoksięgowego* [Principle of Public Credibility of Land and Mortgage Registers and Defective Striking Out of a Land and Mortgage Register Entry], Monitor Prawniczy 15(2014), 803.

21 This principle seems to be the most relevant institution of the entire land and mortgage register system, *Ibid.* 803.

22 *Ibid.*, 803.

## 4    Modern Land Registration Systems. Positive and Negative Registration Systems

Returning to the systems of registration of titles, it must be emphasized that in the majority of European countries, as probably most elsewhere, there are state registers recording rights to real property, constituting a pool of data on the existing and extinguished rights to real property, particulars of the owners, restrictions and encumbrances. One of the classifications of these registration systems is the division into positive and negative systems of title registration. In the negative system, a title proving the existence of a right, entered in the register, is solely proof that the entry exists in the register, while in the case of a positive system, the title emerges as a result of registration. This means that under the latter of these systems, registration expropriates the former owner and guarantees the right to the new owner. A positive system usually involves a state guarantee that the entered title is true. Moreover, in this system, requirements as regards usucaption are more restrictive, rendering the acquisitive prescription of real property unlikely.

In the Polish legal system, even though it provides for a state guarantee as concerns legal titles entered in the register, usucaption is still useful in regard to real estate with unregulated legal status, that is without a set up land and mortgage register.[23] The Polish legislator has in principle adopted the prerequisites of usucaption of Roman law, leaving out only the requirement of just title[24] and admitting the possibility of usucaption in bad faith, although the minimum time for it is very long – 30 years. Considering the obligations of the notary who is required to notify the registry court of the transfer of ownership of real property, there could occur a situation in which an acquirer who is entered, as long as he acts in good faith, could become the registered owner upon recording of the entry, even if the disposing party is not entitled to transfer the

---

23    The lack of a land and mortgage register that is designed for real estate may pose a risk, as such a property will not be subject to the principle of the public trust of the land and mortgage register. Nevertheless, the buyer still has the possibility to check whether the transferor is entitled to transfer the right, among other documents for example: in the act of acquisition of property, the order of the court of acquisition of inheritance, the administrative decision granting the right of perpetual usufruct or the current extract from the land register.

24    Władysław ROZWADOWSKI: *Zasiedzenie nieruchomości w dobrej wierze w prawie cywilnym na tle prawa rzymskiego* [Civil Law Real Property Usucaption in Good Faith in Light of Roman Law] = *W kręgu teoretycznych i praktycznych aspektów prawoznawstwa. Księga Jubileuszowa Profesora Bronisława Ziemianina*: [Theoretical and Practical Aspects of Jurisprudence. Jubilee Book of Professor Bronisław Ziemianin], Maciej ZIELIŃSKI (ed.), Ars boni et aequi, Poznań, 2005, 235 et seq.

title. If however, the acquirer is acting in bad faith, usucaption would be necessary, as in such cases the principle of public credibility of land and mortgage registers would not apply. A similar regulation functions in the German[25] and English law systems, that is the positive system of title registration. Under this system, a person entered in the register acquires ownership, even if they are not the owner, provided that they have been entered for the time specified at the law and throughout this time they held the real property in their interest.

Under § 900 Bürgerliches Gesetzbuch,[26] a person registered as a landowner in the Land Register (Grundbuch) acquires ownership if he or she is registered as owner for 30 years and throughout that period holds that real property in his own or her own interest. Registration, or scriptum, is a requirement for the holder to be registered as the owner and to a large degree probable that he is the owner of the property. If the holder is registered as a co-owner, the owner will only own the part that he possessed. Pursuant to § 900 (1) of the BGB, the period of acquisitive prescription of a real property is calculated according to the rules adopted for the calculation of acquisitive prescription of movable property and is therefore terminated if the objection is raised. Similarly, the Land Registration Act 2002 stipulates that the registration is a sufficient proof of the existence of a legal title to immovable property.

Where a person is entitled to hold and use land on the basis of a title that does not actually exist in the register, Section 900 (2) of the BGB applies. This provision makes it very difficult for a person to be mistakenly registered as owner for a period of 30 years. The reason for such a restrictive regulation is probably the guarantee of the correct entry into Grundbuch, as provided for in the BGB. The subject of the prescription under § 900 BGB (*usucapio secundum tabulas*) may only be a property admitted to trading as a possible object of private property. This condition does not meet, for example, land under inland waterways, which, according to Art. 89 of the German Constitution cannot be private property. Upon fulfillment of the indicated conditions, the holder becomes the immovable property owner by law. If even the registration was wrong in the sense that it would not reflect the true legal situation, then maintaining it for 30 years causes it to be considered true and correct. Of course, this has an impact on the legal situation of the former owner, who can not make a claim for compensation or for unjust enrichment, because the acquisition of real estate under the conditions provided for in § 900 BGB is legal.

---

25 Peter VON BORCH: *Federal Republic of Germany = Legal Aspects of Alien Acquisition of Real Property* Dennis CAMPBELL (ed.), Springer-Science+Bussiness Media, B.V., Dordrecht, 1980, 80.

26 *Bürgerliches Gestesbuch* (BGB), 1896.

England joined the states with a positive real estate registration system as a result of the 2002 reform, when the Land Registration Act 2002 came into force.[27] The act was introduced as a result of the high court case Pye v Graham, as a consequence of which J.A. Pye lost 57 acres of land worth £10m registered for Graham's farm.[28] This case revealed the unfairness of the current regulation, which consisted of a lack of protection against oversight or oversight of the expiry of the time-limit by the registered owner. As a consequence, Pye sued the United Kingdom for the European Court of Human Rights, pointing out that the loss of his property was inconsistent with Art. 1 Protocol No. 1 to the Convention for the Protection of Human Rights and Fundamental Freedoms, and that the UK was guilty of this.

The Court stated that English law was not contrary to the protocol. At the same time, it concluded that few applicant activities could have stopped the course of the term. However, if Pye had asked Graham to rent or pay for land, it would have lost its hostile nature, and even if the latter had not wanted to agree to the land use conditions or would not leave, the term would have been interrupted and Pye could file a lawsuit for the land, which would have prevented him from losing his title.

The Land Registration Act 2002 is intended to prevent deprivation of registered land title, which has so far been poorly documented, leading to many processes and resulted in easy acquisition of property by hostile owners six months after the loss of the property owner. The Office will send a notice to the registered owner and to all other third parties with a legitimate property interest who have three months to respond to the claim and, if appropriate, to have their possession held. If they do not, the application made by the hostile owner will be registered and he will eventually become the property owner.[29] If the owner makes an objection to the registration of the title of the owner, the circumstances indicated in the act which are justifying the registration of the title of the owner are being examined, this means, when the registered proprietor obtains the applicant in circumstances that justify his registration as owner and also other reasons why the applicant should be registered, such as succession, and moreover, when there were reasonable errors in determining the boundaries of the property. If the holder has been denied registration due to

---

27    Amy GOYMOUR: *Mistaken Registrations of Land: Exploding the Myth of "Title By Registration."* The Cambridge Law Journal, 72(2013)/3, 617–650.

28    Oliver RADLEY-GARDNER: *Civilized Squatting*, Oxford Journal of Legal Studies 25(2005)/4, 727–747.

29    Pamela O'CONNOR: *An Adjudication Rule for Encroachment Disputes: Adverse Possession or a Building Encroachment Statute? = Modern Studies in Property Law*, Elizabeth COOKE (ed.), Oxford-Portland, Hart Publishing, 2007, vol. 4, 206.

failure to meet one of the conditions indicated and the landlord has not taken action to recover the property, the holder may submit another application for entry if he or she continues to hold possession for an additional two years. If the possessor retains the property in his possession during that time, he will be entered in the registry regardless of the actions taken by the owner.[30]

## 5      English, German-Swiss and Torrens Group of Title Registration Systems

Countries in which title registration systems are in place are also divided according to another classification: as English,[31] German-Swiss,[32] and *Torrens*.[33] The differences between the three groups may be found especially regarding technical aspects, and specifically the method of describing plots of land and of completing the registration.

In the English group, large topographic maps are used, and the registration may be completed by the parties to the transaction themselves; in the German-Swiss group plots of land are marked based on cadastral maps and the registration is completed by officials (notaries) with relevant statutory authorisation, and under the Torrens system, based on individual survey maps.[34] Some countries chose to employ a system of legal acts registration (*deeds recordation*), which does not confirm the title, but merely shows that a transaction has taken place.[35] Only proof of the fact that a title exists, and not the title itself, is subject to registration. In such case, if an acquirer wants to check whether the disposing party is the owner and is entitled to dispose of the title, he would have to trace the chain of past transactions, all the way down to original

---

30   Simon COOPER: *Regulating fallibility in registered land titles*, Cambridge Law Journal 72(2013)/2, 341–368.

31   This covers England, Ireland, Nigeria and parts of Canada. Jaap ZEVENBERGEN: *Systems of Land Registration. Aspects and Effects*, Netherlands Geodetic Commissiion, Delft, 2002, 52.

32   This group includes Germany, Austria, Alsace-Lorraine, Switzerland, Egypt, Turkey, Sweden, Denmark. This system was adopted toward the end of the 19th century in many countries that had formerly belonged to the historical Austro-Hungarian Empire. Among others in Croatia, Czech Republic, Hungary, Slovakia, Slovenia, Poland and Romania. *Ibid.* 52.

33   *Ibid.*, 57. This group includes Australia, New Zealand., parts of Canada, some states of the USA, Morocco, Tunisia and Syria.

34   *Ibid.*, 51.

35   This is the dominant solution in the USA, Scotland, France, the Netherlands and Republic of South Africa. Cf. *ibid.*

acquisition, similar to the Roman *probatio diabolica*.[36] In many cases, the examination of the past transactions is limited to the time of the statute of limitations on vindication claims. This results from the underlying principle of the deeds recordation model, according to which it is not the right to real property that is subject to registration, but rather the evidence of title, that is an instrument concerning the transfer of rights to a real property or other actions concerning these rights (establishment of encumbrances, etc).

The deeds registration model is the dominant one in the USA. Separate solutions are currently in place only in Louisiana, because of the fact that it belongs to the civil law system, and in a few other states that decided to introduce the Torrens system. Nevertheless, even though the majority of US states have the deeds recordation system whose origins date back to the Massachusetts ordinance of 1640, the state-specific solutions are quite different in terms of details.[37]

However, the characteristic feature of the American deeds recordation model is the fact that official registers in which documents concerning real property titles are kept are not the sole instrument for ensuring the safety of transactions; in reality, one could venture to state that they are of secondary significance in this respect.[38] The fundamental role in ensuring the safety of real property transactions in the USA, and thus the most significant form of safeguarding the interests of parties thereto, is to this day transaction insurance, including, particularly, title insurance.

Considering the solutions adopted in the USA, it must be concluded that owing to the possible necessity of proving the existence of predecessor's rights, usucaption, which is called adverse possession, could lead to the alignment of the facts with the legal status of the real property. At each stage of such an examination, the acquirer could acquire the title from his predecessor as a result of adverse possession, which is possible already upon the lapse of two years in Arizona, while in New Jersey – upon 30.[39] As regards possession, it must be open, so that the potential owner has a chance to react to the trespass. Moreover, it must be continuous and autonomous, i.e. without prior consent of the owner, and

---

36    The legal status of a real property is established through the analysis of rights to which the disposing party is entitled, by tracing the chain of title consisting in proving legal succession, reaching up to a few decades back (between 40 and 60 years depending on the state). Paweł BLAJER: *"Deeds recordation" "title registration": rozwiązania modelowe w zakresie rejestrów nieruchomości w systemie "common law"* ["Deeds Recordation", "Title Registration": Model Solutions Concerning Real Property Registers in the Common Law System], Zeszyty Prawnicze, 13(2004)/4, 64.

37    *Ibid.*

38    Paweł BLAJER: *Notariat łaciński z amerykańskiej perspektywy*, Rejent, 23(2013)/2, 50–59.

39    Kristine S. CHEREK: *From Trespasser to Homeowner: The Case Against Adverse Possession In The Post-Crash World*, Virginia Journal of Social Policy and the Law, 20(2012), 271–321.

also last long enough for the owner's right to press recovery claims to become extinguished.[40]

A different solution that completely makes usucaption of real estate impossible, providing a high assurance of legal certainty and the one of the most widespread real estate title registrations in the world, is provided by the Torrens system.[41] This system is a reference to the German tradition, where entries in the land register (Grandbuch) have a constitutive character. The South Australian Torrens Act of 1858, which introduced the aforementioned system, also relies on a constitutive registration of standardized forms, which, along with a certificate confirming the rights of the seller, are the basis for the registrar to make the relevant entries in the register.[42] The quasi-judge's recorder cancels the seller's certificate at the same time and inserts a new certificate confirming the purchaser's rights. This certificate adequately reflects the legal status of the property, which at the same time makes it impossible to conduct any disputes that would be subject to the legal status of the real estate and claims of others, and in particular the cessation of the real estate. The Torrens system provides protection to any purchaser of property rights under pecuniary title when it acquires these rights from the seller with the appropriate certificate and does not invalidate that protection even to the purchaser's knowledge that the rights do not actually belong to the seller and therefore are referred to in the literature as having a positive character.[43] This broadly defined protection has forced the establishment of an institution to compensate for damages suffered by persons deprived of or restricted in their rights due to erroneous entries in the registry or errors in the content of the certificate. Compensation is paid from the fund affected by the registration fee and can be claimed for a period of six to ten years from the date of the mistake or error.[44]

## 6 Conclusion

Even this short characterisation of a few systems of real property title registration reveals certain conclusions regarding the contemporary function of

---

40 *Ibid.*, 237.

41 L. TING, Ian WILLIAMSON, Donald GRANT, J.R. PARKER: *Understanding the Evolution of Land Administration Systems in Some Common Law Countries*, Survey Review, 35(1999)/272, 83–102.

42 Eugene C. MASSIE: *The Torrens System of Land Registration and Transfer*, The Virginia Law Register 6(1900)/4, 215.

43 Joseph T. JANCZYK: *Land Title Systems, Scale of Operations, and Operating and Conversion Costs*, The Journal of Legal Studies 8(1979)/3, 572.

44 Eugene C. MASSIE: *Perfection of the Torrens System*, The Virginia Law Register 2(1917)/10, 750–771.

usucaption. Firstly, it must be emphasized that usucaption is one of many institutions that can be traced back to Roman law and which withstood the test of time and function to this day in most legal systems. Nevertheless, its modern role is completely different from the one it fulfilled over 2000 years ago. The intensification of legal relations, as well as the possibility of digitalisation of legal documentation, mean that today it is much easier to obtain reliable information on the legal status of real property than it was even 20 years ago. For this reason, the current function of usucaption – a stabilizing one that in a sense guarantees safety of transactions concerning real property – is not as significant for legal transactions. In a time of globalisation and modernisation of regulation using advancement IT technology, all states apply systems that guarantee the certainty of real property titles, such as the positive system of registration in Germany and England or the deeds recordation system in place in the United States of America. However, even there the institution of usucaption has been maintained, even though its legal consequences are at odds with the main purpose of these systems. It has been decided that in extraordinary circumstances,when the owner has lost interest in his real property and someone else has taken possession of it and used it for a sufficiently long time, exercising all the entitlements of a possessor and satisfying all the attendant obligations, the factual state should be sanctioned by granting the legal title to such a possessor. This, however, does not change the fact that the role played by usucaption in these countries is marginal. In countries with a negative system of registration, for example in Poland, the safeguarding function is fulfilled by the institution of public credibility of land and mortgage registers as regards real property with set up land and mortgage registers in case of acquisition from an non-entitled party. There are also other, restrictive rules in place, such as the requirement of *animo domini* or longer usucaption terms of 20 or 30 years for bad faith possessors, which seems to provide owners with sufficient security. Certainly, this is not the same degree of protection as in the countries with positive system of title registration, where the state itself guarantees that the registered titles are true. Nevertheless, in all these countries, the institution of usucaption still aims to cause the alignment of the legal status with the longstanding state of facts, especially in cases where the real property in question does not have a land and mortgage register set up. The significance of usucaption has been downgraded in those countries in which restrictive regulations under the positive system of title registration, combined with a state guarantee, have taken over the function of usucaption which consisted in maintaining certainty as to ownership. Of particular importance seems to be the introduction of this system into English legislation. Thanks to this, the controversial institution of *adverse possessio*, sometimes referred to as real property theft and raising serious moral doubts, has acquired a new, more civilized construction. It is worth mentioning that this modernisation was fashioned after the most restrictive regulation regarding this area, in effect in Germany, where usucaption of real property seems very unlikely. Regardless of this, even in countries where, owing to systems of registration of real property titles, usucaption is not likely, legislators have not chosen to rid the legal order of usucaption completely. In spite of this, the inability to use *usucapio* from the reason of the modernized provisions may lead to the loss of its binding power called *desuetudo*.

### Bibliography

*Biblia Starego i Nowego Testamentu* [Bible of Old and New Testament], Kazimierz JACASZEK (ed.), Warsaw-Poznań 2011.

Paweł BLAJER: *"Deeds recordation" "title registration": rozwiązania modelowe w zakresie rejestrów nieruchomości w systemie "common law"* ["Deeds Recordation," "Title Registration": Model Solutions Concerning Real Property Registers in the Common Law System], Zeszyty Prawnicze, 13(2004)/4, 53–90.

Paweł BLAJER: *Notariat łaciński z amerykańskiej perspektywy*, Rejent, 23(2013)/2, 50–59.

Bürgerliches Gestesbuch (BGB), 1896.

Kristine S. CHEREK: *From Trespasser to Homeowner: The Case Against Adverse Possession In The Post-Crash World*, Virginia Journal of Social Policy and the Law, 20(2012), 271–321.

Joan CHURCH, Christian SCHULZE, Hennie STRYDOM: *Human Rights from a Comparative and International Law Perspective*, Unisa, Praetoria, 2007.

Pierre CLERGEOT: *The Origins of the French General Cadastre*, PSI Cadastre, FIG Working Week 2003.

Simon COOPER: *Regulating fallibility in registered land titles*, Cambridge Law Journal 72(2013)/2, 341–368.

Wojciech DAJCZAK, Tomasz GIARO, Franciszek LONGCHAMPS DE BÉRIER: *Prawo rzymskie. U podstaw prawa prywatnego*, Wydawnictwo Naukowe PWN, Warszawa, 2009.

Györgyo DIÓSDI: *Ownership in Ancient and Classical Roman Law*, Akademiai Kiado, Budapest, 1968.

Gershon FEDER, Akihiko NISHIO: *The benefits of land registration and titling: Economic and social perspectives*, Land Use Policy, 15(1998)/1, 25–43.

*Fontes Iuris Romani anteiustiniani*, Salvatore RICCOBONO et al. (eds.), S.A.G. Barbera, Firenze, 1968.

H. Patrick GLENN: *On Common Laws*, Oxford University Press, Oxford, 2007.

Amy GOYMOUR: *Mistaken Registrations of Land: Exploding the Myth of "Title By Registration."* The Cambridge Law Journal, 72(2013)/3, 617–650.

Tim HANSTAD: *Designing Land Registration Systems for Developing Countries*, American University International Law Review 13(1998)/3, 647–703.

*The Institutiones of Gaius*, Samuel P. SCOTT (transl.) The Central Trust Company, Cincinnati, 1932.

Daniel JAKIMIEC: *Rękojmia wiary publicznej ksiąg wieczystych a wadliwe wykreślenie wpisu wieczystoksięgowego* [Principle of Public Credibility of Land and Mortgage Registers and Defective Striking Out of a Land and Mortgage Register Entry], Monitor Prawniczy 15(2014).

Joseph T. JANCZYK: *Land Title Systems, Scale of Operations, and Operating and Conversion Costs*, The Journal of Legal Studies 8(1979)/3, 569–583.

Hans KIEFNER: *Klassizität der "probatio diabolica"?*, Zetschrift der Savigny Stiftung für Rechtsgeschichte, Romanistische Abteilung 81(1964), 212–232.

Paulus KRUEGER, *Corpus Iuris Civilis*, vol. 2: *Codex Iustinianus*, Apud Weidmannos, Berolini, 1877.

Åke MALMSTRÖM: *The System of Legal Systems. Notes on a Problem of Classification in Comparative Law*, Scandinavian Studies in Law 13(1969), 127–149.

Eugene C. MASSIE: *The Torrens System of Land Registration and Transfer*, The Virginia Law Register 6(1900)/4, 215–221.

Eugene C. MASSIE: *Perfection of the Torrens System*, The Virginia Law Register 2(1917)/10, 750–771.

Codex Theodosianus, Theodore MOMMSEN, Paul M. MEYER (eds.), Berlin 1905.

Pamela O'CONNOR: *An Adjudication Rule for Encroachment Disputes: Adverse Possession or a Building Encroachment Statute?* = *Modern Studies in Property Law*, Elizabeth COOKE (ed.), Oxford-Portland, Hart Publishing, 2007, vol. 4, 197–217.

Hiroshi ODA: *Japanese Law*, London, Butterworths, 1992.

Heinrich Hackfeld PFLÜGER: *Ueber die probatio diabolica*, Archiv für die civilistische Praxis 77(1891), 16–27.

Jerzy PIEŃKOS: *Praecepta iuris*, Iuris, Warsaw-Poznań, 2010.

*Principles, Definitions and Model Rules of European Private Law. Draft Common Frame of Reference*, Christian VON BAR, Eric CLIVE, Hans SCHULTE-NÖLKE (eds.), European Law Publishers, Münich, 2009, vol. 1.

Oliver RADLEY-GARDNER: *Civilized Squatting*, Oxford Journal of Legal Studies 25(2005)/4, 727–747.

Władysław ROZWADOWSKI: *Prawo rzymskie. Zarys wykładu wraz z wyborem źródeł* [Roman Law. An Outline of Lecture with Selection of Sources], Ars boni et aequi, Poznań, 1992.

Władysław ROZWADOWSKI: *Zasiedzenie nieruchomości w dobrej wierze w prawie cywilnym na tle prawa rzymskiego* [Civil Law Real Property Usucaption in Good Faith in Light of Roman Law] = *W kręgu teoretycznych i praktycznych aspektów prawoznawstwa. Księga Jubileuszowa Profesora Bronisława Ziemianina*: [Theoretical and Practical Aspects of Jurisprudence. Jubilee Book of Professor Bronisław Ziemianin], Maciej ZIELIŃSKI (ed.), Ars boni et aequi, Poznań, 2005, 235–258.

Beata RUSZKIEWICZ: *Longi temporis praescriptio jako zarzut długiego okresu posiadania* [Longi temporis praescriptio as a defence of a long period of possession], Zeszyty Prawnicze, 11(2011)/1, 235–248.

Katarzyna SÓJKA-ZIELIŃSKA: *Drogi i bezdroża prawa. Szkice z dziejów kultury prawnej Europy* [On and Off the Paths of Law. Sketches on the History of Europe's Legal Culture], Ossolineum, Wrocław, 2010.

Lisa TING, Ian WILLIAMSON, Donald GRANT, John R. PARKER: *Understanding the Evolution of Land Administration Systems in Some Common Law Countries*, Survey Review, 35(1999)/272, 83–102.

Peter Von BORCH: *Federal Republic of Germany* = *Legal Aspects of Alien Acquisition of Real Property* Dennis CAMPBELL (ed.), Springer-Science+Bussiness Media, B.V., Dordrecht, 1980, 77–89.

Daniel VISSER: *Obligations arising neither from Contract nor from Delict* = *Southern Cross: Civil Law and Common Law in South Africa*, Reinhard ZIMMERMANN, Daniel VISSER (eds.) Clarendon Press, Oxford, 1996, 521–558.

YIFEI Zhang: *The necessity of establishing positive prescription system in China*, Journal of Harbin Institute of Technology 1(2005).

YONGMIN Shin: *Maintenance or Discard on Acquisitive Prescription System: Also on the Missing and Construction of Acquisitive Prescription in Property Law in China*, Journal of Fujian Administration Institute 1(2009).

Jaap ZEVENBERGEN: *Systems of Land Registration. Aspects and Effects*, Netherlands Geodetic Commissiion, Delft, 2002.

CHAPTER 11

# In the Name of the Republic: Family Reform in Late Nineteenth and Early Twentieth-Century France and China

*Mingzhe Zhu*

## 1 Introduction

Usually treated through private law, the institution of the family has great political significance in the construction of regimes. This chapter compares the legal reforms concerning family structure during the republican moments of two countries: France (in the late 19th century) and China (in the early 20th century). The republican militants in both contexts endeavoured to affect the transformation of the traditional organisation of the family, or even more radically, the dissolution of the family structure altogether, for the purpose of strengthening the State's monopoly of powers. In France, family reforms were before all an instrument to laicise the social institutions. The basic structure of masculine dominance in the family persisted through the first decades of the Third French Republic, from 1870 to 1900. In contrast to France, to forge an entirley new nation free from the burden of the past was the leading idea of the Republic of China. It therefore urged wilder conscious judicial measures to eliminate the traditional family model.

On 22 October 1931, nineteen years after the foundation of the Republic of China, a couple settled their divorce agreement in a law firm in Tianjin. This ordinary practice soon became symbolic, because it had been filed by Wanrong (1906–1946), known as Consort Shu, on the grounds that she had suffered "grave injures" by her husband, or the Abrogated Emperor of the Qing Dynasty (Xuantong Emperor, 1906–1967), the last ruling Emperor in China's history. This is the first and the only imperial divorce in China. There are two ways of telling this story as a grand narrative, leaving aside those rumours about jealousy, adultery or even infanticide that interested mostly rumourmongers. Scenario I: a modern woman and subject freed herself from the abusive marital and imperial authority. Scenario II: the traditional virtue and the good social order were in danger because of this rebellious act. Both narratives highlight the fact that double dissolution of the traditional patriarchal family and of the ancient Empire was ongoing. Chinese reformers in the early 20th century, no

© KONINKLIJKE BRILL NV, LEIDEN, 2020 | DOI:10.1163/9789004417274_012

IN THE NAME OF THE REPUBLIC

matter how they behaved in their own families, held the belief that a republican regime could only be built upon the total disposal of the traditional family. Since the drafting of the Chinese Civil Code also took place in these crucial years known as the republican moment in China, such a political agenda transformed into numerous legal reforms. Private law is never free from political constitution of a nation.[1]

This was not an isolated case in modern legal history. Similar ideas had also appeared in revolutionary France and in the founding period of the Third French Republic, namely in the late 18th century and the late 19th century. It might not be simply contractictory that the space reserved for private life and relations had also political significance. The family in modern legal philosophy implies usually respect for family autonomy, patriarchy, as well as mutual care among members.[2] It stands between the State power and individuals. On the scale of classical Confucian moral teachings, on the one hand, the family provides protection to its members and assures the stability of the regime. French and Chinese republicans, seeking to construct modern States, on the other hand, underscore its efforts of overshadowing individual liberties as well as undermining State authority.[3]

The similarity between the French and Chinese revolutionary programmes on the family law leads us to two reflections. First, for what reasons did these republicans believe that the form of the family was crucial to their political agenda and what were the actual effects, in each country retrospectively, of their programmes in family law? This chapter studies in first place the

---

1   In the context of Chinese codification of private law, the relation between private law and the Constitution is particularly disputed. Some civilists still insists on the purity of civil law. Cf. 苏永钦：“现代民法典的体系定位与建构规则”，载《交大法学》（第1卷），上海交通大学出版社2011年版，第59—93页。Others argue that the construction of civil law system is inevitably political. Cf. 刘征峰：“家庭法与民法知识谱系的分立”，载《法学研究》2017年第4期；韩大元：“宪法与民法关系在中国的演变——一种学说史的梳理”，载《清华法学》2016　年第6期；谢鸿飞：“中国民法典的生活世界、价值体系与立法表达”，载《清华法学》2014年第6期；薛军：“，民法—宪法‘关系的演变与民法的转型——以欧洲近现代民法的发展轨迹为中心”，载《中国法学》2010年第1期。

2   张翔：“论我国法律体系中的家与个体自由原则”，《中外法学》2013年第4期。

3   Georges Padoux, French legal consultant for Chinese Republican government, expressed his critiques of the traditional Chinese family in his opinion on the reform of Chinese family law.　Cf.　[法]宝道：“中国亲属法之改造”，张毓昆译，《法学季刊》1936年第1卷1号。

republican discourses, in both languages, to reconstruct the ways in which French and Chinese reformers envisaged the issue in question. Then it will compare the adaptations of Enlightenment ideals of family – a voluntary union of equal and free individuals – in legislation, jurisprudence, and doctrine in each country.

Second, if we go beyond comparative legal history and try to perceive the issue in question from the perspective of transnational legal history, we might revaluate the West/East dichotomy, based on the practice of Enlightenment ideals. The French family regime was modernised rather reluctantly in the 19th century gradually departing the traditional model of family based on patriarchism, interdiction of divorce and the doctrine of legitimacy.[4] But it still served, along with other European laws, as as reference point for China's legal modernisation. Though Chinese lawyers were in many cases more positively disposed toward radical changes than their European counterparts, the achievements of China, its progress, its modernisation, and its legislations were all measured by reference to Europe. Eurocentricism is a reality in China's modernisation.[5] For decades scholars have discussed the "legal transplant" in China, as if it had been a passive vassal of all foreign influence. A less biased or less caricatured story may nevertheless be more complex. This paper shows also the complexity of the transplant of European legal ideals in China, which further suggests that not only do these ideals have a history, they have a world history.

The militants of radical reforms at both ends of the Eurasian continent were not fighting against any kind of family whatsoever. The real enemy was the particular patriarchal family in which the fathers enjoy the highest internal authority that is deemed to last until the end of days. But to what extent can one expect to compare a European story and an oriental passé? If Chinese republicans had an exotic conception of what "traditional family" means that was totally strange to their French forerunners, a comparison between what they achieved can only be a distorted and pointless effort. Should we take caution and remind ourselves of the very first line of Rudyard Kipling's *The Ballad*

---

4  Jean-Paul SARDON: *L'évolution Du Divorce En France*, Population 51(1996)/3, 717–749; Max RHEINSTEIN: *Trends in Marriage and Divorce Law of Western Countries*, Law and Contemporary Problems. 18(1953)/1, 3–19.

5  Cf. Enrique DUSSEL, Javier KRAUEL, Virginia TUMA: *Europe, Modernity, and Eurocentrism*, Nepantla: Views from South, 1(2000)/3, 465–478; Immanuel WALLERSTEIN: *Eurocentrism and Its Avatars: The Dilemma of Social Sciences*, Sociological Bulletin, 46(1997)/1 21–39; Cornel WEST, Bill BROWN: *Beyond Eurocentrism and Multiculturalism*, Modern Philology 90(1993)/1, 142–166.

IN THE NAME OF THE REPUBLIC                                                                257

*of East and West*: "Oh, East is East, and West is West, and never the twain shall meet".[6]

Per the rhetoric of lawyers at the beginning of the 20th century, traditional Chinese society regarded family as the fundamental unity of the society and the guarantor of its intrinsic value.[7] Under the traditional regime, the Chinese family had a chief of the family who not only could dispose of the property of the members but also claim authority over their personal arrangements, such as marriage. A similar conception of family did exist in France. Napoleon remarked in the authority of the First Consul that "civil law provides only three sets of rules of persons: those fixing each individual in a civic society; those regulating the marital relationship; and those regulating the relation between a father and his children."[8] Family law being a part of the law of persons in the French Civil Code, we can also deduce from his remark that family law deals only with two major relations: that between a family and the greater society and that between family members. The primacy of family in Europe might not be as obvious as it was in Ancient China. Still, family laws in most Romano-German legal systems conceive as fundamental notions the legitimacy that decides if a child can legally claim support, education, compensatory allowance; the parental authority that allows a parent to validate or revoke children's acts; the marital authority that guarantees the generations of husbands' privileges over their female counterparts,[9] and the insolubility of marriage that protects the unity from rebellious acts. Despite of all the differences between the conceptions of family in the East and in the West, it seems reasonable to admit that patriarchy and insoluble marriage are crucial elements for traditional family on both sides.

The mutations of property rights and of divorce provide us aspects from which modern researchers can evaluate the family reforms during the revolutionary years. However similar the revolutionary discourses of French and Chinese reformists' purposes may be, a closer account shows that family law reforms in the two countries in their republican moments were accomplished in different mechanisms. In late 19th century France, nominal acceptance of divorce encountered resistance in both practice and doctrine and the equality of property rights was recognised only gradually. Legal institutions,

---

6   My gratitude is to David Shorr of Tel Aviv University who reminded me of this poem.
7   参见[法]宝道："中国亲属法之改造"，张毓昆译，《法学季刊》1936年第1卷1号；胡长清：《中国民法亲属论》，商务印书馆1936年版，第7页；并参见史尚宽：《亲属法论》，中国政法大学出版社2000年版，第6页。
8   Pierre-Antoine FENET: *Précis Historique Sur La Confection Du Code Civil = Recueil Complet Des Travaux Préparatoires Du Code Civil*, Pierre-Antoine FENET (ed.), vol. 1, Videcoq, Paris, 1836.
9   *Cf.* Edward MANSON: *Marital Authority*, Law Quarterly Review 7(1891), 244.

a combination of lent legislations, conservative legal doctrine, and progressive jurisprudence, changed along with social progress. The relationship between the laws and society at the other end of the Eurasian continent was exactly the opposite. In early 20th century China, although the paternal dominance of property remained obvious, the trend toward divorce and the legislative limitation of "family" as a unit demonstrate the governmental determination to modernise society by means of laws.

This chapter, just as the other chapters of this book, provides empirical evidence to the philosophical debate over the nature of law. To better understand the nature of law and legal practice, we shall take the instrumental view of law. In legal philosophy, it means that "law – encompassing legal rules, legal institutions, and legal processes – is consciously viewed by people and groups as a tool or means with which to achieve ends."[10] As a historian, I think it is just to add a verb to Tamanaha's definition: law is not only viewed, but also actually used as a tool. In the particular stories of this chapter, the debates over family reformes reveal the concern of national identies. When women and men of law discuss the institution of marriage, they did not merely due with the value of the marriage as such, but also attacked or defended an essential component of the national identity.

## 2       Family and Republic in Politics

### 2.A       *Secularising the Society to Defend the Republic*
Before the Chamber of representatives, on May the 4 1877, one of the founding members of the Third Republic, Léon Gambetta (1838–1882), put forward one of his most famous slogans: "Clericalism, that is the enemy!".[11] Among few passionate political beliefs an opportunist professed, this was one.[12] The Church was usually described as the allied power of the old elites and notables. The republicans who endorsed the Third Republic were convinced that a Republican regime could only be built by driving out the alliance of all those elements that represented the Old France, the Monarchy, and the Concordat.[13] Although

---

10      Brian TAMANAHA: *Law as a Means to an End*, Cambridge University Press, Cambridge (UK), 2006, 6.

11      The French version is more compelling: "Le cléricalisme, voilà l'ennemi!" *Cf.* Jacqueline LALOUETTE: *Laïcité, anticléricalismes et antichristianisme*, Transversalités, 108(2013), 69–84.

12      Herbert FISHER: *The Republican Tradition in Europe*, G. Putnam's sons, New York-London, 1911, 299.

13      Roger MAGRAW: *France, 1815–1914: The Bourgeois Century*, Oxford University Press, Oxford, 1983, 212.

the nature of French laicity is still under dispute, modern observers accept that the the historical practice of this idea treat the churches as the potential threat to the Republican State and individual liberties of its citizens.[14] Soon after the universal male suffrage was established (1875), the republican government expelled the Jesuits and other religious congregations for their refusal to obtain governmental authorisation to teach (1880), and also introduced the compulsory secular primary school system (1881).

The climax of French laicisation, from a legal point of view, is definitely the 1905 law on the *Separation of the Churches and State*.[15] By putting an end to state finance for ecclesiastical institutions, confiscating the buildings of worship, and banning religious symbols from public places, this law successfully made the republic a laic country where Christian churches and other religious institutions play no significant role in the daily organisation of social and political life. Beside these efforts, discourses concerning ecclesiasticism and the Catholic Church were scandalising. In official textbooks of history, Clovis I, who made huge efforts toward evangelisation, was depicted as a "barbarian," and the historical faults of the Church are depicted because of its strange and inferior nature *vis à vis* Gaulois civilisation.[16]

The struggle against the Catholic Church for the State's monopoly on social and political power also affected domestic administration, for the private domain remained a refuge of the Catholicism. Furthermore, the Catholic Church was the social power that defended most stridently the patriarchal family model. Politicians and lawyers who drafted and validated the Napoleonic Code endorsed the Catholic view of the family, bearing in mind that the majority of the French population was Catholic.[17] A glance at the drafts previous to the final version of the code revealed that a patriarchal view of the family overshadowed the egalitarian alternative as time passed. In the first two drafts by eminent French jurist Jean-Jacques-Régis de Cambacérès (1753–1824), who

---

14  Géraldine MUHLMANN, Claire ZALC: *La laïcité, de la IIIe à la Ve République*, Pouvoirs, 126(2008)/3, 101–114. Cf. Mingzhe ZHU: *On French Laicity in Combat*, Chinese Journal of European Studies, 6(2016), 117–135.

15  Alain BERGOUNIOUX: *La Laïcité, Valeur de La République*, Pouvoirs 75(1995), 17–26.

16  Patrick CABANEL: *Compromis historique et déceptions démocratiques: la laïcité républicaine = Une contre-histoire de la IIIe République*, Marion FONTAINE, Frédéric MONIER, Christophe PROCHASSON (eds.), Cahiers libres, Dévouverte 2013; Perrine SIMON-NAHUM: *La République et les républicains, adversaires du religieux et des religions = Une contre-histoire de la IIIe République...*, *op. cit.*

17  Jean-Etienne-Marie PORTALIS: *Discours Préliminaire Prononcé Par Portalis, Le 24 Thermidor an VIII, Lors de La Présentation Du Projet Arrêté Par La Commission Du Gouvernement = Recueil Complet Des Travaux Préparatoires Du Code Civil...*, vol. 1, *op. cit.*, 463–524.

claimed that husbands ought to administer the property of married women,[18] the community property system was chosen as the legal matrimonial regime, per which, in the name of the equality of spouses, husband and wife would exercise the same rights of governing property. Such an egalitarian arrangement disappeared with the Thermidorian Reaction. In the third Cambacérès project prior to the Reaction, the husband alone enjoyed the right over community property,[19] while the wife was obliged to obtain specific spousal authorisation even when she intended to dispose of her separate property.[20] Then came the Eighteenth of Brumaire that brought Napoleon Bonaparte to power. A rather concise and unfinished project was proposed by Jean-Ignace Jacqueminot (1754–1813). A married woman was obliged to obtain written permission from her husband to be the beneficiary of a grant or an inheritance,[21] no matter which matrimonial regime they had chosen. The principal dispositions of this ephemeral project were then specified in the 1801 project drafted by the famous committee of four, and therefore it entered the final text of the 1804 Civil Code. In the original version of the 1804 Civil Code, the wife owed obedience to her husband[22] and was obliged to follow him to all the places where he may judge it convenient to reside.[23] The husband alone administered the community property.[24] All personal property of the wife was under the administration of her husband.[25] More examples can be named.

Justified by Enlightenment ideals,[26] the Napoleonic Code did not differ significantly from the Ancien Régime in the way it also conceived the marital

---

18  Jean-Jacques-Régis DE CAMBACÉRÈS: *Discours Préliminaire Prononcé Par Cambacérès Au Conseil Des Cinq-Cents, Lors de La Présentation Du Troisième Projet de Code Civil, Faite Au Nom de La Commission de La Classification Des Lois = Recueil Complet Des Travaux Préparatoires Du Code Civil...*, vol. 1, *op. cit.*, 140–177.

19  Art. 293.

20  Art. 295.

21  Art. 58 and art. 111.

22  Art. 213.

23  Art. 214.

24  Art. 1421.

25  Art. 1428.

26  *Cf.* CAMBACÉRÈS: *Discours Préliminaire Prononcé Par Cambacérès Au Conseil Des Cinq-Cents, Lors de La Présentation Du Troisième Projet de Code Civil, Faite Au Nom de La Commission de La Classification Des Lois*; PORTALIS: *Discours Préliminaire Prononcé Par Portalis, Le 24 Thermidor an VIII, Lors de La Présentation Du Projet Arrêté Par La Commission Du Gouvernement*; Jean-Ignace JACQUEMINOT, *Idées Préliminaires Sur Le Projet de Jacqueminot, Présenté Par Jacqueminot, Au Nom de La Section de Législation = Recueil Complet Des Travaux Préparatoires Du Code Civil...*, *op. cit.*, vol. 1, 327–332.

IN THE NAME OF THE REPUBLIC                                                    261

relationship. What is worse, while Catholicism did contribute indeed to the elaboration of family law the moment the code was drafted, nevertheless, the persistence of the traditional form of the family had its roots in revolutionary republicanism as well. The female citizens engaged in social and political movements with whom Condorcet and Sieyès were willing to ally soon turned to be the opposite party of independent and rational males in post-revolutionary discourses.[27] It is also the language of the Enlightenment that placed an emphasis on both nature and physical existence. According to nature, men were stronger, thus able to use their time and capacity more independently.[28] Therefore, the patriarchal regime of the family was based on "the very nature of things."[29] Cambacérès defended still the idea of spousal equality, saying that it was not a violation of egalitarian principles to allow the husband to have higher authority to prevent the happiness of family life from being destroyed by endless disputes, though it was "totally against the laws of nature to let women to administer property."[30] In the preliminary discourse attributed to Jean-Étienne-Marie Portalis (1746–1807), the answer was more straightforward: "the husband is the chief of the family", and "we will tolerate the indiscretion and the triviality of this admirable sex as its graces but cannot encourage the actions that could disturb order or offend decency."[31]

Regarding themselves as the heirs of the 1789 revolution, the Republicans of the Third Republic also inherited the indifference to gender equality.[32] *Le Serment des Horaces* of Jacques-Louis David corresponds well to the French republican spirit: social spheres are divided into the public domain and the private one. While the former belongs to male citizens and their virtues, the latter is the place for females and their weakness. Saying that does not mean that women were to have larger privileges in domestic affairs. On the contrary, at the beginning of the 20th century, the *Code civil annoté* explained that the husband is by nature and by law the chief of family and that the marital authority, being essential to domestic organisation and public order, cannot be modified

---

27  Yvonne KNIBIEHLER: *Les Médecins et La 'nature Féminine' au Temps Du Code Civil*, Annales. Histoire, Sciences Sociales 31(1976)/4, 824–845.

28  Jean-Etienne-Marie PORTALIS: *Présentation Au Corps Législatif, et Exposé Des Motifs Du Mariage = Recueil Complet Des Travaux Préparatoires Du Code Civil…, op. cit.*, vol. 9, 138–181.

29  Jean-Baptiste TREILHARD: *Présentation au corps législatif, et exposé des motifs = Recueil complet des travaux préparatoires du Code civil…, op. cit.*, vol. 9, 556–563.

30  CAMBACÉRÈS: *Discours Préliminaire…, op. cit.*

31  PORTALIS: *Discours Préliminaire…, op. cit.*

32  David DEROUSSIN: *Histoire du droit privé : XVIe–XXIe siècle*, Ellipses Marketing, Paris, 2010, 205.

by matrimonial conventions.[33] The social inferiority of women is indicated in daily language. The feminine term of student, étudiante, in French, did not mean a school girl but the female companion of a male student until the early 20th century. Females could not study subjects.[34]

Anticlerical determination in the last decades of the 19th century, however, led to a profound transformation in the family. Their use of legislative power led to limited recognition of married women's property rights, but significant legislative changes took place with the reintroduction of divorce (1884) and that of greater protection of illegitimate children. Apart from these direct modifications to family law, compulsory public education also shook the statute of family as the last asylum of the religion. In the republican tradition, education was always a public affair.[35] After the Jules Ferry Laws (1881), in practice, the parental authority ceased to entail the full autonomy of parents in deciding what was the proper way to educate their children. The family in the Third Republic was not only a dissolvable subject,[36] but also a unit invaded by public authority.[37]

Girls were progressively admitted to secondary schools in 1880[38] and to higher education in 1919. Gender equality seems to be a side effort of the anticlerical legislations. If young girls must also be brought to public schools as their male counterparts, to be exposed to the republican spirit, there is no reason not to grant to them access to further education.[39] With the successful defense of Sarmiza Bilcescu-Alimăniteanu (1867–1935) as the first female Doctor in Law in Europe or even worldwide (1890) and Jeanne Chauvin (1862–1926) as the first French woman with Doctor in Law (1892), women began to impose their influence in legal practice.[40] And it is Chauvin who wrote in her dissertation on professions accessible to women that the inequalities between sexes

---

33    Article 148.

34    Cf. Carole LÉCUYER: *Une nouvelle figure de la jeune fille sous la IIIe République: l'étudiante*, Clio, 2(1996)/4, 166–176.

35    Cf. Francine MUEL-DREYFUS: *Les instituteurs, les paysans et l'ordre républicain*, Actes de la recherche en sciences sociales, 19(1977)/1, 37–61.

36    GAVOUYÈRE: *Le Mariage Entre Chrétiens (III)*, Revue Catholique Des Institutions et Du Armand Droit 12(1884)/1, 38–61.

37    *Consultations Relatives À La Liberté D'enseignement, Aux Droits Des Pères de Famille et Des Congrégations Religieuses, et À La Loi Jules Ferry*, Revue Catholique Des Institutions et Du Droit 7(1879)/9, 277–283; *Liberté D'enseignement. Les Vrais Principes et Les Vrais Moyens de Défense*, Revue Catholique Des Institutions et Du Droit 7(1879)/12, 357–373.

38    La loi du 21 décembre 1880 sur l'enseignement secondaire des jeunes filles.

39    Cf. LÉCUYER: *op. cit.*

40    Cf. Anne-Laure CATINAT: *Les premières avocates du barreau de Paris*, Mil neuf cent, 16(1998)/1, 43–56.

IN THE NAME OF THE REPUBLIC 263

are originated from the biblical teachings and the Catholicisme. In a republican regime, women would prove their quality no only as wives and mothers, but also as active citizens in society to serve the public.[41]

### 2.B  *Republic Building to Modernise the State*

Like their French equivalents, the first generation of Chinese republicans fought for the renewal of their regime. Meanwhile, aligned with the political ideology which served a modern form of politics in a colonised country, they were unlike those French republicans who worked in what was already a modern context.

Since late Qing dynasty, a series of military defeats against foreign countries, especially that against modernised Japan in 1895 has driven Chinese elites to renew the political regime and laws.[42] The intellectuals in favour of a modern constitution share a view that the effectivity of a new constitutional regime depends on the mentality of the nationals.[43] Making "nationals" therefore became one of the major issues in political polemics. The failure to establish a constitutional monarchy finally led to the 1911 revolution, through which Sun Yat-Sen (1866–1925) and his camarades abolish the monarchy at once. The revolutionaries continued the discourse of national building in the republican regime and they invented a narrative in which familyism, once the central unit of the Confucian society and the foundation of the country, became the major obstacle of this enterprise. For the purpose of the present study, two aspects of familyism can be identified. Firstly, it implies that the basic level of public life is organised by the family, rather than by government agents. It also entails that familial hierarchy has higher moral or ethical values than that of any members as individuals.[44] Individuals were, first and foremost, players of their roles within the family, rather than equals in an indivisible and homogenous nation that forms a State. The duties and rights of each person were to be specified in each particular interpersonal relationship. Although Confucian political philosophy insists that the structure of family is the model for the

---

41  Jeanne CHAUVIN: *Étude historique sur les professions accessibles aux femmes : Influence du sémitisme sur l'évolution de la position économique de la femme dans la société*, Paris, A. Giard & E.Brière, 1892, 285.

42  陈新宇、陈煜、江照信：《中国近代法律史讲义》，九州出版社2016年版，第3–14页。

43  赖骏楠："清末《新民丛报》与《民报》论战中的'国民'议题"，《法学研究》2018年第4期。

44  黄源盛：《中国法史导论》，广西师范大学出版社2014年版，第90页。

governance of the State,[45] implying that the Emperor is the *bonus pater famili-as* in the relationships with his/her subjects, State authority usually did not administer individual affairs.[46] It is only natural that the republicans are against the familyism. There would never be true citizens – equal, homogenous, unified by national identity, and are directly related to the State itself – if the institution of the family were to remain in society.

The political agenda of destroying the family for the sake of the nation was first elaborated in the debates on the draft of a new Penal Code of the Qing Dynasty in the first decade of the 20th century. The traditionalistic bureaucrats insisted that the preservation of the family was the basic subject of law; whereas the reformers fought for freeing individuals and the State from the family.[47] In their discourses, the family prevented individuals not only from fully enjoying their liberties, but also from serving their country as mature citizens. Yang Du (1875–1931), a politician who changed regularly his ideology but a militant for Constitutional monarchy at that time, was one who advanced this argument. In an article published in the *Journal of the Empire*, this constitutionalist claimed that familyism was a true obstacle of statism, which was a doctrine that was believed to be the lead of a strong modern state.

> A State governed by statism must have a direct relationship with its citizens. In our country, in contrast, the direct relationship between the State and an individual rarely exists. Among 400 million subjects, there is not one citizen. Our nationals are divided into two categories: the heads of families and their protégés...The latter category has nothing at all to do with the nation, being remote enough to duties or rights. They are parasites on society and the nation. And the heads of family privatise their public functions to serve the interests of their families...Therefore, to truly strengthen our nation [...] we have no other possibility than to begin by isolating individuals from their families and making them real citizens. This strategy drives us to abolish familyism and to embrace statism.[48]

---

45  Jérôme Bourgon: *Lapsus de Laïus : Entre régicide et parricide, l'introuvable meurtre du père*, Extrême-Orient Extrême-Occident, Hors-série, 2012, 313–339.

46  On the different property rights of family members, Cf. 王帅一：《明月清风——明清时代的人、契约与国家》，社会科学文献出版社2018年版，第49页。

47  陈新宇、陈煜、江照信：《中国近代法律史讲义》，九州出版社2016年版，第168–176页。

48  杨度："论国家主义与家族主义之区别"，载刘晴波主编：《杨度集》，湖南人民出版社1985年版，第529~533页（原载《帝国日报》1910年12月5日）。

IN THE NAME OF THE REPUBLIC

The discourse of Yang Du represents the political awareness of most Chinese republicans of his time. To build a modern republic, they first had to free individuals from the yoke of family. This belief prevailed the first decades of 20th century. The first research completed on the Chinese legal tradition published in 1947 concludes that, in a less biased way, unlike individualistic Occidental laws, ancient Chinese laws granted higher consideration to family.[49] The reformers commonly relied on the legislations of the republican government that formerly embraced individualism. Wang Boqi (1909–1964), formerly a professor of law at National Yunan University and later Minister of Education, is one of the promoters of the individualistic legal philosophy. He argues in an article against familyism and traditionalism:

> Independence of individual personality is the leading idea of our laws. We can even claim that the present laws cannot exist without this idea. By persons, we refer to 45 million individual human beings, who are the foundation of our country, and the nationals by nationalism, the demos of democracy, and people in welfare of people. I dare say that the San Min principles (three principles of the people) could not be realised without essential understanding of the individual person.[50]

It is true that the republican government claimed the *San Min* principles as its official ideology. However, San Min principles, in the eyes of political activists and intellectuals, can only be achieved by individualism.[51] As a result, men and women of law struggled to change the society in which they lived by imposing individualistic laws, willing to totally banish traditional orders and familyism behind them.

> In such orders, there is no place for individuals. Whoever knows no independent personality and position of one's self by law, must not respect the legal personality and position of others, which means the total failure of the present legal system. And in such a complicated society that we are now facing today, it is evidently impossible to restore the governance by rites and the social control by families.[52]

---

49　瞿同祖：《中国法律与中国社会》，中华书局1981年版，第386页。

50　王伯琦：《近代法律思潮与中国固有文化》，清华大学出版社2004年版，第77页。

51　王伯琦："译序"(1936)，载〔法〕路易·若斯兰：《权利相对论》，王伯琦译，中国法制出版社2006年版。

52　王伯琦：《近代法律思潮与中国固有文化》，清华大学出版社2004年版，第76页。

The primary urgency of building a modern state called for a republic that further required a certain degree of individualism to shape the modern mentality of people, turning subjects to citizens. Chinese élites were instrumentalists who remained rather distant from particular ideologies. Rather, they tried to figure out the utility of trends and chose from among them whatever suited their ends, namely, the establishment of modern statehood. Family stood in the way of the journey toward modernity. Politicians of the republic therefore felt obliged to eliminate it by means of laws.

## 3      Adapting Laws to the Society

On the plan of family law, the mutation of the family was achieved by the diminishment of marital authority, the decline of legitimacy regarding children, and the growing recognition of divorce.

### 3.A    *Legislation Oscillating between Revolutionary and Conservative Proposals*

Gender equality in property rights is before all an economic necessity. French industrialisation in the 1850s made female labourers a significant social presence. In urban context, the number of female workers kept growing. In the rural parts, more and more women earning their livings by small commerces in the absence of their husbands who entered into the industrial world. This new social category challenged the regime of marital property as it was regulated in the French Civil Code, which confirmed that under the legal regime of marital property, the husband was to have the exclusive rights to administer it.[53] Insofar as married female labourers were paid, the need to retain and dispose of their salaries according to their own interests and wills became visible. Since the late 19th century, Dr Jeanne Chauvin herself has argued in favour of women's rights over her own salaries.[54] but it was only after long debates on "the question of women" as a part of the discussion on "the social questions",[55] the

---

53      Article 1421.

54      Jeanne CHAUVIN: *Proposition de loi sur la capacité des femmes mariées de disposer du produit de leur travail ou de leur industrie personnels* , Paris, impr. de May et Motteroz, 1893.

55      Some representative texts: Ernest Désiré GLASSON: *Le code civil et la question ouvrière*, Paris, Librairie Cotillon, 1886; Élie BLANC: *La question sociale, principes les plus nécessaires et réformes les plus urgentes: conférence aux Facultés catholiques de Lyon; suivie d'une Esquisse d'un programme électoral; et de l'Examen de quelques opinions économiques*, Paris, V. Lecoffre, 1891; Ernest Désiré GLASSON: *La Codification en Europe au XIXe siècle: état actuel de la question en France et à l'étranger*, Paris, Bureaux de la Revue politique et

IN THE NAME OF THE REPUBLIC                                                                267

Act on Salaries of Married Women was passed on 13 July 1907 under the pressure of left-wing parties. By this Act, married women had the right to keep their salaries as separate goods from the community property. The Act of 1907 also limited the authorisation of husband in regard of the use of the earnings paid to his wife. But these earnings could be used to pay the debts owned for the sake of ménage, and each spouse had the right to bring a demand before a court if the other party failed to participate according to his or her ability to the ménage. As most of the republican legislations in private law during the Third French Republic,[56] the Act of 1907 is a paradoxical combination between liberal temptations and the confirmation of conservative ideas. The total abolishment of marital puissance had to wait until 1938.

The conservative spirit of a republican government was manifested by its reluctance in entitling illegitimate children to parental support and care. Marriage was still understood by the late 19th century as the necessary condition of legitimate birth. Legislation aiming to grant better protection to illegitimate children, who in 1909 constituted 9% of the total birth rate,[57] appealed to a fictional technique that granted them the status as if they were legitimate. From the Act passed on August 17 1897 that imposed the mention of legitimation by marriage on the margin of a birth certificate, to the Act passed in 1912 that obliged the biological father to assume paternal responsibilities, a branch of legislations did seek to legitimise the children of natural birth by returning them under parental authority within a classical marriage.[58] These solutions paradoxically reinforced the traditional understanding of family, which might well have been an unintended consequence. By broadening the scale of children considered as "legitimate," they indeed guaranteed more minors with care. Meanwhile, the notion of legitimacy itself was sheltered from harsh criticism, since the social consequences it might entail were less harmful than they had been. It was as late as in 1970, the difference between legitimate and naturel borned children was removed.

Divorce is another important perspective in the history of French family law. The reestablishment of divorce by legislators of the Third Republic in 1884

---

parlementaire, 1895; Albert MICHEL: *La question sociale et les principes théologiques: justice légale et charité*, Paris, G. Beauchesne, 1921.

56   Cf. Jean-Louis HALPÉRIN: *Un modèle français de droit républicain? = La République et son droit, 1870–1930*, Annie STORA-LAMARRE, Jean-Louis HALPÉRIN, Frédéric AUDREN (eds.), Presses universitaires de Franche-Comté, Paris, 2011, 479–495.

57   Jean-Louis HALPÉRIN: *Histoire Du Droit Privé Français Depuis 1804*, Presses Universitaires de France, Paris, 2001, 222.

58   Social assistance to abandoned children were also new developments in the Third Republic but this article does not intend to fully discuss them.

after its abolition in 1816 was by no means an effort to return to the revolutionary legislation, but merely a legislative response to social demands. A more radical move took place in 1908. The "*séparation de corps*" or legal separation, the alternative to divorce in France under Cannon Law, since the third year after the declaration of legal separation, would automatically convert into divorce following a request filed by one of the parties. The social efforts, however, were not less significant, for the indissolubility of marriage is symbolic for Catholicism, which remained the leading religion in France. Numerous Vatican encyclicals in the 19th century repeatedly condemned divorce and affirmed the notion of the indissolubility of Christian marriage.[59] As a result, French conservatives considered the reintroduction of divorce in 1884 as a grave violation of the liberty of conscience, as well as the end of the family. For this reason, the debates on divorce triggered more theoretical discourses than those on other subjects. The next section will therefore focus on the doctrinal reactions against the reintroduction of divorce.

## 3.B Legal Doctrine Defending the Traditional Model of Family and Society

Since the 1850s, legal doctrine in the French context does not refer to the opinions of each individual scholar, but the sum of common understandings of positive law and the community of jurists.[60] Despite their pretended fidelity to positive laws, the doctrine takes great liberties to comment, criticise or change the rules designed by the legislators. The almost unanimous hostility to divorce was one such example.

One of the first comprehensive comparative studies in law, *Le Mariage civil et le divorce dans les principaux pays de l'Europe* by Ernest Glasson (1839–1907) already drew attention to the "problem" of divorce before its reintroduction in France. The author relied on statistics to show the danger of the dissolution of the family as an inevitable consequence of divorce.[61] The fragility of marriage

---

59    Notably *Acerbissimum* (1852) of Pius IX, *Arcanum Divinae* (1880) and *Rerum novarum* (1891) of Leo XIII.

60    Cf. Pierre-Nicolas BARENOT, Nader HAKIM: *La jurisprudence et la doctrine: retour sur une relation clef de la pensée juridique française contemporaine*, Quaderni Fiorentini per la storia del pensiero giuridico moderno 42 (2012), 251–297; Jacques CHEVALLIER: *Doctrine juridique et science juridique*, Droit et société 50(2002)/1, 103–120; Nader HAKIM: *L'Autorité de la doctrine civiliste française au XIXème siècle*, Paris: Librairie générale de droit et de jurisprudence, 2002; Philippe JESTAZ, Christophe JAMIN: *The Entity of French Doctrine: Some Thoughts on the Community of French Legal Writers*, Legal Studies 18(1998)/4, 415–437; Philippe JESTAZ: Christophe JAMIN, *La doctrine*, Dalloz, 2004.

61    Ernest-Désiré GLASSON: *Le Mariage civil et le divorce dans les principaux pays de l'Europe, précédé d'un aperçu sur les origines du droit civil moderne, étude de législation comparée*, G. Pedone-Lauriel, Paris, 1879.

IN THE NAME OF THE REPUBLIC                                                      269

and of the contract in an era of secularity replaced the religious arguments against the abuse of divorce. Another doctrinal authority, François Gény (1861–1959), even defended the theory of absolute indissolubility by the voice of Cathrein. This full-hearted conservative Catholic author placed the emphasis on the sacramental character of marriage. If divorce did not totally interrupt the education of children, considered as the first ends of marriage, it seriously harmed it. Since people cannot effectively limit the cases of divorce, it seemed to him that the indissolubility without exception was the only way to assure the solid relation that the union needs in order to achieve the purpose of marriage. He also argued that women often suffered from the unjust treatment caused by divorce, ignoring that more than 60% of the divorces were demanded by wives.[62]

Even republican professors such as Henri Capitant (1865–1937) tried to put up more barriers to divorce: "If marriage is a contract, it must not be dissolved by a divorce pronounced by the will of only one party, because this facility of rupture would make it a contract more fragile than other contracts being, in principle, dissolved only by the declaration made by both parties."[63] Students of Portalis saw as he did the value of family for individuals as well as for society. But they to some extent manifested a lack of confidence in the ability of their fellow citizens to see that value. Their writings give a contemporary reader the impression that most marriages in their era caused suffering to the point that countless men and women were longing to put an end to their marriages.

Ernest Glasson and François Gény were "professors of the State." There existed another category of law professor, namely the scholars in the "liberal faculties of law" financed by the Catholic Church. Although they were relatively marginal in the production of doctrine, the teachers in religious institutions usually spoke more freely in their opposition to divorce. Charles Boucaud (1878–1944), an unjustly forgotten author, argued that civil law must respect the indissolubility of marriage between Christians, though the legislators were free to regulate the marriage between persons with other convictions.[64] According to this lecturer in the Catholic faculty of law in Lille, the civil legislators should give to Caesar what is Caesar's, and to God what is God's. Nonetheless, he deliberately allowed Scripture to decide what is God's. Other than this,

---

62   François GÉNY: *Science et Technique En Droit Privé Positif: Nouvelle Contribution À La Critique de La Méthode Juridique*, vol. 2, Paris, Sirey, 1915, 241.

63   Ambroise COLIN, Henri CAPITANT: *Cours élémentaire de droit civil français. Tome 1er*, Paris, Dalloz, 1930, 114.

64   Charles BOUCAUD: *Les droits de l'État et les garanties civiques du droit naturel*, Paris: Bloud, 1908, 72.

Boucaud, in most parts of his work, cited extensively Charles Darwin, Jeremy Bentham and August Comte to justify his claim. This was not an isolated case. "August Comte," argues one of his colleagues, "does not have a different judgement of divorce than Leo XIII."[65] Scientific authorities and religious authorities were thus combined, giving the arguments against divorce more weight in a secularising context.

### 3.C  *Jurisprudence Adopting Social Progress*

Despite the general hostility toward the doctrine on divorce and its influence in legal practice, restricted by the legislative dispositions, case law elaborated the conditions of divorce and adapted them to the social circumstances.[66] Divorce by fault occupied the central place in the evolution, as the only authorised form of divorce in 1884. The Naquet Law considered adultery, condemnation of an afflictive penalty, excess, abuse and cruelty as grounds for divorce. Interpretative efforts on the understanding of different "faults" enumerated by the Code could virtually change the constitutive conditions under which one of the parties had the right to divorce.

It seems in first place that the judicial power had no intention to restrict the definition of cruelty to physical injuries, though it affirmed that isolated but serious physical violent behaviour, even in a private place, could constitute cruelty. Actually, a divorce could be granted without any physical element involved. The judges in the final years of the 19th century tended to recognise profound religious disputes within a marriage as a constitutive condition of cruelty. Grave injury was found in the case where one of the parties refused the religious celebration demanded by the other party[67] or the baptism of their children.[68] The paradox in these interpretations are manifest as they actually ended marriages of the individuals who professed a religion that constantly claimed that the marriage is an eternal engagement. Apart from spiritual harmony within the family, sexual rapport between spouses found also its importance in the procedure. The party was considered at fault if he/she refused to consummate the marriage and this refusal resulted in pain for the other party.[69] The impuissance causing the failure of the consummation of the marriage,

---

65 GAVOUYÈRE, *op. cit.*
66 This section repeats significantly and materially the ideas that Professor David Deroussin argued in his historical account of family law. DEROUSSIN, *op. cit.*, 226–228.
67 Rouen, 29 avril 1910.
68 Req. 30 novembre 1898, *D.* 1899, 1, 358.
69 Cass. 12 novembre 1900, *D.* 1901, 1, 21.

however, could permit the other party to divorce only if this fact is concealed before the marriage or if he/she did not undergo treatment for negligence.[70]

An analysis of the judicial decisions regarding the property rights of married women is necessary to establish a more comprehensive account of family law jurisprudence in late nineteenth-century France. It remains undeniable that the judges, although educated in law faculties – still conservative institutes – employed the legislative instruments which resulted from controversy for the sake of roughly more liberal consequences. French judges seemed to find a way to apply law pragmaticallywhich was guaranteed by the independence of judicial power.[71] Family reforms did not result the hypothetical social upheaval and the French families are not dissolved dramatically. The number of divorces in France grew after 1884 and reached its peak in 1920, amounting to 34,079, and oscillated around 25,000 before the Vichy regime.[72]

## 4 Modernising Society through Laws

In general, progressivist vocabularies shaped Chinese legal discourses concerning the family. But divisions and contestations coexisted as well with collaborations among legislation, doctrine and jurisprudence in China. The first Civil Code of China, intended to guarantee equality between the genders by its arrangement of marital property and of divorce, preserves nonetheless a minimum account of the moral personality of the family.[73] The heads of the family were still deemed to be the governing persons within the boundaries of the family. The persistence of conservative dispositions in legislation failed to prevent lawyers from imposing rules recognised as "modern" on Chinese society. Doctrinal and jurisprudential interpretations of clauses in the Civil Code regarding divorce and the governance of family were in favour of the abolition of the traditional model of a paternalistic and perpetual family.

### 4.A *The Coexistence of Revolutionary and Conservative Propositions in the Civil Code*

The chapter on family or domestic relations in the First Civil Code in China proved the revolutionary ambition of the republican government. It dis-

---

70  Req. 25 janvier 1922.

71  Cf. BARENOT, HAKIM: *op. cit.*

72  SARDON: *op. cit.*, 717–749.

73  陈新宇、陈煜、江照信：《中国近代法律史讲义》，九州出版社2016年版，第226–227页。

tinguishes itself from the former drafts of family laws since the late Qing Dynasty, by promoting gender equality and by reducing the notion of family to a minimal account.[74] The new Civil Code defines family as the union of its members for permenant common life, having only instrumental values.[75] The authority of the head of family can only be exercised in compliance with the interests of other family members, and its content is reduced to certain property rights and the power of requesting a married adult to leave the family.[76] The persistence of paternalistic rules, however, prevented it from going further to the complete abolition of family, which demonstrates the hesitation of revolutionary efforts of Chinese legislators.

Notwithstanding the achronological use of the term, the most important legal persons, namely whoever has the capacity to have legal rights and obligations in civil law, were families until the late 19th century in China. That explains why civil law bore the name "Laws of Families" in ancient régime China, which was also the translation of the Napoleonic Code when Ma Kie-tchong (1845–1900), the first Chinese graduate from Ecole libre des sciences politiques, first introduced it into the Chinese context at the end of the 19th century.[77] The preoccupation with family is not normatively compatible with the modern trends in codification triggered by the French Revolution, although it might actually share the patriarchal ideology with Roman law or even the French civil law. As far as the legal reforms in China tend to transplant European legal institutions, such a preoccupation can hardly avoid the destiny of being replaced by the regime constructed around the individualistic imagination of a natural person.[78] The institutionalisation of individuals as the primary legal

---

74    In a defeated draft in 1928, family even lost its status as the subject of rights.见许莉：
       《<中华民国民法-亲属>研究》，华东政法大学2007年博士论文，第
       25~28页 。
75    Art. 1122.
76    Art. 1152, 1125, and 1128.
77    马建忠：《法律探原》，教育世界社1901年版。
78    The imagination of a person in the French civil code has been controversial in French
       civil law since the 1970s. Some might well argue that the natural persons imagined by the
       Code are reasonable enlightened individuals, while others dispute that a more concrete
       protocol must be taken into account, namely the artisans or in rural areas or bourgeois
       that know the environment in which they live as well as their own affairs. It is nevertheless
       accepted that individuals, rather than other entities, are at the centre of modern civil law.
       André-Jean ARNAUD: *Essai D'analyse Structurale Du Code Civil Français: La Règle Du Jeu
       Dans La Paix Bourgeoise*, Paris, Pichon et Durand-Auzias, 1973.

IN THE NAME OF THE REPUBLIC

273

TABLE 11.1  Comparison of Family Laws in China

| | Ancient Laws | Draft of Civil Code in Qing | Drafts of Civil Law under the Beiyang Government (1912–1928) | Civil Code of the Republic of China (1930–1949) |
|---|---|---|---|---|
| Principles | Sons obeying fathers, and women obeying men | Sons obeying fathers, and women obeying men | Gender equality and individual freedom | Gender equality and individual freedom |
| Property | Disposed of by the head of the family | Privilege of the head of the family | Division between individual and family property | Regime without community |
| Marriage | Consent of the head of the family | Consent of the head of the family until a certain age | Consent of the head of the family until a certain age | Liberal, except under certain conditions where the parents have the right to contest |
| Divorce | Husband's right | Petition plus mutual consent | Petition plus mutual consent | Mutual consent plus petition, with greater protection for wives |

subjects had therefore persisted in the evaluation of the drafts of the civil code in China from the late Qing Dynasty to the Republic.

Every ideology requires numerous institutional arrangements for its realisation. The table above resumes some significant perspectives of subsequent legal reforms that touched the regime of family. Needless to say, such a representation is an oversimplification and it occludes more elements or conflicts than what it can reveal. The intention of presenting this table is to stress the leading political agenda behind the struggle for a modern civil law in republican China. Overgeneralisation seems thus to be an unavoidable price to pay.

As the final result of the struggle, the Civil Code of the Republic of China in 1930 marks a temporary victory of individualism in family law. Its drafters were convinced that "customs and jurisprudence on family and succession are nothing but the reminders of the ancient laws and rites for thousand years, conflicting with the contemporary progress of world and with the political agenda of the governing party".[79]

It is true that this draft was criticised and in the end failed to be approved by the parliament. But the final version of the Code, in defining the institution of family as "cooperation of family members for the purpose of permanent common life",[80] granted the head of the family rights only for the purpose of common family life, which is reduced to certain property rights[81] and the right to demand an adult or married member to depart from his/her household.[82]

The new Civil Code also departed from Chinese tradition in regard to marriage. Marriage was considered in the Code as a contractual act. The statutory regime as to marital property was the union of goods, transplanted, again, from the Swiss Code.[83] Although the husband, in the absence of agreement between the spouses, was held responsible for the disposal of the communal marital property, the wife could keep her separate property.[84] The differentiation between genders disappears in the rules detailing the conditions of divorce, by mutual consent as well as by petition.

### 4.B    *The Dominance of Modernism in Doctrine*

Most leading Chinese civilists embraced the republicans' proposal of gender equality. Unlike their French counterparts, who remained rather distant from the centre of political power and thus constituted a controlling or balancing power on the issue of the interpretation of legislations, Chinese doctrinal authorities often exercised political functions either as the drafters of legislation

---

79    谢振民：《中华民国立法史》，中国政法大学出版社2000年版，第749 页。

80    Art. 1122. The testimonies of members of the drafting panel show that this article and the institution of family in general were inspired by the "Familiengemeinschaft" of the Swiss Civil Code. The Chinese version of this regime contains fewer details regarding the management and disposal of family property.

81    Art. 1152, 1125.

82    Art. 1128. Doctrinal interpretations claim that the head of the family also had the right to decide the domicile of the members.

83    Art. 1005.

84    Art. 1016, 1025, 1026, 1027.

IN THE NAME OF THE REPUBLIC 275

or as ministers.[85] On the one hand, they were at the centre of the creation of norms. On the other hand, they played significant roles in stabilising the agenda of legislators in doctrine.

Professor Hu Changqing (1900–1988), editor in chief of *Law Review*, one of the most eminent journals in the 1930s, and a member of the drafting committee of the Civil Code, expressly defended the individualistic spirit of the new family law. Testifying to the Swiss origin of the "Familiengemeinschaft" regime, he claimed that the idea of family in the Code had nothing in common with that in ancient Chinese laws dominated by familyism. Rather, "to understand the individualism behind our family law, one is already halfway to fully acquiring the knowledge of this Code."[86] This citation appears on the middle of the seventh page of this textbook. Starting with this leading ideology, the author further articulated six particularities of this new family legislation, including (1) the redefinition of domestic relationships, (2) the establishment of gender equality, (3) the consideration of national health, (4) the protection of the property rights of married women, (5) the progressive equalisation of legitimate and illegitimate children, (6) and the encouragement of independence.[87] Although the order of these particularities in Hu's book is almost chaotic, readers can discern three finalities of the family policy of the nationalist party. (1) (5) and (6) intend to shake the foundations of the traditional paternalistic family that denied the independence and the equality of members. (2) and (4) led to the recognition of women's rights with full legal personality. And (6) was used to justify the restrictions concerning the birth of children, such as marital age, interdiction of marriage within the family, etc. A similar idea repeated in the textbook on family law by Professor Shi Shangkuan (1898–1970),[88] also a member of the drafting committee, and the first author who completed a collection of textbooks that covered all books of the Code.

It seems that the regime of divorce through petition should be a particular perspective that permits modern observers to examine how those abstract principles turn into specific rules through doctrinal interpretation. As stated before, ancient Chinese laws granted husbands the privilege to banish their wives under seven circumstances, and wives could only refuse to depart from the domicile when any of three conditions were fulfilled. The Code already

---

85 A brief and rough sociological explanation can be found in my article on the creative transplant of French legal doctrine in China. 朱明哲：“东方巴黎——略论二十世纪上半叶法国法学在中国的传播”，《北大法律评论》2014年第2期。
86 胡长清：《中国民法亲属论》，第7页。
87 胡长清：《中国民法亲属论》，第7~10页。
88 史尚宽：《亲属法论》，中国政法大学出版社2000年版第6~8页。

abolished the distinction between genders in both divorce by mutual consent and by petition, which embodied the principle of gender equality. Article 1052 having listed causes of divorce by petition,[89] the doctrine and the jurisprudence interpret cruelty, wilful desertion, and incurable illness in a larger sense to *de facto* facilitate the divorce. From the standpoint of legislative techniques, there is the enumeration of causes without a general clause allowing further interpretations for the sake of particular situations. Under such a condition, interpreters, be they law professors or judges, are free to adapt the less concrete terms to the individual cases they encounter.

Two aspects of doctrinal interpretations worth mentioning, even briefly. Not only do they shed light on the previously ignored dimensions of the regulations of divorce, but they also illustrate the active efforts of the doctrine. The first is judicial interventions on domestic sexual behaviours. The refusal of sexual intercourse without due cause, forceful sexual intercourse, as well as forceful and unnatural sexual intercourse[90] are all considered as cruel behaviours.[91] Proponent law professors further adopted the broader interpretation of "incurable illness" to include the permanent impuissance of sexual performance.[92] The second is the discussion on indignity. Indignity is an independent cause of divorce in the French Civil Code, while it is not in China. Nevertheless, prevailing Chinese civilists, almost unanimously, interpreted cruelty to include indignity that can be referred to a wide range of emotional abuse.

These doctrinal articulations of cruelty reveal the jurists' ambition to change society by law. It was still the first decades of the 20th century, when wives' duty to consent to sexual intercourse requested by the husbands was commonly accepted.[93] In this context, the interventions in domestic sexual practice provided wives with the possibility to escape marriages. The willingness to take the legislative function to formerly institutionalise indignity as a cause of divorce also demonstrates this consideration. In an époque where the greater public knew only physical abuse, the doctrine was a leap forward to granting

---

89 Namely, (1) polygamy, (2) adultery, (3) cruelty, (4) abuse between the wife and the relatives by blood of the husbands, (5) wilful desertion, (6) intention of murdering the other party, (7) incurable illness, (8) mental disorder, (9) disappearance more than three years, and (10) imprisonment.

90 二十一年院字第650号。

91 史尚宽：《亲属法论》，中国政法大学出版社2000年版第474~475页。

92 史尚宽：《亲属法论》，中国政法大学出版社2000年版第482页。

93 On the judicial changes in the past decades, Cf. *R. v. R.* [1991] 2 W.L.R. 1065 which constructed also a historical review of the marital sexual abuse in England and Scottland, and CR v. United Kingdom, (1996) 21 E.H.R.R. 363. Disputes on the criminality of marital sexual abuses in early 20th century in China, 见葛佛民："夫对于妻，以强暴胁迫强求性交，是否构成强奸罪"，载《法律评论》第597页。

IN THE NAME OF THE REPUBLIC

greater protection to victims of domestic violence. And the jurists did not even wait for the judicial procedure but turned to foreign case laws and doctrinal interpretations to justify their own dogmatic work.

### 4.C  *The Dissolution of the Traditional Family through Judicial Activism*

Politicisation of judicial power was an evident phenomenon in the republican government. The fundamental text that elaborated the political control of the Nationalist party over judicial power was published in 1929, and the author was Wang Chonghui (1881–1958), who earned his doctorate from Yale Law School and was the Minister of Justice at that time.[94] His successor at the Ministry of Justice, Ju Zheng (1876–1951) further developed this idea in 1935 by stabilising the essential claim that "all judges must full-heartedly accept the political directions of the ruling party and realise them in each individual judgement".[95] Another legal theorist of the Nationalist Party, Zhang Zhiben (1881–1976), the President of Chaoyang University in Beijing, systematised what has been claimed by Ju Zheng and Wang Chonghui, and considered the political control of judicial power as a fundamental principle of all jurists.[96] The theoretical articulation was combined with political arrangements of personnel in regional jurisdictions. The presidents of local and national courts had to be approved members of the Nationalist Party. In this circumstance, courts of the Republic of China failed to constitute a balancing power in regard to political decisions. The procedures of divorce were not exceptional.

Following exactly the direction of the Nationalist Party, regional courts often judged in favour of divorce, which is shown by the growing number of divorces in cities. An observer of Beijing urban society already noticed in 1928

TABLE 11.2  Divorces in Beijing from 1917 to 1928[a]

| 1917 | 1918 | 1919 | 1920 | 1921 | 1922 | 1923 | 1924 | 1925 | 1926 | 1927 | 1928 |
| --- | --- | --- | --- | --- | --- | --- | --- | --- | --- | --- | --- |
| 28 | 26 | 22 | 44 | 38 | 35 | 48 | 54 | 51 | 63 | 62 | 64 |

a 吴至信："最近十六年之北平离婚案"，载李文海主编：《民国时期社会调查丛编-婚姻家庭卷》，福建教育出版社2005年版。

---

94 王宠惠："今后司法改良之方针一"，《法律评论》第6卷21号，1929年3月。
95 居正："司法党化问题"，《东方杂志》32卷第10号，1935年5月。
96 张之本："中华民国法学会之使命"，《中华法学杂志》第1卷1号，1936年9月。

that the frequency of divorces in the Capital kept growing, even before the Civil Code. (Table 11.2)

The year of 1928 marks a dramatic growth in the divorces in court. In Beijing, from October 1929 to September 1930, 974 demands of divorce were brought before the judicial authorities, of which 611 were approved.[97] In Shanghai, the total number of divorces in 1929 was 645 and in 1930, 853. The popularity of divorce was not an isolated phenomenon of modernised urban regions. In Guangxi province, where most of the areas area is rural in nature, 627 divorce petitions were filed in court by wives.[98]

Indeed, the female parties were more likely to appeal to their rights of divorce that previous generations of women had never known. In both Beijing and Tianjin, most of the cases were brought by wives.

TABLE 11.3 Divorces claimed by the wives in Beijing and Tianjin

| Jurisdiction | Year | Cases of divorce demanded by women | Percentage |
| --- | --- | --- | --- |
| Beijing | 1917–1918 | 30 | 55.5 |
| | 1919–1920 | 39 | 59.1 |
| | 1921–1922 | 46 | 63.0 |
| | 1923–1924 | 55 | 53.9 |
| | 1925–1926 | 72 | 63.2 |
| | 1927–1928 | 84 | 66.7 |
| | 1929–1930 | 150 | 76.0 |
| | 1931–1932 | 304 | 81.0 |
| | 1933 | 135 | 75.4 |
| | 1934 | 171 | 75.0 |
| Tianjin | 1926 | 7 | 29.2 |
| | 1927 | 20 | 62.5 |
| | 1928 | 22 | 62.8 |
| | 1929 | 60 | 76.9 |
| | 1930 | 82 | 73.2 |
| | 1933 | 60 | 70.6 |
| | 1934 | 52 | 69.3 |

---

97  沈登杰，陈文杰："中国离婚问题之研究"，《东方杂志》1935年。
98  冰莹："广西的农村妇女"，《妇女生活》第2卷第1期。

Feminist propaganda during the republican moment was no doubt the major dynamic that pushed Chinese women to free themselves from unhappy marriages. The statistics indicate also that the courts became the field on which the liberation of women was pursued. Indeed, economic developments contributed to the awareness of gender equality, as manufacturers began to recruit women labourers, which increased the economic independence of urban women. But the sharp increase in divorces around 1930 can only be explained by the effects of legal reforms. Laws narrated an imaginary space in which men and women are all equal and independent individual nationals. Chinese society in the first half of the 20th century, in contrast, was still a sexist life space where women were *de facto* under men's domination from almost every perspective. Divorced women freed from the yoke of marriage found themselves often exposed to social pressures and economic difficulties.[99] The social consequences of legal reforms remain to be further examined. But the society has already changed, since its applicable norms of judgement change and the cadre that applies these norms shares the same values with their drafters. Legislative power, doctrinal authority, and judicial practice finally managed to collaborate to achieve the ends to build a modern nation-state by smashing the traditional family.

## 5 Conclusion

Reformists and revolutionaries sought to destroy the family, an ancient social institution protected by customs and traditional values. After long struggles to reform family laws, it is fair to say that the domestic administrations of both nations were renewed. Along with other measures, France has become a lay society in which the Catholic Church has only symbolic power, which was recently demonstrated by the inability of conservative power to stop "marriage for all." And individuals in post-revolutionary China, though under other restrictions, have been freed from the yoke of family for decades. In recent years, more and more discourses are expressed in China for the purpose of restoring the family value. Official press is content to represent the President himself as a family man. We are at the frontiers of witnessing another reform of the family in China.

Indeed, the mutation of laws touching the family is but one of examples where the law is used to achieve certain goal. We must reject the temptation to

---

99　朱汉国："从离婚诉讼案看民国时期婚姻观的演进"，《河北学刊》2013年11月。

conclude that the legal institutions of a jurisdiction can be reduced to a consciously designed instrument. Because there is hardly any "Grand Design" in the production of norms, if we understand a legal proposition as a synthesis of normative statements from various sources of law. But legislators, judges, avocates, and scholars of law are aware of the practical outcome of their propositions of law. And they consciously use their symbolic power to shape the law according to the purpose they have in mind. The family reforms in France and in China were originally triggered by the political agenda of creating a new republican national identity. Catholicism ceases from being the dominant feature of the French society, and confusian teachings stop governing the Chinese people. The republicans in both countries successed to a large extend, but in different ways. We can indeed change the law or the national identity, but neither of them can be determined by one body.

## Bibliography

André-Jean ARNAUD: *Essai D'analyse Structurale Du Code Civil Français: La Règle Du Jeu Dans La Paix Bourgeoise*, Paris, Pichon et Durand-Auzias, 1973.

Pierre-Nicolas BARENOT, Nader HAKIM: *La jurisprudence et la doctrine: retour sur une relation clef de la pensée juridique française contemporaine*, Quaderni Fiorentini per la storia del pensiero giuridico moderno 42 (2012), 251–297.

Alain BERGOUNIOUX: *La Laïcité, Valeur de La République*, Pouvoirs 75(1995), 17–26.

Élie BLANC: *La question sociale, principes les plus nécessaires et réformes les plus urgentes: conférence aux Facultés catholiques de Lyon; suivie d'une Esquisse d'un programme électoral; et de l'Examen de quelques opinions économiques*, Paris, V. Lecoffre, 1891.

Charles BOUCAUD: *Les droits de l'État et les garanties civiques du droit naturel*, Paris: Bloud, 1908.

Jérôme BOURGON: *Lapsus de Laïus : Entre régicide et parricide, l'introuvable meurtre du père*, Extrême-Orient Extrême-Occident, Hors-série, 2012, 313–339.

Patrick CABANEL: *Compromis historique et déceptions démocratiques: la laïcité républicaine = Une contre-histoire de la IIIe République*, Marion FONTAINE, Frédéric MONIER, Christophe PROCHASSON (eds.), Cahiers libres, Dévouverte 2013.

Jean-Jacques-Régis DE CAMBACÉRÈS: *Discours Préliminaire Prononcé Par Cambacérès Au Conseil Des Cinq-Cents, Lors de La Présentation Du Troisième Projet de Code Civil, Faite Au Nom de La Commission de La Classification Des Lois = Recueil Complet Des Travaux Préparatoires Du Code Civil*, Pierre-Antoine Fenet (ed.), Videcoq, Paris, 1836, vol. 1, 140–177.

Anne-Laure CATINAT: *Les premières avocates du barreau de Paris*, Mil neuf cent, 16(1998)/1, 43–56.

Jeanne CHAUVIN: *Étude historique sur les professions accessibles aux femmes : Influence du sémitisme sur l'évolution de la position économique de la femme dans la société*, Paris, A.Giard & E.Brière, 1892.

Jeanne CHAUVIN: *Proposition de loi sur la capacité des femmes mariées de disposer du produit de leur travail ou de leur industrie personnels*, Paris, impr. de May et Motteroz, 1893.

Jacques CHEVALLIER: *Doctrine juridique et science juridique*, Droit et société 50 (2002) /1, 103–120.

Ambroise COLIN, Henri CAPITANT: *Cours élémentaire de droit civil français. Tome 1$^{er}$*, Paris, Dalloz, 1930.

*Consultations Relatives À La Liberté D'enseignement, Aux Droits Des Pères de Famille et Des Congrégations Religieuses, et À La Loi Jules Ferry*, Revue Catholique Des Institutions et Du Droit 7(1879)/9, 277–283.

David DEROUSSIN: *Histoire du droit privé: XVIe–XXIe siècle*, Ellipses Marketing, Paris, 2010.

Enrique DUSSEL, Javier KRAUEL, Virginia TUMA: *Europe, Modernity, and Eurocentrism*, Nepantla: Views from South, 1(2000)/3, 465–478.

Pierre-Antoine FENET: *Précis Historique Sur La Confection Du Code Civil* = Pierre-Antoine FENET: *Recueil Complet Des Travaux Préparatoires Du Code Civil*, Videcoq, Paris, 1836, vol. 1.

Herbert FISHER: *The Republican Tradition in Europe*, G. Putnam's sons, New York-London, 1911.

GAVOUYÈRE: *Le Mariage Entre Chrétiens (III)*, Revue Catholique Des Institutions et Du Armand Droit 12(1884)/1, 38–61.

François GÉNY: *Science et Technique En Droit Privé Positif: Nouvelle Contribution À La Critique de La Méthode Juridique*, Paris, Sirey, 1915, vol. 2.

Ernest Désiré GLASSON: *Le code civil et la question ouvrière*, Paris, Librairie Cotillon, 1886.

Ernest Désiré GLASSON: *La Codification en Europe au XIXe siècle: état actuel de la question en France et à l'étranger*, Paris, Bureaux de la Revue politique et parlementaire, 1895.

Ernest-Désiré GLASSON: *Le Mariage civil et le divorce dans les principaux pays de l'Europe, précédé d'un aperçu sur les origines du droit civil moderne, étude de législation comparée*, G. Pedone-Lauriel, Paris, 1879.

Nader HAKIM: *L'Autorité de la doctrine civiliste française au XIXème siècle*, Paris: Librairie générale de droit et de jurisprudence, 2002.

Jean-Louis HALPÉRIN: *Histoire Du Droit Privé Français Depuis 1804*, Presses Universitaires de France, Paris, 2001.

Jean-Louis HALPÉRIN: *Un modèle français de droit républicain?* = La République et son droit, 1870–1930, Annie STORA-LAMARRE, Jean-Louis HALPÉRIN, Frédéric AUDREN (eds.), Presses universitaires de Franche-Comté, 2011, 479–495.

Jean-Ignace JACQUEMINO: *Idées Préminimaires Sur Le Projet de Jacqueminot, Présenté Par Jacqueminot, Au Nom de La Section de Législation = Recueil Complet Des Travaux Préparatoires Du Code Civil*, Pierre-Antoine FENET (ed.), Videcoq, Paris, 1836, vol. 1, 327–332.

Philippe JESTAZ, Christophe JAMIN: *The Entity of French Doctrine: Some Thoughts on the Community of French Legal Writers*, Legal Studies 18(1998)/4, 415–437.

Philippe JESTAZ: Christophe JAMIN, *La doctrine*, Dalloz, 2004.

Yvonne KNIBIEHLER: *Les Médecins et La "nature Féminine" au Temps Du Code Civil*, Annales. Histoire, Sciences Sociales 31(1976)/4, 824–845.

Jacqueline LALOUETTE: *Laïcité, anticléricalismes et antichristianisme*, Transversalités, 108 (2013), 69–84.

Carole LÉCUYER: *Une nouvelle figure de la jeune fille sous la IIIe République : l'étudiante*, Clio 2(1996)/4, 166–176.

*Liberté D'enseignement. Les Vrais Principes et Les Vrais Moyens de Défense*, Revue Catholique Des Institutions et Du Droit 7(1879)/12, 357–373.

Roger MAGRAW: *France, 1815–1914: The Bourgeois Century*, Oxford University Press, Oxford, 1983.

Edward MANSON: *Marital Authority*, Law Quarterly Review 7(1891), 244–255.

Albert MICHEL: *La question sociale et les principes théologiques: justice légale et charité*, Paris, G. Beauchesne, 1921.

Francine MUEL-DREYFUS: *Les instituteurs, les paysans et l'ordre républicain*, Actes de la recherche en sciences sociales, 19(1977)/1, 37–61.

Géraldine MUHLMANN, Claire ZALC: *La laïcité, de la IIIe à la Ve République*, Pouvoirs, 126(2008)/3, 101–114.

Jean-Etienne-Marie Portalis: *Discours Préliminaire Prononcé Par Portalis, Le 24 Thermidor an VIII, Lors de La Présentation Du Projet Arrêté Par La Commission Du Gouvernement = Recueil Complet Des Travaux Préparatoires Du Code Civil*, Pierre-Antoine FENET (ed.), Videcoq, Paris, 1836, 463–524, vol. 1.

Jean-Etienne-Marie PORTALIS: *Présentation Au Corps Législatif, et Exposé Des Motifs Du Mariage = Recueil Complet Des Travaux Préparatoires Du Code Civil*, Pierre-Antoine FENET (ed.), Videcoq, Paris, 1836, 138–181, vol. 9.

Max RHEINSTEIN: *Trends in Marriage and Divorce Law of Western Countries*, Law and Contemporary Problems 18(1953)/1, 3–19.

Jean-Paul SARDON: *L'évolution Du Divorce En France*, Population 51(1996)/3, 717–749.

Perrine SIMON-NAHUM: *La République et les républicains, adversaires du religieux et des religions = Une contre-histoire de la iiie République*, Marion FONTAINE, Frédéric MONIER, Christophe PROCHASSON (eds.), Cahiers libres, Dévouverte 2013.

Brian TAMANAHA: *Law as a Means to an End*, Cambridge University Press, Cambridge (UK), 2006.

Jean-Baptiste TREILHARD: *Présentation au corps législatif, et exposé des motifs = Recueil Complet Des Travaux Préparatoires Du Code Civil*, Pierre-Antoine FENET (ed.), Videcoq, Paris, 1836, vol. 9, 556–563.

Immanuel WALLERSTEIN: *Eurocentrism and Its Avatars: The Dilemma of Social Sciences*, Sociological Bulletin 46(1997)/1 21–39.

Cornel WEST, Bill BROWN: *Beyond Eurocentrism and Multiculturalism*, Modern Philology 90(1993)/1, 142–166.

Zhu MINGZHE: *On French Laicity in Combat*, Chinese Journal of European Studies 6(2016), 117–135.

苏永钦：《现代民法典的体系定位与建构规则》，载《交大法学》（第1卷），上海交通大学出版社2011年版，第59—93页。

刘征峰：《家庭法与民法知识谱系的分立》，载《法学研究》2017 年第4期。

韩大元：《宪法与民法关系在中国的演变———一种学说史的梳理》，载《清华法学》2016年第6期。

谢鸿飞：《中国民法典的生活世界、价值体系与立法表达》，载《清华法学》2014年第6期。

薛军：《"民法—宪法"关系的演变与民法的转型——以欧洲近现代民法的发展轨迹为中心》，载《中国法学》2010年第1期。

张龑：《论我国法律体系中的家与个体自由原则》，《中外法学》2013年第4期。

[法]宝道："中国亲属法之改造"，张毓昆译，《法学季刊》1936，第1卷1号。

胡长清：《中国民法亲属论》，商务印书馆1936年版。

史尚宽：《亲属法论》，中国政法大学出版社2000年版。

陈新宇、陈煜、江照信：《中国近代法律史讲义》，九州出版社2016年版。

赖骏楠：《清末<新民丛报>与<民报>论战中的"国民"议题》，《法学研究》2018年第4期。

黄源盛：《中国法史导论》，广西师范大学出版社2014年版。

王帅一：《明月清风——明清时代的人、契约与国家》，社会科学文献出版社2018年版。

陈新宇、陈煜、江照信：《中国近代法律史讲义》，九州出版社2016年版，第168–176页。

杨度：《论国家主义与家族主义之区别》，载刘晴波主编：《杨度集》，湖南人民出版社1985年版，第529~533页（原载《帝国日报》1910年12月5日）。

瞿同祖：《中国法律与中国社会》，中华书局1981年版，第386页。

王伯琦：《近代法律思潮与中国固有文化》，清华大学出版社2004年版，第77页。

王伯琦："译序"（1936），载〔法〕路易·若斯兰：《权利相对论》，王
　　伯琦译，中国法制出版社2006年版。

王伯琦：《近代法律思潮与中国固有文化》，清华大学出版社2004年版，
　　第76页。

陈新宇、陈煜、江照信：《中国近代法律史讲义》，九州出版社2016年版，
　　第226-227页。

许莉：《<中华民国民法-亲属>研究》，华东政法大学2007年博士论文。

马建忠：《法律探原》，教育世界社1901年版。

谢振民：《中华民国立法史》，中国政法大学出版社2000年版

王宠惠：《今后司法改良之方针一》，《法律评论》第6卷21号，1929年3
　　月。

居正：《司法党化问题》，《东方杂志》32卷第10号，1935年5月。

张之本：《中华民国法学会之使命》，《中华法学杂志》第1卷1号，1936年
　　9月。

吴至信：《最近十六年之北平离婚案》，载李文海主编：《民国时期社会
　　调查丛编-婚姻家庭卷》，福建教育出版社2005年版。

沈登杰，陈文杰：《中国离婚问题之研究》，《东方杂志》1935年。

冰莹：《广西的农村妇女》，《妇女生活》第2卷第1期。

朱汉国：《从离婚诉讼案看民国时期婚姻观的演进》，《河北学刊》2013年
　　11月。

CHAPTER 12

# The Private Law Codification as an Instrument for the Consolidation of a Nation from Inside: Estonia and Latvia between Two World Wars

*Marju Luts-Sootak, Hesi Siimets-Gross and Katrin Kiirend-Pruuli*

## 1 Introduction[1]

With the Russian Empire crumbling during the First World War, many nations, including Estonians, were presented with an unprecedented opportunity to establish their own state and decide independently how to transform their legal systems.[2] Estonian Republic, which had declared independence in 1918 and, after winning its War of Independence, secured power in 1920. Similar to the southern neighbour, Republic of Latvia, Estonia had to deal with the legal heritage of the Russian Empire's Baltic provinces.

It would be reasonable to take a comparative look to the ways and solutions of independent legal development of two nations – Estonia and Latvia – who had partially had very similar earlier history and who had the same starting position after WWI. One should recognise, that the similarity in earlier history stemmed from the influence of the German-speaking upper classes – the nobility, bourgeoisie and Evangelical clergy. Until 1816/1817/1819 (depending of the province) the lower class – Estonian and Latvian peasants – were serfs and had only a century to build up their nation and become able to build a national state afterwards. Private law as the law of legal relations of every person's should be a good point of reference also for identity building processes. First, we will characterise the legal heritage in private law and the ways, how both young states dealt with them. Second, we will compare the ways to overcome the premodern obstacles that were incorporated in old law, and how they developed a new private law. It can be said beforehand that both countries hoped to reach a new level by the means of codification of private law. There is

---

1    The research for this article has been supported by Estonian Research Council (IUT20-50).
2    On the general history, cf. e.g. Andres KASEKAMP: *A History of the Baltic States,* Palgrave Macmillan, New York, 2010, 1–90; for an overview of the legal history of Estonia and other Baltic States after WWI cf. Toomas ANEPAIO: *Die rechtliche Entwicklung der baltischen Staaten 1918–1940 = Modernisierung durch Transfer zwischen den Weltkriegen,* Tomasz GIARO (ed.), Vittorio Klostermann, Frankfurt a.M., 2007, 7–30.

nothing new – also the 19th century consolidation of big nations was accompanied or even preceded by the codification of private law. However, Estonia and Latvia had already established their statehood and were facing the question what to do with private law. Finally, we will examine more thoroughly how did different countries tackle this issue and what were the results.

Before the substantive analysis, it should be noted that Estonian and Latvian are completely different and either nation do not understand each other's language without prior learning. As both nations were and still are small in numbers, either of them has not been very motivated to learn each other's language – learning the languages of bigger nations has always seemed more attractive and opened up more opportunities.

## 2    Private Law of Former Baltic Provinces in Republics of Estonia and Latvia

In several European countries, private law was unified through codification. The codifications in the 19th century were mostly accompanied by the modernisation of society and law. Although private law in the Baltic provinces, subsequently Estonian and Latvian territory, was already codified into the "*Liv-, Est-und Curlaendisches Privatrecht*" of 1864/65 (Baltic Private Law Code; henceforth: BPLC)[3] in the middle of the 19th century, it failed to fulfil one of the most important tasks of modern codification: unifying the particular laws of different provinces and different estates into a single, substantially coherent, corpus of law. The BPLC was a code only for upper classes whereas the majority of the

---

3    *Provincialrecht der Ostseegouvernements. Dritter Theil. Privatrecht. Liv-, Est- und Curlaendisches Privatrecht.* Zusammengestellt auf Befehl des Herrn und Kaisers Alexander II, Buchdruckerei der Zweiten Abtheilung Seiner Kaiserlichen Majestät Eigener Kanzlei, St. Petersburg, 1864. For older research literature, cf. Barbara DÖLEMEYER: *Das Privatrecht Liv-, Est- und Kurlands von 1864.* = *Handbuch der Quellen und Literatur der neueren europäischen Privatrechtsgeschichte*, Helmut COING (ed.), vol. 3/2, Beck, München, 1982, 2078 ff; for the recent Estonian research: Marju LUTS: *Modernisierung und deren Hemmnisse in den Ostseeprovinzen Est-, Liv- und Kurland im 19. Jahrhundert = Modernisierung durch Transfer* im 19. und frühen 20. Jahrhundert, Tomasz Giaro (ed.), Vittorio Klostermann, Frankfurt a.M., 2006, 159–200; Marju LUTS-SOOTAK: *Das Baltische Privatrecht von 1864/65 – Triumphbogen oder Grabmal für das römische Recht im Baltikum?* Zeitschrift für Ostmitteleuropa-Forschung, 58(2009), 357–379; Hesi SIIMETS-GROSS: *Das Liv-, Est- und Curlaendische Privatrecht (1864/65) und das römische Recht im Baltikum,* Tartu University Press, Tartu, 2011; Hesi SIIMETS-GROSS: *Das Liv-, Esth- und Curlaendisches Privatrecht (1864/1865) – die einzige Quelle des Privatrechts? = Einheit und Vielfalt in der Rechtschichte im Ostseeraum. Sechster Rechtshistorikertag im Ostseeraum, 3.-5. Juni 2010 Tartu (Estland)/Riga (Lettland)*, Marju LUTS-SOOTAK, Sanita OSIPOVA, Frank L. SCHÄFER (eds.), Lang, Frankfurt a.M., 2012, 275–285.

ESTONIA AND LATVIA BETWEEN TWO WORLD WARS 287

population, around 95%, consisted of peasants to whom this code was not applicable. In Estonia and in the northern part of Livonia, they were Estonians; in the southern part of Livonia and in Courland, they were Latvians. Therefore, the voluminous BPLC of 1864 was originally applicable to approximately 5% of the population, or to ca. 180,000 people. One of the 4,636 articles of the Code expressed the dependence of private law norms and relations on the estate of persons (Art. XXVIII).[4] Along with the different estates, the BPLC also acknowledged a large number of private law institutions, which were characteristic of pre-modern private law.[5]

When the Estonian Republic was established, even before the constitution was promulgated on June 15, 1920, the Estonian Constituent Assembly passed the Law for Abolishing Estates.[6] The first clause of this law was following: "All estates are abolished in the democratic Republic of Estonia." For private law, this meant that the prerequisite for modern private law, universal and equal legal capacity, was acknowledged. A short sentence on abolishing estates had to establish a framework of constitutional law so that on this basis it would be possible to provide a modern, free and equal private law of free and equal persons. However, the modernisation and the homogenisation of private law came to a standstill at the beginning of the 1920s. The same law for abolishing the estates was utilised to declare that the BPLC would be the "only legal act for private law" in the Republic of Estonia. Thus Estonia retained the (Baltic-)German legal tradition and the laws that previously had only regulated the nobility's private legal relations were now applied to the whole population. The law for abolishing the estates emphasised specifically that the norms of land laws applied to citizens in the countryside and norms of town laws applied to people in towns. There were exceptions: for example, for the population inhabiting the towns' patrimonial manors, town law applied. On the other hand, on former manor properties, which had, during the agglomeration, become parts of towns in terms of administration, land law still applied. The law for abolishing the estates specifically reaffirmed all of this, as even the fact that in territories formerly belonging to the governorates of St. Petersburg and Pskov, which had become Estonian as a result of the victorious War of Independence against

---

4   Cf. in detail Marju LUTS: *Private Law of the Baltic Provinces as a Patriotic Act*, Juridica International 5(2000), 157–167.

5   For examples cf. Marju LUTS: *Modernisierung..., op. cit.,* 183–190; on the application of the pre-modern legal pluralism and institutes in court practice cf. Marju LUTS-SOOTAK: *Die baltischen Privatrechte in den Händen der russischen Reichsjustiz = Rechtsprechung in Osteuropa. Studien zum 19. und frühen 20. Jahrhundert*, Zoran POKROVAC (ed.), Vittorio Klostermann, Frankfurt a.M., 2012, 296–370.

6   Riigi Teataja [State Gazette] 129–130(1920), 254.

the Red Army, Part 1 of Volume 10 of the Code of the Russian Empire still applied. Latvia acted the same way. The laws of Russian empire stayed in force[7] in the same manner as in Estonia: BPLC was declared to regulate all private law relations of all inhabitants everywhere, where BPLC itself was formerly in force, and in Latgale, in the eastern part of Latvia, the Part 1 of Volume 10 of the Code of the Russian Empire remained applicable.[8] Since the middle of the 19th century the so called peasant laws regulated the private law relations for most of the population. The peasant law of the governorate Estonia from 1856 was valid in North-Estonia; in South-Estonia the peasant legal relations were regulated by the peasant law of the governorate Livonia from 1849/60 – valid also for North-Latvia as southern part of the governorate Livonia. In South-Latvia the peasant law of Courland from 1817 was valid. In the Eastern borderlands of Estonia as well of Latvia, the Russian peasant laws from 1861 were valid. Both republics abolished all those peasant laws in order to groom the population – still consisting mostly of peasants – and in the interest of uniting and consolidating the nation.[9]

It could be asked, what the alternatives to such a solution could have been. For example, when the Soviet Union occupied the Baltic States in 1940, one of the first things that was done was to abolish the entire existing legal system step by step in a very short time. In its place, the Soviet legal system was applied immediately.[10] This was not an option for the Republic of Estonia or Latvia after WWI – different from Soviet Union in 1940, until that time, there was no organisation or territory where an own Estonian or Latvian legal system could have been developed and then presented to the newly-established Republics. A newer foreign civil code could have been used as a substitution, overtaking the German BGB or the Swiss ZGB, for example. The Estonian

---

7   The law on the validity of former Russian laws, 5.12.1919; cf. in detail Philipp SCHWARTZ: *Lettland: Das Lettländische Zivilgesetzbuch vom 28. Januar 1937 = „Nichtgeborene Kinder der Liberalismus"? Zivilgesetzgebung im Mitteleuropa der Zwischenkriegszeit,* Martin LÖHNIG, Stephan WAGNER (eds.), Mohr Siebeck, Tübingen, 2018, 318.

8   *Ibid.,* 319–320.

9   This did not go wholly without problems. For Estonia cf, in detail Marju LUTS-SOOTAK, Hesi SIIMETS-GROSS, Katrin KIIREND-PRUULI: *Estlands Zivilrechtskodifikation – ein fast geborenes Kind des Konservatismus = Nichtgeborene Kinder...,* op. cit., 283–284; for Latvia cf. Philipp SCHWARTZ: *Das Lettländische Zivilgesetzbuch vom 28. Januar 1937 und seine Entstehungsgeschichte,* Shaker Verlag, Aachen, 2008, 26–27.

10   Dietrich A. LOEBER: *Kontinuität im Zivilrecht nach Wiederherstellung staatlicher Unabhängigkeit – Zu den Zivilgesetzbüchern von Lettland (1937), Estland (1993) und Litauen (2000) = Aufbruch nach Europa: 75 Jahre Max-Planck-Institut für Privatrecht,* Jürgen BASEDOW et al. (eds.), Mohr Siebeck, Tübingen, 2001, 945. Cf. for the context KASEKAMP, *op. cit.,* 124–131.

Constituent Assembly even considered this solution in 1920, and later the Estonian Conference of Jurists in 1926 as well the commission for drafting the Civil Code in 1927.[11] The German BGB was refused not only for historical and political reasons as the law of still unpopular Germans, but also evaluated as too technical and complicated for the Estonians – mostly still the people of peasants. The Swiss ZGB was seen as a code that would have been more suitable for simple nature of Estonian and Latvian people, but in every case too distant and completely unknown also for lawyers. The most important argument was, however, that these legal systems lacked decent local court practices, as well as higher instances. The idea to apply the draft of the Russian Empire's modern civil code dating from 1905[12] was abandoned for the same reason. Thus, using the BPLC was supported by pragmatism – local courts had already applied the BPLC for half a century and there were already a considerable number of explanations available from the higher court of the Russian Empire – the Governing Senate.[13] Although its justice apparatus disappeared with the Empire and the Senate's decisions were no longer formally binding, they were still accepted in Estonian and Latvian courts. As late as 1932, a collection[14] was issued in Riga containing the decisions made by the Senate in applying the BPLC.

---

11    Cf. in detail for the arguments *pro* and *contra* LUTS-SOOTAK, SIIMETS-GROSS, KIIREND-PRUULI: *Estlands Zivilrechtskodifikation...*, *op. cit.*, 292–293; SCHWARTZ: *Das Lettländische Zivilgesetzbuch...*, *op. cit.*, 34–36.

12    It was the most „western" and modern draft in the history of civil law codification in Russian Empire. Cf. in detail and for further literature Martin AVENARIUS: *Fremde Traditionen des römischen Rechts. Einfluß, Wahrnehmung und Argument des „rimskoe pravo" im russischen Zarenreich des 19. Jahrhunderts*, Wallstein, Göttingen, 2014, 521–578.

13    On the Senate's role and impact in general and especially in private law cf: Samuel KUCHEROV: *Courts, lawyers and trials under the last three tsars*, Greenwood Press, New York, 1953 (re-print Westport 1974); William Elliot BUTLER: *The Role of Case-Law in the Russian Legal System = Judicial Records, Law Reports and the Growth of Case Law*, J.H. BAKER (ed.), Dunker & Humblot, Berlin 1989, 338–352; William W. WAGNER: *The Civil Cassation Department of the Senate as an Instrument of Progressive Reform in Post-Emancipation Russia: The Case of Property and Inheritance Law*, Slavic Review, 42(1983), 36–59; in German: Jörg BABEROWSKI: *Das Justizwesen im späten Zarenreich 1864–1914. Zum Problem von Rechtsstaatlichkeit, politischer Justiz und Rückständigkeit in Rußland*, Zeitschrift für neuere Rechtsgeschichte, 1(1991), 156–172; Jörg BABEROWSKI: *Autokratie und Justiz. Zum Verhältnis von Rechtsstaatlichkeit und Rückständigkeit im ausgehenden Zarenreich 1864–1914*, Vittorio Klostermann, Frankfurt a.M., 1996; on the Senate's role in administrative law and the judiciary, Peter LIESSEM: *Verwaltungsgerichtsbarkeit im späten Zarenreich: Der Dirigierende Senat und seine Entscheidungen zur russischen Selbstverwaltung (1864–1917)*, Vittorio Klostermann, Frankfurt a.M., 1996.

14    Сборник решений Гражданского и общего собрания 1-го и Кассационного департаментов бывшего Правительствующего сената, разъясняющих законоположения, действующие в западной Латвии и в Эстонии [Collection of

290                  LUTS-SOOTAK, SIIMETS-GROSS AND KIIREND-PRUULI

Accordingly, it seems that this German past was seen as "local" and as such part of national legal identity. This is even more surprising if we consider the fact that until that moment, the BPLC was the code valid only for the German-speaking upper class, applying to Estonian and Latvian peasants only on a subsidiary basis. From the middle of the 19th century – the time of Estonian and Latvian history which is called National Awakening – the ideologies of both nations towards the Germans was quite hostile,[15] as the local nobility consisted mainly of Germans with a very few exeptional Swedes and Russians. German was the local *lingua franca*, but thus approximately 100 Estonians, who already had higher legal education, had studied mostly in both Russian capitals: first at all in St. Petersburg[16] but also in Moscow. So the understanding of the BPLC as part of Estonian national identity by local lawyers is quite surprising, to say the least. For Latvia it is not so surprising. Former Livonian, now Latvian, capital Riga was the biggest city of the Baltic area and the concentration of lawyers was the highest one. Also the Latvians, who went to the university for to study law, studied mostly at the University of Tartu in current Estonia, where the BPLC was teached as local law. Also the (Baltic-)German and local Russian lawyers practiced mostly in Riga and they formed also a prominent part of the reformers of Latvian civil law.[17]

However, the imposition of the BPLC was in Estonia as well as in Latvia seen from the beginning as an *improvisorium* as the local but alien nature of the code was acknowledged and it was even available only in foreign languages (German and Russian).[18] An official Estonian translation never followed, only some parts were published in inofficial translations. The complete but not

---

       the Decisions of Civil Cassation Department and General Panel and the 1st Cassation Department of the former Governing Senate, explaining the rules applicable in Western Latvia and in Estonia], L. KANTOR (ed.), Jurist, Riga 1932.

15     Cf. for national awakening and the national narrative, by Estonians and Latvians first at all against Germans, by Lithuanians against their Polish upper classes KASEKAMP: *op. cit.,* 76–82; more in detail Toivo U. RAUN: *Estonia and the Estonians,* 2nd ed., Hoover Institution Press, Stanford, 2001, 57–80; Andrejs PLAKANS: *The Latvians. A Short History,* Hoover Institution Press, Stanford, 1995, 89–111.

16     Raimo PULLAT: *Estnische Juristen in St. Petersburg bis 1917 = Buch und Bildung im Baltikum: Festschrift für Paul Kaegbein zum 80. Geburtstag,* Heinrich BOSSE, Otto-Heinrich ELIAS, Robert SCHWEITZER (eds.), LIT, Münster, 2005, 555–579.

17     For national background of members civil law drafting commissions in Latvia cf. SCHWARTZ: *Lettland..., op. cit.,* 324–333.

18     Although the original language of the BPLC was German, the code was translated into Russian and translation was promulgated in the same time (1864) as the German original. Since 1870, according to one decision of Governing Senate, in the case of textual differences the Russian translation had to prevail. Cf. for details: LUTS-SOOTAK, *Das Baltische Privatrecht..., op.cit,* 365.

ESTONIA AND LATVIA BETWEEN TWO WORLD WARS

official Latvian translation of BPLC was published already in 1885.[19] In 1928, a new Latvian translation of BPLC was published as "Latvian civil laws"[20] – a peculiar compilation, were the articles concerning Estonian governorate and Estonian part of Livonia were left out and the original numbers of articles of BPLC replaced with new ones. So the number of articles was reduced from 4636 to 4079. Although Latvia had the consolidated law code on the valid civil law in Latvian, the preparation for a new civil code was never disgarded and the drafting of own civil code was, very similarly to the contemporary Estonia, seen as the ultimate goal.

## 3    The Drafting of the Civil Codes in Estonia and Latvia

The first attempt to draft a Civil Code for the Republic of Estonia was already made in 1919 when the Constituent Assembly was presented with two parts of the Civil Code – the General Part, and Family Law, and there were plans to use the system of five books to discuss the other books.[21] Apparently the opposition to the German BGB as example was also not enough to hinder adoption, without objection, of the five-book system, composed by 19th century German private law scholars and applied in the German BGB from 1896/1900. Therefore, the question arose as to whether to rely on the BPLC and make necessary amendments or to draft a completely new code. When considering the system of the new code, the decisive difference would have been to add the general part because the other four books were already present in the BPLC.[22]

A member of the Constituent Assembly and, later, a professor of Estonian legal history at the University of Tartu, and important politician, Jüri Uluots (1890–1945) emphasised that the principles of the private law had stood for millennia, influencing the nation's life as a whole. He thought that it was not yet the right time to create a Civil Code – the land question and abolition of the

---

19    *Vidzemes ur Kurzemes Privāttiesību likumu grāmata*, Zimmermann, Liepaja, 1885. In title only Livonia and Courland are mentioned, in text the articles concerning the Estonian governorate are also included.

20    *Vietējo Civillikumu kopojums*, Valtera un Rapas, Riga, 1928.

21    *Asutawa Kogu koosolek, 8. juuli 1919, Asutava Kogu protokoll nr 33* (6) [Meeting of the Constituent Assembly, July 8, 1919, Records of the Constituent Assembly No. 33 (6)]. The Civil Code draft was discussed as the third order of business according to the agenda, columns 233–279.

22    The order of books was, admittedly, different from the German BGB: in the BGB there is the General Part, the Law of Obligations, Property Law, Family Law and Inheritance Law; in the BPLC they were Family Law, Property Law, Inheritance Law and in last place the "Law of Demands," as counterpart to the Law of Obligations.

estates were still undecided and needed more attention.[23] His opinion won the day: although there is a draft act for the Civil Code in the materials of the Constituent Assembly, it was never, in essence, taken under discussion and no decision was made on it. The private law or the new and unified Civil Code was not yet understood as a tool to create or to preserve national unity. During the discussions in the Constituent Assembly these questions were not raised. National identity was to be created by the new and very modern Constitution[24] and the Land law.[25]

Also the Constituent Assembly of Latvia solved only the issue of land and adopted the Constitution, leaving aside civil law for the time being. Already in August 1920, Vladimir Bukovsky (1867–1937), the former judge of Riga Circuit Court and the future professor of the University of Latvia, received an invitation from the Minister of Justice to set up a commission for the purpose of drafting a new Civil Code of Latvia. The Ministry also prescribed the content of the work: to harmonise and simplify the already valid BPLC. Without a doubt, Bukovsky was the best choice for this task, namely because he was the author of the only complete commentary[26] of the BPLC. Although Bukovsky's commission had not finished the aforementioned first task, in 1922, it was entrusted with an additional task to prepare a law for the harmonisation of the private law valid in Latgale with the law valid in other parts of Latvia.[27]

In Estonia the next attempt to create a new Civil Code was made also in 1920, already at the beginning of year. Analysing the valid family law and preparing the law of marriage, a decision was reached that it would be more suitable to develop a modern Civil Code "without wasting time on modernising the BPLC, which is boring to the core."[28] Thus, Estonia's codification efforts

---

23    *Asutawa Kogu koosolek, 8. juuli 1919. Asutava Kogu protokoll nr 33* (6) [Meeting of the Constituent Assembly, July 8, 1919. Records of the Constituent Assembly], column 262.

24    Cf. more about the Estonian Constitution of 1920: Hesi SIIMETS-GROSS, Marelle LEPPIK: *Estonia: First Landmarks of Fundamental Rights = First Fundamental Rights Documents in Europe*, Markku SUKSI, Kalliope AGAPIOU-JOSEPHIDES, Jean-Paul LEHNERS, Manfred NOWAK (eds.), Intersentia, Cambridge-Antwerp-Portland, 2015, 304–307.

25    Cf. more about the so-called land question and land reform in Estonia Marju LUTS-SOOTAK: *Pre-modern divided ownership in the modern legal history of Estonia = Legal pluralism – cui bono?*, Marju LUTS- SOOTAK, Irene KULL, Karin SEIN, Hesi SIIMETS-GROSS (eds.), Tartu University Press, Tartu, 2018, 108–110.

26    Vladimir BUKOVSKY: Сводъ гражданскихъ узаконеній губерній прибалтийскихъ [Code of Civil Laws of Baltic Governorates], vol. 2, Hempel & Co, Riga, 1914.

27    SCHWARTZ: *Lettland...*, *op. cit.*, 324–325.

28    Estonian National Archives (ENA) ERA.76.5.1, *Ministri päevakäsk ning kirjavahetus kodifikatsiooniosakonna liikme Igor Tjutrjumov'i määramise kohta tsiviilseaduse eelnõu väljatöötajaks koos abijõududega. 15.01.1920 kiri nr 97* [The Minister's directive of the day and correspondence with the member of the codification department Igor Tyutryumov on his

were started with the decision to leave behind the pre-modern BPLC, whereas Latvia had decided at the same time to merely modify the BPLC.

The new Estonian Civil Code had to be drafted by a commission of several Russian lawyers, who had after the Bolshevik revolution in Russia, gone in exile to Estonia and worked there.[29] This commission was led by a Russian legal scholar and former member of the Senate and future professor of the University of Tartu, Igor Tyutryumov (1865–1943). He was already known as the author of the most significant commentary on the draft of the Russian Civil Code from 1905[30] and knew it very well. So Tyutryumov was the most suitable person to draft a new civil code for Estonia. Whether his commission took as a model the draft of Russian Code of 1905 or the civil law part of the Code of the Russian Empire,[31] is not known. There is no specific sign of the results of the commission's work. By the end of 1920, the commission had been dissolved again because of the revelation that one of the members of the commission was working against the Republic of Estonia by spreading communist propaganda.[32]

At the first Conference of the Estonian Lawyers in April 1922, a member of parliament at the time and former minister of justice Jüri Jaakson (1870–1942) described the situation and stressed following points. First, the legal order in

---

appointment of drafter of the Civil Code draft act with additional help. January 15, 1920, letter no. 97].

29    *Ibid.*

30    Гражданское уложение: проект Высочайше учрежденной Редакционной комиссии по составлению Гражданского уложения с объяснениями, извлеченными из трудов Редакционной комиссии [Civil Code: Draft of Project Committee for the Completing of Civil Code, confirmed by Zar, with Explanations from Works of Members of Project Committee], I. TYUTRYUMOV (ed.), [s.n.] St. Petersburg, 1910, reprint Wolters Kluwer Russia, Moskva, 2007, 2 vols.

31    The editor of this most important commentary was the same Igor Tyutryumov: Законы гражданские (Свод зак. Т. *X*, ч. *1*, изд. *1900* г. по Прод. *1906* и *1908* гг.) с разъяснениями Правительствующего Сената (Гражд. Кассац., *1* и *2* Департаментов, Первого Общего Собр. и Общ. Собр. *1*, *2* и Кассац. Департ. по *1* сентября *1910* г.) и комментариями русских юристов, извлеченными из научных и практических трудов по гражданскому праву и судопроизводству (по *1* июля *1910* г.) [Civil Laws (Collection of Laws, vol. 10, Part 1, ed. 1900 according to the installments of 1906 and 1908) with Explanations of the Governing Senate (Civil Cassation Department, 1st and 2nd Department, First General Panel and General Panel of 1st and 2nd Cassation Department until 1910 September 1st) and Commentaries of Russian Jurists from Scholarly and Practical Works about the Civil Law and Procedure (until 1910 July 1st).], Igor TYUTRYUMOV (ed.), 3. ed., Zakonovedenye, St.Petersburg, 1911; reprint Statut, Moskva, 2004.

32    ENA ERA.76.2.333, *Kirjavahetus Eesti tsiviilseaduse eelnõu väljatöötamise ning sama komisjoni isikulise koosseisu küsimuses* [Correspondence on drafting the Civil Code and about the same commission's personnel]. January 15, 1920 – March 3, 1921.

Estonia had been modernised through the constitution and other statutes, but civil law had stacked up to the norms of premodern law. The main problem was caused by the particularism and pluralism of the BPLC which had been a compilation of all local and territorial particularities and has had many amendments, even afterwards by different rulers.[33] The legal particularism caused, secondly, individual problems in practice as the movement of spouses from one part of the town to another could mean the movement from an area that was regulated by town law to an area regulated by land law. Through this, for example, the hereditary system and norms changed, and the spouse could inherit less than before. The intensity of movements from land to town had increased "in an unprecedented manner." Therefore, the problems arising from the particularism of private law were in Jaakson's opinion more individual and practical, not national or ideological in a broader sense. Even more, particularism was not considered as an obstacle to the unification of the nation or the Estonian state.[34] In addition, Jaakson brought up the question of languages – now more clearly than in the Constituent Assembly: "although Estonians are generally literate, the majority understands only their mother tongue." As the BPLC was available only in German and Russian, the people often could not understand it.[35]

Despite all the criticism directed at the BPLC, Jaakson thought that at first, similarly to the solution of Latvia, quick and essential changes must be made namely in this code, it must be translated into Estonian and such "cleaned" BPLC must be set in force in the whole territory of the Republic of Estonia, including the border areas received from Russia.[36] Although there were not so many German lawyers in Estonia if compared to Latvia, the BPLC was the most familiar code in Estonian legal practice and Jaakson's proposal relied on this pragmatic consideration.

In Latvia, the work of the first comission was stopped 1923 and attention was turned to other laws, inter alia, to those which amended the private law in force in several parts of family and inheritance law, law of contracts, property law etc.[37] At the same time in Estonia, by the decision of the government from November 7, 1923, a special commission was established, next to the

---

33   Jüri JAAKSON: *Ettekanne Õigusteadlaste päevadel* [Speech during the Estonian Lawyers Conference] (1922) = *Õigusteadlaste päevad 1922–1940. Protokollid* [Conferences of Estonian Lawyers 1922–1940. Records], Jaanika ERNE (ed.), Juura, Tallinn, 2008, 26–34.

34   *Ibid.*, 26, 32–34.

35   *Ibid.*, 35–37.

36   *Ibid.*, 37–38.

37   SCHWARTZ: *Das Lettländische Zivilgesetzbuch...*, *op. cit.*, 68–77, 82–110.

ESTONIA AND LATVIA BETWEEN TWO WORLD WARS 295

codification department, which was supposed to draft the Civil Code.[38] This commission had the task of developing the new code on the basis of the BPLC. The commission continued their work until 1935. Their first results – Inheritance Law, the General Part of the Civil Code, as well as the Family Law – were published in print for public commentary quite quickly: in 1925 and in 1926.[39] These drafts were heavily criticised by the public and finally the Minister of Justice decided to convene a high-profile meeting to discuss the reform of the Civil Code. The meeting was held in 1927 and there were seventeen active lawyers and seven members of the drafting commission of the Civil Code draft act present. The discussion was, again, about suitable models for the new code, but all in all the decision was made for the BPLC, with which the people were supposedly already familiar and for which better conditions were supposedly in place.[40] Only at the end of the meeting did Jüri Jaakson once again draw attention to the fact that the civil code in force was available only in German and Russian, not in Estonian, and that this problem should not be allowed to continue.[41] The translation of the whole BPLC was not really discussed, only the question of whether, with changed parts in the BPLC, the part still in force from the BPLC should also be translated. Jüri Uluots remarked that in the near future the number of young lawyers who did not understand Russian would grow considerably, so legislation in Estonian was very much needed. As the meeting had already lasted for hours, this question was set aside.[42] The problem concerning the language of the BPLC was in that context seen as an everyday problem concerning legal practice, not a question of national ideology or identity.

---

38    ENA ERA.76.2.334, *Kirjavahetus tsiviilseadustiku eelnõu väljatöötamiseks vastava komisjoni moodustamise, komisjoni koosseisu ja selle liikmetele tasumaksmise küsimuses* [Correspondence on forming a comission to draft a Civil Code, on the personnel of this commission and on the salary of the members of this commission], October 26, 1923 – March 11, 1927.

39    *Tsiwiil seadustik: pärandusõigus: eelkawa* [Civil Code: Inheritance Law: Draft], Tallinna Eesti Kirjastus-Ühisus, Tallinn, 1925; *Tsiviilseadustik. Üldosa ja perekonnaõigus: eelkava* [Civil Code. General Part and Family Law: Draft], Tallinna Eesti Kirjastus-Ühtsus, Tallinn, 1926.

40    ENA ERA.76.2.347, *Tsiviilseaduste reformeerimise küsimuse selgitamise nõupidamise protokolli ärakiri* [Apograph of the stenographic record of the meeting to clear the question of reforming civil law], October 9, 1927, 50–52.

41    ENA ERA.76.2.299, *Stenogramm Kohtuministeeriumi poolt kokkukutsutud nõupidamisest tsiviilseaduste reformimise küsimuse selgitamiseks: 9. oktoobril 1927 a. kl. 11 Riigikogu hoones* [Stenographic record of a meeting, summoned by the ministry of Justice, to clear the questions of reforming the civil laws: 1927 October 9th, 11 o'clock in the building of the Parliament], 62.

42    *Ibid.*, 63–64.

Exactly at the time when Estonia came to the conclusion, with resignation, that the only feasible way was to harmonise and simplify the valid BPLC, in Latvia, professor Vasily Sinaisky (1876–1949) submitted an alternative proposal to prepare a completely new and original Civil Code for Latvian Republic. According to the opinion of Sinaisky, the BPLC was so outdated that its harmonisation would not achieve the desired objective, i.e. the Civil Code with a modern content. Actually, Sinaisky did not mean to prepare an entirely original code, he recommended to use Swiss Civil Code as an example. In Latvia, only this code from all possible foreign examples was considered, but one of the reasons for the country to have its own codification was the "danger for the reputation and self-confidence of the Latvian state," while another was the continuity of the law.[43] Although Sinaisky stated that a group of Latvian lawyers had prepared an entire draft code under his guidance, nobody has been able to find the text of this code to this day.[44] More likely, it was probably just an idea that did not reach the level of a complete draft – similarly, the idea to enforce Swiss Civil Code was rejected in Estonia at the same time.

Ten years on since the announcement of their independent states, the commissions within the Ministries of Justice both in Estonia and Latvia continued to develop new codes from the basis of the valid BPLC. In addition, Baltic German lawyers came up with a new idea for shaping the private law of two states: new codes must be jointly prepared for both countries and they must be identical.[45] In 1928, the first conference of Baltic lawyers (Ger. Erste Baltische Juristenkonferenz) was held in Tartu. The purpose of the conference was to give an overview of the legal developments, which had taken place in both countries so far. Besides, a close cooperation aimed at harmonising laws or even developing joint legislation was planned for the future. However, it was just a private initiative of Baltic German lawyers, which had no state support or a higher visibility to Estonian and Latvian national or legal communities. It is also possible that the orientation to harmonising the entire legal order of these countries and not concentrating on one specific branch of law – private law – turned out to be the final straw. The Commercial and Industrial Chambers of

---

43 According to Herman Apsītis (1893–1942), a lawyer and Minster of Justice after the Ulmanis coup, who was one of the drafters and promoters of the Latvian new Civil Code 1937/38. SCHWARTZ: *Das Lettländische...*, *op. cit.*, 34–35.

44 SCHWARTZ: *Lettland...*, *op. cit.*, 327.

45 Cf. conference report *Rechtsangleichung der Baltischen Staaten Lettland-Estland*, Rigasche Zeitschrift für Rechtswissenschaft, 1927/28, 286–288 and proceedings *Baltische Rechtsangleichung. 10 Jahre Gesetzgebung Estlands und Lettlands: Baltische Rechtsangleichung. Referate des I. Baltischen Juristenkonferenz zu Dorpat (1928)*, Wassermann, Reval, 1929.

ESTONIA AND LATVIA BETWEEN TWO WORLD WARS

both countries were in favour of the idea of harmonisation submitted by Baltic Germans, but their interest was directed toward a wider regional cooperation in trade and industry. From 1928 to 1934, five conferences were organised, in which participated also the representatives of Lithuania, in addition to the participants from Estonia and Latvia and ultimately, some harmonisations were made in patent and copyright law, commercial registry law and labour law, as well as in civil execution proceeding.[46] As a result of these Baltic cooperation projects, the core private law was disregarded in the end.

Official commissions worked more or less at the same pace in Latvia and Estonia: by 1935, most pre-drafts of individual parts of codes were completed and published in both countries. In Estonia, the work with these documents went on and in 1936, a full draft of Civil Code with all five books – General Part, Family Law, Property Law, Inheritance Law, Law of Obligations – was completed.[47] Despite the fact that in 1935, Latvia decided to discontinue the modification of the valid BPLC and start to prepare a completely new code,[48] the draft that was completed by 1936 relied on the previous work and thus the Latvian draft of 1936 was, above all, a processed version of the BPLC. Although both countries relied on the valid BPLC, they ended up with different results: in Estonia, a five-book-system along with general part originating from German law was transposed, but not in Latvia; regarding the property law, Estonia's draft relied much more on the BPLC, whereas in Latvia, an essential reform in this field had already been implemented in 1925 with the so-called Bukovsky's amendment and its modern solutions were adhered to in the further codification process; out of the plentiful choice of the law of obligations of the BPLC, Estonia and Latvia cherry-picked next to the same also different things. In the research work made so far, no detailed comparison has been made between the drafts of Estonia and Latvia. At first sight, it seems that the reasons behind different results, which were achieved from the same starting position and even on the basis of substantially identical material, are more likely pragmatic choices, the education of referents and personal preferences, and not national characteristics or the efforts to form an identity.

---

46   Cf. more Wilm SCHARLEMANN: *Privatrechtsentwicklung im Baltikum zwischen nationaler Souveränität, regionaler Kooperation und europäischer Integration = Europa und seine Regionen. 2000 Jahre Rechtsgeschichte*, Andreas BAUER, Karl H.L. WELKER (eds.), Böhlau, Köln et al., 2007, 673–677.

47   *Tsiviilseadustiku 1936. aasta eelnõu*, [Civil Code draft act of 1936], [s. n.], Tallinn, 1936.

48   Cf. in detail SCHWARTZ: *Lettland..., op. cit.*, 330–331.

## 4 Estonian and Latvian Autocratic Turns and Private Law Codifications

Already before the finalising the drafting of Civil Codes, in both states – Estonia and Latvia – the autocratic coup d'etat was carried out: in March 1934 in Estonia and in May 1934 in Latvia. In both countries, the turn towards authoritarian regimes resulted in a turn towards a nationalistic discourse, emphasising the ideology of consolidation of the country's main nation and in certain aspects a genuine limitation of minority nations' rights.[49] However, the attitude of autocratic rulers in Estonia and Latvia towards the private law or towards the law as a whole was different. Latvian President Kārlis Ulmanis (1877–1942) who staged a coup in Latvia dissolved the parliament and neglected to set up a new chamber of representatives. He did place great emphasis on Latvia's own Civil Code, rapidly constituted a new commission and approved its work in his own name day on January 28th 1937. Thus, a new Latvian national Civil Code entered into force in 1938, officially called the Civillikums (Civil Code); in celebration speeches, however, it was called the "Code Ulmanis." Dictatorships can be highly efficient in the short-term. However, even if the Civillikums was praised as a new and original code, "a new, Latvian way" that was a sign of the end of foreign power and oppression, it was basically a renewed and cleansed version of the BPLC.[50] "Code Ulmanis" refers directly to Code Napoléon – also Ulmanis wanted to be a great ruler and legislator, above all in civil law.

Having seized power in Estonia, President Konstantin Päts (1874–1956) also dissolved the parliament, but he did not set the existing draft of Civil Code into force. Instead of civil law he turned his attention more to the public law. The new constitution was prepared and approved in 1937 and 1938 also the Parliament was re-established, which, however, was composed on different principles than those of its predecessors. Another new commission was formed in 1938 to finalise the Civil Code in Estonia and in 1939 the new draft, still on the basis of the former one, was approved by the government of the Republic and presented for the discussions ot the Parliament.

Meanwhile, it would be false to claim that quotidian life and public discussion in Estonia returned to "normal democracy" and liberal discourse. We will observe some moments of the relationship between private law and the nation that emerged in the reform discourse and legal reality in Estonia in the second half of the 1930s, after the coup.

---

49    KASEKAMP: *op. cit.*, 109–112.
50    SCHWARTZ: *Das Lettländische...*, *op. cit.*, 246, 248.

ESTONIA AND LATVIA BETWEEN TWO WORLD WARS                                     299

The narrative of renewal of civil law was changed if we compare it with the pragmatic and liberal one in 1920s. Jüri Uluots, still the leading person by the drafting of Civil Code, wrote that the draft of the Civil Code was based on four important principles that were also emphasised in the preamble of the Estonian Constitution: justice, law, freedom and "the general welfare of present and future generations."[51] In 1939, Ernst Ein (1898–1956), professor of Roman law at the Estonian National University in Tartu, wrote an article about the inheritance law in the draft of the Civil Code.[52] According to Ein, the principle of justice was, above all, related to the fact that for once, the principle of justice postulated in the Republic of Estonia would be executed in private law, where the differences between the laws of town and country, as well as differences between former governorates of Estonia and Livonia, would be abolished and all citizens could enjoy the same private law. However, Ein mentioned providing all citizens with the same private law only as a second point. First place was given to the "consolidation of a nation from inside," predisposed by unified private law: "As local dialects disappear and a homogeneous official language takes its place, which helps the isolated parts of our nation come together, so a unified law enables a legal traffic between those parts."[53] The idea of using a unified private law to achieve national unity was no novelty.[54] This idea had for example already been expressed by a professor of the University of Heidelberg, Anton Justus Friedrich Thibaut (1772–1840), during the prime of the German national awakening in 1814. Thibaut's essay "On the Necessity of a General Civil Code in Germany"[55] launched the most famous scientific dispute in German legal history – the so-called codification dispute (Ger. *Kodifikationsstreit*).[56]

---

51    Jüri ULUOTS: *Seletuskiri Tsiviilseadustiku 1935. a. eelnõu nelja esimese raamatu juurde* [Explanatory Memorandum to the First Four Books of the Civil Law Code of 1935], [s. n.] Tartu, 1936, 6–7. Both Estonian constitutions, from 1920 and from 1937 had in the preamble the same wording. *Eesti Vabariigi Põhiseadus* [Constitution of the Republic of Estonia], Riigi Teataja [State Gazette, RT], 113/114(1920), 897. In English published as *The Constitution of the Esthonian Republic (Passed by the Constituent Assembly on the 15th of June 1920)*, Ühiselu, Tallinn, 1924.

52    Ernst EIN: *Pärimisõigus Tsiviilseadustiku eelnõus* [Inheritance law in the draft of Civil Code], Õigus 4(1939), 177–188.

53    *Ibid.*, 181.

54    Cf. for the Spanish example Aniceto MASFERRER: *Codification as nationalisation or denationalisation of law: the Spanish case in comparative perspective*, Comparative Legal History 2(2016), 100–130.

55    Anton Justus Friedrich THIBAUT: *Ueber die Nothwendigkeit eines allgemeinen bürgerlichen Rechts für Deutschland*, Zimmer, Heidelberg, 1814.

56    The most important works in this dispute have been re-published in *Thibaut und Savigny. Ihre programmatischen Schriften*, Hans HATTENAUER (ed.), Vahlen, München, 1973; 2nd. ed. 2002.

However, Thibaut's adversary, Friedrich Carl von Savigny (1779–1861), triumphed in this dispute. In his metaphysical teaching of "the spirit of the people" (Ger. *Volksgeist*)[57] and the "indwelling silently working forces"[58] that shape the common conviction of the people also for law,[59] Savigny contributed i.a. to the evolution of German nationalism. His works were also one of the sources of National Socialist ideology when it came to power in Germany in 1933.[60] However, in 1939, the ideology of national consolidation, even by the codification of private law, shone with a completely new and different light compared to the situation in 1814. By 1939, while Ernst Ein was still hopefully waiting for Estonian national entity to coalesce with the help of unified private law, many things had already happened: Austria had been unified with Germany, Czechoslovakia had been divided, and ensuring the "purity" of the German national body from Jewish blood, rather than just property and civil rights, was in full process.

The Estonian people, nation or nationality, whose consolidation had to be assisted by unified private law, were far from being a simply empirical collection of people called Estonians. "True" Estonians had to be healthy and hard working. To achieve these objectives private law had to be of assistance in some ways, and when necessary the state could use norms of coercion belonging to public law. Jüri Uluots claimed in the explanatory memorandum to the Civil Code that everything hindering the homogenisation had to be eliminated, but in certain circumstances and in certain areas, exceptions might equally prove necessary. Greater exceptions from a unitary and homogenised private law had to remain tasks for special laws. Meanwhile, the Civil Code had to be only the core of the civil law.[61] When Uluots was talking about "removing" excessive material or material that hindered homogenisation, then that is how it should be understood. In 1939, together with the draft of the Civil Code, the Parliament also received a separate draft that "demanded the largest exception" – a draft for the "Act on the Inheritance of Farmsteads."[62] The necessity for a

---

57    Locus classicus: Friedrich Carl VON SAVIGNY: *System des heutigen römischen Rechts*, vol. 1, Veit, Berlin 1840, 14.

58    Friedrich Carl VON SAVIGNY: *Vom Beruf unsrer Zeit für Gesetzgebung und Rechtswissenschaft*, Mohr und Zimmer, Heidelberg, 1814, 13–14; cf. also SAVIGNY: *System..., op. cit.*, 14.

59    Cf. SAVIGNY: *System... op. cit.*, 14.

60    Cf. the relevant differentiation by Joachim RÜCKERT: *Das „gesunde Volksempfinden" – eine Erbschaft Savignys?* Zeitschrift der Savigny-Stiftung für Rechtsgeschichte, Germanistische Abteilung, 103(1986), 199–246.

61    ULUOTS: *Seletuskiri..., op. cit.*, 6–7.

62    *Talundite pärimise seadus. Vabariigi Valituse ettepanek* [Act on the Succession of Farmsteads. Proposal of the Government of the Republic], 11.12.1939. Text with an explanatory memorandum is published in *Riigivolikogu stenograafiliste aruannete lisad. I koosseis, v ja

ESTONIA AND LATVIA BETWEEN TWO WORLD WARS 301

separate system to limit the freedom to command or to testate was explained by several social and economic arguments, among others by the nation's vitality. Jüri Uluots expressed himself clearly in the presentation at the Thirteenth Conference of Estonian Lawyers in April 1939:

> From now on the farms' social importance will be taken into consideration. If the towns fail to provide an increase in population, then the nation's vitality will come from the countryside. The countryside is the natural reservoir for the increase of the population, the city destroys the nation's vitality. /.../ The legislation has to provide that the nation's increase hubs remain healthy and vital and their urbanisation has to be hindered using legal methods in order to preserve the nation's future.[63]

The latter was one of the arguments that were used to justify intervention in the unified inheritance system and in the freedom to testate. The same social economic and eugenic–demographic arguments were used to impose the land heritage law[64] in Nazi Germany in 1933. The introduction of this law claimed that the government's intent was to ensure the peasantry as the "spring of blood of the German nation."[65] A large number of small and medium sized farms, divided evenly throughout the country, was supposedly the "best guarantee for the preservation of a nation's and country's health,"[66] for the Estonian people, who were perceived to be very similar to the German people of the day. In the Estonian discussion on the privileged succession of farmsteads, Germany was always mentioned as the primary example of a modern model of how to create a societally and legally special situation for the succession of

---

VI istungjärk 1939/1940 [Appendixes for the stenographic reports of the Chamber of Deputies. I composition, V and VI sessions 1939/1940], [s. n.], Tallinn, 1940, 125–147.

63 Jüri ULUOTS: *Talundite pärimine* [The succession of farmsteads], Õigus 7(1939), 324.

64 *Reichserbhofgesetz vom 29. September 1933*, Reichsgesetzblatt, 1(1933), 685. On this law in the German context cf. Jürgen WEITZEL: *Sonderprivatrecht aus konkretem Ordnungsdenken: Reichserbhofrecht und allgemeines Privatrecht 1933–1945*, Zeitschrift für Neuere Rechtsgeschichte, 14(1992), 55–79.

65 Cf. "Die Reichsregierung will unter Sicherung alter deutschen Erbsitte das Bauerntum als Blutquelle des deutschen Volkes erhalten. ... Es solle auf eine gesunde Verteilung der landwirtschaftlichen Besitzgrößen hingewirkt werden, da eine große Anzahl lebensfähiger kleiner und mittlerer Bauernhöfe, möglichst gleichmäßig über das ganze Land verteilt, die beste Gewähr für die Gesunderhaltung von Volk und Staat bildet." So the Introduction to the German *Reichserbhofgesetz*.

66 ULUOTS: *Talundite..., op. cit.*, 324.

farmsteads.[67] After Germany the USSR was cited, where agricultural land was also subject to a legally special regime and separate agrarian legislation.

By 1939, the German solution had already shown its economically darker side. The explanatory memorandum added to the draft of Estonian government explained the German law thoroughly, but for Estonia a different solution was sought. Both the German as well as the Soviet etatistic-authoritarian versions were cast aside. At the same time, the Estonian legislature was reluctant to remain in a Western European liberal-individualistic position. Thus, an intermediate solution was sought and countries in which such models had already been implemented were mentioned: Switzerland, Hungary, Norway and, by 1939, the already "former" Austria and Czechoslovakia.[68] So the Estonian solutions in the draft of the act on farmstead succession were actually substantially less radical and granted more economic freedom to the testator and the inheritor. In addition, the Estonian legislature did not foresee special courts or supervisory institutions for farmstead succession. The general aim – caring for the nation's physical well-being by favouring the lifestyle in the countryside, was the same in Estonia as it was in Nazi Germany. Although the so-called settler farmsteads[69] had been actively built in Estonia since the 1920s, from the resources gained from country manors with the land reform, this trend took flight on another level after the coup in 1934.[70] The state's propaganda machine contributed by creating an image of a "normal" or "true" Estonian family who lived off their small one-horse farm or their slightly larger two-horse farm. In any case, the farmstead, which took the whole family's time and strength, had to feed them and ensure healthy sleep after a hard but joyful day in the wholesome country air. The town, where people went about more often and could

---

67    Already in the early phase of the abovementioned plans (when there was a considerable uncertainty whether a separate inheritance law for farmsteads would be drafted for Estonia) the relevant German legislation was introduced in depth in legal literature, all the while placing it in a historic and internationally comparative context: Elmar ILUS: *Talundi eelispärimisõigus* [Privileged succession of farmstead], Õigus 9–10(1936), 409–436.

68    *Seletuskiri – Riigivolikogu stenograafiliste aruannete lisad. I koosseis, V ja VI istungjärk 1939/1940* [[Explanatory memorandum – Appendixes to the stenographic reports of the Chamber of Deputies. I composition, V and VI sessions 1939/1940], Tallinn, 1939, 136.

69    New farmsteads established after 1919 land reform on land, that previously was part of large manors. Usually these farmsteads were quite small and economically not very profitable.

70    Elo LUTSEPP: *Asunduspoliitikast Eesti Vabariigis: Asundusameti tegevus 1929–1941* [The policy of settlement in the Republic of Estonia: the activities of the Settlement Committee in 1929–1941], Ajalooline Ajakiri/The Estonian Historical Journal 3–4/(2007), 443–460, especially 455–457; English summary: 460–462.

ESTONIA AND LATVIA BETWEEN TWO WORLD WARS 303

spread political and state-critical ideas more easily, was considered, in contrast, unhealthy and decadent – the seedbed of sloth and laziness.

Estonians had not only to be healthy but also hard-working people. Those who strayed from this maxim had to be forced. On July 7, 1938 the president Konstantin Päts issued a decree commanding the establishment of a camp for the work-shy,[71] to forcefully "teach, provide practice and put into use the able work-shy." All 18–60-year-olds who had not lost more than 60% of their normal working ability were eligible for these involuntary work studies. The able person who was unemployed because of neglect for work and who was without income had to spend six months to three years in the labour camp. People who were actively employed could also be sent to the camp if they "wasted" their salary or other income on alcohol or narcotic substances. It was unimportant if they threatened their family's well-being, it was enough if they were living in "extreme poverty." When the Estonian president entered this decree into force in July 1938, in April and June of the same year Germany had already seen two waves of the so-called action *Arbeitsscheu Reich*, which had already sent approximately 10,000 people to concentration camps to learn and practice work.[72] The treatment of social "parasites" by Estonia's neighbour, the Soviet Union, is well known. Article 12 of the Stalinist constitution declared: "In the U.S.S.R. work is a duty and a matter of honour for every able-bodied citizen, in accordance with the principle: 'He who does not work, neither shall he eat.'" In reality, the Soviet work-shy were not only removed from the dinner table, they were also removed from society – there were enough places and work for them with other "enemies of the people" in the Gulag. In the Stalinist empire, rather than sending them to the camps by the thousands, they were sent there by the millions.

Indeed, Estonian dimensions were different from these large countries. Up to June 1940, only 129 "work-shy" people had been sent to the work camp,

---

71    *Tööpõlgurite töölaagrite seadus* [Statute of Camps for work-shy persons], Riigi Teataja [State Gazette] 1938, 62, 614.

72    Cf. in general Wolfgang AYAß: *„Asoziale" im Nationalsozialismus*, Klett-Cotta, Stuttgart, 1995 and the proceedings *Ausgesteuert – ausgegrenzt ... angeblich asozial*, Anne ALLEX, Dietrich KALKAN (eds.), AG SPAK Bücher, Neu-Ulm, 2009; focused on a separate action Wolfgang AYAß: *„Ein Gebot der nationalen Arbeitsdisziplin." Die Aktion „Arbeitsscheu Reich" 1938* = Beiträge zur nationalsozialistischen Gesundheits- und Sozialpolitik, vol. 6: *Feinderklärung und Prävention. Kriminalbiologie, Zigeunerforschung und Asozialenpolitik*, Rotbuch Verlag, Berlin, 1988, 43–74; an important collection of documents: *„Gemeinschaftsfremde." Quellen zur Verfolgung von „Asozialen" 1933–1945*, Wolfgang AYAß (ed.): *Materialien aus dem Bundesarchiv*, vol. 5, Bundesarchiv, Koblenz, 1998.

which started its work on August 1, 1938.[73] In order to arrest the homeless or work-shy and force them to work, Estonia's first camp-type detention facility was established. About two years later, the Soviet occupation found it easy to integrate this facility into the Soviet prison system, which consisted mostly of camp-type detention facilities. Many Estonians, forced to endure hard labour, were sent to prison camps situated very far from Estonia, mainly in Siberia. Similar camp for work-shy was not established in Latvia in 1930s but this did not save them and other nationalities of the Soviet Union from prison camps in Siberia.

The Soviet occupation reached Estonia in Juny 1940, before Parliament of Estonia had finalised the discussions on the draft of Civil Code. Contrary to the Latvia, Estonian Civil Code never was adopted. Under the soviet rule the whole legal system both, in Estonia as well in Latvia, was completely abolished, including the laws concerning private law. The substitute, the Civil Code of the Russian Soviet Federated Socialist Republic, was very rapidly translated into Estonian and Latvian and introduced already since the beginning of 1941.

## 5    Conclusion

Although the codification of private law at least in Estonia was originally not motivated by the will to consolidate the nation and shape the people's legal identity using the tool of codified private law, there was a change in the wake of the nationalistic ideology of the 1930s. Moreover, the purpose of uniting and teaching the nation was to be fulfilled not only by codified private law but even more by the special laws. These were to be separate from the core civil law and the state was planning to use them – or was already using – to interfere into the private autonomy of individuals. This was not a unique Estonian fenomenon but widespread in Europe of the 1930s: in Germany, Italy etc, also in the sister-state Latvia.

After the coups d'etat from year 1934, the authoritarian rulers in Latvia and Estonia had different attitude to the legal order and codification of private law. Latvian president Kārlis Ulmanis used the consolidated power to show himself as a great legislator and adopted quickly the Civil Code as "Code Ulmanis." Estonian president Konstantin Päts relied on the securing his power by the new constitution and building up the parliament in a new constellation with two chambers. The parliamentary discussions take the time, in two chambers

---

73    Uno ILM: *Tööpõlgurid Harkus* [Work-shy Persons in Harku], Politsei 5(1998), 10–11.

ESTONIA AND LATVIA BETWEEN TWO WORLD WARS

even more, and so the Estonian parliament had before the Soviet occupation not enough time to adopt the Civil Code.

## Bibliography

### Archival Sources

Rahvusarhiiv [Estonian National Archive], ERA.76.2.299, *Stenogramm Kohtuministeeriumi poolt kokkukutsutud nõupidamisest tsiviilseaduste reformimise küsimuse selgitamiseks: 9. oktoobril 1927 a. kl. 11 Riigikogu hoones* [Stenographic record of a meeting, summoned by the ministery of Justice, to clear the questions of reforming the civil laws: 1927 October 9th, 11 o'clock in the building of the Parliament].

Rahvusarhiiv, ERA.76.2.333, *Kirjavahetus Eesti tsiviilseaduse eelnõu väljatöötamise ning sama komisjoni isikulise koosseisu küsimuses* [Correspondence on drafting the Civil Code and about the same commission's personnel], January 15, 1920 – March 3, 1921.

Rahvusarhiiv, ERA.76.2.334, *Kirjavahetus tsiviilseadustiku eelnõu väljatöötamiseks vastava komisjoni moodustamise, komisjoni koosseisu ja selle liikmetele tasumaksmise küsimuses* [Correspondence on forming a comission to draft a Civil Code, on the personnel of this commission and on the salary of the members of this commission], October 26, 1923 – March 11, 1927.

Rahvusarhiiv, ERA.76.2.347, *Tsiviilseaduste reformeerimise küsimuse selgitamise nõupidamise protokolli ärakiri* [Apograph of the stenographic record of the meeting to clear the question of reforming civil law], October 9, 1927.

Rahvusarhiiv, ERA.76.5.1, *Ministri päevakäsk ning kirjavahetus kodifikatsiooniosakonna liikme Igor Tjutrjumov'i määramise kohta tsiviilseaduse eelnõu väljatöötajaks koos abijõududega. 15.01.1920 kiri nr 97* [The Minister's directive of the day and correspondence with the member of the codification department Igor Tyutryumov on his appointment of drafter of the Civil Code draft act with additional help, January 15, 1920, letter no. 97].

### Literature

Toomas ANEPAIO: *Die rechtliche Entwicklung der baltischen Staaten 1918–1940 = Modernisierung durch Transfer zwischen den Weltkriegen*, Tomasz GIARO (ed.), Vitorio Klostermann, Frankfurt a.M., 2007, 7–30.

*Asutava Kogu protokollid, 11 istungjärk* [Records of the Constituent Assembly, 11 session] June 17 – December 20, 1919, records no. 28–97, Täht, Tallinn, 1920.

*Ausgesteuert – ausgegrenzt ... angeblich asozial*, Anne ALLEX, Dietrich KALKAN (eds.), AG SPAK Bücher, Neu-Ulm, 2009.

Martin AVENARIUS: *Fremde Traditionen des römischen Rechts. Einfluß, Wahrnehmung und Argument des „rimskoe pravo" im russischen Zarenreich des 19. Jahrhunderts*, Wallstein, Göttingen, 2014.

Wolfgang: Ayaß, *„Asoziale" im Nationalsozialismus*, Klett-Cotta, Stuttgart, 1995.

Wolfgang: Ayaß, *„Ein Gebot der nationalen Arbeitsdisziplin." Die Aktion „Arbeitsscheu Reich" 1938 = Beiträge zur nationalsozialistischen Gesundheits- und Sozialpolitik*, vol. 6: *Feinderklärung und Prävention. Kriminalbiologie, Zigeunerforschung und Asozialenpolitik*, Rotbuch Verlag, Berlin, 1988, 43–74.

Jörg Baberowski: *Autokratie und Justiz. Zum Verhältnis von Rechtsstaatlichkeit und Rückständigkeit im ausgehenden Zarenreich 1864–1914*, Vittorio Klostermann, Frankfurt a.M., 1996.

Jörg Baberowski: *Das Justizwesen im späten Zarenreich 1864–1914. Zum Problem von Rechtsstaatlichkeit, politischer Justiz und Rückständigkeit in Rußland*, Zeitschrift für neuere Rechtsgeschichte 1(1991), 156–172.

*Baltische Rechtsangleichung. 10 Jahre Gesetzgebung Estlands und Lettlands: Baltische Rechtsangleichung. Referate des I. Baltischen Juristenkonferenz zu Dorpat (1928)*, Wassermann, Reval, 1929.

Vladimir Bukovsky: *Сводъ гражданскихъ узаконений губерний прибалтийскихъ* [Code of Civil Laws of Baltic Governorates], Hempel & Co, Riga, 1914, vol. 2.

William Elliot Butler: *The Role of Case-Law in the Russian Legal System = Judicial Records, Law Reports and the Growth of Case Law*, J.H. Baker (ed.), Dunker & Humblot, Berlin 1989, 338–352.

Barbara Dölemeyer: *Das Privatrecht Liv-, Est- und Kurlands von 1864. = Handbuch der Quellen und Literatur der neueren europäischen Privatrechtsgeschichte*, Helmut Coing (ed.), Beck, München, 1982, vol. 3, Part 2, 2076–2090.

*Eesti Vabariigi Põhiseadus* [Constitution of the Republic of Estonia], Riigi Teataja [State Gazette, RT], 113/114(1920).

Ernst Ein: *Pärimisõigus Tsiviilseadustiku eelnõus* [Inheritance law in the draft of Civil Code], Õigus 4(1939), 177–188.

*„Gemeinschaftsfremde." Quellen zur Verfolgung von „Asozialen" 1933–1945*, Wolfgang Ayaß (ed.): *Materialien aus dem Bundesarchiv*, Bundesarchiv, Koblenz, 1998, vol. 5.

*Гражданское уложение: проект Высочайше учрежденной Редакционной комиссии по составлению Гражданского уложения с объяснениями, извлеченными из трудов Редакционной комиссии* [Civil Code: Draft of Project Committee for the Completing of Civil Code, confirmed by Zar, with Explanations from Works of Members of Project Committee], Igor Tyutryumov (ed.), [s.n.] St. Petersburg, 1910, reprint Wolters Kluwer Russia, Moskva, 2007, 2 vols.

Uno Ilm: *Tööpõlgurid Harkus* [Work-shy Persons in Harku], Politsei 5(1998), 10–11.

Elmar Ilus: *Talundi eelispärimisõigus* [Privileged succession of farmstead], Õigus 9–10(1936), 409–436.

Jüri Jaakson: *Ettekanne Õigusteadlaste päevadel* [Speech during the Estonian Lawyers Conference] (1922) = *Õigusteadlaste päevad 1922–1940. Protokollid* [Conferences of

Estonian Lawyers 1922–1940. Records], Jaanika ERNE (ed.), Juura, Tallinn, 2008, 25–38.

Andres KASEKAMP: *A History of the Baltic States,* Palgrave Macmillan, New York, 2010.

Samuel KUCHEROV: *Courts, lawyers and trials under the last three tsars*, Greenwood Press, New York, 1953 (re-print Westport 1974).

Peter LIESSEM: *Verwaltungsgerichtsbarkeit im späten Zarenreich: Der Dirigierende Senat und seine Entscheidungen zur russischen Selbstverwaltung (1864–1917),* Vittorio Klostermann, Frankfurt a.M., 1996.

Dietrich A. LOEBER: *Kontinuität im Zivilrecht nach Wiederherstellung staatlicher Unabhängigkeit – Zu den Zivilgesetzbüchern von Lettland (1937), Estland (1993) und Litauen (2000) = Aufbruch nach Europa: 75 Jahre Max-Planck-Institut für Privatrecht*, Jürgen BASEDOW et al. (eds.), Mohr Siebeck, Tübingen, 2001, 943–954.

Marju LUTS: *Modernisierung und deren Hemmnisse in den Ostseeprovinzen Est-, Liv- und Kurland im 19. Jahrhundert = Modernisierung durch Transfer zwischen den Weltkriegen,* Tomasz GIARO (ed.), Vittorio Klostermann, Frankfurt a.M., 159–200.

Marju LUTS: *Private Law of the Baltic Provinces as a Patriotic Act,* Juridica International 5(2000), 157–167.

Marju LUTS-SOOTAK: *Das Baltische Privatrecht von 1864/65 – Triumphbogen oder Grabmal für das römische Recht im Baltikum?,* Zeitschrift für Ostmitteleuropa-Forschung 58(2009), 357–379.

Marju LUTS-SOOTAK: *Die baltischen Privatrechte in den Händen der russischen Reichsjustiz = Rechtsprechung in Osteuropa. Studien zum 19. und frühen 20. Jahrhundert,* Zoran POKROVAC (ed.), Vittorio Klostermann, Frankfurt a.M., 2012, 296–370.

Marju LUTS-SOOTAK: *Pre-modern divided ownership in the modern legal history of Estonia = Legal pluralism – cui bono?,* Marju LUTS-SOOTAK, Irene KULL, Karin SEIN, Hesi SIIMETS-GROSS (eds.), Tartu University Press, Tartu, 2018, 94–113.

Marju LUTS-SOOTAK, Hesi SIIMETS-GROSS, Katrin KIIREND-PRUULI: *Estlands Zivilrechtskodifikation – ein fast geborenes Kind des Konservatismus = „Nichtgeborene Kinder der Liberalismus"? Zivilgesetzgebung im Mitteleuropa der Zwischenkriegszeit,* Martin LÖHNIG, Stephan WAGNER (eds.), Mohr Siebeck, Tübingen, 2018, 273–316.

Elo LUTSEPP: *Asunduspoliitikast Eesti Vabariigis: Asundusameti tegevus 1929–1941* [The policy of settlement in the Republic of Estonia: the activities of the Settlement Committee in 1929–1941], Ajalooline Ajakiri/The Estonian Historical Journal 3–4/ (2007), 443–460.

Aniceto MASFERRER: *Codification as nationalisation or denationalisation of law: the Spanish case in comparative perspective,* Comparative Legal History 2(2016), 100–130.

Andrejs PLAKANS: *The Latvians. A Short History*, Hoover Institution Press, Stanford, 1995.

*Provincialrecht der Ostseegouvernements. Dritter Theil. Privatrecht. Liv-, Est- und Curlaendisches Privatrecht*, Buchdruckerei der Zweiten Abtheilung Seiner Kaiserlichen Majestät Eigener Kanzlei, St. Petersburg, 1864.

Raimo PULLAT: *Estnische Juristen in St. Petersburg bis 1917 = Buch und Bildung im Baltikum: Festschrift für Paul Kaegbein zum 80. Geburtstag*, Heinrich BOSSE, Otto-Heinrich ELIAS, Robert SCHWEITZER (eds.), LIT, Münster, 2005, 555–579.

Toivo U. RAUN: *Estonia and the Estonians*, 2nd ed., Hoover Institution Press, Stanford, 2001.

*Rechtsangleichung der Baltischen Staaten Lettland-Estland*, Rigasche Zeitschrift für Rechtswissenschaft, 2(1927/28)/4, 286–288.

*Reichserbhofgesetz vom 29. September 1933*, Reichsgesetzblatt, 1(1933) 685.

*Riigivolikogu stenograafiliste aruannete lisad* [Appendixes to the stenographic reports of the Chamber of Deputies]. I composition, V and VI sessions 1939/1940, Riigi Trükikoda, Tallinn, 1939.

Joachim RÜCKERT: *Das „gesunde Volksempfinden" – eine Erbschaft Savignys?* Zeitschrift der Savigny-Stiftung für Rechtsgeschichte, Germanistische Abteilung, 103(1986), 199–246.

*Seisuste kaotamise seadus* [Law for Abolishing Estates], Riigi Teataja [State Gazette] 129–130(1920), 254.

*Сборник решений Гражданского и общего собрания 1-го и Кассационного департаментов бывшего Правительствующего сената, разъясняющих законоположения, действующие в западной Латвии и в Эстонии* [Collection of the Decisions of Civil Cassation Department and General Panel and the 1st Cassation Department of the former Governing Senate, explaining the rules applicable in Western Latvia and in Estonia], L. KANTOR (ed.), Jurist, Riga 1932.

Wilm SCHARLEMANN: *Privatrechtsentwicklung im Baltikum zwischen nationaler Souveränität, regionaler Kooperation und europäischer Integration = Europa und seine Regionen. 2000 Jahre Rechtsgeschichte*, Andreas BAUER, Karl H.L. WELKER (eds.), Böhlau, Köln et al., 2007, 657–680.

Philipp SCHWARTZ: *Lettland: Das Lettländische Zivilgesetzbuch vom 28. Januar 1937 = „Nichtgeborene Kinder der Liberalismus"? Zivilgesetzgebung im Mitteleuropa der Zwischenkriegszeit*, Martin LÖHNIG, Stephan WAGNER (eds.), Mohr Siebeck, Tübingen, 2018, 317–358.

Philipp SCHWARTZ: *Das Lettländische Zivilgesetzbuch vom 28. Januar 1937 und seine Entstehungsgeschichte*, Shaker Verlag, Aachen, 2008.

Hesi SIIMETS-GROSS: *Das Liv-, Est- und Curlaendische Privatrecht (1864/65) und das römische Recht im Baltikum*, Tartu University Press, Tartu, 2011.

Hesi SIIMETS-GROSS: *Das Liv-, Esth- und Curlaendisches Privatrecht (1864/1865) – die einzige Quelle des Privatrechts? = Einheit und Vielfalt in der Rechtschichte im Ostseeraum. Sechster Rechtshistorikertag im Ostseeraum, 3.–5. Juni 2010 Tartu (Estland)/*

ESTONIA AND LATVIA BETWEEN TWO WORLD WARS 309

*Riga (Lettland)*, Marju LUTS-SOOTAK, Sanita OSIPOVA, Frank L. SCHÄFER (eds.), Lang, Frankfurt a.M., 2012, 275–285.

Hesi SIIMETS-GROSS, Marelle LEPPIK: *Estonia: First Landmarks of Fundamental Rights* = *First Fundamental Rights Documents in Europe*, Markku SUKSI, Kalliope AGAPIOU-JOSEPHIDES, Jean-Paul LEHNERS, Manfred NOWAK (eds.), Intersentia, Cambridge-Antwerp-Portland, 2015, 295–308.

*Temporary Administrative Laws of Interim Government*, Riigi Teataja [State Gazette] 1918, 1.

*The Constitution of the Esthonian Republic (Passed by the Constituent Assembly on the 15th of June 1920)*, Ühiselu, Tallinn, 1924.

*Thibaut und Savigny. Ihre programmatischen Schriften*, Hans HATTENAUER (ed.), Vahlen, München, 1973; 2nd. ed. 2002.

Anton Justus Friedrich THIBAUT: *Ueber die Nothwendigkeit eines allgemeinen bürgerlichen Rechts für Deutschland*, Zimmer, Heidelberg, 1814.

*Tööpõlgurite töölaagrite seadus* [Statute of Camps for work-shy persons], Riigi Teataja [State Gazette] 1938, 62, 614.

*Tsiviilseadustiku 1936. aasta eelnõu*, [Civil Code draft act of 1936], [s. n.], Tallinn, 1936.

*Tsiwiil seadustik: pärandusõigus: eelkawa* [Civil Code: Inheritance Law: Draft], Tallinna Eesti Kirjastus-Ühisus, Tallinn, 1925.

*Tsiviilseadustik. Üldosa ja perekonnaõigus: eelkava* [Civil Code. General Part and Family Law: Draft], Tallinna Eesti Kirjastus-Ühtsus, Tallinn, 1926.

Jüri ULUOTS: *Seletuskiri Tsiviilseadustiku 1935. a. eelnõu nelja esimese raamatu juurde* [Explanatory Memorandum to the First Four Books of the Civil Law Code of 1935], [s. n.] Tartu, 1936.

Jüri ULUOTS: *Talundite pärimine* [The succession of farmsteads], Õigus 7(1939), 322–327.

*Vidzemes ur Kurzemes Privāttiesību likumu grāmata* [Private Law Act of Livland and Courland], Zimmermann, Liepaja, 1885.

*Vietējo Civillikumu kopojums* [A collection of local civil laws], Valtera un Rapas, Riga, 1928.

VON SAVIGNY, Friedrich Carl: *System des heutigen römischen Rechts*, vol. 1, Veit, Berlin 1840.

VON SAVIGNY, Friedrich Carl: *Vom Beruf unsrer Zeit für Gesetzgebung und Rechtswissenschaft*, Mohr und Zimmer, Heidelberg, 1814.

William W. WAGNER: *The Civil Cassation Department of the Senate as an Instrument of Progressive Reform in Post-Emancipation Russia: The Case of Property and Inheritance Law*, Slavic Review, 42(1983), 36–59.

Jürgen WEITZEL: *Sonderprivatrecht aus konkretem Ordnungsdenken: Reichserbhofrecht und allgemeines Privatrecht 1933–1945*, Zeitschrift für Neuere Rechtsgeschichte, 14(1992), 55–79.

*Законы гражданские (Свод зак. Т. X, ч. 1, изд. 1900 г. по Прод. 1906 и 1908 гг.) с разъясн ениями Правительствующего Сената (Гражд. Кассац., 1 и 2 Департаментов, Первого Общего Собр. и Общ. Собр. 1, 2 и Кассац. Департ. по 1 сентября 1910 г.) и комментариями русских юристов, извлеченными из научных и практических трудов по гражданскому праву и судопроизводству (по 1 июля 1910 г.)* [Civil Laws (Collection of Laws, vol. 10, Part 1, ed. 1900 according to the installments of 1906 and 1908) with Explanations of the Governing Senate (Civil Cassation Department, 1st and 2nd Department, First General Panel and General Panel of 1st and 2nd Cassation Department until 1910 September 1st) and Commentaries of Russian Jurists from Scholarly and Practical Works about the Civil Law and Procedure (until 1910 July 1st)], Igor TYUTRYUMOV (ed.), 3. ed., Zakonovedenye, St.Petersburg, 1911; reprint Statut, Moskva, 2004.

CHAPTER 13

# Reluctant Legal Transplant: United States Moral Rights as Late 20th Century Honor Law

*Steven Wilf*

## 1 Introduction

Moral rights might be considered an accidental doctrine in United States intellectual property law. Enacted in 1990, the United States Visual Artists Rights Act (VARA) was intended to provide artists with the moral rights of attribution and integrity.[1] VARA granted creators the right to determine the fate of their art works even after their sale to others – to ensure that their names would remain identified with their artwork and that these works might be neither altered nor destroyed by others. The idea of moral rights (*droit moral*) originated in nineteenth-century France and stood in sharp contrast to existing common law property principles of free alienability and absolute dominion. Purchasers traditionally might dispose of owned intellectual property without any of the impediments imposed by VARA. Nevertheless, Congress passed VARA as a condition of the United States becoming a signatory of the Berne Convention for the Protection of Literary and Artistic Works, the preeminent treaty governing copyright across the globe, after nearly a century of remaining aloof.[2] Berne Convention accession required the United States to adapt its moral rights provision, Article 6*bis*. This provision required member states to protect moral rights – including attribution and integrity – in addition to intellectual property economic rights.

VARA appears at a superficial examination to be a classic importation of civil law norms into a common law framework. But did legislating VARA truly constitute a transplant of continental European legal principles into United States intellectual property law? How are legal transplants – much like their medical analogues – incorporated by a jurisdiction's *corpus juris* over time?

---

1  Visual Artists Rights Act (VARA) of 1990, Public Law 101–650, *The United States Status at Large*, 5128–5129, 104 (codified at *Code of Laws of the United States of America*, Title 17 [U.S.C. 17], 106A).

2  Roberta KWALL: *The Soul of Creativity: Forging A Moral Right Law For The United States*, Stanford University Press, Stanford, 2009, 23–31.

And what might such histories tell us about the dangers, complexities, and possibilities inherent in adopting legal norms from other systems in our ever more global legal landscape? These issues were hardly raised when VARA entered into United States law for pragmatic reasons as a prerequisite to the United States joining the Berne Convention. This essay is a retrospective attempt over twenty-five years later to deploy the optic of legal historians to evaluate one of the earliest and most notable adoptions of foreign legal principles into United States intellectual property law.

It is possible to view VARA as a watershed moment, a coming of age of United States law as it reached beyond its borders to adapt a transnational norm. VARA might be seen as the harbinger a much broader harmonisation of global intellectual property, and perhaps even a signal beginning to bridging the chasm between common law and civil law systems in general. Yet for both promoters and detractors VARA has proved enigmatic.[3] This essay seeks to scrutinize VARA's historical course as a legal transplant a quarter of a century after its implementation. It identifies VARA as a reluctant legal transplant. Characterizing VARA as fraught – I could equally have used other adjectives such as partial, impaired, or even compromised – suggests how legal transplantation takes place at a variety of levels: jurisprudential, statutory, judicial, and the social historical incorporation of VARA into the strategies of artists themselves. Ex post justifications by supporters have been diffuse and often unconvincing. Proposing multiple reasons – such as safeguarding creator dignity, seeing the artist as subject to emotional injury if his or her work would be damaged, identifying the artist as a fiduciary protecting the art work itself for posterity, and placing VARA in a human rights skein – suggests the lack of agreement upon the law's philosophical grounding.[4] More importantly, Congress was skeptical

---

3  David E. SHIPLEY: *The Empty Promise of VARA: The Restrictive Application of a Narrow Statute*, Mississippi Law Journal 83(2014), 985–1048 (underscores the minimal difference VARA has made in protecting artists), Sonya G. BONNEAU: *Honor and Destruction: The Conflicted Object in Moral Rights Law*, St. John's Law Review 87(2013), 47–105 (argues VARA is directed towards the art object rather than extending moral rights to artists), Xiyan TANG: *The Artist as Brand: Towards a Trademark Conception of Moral Rights*, Yale Law Journal 122(2012), 218–257 (VARA protections inadequate in the face of mass commodisation of modern art), Nathan M. DAVIS: *As Good as New: Conserving Artwork and the Destruction of Moral Rights*, Cardozo Arts & Enterteinment Law Journal 215(2011), 29–65 (application of VARA is inconsistent and unpredictable), Amy ADLER: *Against Moral Rights,* California Law Review 97(2009), 263–299 (VARA is antithetical to the development of modern art forms calls for abolition of moral rights).

4  Ilhyung LEE: *Toward an American Moral Rights in Copyright*, Washington & Lee Law Review 58 (2001), 795–854 (viewing for moral rights as dignity rights), DAVIS: *op. cit.* (underscoring the tension between the artist stake in preservation and the public's), KWALL: *op. cit.*, 133–146 (relating artistic authorship to human rights). Although France was progenitor of artist

UNITED STATES MORAL RIGHTS AS LATE 20TH CENTURY HONOR LAW 313

of importing *droit moral*. VARA therefore cabined the appropriation of moral rights in a variety of ways. Its circumscribed scope narrowed subject matter even within the ambit of the slender category of visual works of art, truncated moral rights to only attribution and integrity, vested rights solely in living creators (a term more restricted than its continental European counterparts), and, most controversially, permitted artists to waive their VARA rights.[5] Indeed, a significant number of critics view the United States minimal compliance approach to moral rights as meaning that the United States is truly non-compliant with Berne Convention 6*bis*.[6] Jane Ginsburg has called the United States compliance with 6*bis* a mere "fig leaf."[7]

Courts further narrowed VARA. During the last quarter of a century, courts dismissed the concept of site specific art and denied VARA protection to works failing to show recognized stature. Judges have treated VARA as a disfavored legal doctrine, and, not surprisingly, artists have lost a significant number of law cases brought. While not directly addressing VARA, two United States Supreme Court cases *Dastar* and *Reid* underscore the adverse response of courts to moral rights restricting the economic rights of property owners. Even artists themselves have shown little enthusiasm for VARA. Survey evidence

---

moral rights in Europe, and claimed that such rights were intrinsic, natural rights possessed by creators, it was German law, not French law that seems to have determined VARA's particular concern with dignitary law. France extends moral rights in perpetuity. In Germany, the duration of rights is circumscribed much in the same fashion as economic copyright rights, and is limited to a term of the life of the creator plus seventy years. Similarly, VARA – even more circumscribed – limits conferred rights to the life of the creator. Such limitations suggest a concern with reputation when the dignity of the artist might be personally effected by the emotional injury caused by destruction of a work.

5  Compare the willingness 5 (2011) of Congress to accept Congressional enactment of lengthier copyright terms even if extending the duration of copyright raises constitutional issues since it requires allowing private parties to protect works that already have entered the public domain. Cf. *Eldred v. Ashcroft*, U.S. 537 (2003), 186 (recognizing Congressional power to extend retrospectively the copyright term) and *Golan* v. *Holder*, U.S. 565 (2012) (recognizing restoration of copyright for works situated in the public domain).

6  Adrian ZUCKERMAN, Annemarie SEDORFE: *Do US Property Concepts Prevent VARA From Implementing the Berne Convention?*, Dublin University Law Journal 26(2004), 172–199 (evaluating VARA's compliance with the Berne Convention).

7  Jane GINSBURG: *The Right to Claim Authorship in U.S. Copyright and Trademarks Law*, Houston Law Review, 41(2004), 263–307. Another prominent copyright scholar, David Nimmer, has called the United States moral rights regime, "a stretch" to claim compliance with the Berne Convention's 6*bis* provision. David NIMMER: *The Moral Imperative against Academic Plagiarism (without a moral right against passing off)*, DePaul Law Review 54(2004), 1–22. The official position of the United States is that a "composite of laws" provide "the kind of protection envisioned by Article 6*bis*." *Senate Report* 100–352 (1988).

suggests that asymmetrical bargaining positions and an uncertain, conflicted relationship to the commercialisation of art has left artists with an ambiguous relationship to VARA rights.

This essay examines the various ways that VARA became a fraught legal transplant. In our increasingly global jurisprudence, legal transplantation has become a commonplace. However, as in the case of VARA the appropriation of non-indigenous legal norms might take place differently at various levels – legislature, court, and social fabrication. A transplant could be met with a peculiar mix of valorisation and resistance, and appropriation of new legal doctrine occurs over an extended period of time. In some ways, all three approaches are true for VARA.

Part 1 of this essay, Uncertain Genealogies, addresses the problem VARA faced as a foreign transplant into American intellectual property law. Linking VARA and moral rights to membership in the Berne international system of copyright underscored its troubling lineage. It *was* alien to common law jurisprudence. Congress imposed a series of restrictions that made VARA neither an exemplar of continental European *droit moral* nor an ordinary inhabitant of America's common law jurisprudence. Courts, moreover, established an unfriendly copyright ecosystem surrounding VARA. In Part 2, I interrogate the core concept from Berne Article 6*bis* that VARA is a dignity law. Yet the linking of honor to the artistic work itself created dilemmas. The granting of reputational safeguards in a flexible fashion produced uneven, often discretionary decisions about the status of an artist. It juxtaposed intangible *Dignitas* to cognizable economic costs. VARA conceived of an honor law that did not flow from the artist's status – but is imposed by law. And the very notion of waiving moral rights suggests that these rights are not inherent or natural rights.

Cabined by Congress, circumscribed by courts, remaining outside the fold of popular common law intuitions that owners should be able to freely dispose of their property, and ignored by the very artists it sought protect, VARA appears to be not simply a fraught transplant – but a marginal one as well. Yet VARA might not be as unrooted a parvenu legalism as the statute first appears. Ironically, the notion of moral rights has slowly seeped into the fabric of United States intellectual property law. This essay will conclude with one such example – a surprising surfacing of VARA rights in circumstances far afield from the statutory scope of VARA itself. The checkered history of VARA provides all sorts of lessons about the historical permeability of legal systems such as common and civil law. Legal transplants, I suggest in my conclusion, might prove remarkably durable if one examines them over time.

## 2 Uncertain Genealogies

Traditional narratives of the genealogy of moral rights commonly trace a seamless arc from continental Europe to the United States. The French invented *droit moral* – much as they have the Rights of Man or Impressionism – and an increasingly global United States incorporated these rights within its own copyright framework as VARA. Yet legal transplants are seldom so uncomplicated. Congress did not adopt the entirety of moral rights for artists as conceived within continental jurisprudence. Courts found ways to compartmentalize moral rights and reduce their impact on economic rights. Most significantly, an undercurrent of reaction to moral rights in a variety of forms of discourse from law reviews to judicial dicta identified distinctions between European moral rights norms and United States intellectual property norms. As a fraught transplant, of course, VARA's enactment could hardly have been straightforward. A more accurate genealogy must step beyond mere incorporation into the federal statutory code, and interrogate ambivalence, antipathy, silo strategies, critiques, and the reassertion of how United States intellectual property jurisprudence might diverge from the cultural matrix of European moral rights.

### 2.A    *European Beginnings*

If VARA was a reluctant transplant, this was in part due to the legal archipelagoes of intellectual property remaining separate for such a very long stretch of time. Intellectual property law was traditionally territorial law.[8] The earliest modern copyright and patent statutes, which were enacted in Britain (the Statute of Anne, 1710 for copyright and the Statute of Monopolies, 1624 for patent) were designed to benefit citizens. In the United States, the Copyright Act of 1790 and its progeny were specifically intended to provide royalties only to citizen authors. The goal was to produce a national literature in English and to disseminate knowledge to an informed citizenry. Perhaps favoring the latter goal, the United States was still largely a copyright pirate nation until the very end of the nineteenth century, reprinting works of British authors without the payment of royalties.[9] The controversy over international protection for copyright was particularly intense in America, and the passage of the Chase Act of

---

8    Steven WILF: *Intellectual Property = A Companion to American Legal History*, Sally E. HADDEN, Alfred L. BROPHY (eds.), Wiley-Blackwell, Oxford, 2013, 441–459.

9    Steven WILF: *Copyright and Social Movements in Late-Nineteenth Century America*, Theoretical Inquiries in Law 12(2011), 123–160.

1891, which provided for limited rights to foreign authors, was passed with difficulty over significant opposition.[10]

It was America's commitment to copyright piracy – more than any uneasiness with continental European copyright doctrines – that made the United States reluctant to join the growing movement to establish international copyright norms. Yet the rise of the industrial book and cross-border exchange of manufacturing technologies after the Industrial Revolution led to increasing concern with the protection of knowledge across national borders. French theories of creator rights as natural rights provided the grounding for internationalizing intellectual property. Emerging from Enlightenment conceptions of natural rights, the idea of inherent rights dovetailed neatly with the valorisation of creators in the age of the romantic author. Victor Hugo and his organisation promoting international protection of author rights, *Association Littéraire et Artistique*, fostered French ideas of author's rights (*droit d'auteur*).

The *Association Littéraire et Artistique* formed the basis of the Berne Convention. Founded on September 9, 1886, the Berne Convention included France, Britain, Germany, Spain, and Italy as well as a handful of nations outside of Europe. Berne already had to bridge the philosophical difference between French conceptions of authorial rights as the natural right of a creator and utilitarian Anglo-Saxon legal notions of copyright as a utilitarian means of promoting the making of useful knowledge.[11] Prior to the Chase Act of 1891, of course, the United States was unwilling to grant copyright rights to noncitizens. But even after the statute's passage, America stood aloof from the Berne Convention. It sought to construct a Pan-American copyright system, uniting countries in the New World, in a system closer to that of United States copyright. The United States stood aloof from the Berne Convention on the basis of the changes that would be required in shifting from a registration and notice system of copyright formalities to one where copyright protection is granted simply when the expression is fixed. This substantial disagreement about basic requirements for copyright, of course, reflected the philosophical difference in United States economic rights granted by the state upon registration and the natural rights of creators in their creations. Moreover, in the matter of moral rights, the Inter-American Convention on the Rights of the Author

---

10   *International Copyright Act of 1891*, Ch. 565, *The United States Status at Large* n. 1106, 26.

11   Jane GINSBURG: *A Tale of Two Copyrights: Literary Property in Revolutionary France and America*, Tulane Law Review 64(1990), 993–996, Justin HUGHES: *The Philosophy of Intellectual Property*, Georgia Law Journal 77(1988), 287–304; Carla HESSE: *Enlightenment Epistemology and the Law of Authorship in Revolutionary France 1777–1793*, Representations 30(1990), 109–137.

UNITED STATES MORAL RIGHTS AS LATE 20TH CENTURY HONOR LAW          317

in Literary, Scientific, and Artistic Works (1946) promoted by the United States, sought to provide a truncated form of moral rights. It afforded suit for damages if the paternity of a work was altered, but pointedly rejected Berne Article 6*bis* language protecting against modifications prejudicial to the "honor or reputation of the author."[12]

French copyright theory presumed that moral rights and economic rights were protected by distinct regimes.[13] The imposition of moral rights as a requirement of the Berne Convention was introduced in the Rome Conference of 1928, which took place in Mussolini's Italy. According to Peter Baldwin, moral rights in the form of the Berne Convention's article 6*bis*, was based on a showcase Italian fascist model enacted in 1925. The Italian act protected rights of attribution, integrity, honor and reputation, and included a right of withdraw. Heirs could be designated as recipients of rights.[14] Moral rights, at least in this incarnation, were closely linked to fascist concerns with mass consumer culture. Authors and artists with appropriate themes were seen as the bulwark of a national culture against international and modernist forms. Moral rights stood against the demands of market economics.[15] However, even though the Berne convention included after the 1928 Rome Conference moral rights for creators, it determined in 6*bis* to leave implementation to signatory states.[16]

Indeed, this may have reflected – and brought about – the significant variation in the national treatment of moral rights. Moral rights in France are applied to a broad range of the arts, and are perpetual, inalienable (cannot be waived), and imprescriptible.[17] They may be transmitted *mortis causa* to the creator's heirs.[18] And they are protected even if the work itself falls into the public domain.[19] In Italy, the government, and not simply the artist, might

---

12    The Inter-American Convention on the Rights of the Author in Literary, Scientific, and Artistic Works (1946), Article 11. *The Inter-American Copyright Convention: Its Place in United States Copyright Law*, Harvard Law Review 60(1947), 1336, note 53.

13    French moral rights are protected through a distinct part of the statutory code, *Code de la propriété intellectuelle*, art. L 121-1-2.

14    Peter BALDWIN: *The Copyright Wars: Three Centuries Of Transatlantic Battle*, Princeton University Press, Princeton, 2014.

15    6*bis* begins by stating that moral rights operate "independently of the author's economic rights, and even after the transfer of the said rights," *Berne* Convention for the Protection of Literary and Artistic Works, art. 6*bis*, Sept. 9, 1886, League of Nations Treaty Series n. 123, 233 [hereinafter Rome Revision] (as revised in Rome on June 2, 1928).

16    *Ibid.*

17    Code de la propriété in intellectuelle, art. L121-1.

18    *Ibid.*

19    *Pierro Hugo v. Société Plon*, Cour de cassation – Première chambre civile, Arrêt n° 125 du 30 janvier 2007 (04-15.543).

litigate to enforce moral rights.[20] Almost every other jurisdiction that has adopted moral rights in intellectual property has a broader definition of those rights than the United States. Other countries do have mechanisms for balancing moral and competing economic rights – and the rights of artists as opposed to the rights of the public. The Netherlands, for example, requires reasonable execution of these rights.[21] If the United States had joined the Berne Convention in the late nineteenth century, it might have developed its own approach to moral rights. But the United States had remained detached from the broader international copyright movement with its commitment to moral rights. In part this was due the continuing copyright piracy through until the 1890s, in part to its insistence in constructing an alternative Pan-American system, and in part due to the obstacles of the United States joining Berne in the midst of two World Wars, a growing isolationist movement by the 1920s, and the disconcerting global milieu torn between fascism and communism. But, whatever the reasons, by the time the United States became a Berne signatory in the late 1980s, a more complex jurisprudence of moral rights had emerged that seemed particularly outlandish to those accustomed to common law copyright.

### 2.B    *Congressional Reluctance*
Ironically, moral rights – which often stand as a counterpoint to economic rights – were adopted by America for purely economic and pragmatic reasons. During the late twentieth century, slumping exports in various industrial sectors led the United States to seek membership in the Berne Convention. Founded in 1886, the Berne Convention for the Protection of Literary and Artistic Works is the largest and oldest international agreement covering copyright, and includes a mandatory moral rights provision.[22] VARA entered into law two years after the United States in 1988 became a participant in the Berne Convention around a hundred years after the organisation was founded.[23] In

---

20    Protezione del diritto d'autore e di altri diritti connessi al suo esercizio, Legge 22 aprile 1941, n. 633, art. 23 Gazzetta Ufficiale della Repubblica Italiana, n. 163, R. KWALL: *op. cit.*, *supra* note 1 at 47.

21    Wet van 23 september 1912, houdende nieuwe regeling van het auteursrecht, Staatsblad 2015, art. 25 (a)-(d).

22    Berne Convention for the Protection of Literary and Artistic Works, art. 6*bis* (1), Sept. 9, 1886, *as revised* July 24, 1971, *and as amended* Sept. 28, 1979, which mandates, in relevant part: "Independently of the author's economic rights, and even after the transfer of the said rights, the author shall have the right to claim authorship of the work and to object to any distortion, mutilation, or other modification of, or other derogatory action in relation to, the said work, which would be prejudicial to his honor or reputation."

23    Berne Convention Implementation Act of 1988, Public Law 100–568, 102 *The United States Status at Large*, 2853, 102.

order to become a signatory of Berne, the United States had to shift from a registration system to one which provides copyright for a work without formalities simply by having it fixed in a tangible medium of expression, and to provide moral rights to creators.

The publishing and entertainment industries vehemently opposed the adoption of moral rights on the eve of the United States ascension to Berne.[24] Nevertheless, much of this discussion occurred as lobbying and there was little public debate. According to Roberta Kwall, a number of Republican senators were reluctant to pass VARA. On the last day of the 101st Congress in 1990, however, VARA was enacted as part of a deal that permitted eighty-five new federal judgeships.[25] Congressional disinclination towards VARA has been a core feature of the statute's existence. Beyond the legislative narrowing of moral rights that will be discussed below, it is telling that in the last few decades when the United States has promoted bilateral and multilateral trade agreements as a mechanism to enforce international intellectual property rights it has included moral rights in none of these treaties. Moral rights were not included in the Trade-Related Aspects of Intellectual Property Rights Agreement (TRIPS) of 1994, in the ill-fated Anti-Counterfeiting Trade Agreement (ACTA), nor in the proposed Trans-Pacific Partnership (TPP) agreement.

VARA has been narrowed in almost every fashion. Unlike in many European countries, it does not apply to deceased artists.[26] The recognized stature requirement, which will be discussed below, excludes the protection of graffiti art, tattoos, and various forms of street art.[27] Limited to certain forms of high art works, but also fails to provide coverage for found art (*objet trouvé*), applied art – which decorates everyday objects to render them aesthetically pleasing,[28]

---

24   KWALL: *op. cit.*, 28.

25   *Ibid.*

26   Seth TIPTON: *Connoisseurship Corrected: Protecting the Artist, the Public and the Role of Art Museums through the Amendment of VARA*, Rutgers Law Review 62(2009), 269–303 (extending rights to deceased artists would prevent misattribution).

27   John BICKNELL: *Is Graffiti Worthy of Protection? Changes within the Recognized Stature Requirement of the Visual Artists Rights Act*, Tulane Journal of Technology & Intellectual Property 17(2014), 337–352, *Cohen v. G & M Reality L.P.*, F. Supp. 2d 212 (E.D.N.Y. 2013), 988 (finding wall with graffiti as transitory and therefore precluding injunctive relief to prevent its slated demolition), Christine LESICKO: *Tattoos as Visual Art: How Art Fits in the Visual Artists Rights Act*, *IDEA* – The Intelectual Property Law Review 53(2013), 39–62 (VARA should apply to tattoos in a certain number of cases), Griffin M. BARNETT: *Recognized Stature: Protecting Street Art as Cultural Property*, Chicago-Kent Journal of Intellectual Property 12(2013), 204–216 (calling for amending VARA to include street art). *Reece v. Marc Ecko Unltd*, 2011 WL 4112071, (S.D.N.Y. 2011), (finding graffiti art unprotectable under VARA).

28   *Cheffins v. Stewart 2011*, F. 3d 825 (2016), 588, (determining that a replica of a 16th century Spanish galleon to school bus was applied art outside of VARA's ambit).

generative art based upon algorithms, visual art including films,[29] living art,[30] conceptual art,[31] unfinished works,[32] textile artists,[33] and digital works.[34] The definition of a work of visual art under VARA is dependent upon a statutory definition more broadly applicable in the 1976 Copyright Act, and includes "a painting, drawing, print, or sculpture" or a still photograph, either as a single copy or in a limited edition of copies.[35] It specifically excludes any "poster, map, globe, chart, technical drawing, diagram, model, applied art, motion picture or any other audiovisual work, book, magazine, newspaper periodical, database, electronic information service, electronic or similar publication." Advertising and promotional materials are also excluded from VARA protection.[36] Photographic images might be protected – but only if they are produced for exhibition purposes, and signed and number by the photographer in a limited edition of less than two hundred copies. Such a list suggests that Congress hewed to a definition of Mandarin art that is remarkably old-fashioned. Art is not functional. Art is not ephemeral. Art is displayed through the deployment of traditional materials such as ink and paper.

## 3    Creating the Jurisprudential Ecosystem

United States copyright law has traditionally been identified as utilitarian.[37] It provides economic incentives for the creation and dissemination of expression.

---

29    *Garcia v. Google*, F.3d 1258 (2014) (absence of moral rights in films).

30    *Kelley v. Chicago Park District*, F. 3d 290 (7th Cir. 2011, 635) (holding that an artist's wildflower garden lacked authorship and stable fixation to fall within the scope of VARA).

31    Charles CRONIN: *Dead on the Vine: Living and Conceptual Art and VARA*, Vanderbilt Journal of Entertainment and Technology Law, 12(2010), 209–243, *Kleinman v. City of San Marcos*, 597 F. 3d 323 (5th Cir. 2010) (finding a colorfully painted junked automobile reconfigured as a cactus planter unworthy of VARA protection).

32    *Massachusetts Museum of Contemporary Art v. Buchel*, F.3d 38 (1st Cir. 2010, 593) (VARA is inapplicable to unfinished works).

33    Michelle MORAN: *Quilt Artists: Left Out in the Cold by the Visual Artists Rights Act of* 1990, Marquette Intellectual Property Law Review 14(2010), 393–409 (textile artists disfavored by judicial interpretation of VARA).

34    SHIPLEY: *op. cit.*, 985–1048 (applying narrow definitions denies reasonable moral rights claims even for visual artists), Llewellyn Joseph GIBBONS: *Visual Artists Rights Act (VARA) and the Protection of Digital Works of Photographic Art*, North Carolina Journal of Law and Technology 11(2010), 531–553 (VARA would need to be amended to include digital works in its scope). *Teter v. Glass Onion, Inc.*, F. Supp. 2d 1138 (W.D. Mo. 2010, 723) (digital images of art are not entitled to VARA protection).

35    U.S.C. 17 (1994), § 101.

36    *Ibid.*

37    Robert MERGES: *Justifying Intellectual Property*, Harvard University Press, Cambridge (MA), 2011, 2–4.

The 1976 Copyright Act grants creators exclusive rights to reproduce, distribute, and create derivative works such as sequels or treatment in other media (a novel made into a film). Affording such rights to authors and artists was intended to establish pecuniary rewards that would provide economic security for authors and their dependents. Certain provisions of the 1976 Copyright Act, notably compulsory licenses and the fair use affirmative defense which permits users the adverse use of copyrighted material under certain circumstances, expressly *limit* the rights of authors and artists. United States copyright law is not only interested in creating expression, but also disseminating this expression broadly to readers and audiences.

By extending artist control over their works even after sale, VARA seemed intuitively at odds with the goal of dissemination. Through a steady stream of cases courts have sought to hone what was an often ambiguous statute. These decisions have focused on defining rights to attribution and integrity as set out by Congress. Yet VARA has operated in a copyright law ecosystem that had addressed artist rights outside of visual works of art that lay specifically within the ambit of VARA. Two major Supreme Court cases, *Dastar v. Twentieth-Century Fox* (2003) and *Community for Creative Non-Violence v. Reid* (1989) have contributed to VARA's identity as a disfavored doctrine.[38]

In *Dastar* the issue was the persistence of a right of attribution after a work had entered into the public domain. The exclusive rights to Dwight D. Eisenhower's first-person book on World War II, *Crusade in Europe* (1948) were purchased by Twentieth-Century Fox studios to create a twenty-six episode television series by the same name. Although Doubleday renewed the copyright on Eisenhower's book, Fox failed to renew the copyright on the video version and it entered the public domain in 1977. In 1988, Fox reacquired television rights to the book. Dastar in 1995 purchased the tangible videotapes to the original Fox series, and edited these to about half the length. It broadcast these as *World War II Campaigns in Europe* identifying Dastar as the producer. No credit was given to Fox. As audiovisual works, Fox could not sue for the deprivation of moral rights under VARA. Instead, Fox claimed that the lack of attribution was reverse passing off in violation of trademark law under the Lanham Act by creating confusion as to the source of goods. The Supreme Court, however, decided that no right of attribution exists for once copyrighted material that now passes into the public domain. What is important about this case is not its effect on VARA itself since this was not a case brought under VARA. Instead, its salience lies in the dicta hostile to moral rights in

---

38    *Dastar Corp. v. Twentieth Century Fox Film Corp.,* U.S. 23 (2003), *Community for Creative Non-Violence v. Reid,* U.S. 490 (1989), 730.

322          WILF

general. Justice Antonin Scalia held that the absence of moral rights language as used in VARA suggests that Congress had no intention of establishing moral rights in uncopyrighted material. Moral rights are purely positive law.[39] Moreover, Justice Antonin Scalia points out, attribution might be a two-edged sword. If Fox was identified with a truncated, perhaps even mutilated version of its original television production it might have a negative impact on its reputation.[40]

If *Dastar* simply provided an oblique critique of moral rights in VARA – its dicta underscoring the claim that moral rights are not natural rights and Congress sought to limit *droit moral* as positive law – *Reid* is completely silent about moral rights and nevertheless had a major impact on its implementation. In this case, James Earl Reid, a sculptor, was commissioned to create a work depicting the plight of the homeless – a modern nativity scene on a steam grate – by a charity, the Community for Creative Non-Violence. Neither Reid nor Creative Non-Violence had negotiated over ownership of the copyright in the sculpture. The Court deployed an eleven factor test based upon common law principles of agency to determine whether Reid was an independent contractor (and the copyright belonged to the artist) or whether Reid was an employee and the copyright would be retained by the employer as a work-made-for hire.[41] These factors included control over the manner and means of the artistic production such as the location of the workshop, the duration of the relationship, and the skill necessary for the endeavor.[42]

The Supreme Court plumbed the legislative history of the statutory definition of work-made-for-hire and concluded that it reflected Congress's historic compromise between the interests of creators and those belonging to copyright industries.[43] The *Reid* test – multifactorial with no single factor dispositive – may have seemed a fair balancing of interests. Nevertheless, since VARA includes an exception for works-made-for-hire, it provides (as with waiver) a ready escape hatch to sidestep VARA's moral rights.[44]

---

39    *Dastar Corp. v. Twentieth Century Fox Film Corp.*, U.S. 23 (2003), 539.

40    Justin HUGHES: *American Moral Rights and Fixing the Dastar "Gap,"* Utah Law Review (2007), 659–755 (Dastar endangers that patchwork protection that permits the United States to claim 6*bis* compliance).

41    A work-made-for-hire is defined by the 1976 Copyright Act, U.S.C. 17 (1994), § 101.

42    *Community for Creative Non-Violence v. Reid*, U.S. 490 (1989), 752.

43    *Ibid.*, 748.

44    U.S.C. 17 (1994), § 106A (c) (3). On VARA's work-made-for-hire exception, cf. *Carter v. Helmsley-Spear*, F. 3d 77 (2d Cir. 1995) (applying Reid Test to find a work of art unprotected under VARA as a work-made-for-hire).

# UNITED STATES MORAL RIGHTS AS LATE 20TH CENTURY HONOR LAW 323

## 4 VARA and Artist Honor in an Age of Digital Reproduction

VARA's twin rights – attribution and integrity – are closely interrelated. Attribution, the right to be recognized as the work's creator, underscores the importance of reputation in the world of art. While VARA does not protect the right to be anonymous since this would mean shedding artistic identity, it does seek to ensure that an artist's name cannot be removed from a work of art within the scope of VARA or the artist's identity substitute with another. Integrity might be seen as the other side of attribution. A painting or a sculpture that is altered in some fashion without the artist's authorisation – and VARA ignores whether this change might be an improvement – misrepresents the artistic will of the creator. Yet the name and the object are ultimately proxies for artist dignity.[45] Following the Berne Convention's Article 6*bis*, it clearly enunciates the purpose of the integrity right as preventing modifications "that would be prejudicial to his or her honor or reputation."[46]

Such solicitude towards reputation is puzzling. While other forms of dignity – such as aristocratic titles in the Title of Nobility Clause – are disfavored by the Constitution, artists are granted reputational protection grounded upon their occupational status.[47] Protection of reputation is limited, of course, only to the artistic object itself. Artists in the United States cannot prevent unfavorable reviews of their work nor can they halt exhibitions which critique as much as display art. Nevertheless, *Dignitas* under VARA is intimately connected to rank and status.[48] It is not the universal claim to inviolable human dignity as can be found in the German *Grundgesetz* Article 1.

### 4.A Mandating Honor and Mandarin Art: VARA in the Skein of Human Dignity

The Visual Artists Rights Act of 1990 (VARA) amends the United States Copyright Act to bestow moral rights upon artists who produce a work of "recognized stature" within certain categories of visual art such as painting, drawing, print, or sculpture, which are produced as two hundred or fewer copies. These copies must bear the artist's signature and be consecutively numbered.

---

45 BONNEAU: *op. cit.*, (VARA's focus on the object of protection hamstrings its recognition of artist moral rights). Elizabeth M. BOCK: *Using Public Disclosure as the Vesting Point for Moral Rights under the Visual Rights Act*, Michigan Law Review 110(2011), 153–174 (rather than protecting unfinished works VARA should vest when art is presented to the public).

46 U.S.C. 17, § 106A (a) (3). The terms, *prejudice* and *honor* are not defined by the statute.

47 United States Constitution, Art. I, Sec. 9, cl. 8.

48 For a philosophical treatment of this issue, cf. Jeremy WALDRON: *Dignity, Rank, & Rights*, Oxford University Press, Oxford, 13–46.

It specifically excludes various works, including maps, technical drawings, and illustrations used for advertising.[49]

Recognized stature, of course, reflects Mandarin artistic categories. Courts have employed a test asking whether a work is "meritorious" and whether it is "recognized by experts, other members of the artistic community, or by some cross-section of society."[50] Beyond the formal exclusions listed in the statute, it does not include tattoo art or graffiti or many forms of modern multi-media and appropriation artistic genres.[51] Moreover, VARA protection does not apply to transitory works of art.[52] Unfinished works – even if masterpieces, those not yet exhibited, or those – like the case of a sculpture displayed in an inaccessible backyard – where the public has not yet viewed the work may be considered lacking in recognized stature.[53] A work of recognized stature, of course, is highly dependent upon the reputation of a particular artist. A Matisse, even a mediocre Matisse, might have recognized stature in the art world. VARA was seen as a counterpoint to untrammeled commodification of art. But the most readily available metric for recognized status might well be the market value of the art work.

But it is more striking that it violates a principle of aesthetic neutrality established in copyright in Justice Oliver Wendell Holmes's 1903 decision, *Bleistein v. Donaldson Lithographing Company*, where the Supreme Court decided that a poster advertising a circus might be afforded the same protection as the etchings of a modern-day Rembrandt.[54] "Meritorious" is a particularly slippery judgment which places courts in the unenviable position of trying to determine what constitutes art. In the 2003 case *Pollara v. Seymour*, for example, the court decided that a hand-painted banner used as part of an effort to mobilize

---

49  U.S.C. 17, § 106(A) (2003).

50  *Carter v. Helmsley-Spear*, F. Supp. 861 (S.D.N.Y. 1994), 325. There is some question as to what constitutes recognition, *Martin v. City of Indianapolis*, F. Sup. 982 (S.D. Ind. 1997), 630–631 (newspaper reports suggests newsworthiness).

51  ADLER: *op. cit.* (opposing moral rights because they create limitations on artist creativity). Robert C. BIRD, *Moral Rights: Diagnosis and Rehabilitation*, American Bussiness Law Journal 46(2009), 407–452 (argues against the notion that moral rights are incompatible with United States legal theory).

52  *Cohen v. G & M Realty L.P.*, F. Supp. 988 (E.D.N.Y. 2013) (denying injunction to prevent destruction of building with wall art because of their transient nature).

53  *Scott v. Dixon*, F. Supp. 2d 309 (E.D.N.Y. 2004), 396–399 (substantial hedges ensured backyard sculpture invisible to public).

54  *Bleistein v. Donaldson Lithographing Company*, U.S. 188 (1903), 251. Christopher J. ROBINSON: *The "Recognized Stature" Standard in the Visual Artists Rights Act*, Fordham Law Review 68(2000), 1965 (arguing that recognized stature requires courts to make aesthetic determinations).

UNITED STATES MORAL RIGHTS AS LATE 20TH CENTURY HONOR LAW          325

support for legal privileges for the underserved constituted applied art and did not fall within the ambit of VARA.[55] In a recent case, *Cheffins v. Stewart*, an artist created a replica of a sixteenth-century Spanish galleon called La Contessa around the frame of a school bus for the Burning Man festival. The court decided it was merely applied art since it retained the practical function of transportation.[56] VARA has the ironic effect of determining what is *not* art – thereby by lessening the stature of the artists who produced these works.

Moreover, the United States waiver provision stands in opposition to the conception of moral rights as natural, inalienable rights granted to creators.[57] A number of other legal systems understood *droit moral* as rights that cannot be waived by contractual agreement or alienated. Japan's copyright statute, for example, identifies moral rights as inalienable.[58] Even within the limited Congressional discussion at the time of VARA's passage, questions were raised about the feasibility of the waiver provision. Artists are often in a notoriously precarious bargaining position when selling their works. Indeed, moral rights in general and *droit de suite* (which allows artists to receive a certain percentage of windfall profits made when a work originally sold by the artist for a low price is subsequently resold for much higher prices later) in particular, are intended to address asymmetrical bargaining power in art sales.

Concerned about this issue, Congress ordered the Copyright Office to conduct a survey to ascertain the impact of the waiver provisions.[59] The Copyright Office has performed two surveys, 1995 (shortly after VARA was enacted) and 2003. The survey data suggests that at both times around 70% of artists were aware of VARA and few had been asked to waive their rights.[60] While still a comparatively small a group, the number of artists who were willing to waive

---

55    *Pollara v. Seymour*, F.3d 344 (2d Cir. 2003), 265.

56    *Cheffins v. Stewart*, F. 3d 825 (2016), 588.

57    Section 106A (1) of the 1976 Copyright Act provides that an artist might waive moral rights if consent is manifested through signing a written agreement. In the case of a co-authored work, one artist's waiver establishes a waiver for all the co-creators of the work. According to the statute, the rights conferred by VARA might not be transferred even though they may be waived.

58    著作権法 [Copyright Act], Act. No. 65 of 2010, arts 18–20, translated in Copyright Research and Information Center (cric.or.jp/english/clj/doc/20151001_October, 2015_Copyright_Law_of_Japan.pdf). Brazil also provides for inalienable moral rights, Law No. 9.610, February 19, 1998, Part 3, Ch. 2, 27.

59    Cf. *House Report*, No. 10–514, 101st Cong. 2d Sess. (1990), 22.

60    RayMing CHANG: *Revisiting The Visual Rights Act of 1990: A Follow-Up Survey About Awareness and Waiver*, Texas Intellectual Property Law Journal 13(2005) 152.

their rights doubled between 1995 and 2003.[61] Nevertheless, these surveys suggest an irony: artist concern with reputation might be less than the solicitude shown by VARA itself. And if this is true for artists, might not the same lack of awareness be true for the public as well? One court even has suggested that VARA is so poorly known that the destruction of a work of art might not be willful.

### 4.B    *Sites of Reputation*

By bestowing rights only upon those producing a work of recognized stature, VARA deployed the artistic object to define those artists with sufficient rank to have their dignity safeguarded. Yet the object itself might create conflicts with traditional property rights. Particularly in the area of site specific art VARA proved to be a locus of contention as much as it was a grant of trumping dignity rights. Three competing interests are asserted by stakeholders over a work of art: (1) the artist – who might assert moral rights under VARA for attribution and integrity; (2) the traditional rights of property owner to control property; and (3) cultural value to the public in preserving and providing access to works of art.[62] The problem of competing interests is especially apparent in the area of site specific art.[63] Site specific art might be defined as art where the location constitutes a fundamental element of the work. Generally, site specific art, often sculpture, has been designed for a particular setting. In the most famous of the site-specific art VARA cases, Richard Serra the removal of his sculpture *Tilted Arc* from its location on the plaza in front of the Federal Office Building in downtown Manhattan. The work was originally commissioned by the United States Service Commission for use in this particular site. Although Serra ultimately lost in the courts, the public and protracted legal battle serves as

---

61   *Ibid.*

62   Natalie THURSTON: *Buyer Beware: The Unexpected Consequences of the Visual Artists Rights Act*, Berkeley Technology Law Journal 20(2005), 702.

63   Virginia M. CASICIO: *Hardly a Walk in the Park: Courts' Hostile Treatment of Site-Specific Works under VARA*, DePaul Journal of Art, Technology and Intellectual Property Law 20(2009), 167–197 (criticizing the failure of VARA to extend to site-specific works), Lauren Ruth SPOTTS: *Phillips has Left VARA Little Protection for Site-Specific Artists*, Journal of Intellectual Property Law 16(2009)/2, 297–322 (amending VARA to include site-specific art might balance the interests of private owners and the public at large), Anne Belle Wilder NORTON: *Site-Specific Art Gets a Bum Wrap: Illustrating the Limitations of the Visual Artists Rights Act of 1990 through a Study of Christo and Jean-Claude's Unique Art*, Cumberland Law Review 39(2008–2009), 749–784 (absence of site-specific protection in VARA poses problems for planning creation of art work).

UNITED STATES MORAL RIGHTS AS LATE 20TH CENTURY HONOR LAW 327

perhaps the best articulations of Serra's position that for sculptures seen by the artist as site-specific, "to remove the work is to destroy the work."[64]

Sculpture's function is to define the surrounding space. But defining the extent of this impact can be daunting. Is the site the immediate backdrop? Does it consist of any landscape that follows a sculpture's sight line? Or, alternatively, might the location for site specific art include an entire surrounding park or garden? Fixing the area around a sculpture, and not simply protecting the integrity of the object itself, would have significant impact on fluid, constantly changing cityscapes.

Courts, however, have been unsympathetic to claims of protection under for VARA for site specificity. In *Phillips v. Pembroke Real Estate*, the First Circuit rejected the artist's claims that commissioned sculptures could not be relocated in the process of renovating a Boston Park. The court held that "not only would Pembroke's ability to move [Phillips'] work or alter Eastport Park be subject to Phillips' approval, but also the owners of nearby property who had nothing to do with the purchase or installation of Phillips' works would be subject to claims that what they do with *their* property has somehow affected the site and has, as a result, altered or destroyed Phillips' works." According to the decision, "statutes which invade the common law are to be read with a presumption favoring the retention of long-established and familiar principles, except when a statutory purpose to the contrary is evident."[65] The use of the term *invade* is remarkable. It suggests that VARA's outsider origins renders it disfavored in the face of competing claims of property rights rooted in common law.

## 5 Conclusion: Towards an Archeology of Legal Transplant

When Alan Watson coined the term legal transplant to refer to explore the phenomenon of law created in one country and transferred to another, he simply noted what any legal historian of Roman law's reception in nineteenth-century Europe knew: legal systems were less autonomous and more adaptive than previously described.[66] More recently, Pierre Legrand has challenged the idea that transplants prompt legal change because transplants are altered and

---

64 Francesca GARSON: *Before that Artist Came Along, It was Just a Bridge: The Visual Artists Rights Act and the Removal of Site-Specific Artwork*, Cornell Journal of Law and Public Policy 11(2001), 206.

65 *David Phillips v. Pembroke Realty*, 449 F.3d 128 (1st Cir. 2006) quoting *United States v. Texas*, 534; S. Ct. 113, 1631; L. Ed. 2d 123 (1993), 245.

66 Alan WATSON: *Legal Transplants: An Approach to Comparative Law*, 2d ed., University of Georgia Press, Athens, 1993; Michael GRAZIADEI: *Comparative Law ad the Study of*

adapted in their new environment. Law, as Legrand sees it, largely reflects existing mores and legal structures.[67]

By all accounts, VARA seems to support Legrand's position. VARA was never intended to constitute a serious reform of United States intellectual property law – and was instead meant simply to ensure United States compliance with the Berne Convention – then it is not surprising that it appears to skeptics as "an unwanted statutory child ... never intended to protect artists' rights broadly."[68] From its very beginning it was a fraught transplant: grounded on quicksand justifications, fitted into a straightjacket of exemptions by Congress, situated in an unfriendly legal ecosystem by two major decisions in copyright law, often cabined by courts in the course of litigation as they sought to impose the legislature's intent moral rights be limited in their application, evoking archaic notions of dignity founded upon rank and status, often in conflict with economic rights – especially in the case of site-specific art, evoking little interest in the artist community, and subject to waiver in the course of asymmetrical bargaining over the disposition of art.

Yet all of the debates about defining works of visual art, site-specific art, recognized stature, what might be prejudicial to artist honor or reputation, attribution and integrity, art as promotion versus art for its own sake, exhibition permanence and all sorts of other legal issues addressed in law reviews and courts has created over the past quarter of a century a dense layering of jurisprudence. A legal transplant only begins with adoption of a statue. More striking is the accretion of strata of norms and interpretations in the fashion of a coral reef – and this, rather than the medical metaphor of transplants – might be the more apt comparison.

VARA has slowly become part of the United States legal landscape in surprising ways. The right of attribution has appeared in places far afield from VARA. An appellate court determined that removing CMI (Copyright Management Information) from a photograph constitutes a copyright violation under the Digital Millennium Copyright Act.[69] Such a removal would prevent a functioning right of attribution. Might we be backing into a right of attribution by

---

     *Transplants and Receptions* = *Oxford Handbook of Comparative Law*, Mathias REIMANN, Reinhard ZIMMERMANN (eds.), Oxford University Press, Oxford, 2006, 441–475.

67    Pierre LEGRAND: *The Impossibility of Legal Transplants*, Maastricht Journal of European and Comparative Law 4(1997), 111–124.

68    Monica PA, Christopher J. ROBINSON: *Making Lemons out of Lemons: Recent Developments in the Visual Artists Rights Act,* Landslide 3(2009), 22, 24.

69    *Murphy v. Millennium, Radio Group LLC*, F.3d 650 (3d Cir. 2011), 295 (CMI removal encompassed by 17 U.S.C. § 1202).

# UNITED STATES MORAL RIGHTS AS LATE 20TH CENTURY HONOR LAW

responding to corporate interests in retaining notice – but drawing upon the language of moral rights? A quarter of a century is a remarkably short amount of time to know whether an accidental tourist of a law might remain in the United States for a longer, more rooted stay.

## Acknowledgements

This chapter was researched when I was Abraham L. Kaminstein Scholar in Residence, at the United States Copyright Office. While the views expressed in the chapter are completely my own and do not reflect the Copyright Office, I would like to thank the Office's extraordinary lawyers and its Register of Copyrights, Karyn A. Temple.

## Bibliography

### Cases

*Bleistein v. Donaldson Lithographing Company*, U.S. 188 (1903).

*Carter v. Helmsley-Spear*, F.3d 71 (2d Cir. 1995).

*Carter v. Helmsley-Spear*, F. Supp. 861 (S.D.N.Y. 1994).

*Cheffins v. Stewart*, F. 3d 825 (2016), 588.

*Cohen v. G & M Reality L.P.*, F. Supp. 2d 212 (E.D.N.Y. 2013).

*Community for Creative Non-Violence v. Reid,* U.S. 490 (1989).

*David Phillips v. Pembroke Realty*, 449 F. 3d 128 (1st Cir. 2006).

*Dastar Corp. v. Twentieth Century Fox Film Corp.,* U.S. 23 (2003).

*Eldred v. Ashcroft*, U.S. 537 (2003).

*Garcia v. Google*, F.3d 1258 (2014).

*Golan* v. *Holder*, U.S. 565 (2012).

*Kleinman v. City of San Marcos*, F. 3d 323 (5th Cir. 2010).

*Martin v. City of Indianapolis*, F. Sup. 982 (S.D. Ind. 1997).

*Massachusetts Museum of Contemporary Art v. Buchel*, F.3d 38 (1st Cir. 2010).

*Murphy v. Millennium, Radio Group LLC*, F.3d 650 (3d Cir. 2011).

*Pierro Hugo v. Société Plon*, Cour de cassation – Première chambre civile, Arrêt n° 125 du 30 janvier 2007 (04-15.543).

*Pollara v. Seymour*, F.3d 344 (2d Cir. 2003).

*Reece v. Marc Ecko Unltd, 2011 WL 4112071* (S.D.N.Y. 2011).

*Scott v. Dixon*, F. Supp. 2d 309 (E.D.N.Y. 2004).

*Teter v. Glass Onion, Inc.*, F. Supp. 2d 1138 (W.D. Mo. 2010).

## Literature

Amy ADLER: *Against Moral Rights,* California. Law Review 97(2009), 263–299.

Peter BALDWIN: *The Copyright Wars: Three Centuries Of Transatlantic Battle*, Princeton University Press, Princeton, 2014.

Griffin M. BARNETT: *Recognized Stature: Protecting Street Art as Cultural Property*, Chicago-Kent Journal of Intellectual Property 12(2013), 204–216.

*Berne* Convention for the Protection of Literary and Artistic Works, Sept. 9, 1886, *League of Nations Treaty Series* 123.

John BICKNELL: *Is Graffiti Worthy of Protection? Changes within the Recognized Stature Requirement of the Visual Artists Rights Act,* Tulane Journal of Technology & Intellectual Property 17(2014), 337–352.

Robert C. BIRD, *Moral Rights: Diagnosis and Rehabilitation*, American Bussiness Law Journal 46(2009), 407–452.

Elizabeth M. BOCK: *Using Public Disclosure as the Vesting Point for Moral Rights under the Visual Rights Act*, Michigan Law Review 110(2011), 153–174.

Sonya G. BONNEAU: *Honor and Destruction: The Conflicted Object in Moral Rights Law*, St. John's Law Review 87(2013), 47–105.

Virginia M. CASICIO: *Hardly a Walk in the Park: Courts' Hostile Treatment of Site-Specific Works under VARA,* DePaul Journal of Art, Technology and Intellectual Property Law 20(2009), 167–197.

RayMing CHANG: *Revisiting The Visual Rights Act of 1990: A Follow-Up Survey About Awareness and Waiver*, Texas Intellectual Property Law Journal 13(2005) 129–171.

Code de la propriété intellectuelle.

*Copyright Act of 1976, Code of Laws of the United States of America*, Title 17.

Charles CRONIN: *Dead on the Vine: Living and Conceptual Art and VARA*, Vanderbilt Journal of Entertainment & Technology Law, 12(2010), 209–243.

Nathan M. DAVIS: *As Good as New: Conserving Artwork and the Destruction of Moral Rights*, Cardozo Arts & Enterteinment Law Journal 215(2011), 29–65.

Francesca GARSON: *Before that Artist Came Along, It was Just a Bridge: The Visual Artists Rights Act and the Removal of Site-Specific Artwork*, Cornell Journal of Law and Public Policy 11(2001), 203–244.

Llewellyn Joseph GIBBONS, *Visual Artists Rights Act (VARA) and the Protection of Digital Works of Photographic Art*, North Carolina Journal of Law and Technology 11(2010), 531–553.

Jane GINSBURG: *The Right to Claim Authorship in U.S. Copyright and Trademarks Law*, Houston Law Review, 41(2004), 263–307.

Jane GINSBURG: *A Tale of Two Copyrights:* Literary Property in Revolutionary France and America, Tulane Law Review 64(1990), 993–1031.

Michael GRAZIADEI: *Comparative Law ad the Study of Transplants and Receptions = Oxford Handbook of Comparative Law*, Mathias REIMANN, Reinhard ZIMMERMANN (eds.), Oxford University Press, Oxford, 2006, 441–475.

Carla HESSE: *Enlightenment Epistemology and the Law of Authorship in Revolutionary France 1777–1793*, Representations 30(1990), 109–137.

*House Report*, No. 10–514 (1990).

Justin HUGHES: *American Moral Rights and Fixing the Dastar "Gap,"* Utah Law Review (2007), 659–755.

Justin HUGHES: *The Philosophy of Intellectual Property,* Georgia Law Journal 77(1988), 287–304.

International Copyright Act of 1891, Ch. 565, *The United States Status at Large,* n. 1106.

Roberta KWALL: *The Soul of Creativity: Forging A Moral Right Law For The United States,* Stanford University Press, Stanford, 2009.

Ilhyung LEE: *Toward an American Moral Rights in Copyright,* Washington & Lee Law Review 58(2001), 795–854.

Pierre LEGRAND: *The Impossibility of Legal Transplants,* Maastricht Journal of European and Comparative Law 4(1997), 111–124.

Christine LESICKO: *Tattoos as Visual Art: How Art Fits in the Visual Artists Rights Act, IDEA* – The Intelectual Property Law Review 53(2013), 39–62.

Robert MERGES: *Justifying Intellectual Property,* Harvard University Press, Cambridge, 2011.

Michelle MORAN: *Quilt Artists: Left Out in the Cold by the Visual Artists Rights Act of 1990,* Marquette Intellectual Property Law Review 14(2010), 393–409.

David NIMMER: *The Moral Imperative against Academic Plagiarism (without a moral right against passing off),* DePaul Law Review 54(2004), 1–22.

Anne Belle Wilder NORTON: *Site-Specific Art Gets a Bum Wrap: Illustrating the Limitations of the Visual Artists Rights Act of 1990 through a Study of Christo and Jean-Claude's Unique Art,* Cumberland Law Review 39(2008–2009), 749–784.

Monica PA, Christopher J. ROBINSON: *Making Lemons out of Lemons: Recent Developments in the Visual Artists Rights Act,* Landslide 3(2009), 22.

Protezione del diritto d'autore e di altri diritti connessi al suo esercizio, Legge 22 aprile 1941, n. 633, *Gazzetta Ufficiale della Repubblica Italiana,* n. 163.

Christopher J. ROBINSON: *The "Recognized Stature" Standard in the Visual Artists Rights Act,* Fordham Law Review 68(2000), 1935–1976.

*Senate Report* 100–352 (1988).

David E. SHIPLEY: *The Empty Promise of VARA: The Restrictive Application of a Narrow Statute,* Mississippi Law Journal 83(2014), 985–1048.

Lauren Ruth SPOTTS: *Phillips has Left VARA Little Protection for Site-Specific Artists,* Journal of Intellectual Property Law 16(2009)/2, 297–322.

Xiyan TANG: *The Artist as Brand: Towards a Trademark Conception of Moral Rights,* Yale Law Journal 122(2012), 218–257.

*The Inter-American Copyright Convention: Its Place in United States Copyright Law,* Harvard Law Review 60(1947), 1329–1339.

Natalie THURSTON: *Buyer Beware: The Unexpected Consequences of the Visual Artists Rights Act*, Berkeley Technology Law Journal 20(2005), 701–721.

Seth TIPTON: *Connoisseurship Corrected: Protecting the Artist, the Public and the Role of Art Museums through the Amendment of VARA*, Rutgers Law Review 62(2009), 269–303.

*Visual Artists Rights Act of 1990*, Public Law 101–650, *The United States Status at Large*, n. 104 (*Code of Laws of the United States of America*, Title 17).

Jeremy WALDRON: *Dignity, Rank, & Rights*, Oxford University Press, Oxford, 2012.

Wet van 23 september 1912, houdende nieuwe regeling van het auteursrecht, *Staatsblad* 2015.

Alan WATSON: *Legal Transplants: An Approach to Comparative Law*, 2d ed., University of Georgia Press, Athens, 1993.

Steven WILF: *Copyright and Social Movements in Late-Nineteenth Century America*, Theoretical Inquiries in Law 12(2011), 123–160.

Steven WILF: *Intellectual Property = A Companion to American Legal History*, eds. Sally E. HADDEN, Alfred L. BROPHY, Wiley-Blackwell, Oxford, 2013, 441–459.

Adrian ZUCKERMAN, Annemarie SEDORFE: *Do US Property Concepts Prevent VARA From Implementing the Berne Convention?*, Dublin University Law Journal 26(2004), 172–199.

著作権法, Act. No. 65 of 2010, Copyright Research and Information Center.

# Index of Names

A. Bielski 145
A. John Simmons 61, 62, 71
A.W.B. Simpson 77, 82, 109
Abraham L. Kaminstein 329
Adele Bianchi Robbiati 113, 137
Adrian Belton 114, 139
Adrian Zuckerman 313, 332
Adriano Cavanna 113–115, 127, 132, 135
Adrien Duport 53, 54
Ágnes R. Várkonyi 29, 35, 47
Agustin Parise 9, 24
Ajay K. Mehrotra 86, 107
Âke Malmström 237, 252
Akihiko Nishio 242, 252
Alain Bergounioux 259, 280
Alain Wijffels 4, 24
Alan Rodger 92, 95, 108, 228, 229, 236
Alan Watson 327, 332
Albert Michel 267, 282
Alberto Cova 117, 135
Alberto Sciumè 116, 118, 122–124, 126, 127, 141
Aldo Mazzacane 114, 138
Alessandro Somma 114, 140
Alexis Albarian 8, 24
Alexis de Tocqueville 171
Alfred L. Brophy 315, 332
Algerson Sidney 55
Allen Jayne 54–56, 62, 70
Amasa A. Redfield 178, 190
Ambroise Colin 269, 281
Amy Adler 312, 324, 330
Amy Goymour 246, 252
Andrea Appiani 111
Andreas Bauer 297, 308
André-Jean Arnaud 273, 280
Andrejs Plakans 290, 307
Andres Kasekamp 285, 288, 290, 298, 307
Andrew Burrows 233, 236
Andrew III of Hungary 27
Andrew Johnston 103, 106
Andrzej Birch Evans 154
Angela Valente 113, 141
Anicteto Masferrer 3, 4, 24, 77, 107, 299, 307
Anna Eleonora Esterházy 39, 40, 42, 43
Anna Eleonora Pálffy 36

Anna Fundárková 28, 32, 45, 46
Anna Klimaszewska 6, 8, 9, 18, 20, 23–25, 73, 104, 106, 143, 148, 162
Anna Margaretha Desanna et Rhodi 36
Annamaria Monti 18, 20, 111
Anne Allex 303, 305
Anne Belle Wilder Norton 326, 331
Anne Lefebvre-Teillard 124, 138
Anne-Laure Catinat 262, 281
Annemarie Sedorfe 313, 332
Annie Stora-Lamarre 267, 282
Anthony F.C. Wallace 51, 72
Anthony Musson 4, 24
Anton Esterházy 40
Anton Justus Friedrich Thibaut 299, 309
Antonello Mattone 120, 137, 141
Antoni Kiesewetter 158
Antoni Matakiewicz 150, 151
Antonia Czobor 42
Antonia Ratouit de Souches 42
Antonin Scalia 322
Antonino De Francesco 112, 135
Antonio Aldini 116, 124
Antonio Grilli 111, 114, 137
Antonio Guarino 195, 210
Antonio Padoa-Schioppa 118, 124, 125, 128–130, 132, 139
Aristotle 55
Armand Thomas Hue de Miromesnil 120
Arnold Vinnius 216, 217, 236
Arthur Eric Fairchild 230
Arthur Goldhammer 90, 108
Arturo Brienza 118, 134
Ascanio Baldasseroni 122, 123, 134
Attila Menyhárd 30, 45
August Comte 270
Aurelio Lepre 113, 138
Avner Greif 87, 106

Balázs Pálvölgyi 17
Balthazard-Marie Emerigon 122, 129, 136
Barbara Dölemeyer 114, 140, 286, 306
Barna Mezey 30, 45
Bart Wauters 2, 7, 8, 16, 20, 25, 49
Basil Kennett 60

## INDEX OF NAMES

Beata J. Kowalczyk  19, 237
Beata Ruszkiewicz  241, 253
Béatrice Fourniel  128, 137
Béla III of Hungary  32
Béla Radvánszky  38, 47
Benjamin Hawkins  51
Benjamin Thompson  61, 71
Benvenuto Stracca  118, 121, 141
Bernard Bailyn  52, 56, 62, 70
Bernard Schwartz  166–171, 190
Bertrand Badie  8, 9, 23
Bill Brown  256, 283
Bing Ying  278, 284
Biondo Biondi  196, 210
Boris Kozolchyk  75, 107
Brian Tamanaha  258, 283
Brian Tierney  61, 72
Bronisław Pawłowski  144, 163
Bulgarus  200

Caracalla  241
Carla Hesse  316, 331
Carla Rahn Phillips  85, 108
Carlo Capra  112, 113, 117, 134, 139
Carlo Ghisalberti  113, 114, 137
Carlo Targa  121, 122, 141
Carlo Zaghi  113, 142
Carlos Petit  112, 120, 140
Carole Christen  113, 138
Carole Lécuyer  262, 282
Catherine MacMillan  77, 95, 96, 107
Charles Abbott  89, 94, 104
Charles Bonaventure Marie Touller  158, 163
Charles Boucaud  269, 270, 280
Charles Cronin  320, 330
Charles Darwin  270
Charles Donahue, Jr.  118, 136
Charles H. Monro  231, 236
Charles Lowell  173–175, 190
Charles M. Haar  170, 189
Charles Montesqui  11, 120, 122
Charles VI (III), Holy Roman Emperor  32
Charles Warren  166, 190
Chen Wenjie  278, 284
Chen Xinyu  263, 264, 271, 283, 284
Chen Yu  263, 264, 271, 283, 284
Christian M. Burset  80, 100, 105
Christian Schulze  237, 251

Christian von Bar  237, 253
Christine Lesicko  319, 331
Christoph Erdődy  36, 43
Christoph Krampe  228, 235
Christophe Jamin  268, 282
Christophe Prochasson  259, 280, 283
Christopher J. Robinson  324, 328, 331, 332
Christopher Pierson  57, 71
Cicero  55
Claire Zalc  259, 282
Claude Etienne Delvincourt  129, 135, 136
Claude-Alphonse Delangle  130, 135
Clifford Ando  194, 210
Clovis I  259
Colin Blackburn  94–96, 105
Condorcet  261
Constantine the Great  239, 241
Corinne Saint-Alary-Houin  124, 134, 137, 139, 141
Cornel West  256, 283
Crawford B. Macpherson  56, 58, 71
Cristina Ciancio  128, 135

d'André  49, 66
Dale Van Kley  52, 71
Damiano Canale  4, 23
Daniel J. Boorstin  167, 173, 189
Daniel Jakimiec  243, 252
Daniel Klimchuk  60, 71
Daniel Visser  238, 253
Dave De ruysscher  90–92, 101, 105
David Armitage  79, 104
David Deroussin  261, 270, 281
David E. Shipley  312, 320, 332
David Graeber  76, 83, 87, 97, 100, 101, 106
David Hume  55
David Ibbetson  194, 210, 228, 229, 235
David Johnston  233, 236
David Lieberman  92, 102, 107
David M. Walker  223, 224, 236
David Nimmer  313, 331
David Phillips  327, 329
David S. Bogen  168, 189
David Shorr  257
David Sugarman  79, 95, 100, 106, 109
Dennis Campbell  245, 253
Diana Duchonová  32, 45
Dietrich A. Loeber  288, 307

INDEX OF NAMES 335

Dietrich Kalkan 303, 305
Diocletian 198, 220
Domenico Alberto Azuni 123–125, 127, 134
Domenico Balì 130, 134
Dominique Fenouillet 204, 211
Domokos Kosáry 29, 31, 33, 45
Donald Grant 249, 253
Donald O. Wagner 81, 110
Dr Bowman 181, 182, 184, 185
Dr Brown 184
Dr Coffin 181, 182
Duke of Alguillon 53
Duncan Forbes 57, 70
Dwight D. Eisenhauer 321

E.J.H. Schrage 193, 195, 205, 210
Eduardo M. Peñalver 58, 70
Edward A. Purcell Jr. 81, 103, 108
Edward Cavanagh 76, 105
Edward Coke 63, 218
Edward Manson 257, 282
Edwin Matthews 230
Elemér Balogh 30, 45
Élie Blanc 266, 280
Elio Tavilla 115, 138
Elisabeth Lobenwein 34, 46
Elizabeth A. Martin 220, 236
Elizabeth Cooke 246, 252
Elizabeth M. Bock 323, 330
Ellen F. Paul 55, 72
Elmar Ilus 302, 306
Elo Lutsepp 302, 307
Emile Clavel 49, 70
Émile Laurent 49, 70
Émile Vincens 158, 163
Emily Erikson 87, 106
Emily Kadens 92, 106, 107
Emma Bartoniek 29, 44
Emma Iványi 34, 45
Emőd Veress 148, 162
Endre Arató 34, 44
Engels 78
Ennio Cortese 120, 137, 141
Enrico Pattaro 4, 23
Enrique Dussel 256, 281
Eric Clive 237, 253
Eric Descheemaeker 223, 235
Ernest Lamè-Fleury 156, 162

Ernest-Désiré Glasson 266, 268, 269, 281
Ernst Ein 299, 300, 306
Erzsébet Rákóczi 34
Ettore Dezza 115, 136
Eugene C. Massie 249, 252
Ewan McKendrick 74, 107

Fabien Valente 124, 141
Ferdinand I, Holy Roman Emperor 27, 28, 32, 33
Ferdinand Karl Aspremond-Lynden 41
Ferdinando Mazzarella 121, 131, 139
Ferenc Eckhart 30, 44
Ferenc Esterházy 34
Ferenc II Rákóczi 27
Ferenc Károlyi 34
Fernand Braudel 73, 74, 76, 82–90, 92, 96, 97, 99, 101–103, 105
Fernando Mazzocca 113, 139
Filippo Ranieri 115, 140
Forrest McDonald 54
Fortuné Anthoine de Saint-Joseph 130, 137
Francesca Garson 327, 331
Francesco Mastroberti 114, 138
Francine Muel-Dreyfus 262, 282
Francis Hutcheson 55
Franciszek Buchelt 150
Franciszek Ksawery Kossecki 152, 153
Franciszek Longchamps de Bérier 238, 252
Franco Della Peruta 113, 139
François Gény 268, 281
Francois Xavier Martin 166, 189
Frank L. Schäfer 286, 309
Frank Trentmann 81, 84, 85, 87, 89, 108, 109
Franz Folch de Cardona 42
Franz Wieacker 132, 133, 142
Frédéric Audren 267, 282
Frédéric Monier 259, 280, 283
Frederick H. Lawson 224, 235
Frederick Parker Walton 218, 236
Frederick Pollock 87, 95, 108
Frederick Rockwell Sanborn 101, 108
Frederick Silver 99, 109
Frederick W. Maitland 95, 108, 217, 236
Friedrich Carl von Savigny 300, 309
Fryderyk Łubieński 145, 147
Fryderyk Skarbek 145, 163

## INDEX OF NAMES

G.R. Rubin   79, 95, 100, 106, 108, 109
Gábor Béli   32, 45
Gábor Máthé   30, 45
Gabriel Massé   132
Gaetano Del Re   130, 135
Gaetano Marré   129, 138
Gaius   194, 196, 201, 214, 218, 240
Garry Wills   56, 72
Gavouyère   262, 270, 281
Geoffrey MacCormack   228, 236
Geoffrey Samuel   75, 108
George Joseph Bell   95, 104, 229
Georges Martyn   4, 24
Georges Padoux   254, 255, 257, 283
Georges Ripert   133, 140
Géraldine Muhlmann   259, 282
Gerd Bender   9, 24
Gerhard Ammerer   34, 46
Gerhard Otte   201, 211
Gershon Feder   242, 252
Géza Pálffy   28, 33, 46
Gian Savino Pene Vidari   128, 140
Giorgio Zordan   121, 142
Giovanni Falcone   194, 210
Giovanni Finazzi   198, 210
Giovanni Tarello   119, 141
Giovanni Varanese   208, 211
Gisbert(us) Voetius   216
Giuseppe Compagnoni   123
Giuseppe De Stefani   123–125
Giuseppe Lorenzo Maria Casaregi   118, 134
Giuseppe Luosi   122–124
Gopal Sreenivasan   56, 72
Gordon S. Wood   51, 72, 172
Graeme J. Milne   75, 87, 89, 98, 100, 107
Graham   246
Grant Gilmore   81, 106
Gregory S. Alexander   58, 70, 171, 189
Griffin M. Barnett   319, 330
György Bónis   32, 44
György Jancsó   35, 36, 45
György Spira   35, 44
Györgyo Diósdi   240, 252
Győző Cholnoky   30, 44
Győző Ember   33, 45

H. Patrick Glenn   237, 252
H.W. Woolrych   94, 110

Han Dayuan   255, 283
Hanamel   242
Hans Ankum   203, 210
Hans Hattenauer   299, 309
Hans Kiefner   240, 252
Hans Koch   29
Hans Schulte-Nölke   237, 253
Harold J. Berman   6, 7, 23
Harry Dondorp   193, 203, 205, 210
Hasso Hofmann   4, 23
Hector MacQuinn   233
Heikki Pihlajamäki   3, 4, 11, 13, 23–25, 75, 77,
   92, 108, 118, 137
Heinrich Bosse   290, 308
Heinrich Hackfeld Pflüger   240, 253
Heinz Mohnhaupt   114, 140
Helen Scott   223, 231, 235, 236
Helena Żółtowska   158
Helmut Coing   128, 139, 286, 306
Hennie Strydom   237, 251
Henri Capitant   269, 281
Henry Bracton   217
Henry E. Smith   61, 71
Henry Goudy   215, 235
Henry Home, Lord Kames   55
Henry S. Maine   3, 24
Herbert F. Jolowicz   225, 235
Herbert Fisher   258, 261
Herman Apsītis   297
Herwig Wolfram   28, 47
Hesi Siimets-Gross   21, 285, 286, 288, 289,
   292, 307–309
Hiroshi Oda   238, 252
Hooker   60
Howard Dickman   55, 72
Hu Changqing   257, 275, 283
Huang Yuansheng   263, 284
Hugo(nis) Grottii (Grotius)   19, 60, 64, 70,
   203, 204, 210, 216
Hugolini (Hugolinus) de Presbyteris   202,
   210

Ian McLean   67, 71
Ian Williamson   249, 253
Ignacy Neumark   151, 154
Ignacy Stawiarski   145
Igor Moullier   113, 138
Igor Tyutryumov   293, 305, 306, 310

# INDEX OF NAMES

Ildikó Horn 31, 47
Ilhyung Lee 312, 331
Immanuel Wallerstein 256, 283
Imre Képessy 16
Iren Kull 292, 307
Irén Őriné Bilkei 32, 46
István Fazekas 28, 32, 45, 46
István György Tóth 33, 46
István Kajtár 32, 45
István Monok 31, 46
Italo Birocchi 120, 137, 141
Iván Berkeszi 34, 44
Ivan Kosnica 21
Ivan Paskevich 148

J. Devlin 99
J. Kerr 96
J.B. Scott 203, 210
J.B. Sirey 127, 157, 158, 160, 163
J.C. Ledlie 220, 236
J.H. Plumb 81, 107
J.M. Kelly 1, 24
J.W. Smith 94, 95, 109
J.Y. Pye 246
Jaanika Erne 294, 307
Jaap Zevenbergen 247, 253
Jacqueline Lalouette 258, 282
Jacques Chevallier 268, 281
Jacques Cujas 121
Jacques Savary 116, 121, 129, 141
Jacques-Louis David 111, 261
Jakob Wührer 33, 47
Jamens Harrington 55
James Balfour 221
James Earl Reid 322
James Gordley 77, 106
James Madison 167
James Oldham 92, 108
James Penner 61, 71
James Stephen Rogers 76, 80, 81, 84, 89, 90, 92, 93, 101, 108
James Tracy 84, 85, 92, 104, 108, 109
James Tully 72
James Willard Hurst 170, 171, 190
Jan Chryzostom Kijewski 150
Jan Dawid Ebert 154
Jan Halberda 215, 235
Jan Hallebeek 193, 195, 196, 198, 202, 203, 210

Jan Nepomucen Kwilecki 150
Jan Wincenty Bandtkie 153, 154
Jane Ginsburg 313, 316, 331
Jani Kirov 9, 24
Janka Teodóra Nagy 38
Javier Krauel 256, 281
Jean Barbeyrac 60, 64
Jean Etienne-Marie Portalis 259–261, 269, 282
Jean Hilaire 118–120, 126–128, 138, 153, 161
Jean M. Yarbrough 55, 72
Jean-Baptiste Duvergier 153, 156, 158, 161, 163
Jean-Baptiste Treilhard 261
Jean-Guillaume Locrè 126, 129, 130, 138, 156, 162
Jean-Ignace Jacqueminot 260, 282
Jean-Jacques Burlamaqui 55, 61–63, 70
Jean-Jacques Clere 53, 70
Jean-Jacques Rousseau 30
Jean-Jacques-Régis de Cambacérès 259–261, 280
Jean-Louis Halpérin 4, 5, 13, 24, 25, 115, 138, 267, 282
Jean-Luc Chappey 113, 138
Jean-Marie Pardessus 126, 127, 129, 139
Jeanne Chauvin 262, 263, 266
Jean-Paul Lehners 292, 309
Jean-Paul Sardon 256, 271, 283
Jean-Pierre Allinne 128, 134
Jenő Szűcs 29, 30, 47
Jeremiah 241
Jeremy Bentham 167, 270
Jeremy Waldron 56, 58–60, 72, 323, 332
Jeroen S. Kortmann 230, 235
Jérôme Bourgon 264, 280
Jerome Huyler 56, 57, 70
Jérôme Marie Champion de Cicé 67
Jérôme Mavidal 49, 70
Jerzy Jedlicki 10, 14, 24
Jerzy Pieńkos 240, 253
Jiang Zhaoxin 263, 264, 271, 283, 284
Jiří Brňovják 15, 20
Jo Guldi 79, 104
Joachim Rückert 300, 308
Joan Church 237, 251
Johann Gottfried Herder 30, 45
Johann Gottlieb Heinecke (Heineccius) 129, 138, 216, 217, 225, 235

# INDEX OF NAMES

Johann Pálffy 36, 40, 42, 43
Johann von Müller 30, 45
Johannes W. Flume 131, 136
John Adams 51
John Bicknell 319, 330
John Brewer 81, 92, 107
John Cockerill 151–153
John Erskine 218, 220, 222, 223, 226, 229, 235
John Faxon 174–176
John G.A. Pocock 51, 55, 56, 71
John H. Baker 80, 94, 102, 104, 289, 306
John H. Raach 184, 190
John J. Elwell 177, 179, 189
John Locke 50, 55–61, 62, 64, 69, 71
John Ordronaux 184, 185, 190
John R. Parker 249, 253
John Rodman 153, 163
John Salter 61, 71
John W. Cairns 216, 217, 234, 235
Jon R. Waltz 181, 190
Jonathan M. Miller 147, 163
Jörg Baberowski 289, 306
Joseph Chitty 94, 102, 105
Joseph Esterházy 36
Joseph II, Holy Roman Emperor 30, 119
Joseph T. Janczyk 249, 252
Jousse 129
Joyce Appleby 63, 70
Józef de Geppert 158
Józef Dyzmański 151, 154
Józef Morris 154
Józef Zwierzyna 158
József Holub 37, 45
József Perényi 29, 46
Ju Zheng 277, 284
Judah Benjamin 95, 96, 104
Judge Chalmers 95, 105
Judit Beke-Martos 9, 21
Judith Flanders 88, 106
Julian 230
Julian Hoppit 98, 100, 106
Julien Boyd 51, 71
Jürgen Basedow 288, 307
Jürgen Weitzel 301, 309
Jüri Jaakson 293–295, 306
Jüri Uluots 291, 295, 299–301, 309
Justin Hughes 316, 322, 331

Justin Simard 80, 101, 109
Justinian 194, 195, 197, 239

Kaius Tuori 194, 210
Kalliope Agapiou-Josephides 292, 309
Kálmán Kulcsár 4, 7, 8, 10, 24
Karel Vocelka 28, 47
Karin Sein 292, 307
Karl H.L. Welker 297, 308
Karl Nickerson Llewellyn 75, 81, 107
Karl Polanyi 76, 108
Kārlis Ulmanis 298, 304
Karol Fryderyk Wojda 144
Karol Księżyk 153
Karol Ludwik Hamann 153
Károly Kisteleki 30, 45
Karyn A. Temple 329
Katalin Péter 28, 47
Katalin Toma 31, 47
Katarzyna Hügerle 158
Katarzyna Sójka-Zielińska 237, 253
Katrin Kiirend-Pruuli 21, 285, 288, 289, 307
Kazimierz Jacaszek 242, 251
Kenneth A. DeVille 177–179, 189
Kenneth McK. Norrie 221, 224, 236
Kenneth Reid 216, 235, 236
Kjell A. Modéer 77, 107
Klaus Luig 220, 235
Konstantin Päts 298, 303, 304
Kristine S. Cherek 248, 251
Krystian Bichterl 151

L. Kantor 290, 308
L.J. Donaldson 96
L.M. Devilleneuve 163
Lafayette 53
Lai Junnan 263, 284
Lajos Gecsényi 33, 45
Lajos Merényi 34, 46
Lajos Rácz 30, 47
László Katus 30, 45
Laura Moscati 127, 139
Lauren Ruth Spotts 326, 332
Lawrence M. Friedman 80, 81, 96, 106, 164, 166–169, 171, 172, 189
Lech Mażewski 148, 162
Lena Foljanty 111, 137
Lenin 78

## INDEX OF NAMES

Leo XIII   270
Leon Gambetta   258
Leoni Levi   95, 96, 107
Leopold Graf Pálffy   42
Leopold I, Holy Roman Emperor   32
Letizia Vacca   193, 210
Lipót Kollonich   34
Lisa Ting   249, 253
Liu Zhengfeng   255, 283
Llewellyn Joseph Gibbons   320, 331
Lloyd S. Kramer   12, 24
Lord Atkin   227, 228, 230
Lord Bankton   222
Lord Bolingbroke   55
Lord Buckmaster   228
Lord Clauson   214
Lord Denning   229
Lord Denning   229, 230, 233
Lord Dundas   215
Lord Ellenborough   218
Lord Forbes   215
Lord Fraser of Tullybelton   226, 227
Lord Herschell   95
Lord Inglis   226
Lord Klirbardon   222, 223, 226
Lord Mackay   224
Lord Macmillan   215–218, 223, 225, 227–229
Lord Mance   233, 236
Lord Mansfield   92, 94
Lord Methuen   85
Lord Reid   222
Lord Rodger of Earlsferry   228, 230–233
Lord Stair   216, 222, 229
Lord Thankerton   215
Lord Wilberforce   224, 225
Lord Wright   218
Louis II of Hungary   27
Lucio Valerio Moscarini   206, 211
Ludwig Ernst Batthyány   40
Ludwig Schnorr von Carolsfeld   203, 210
Ludwik Hirschman   150
Luigi Berlinguer   117, 118, 122–124, 126, 134
Luigi Marco Bassani   50, 54, 56, 62, 70
Luigi Pepe   127, 141
Łukasz J. Korporowicz   19, 212

M. Skrzypiński   145
M. Stokowski   145

M. Wlassak   225
M.C. Mirow   9, 24
M.R. Denning   96
Ma Jianzhong   272, 284
Ma Kie-tchong   272
Maciej Zieliński   244, 253
Mackenzie Dalzell Chalmers   143, 160
Maja Maciejewska-Szałas   16
Manfred Nowak   292, 309
Manuel Guţan   3, 8–10, 12, 13, 24
Marc D. Ginsberg   177, 189
Marceli Handelsman   145, 161
Marcin Michalak   19, 164
Marcin Schestarum   158
Marco Nicola Miletti   120, 137, 141
Marek Starý   15, 20
Marelle Leppik   292, 309
Margaret Elizabeth Stewart   213, 214
Maria Anna Althann   42
Maria F. Cursi   233, 235
Maria Gigliola di Renzo Villata   115, 136
Mária Homoki-Nagy   30, 45
Maria Malatesta   114, 139
Maria Octavia von Gilleis   36
Mária Ormos   33, 45
Maria Theresa   32, 33
Mario Ascheri   112, 134
Mario Stella Richter Jr.   133, 141
Mario Talamanca   193, 198, 211
Marion Fontaine   259, 280, 283
Marjorie Carvalho de Souza   9, 18, 20
Marju Luts (Luts-Sootak)   21, 285–290, 292, 307, 309
Mark Godfrey   11, 23
Markku Suksi   292, 309
Markus D. Dubber   11, 23
Márkus Dezső   27, 47
Martin Belov   7, 23
Martin Löhnig   288, 307, 308
Martin Scheutz   33, 34, 46, 47
Martinus Gosia   202, 203
Marx   78
Mary Helen Stewart   213
Mary Margareth Stubenberg   36, 40, 41
Massimo Brutti   194, 210
Massimo Tita   120, 126, 128, 141
Mathias Reimann   77, 106, 328, 331
Matthew H. Kramer   56, 71

340 INDEX OF NAMES

Maura Fortunati  122, 125, 137
Maurice Eugen Lang  167, 190
Max Rheinstein  256, 282
Maximian  220
Melchiorre Roberti  114, 116, 139
Merrill Jensen  52, 72
Micajah Hawks  174, 175
Michael Broers  113, 134
Michael E. Tigar  102, 109
Michael Esterházy  36
Michael G. Bridge  88, 92, 94, 96, 105
Michael Graziadei  327, 331
Michael Stolleis  3, 4, 9, 24
Michael Zuckert  56, 72
Michał Gałędek  1, 3, 4, 6, 8, 9, 11, 13, 15, 17, 20,
    23–25, 73, 104, 106, 158
Michele Agresti  130, 134
Michele Costi  130, 135
Michele De Jorio  120, 121, 135
Michelle Moran  320, 331
Milo A. McClelland  178, 190
Mirabeau  66
Monica Pa  328, 331
Morton J. Horwitz  82, 106, 165, 170, 189
Morton White  55, 56, 62, 72
Mougin  49, 66

Nader Hakim  268, 271, 280, 282
Napoleon I  111–117, 120, 121, 123–129, 133, 143,
    242, 257, 260
Natalie Thurston  326, 332
Nathan M. Davis  312, 330
Neil McKendrick  81, 107
Niall Ferguson  76, 106
Niall R. Whitty  219, 236
Nicholas Esterházy  34
Nicholas Pálffy  42, 43
Niels Steensgaard  84, 85, 109
Nóra G. Etenyi  31, 47

Oliver Radley-Gardner  246, 253
Oliver Wendell Holmes  324
Olivier Moréteau  8, 24, 77, 107
Orazio Condorelli  203, 210
Oswald Redlich  33, 46
Otto-Heinrich Elias  290, 308

P.G.B. McNeil  222, 236

Pál Fodor  33, 46
Pamela O'Connor  246, 252
(Pallas) Athena  143
Paolo Castrovano  207
Paolo Ungari  125, 141
Paolo Vergani  125
Paolo Voci  195, 211
Pasquale Stanislao Mancini  131
Patrick Cabanel  259, 280
Patrick Devlin  88, 105
Patrick Riley  4, 23
Paul Carl Pálffy  34–36
Paul Hazard  10, 24
Paul J. Du Plessis  194, 210, 233
Paul Johnson  97, 108
Paul Karl Pálffy  40, 41
Paul Langford  82, 97, 101, 107
Paul M. Meyer  252
Paul Mitchell  88, 107
Paul Starr  184, 190
Paul Vinogradoff  215, 235
Paul(us) Krueger  198, 211, 252
Pauline Rémy-Corlay  204, 211
Paulus  196, 201, 214, 231, 232
Paulus Voet  216
Paweł Blajer  248, 251
Pélérin  49, 66
Percy H. Winfield  215, 236
Perrine Simon-Nahum  259, 283
Peter Baldwin  317, 330
Peter Birks  88, 105
Peter G. Stein  5, 15, 24, 234
Peter Garnsey  51, 70
Peter Liessem  289, 307
Peter Von Borch  245, 253
Petter Korkman  61–63, 70–72
Philip W. Thayer  99, 109
Philipp Schwartz  288–290, 292, 294,
    296–298, 308
Philippe Jestaz  268, 282
Philippe Joseph Gorneau  124
Philippe Nelidoff  127, 139
Philippe-Antoine Merlin  157, 162
Piergiorgio Peruzzi  115, 140
Piero Del Negro  127, 141
Pierre Clergeot  242, 251
Pierre Legrand  327, 328, 331
Pierre-Antoine Fenet  257, 281–283

## INDEX OF NAMES

Pierre-Nicolas Barenot   268, 271, 280
Piotr Steinkeller   150
Plautius   231
(Pope) Pius VII   125
Pompeo Baldasseroni   122, 123, 125, 134

Qu Tongzu   265, 284
Quintus Mucius Scaevola   196

R.C. van Caenegem   11, 12, 22, 25
R.K. Ramazani   67, 71
Rabaud de Saint-Étienne   53, 66
Rafe Blaufarb   52, 70
Raimo Pullat   287, 308
Ray B. Westerfield   96, 110
Ray Forrest Harvey   62, 70
RayMing Chang   325, 330
Reinhard Zimmermann   77, 94, 106, 110, 132,
      142, 193, 195, 198, 205, 211, 216, 223, 233,
      235, 236, 238, 253, 328, 331
Rena Van den Bergh   205, 210
René Josué Valin   122, 129, 142
René-Marie Rampelberg   204, 211
Riccardo Ferrante   124, 127, 128, 136
Richard A. Epstein   56, 70
Richard Ashcraft   56, 70
Richard Harrison Shryock   184, 190
Richard P. Applebaum   87, 108
Richard Serra   326, 327
Richard Tuck   60, 61, 70, 72
Robert B. Ferguson   88, 92, 100, 106
Robert Bell   182, 189
Robert Black   221, 234
Robert C. Bird   324, 330
Robert Fatton Jr.   67, 71
Robert Feenstra   216, 23
Robert Joseph Pothier   129, 204, 211
Robert Lamb   61, 71
Robert Merges   320, 331
Robert Nozick   56, 71
Robert Schweitzer   290, 308
Robert Weisberg   100, 110
Roberta Kwall   311, 312, 318, 319, 331
Robin Evans-Jones   228, 229, 235
Roderick Floud   97, 108
Rodolfo Batiza   6, 23
Rodolfo Sacco   78, 108, 192, 211
Rodolfo Savelli   118, 141

Roger Magraw   258, 282
Ron Harris   87, 106
Roscoe Pound   164–166, 170, 172, 190
Roy Goode   74, 75, 80, 88, 92,
      95, 106
Rudolph Sohm   220, 236
Rudyard Kipling   255
Rufus James Trimble   97, 101, 109
Russo Ruggeri   198, 210, 211

S. Jarociński   145
Sally E. Hadden   315, 332
Salvatore Riccobono   252
Sampsa Samila   87, 106
Samuel Kucherov   289, 307
Samuel P. Scott   252
Samuel Pufendorf   55, 60, 64, 71
Sándor Károlyi   34
Sanita Osipova   286, 309
Sara Pennell   89, 108
Sara Pilloni   19, 191
Sarmiza Bilcescu-Alimăniteanu   262
Saverio Gentile   116, 128, 129, 137
Sean Thomas   18, 21, 25, 73, 81, 85, 88,
      95, 109
Septiumius Severus   241
Serge Dauchy   4, 24, 118, 137
Sergio Zaninelli   117, 135
Seth Tipton   319, 332
Shen Dengjie   278, 284
Shi Shangkuan   275, 276, 283
Siân Reynolds   76, 82, 83, 105
Sièyes   67, 261
Sigismondo Scaccia   118, 129, 141
Simon Cooper   247, 252
Simon Lavis   17
Sonya G. Bonneau   312, 323, 330
Stanisław Staszic   145
Stanisław Zawadzki   146, 163
Stanley N. Katz   51, 52, 71
Stefania Gialdroni   118, 137
Stephan Wagner   288, 307, 308
Stephen Buckle   57, 60, 61, 70
Stephen Quinn   96, 97, 108
Stephen Werbőczy   27, 28, 37, 38
Steven Forde   61, 70
Steven Wilf   17, 18, 311, 315, 332
Sun Yat-Sen   263

## 342     INDEX OF NAMES

Susan Staves   92, 107
Susanne Maria Pálffy   36, 43

T.A.J. McGinn   233, 236
T.C. Smout   216, 235
Tadeusz Maciejewski   16
Tadeusz Mencel   144, 163
Tammo Wallinga   200, 201, 211
Teodor Weichhan   151, 154
Terence Ball   63, 70
Theodor Mayer   33, 46
Theodor Mommsen   198, 211, 252
Theodosius   239, 242
Theresa Erdődy   40
Theresa Esterházy   41
Theresia Kinsky   40
Thomas B. Allen   166, 189
Thomas B. Smith   223, 236
Thomas Duve   111, 115, 136
Thomas E. Kaiser   52, 71
Thomas Fox   230
Thomas G. Shearman   178, 190
Thomas Hobbes   55
Thomas Jefferson   49–52, 54–56, 62, 63, 70
Thomas Mohr   17
Thomas Nugent   62, 70
Thomas Piketty   90, 108
Thomas Winkelbauer   27, 28, 33, 47
Tim Hanstad   242, 252
Toivo U. Raun   290, 308
Tomasz Byszewski   145
Tomasz de Ruhmfeld Chromy   158
Tomasz Giaro   238, 252, 285, 305, 307
Tomasz Moore Evans   154
Tony Weir   132, 142
Tullio Ascarelli   133, 134

Ugo Petronio   117, 140
Ulpian(us)   195, 231
Ulrich Manthe   228, 235
Umberto Santarelli   118, 141
Uno Ilm   304, 306

V.A.D. Dalloz   157
Vasily Sinaisky   297
Victor Hugo   316
Vincenzo Bartolucci   125
Virginia M. Casicio   326, 330

Virginia Tuma   256, 281
Virginie Martin   113, 138
Virpu Mäkinen   61, 62, 71, 72
Viscount Simon   214
Vito Piergiovanni   118, 119, 136, 140, 141
Vladimir Bukovsky   292, 297, 306
Volkmar Gessner   87, 109

W. Lalewicz   145
Walenty Skorochód-Majewski   145
Walter Bayer   205, 210
Walter G. Becker   203, 210
Wang Boqi   265, 284
Wang Chonghui   277, 284
Wang Shuaiyi   264, 284
Wanrong (Consort Sku)   254
Ward Barrett   86, 104
Warren Swain   73, 109
Whipple   174, 175
Wilhelm Brauneder   39, 44
Wilhelm Studemund   198, 211
Wilhelmus de Cabriano   200
William A. Hunter   219, 226, 235
William B. Scott   51, 52, 55, 71
William Blackstone   50, 55, 63–66, 70, 182, 189
William E. McCurdy   97–99, 107
William E. Scheuerman   87, 108
William Elliot Butler   289, 306
William L.F. Felstine   87, 109
William Mitchell   101, 107
William Searle Holdsworth   218, 219, 235
William Tilghman   169
William W. Buckland   215, 225, 230, 234
William W. Story   95, 109
William W. Wagner   289, 309
Wilm Scharlemann   297, 308
Władysław Rozwadowski   240, 244, 253
Wojciech Dajczak   238, 252
Wojciech Konrady   151
Wolfgang Ayaß   303, 306
Woods   181
Wu Zhixin   277, 284

Xavier Prévost   121, 140
Xie Hongfei   255, 283
Xie Zhenmin   274, 284
Xiyan Tang   312, 332

# INDEX OF NAMES

343

Xu Li   272, 284
Xuantong   254
Xue Jun   255, 283

Yang Du   264, 284
Yasutomo Morigiwa   4, 24
Yongmin Shin   238, 253
Yvonne Knibiehler   261, 282

Zeus   143
Zhang Yan   255, 283

Zhang Yifei   238, 253
Zhang Zhiben   277, 284
Zhu Hanguo   279, 284
Zhu Mingzhe   16, 20, 254, 259, 283
Zoltán Ács   29, 44
Zoltán Fallenbüchl   33, 45
Zoltán Kérészy   45
Zoran Pokrovac   287, 307
Zsuzsanna Peres   8, 16, 24, 26, 32, 35, 38, 45–47

# Index of Subjects

Application of Law (Principles,
    Provisions)   1, 17, 144, 150, 157, 159
  Application of Artist Rights Act   312
  Application of the Contract   208
  Application of the Contractual Liability
    Rules   207, 208
  Application of French Commercial
    Code   150, 154
  Application in Court Practice   289
  Application of Moral Rights   328
  Application of the Relativity of
    Contracts   209
  Application of the Usucaption   238, 239
(Hungarian) Aristocracy   26–28, 31, 35, 39,
    40, 43, 44

Civil
  Civil Case   157, 158
  Civil Code(s)/Codifications   21, 73, 131,
    194, 204, 288, 295
  Austrian Civil Code (ABGB)   36, 130,
    238, 240
  Baltic Private Law Codes
    (BPLC)   286–298
  Civil Code of the Republic of
    China   255, 271–275, 278
  Estonian Draft Civil Code   21, 289,
    291–293, 295, 297–300, 304, 305
  French Civil Code (*Code civil*, Code
    Napoleon, Napoleonic Code)   116,
    128, 130, 132, 133, 144, 146, 147, 204,
    206, 257, 259, 260, 266, 272, 275, 298
  German Civil Code (BGB)   204, 205,
    207, 238, 245, 288, 289, 291
  Italian Civil Code   206
  Polish Civil Code   238, 240
  Latvian Civil Code   292, 296, 298
  Draft Civil Code of Rome
    Republic   115
  Draft Civil Code of Russian
    Empire   289, 293
  Civil Code of the Russian Soviet
    Federated Socialist Republic   304
  Swiss Civil Code   274, 296
  Civil Company   158
  Civil Court (Tribunal)   154, 155, 218

Civil Form of Assythment   233
Civil Government   57, 69
*Ius Civile*   240
Civil Law (System(s))   4, 91, 131, 191, 200,
    207–209, 230, 248, 255, 257, 269,
    272–274, 290, 292, 294, 298, 299, 304,
    311, 312, 314
Civil Legislators   270
Civil Privileges   65
Civil Procedure   114, 131
  Austrian Civil Procedure   130
  French Code of Civil Procedure   144
Civil Reparation   223
Civil Right(s)   64, 65, 300
Civil Rota's Case Law   119
Civil Society(ies)   58, 61, 64, 66, 68
Civilists (Civil Lawyer)   75, 255, 274, 276
Civilisation   3, 4, 10
  Material Civilisation   73, 76, 82, 85, 86,
    89, 91, 96, 103
Codification(s)   3–5, 11, 21, 37, 92, 120, 123,
    125, 131, 143, 167, 204, 206, 272, 286,
    295–297
  Austrian Codification   206
  Chinese Private Law Codification   255
  Civil Law Codifications   194, 204
  Codification Dispute   299
  Codification Ideas
  Commercial Law Codification   133
    Commercial Law Codification in
      Italy   120, 121, 123, 125, 131
    Neapolitan Commercial Law
      Codification   120, 129
    Venetian Commercial Law
      Codification   120, 121
  (European) Codification Movement   4,
    167, 168, 187
  French (Napoleon's) Codification   6, 115,
    116, 123, 126
  Hungarian Private Law Codification   35
  Italian Codification   115, 206
  National Codification   131
  Private Law Codification   285, 286, 298,
    300, 304
  Estonian Private Law Codification   21,
    292

# INDEX OF SUBJECTS

Russian Civil Law Codification   289
Tuscanian Private Law Codification   129
Commercial
  Commercial Act(s)   147, 155, 156, 158
  Commercial Actions   99
  Commercial Activity (ies)   83, 84, 92, 102,
    147, 150
  Commercial Actors   79
  Commercial Agreements   90
  Commercial Behaviour   79
  Commercial Case Law   120, 123, 126, 128,
    130
  Commercial (Character/Nature of) Case
    (s)   154, 155, 157, 158
  Commercial Circulation   101
  Commercial Classes   82
  Commercial Claims   93
  Commercial Clubs   99, 100
  Commercial Code(s)   128, 131, 144
    Draft(s) (Project(s), Proposal(s) for a
      Codification) of Italian Commercial
      Code   116, 117, 120–123, 127
    French Commercial Code (Code de
      commerce)   111, 116, 117, 120,
      124–129, 132, 133, 143–147, 149, 150,
      152–156, 158, 159
    German Commercial Code
      (ADHGB)   131, 132
    Italian Commercial Code   132
    Piedmont Commercial Code   132
  Commercial Company (ies)   125,
    158
  Commercial Complexity   89
  Commercial Connectivity   76
  Commercial Context(s)   93, 100
  Commercial Courts (Tribunals)   128,
    154, 155Commercial Financing   96
  Commercial Goods   95
  Commercial Growth   89
  Commercial Guilds   114, 116
  Commercial Honour   99
  Commercial Innovations   91
  Commercial Institutions   80
  Commercial Instruments   88
  Commercial Interaction   76
  Commercial Judges   126
  Commercial Jurisdiction   74, 155
  Commercial Law   18, 74, 75, 77–80, 88, 91,
    92, 94–96, 102, 103, 114, 117–123, 125, 127,
    129–133, 143, 147, 149, 154, 158, 159

  Customary Commercial Law   121
  Commercial Law Doctrine   120, 123,
    130
  English Commercial Law   18, 21,
    73–76, 80, 81, 92, 101, 102
  French Commercial Law   18, 112, 126,
    128, 144
  Italian Commercial Law   18, 112, 116,
    119, 121, 126, 131
  Mercantile Commercial Law   121
  Polish Commercial Law   159
  Commercial Law School(s)
    (classes)   127, 128
  Commercial Law Science   149
  Commercial Lawyer   74
  Commercial Legislation   117, 118, 125, 132
  Commercial Letter of Credit   97
  Commercial Life   81, 88
  Commercial Maritime Law   120
  Commercial Matters   145
  Commercial Mechanisms   73, 102
  Commercial Network   97, 103
  Commercial Paper(s)   84, 87, 89, 93, 118
  Commercial Perspectives   96
  Commercial Policy   81
  Commercial Practice(s)   73, 75, 81, 90–92,
    96–98, 100, 101, 119
  Commercial Registry Law   297
  Commercial Relations (ships)   95, 146,
    159
  Commercial Revolution   83
  Commercial Routes   117, 118
  Commercial Rules   118
  Commercial Sales Ethic   94
  Commercial Setback   98
  Commercial System   96
  Commercial Systems of Circuits   97
  Commercial Texts   94
  Commercial Thought   92
  Commercial Transactions   89, 118
  Commercial Treatment of Money   94
  Primitive Non-Commercial Societies   76
  Pro-Commercial Judicial Attitude   92
Comparative
  Comparative Analysis (Research)   16, 19,
    77, 78, 192, 239
  Comparative Approach   191, 212
  Comparative Context   16, 302
  Comparative Issues   209
  Comparative Law   78

## INDEX OF SUBJECTS

Comparative (cont.)
    Comparative Legal History   77, 78, 191, 233, 256
    Comparative Look (Reflection)   19, 285
    Comparative Perspective   21, 204
Comparative Point of View   112, 191, 193
    Comparative Studies in Law   268
    Comparatively Used   219
Consolidation of a Nation (Community)   2, 12, 21, 285, 286, 298–300
Contract(s)   35, 36, 38, 86, 150–152, 154, 191, 196, 197, 206–209, 241, 269
    Breach of a Contract   231
    Contract Formalities   102
    Judicial Contract   218
    Contract Law (Contractual Law, Law of Contracts)   191, 193, 194, 208, 294
        English Contract Law   77, 82
        European Contract Law   192, 196
        French Contract Law   206
        German Contract Law   205
        Roman Law of Obligations and Contracts   200
    Marriage Contract(s)   39, 49
    Quasi-Contract   225
    Prenuptial Contracts   39
    Relativity of Contract(s)   191–193, 203–205, 207, 209
    Sale(s) Contract   99, 199
    Contract of a *stipulation*   195
    Third-Party Contract(s)   19, 193, 197, 198, 203–209
    Valid Contract   208
Contractual
    Contractual Act   274
    Contractual Agreement   325
    Contractual Character   225
    Contractual Concept   225
    Contractual Effects   206
    Contractual Institute   204, 207
    Contractual Liability   207–209
    Quasi-Contractual Nature   225
    Contractual Obligation   194, 202
    Contractual Praxis   199
    Contractual Protection   191
    Contractual Structure   203, 207
    Contractual Subject   207
    Contractual System   203, 204
    Contractual Third-Party   191

Counter-dowry (*Werlag*)   38–41
Culture   7, 9, 14, 15, 101, 317
    Legal Culture   2, 6, 10, 11, 13, 18, 23

Declaration
    French Declaration of the Rights of Man and of the Citizen of 1789   49, 52, 54, 66, 67, 69, 114
    US Declaration of Independence   49, 50, 52, 54, 55, 63, 67–69, 164
    Virginia Declaration of Rights   50
Decodification   148

Enlightenment   2–6, 8, 10, 11, 13–15, 20, 22, 30, 49, 54, 56, 120, 121, 256, 260, 261, 316

Family   16, 33, 34, 37, 38, 40, 41, 89, 176, 221, 254–259, 261–275, 277, 279, 280, 302
    Family Autonomy   255
    Conception (Idea) of Family   257, 275
    Head (Chief) of Family   261, 264, 271–274
    Family Law(s) (Legislation)   255, 257, 261, 262, 266, 268, 270–272, 274, 275, 279, 291, 292, 294, 295, 297
    Family Life   261, 274
    Family Members   257, 272, 274
    Patriarchal Family   256, 259, 271
    Family Policy   275
    Family Property   37, 273, 274
    Family Regime   256, 261, 274
    Family Reform(s)   254, 257, 258, 271, 280
    Family Structure   254, 263
    Traditional Family   254–256, 268, 271, 277, 279
    Family Value   269, 279

Implementation
    Implementation of Codification (Codes)   3, 73, 114–117, 126, 127, 155
    Implementation of Constitutionalist Ideas   3
    Implementation of Common Law   164, 170
    Implementation of Courts   128
    Implementation of Ideological Aim(s)   1, 3, 7, 12
    Implementation of Legal Norms (Principles)   19, 121
    Implementation of Mining Law   156

INDEX OF SUBJECTS 347

Implementation of True Justice 166
Implementation of Visual Artists Rights
Act 312, 317, 322
Inheritance Law (Provisions, Rules) 41, 171,
220, 291, 294, 295, 297, 299, 302
Instrumentality of Law 16, 49
Law as an Instrument 2, 3, 12, 16, 20, 21,
49, 165, 173, 188, 285
Legal Instrumentalism 1, 16, 17, 164, 192,
209

Judgment(s) 155, 213–215, 217, 218, 223, 224,
227–230, 324
Jurisprudence 207, 209, 256, 274,
276, 328
American Jurisprudence 181
Chinese Jurisprudence 271
Common Law Jurisprudence 314
Continental Jurisprudence 315
French Jurisprudence 271
Global Jurisprudence 314
Intellectual Property Jurisprudence
315
Moral Rights Jurisprudence 318
Progressive Jurisprudence 258, 270
Roman Jurisprudence 19
Scottish Jurisprudence 219

Language(s) 29, 31, 32, 43, 183, 261, 262, 286,
290, 295, 299, 317
Chinese Language 256
French Language 34, 145, 256
German Language 32–34, 290, 294
Hungarian Language 29, 31, 34, 43, 44
Jurisprudential Language 90
Latin Language 31, 33
Legal Language 124
Moral Rights Language 322, 329
Polish Legal Language 159
Russian Language 290, 294
Law
American Law 170, 171, 173
Austrian Law(s) 36, 130, 238
Chinese Law(s) 265, 275
Common Law 7, 19, 52, 63, 94, 133,
164–173, 182, 183, 185–188, 217, 220, 238,
240, 311, 312, 314, 318, 322, 327
Continental Law 7, 19
Customary Law 38, 39, 116, 133, 172

English Law 21, 73, 76, 79, 81, 82, 92–96,
102, 164–171, 173, 181–183, 186–188, 212,
218, 229–231, 245, 246
European Laws 256
French Law(s) 114, 127, 130, 208
German Law(s) 149, 238, 297, 302, 313
Hungarian Law(s) 17, 26, 35, 36, 38–40
Italian Law 130
Polish Law 18, 238, 243
Roman Law 6, 19, 94, 120, 129, 191–201,
204, 207–209, 212–223, 225–230, 232,
233, 237–240, 242, 244, 260, 272, 299,
327
Russian Laws 288
Scottish Law 215, 219, 228
Swiss Law 238
Lawyers
American Lawyers 168
Chinese Lawyers 256
English Lawyers 217, 229
German Lawyers 290, 294, 296
Russian Lawyers 290, 293
Scottish Lawyers 216, 222, 227
Legislation 19, 75, 143, 149, 156, 167,
171, 207, 256, 258, 265–267, 271, 275,
296, 301
Agrarian Legislation 302
Anticlerical Legislations 262
Austrian Legislation 240
Chinese Legislation 256
Commercial Legislation 117, 118, 125, 132,
159
English Legislation 251
Estonian Legislation 295
Family Legislation 275
Foreign Legislations 132
French Legislation 158, 159
German Legislation 302
Italian Legislation 125
Native American Legislation 166
Republican Legislations 265, 267
Revolutionary Legislation 268
Liability 75, 95, 118, 152, 153, 177, 185, 195, 207,
222, 223, 228, 230, 231
Acquilian Liability 227, 228, 231
Contractual Liability 191, 207–209
Criminal Liability 222
Delictual (Tortious) Liability 19, 212, 213,
215, 224, 227–232

# INDEX OF SUBJECTS

Liability (cont.)

Doctors' (Physcians) Liability   19, 165, 173, 179, 181–183, 187, 188

Locality Rule   165, 173, 187, 188

*Longue Durée*   73–77, 79, 80, 84, 85, 88, 100

Marital

Marital Property   36–38, 42, 266, 271, 274

Marital Remuneration (*paraphernal, dos*)   37, 38, 41

(Medical) Malpractise   164, 165, 173, 174, 178, 182, 183, 187, 188, 208

Modernisation   1, 2, 4, 7, 10, 12, 13, 15, 16, 22, 73, 74, 83, 131, 159, 213, 239, 250, 251, 256, 286, 287

Morning Gift (*Morgengabe*)   38, 39, 41

Napoleonic

Napoleonic codification   6

Napoleonic Code   206, 259, 260, 272

Napoleonic Era   127

Napoleonic Law Schools   127

Napoleonic Wars   111

National Identity   1, 10, 12, 15, 20, 26, 30, 73, 112, 258, 264, 280, 290, 292, 295

American Identity   165

Artistic Identity   323

Community Identity   9, 22, 23

Croatian Legal Identity   21

To Cultivate and Develop Identity   1

To Form Identity   297

Hungarian National Identity   21, 30

Identity Aims   1

Identity Building Processes   285

Identity Expectations of the Society   10

Identity Requirements   15

Juridical Identity   133

Legal Identity   21, 304

National Identity Ideology   1, 2

National Legal Identity   12, 21, 212, 290

Republican National Identity   280

VARA's Identity   321

Negligence   176–178, 215, 222, 227, 228, 233, 271

Law of Obligations   193, 196, 200, 208, 291, 297

Quarter (*quarta puellaris*)   37

Prenuptial Agreement   26, 35, 36, 39–43

Private Law

Property   38, 49, 50, 52, 54, 55, 57, 58, 62–66, 68, 69, 81, 82, 86, 88, 92, 94–97, 103, 152, 191, 221, 244–247, 249, 257, 258, 260, 261, 273, 300, 314, 326, 327

Common Property   39

Community Property   260, 267

Property Concept   16, 54, 69, 81, 95

Family Property   37, 273, 274

Head of the Family Property Rights   274

Husband's Property   41

Immovable Property   245

Individual Property   273

Intellectual Property   311, 312, 314–316, 318

Intellectual Property Law   311, 312, 314, 315, 328

Intellectual Property Rights   311, 319

Property Law   94, 294, 297, 311

Marital Property   36, 37, 42, 266, 271, 274

Marital Property Law   17

Marital Property Provisions   26, 38, 39

Marital Property Rights   16, 37

Married Women Property   40, 260, 262

Married Women Property Rights   271, 275

Movable Property   40, 55, 245

Property Owner   35, 59, 245, 246, 313, 326

Private Property   50, 52, 55–57, 59, 61, 64–66, 68, 81, 241, 245

Pledged Property (pignus)   220

Real Property   152, 238, 239, 241–245, 248, 250, 251

Property Rights   36, 51–53, 58, 62, 63, 68, 69, 171, 243, 249, 257, 266, 313, 326, 327

Property Rights of Family Members   264, 272

Separate Property of the Wife   260, 274

Property Theory   2, 49, 56, 63, 69

Republican   169, 274, 279, 319

Republican China   274

Republican Discourse   256

Republican Government   52, 255, 259, 265, 267, 272, 277

Republican Legislations   267

# INDEX OF SUBJECTS

Republican Militants  254
Republican Moment(s)  16, 254, 255, 257
Republican National Identity  280
Republican Professors  269
Republican Reality  169
Republican Regime  255, 258, 263
Republican Senators  319
Republican Society  166
Republican Spirit  261, 262
Republican State  259
Republican System  187
Republican Tradition  262
Republicans  255, 256, 258, 261, 263–265, 274, 280
Republicanism  51, 261
Revolution  2, 6, 7, 49, 54
  Age of Revolution  5
  American Revolution  2, 16, 49, 51, 166, 168, 173
  French Revolution  2, 16, 30, 49, 112, 113, 115, 120, 167, 261, 272
  Bolshevik Revolution  293
  Commercial Revolution  83
  Industrial Revolution  86, 92, 316
  Enlightenment Revolution  2, 4, 8
  Legal Revolution  8, 11
  National Revolutions  6
  Political Revolution  49
  Revolutions of 1848  37
Rights
  Acquired Rights  62
  Artist (s') Rights  313–314, 318, 321, 323, 328
  Author Rights  316
  Civil Rights  300
  Citizens Rights  3
  Copyright Rights  313, 316
  Creator(s) Rights  316, 325
  Dignity Rights  312, 326
  Economic Rights  311, 313, 315–318, 328
  Family Rights  274
  Feudal Rights  53
  Human Rights  10, 312
  Inherent Rights  316
  Inviolable Right(s)  53, 66
  Rights of Man  49
  Minority Nations' Rights  29, 298

Moral Rights  18, 58, 311–323, 325–326, 328, 329
Natural Rights  52, 56, 62, 64, 313, 314, 316, 322
Political Rights  64
Property Rights  16, 36, 37, 51–53, 58, 62, 63, 68, 69, 171, 249, 257, 260, 262, 264, 266, 271, 272, 274, 275, 319, 326, 327
Purchaser's (Seller's) Rights  249
Third-Party Rights  198
Unmarried Woman Rights  37
Violable Right(s)  49, 52, 69, 168
Widow's Rights  37
Women's Rights  37, 266, 275
(Legal) Transplant  18, 19, 256, 312, 314, 327, 328
  Continental European Legal Principles Transplant  311
  Delictual Liability Transplant  230
  European Legal Ideals Transplant  256
  European Legal Institutions Transplant  272
  Foreign (Legal) Transplant  314
  Fraught (Legal) Transplant  314, 315, 328
  French Legal Doctrine Transplant  275
  Reluctant (Legal) Transplant  311, 312, 315

School
  Historical School of Law  11
  French Law Schools  127
  Italian Law Schools  127
  Medieval School of Roman Law  19
  Polish School of Commercial Law  158
  Pandectist School  240
  School of Medicine  182
School of Practice Doctrine  165, 173, 181, 186–188
School of Treatment  188
Science(s)  143, 178, 186, 188
  Commercial Law Science  119, 149
  Comparative Law Science  78
  Development of Science  2
  French Legal Science  126
  Legal (Juridical) Science  4, 5, 19, 118, 144, 147, 148, 150, 194
  Medical Science(s)  179, 184
  Polish Legal Science  159
  Political Science  5

Science(s) (cont.)

*Stipulation alteri*   191, 193–197, 200, 202–205, 207

Title Registration System(s)   238, 239, 241, 242, 244–248, 250, 251

Tort Law   233

Usucaption (*usucapio*)   237–241, 243–245, 248–251

Widow's Remuneration   35, 41

# Index of Places

Alps 118
Alsace-Lorraine 247
America 50, 84, 166, 169, 170, 172, 315, 316, 318
   Latin America 8
   North America 49, 57, 69, 164
   South America 9, 18
Amsterdam 79, 85, 90, 96, 119
Antwerp 79, 90, 91, 102
Archangel 227
Arizona 248
Asia 84
Australia 247
Austria 19, 34, 247, 300, 302
Austro-Hungarian Empire 247

Baltic Sea 86
Baltic area (Baltic provinces, Baltic States) 285, 286, 288, 290
Beijing 254, 277–279
Berne 312–314, 316–319, 323, 328
Bologna 128, 200
Boston 175, 178, 188
Boston Park 327
Bratislava (Pozsony) 27, 32, 34
Brazil (Republic of Brazil) 9, 18, 325
Britain 86, 96, 101, 103, 315, 316
British Empire 17
British Isles 170, 184
Buda 27
Budapest 43
Bydgoszcz 154

Cambridge (UK) 184
Canada 247
Carrara 122
Champagne 84
Chelmsford 179
China (Republic of China) 16, 238, 254–258, 271–277, 279, 280
Cisalpine Republic 113, 122
Courland 287, 288, 291
Croatia 247
Czech Lands (Bohemian Crown Lands, Czech Republic) 14, 247
Czechoslovakia 300

Dąbrowa 155, 158
Denmark 247
Dundee 227

East (Atlantic) Coast 172, 178
Eastport 174
Eastport Park 327
Edinburgh 233
England 50, 74, 77, 82, 92, 94, 98, 102, 119, 164, 166–170, 172, 184, 185, 187, 212, 218, 224, 233, 246, 247, 250, 276
Egypt 247
Estonia (Estonian territory, Republic of Estonia) 285–288, 290–294, 296–299, 302, 304
Esztergom 33, 34
Eurasia 256, 258
Europe 6, 7, 10, 13, 16, 18, 19, 21, 42, 57, 73, 79, 84, 92, 101, 132, 133, 167, 168, 187, 238, 242, 256, 257, 262, 304, 313, 315, 316, 327
   Central-Eastern Europe 8, 9, 18
   Continental Europe 7, 133, 238, 315
   Western Europe 3, 6, 8
European Union 237

Falkirk 224
Florence 125
France (French Empire, French Republic) 16, 19, 49, 52–54, 69, 113, 115, 116, 119, 120, 124–129, 132, 133, 146, 153, 154, 156, 167, 168, 187, 242, 247, 254, 255, 257, 258, 261, 267, 268, 271, 279, 280, 311–313, 316, 317
Frankfurt 119

Galicia (in Poland) 148, 149
Gdańsk 15, 28, 103
Gdynia 15
Genoa (Republic of Genoa) 79, 113, 119, 124, 125, 128, 129
Georgia 51
Germany 19, 90, 119, 247, 250, 251, 299–304, 313, 316
Great Britain (Kingdom of Great Britain) 95, 164–166, 168, 169
Guangxi 278

## INDEX OF PLACES

Holland  119
Hungary (Kingdom of Hungary)  9, 16, 21, 27, 29, 32, 33, 36, 38, 39, 41–43, 247, 302

Iowa  181–183, 185, 186
Ireland  247
Italian Mediterranean  84
Italy (Italian territories, Italian Republic, Kingdom of Italy, Italian Pennisula)  18, 19, 84, 90, 101, 111–132, 304, 316, 317

Japan  238

Kalisz  154
Kosice  34
Krakow (Republic of Krakow)  143, 148, 150, 151, 154, 155, 158

Latvia (Latvian territory, Republic of Latvia)  285, 286, 288, 290–294, 296–298, 304
Lille  270
Liverpool  89
Lithuania  297
Livonia  287, 288, 291
Lombardy (Kingdom of Lombardy-Venetia)  112, 119, 130, 131
London  73, 79, 85, 91, 96, 176, 183–185, 213
Louisiana  248
Low Countries  84
Lubec  174
Lvov  148
Lyon  119

Maine  174
Manhattan  326
Massa  122
Massachussetts  50, 175, 179–181, 248
Mediterranean Sea  118
Milan  113, 117, 121
Mohács  27
Morocco  247
Moscow  290
Mougin  49

Naples (Kingdom of Naples)  113, 114, 116, 119, 120, 126, 129
Netherlands  216, 247, 318

New Hampshire  50
New Jersey  248
New Zealand  247
Nigeria  247
North Sea  85
Norway  302

Ohio  169, 177
Oxford  184

Papal States  113, 125, 130
Paris  112, 117, 127, 129, 164
Parma (Duchy of Parma)  113, 129
Pavia  127
Pennsylvania  50, 169
Philadelphia  164
Piacenza (Duchy of Piacenza)  113
Piedmont  113, 129, 131, 132
Poland (Kingdom of Poland, Congress Poland, Polish territories)  9, 15, 18, 143, 146–149, 153, 154, 156, 158, 159, 247, 250
Portland  173
Grand Duchy of Poznań  148
Prussia  149, 154
Przedbórz  152
Pskov  287

Riga  289, 290, 292
Romania  247
Rome  126, 317
Ancient Rome (Roman Republic)  115, 194, 197, 199, 237, 240
Russia (Russian Empire, Russian Soviet Federated Socialist Republic)  148, 149, 285, 288, 289, 293, 294, 304

Sardinia (Kingdom of Sardinia)  123, 130, 132
Scotland  92, 202, 212, 215–218, 222, 224, 247, 317
Shanghai  278
Slovakia  27, 247
Slovenia  247
Republic of South Africa  238, 247
South Carolina  51
Soviet Union (USSR)  288, 302–304
Spain  112, 113, 120, 316
St. Petersburg  287, 290
St. Pölten  34
Sweden  247

INDEX OF PLACES 353

Switzerland 247, 302
Syria 247

Tartu 290, 291, 293, 299
Tel Aviv 257
Tianjin 247, 278, 279
Transylvania (Principality of
Transylvania) 27
Tunisia 247
Turin 128
Turkey 247
Tuscany (Duchy of Tuscany) 113, 119,
122, 129

United Kingdom 212, 228, 246
United States of America 3, 18, 19, 50, 54, 101,
164, 165, 167–170, 172, 173, 178, 184–188,
247, 248, 250, 311–326, 328, 329

Utrecht 216

Venice (Venetian Republic) 79, 103, 119–121,
125, 127
Vichy 271
Vienna 26–35, 43, 130, 131, 143, 146
Virginia 52

Duchy of Warsaw 143–149, 154
Warsaw 151, 153, 154
Wieliczka 158

Yunan 265

Printed in the United States
By Bookmasters